[編著] 牧野成一
Seiichi Makino
岡まゆみ
Mayumi Oka

日英共通
メタファー辞典
A Bilingual Dictionary of
English and Japanese
Metaphors

Kurosio

序　文

　みなさんは「比喩／メタファー」と聞くと、なんだか文学的な小難しいもののような印象を持っていませんか。比喩というのは簡単に言うと「喩え」のことで、「ある概念を身近なわかりやすいものに喩えて表現する」という働きを持っています。そして、日常の言語生活に深く浸透していて、人々の相互理解を深めるため、また表現を豊かにするために大切な役割を果たしています。

　本書の企画の出発点は、日本語と英語に共通の概念を持った比喩表現が多く存在することに気付いたことでした。言語が違っても同じ表現で同じ意味を表すことができれば、翻訳して使うだけで語彙数や表現力が倍加するのではないか。ならば、言語を対照しながら学習できる辞書があったら、語学学習に苦しんでいる人、表現力を磨きたいと思っている人々の役に立つに違いない！と考えたのがきっかけです。そこで、日英語共通の比喩表現を集め執筆を始めたのですが、道のりは想像以上に険しいものでした。

　振り返ると、本書の企画が始まり完成するまでに 20 年近くの年月が過ぎ去ろうとしています。その間にはアメリカの同時多発テロ (9.11) があり、世界経済がリーマンショックにみまわれ、日本では東日本大震災 (3.11) が起こり、そして、テロが日常の出来事のようになってしまうなど、世界情勢が著しく変化を遂げました。それと共に、人々が口にする言葉も随分変化したと思います。

　本書で取り上げた項目や例文も、時代の変化に合わせ、当初の原型をとどめないほどに書き換えたものもあります。しかし、言葉の持つ力「言霊」は、歳月を超えて脈々と生き続けていることを、本書の執筆を通して実感しました。比喩はそれぞれの言語で、文化や歴史、人々の生活を通して独自に創り上げられ、生き続けています。そして、それぞれの表現が根底で共通しているということは、チョムスキーの言う人間の言語の普遍性の証拠にもなると思います。「文化や言葉は違っても共通の比喩が存在する」のは、人間の思考に流れる概念にあまり差異がないことを示唆していると言えるでしょう。

　今現在、日本語や英語を学んでいる皆さん、もっと語彙・表現力を磨きたいと思っている皆さん、この辞典を大いに活用して、日英語の比喩力、表現力を身につけてください。本書は日英語の違いではなく共通点に視点をあてているので、自分の言語を下敷きにして学ぶことができます。ゼロから覚える必要がなくて学習効率もいいですし、言いたいことを何かに喩えて言い表すことで、表現力も間違いなく上達するはずです。

　最後になりますが、綿密な英語校正のみならず内容にも洞察に富んだコメントをしてくださったグレン・ラシュリーさんに心から感謝します。グレンさんの協力なくしては、英語ページの充実はありえませんでした。また、くろしお出版編集部の市川麻里子さん、斉藤章明さん、荻原典子さん、坂本麻美さん、金髙浩子さんには、大変な編集作業を献身的に続けてくださったことに深くお礼を申し上げます。本書が我々の願いをのせて世界に羽ばたいていってくれることを願っています。

2017 年 10 月吉日

牧野成一、岡まゆみ

Preface

What comes to mind when you hear the word "metaphor"? In a basic sense, metaphors are comparisons that we make to express concepts in terms that are familiar and easy to understand. They have suffused every aspect of our daily lives and play a vital role in deepening mutual understanding between people and enriching the language we use to communicate.

This work was inspired by the realization that English and Japanese share a multitude of conceptually analogous metaphorical expressions. It occurred to us that learning to convey the same meaning in a different language using similar expressions could greatly enhance one's vocabulary and fluency. In which case, we thought, a dictionary that allows readers to advance their studies and improve their fluency while comparing the two languages side by side would certainly come in handy. And so we set about the task of compiling metaphorical expressions shared by both languages and presenting them in coherent form. Little did we realize that the journey was to be much more arduous than we expected.

Looking back, it has been nearly 20 years since we began working on this dictionary, and much has transpired in that time. From the events of 9/11 to the turmoil of the global financial crisis, the 2011 Tōhoku earthquake and tsunami, and the daily reality of terrorism, the world today is radically different than it was two decades ago. And along with this transformation came a considerable shift in the way people express themselves.

As a result, several of the entries and examples contained in this work needed to be completely revamped due to the change in global circumstances. Yet the experience of creating this dictionary has made us feel more strongly than ever that language is a living, breathing entity whose spirit persists throughout the ages. Each language's metaphorical expressions are imbued with the unique culture, history, and life experiences of their users. The fact that many of these figures of speech share the same underlying meaning across different languages lends credence to Chomsky's theory on the universal aspects of human language. For if the same metaphorical expressions exist across multiple cultures and languages, perhaps there are no major distinctions in the underlying conceptual framework that shapes our way of thinking.

So if you're a student of English or Japanese striving to increase your vocabulary and polish your language skills, use this dictionary to help you integrate figurative expressions into your speech and refine your ability to express your thoughts. As this work focuses on the similarities rather than the differences between the two languages, you can use your own native language as a base to assist your comprehension of the material. And since there's no need to start from scratch, you should find that your studies proceed at a rapid rate. We are confident that learning to convey your thoughts using figurative expressions will increase your linguistic dexterity.

Last but not least, we would like to extend our heartfelt gratitude to Glenn Lashley for his painstaking efforts during the editorial process as well as the rich insight he provided into the material. Without his contributions, the English portion of this work would not have come to fruition. We would also like to express our sincere thanks to Mariko Ichikawa, Fumiaki Saito, Noriko Ogiwara, Asami Sakamoto, and Hiroko Kanetaka of the Kurosio editorial staff for the tireless dedication they displayed every step of the way. It is our hope that this dictionary finds a home on bookshelves all across the world.

October 2017
Seiichi Makino, Mayumi Oka

比喩とは

　本書の書名にある「メタファー /metaphor」という言葉の語源は古典ギリシャ語の「メタ（に）＋フェレイン（運ぶ、移す）」（meta + pherein）です。日本語のタイトルの「メタファー」は英語からの借用語で比喩全般を指す時に使われます。また、英語のタイトルの metaphor は本来の意味は「隠喩」ですが、比喩表現のほとんどが隠喩であることから、英語でも metaphor というと普通、比喩的な表現を指すことが多いです。

　「比喩」というのは、抽象的な概念や言語化しにくい物事をわかりやすく表すために、身近な物や生き物、具体的な事柄を喩えに使って、言語上に移し替えた表現のことです。例えば、ドイツの詩人ハインリッヒ・ハイネ（1797-1856）の詩に「君は花のようだ」（Du bist wie eine Blume）という有名な一節があります。ただ単に「君は本当にきれいだね」と告げるより、「君は花のようにきれいだね」の方が、より視覚的で人の感情に訴える力を持っています。また、「人生は旅だ」という一節は、人生という抽象的な概念を一言で簡潔に言い尽くしています。この二つの文が意味するところはおそらく万国共通でしょう。

　人間はコミュニケーションを円滑にするために、また言葉を使ってお互いを理解し合うために、ほとんど無意識のうちに比喩を使って生きています。その中には様々な言語、文化、歴史の中で独自に生まれたにも関わらず、共通の概念に根ざしているものが多くあります。そして、それらの多くが日常的な慣用句として用いられているのです。一方で、詩人や作家たちが独創的に創り出す比喩もまた、無限に存在します。それらの創造的比喩には個人の認知の仕方と表現の嗜好が反映されていて、一般に用いられている慣用的な比喩とは異なります。しかし、慣用句でも個人の創作でも、比喩が人間の言語活動に重要な役割を果たしていることは明らかです。

　本書では、日英語の共通の慣用的比喩表現を以下の6種類に分類しました。

1	**直喩** simile	日本語では「よう / みたい」、英語では 'as/like' で表されるされる表現。多数の例があり日英語で共通の概念を持つものが多い。 　**例** 炭のように黒い／ (as) black as coal，鳥のように自由／ (as) free as a bird
2	**隠喩** metaphor	抽象的でわかりにくい概念や、説明しにくい物事を具体的でイメージしやすい言葉に置き換えて表現する。 ① 視覚的類似性を表す表現 　**例** 犬かき＝犬のような泳ぎ方／dog paddle 　　　綿あめ＝綿のような形をしたあめ／cotton candy ② 概念領域が近い表現 　**例** 水と油／oil and water ＝考えや性質が合わず、絶対に交わらない 　　　波長が合う／be on the same wavelength ＝考え方や感じ方がよく似ている ③ 語彙の基本的意味を抽象的に発展させていく表現 　**例** 川の流れ→空気の流れ→時代の流れ 　　　家が近い→年が近い→考えが近い ④ 字義通りの意味と抽象的意味と二重の機能を持つ表現 　**例** 川が {深い / 浅い} vs. 考えが {深い / 浅い} 　　　飲み物が {温かい / 冷たい} vs. 人柄が {温かい / 冷たい}

4

3 提喩
synecdoche

包含関係で表される比喩、つまり一部で全体を表したり、全体で一部を表すような表現。

・全体で一部を表す＝「花見をする」の「花」は桜を表していて、バラや百合など他の花を指しているわけではない。
・一部で全体を表す＝「人はパンだけで生きているわけではない」の「パン」は食べ物全体を表していてパンだけを指しているわけではない。
例 公共の目／public eye，鍋釜／pots and pans

4 換喩
metonymy

外側で中の部分も意味する表現。或いは外から見える動作が内面の気持ちを表す表現。

①やかんが沸騰する＝外側の容器であるやかんが沸騰しているのではなく、やかんの中に入っている水が沸騰している。
丼を食べた＝外側の容器である丼を食べたのではなく、中に入っているご飯料理を食べた。
例 新しい血／new blood，頭数／head count
②唇を噛む：唇を噛んでいるというソトから見える動作が、悔しいという内面の気持ちを表している。例 唇を噛む／bite one's lip
手元に置く：ある物や人を自分のそばに置くというソトから見える動作が、その物や人を大切だと思っている内面の気持ちを表している。
例 手元に置く／keep s.t. on hand

5 擬人化
personification

人間でないものを人間のように描写する表現
例 金がものを言う／Money talks.，ビンの首／neck of a bottle，
机の脚／desk('s) legs，時がいやしてくれる／Time is a great healer.

6 共感覚
synesthesia

身体的、感覚的な経験に根ざす表現。共感覚とは人間の五感（視覚、聴覚、触覚、味覚、嗅覚）を表す心理学の言葉。
例 甘い声／sweet voice ＝甘くておいしいと感じた味覚が、
聴いて心地よいと感じる聴覚に転移した表現
苦い経験／bitter experience ＝苦いと感じた味覚と、大変で苦しい経験が
結びついた表現

　本書では、日英語で意味と形が類似している比喩に焦点を置いて見出し項目を作成しましたが、それぞれの類似の程度は様々です。完全に共通しているものもあれば、意味や用法が若干違うものなど、いろいろなタイプのものがあります。それらについては解説や関連語に説明を入れました。そして、日英語で形は似ていても意味が違う項目を「同形異義語」として取り上げました。また、見出し項目には、慣用的表現だけでなく、ことわざや故事成語、格言や成句、四字熟語なども入れました。

　外国語を学ぶ時は両方の言語の違いが注目されがちですが、共通点に目を向けることも言語習得の大きな助けとなります。この辞典は言葉を引くだけでなく、読み物としても楽しんでみてください。日英語でどんな概念が共通しているかを知るのはとても面白いですし、生きた例文や様々な視点に立った解説は言語の知識を豊かにします。本書がみなさんの日英語のレベルを上達させ、言語知識を深め、そして比喩力をつけることを願っています。

本書の使い方

1) 本書では、日本語と英語の比喩表現を、左頁に英語、右頁に日本語で紹介、解説しています。
2) 掲載は英語アルファベット順。日本語は五十音順索引を参照してください。
3) 以下の二つの分類（日英共通比喩表現（695組）、同形異義語（45組））に分けて解説しています。

【日英共通比喩表現】：日本語と英語で、その形や比喩的意味がよく似ているものを「共通比喩表現」として左右の頁に並べて掲載しました。ただ、異なる言語であり、意味や用法については完全に一致していない部分もあるため、その共通点と共通しない点については解説で具体的に説明しています。

【同形異義語】：日本語と英語で、形はよく似ているが、比喩的な意味が異なる表現を「同形異義語」として左右の頁に並べて掲載しました。

見出し：比喩表現の見出し。

定義：字義通りの意味ではなく比喩的な意味。

例文：会話例と通常例文があります。会話例では、日常会話に自然に含まれている比喩表現を、通常例文では、時事的なものから文学的なものまで多様な例文を紹介しています。

関連語：見出しと置き換えられる同義表現や、一部を置き換えて使える表現、意味は似ているがニュアンスが異なる表現などを紹介しています。例文で具体的な用例を示しました。

反意語：見出しと反対の意味を持つ表現。例文で具体的な用例を示しました。

品詞　比喩の種類

見出し　●**規則を曲げる**　phr.　隠喩

定義　●ルールを（誰かの利益になるよう）勝手に変える

関連語見出し　関 規則を[破る／犯す]

反意語見出し　反 規則に従う，規則を守る

例文
●マイク：この夏、休暇を3週間とってもよろしいでしょうか。
課長：いや、君だけのために規則を曲げるわけにいかないんだ。
(a) 状況に適応するために規則を曲げなければならない時が来るだろう。
(b) 試合の規則通りだと勝てない場合、彼は自分が勝つために規則を曲げるだろう。

解説
●日本語の「曲げる」は法律、事実、自説を直接目的語としてとるが、英語の場合、自説には bend は使われない。change (one's own) view となる。
(1) a. 法律を曲げる
　　pervert the law, bend the law

関連語
●break the rules と violate the rules はそれぞれ、「規則を破る」と「規則を犯す」に対応する。動詞 break「破る」も violate「犯す」も比喩的に使われている。
(1) この寮の規則を破ったら、もう住めなくなる。
　　If you break the dormitory rules, you will be asked to move out.

反意語
●日英語の反意語は、それぞれ、「規則に従う」「規則を守る」と [obey/observe/stick to/play by] the rules である。　　ANT(1)

反意語例文への参照
※英語頁を参照

同形異義語

見出し　●**足を引っぱる**　／ phr. ／ 隠喩

定義　●だれかの成功や、何かの進行の邪魔をする
to impede s.o.'s success or progress

例文
●彼の行動はひとりよがりで、いつもチームの足を引っぱってしまう。
He always does things his own way and ends up holding his team back.

7

凡　例

●略語・記号

例 文	例文（日本語）
Examples	例文（英語）
解 説	日本語の解説
Notes	英語の解説
関 関連語	関連語（日本語） 関連語の解説・例文
REL REL	関連語 related words（英語） 関連語の解説・例文
反 反意語	反意語（日本語） 反意語の解説・例文
ANT ANT	反意語 antonym words（英語） 反意語の解説・例文
同形異議語	同形異議語（日本語）
homograph	同形異議語（英語 homograph）
─📖 Note(1)	英語頁 Note の例文(1)を参照
─📖 REL(1)	英語頁 REL の例文(1)を参照
─📖 ANT(1)	英語頁 ANT の例文(1)を参照
📖─解説(1)	日本語頁、解説例文(1)を参照
📖─関連語(1)	日本語頁、関連語例文(1)を参照
📖─反意語(1)	日本語頁、反意語例文(1)を参照
s.t.	something（何か）
s.o.	someone（誰か / 人）
lit.	literally（字義通りの意味）
i.e.	id est（すなわち）
×	間違った用例
?	少し不自然な用例
??	間違いではないが、かなり不自然な用例
→(a)	例文(a)を参照
LOOK	その見出しを参照

（ ） 英語の見出し内	接続する前置詞など。省略可能 例）(as) black as coal
（ ） 日本語の見出し内	接続する助詞など。省略可能 例）(〜と)波長が合う
（ ） 解説内	直前の単語の意味を表す。例）oriru (come down)、「インク」(ink)
" " 解説内	直前のフレーズの意味を表す。
{ X/Y }	X あるいは Y。置き換え可能

●表記

イタリック	英語見出しを表す 例）break the rules
斜体	日本語見出しを表す 例）kisoku o mageru

●品詞

phr.	句、フレーズ	例）全身を耳にする
n. phr.	名詞句	例）血と汗と涙
n.	名詞	例）ひよこ
v.	動詞	例）攻撃する
comp. n.	複合名詞	例）視点
comp. v.	複合動詞	例）燃え尽きる
adj.	形容詞	例）breathtaking
adj. (i)	イ形容詞	例）冷たい
adj. (na)	ナ形容詞	例）無神経（な）
adj. (i). phr.	イ形容詞句	例）(〜に)弱い
adv.	副詞	例）文字通り（に）
adv. phr.	副詞句	例）by a nose
comp. adj.	複合形容詞	例）deep-rooted
comp. adj. (i)	複合イ形容詞	例）根深い
comp. adj. (na)	複合ナ形容詞	例）冷血（な）
comp. adv.	複合副詞	例）手近に
prep.	前置詞	例）beyond

●会話文登場人物

鈴木（夫）	Mr. S	鈴木家の夫・父	カレン	Karen	英語教師、鈴木家の友人
鈴木（妻）	Mrs. S	鈴木家の妻・母	マイク	Mike	会社員、鈴木家の友人
健太	Kenta	鈴木家の息子（大学生）	課長	Section Chief	会社員
さや	Saya	健太の友人	同僚	Colleague	会社員

What Are Metaphors?

The word *metaphor* in the title is derived from the Greek words *meta* and *pherein*, which together mean "to carry over; to transfer." *Metafaa*, used in the Japanese title, is derived from *metaphor* and employed as a general term that denotes all types of figurative expressions. While *metaphor* primarily refers to words or phrases used to represent something other than their literal meanings, considering that most figures of speech are metaphors, this word is often used in the more general sense of "a figurative expression."

Metaphors are expressions that take abstract concepts and phenomena that are difficult to put into words and transpose their meanings onto familiar objects, creatures, and other concrete matters, thereby making them easier to understand. One famous example is the line *Du bist wie eine Blume* (You are so like a flower) from the poem of the same name by German poet Heinrich Heine (1797-1856). The visual imagery and emotional force of this expression creates a more powerful effect than simply saying "you are very beautiful." Another example is "life is a journey," which distills the abstract concept of life into a simple expression. Both examples convey meanings that are presumably universal.

People employ metaphors almost unconsciously to ensure smooth communication and foster mutual understanding. And while these metaphors may have originated in different linguistic, cultural, and historical contexts, many of them are rooted in the same underlying concepts. Several find use in our daily lives as idiomatic expressions, while creative individuals such as poets and authors invent countless other original expressions as well. These original creations reflect the unique perceptions and expressive tendencies of their creators, which sets them apart from commonly used idiomatic expressions. However, whether they be idioms or personal inventions, it is clear that metaphors play an indispensable role in human communication.

This work focuses on the following six categories of common figurative expressions shared between English and Japanese.

1 Simile	An expression that uses *yō/mitai* in Japanese or *as/like* in English. There are many examples of this type of expression, and several of these share the same concept in both languages. **e.g** (as) black as coal ／炭のように黒い, (as) free as a bird ／鳥のように自由
2 Metaphor	An expression that uses concrete images to represent complex, abstract ideas and phenomena that are difficult to explain in words. ① Expressions that convey visual similarity **e.g** dog paddle ／犬かき = swimming like a dog cotton candy ／綿あめ = candy that looks like cotton ② Expressions that convey conceptual similarity **e.g** oil and water ／水と油 = having thoughts and personalities that don't match at all be on the same wavelength ／波長が合う = thinking and feeling the same way ③ Expressions that employ terms' literal meanings in figurative fashion **e.g** Flow of a river → airflow → flow of time The house is close → close in age → their ideas are close ④ Expressions that function both literally and figuratively **e.g** The river is {deep/shallow} / someone's thinking is {deep/shallow} The drink is {warm/cold} / someone's personality is {warm/cold}

3 Synecdoche	A figurative expression that is conveyed via a relationship of inclusion; that is, expressing the whole in terms of a part or a part in terms of the whole.

- *Flower viewing* expresses a part in terms of the whole, since *flower* is used to represent cherry blossoms specifically and not other flowers such as roses and lilies.
- *Man cannot live on bread alone* expresses the whole in terms of a part, since *bread* is used to represent all food, not just bread.

e.g. public eye ／公共の目, pots and pans ／鍋釜

4 Metonymy	An expression that represents the interior via the exterior or internal emotions via external gestures.

① *The kettle is boiling*: The kettle (the external container) is not itself boiling; rather, the water inside the kettle is boiling.

I ate a bowl (of something): One did not eat the bowl (the external container) itself, but rather the food inside the bowl.

e.g. new blood ／新しい血, head count ／頭数

② *Bite one's lip* = The external act of biting one's lip signifies internal frustration.

e.g. bite one's lip ／唇を噛む

Keep something on hand = The external act of keeping someone or something close by signifies the importance that one attaches to that person or thing. **e.g.** keep s.t. on hand ／手元に置く

5 Personification	Describes an expression in which human characteristics are assigned to a non-human entity.

e.g. Money talks. ／金がものを言う, neck of a bottle ／ビンの首
desk('s) legs ／机の脚, Time is a great healer. ／時がいやしてくれる

6 Synesthesia	Describes an expression rooted in a physical or sensory experience. Synesthesia is a psychological term that is related to the five human senses (sight, hearing, touch, taste, and smell).

e.g. Sweet voice ／甘い声 = This expression transfers the gustatory sensation of tasting something sweet and delicious to the auditory sensation of hearing a pleasant sound.

Bitter experience ／苦い経験 = This expression links the experience of tasting something bitter to the experience of enduring a difficult, distressing situation.

While this work focuses on English and Japanese expressions whose forms and meanings resemble one another, there are varying degrees of resemblance. Some entries are nearly identical, while others have slight differences in meaning and usage. These differences are addressed via the explanations and related expressions. Entries that are similar in form but different in meaning are treated as homographs. In addition, entries consist not only of idiomatic expressions, but also various types of proverbial expressions.

When studying a foreign language, it is common to focus on the differences between your native tongue and the language of study, but examining the similarities can greatly enhance language acquisition as well. Try treating this dictionary as reading material rather than simply as a reference. It is quite fascinating to learn just how much English and Japanese have in common, and the various examples and explanations provided are sure to enrich your language-learning experience. We hope this work improves your English and Japanese skills, deepens your linguistic knowledge, and helps you weave figurative expressions into your daily conversations.

Using the Dictionary

1) In this text, the English expressions and explanations are listed on the left, while the corresponding Japanese is listed on the right.
2) Entries are ordered according to the English alphabet. The Japanese entries can be looked up in the Japanese syllabary index.
3) The entries are divided into two categories: shared metaphorical expressions (695 pairs) and homographs (45 pairs).

[Shared Metaphorical Expressions]: English and Japanese expressions whose form, figurative meaning, and other elements resemble one another are considered "shared metaphorical expressions" and listed side by side. However, as there are often differences in meaning and usage arising from the differences in the languages, details pertaining to each entry are provided in the Notes section.

[Homographs]: English and Japanese expressions that resemble one another in form but not figurative meaning are considered "homographs" and listed side by side.

Main Entry: The metaphorical expression being examined.
Definition: The figurative meaning of the expression (as opposed to the literal meaning).
Examples: There are example dialogues and example sentences. The dialogues usually feature expressions that come up naturally in daily conversation, while the example sentences feature a variety of usages ranging from the topical to the philosophical.
Related Expressions: Related expressions include those that have the same meaning as the main entry and can replace it freely, expressions that can replace the main entry in certain situations, expressions with similar meanings but differences in nuance, and so on. Examples of usage are included as well.
Opposite Expressions: Expressions with meanings that are opposite that of the main entry. Examples of usage are included as well.

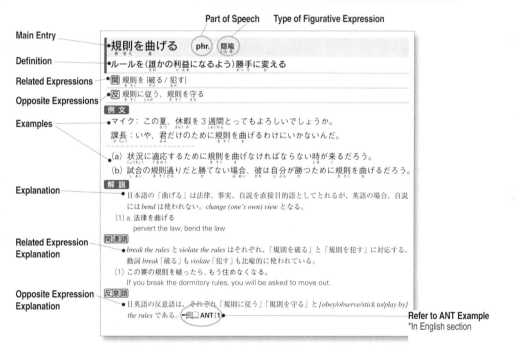

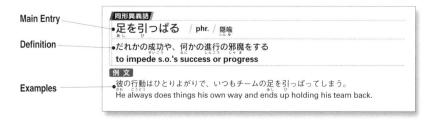

13

Usage Guide

● Abbreviations/Symbols

例 文	Japanese Examples
Examples	English Examples
解 説	Japanese Explanation
Notes	English Explanation
関 **関連語**	Japanese Related Expressions Related Expression Explanation/Examples
REL **REL**	English Related Expressions Related Expression Explanation/Examples
反 **反意語**	Japanese Opposite Expressions Opposite Expression Explanation/Examples
ANT **ANT**	English Opposite Expressions Opposite Expression Explanation/Examples
同形異義語	Japanese Homograph
homograph	English Homograph
➡📖 Note (**1**)	Refer to English Note Example (1)
➡📖 REL (**1**)	Refer to English REL Example (1)
➡📖 ANT (**1**)	Refer to English ANT Example (1)
📖➡解説 (**1**)	Refer to Japanese Note Example (1)
📖➡関連語 (**1**)	Refer to Japanese REL Example (1)
📖➡反意語 (**1**)	Refer to Japanese ANT Example (1)
s.t.	Something
s.o.	Someone
lit.	Literally
i.e.	id est (Latin for "that is")
×	Incorrect usage
?	Somewhat unnatural usage
??	Very unnatural usage
→ (a)	Refer to Example (a)
LOOK▶	Refer to the entry indicated

( ) used inside an English entry	Indicates prepositions and other elements that can be omitted e.g. (as) black as coal
( ) used inside a Japanese entry	Indicates particles and other elements that can be omitted e.g. (〜と)波長が合う
( ) used inside an explanation	Defines the preceding element e.g. *oriru* (come down),「インク」(ink)
" " used inside an explanation	Defines the preceding element
{ X/Y }	X or Y. Interchangeable

● Type Style

Italics	Indicates an English expression e.g. *break the rules*
Slanted	Indicates a Japanese expression e.g. *kisoku o mageru*

● Parts of Speech

phr.	Phrase	e.g. be all ears
n. phr.	Noun Phrase	e.g. blood, sweat, and tears
n.	Noun	e.g. chicken
v.	Verb	e.g. attack
comp. n.	Compound Noun	e.g. viewpoint
comp. v.	Compound Verb	e.g. bad-mouth
adj.	Adjective	e.g. breathtaking
adj. (i)	i-adjective	e.g. 冷たい
adj. (na)	na-adjective	e.g. 無神経(な)
adj. (i). phr.	i-adjective phrase	e.g. (〜に)弱い
adv.	Adverb	e.g. literally
adv. phr.	Adverb Phrase	e.g. by a nose
comp. adj.	Compound Adjective	e.g. deep-rooted
comp. adj. (i)	Compound i-adjective	e.g. 根深い
comp. adj. (na)	Compound na-adjective	e.g. 冷血(な)
comp. adv.	Compound Adverb	e.g. 手近に
prep.	Preposition	e.g. beyond

● Dialogue Characters

鈴木（夫）	Mr. S	Mr. Suzuki. Kenta's father and Mrs. Suzuki's husband	カレン	Karen	English teacher, friends with the Suzukis
鈴木（妻）	Mrs. S	Mrs. Suzuki. Kenta's mother and Mr. Suzuki's wife	マイク	Mike	Company employee, friends with the Suzukis
健太	Kenta	Son of Mr. and Mrs. Suzuki (college student)	課長	Section Chief	Company employee
さや	Saya	Kenta's friend	同僚	Colleague	Company employee

15

ABCs of ~, the / n. phr. / metaphor

(to know) the basics of s.t.

Examples

Saya: Kenta, can you show me how to work this computer?

Kenta: You know, these sorts of things are like the ABCs of using a computer.

Saya: You're pretty good with computers, aren't you?

Kenta: I suppose.

- -

(a) She doesn't even know the ABCs of dancing, yet she thinks she's a pro.

(b) That producer doesn't even know the ABCs of filmmaking.

Note

The English and the Japanese use the first three entries of the alphabet and the Japanese syllabary, respectively. The older *hiragana* arrangement (as opposed to the newer *A-I-U-E-O* order) is based on a poem traditionally ascribed to the Buddhist monk *Kūkai* (774-835). It goes like this: *I-RO-HA-NI-HO-HE-TO-CHI-RI-NU-RU-(W)O-WA-KA-YO-TA-RE-SO-TSU-NE-NA-RA-MU-U-(W)I-NO-O-KU-YA-MA-KE-FU-KO-E-TE-A-SA-KI-YU-ME-MI-SHI-(W)E-HI-MO-SE-SU.* The translation is as follows: "The colors blossom, scatter and fall. In this world of ours, who lasts forever? Today let us cross over the remote mountains of life's illusions, and dream no more shallow dreams nor succumb to drunkenness."

ache in one's heart / n. phr. / metaphor

psychological suffering

REL heartache

Examples

(a) The tears in my eyes I can wipe away, but the ache in my heart will always stay.

(b) Losing a child is the most painful tragedy a parent can suffer. There's a constant ache in my heart.

(c) After she broke up with her first love, she thought that the ache in her heart would never heal.

Note

The English sounds like it could describe either a mental or a physical condition, but the Japanese does not. This is because *heart* can mean either "the organ in one's chest that pumps blood" or "the seat of one's {thoughts/feelings}," whereas *kokoro* can only refer to the latter. To refer to physical pain in one's heart, one must use *shinzō no itami* (pain in the heart [organ]).

REL

1. The Sino-Japanese *shintsū* is used in formal written Japanese. 📖→ 関連語(1)
2. The English has the REL *heartache*.

A

（〜の）イロハ / phr. 隠喩（いんゆ）

何（なに）かの基本（きほん）を知（し）っている

例文

さや：健太（けんた）、ちょっとこのコンピュータの操作（そうさ）について、教（おし）えて。

健太（けんた）：あ、なんだ。こんなのコンピュータのイロハだよ。

さや：健太（けんた）はコンピュータが強（つよ）いわね。

健太（けんた）：まあね。

- -

（a）彼女（かのじょ）はダンスのイロハも知（し）らないのに、自分（じぶん）はダンスがうまいと思（おも）っている。

（b）そのプロデューサーは映画製作（えいがせいさく）のイロハも知（し）らない。

解説

日英語（にちえいご）はそれぞれアルファベットと平仮名（ひらがな）いろはにほへと…、の最初（さいしょ）の3文字（もじ）を使（つか）っている。新（あたら）しい平仮名（ひらがな）の順序（じゅんじょ）（あ－い－う－え－お）に対（たい）して、この古（ふる）い平仮名（ひらがな）の順序（じゅんじょ）は僧侶空海（そうりょくうかい）（774-835）の作（さく）とされている「いろは歌（うた）」に基（もと）づいている。この歌（うた）は「いろ（色）はにほ（匂）へとちり（散）りぬるをわか（我）よ（世）たれ（誰）そつね（常）ならむうゐ（有為）のおくやま（奥山）けふ（今日）こ（越）えてあさ（浅）きゆめ（夢）み（見）しゑひ（酔）もせす」である。

心（こころ）の痛（いた）み / n. phr. 隠喩（いんゆ）

心理的（しんりてき）な苦（くる）しみ

関 心痛（しんつう）

例文

（a）目（め）の涙（なみだ）はふくことができるが、心（こころ）の痛（いた）みはいつまでも残（のこ）る。

（b）子供（こども）を失（うしな）うことは親（おや）にとっては最（もっと）もつらい悲劇（ひげき）です。私（わたし）はいつまでも心（こころ）が痛（いた）みます。

（c）初恋（はつこい）が終（お）わってしまった後（あと）、彼女（かのじょ）は心（こころ）の痛（いた）みは決（けっ）して癒（い）えることはないと感（かん）じた。

解説

英語（えいご）は心身両面（しんしんりょうめん）のことを言（い）っているように聞（き）こえるが、日本語（にほんご）ではそうは聞（き）こえない。なぜならば、*heart* は"心臓（しんぞう）"と"心（こころ）"の二（ふた）つの意味（いみ）で使（つか）われるのに対（たい）して、日本語（にほんご）では気持（きも）ちを表（あらわ）す「心（こころ）」を使（つか）っていて、「心臓（しんぞう）の痛（いた）み」と言（い）えば"心臓器官（しんぞうきかん）の痛（いた）み"でしかないからである。

関連語

1．日本語（にほんご）には漢語系（かんごけい）の「心痛（しんつう）」という言葉（ことば）もあるが、これは堅（かた）い書（か）き言葉（ことば）として使（つか）われる。

（1）目（め）の涙（なみだ）はふくことができるが、｛心（こころ）の痛（いた）み / 心痛（しんつう）｝はいつまでも残（のこ）る。（→(a)）

2．英語（えいご）にも *heartache* という関連表現（かんれんひょうげん）がある。

17

Achilles' heel / comp. n. / metaphor

{s.o./s.t.}'s most vulnerable spot

Examples
- (a) His strong sense of responsibility is his Achilles' heel.
- (b) When it comes to America's prosperity, the international value of the dollar is most likely to be its Achilles' heel.
- (c) That politician's Achilles' heel is his pride. He gets very angry if anyone criticizes his behavior.

Notes
1. This phrase refers to Achilles, the hero of Homer's *Iliad*, whose only vulnerable spot was his heel. He killed Hector but was himself killed by Paris, who shot a poison arrow into the Greek warrior's heel.
2. The Japanese is very likely a translation of the English.

act of God, an / n. phr. / metaphor

an uncontrollable natural force

Examples
- (a) The defendant claimed the accident was "an act of god."
- (b) The fine print states that the insurance company doesn't have to pay if the disaster is "an act of god."

Note
The Japanese expression can be used to imply not only an uncontrollable natural force, but also divine powers. 📖→解説(1)

add fuel to the fire / phr. / metaphor

to do s.t. that worsens a situation

REL fan the flames; pour oil on the fire

Examples
Mr. S: The Tanakas are finally getting divorced.

Mrs. S: So I heard. And after all that advice you gave them!

Mr. S: Well, it looks like all I did was add fuel to the fire.

- (a) The mass media's sharp criticism of the terrorists only added fuel to the fire.
- (b) During the debate, the professor's critical remarks only added fuel to the fire.
- (c) The policemen tried to contain the riot, but they only ended up adding fuel to the fire.

A

（〜の）アキレス腱 n. phr. 隠喩

{人／組織}の一番の弱点

例文

(a) 彼のアキレス腱は責任感が強すぎるところだ。

(b) ドルの国際的価値が、アメリカの繁栄のアキレス腱になる可能性が最も大きい。

(c) その政治家のアキレス腱は自尊心だ。彼は自分の行動を批判されるとひどく腹をたててしまう。

解説

1. この表現の出所は、ホメロスの『イリアッド』に出てくるギリシャの英雄アキレスである。彼はかかと以外は弱点がなかった。ヘクトルを殺し、自分自身もパリスの毒矢にかかとを撃たれて死んだという。

2. 日本語は英語からの翻訳の可能性が高い。

神の仕業 n. phr. 隠喩

人間がコントロールできない自然の力の働き，人間を超えた能力

例文

(a) 弁護側は、その事故は神の仕業だと主張した。

(b) その細かい条項には、災害が「神の仕業」なら保険会社は支払う必要はないと書かれている。

解説

日本語の比喩的意味には英語のように、ただ"人間にコントロールできない自然の力"という意味だけでなく"神のような能力"という意味もある。

(1) モーツァルトの作った曲は神の仕業としか思えない。
Mozart's compositions are {divinely inspired/ˣan act of god}.

火に油を注ぐ phr. 隠喩

何かをすることで状況を悪化させる

例文

鈴木(夫)：田中君夫婦は結局、離婚することになったよ。

鈴木(妻)：そうらしいわね。せっかくあなたがいろいろ助言してあげたのに。

鈴木(夫)：う〜ん、どうもそれが火に油を注ぐ結果になってしまったようだね。

(a) マスコミの痛烈なテロ批判が、テロリストの活動の火に油を注ぐことになった。

(b) 教授の批判的なコメントで、論争の火に油が注がれた。

(c) 警官は乱闘の鎮圧をしようとしたが、かえって火に油を注ぐ結果となった。

19

Note

The components of the Japanese and English expressions are different: *add* versus *sosogu* (to pour) and *fuel* versus *abura* (oil). However, taken as a whole, each expression conveys the same figurative meaning.

REL

The English has two RELs: *fan the flames* and *pour oil on the fire*. The latter is much closer to the Japanese expression, but this English expression is used much less frequently than *add fuel to the fire*.

(1) During the debate, the professor's critical remarks only {added fuel to the fire/fanned the flames/poured oil on the fire}. (→ (b))

---

against the tide (of ~) phr. metaphor

to oppose that which is generally accepted

ANT ~ with the tide

Examples

Saya: So you're gonna vote for the Green Party, huh?

Kenta: Yep. You're not gonna get on my case, are you?

Saya: Of course not. If that's what you believe, then go for it.

Kenta: Thanks. It's not easy going against the tide of public opinion.

- - - - - - - - - - - - - - - - - -

(a) To implement health policies that favor the poor, it is necessary to swim against the tide of politics.

(b) His refusal to use computers goes against the tide of the times.

Notes

1. The verb before *against the tide (of ~)* is usually either *swim* or *go*, but other verbs such as *fight* are occasionally used as well. Among these verbs, *swim* is most frequently used because of its close association with *tide* in English. The noun *tide* can be replaced by *flow* or *current* while maintaining the same figurative meaning.

(1) Going against the {tide/flow/current} is never easy. It makes us look strange and out of step with the mainstream.
流れに逆らうことはとても不愉快なことです。変わり者で、主流からそれているように見えるからです。

2. In the Japanese, the verb is *sakarau* (vt., to go against).

ANT

The English ANT uses the preposition *with* instead of *against,* as shown in (1), and the Japanese ANT uses the verb phrase *saosasu* (to pole a boat). 📖➡ 反意語(**1**)

解 説

日英語の語構成は、*add*（加える）と「注ぐ」、*fuel*（燃料）と「油」で基本義が違うが、全体としての比喩の意味は同じである。

関連語

英語には、*fan the flames* と *pour oil on the fire* の2種類の関連表現がある。*pour oil on the fire* のほうが日本語の形にはるかに近いが、この表現は *add fuel to the fire* よりもはるかに使用頻度が低い。 ▬📖 REL (1)

流れに逆らう　phr.　隠喩

{一般的に認められている考え方 / 世論}に反対する

反 流れにさおさす

例 文

さや：緑の党に投票するの？

健太：うん。文句なんか言わないよね。

さや：もちろんよ。健太がいいと思っているんならそうしたらいいじゃない。

健太：どうもありがとう。世間の流れに逆らうって易しくないけどね。

(a) 貧しい人々に配慮した医療政策を実行するためには、政治の流れに逆らわなければならない。

(b) 彼は時代の流れに逆らって、コンピュータは一切使わない。

解 説

1. 英語の *against the tide (of ~)* の前に来る動詞は *swim* か *go* で、ときには *fight* となる。しかし *tide*（潮の流れ）との関連で、一番使用頻度が高い動詞は *swim*（泳ぐ）である。英語の名詞 *tide* は *flow*、*current* のいずれとも、同じ比喩的意味で置き換えられる。 ▬📖 Note (1)

2. 日本語の動詞は「逆らう」である。

反意語

英語の反意表現は前置詞 *against* が *with* になり、日本語の反意表現は動詞「逆らう」が「さおさす」に変わる。

(1) 流れにさおさすほうが常に安全だ。世の中と違うことをすれば、責任も、義務も、さらには問題まで出てきてしまう。

It is always safer to swim with the tide; being different may invite responsibility, accountability, and even trouble.

ahead of the times / phr. / metaphor

to do s.t. remarkable before everyone else

ANT behind the times

Examples

Mike: How was the meeting?

Colleague: Oh, you know, just the usual spiel from the department chief: "We need to develop merchandise that's ahead of the times!"

Mike: Figures.

(a) His research is always ahead of the times.

(b) Her designs were so ahead of the times that the general public wouldn't accept them.

(c) In order to stay ahead of the times, universities have to constantly improve their curriculum, research, and facilities.

Note

This is a case where a spatial expression is used metaphorically as a temporal expression. *Ahead* means "in a forward direction," and *saki* means "the end of a stick or stick-like object."

A N T

The English and Japanese ANTs are *behind the times* and *jidai {okure ni naru/ni okureru}*, respectively. 📖─ 反意語(1)

alarm, {an/the} / n. / metaphor

a warning

Examples

(a) The politician sounded the alarm over rising levels of intolerance among citizens.

(b) The report about the presence of 1.2 billion homeless throughout the world should set off alarm bells in every community.

(c) Global warming is making people sound the alarm on how we produce and use energy.

Notes

1. The verb that goes with *alarm* is *sound*, and the verb that goes with *kēshō* is *narasu* (vt., to sound).

2. *Kēshō* is a Sino-Japanese compound that means "alarm bell."

A

時代の{先 / 先端}を行く　　phr.　隠喩

誰よりも早く何か驚くべきことをし始める

反 時代遅れになる，時代に遅れる

例文

マイク：会議、どうだった？

同僚：いつもと同じ部長の訓示。時代の先端を行く商品開発を心がけろって。

マイク：相変わらずだね。

- (a) 彼の研究はいつも時代の {先 / 先端} を行っている。
- (b) 彼女のデザインは、当時は時代の {先 / 先端} を行き過ぎていて、一般の人には受け入れられなかった。
- (c) 時代の {先 / 先端} を行くために、大学はカリキュラム、研究内容、研究設備を改善しなければなりません。

解説

この表現は、空間表現が比喩的に時間表現として使われている。日本語の「先」と英語の *ahead* は、それぞれ、"棒(のようなもの)の先端の部分"と"前方"を意味する。

反意語

日英語の反意表現は、それぞれ、「時代 {遅れになる / に遅れる}」と *behind the times* である。

- (1) 今の時代はよほど注意していないと時代{遅れになって / に遅れて}しまう。
  It's important not to fall behind the times.

警鐘　　comp. n.　隠喩

警告をすること

例文

- (a) 政治家は市民の寛容さが下がってきていると警鐘を鳴らしている。
- (b) 世界に 12 億のホームレスの人々がいることにどのコミュニティも警鐘を鳴らすべきだ。
- (c) 地球温暖化はエネルギーの生産法や使い方に警鐘を鳴らしている。

解説

1. 例文にあるように、「警鐘」は動詞「鳴らす」と一緒に使われ、*alarm* は動詞 *sound* と一緒に使われることが多い。
2. 「警鐘」は漢語系複合語で、英語の *alarm bell* に当たる。

23

all eyes are on ~ / phr. / metaphor

everybody is paying attention to {s.o./s.t.}

Examples

(a) All eyes were on you when you walked out on stage in the final round of the beauty pageant.

(b) With the fate of its economy hanging in the balance, all eyes appear to be on Japan.

(c) All eyes were on Washington D.C. as the new leaders took office.

Note

The English uses the verb *be*, while the Japanese uses the verb *sosogareru*, which is the passive form of *sosogu* (to pour).

All roads lead to Rome. / phr. / metaphor

no matter what method one uses, the result will be the same

Examples

(a) There are about ten ways to solve this math problem, so it doesn't matter which method you use. As they say, "All roads lead to Rome."

(b) There are all sorts of ways to attain proficiency in a foreign language. In the end, all roads lead to Rome.

Notes

1. This proverb was originally written by La Fontaine, a French poet (1621–1695), in his *The Fables* (1668). Both the English and the Japanese are translations of this French proverb.

2. The Japanese verb *tsūzu* is an archaic form of *tsūjiru* (vi., to lead to ~).

homograph

along the same lines / phr. / metaphor

in the same way
同じように

Example

He and I were thinking along the same lines with regards to the plan.
彼と私はその計画に関して同じように考えていた。

（〜に）すべての目が注がれる　phr.　隠喩

誰もが{誰か / 何か}に注意を払っている

例文

（a）あなたがミスコンテストの最終ラウンドでステージに出てきたとき、すべての人の目があなたに注がれたんですよ。

（b）日本の経済状況はどうなのだろうか。すべての目が日本に注がれているようだ。

（c）新しい指導者たちが仕事につき、すべての目が首都ワシントンに注がれた。

解説

英語の動詞は be だが、日本語の「注がれる」は「注ぐ」の受け身形である。

すべての道はローマに通ず　phr.　隠喩

どのような手段を取っても結果は同じだ

例文

（a）この数学の問題の解答法は 10 ぐらいある。だから、どの解答法を使おうとかまわない。「すべての道はローマに通ず」、というわけだ。

（b）「すべての道はローマに通ず」と言うように、外国語の上達には色々な方法があるのです。

解説

1．このことわざは、もともとはフランスの詩人ジャン・ド・ラ・フォンテーヌ（1621-1695）が『寓話』（1668）の中に書いたものである。日英語ともにそのフランス語からの翻訳である。

2．日本語の動詞「通ず」は「通じる」の文語体である。

同形異義語

{同一線上に / 同じ線で}ある　phr.　隠喩

同じ主義や考えを持つ, 同じことである
to have the same idea; for s.t. to be the same

例文

地球温暖化と自然災害の増加を同一線上で語る人は多いが、あまり関連がないという説を唱える学者もいる。

Many people think global warming and the rising frequency of natural disasters are closely related, but there are also scholars who claim that they aren't related.

attack / v. / metaphor

to strongly criticize {s.o./s.t.}

Examples

Mr. S: The media attacked him pretty harshly because of his alleged infidelity, right?

Mike: True, but he managed to neutralize the attacks and leave behind an impressive presidential legacy.

- -

(a) The students sharply attacked the school administration's unfair policies.

(b) Though the country's development of new nuclear weapons was attacked by the rest of the world, it refused to change course.

Notes

1. The basic meaning of both *attack* and *kōgeki-suru* is "for someone to use physical force against {s.o./s.t.}," and both can be used figuratively to mean "to strongly criticize {s.o./s.t.}."

2. The Sino-Japanese compound for *attack* is 攻撃 (*kōgeki*), but when it means "to attack {s.o./s.t.} verbally," it is sometimes written as 口撃. The pronunciation is the same, but the meaning changes to "mouth + attack." This visual pun results from the use of homophonous *kanji* with different meanings. Another example is 痛勤 (*tsūkin*, "painful commuting") being used instead of 通勤 (*tsūkin*, commuting).

awake to ~ / phr. / metaphor

to realize the value or necessity of s.t. for the first time

REL be awakened to ~; wake up to ~

Examples

Karen: You know, recently I've actually started to like natto.

Mike: Really? I still can't stand it. I guess you've finally awoken to the appeal of the Japanese palate, huh?

- -

(a) I've always enjoyed playing the piano, but lately I've awoken to the joys of teaching others how to play.

(b) Ever since Asia awoke to the importance of science, it has made enormous progress.

Note

Mezameru is a compound verb derived from *me* (eye) and *sameru* (to wake up) that is mainly used in written Japanese. Likewise, in English, *awake* is used primarily in written language and is usually replaced by *wake up* in spoken language. 📖→ REL(1)

REL

In English, *be awakened to ~* is often used as well.

(1) In my junior year of college, I {awoke/was awakened/woke up} to the fact that there was a lot about Japan I did not know.

大学3年生のときに、日本についてほとんど知らないということに {気づいた/ ˟目覚めた}。

A

攻撃する　/ v.　隠喩

相手を強く非難する

例 文

鈴木（夫）：彼は、不倫疑惑でメディアに激しく攻撃されたね。

マイク：ええ、でもその攻撃をかわしきって、最も有能な大統領の一人になりましたね。

- -

（a）学生たちは学校側の不公平なやり方を鋭く攻撃した。

（b）新たな核開発に関して各国の攻撃を受けたにも関わらず、その国は方針を改めることはなかった。

解 説

1．「攻撃する」と *attack* の基本義はいずれも "{誰か}が{誰か／何か}に物理的な力を行使する" だが、両方とも "相手を強く非難する" という比喩的意味も持っている。

2．「攻撃」は「口撃」と書かれることもあるが、これは漢字の同音異義語を使った視覚的洒落の例である。「通勤」をもじった「痛勤」もその一例である。

目覚める　/ comp. v.　隠喩

何かの価値や必要性にはじめて気がつく

関 目が覚める

例 文

カレン：私、最近、納豆が好きになってきてね。

マイク：え、うそ。僕はまだだめだな。カレンはついに日本の味に目覚めたってわけだね。

- -

（a）私は長年ピアノを弾くのを楽しんできたが、最近、人に弾き方を教えるのもおもしろいということに目覚めた。

（b）アジアが科学の重要性に目覚めて以来、その後の進歩は大変速かった。

解 説

日本語の「目覚める」は「目」＋「覚める」の複合動詞で、主に書き言葉で用いられる表現である。英語でも *awake* は書き言葉的で、話し言葉では *wake up* となる。　REL**(1)**

関連語

英語では *awake to ~* と並んで *be awakened to ~* もよく使われる。　REL**(1)**

27

baby talk / comp. n. / metaphor

speech used by babies or very young children

Example

My six-year-old daughter still uses baby talk. I am worried that she will be laughed at in elementary school.

~ back / comp. v. / metaphor

to respond to s.o.'s action with the same action

Examples

Mrs. S: I was watching a program about a school visit on TV today, and it really surprised me. Today's students have no qualms about talking back to the teacher, it seems.

Kenta: You've got that right.

- - - - - - - - - - - - - - - - - - - -

(a) Never hit your child back just because he hits you. This teaches children that using violence is okay.

(b) Large black eyes stared back at me angrily.

Notes

1. In both English and Japanese, the spatial terms *back* and *kaesu* (to cause {s.t./s.o.} to move back to its original location) are used figuratively to mean "to respond to s.o.'s action with the same action."

2. In English, some psychological verbs such as *hate* and *love* can be used with *back*, but in Japanese, these verbs cannot be used with *kaesu*.

(1) a. His eyes shone with hate, and for an instant I hated him back.
   彼は目で私に憎しみを表した。瞬間私は彼を{憎んだ/[×]憎み返した}。
   b. She loved me, and I loved her back.
   彼女は私を愛してくれ、私も彼女を{愛した/[×]愛し返した}。

3. *Kaesu* is mainly used when the repeated action is a negative one. 📖→解説(2)

4. *Back* is an adverb that is typically used with verbs such as *hit* (as shown in [a]), *stare* (as shown in [b]), *swear*, *talk*, and *answer*, among others. By contrast, *kaesu* can be used not only with communication-related verbs, but also regular verbs. 📖→解説(3)
   Additionally, the verb used in the verbal compound must be a reciprocal verb. That is why *tabe-kaesu*, *utai-kaesu*, and *asobi-kaesu* are all unacceptable.

back / n. / personification

the part of a seat supporting the back

Example

Piano players usually sit on benches that don't have backs.

28

赤ちゃん言葉 /n. phr. | 隠喩

赤ちゃんや幼児の（甘えたような）話し方

例文

うちの娘は、6歳になってもまだ赤ちゃん言葉で話している。小学校に行ってみんなに笑われるのではないかと心配だ。

～返す comp. v. | 隠喩

相手から受けた行為に対して同じ行為をこちらからする

例文

鈴木（妻）：今日、学校訪問のテレビ見てて、驚いたわ。最近の子は先生に平気で言い返すのね。

健太：ほんとにそうだね。

(a) 子供に殴られたからといって殴り返してはいけません。そんなことをすれば暴力をふるってもかまわないと子供に教えることになるからです。

(b) 大きな黒い目が怒って私をにらみ返した。

解説

1. 日英語とも、「返す」と *back*（うしろの空間へ）という空間的な表現が、"誰かが行った行為と同じ行為を繰り返す"という比喩的な意味で使われている。

2. 英語では *hate* や *love* といった心理的な動詞が *back* と結びつくが、日本語ではこのような動詞は「返す」とは結びつかない。 ➡📖 Note (1)

3. 日本語では「返す」は好ましくない行為に対して使われることが多い。

(2) 私は大勢の人にほめられましたが、その人たち{のこともほめました/ ?にもほめ返しました}。
A lot of people praised me, and I praised them back.

4. 英語の *back* は、(a) の *hit*、(b) の *stare* のほか、*swear*、*talk*、*answer* などと使われる副詞であるが、日本語の「返す」はそれ以外の動詞とも結び付き反復行為を表現する場合もある。

(3) その本を何度も読み返した。
I read the book again and again.
また、この動詞複合語で使われる動詞は「相互性」がある動詞に限られているので、「食べ返す」「歌い返す」「遊び返す」などはすべて×となる。

（椅子の）背（もたれ） n. phr. | 擬人化

椅子の背中をもたせかける部分

例文

ピアノを演奏するときは、ふつう背もたれのない椅子に座る。

backroom ~ comp. n. / metaphor

s.t. done in secret (and sometimes illegally) by influential persons

REL backroom politics

Examples

(a) Backroom dealings often involve money.

(b) That man never agrees to any kind of backroom deal.

(c) In every society, there is always some degree of backroom dealings in business and politics.

Notes

1. In English and Japanese, *back* and *ura* are used figuratively to refer to unexposed, invisible, dark, or secretive spaces in which some activity (often illegal) occurs.
2. In Japanese, *ura-torihiki* (lit. "back-dealing") is used; *ura-beya no torihiki* is incorrect.

REL

Both English and Japanese also have the expression *backroom politics*, which means "politics that is done in secret."

bad apple comp. n. / metaphor

a person who is a bad influence on others

Example

He's a bad apple. His lazy attitude has a bad influence on other members of the staff.

bad dream, a comp. n. / metaphor

s.t. terrible that s.o. experiences

REL nightmare

Examples

Saya: Kenta, did you hear? Apparently our econ professor is really strict and gives out a lot of Fs.

Kenta: Are you serious? If I get any more Fs, I won't be able to graduate. This whole situation's like some bad dream...

Saya: You'll be fine. There's still time. You'll just have to work hard.

- -

(a) I was all alone during the storm last night. All that unbelievable thunder and rain and wind—it was like a bad dream or something.

(b) When we lost our home to flooding last year, it was like a bad dream. We had nowhere to go until my aunt finally took us in.

Note

The non-Sino-Japanese form of the Sino-Japanese compound *akumu* (*aku* [evil] + *mu* [dream]) is *warui yume* (bad dream). However, *warui yume* is not often used metaphori-

裏取り引き / comp. n. 隠喩

大物の隠れた（時に非合法な）取り引き

関 密室政治

例文

(a) 裏取引というものには、たいていお金が絡むものだ。

(b) 彼はぜったい裏取り引きには応じない人だ。

(c) 人間の社会では、ビジネス界と政界との何らかの裏取り引きが常につきものだ。

解説

1. 日英語ともに「裏」/back が、人に見えない、暗い、秘密の空間を示す場所、あるいは秘密裏に（時に非合法に）事が行われる空間として比喩的に使われている。

2. 日本語では通例「裏取り引き」と言い、英語のように「裏部屋の取り引き」とは言えない。

関連語

日英語ともに、見えない部屋で政治がひそかに行われることを意味する「密室政治」ということばがある。

腐ったリンゴ / n. phr. 隠喩

周りに悪影響を与える人

例文

彼は腐ったリンゴだ。あのやる気のない態度がまわりの社員にも悪影響を及ぼしている。

悪夢 / comp. n. 隠喩

誰かが経験する恐ろしいこと

例文

さや：健太、聞いた？　経済学の教授、厳しいから不可をいっぱい出すらしいよ。

健太：えっ、これ以上不可もらったら、卒業できなくなっちゃう。悪夢だよ。

さや：まだ時間があるから、がんばれば大丈夫よ。

- -

(a) ゆうべはたった一人で嵐の真っ直中にいた。信じられないような雷や雨や風で、まるで悪夢のようだった。

(b) 去年、洪水で家を失った時は、悪夢のようだった。おばが私達を引き取ってくれるまで、どこにも行くところがなかった。

解説

「悪夢」の非漢語表現は「悪い夢」であるが、この表現は比喩的な意味ではあまり使われない。

関連語

英語の関連表現は nightmare（night（夜）+ mare（妖魔））で、日本語では「悪夢」か「夢魔」に当たる。意味としては bad dream よりも悪い夢である。 ▶📖REL（1） cally.

REL

The English REL, *nightmare* (*night* + *mare* [spirit]), corresponds to *akumu* or *muma* (*mu* [dream] + *ma* [devil/evil]) in Japanese. Note that *nightmare* is considered worse than a bad dream, as shown in (1).

(1) Last year's bad dream has become this year's nightmare.
去年の悪夢が今年の夢魔になった。

bad-mouth / comp. v. / metonymy

to say malicious things about s.o. else behind {his/her} back

REL have a foul mouth; have a {sharp/spiteful/malicious} tongue

Examples

Karen: Hey Saya, did you hear Kenta failed his econ exam?

Kenta: Hey guys!

Saya: O-oh, hey Kenta! What's up?

Kenta: Why'd you guys suddenly stop talking? You weren't bad-mouthing me, were you?

Karen: Guilty as charged! Guess we can't fool you, huh?

- -

(a) Tom bad-mouthed Billy to all his friends.

Note

This structure can take the form of *bad-mouth s.o. to s.o. else* and *dareka no waru-kuchi o hoka no hito ni iu*, as shown in (a).

REL

1. The English RELs are *have a foul mouth*, which means "often uses foul language," and *have a {sharp/spiteful/malicious} tongue*, which means "prone to bad-mouthing others."

(1) That child has such a foul mouth. Where did he learn those bad words?
あの子はしょっちゅう汚い言葉を話している。どこでこんな言葉を覚えたのだろう？

(2) Mary has such a spiteful tongue. She's always saying mean things about people she doesn't like.
マリは本当に口が悪いわよね。好きじゃない人について悪口ばっかりだし。

2. The Japanese REL is *kuchi ga warui*, which means "prone to speaking harshly about {people/things}." 📖→関連語(3)

bad name / comp. n. / metaphor

a bad reputation

Examples

(a) A few rowdy fans give ice hockey a bad name.

(b) That movie really gives Wall Street a bad name.

B

悪口を言う / phr. 換喩
わるくち い かんゆ

他人について悪意のあることを直接ではなく陰で言う
たにん あくい ちょくせつ かげ い

関 口が悪い
くち わる

例文

カレン：ね、さや、健太が経済学のテスト、不合格だったって聞いた？
けんた けいざいがく ふごうかく き

健太：おっす！
けんた

さや：あら、健太、元気？
けんた げんき

健太：なんだよ。急に話やめちゃって。もしかして、僕の悪口を言ってた？
けんた きゅう はなし ぼく わるくち い

カレン：よくわかったわね。くしゃみしてたでしょ。

- -

（a）トムはビリーの悪口を友達みんなに言った。
わるくち ともだち い

解説

この表現は(a)のように、「誰かの悪口を他の人に言う」 *bad-mouth s.o. to s.o. else* となること
がある。

関連語

1. 英語の関連表現として *have a foul mouth*（しょっちゅう汚い言葉を使う）と *have a {sharp/ spiteful/malicious} tongue*（{鋭い/悪意に満ちた/意地の悪い}言葉を人に使いがちだ）という意味の表現がある。→📖 **REL(1)(2)**

2. 日本語には関連表現として"人や物に関してきつく言いがちだ"という意味の「口が悪い」という表現がある。

（3）彼女はひどく口が悪いから、あまり気にしない方がいいよ。
She has quite a sharp tongue. Try not to let it get to you.

汚名 comp. n. 隠喩
おめい いんゆ

不名誉
ふめいよ

関 悪名
あくめい

例文

（a）一部のあばれ者のファン達が、アイスホッケーに汚名を着せてしまった。
いちぶ もの たち おめい き

（b）その映画のせいでウォール・ストリートは汚名を着せられた。
えいが おめい き

33

Note

Omē can be used when describing criminal behavior, such as in *satsujinhan no omē o kiserareru* (to be branded a murderer). 📖—解説(1)

REL

The Japanese has the REL *akumē*, which means "bad reputation." It can be used in expressions such as *akumē ga takai* (notorious) and *akumē ga todoroku* (to be considered notorious). ×*Omē ga takai* and ×*akumē o kiserareru* cannot be used. 📖—関連語(1)

---

bald mountain   comp. n.   metaphor

a mountain that lacks trees and plants

Example

Due to fewer trees being planted, the number of bald mountains has increased, which has resulted in a higher frequency of landslides.

---

bare bones of ~, the   n. phr.   metaphor

the essential parts of s.t.

REL core

Examples

(a) Don't tell me every detail. Just tell me the bare bones of the story.

(b) It appears that the two countries have not agreed on how to make the bare bones of the treaty public.

(c) Explain the bare bones of your thesis to me.

Note

Bones is used metaphorically in English and Japanese to mean "the essential parts of s.t." The adjective *bare* in the English emphasizes the existence of only the essentials. The Japanese refers only to *kosshi*, or bones.

REL

The RELs *core* and *kakushin* can be used instead of *bare bones* and *kosshi*, respectively.

(1) Don't tell me every detail. Just tell me the {bare bones/core} of the story.
細部をくどくど言わなくていい。話の {骨子／核心} を知りたいだけなんだ。(→(a))

---

bare one's teeth（牙をむく）→ {show/bare} one's teeth

Barking dogs {never/seldom} bite.   phr.   metaphor

s.o. who makes a lot of threats rarely acts on them

Examples

Saya: Why's he always yelling at us? He's so scary.

Kenta: Barking dogs never bite, you know. I bet you he's actually a coward.

解説

日本語の見出し「汚名」は、「殺人犯の汚名を着せられる」などのように犯罪性のある場合にも使われる。

(1) 私は何もしていないにも関わらず、殺人犯の汚名を着せられた。
I've been branded a murderer even though I'm innocent.

関連語

日本語の関連表現に「悪名」がある。「悪名」は"悪い評判"という意味で、「悪名が高い」「悪名がとどろく」のように使われる。「[×]汚名が高い」「[×]汚名を着せられる」とは言えない。

(1) 日本で最も {悪名 / [×]汚名} の高い泥棒は、石川五右衛門である。
Ishikawa Goemon is the most infamous thief in Japanese history.

禿げ山　/ comp. n.　隠喩

草木が生えていない山

例文

植樹を怠ったため、禿げ山が増えて、山崩れの被害も増大した。

骨子　/ n.　隠喩

要点，一番大事な部分

関 核心

例文

(a) 細部をくどくど言わなくていい。話の骨子を知りたいだけなんだ。
(b) その条約の骨子の公表については、両国の意見が一致しないようだ。
(c) あなたの論文の骨子を私に説明してください。

解説

日英語の共通項は「骨」で、"主要な部分"という比喩的意味になっている。英語の形容詞の *bare*（むき出しの）は本質的要素のみを強調するために使われている。日本語の「骨子」は骨を指しているにすぎない。

関連語

日英語とも、「核心」と *core* という関連表現があり、自由に置き換えることができる。

➡️ REL (1)

吠える犬は噛まない　/ phr.　隠喩

強がった口をきく人はかえって怖くない

例文

さや：あの人、いつも怒鳴ってて、ほんと、怖いね。
健太：「吠える犬は噛まない」ってね。案外、臆病で気が弱いかも。

(a) The saying "barking dogs never bite" is true. It's the ones who don't bark who are the most dangerous.

(b) He's always yelling, but barking dogs seldom bite, you know.

Notes

1. The Japanese version of the proverb is most likely borrowed from English.
2. The English uses *never/seldom*, but the Japanese does not need to use *kesshite ~ nai* or *mettani ~ nai*.

be a fetter on ~   *phr.*   metaphor

to restrain s.t.

REL   be a shackle on ~

Examples

(a) They opposed the expansion of slavery, but only because it was a fetter on the development of capitalism.

(b) This country's constitution will end up being a fetter on its development.

(c) The current exchange rate is a fetter on business development.

Note

In Japanese, the particle *to* sounds more formal and is more likely to be used in written-Japanese than *ni*. 📖→解説(1)

REL

In English, *fetter* can be replaced by *shackle* without a change in meaning. It should be noted, however, that neither the main entry nor the REL appears to be used very frequently.

(1) They opposed the expansion of slavery, but only because it was a {fetter/shackle} on the development of capitalism. (→(a))

be a litmus test for ~   *phr.*   metaphor

s.t. that reveals the true nature of {s.t./s.o.}

Examples

(a) Emergencies such as terrorist attacks and natural disasters are a litmus test for the competency of the government.

(b) The ability to attract talent is a litmus test for the health of a company.

(c) Up through about the 80s, college was a litmus test for a person's ability to think.

Notes

1. In Japanese, the expression *ritomasu-shikenshi* (litmus paper) is used, as opposed to *ritomasu-shiken* (litmus test).
2. The Japanese is most likely a translation of *litmus test*.

(a) 「吠える犬は噛まない」ということわざは正しい。歯をむき出しにしない人が一番危険かもしれないのだ。

(b) 彼はいつも怒鳴っているけれど、吠える犬はめったに噛まないんだよね。

解説

1. 日本語は英語からの翻訳の可能性が高い。

2. 英語では *[never/seldom]* を使うが、日本語では「決して〜ない」「めったに〜ない」はなくてもよい。

（〜の）足かせ{に / と}なる　phr.　隠喩

何かを束縛するものになる

例文

(a) 彼らは奴隷制度の拡大に反対したが、その理由はそれが資本主義の発展の足かせとなったからである。

(b) この国の憲法はこの国の将来の発展の足かせとなるだろう。

(c) 現在の為替レートは商業発展の足かせとなっている。

解説

日本語の助詞の「と」は「に」より書き言葉的である。

(1) 現在の為替レートは商業発展の足かせ{と / に}なっている。(→(c))

関連語

英語では *fetter* を *shackle* に置き換えても意味は変わらないが使用頻度は低い。━📖REL(1)

（〜の）リトマス試験紙（だ）　phr.　隠喩

{誰か / 何か}の本性を明らかにするもの

例文

(a) テロや自然災害などの緊急事態は、政府の能力を試すリトマス試験紙となる。

(b) 才能ある人を引き込む力は、会社の活力のリトマス試験紙だ。

(c) 80年代までは、大学は人間の思考力のリトマス試験紙だった。

解説

1. 日本語は「リトマス試験」ではなく「リトマス試験紙」を使う。

2. 日本語は英語からの翻訳の可能性が高い。

be a puppet / phr. / metaphor

to be s.o. who does what {he/she} is told to do by {s.o. else/an organization} behind {him/her}

Examples

Mr. S: This governor is a puppet of the local business community. He's like putty in their hands.

Mrs. S: I agree. He doesn't listen to the people at all.

(a) Was the Emperor the mastermind behind the war in the Pacific, or was he merely a puppet?

(b) Humankind was not merely a puppet of the Creator, but was given free will and the ability to make decisions.

Note

Both the English and Japanese often co-occur with *merely* or ~ *ni suginai* (merely), but they can be used without these words, as shown in the dialogue and (b).

be a wolf in sheep's clothing / phr. / metaphor

for {s.o./s.t.} to look {gentle/beneficial} but be {scary/harmful} in reality

Examples

(a) John is as charming as they come. But if ever there was a wolf in sheep's clothing, this man is it.

(b) Someone who seems altruistic could very well be a wolf in sheep's clothing.

(c) It took seven years before I realized that the lawyer was really a wolf in sheep's clothing.

Notes

1. *Hitsuji no kawa o kabutta ōkami* (a wolf covering its body with sheep's skin) is slightly different from the English in that *skin* is used instead of *clothing*. *A wolf in sheep's skin* and *hitsuji no koromo o kita ōkami* (a wolf wearing sheep's clothing) are also used, albeit quite rarely.

2. In English, the metaphor is applicable not only to people, but also inanimate objects. The Japanese, however, is used only in reference to people.

(1) This treaty is a wolf in sheep's clothing.
    この条約は{見せ掛け/ˣ羊の皮をかぶった狼}だ。

3. Both the English and Japanese come from the New Testament of the Bible: "Beware of false prophets, which come to you in sheep's clothing, but inwardly they are ravening wolves" (Matthew 7:15).

操り人形（だ） / comp. n. / 隠喩

人や組織の言いなりになって行動する人

例文

鈴木（夫）：今度の知事は、まったく地元経済界の操り人形だね。彼らの言いなりだ。

鈴木（妻）：ほんと、私達市民のことはそっちのけよね。

(a) 天皇は大平洋戦争の指導者だったのか、それとも操り人形にすぎなかったのだろうか。

(b) 人間はただ創造主の操り人形だったわけではない。自由意志と決断する能力を与えられたのだ。

解説

この表現は「〜にすぎない」と *merely* が共に使われることが多いが、会話例や(b)のように省略することもできる。

羊の皮をかぶった狼 / n. phr. / 隠喩

外見はやさしそうに見えるけれど、本当は怖い人

例文

(a) ジョンはどこから見ても魅力がある。しかし、羊の皮をかぶった狼がいるとしたら、この男こそそうだ。

(b) 利他的な人が、実は羊の皮をかぶった狼であるということはあり得る。

(c) 私が信用していた弁護士が、実は羊の皮をかぶった狼だったことがわかるのに、7年もかかってしまった。

解説

1. 日本語では「皮」(skin)を使うのに対して英語では *clothing*（衣）を用いる点が異なっているが、日本語でも「皮」を「衣」にした「羊の衣を着た狼」といった例が、また英語でも *clothing* を *skin* にした *a wolf in sheep's skin* といった例が、それぞれ稀にみられる。
2. 英語は人間だけでなく無生物にも使えるが、日本語は人間に限られている。 ➡📖 **REL(1)**
3. 日英語とも新訳聖書(マタイ伝 7:15)の「にせ預言者に警戒せよ。彼らは羊の皮を着てあなたがたのところに来るが、その内側は強欲な狼である」が出典である。

| homograph |

be afraid of one's own shadow / phr. / metaphor

to be easily or frequently scared
すぐに、簡単に不安を感じる

| Example |

My brother hates haunted houses—he's afraid of his own shadow.
弟は、とても怖がり屋なのでお化け屋敷が大嫌いだ。

be all ears / phr. metaphor

to be eager to listen to {s.t./s.o.}

| Examples |

(a) When the famous businessman started talking about how he became successful, everyone was all ears.

(b) When the guy I liked started talking about the type of girl he likes, I was all ears.

(c) When our teacher said that he had exciting news, we were all ears.

| Notes |

1. The English and Japanese expressions are different in form, but identical in metaphorical meaning: "to be eager to listen to {s.t./s.o.}." The difference is that in English, one *is all ears*, whereas in Japanese, one causes one's entire body to become ears.

2. The Japanese can take the form of *zenshin o mimi ni shite kiku*, where *kiku* means "to listen to ~," as shown in (b) and (c).

3. The English is used to indicate strong interest in what someone is about to say.
   (1) Hey, tell me about your trip. I'm all ears.
   ねえ、旅行どうだった？ {すごく聞きたいな。/ ˣ私は全身を耳にするわ。}

4. The Japanese can be used when one listens attentively to something, such as noise or music. 📖—解説(2)

be an antidote to ~ / phr. metaphor

for s.t. to be a solution to s.t. negative

| Examples |

(a) Laughter is an antidote to apprehension.

(b) Exercise is an antidote to depression.

(c) Knowledge is the antidote to fear.

| Note |

In the English, if the preposition *to* is replaced by *for*, the phrase is very seldom used metaphorically.

(1) This injection is an antidote for scorpion poison.
この注射は、サソリの毒の解毒剤です。

同形異義語

（〜の）影におびえる　/ phr. / 隠喩

衝撃的な経験のために {誰か / 何か} に恐れを抱く
to fear {s.o./s.t.} that has caused a traumatic experience

例文

武は、いじめっこの影におびえて、学校を休むようになってしまった。
Takeshi is so afraid of the bully that he stopped going to school.

全身を耳にする　phr.　隠喩

何かを熱心に聞く

例文

(a) 著名なビジネスマンが、どうやって成功したかについて話し出したとき、人々は全身を耳にした。

(b) 憧れの人が、好きな女性のタイプについて話し出したとき、私は全身を耳にして聞いた。

(c) 先生が「すごいニュースがあるよ」と言ったとき、僕達は全身を耳にして聞いていた。

解説

1. 英語と日本語とでは形は違うが "誰かが何かを熱心に聞く" という意味は同じである。英語が be all ears（人が耳だけになる）であるのに対して、日本語は「全身を耳にする」という点で異なる。

2. 日本語は (b)(c) のように「全身を耳にして聞く」という形になることがある。

3. 英語では、誰かがこれから話す事に強い興味がある時に使う。　Note(1)

4. 日本語では物音や音楽などを、注意深く熱心に聞くときにも使用できる。

(2) 夜中に外で物音がしたので、全身を耳にした。
I heard a noise outside at night, so I pricked up my ears.

（〜の）解毒剤（だ）　phr.　隠喩

何かが何か悪いものやことの解決法になる

例文

(a) 笑いは心配の解毒剤だ。

(b) 体を動かすことは、落ちこんだ時の解毒剤です。

(c) 知識は恐怖の解毒剤です。

解説

英語の前置詞の to を for に変えると比喩的解釈は非常にまれになる。　Note(1)

{be/go} beyond a joke   *phr.*   **metaphor**

for s.t. to stop being funny and become a serious matter

Examples

(a) I thought it was beyond a joke that they got married the day after they met, but I guess some things are just meant to be.

(b) The audience may have loved his talk, but it was extreme and went beyond a joke at points, and some people were undoubtedly hurt.

Note

Both the English and Japanese use a spatial term: the preposition *beyond* in the English and a verb *sugiru* (to go beyond a point) in the Japanese. Both share the figurative meaning of a joke that goes beyond the territory acceptable for an ordinary joke.

REL

In Japanese, there is the related expression *jōdan ni mo hodo ga aru* (even jokes have limits), which can replace *jōdan ga sugiru* without changing the meaning.

be born under a lucky star   *phr.*   **metaphor**

to be provided from birth with everything that will make one happy; to be very fortunate

REL	be born with a silver spoon in one's mouth
ANT	be born under an unlucky star

Examples

(a) You were born under a lucky star. You're going to meet the love of your life soon.

(b) She must have been born under a lucky star. Not only was she blessed with success as an international supermodel, but she was also blessed with a wonderful family.

Note

The Japanese is likely to be a translation of the English.

REL

The REL *be born with a silver spoon in one's mouth* can express a figurative meaning similar to that of *be born under a lucky star*, though it specifically refers to being born into wealth and privilege. Furthermore, the subject of the REL is usually s.o. other than the speaker. There is no Japanese equivalent for this English expression.

(1) a. She was born {under a lucky star/with a silver spoon in her mouth}.
　　彼女は幸せの星のもとに生まれた。

　　b. I was born {under a lucky star/ ˣwith a silver spoon in my mouth}.
　　私は幸せの星のもとに生まれた。

ANT

The ANTs of *be born under a lucky star* and *shiawase no hoshi no moto ni umareru* are *born under an unlucky star* and *fukō no hoshi no moto ni umareru*, respectively.

反意語(1)

42

冗談が過ぎる /phr. 隠喩

{いたずら / たわむれ / からかい}などが我慢できないほどだ

関 冗談にもほどがある

例文

(a) 初めて会った次の日に結婚するなんて、冗談が過ぎると思ったけど、でも、人生には運命の出会いってのもあるからね。

(b) いくら観客が喜ぶと言っても、彼の話は過激で冗談が過ぎる。傷付く人もいるはずだ。

解説

日英語とも空間表現の動詞「過ぎる」と前置詞の beyond(〜の先に)を使っている。両方とも「冗談」として受け入れられる領域を越えているという比喩的な意味を持っている。

関連語

日本語には「冗談にもほどがある」という関連表現があり、「冗談が過ぎる」と意味を変えずに置き換えることができる。

幸せの星のもとに生まれる /phr. 隠喩

幸せになる条件をすべて与えられて生まれてくる

反 不幸の星のもとに生まれる

例文

(a) あなたは幸せの星のもとに生まれたのです。あなたはもうすぐ、生涯の恋人に出会うでしょう。

(b) 彼女は幸せの星のもとに生まれたにちがいない。国際的なスーパーモデルとしてすばらしい成功をおさめたし、すばらしい家庭にも恵まれた。

解説

日本語は英語からの翻訳の可能性が高い。

関連語

英語には *be born with a silver spoon in one's mouth*(lit. 銀のさじをくわえて生まれてくる)という関連表現があり、見出しと比喩的に近い意味を持っている。しかし、この表現は"富と特権のある家庭に生まれる"という特定の意味がある。さらに、この表現の場合、主語は話し手以外の人でなければならない。日本語にはこの英語に対応する表現はない。 REL (1)

反意語

日英語の反意表現は、「不幸の星のもとに生まれる」と *be born under an unlucky star* である。

(1) あなたは運命の女神に微笑みかけられたことがない、つまり、不幸の星のもとに生まれたと思いますか。

Do you ever feel like fate has never smiled on you—like you were born under an unlucky star?

43

be buried in ~ / phr. / metaphor

for s.t. to be hidden; to be overwhelmed by a large amount of s.t.

Examples

(a) There are many mysteries buried in history.

(b) I'm buried in Japanese homework, so I can't hang out with my friends.

(c) Unfortunately, most of her work is buried in the pages of obscure papers.

Notes

1. The basic meaning of *be buried* and *umoreru* is "for s.t. to be physically placed into a hole and concealed with dirt, etc."

2. The English can be used to describe someone who is buried in a grave, but the Japanese cannot.

(1) Sartre is buried at the Montparnasse Cemetery in Paris.
サルトルはパリのモンパルナス墓地に{埋葬されている/ˣ埋もれている}。

be {burned/burnt} out / phr. / metaphor

to be exhausted due to excessive engagement in an activity

Examples

Saya: Mike, you haven't been looking so good these days. Did something happen at work?

Mike: It's just that work's been really busy, so I'm completely burnt out.

- - - - - - - - - - - - - - - - - - -

(a) If you feel burnt out, you should take a few days off and vacation abroad.

(b) The number one sign that you are burned out because of work is feeling that you simply don't want to work anymore.

(c) I've gotta work, fix meals, help the kids with homework, listen to my husband complain—I'm completely burned out!

Note

Burnt out is colloquial, but *moe-tsukiru* is not.

be calculating / phr. / metaphor

shrewd or cunning, especially in a {selfish/scheming} way

Examples

Saya: The other day, Sato said he'd give me a ride if I helped pay for gas.

Karen: Even though he was going by his girlfriend's house anyway? Why does he always have to be so selfish and calculating?

- - - - - - - - - - - - - - - - - - -

(a) Yamada is a flawed character in that he is calculating and somewhat mean.

(b) He is calculating and rational; he only performs actions that are necessary for accomplishing his goal.

埋もれる / v. / 隠喩

何かが世の中に知られていない，量が多すぎて、身動きが取れない

例文

(a) 歴史に埋もれている多くの謎がある。

(b) 僕は日本語の宿題の山に埋もれていて、友達に会う時間もない。

(c) 残念なことに彼女の論文の大半は、あまり知られていない論集の中に埋もれている。

解説

1. 日本語の動詞「埋もれる」と英語の動詞 *be buried* の基本義はどちらも "何かが穴の中に置かれ、土のようなもので覆い隠されている" である。

2. 英語では、誰かが墓に埋葬されているときにも使えるが、日本語では使えない。

→📖Note(1)

燃え尽きる / comp. v. / 隠喩

やり甲斐のある事を継続し熱中してやり過ぎたため、疲れ切っている

例文

さや：マイク、このごろ、あまり元気ないわね。会社で何かあったの？

マイク：仕事が忙しすぎてね。ちょっと燃え尽きたって感じかな。

(a) もし燃え尽きたと思ったら、休暇を取って海外旅行に出かけたほうがいいですよ。

(b) もう仕事はしたくないと思うことが、仕事に燃え尽きた一番の証拠だ。

(c) 私は仕事をして、食事を作り、子供達の宿題を見てやったり、夫の不平を聞いてやったりして燃え尽きちゃうんです。

解説

英語の *burnt out* はくだけた表現だが、日本語の「燃え尽きる」はそうではない。

計算高い / comp. adj. (i) / 隠喩

損得に敏感な

[関] 打算的な，勘定高い

例文

さや：佐藤君ったらこの間、車で送ってやるからガソリン代出せなんて言うのよ。

カレン：どうせ帰りに彼女の家に寄るくせに。相変わらず計算高いわね。

(a) 山田は計算高くやや意地が悪いという点で性格に問題がある。

(b) 彼は計算高く合理的だ。目標達成に必要な行動しかとらない。

[R][E][L]

The Japanese can be replaced with the RELs *dasan-tekina* and *kanjō-dakai*. 📖➝関連語(1)

be cancerous to ~ / phr. / metaphor

for s.t. to be damaging to {a system/institution}

Examples

(a) The current campaign finance system is cancerous to the underpinnings of a fair and free society.

(b) This intense work schedule is cancerous to my lifestyle.

(c) Social maladies such as drug addiction and terrorism are cancerous to society.

Note

The only difference between the English and Japanese is that the English uses an adjective, *cancerous*, whereas the Japanese uses a noun, *gan* (cancer).

be crowned with victory / phr. / metaphor

to win after remarkable {activity/efforts/hardships}

Examples

(a) Nine years passed before the movement for democracy was crowned with victory.

(b) Finally came a great battle where he led a desperate charge and was crowned with victory.

(c) If you want to be crowned with victory in life, you have to believe in yourself and work as hard as you can.

Notes

1. *Crown* means "an imperial headdress," and *ēkan* (*ē* [glorious] + *kan* [crown]) means "glorious headdress," so *crown* is the common feature in these two expressions.

2. The Japanese verb *eru* (to obtain) is a verb used in formal speech or written Japanese.

be dead / phr. / metaphor

describes a machine, etc., that has suddenly stopped working

Example

My mobile phone is dead. The battery may be running out.

関連語

例文の「計算高い」はすべて「打算的な」と「勘定高い」で置き換えられる。

(1) 山田は{計算高く/打算的で/勘定高く}、やや意地が悪いという点で性格に問題がある。(→(a))

（〜にとって（の））癌（だ） phr. 隠喩

何かが{組織/機関}にとって大きな障害となっている

例文

(a) 現在の選挙資金集めの方法は不公正で、自由な社会の支柱にとって癌である。

(b) このような過度の多忙さは、幸福な生活設計にとって癌である。

(c) 麻薬中毒やテロリズムのような社会の病弊は、社会にとっての癌である。

解説

英語と日本語の違いは、日本語が名詞「癌」を、英語が形容詞 *cancerous* を使っている点である。

勝利の栄冠を得る phr. 隠喩

著しい{活動/努力/苦労}などで勝つ

例文

(a) 民主化の運動が勝利の栄冠を得るのに9年かかった。

(b) 最後に大きな戦闘があり、彼は必死の攻撃をしかけて勝利の栄冠を得た。

(c) 人生で勝利の栄冠を得るためには、自分を信じて切磋琢磨するしかない。

解説

1. 「栄冠」は"栄誉ある冠"、*crown* は"王冠"ということで"冠"が共通の意味になっている。

2. 日本語の動詞「得る」は書き言葉か、かたい話し言葉で使われる。

死んだ v. 隠喩

機械などが突然機能しなくなること

例文

携帯が死んだ。バッテリーがなくなったのかなあ。

be drawn into ~ / phr. / metaphor

to be made to get involved in or take an interest in s.t.

Examples

Karen: Saya, have you seen this movie?

Saya: Nope, not yet. I hear it's good.

Karen: It's really good. The children are such great actors, you just get drawn into it.

Saya: In that case, maybe I'll go see it this weekend.

- - - - - - - - - - - - - - - - - - - -

(a) The audience was drawn into the musician's marvelous performance.

(b) He was drawn into the discussion on genomics.

Notes

1. *Be drawn into ~* and *(~ ni) hiki-komareru* are the passive forms of *draw into* and *hiki-komu*, respectively.
2. The English can be used when s.o. is made to get involved in s.t. negative, as shown in (1), but the Japanese cannot be used in such a context.

(1) Catholic schoolchildren were drawn into the Northern Ireland conflict.
カトリックの学校の子供達は北アイルランドの紛争に {巻き込まれた/ ×引き込まれた}。

be easy on ~ / phr. / metaphor

for {s.o./s.t.} to be {gentle/kind} toward {s.o./s.t.}

Examples

(a) The color green is supposed to be easy on the eyes.

(b) Cyclists, kayakers, bird-lovers, and the like are easy on the environments they visit.

(c) Baroque music is easy on the ears.

(d) This soap has a refreshing scent and is easy on the skin.

Note

For many Japanese people, when s.t. is easy to do, it is natural to think of it as being "kind." This is a case of personification. In Japanese, the meanings "easy (to do); simple" and "not strict; gentle and kind" are distinguished by the kanji 易しい and 優しい, respectively. 📖➡解説(1)

（〜に）引き込まれる　phr.　隠喩

何かに心を引き寄せられる

例文

カレン: さや、この映画見た？

さや: ううん、まだ。いいらしいね。

カレン: うん、すっごくいいよ。子供達の演技がすばらしくって、思わず引き込まれちゃうの。

さや: そう。じゃ、今週末、見に行ってみようかな。

- -

（a）聴衆は、この芸術家がコンサート中に起こした奇跡的な魔力に引き込まれた。

（b）彼はゲノム学の議論に引き込まれた。

解説

1. 「（〜に）引き込まれる」も be drawn into 〜 も、それぞれ「引き込む」と draw into の受け身形である。

2. 英語では誰かが悪い状況に巻き込まれる場合にも使えるが、日本語では使えない。

→📖 Note（1）

（〜に）優しい　phr. adj. (i)　隠喩

{誰か / 何か}にとって{快適である / 刺激がない}，悪い影響を及ぼさない

例文

（a）緑色は目に優しいとされている。

（b）サイクリングやカヤックを楽しむ人、野鳥愛好家などは、環境に優しい人たちだ。

（c）バロック音楽は耳に優しい。

（d）このせっけんは匂いがさわやかで、お肌に優しいです。

解説

何かをするのが簡単でしやすいとき、その何かが自分にやさしいと感じる日本人は多い。これは擬人化の例である。日本語では、「やさしい」は漢字で「優しい」と「易しい」と表記するが、前者は「厳しくない、おだやかである、気持ちが温かい」という意味で、後者は、「難しくない、しやすい、簡単」という意味である。

（1）a. みちこさんはとても優しい人だ。

Michiko is a very kind person.

b. 昨日の試験はとても易しかった。

Yesterday's examination was very easy.

49

be engraved in ~ / phr. / metaphor

for s.t. to be embedded deeply in one's {mind/memory}

Examples

(a) My mentor's words are deeply engraved in my mind.

(b) That horrible event will be engraved in my memory until I die.

(c) Trauma is an emotional response caused by a terrible event engraved in one's memory.

---

homograph

be in deep water / phr. / metaphor

to get into serious {trouble/difficulty}
大変困る
たいへんこま

Example

I knew I was in deep water when I deleted the document by mistake.
文書を間違って消してしまい、とても困った。
ぶんしょ　まちが　　け　　　　　　　　　　こま

---

be in the red / phr. / synesthesia

to be in debt

[ANT] be in the black

Examples

Collegue: Hey, Mike. Do you wanna go get a drink?

Mike: Sorry, I'm gonna have to pass. I'm in the red this month. I might not even be able to pay my rent.

Collegue: That's because you waste your money on expensive cars.

- -

(a) It became clear that the government was in the red by about $10 billion.

(b) The simple fact is that the healthcare system for the elderly is in the red, and it has only been getting worse.

Notes

1. It is very likely that the Japanese version of this expression was introduced when people in Japan adopted the Western practice of using red ink in bookkeeping to indicate losses.
2. Both the English and Japanese expressions can be considered a kind of "synesthesia" in that the visual color *red* is transferred to the non-visual semiotics of monetary loss.

[A][N][T]

The ANTs of *be in the red* and *akaji* are *be in the black* and *kuroji*, respectively.

(1) That computer manufacturer is operating in the black.
そのコンピュータ会社の経営は黒字だ。

50

刻み付けられる comp. v. 隠喩

誰かの心や記憶に強く印象を残す

例文

(a) 恩師の言葉は、深く心に刻み付けられている。

(b) あの恐ろしい出来事は、死ぬまで記憶に刻み付けられるだろう。

(c) トラウマとは、人の記憶に刻み付けられた恐ろしい出来事で起きる情緒的反応のことである。

同形異義語

深みにはまる phr. 隠喩

関係が親密になって抜け出せない{状況 / 立場}になる
to be deeply involved in a bad relationship and unable to end it

例文

彼女は課長と不倫の関係になり、深みにはまってしまった。
She had an affair with the section chief and just couldn't bring herself to end it.

赤字 comp. n. 共感覚

{経営 / 財政}的に損失が出ている状態

反 黒字

例文

同僚：マイク、飲みにいこうか。

マイク：だめだめ、今月は赤字で家賃も払えないくらいなんだから。

同僚：あんな高い車、買うからだよ。

- - - - - - - - - - -

(a) 政府財政は約 100 億ドルの赤字であることが明らかになった。

(b) 事実を簡単に言えば、老人医療保険制度は赤字で、それもますますひどくなっている。

解説

1. 日本語はおそらく、西洋の簿記にならって損失額を赤インクで示したことが始まりとなったのであろう。

2. 日英語とも視覚的な色彩の「赤」が、非感覚的で記号論的な"負債"という意味になっている点で一種の共感覚現象といえるだろう。

反意語

日英語の反意表現は、それぞれ、「黒字」と *be in the black* である。 ➡ ANT(1)

| homograph |

be in the same boat / phr. / metaphor

to be in the same unpleasant or difficult situation
同じ悪い状況に{ある / いる}

Example

Don't complain about your salary. We're in the same boat.
給料のことについて不平を言うなよ。僕らは同じ状況なのだから。

be intoxicated with victory / phr. / metaphor

to be extremely happy with a victory

Example

The night the Red Sox won the World Series for the first time in 86 years, they were so intoxicated with victory that they drank one victory toast after another.

be mad about ~ / phr. / metaphor

to be carried away by strong interest in {s.t./s.o}

REL be crazy about ~

Examples

Kenta: Saya, are you eating that ice cream again?

Saya: Yep! I'm simply mad about the taste. I wanna try all the flavors.

Kenta: Don't overdo it!

- -

(a) My older brother is mad about you.

(b) Everyone here is mad about music.

(c) He's mad about Star Wars. He's got tons of action figures.

REL
1. The related expression *be crazy about* ~ is more frequently used than *be mad about* ~, but the degree of enthusiasm or interest it expresses is somewhat lower. Likewise, the Japanese has the REL *(~ ni) muchū da*, which is more frequently used than *~ ni kurutte iru* and does not have as negative a connotation. 📖➡関連語(**1**)
2. In spoken Japanese, the expression *(~ ni) hamatte iru* is frequently used. It can be used with anything but people. So all uses of *(~ ni) kurutte iru* can be replaced by *(~ ni) hamatte iru* except for (a). 📖➡関連語(**2**)

52

同形異義語

呉越同舟 ｜ comp. n. ｜ 隠喩

敵同士が同じ場所にいあわせる，困難な状況で共に協力し合う
for enemies to be in the same place; to cooperate in a difficult situation

例文

ライバル同士の二人の社長が同じパーティにいあわせ、まさに呉越同舟だった。
I heard that those two CEOs happened to attend the same party. It's like two enemies suddenly found themselves stuck with one another.

勝利に酔う ｜ phr. ｜ 隠喩

勝ったことを非常に喜ぶ

例文

86年ぶりにワールドシリーズを制した晩、レッドソックスの選手は勝利に酔いしれて何度も乾杯をした。

(〜に)狂っている ｜ phr. ｜ 隠喩

{何か / 誰か}に強い関心があってその気持ちを抑えられない

関 (〜に)夢中だ，(〜に)はまっている

例文

健太：さや、また、そのアイスクリーム、食べてるの？
さや：そ、私、最近この味に狂ってるのよ。全種類制覇が目標なの。
健太：食べ過ぎるなよ！

(a) 兄貴は君に狂っているんだ。
(b) ここでは誰もが音楽に狂っている。
(c) 彼は「スターウォーズ」に狂っていて、スターウォーズ関係のおもちゃをたくさん持っている。

関連語

1. 日本語では、「(〜に)夢中だ」という関連表現があり、「(〜に)狂っている」ほど否定的な意味合いはなく、使用頻度もはるかに高い。また、英語には *be crazy about ~* という関連表現がある。これは *be mad about ~* よりかなり使用頻度が高いが、熱意や興味の程度はやや低い。

(1) a. 彼は今はコンピュータの勉強に {夢中だ /?? 狂っている}。
　　 He's {mad/crazy} about computer science.
　 b. 兄貴は君に {狂っている / 夢中な} んだ。(→(a))
　　 My older brother is {mad/crazy} about you.

2. 日本語の話し言葉には「(〜に)はまっている」という表現があり、人以外の対象なら何にでも使える。従って、会話例と(b)(c)の「狂っている」はすべて「はまっている」と置き換えることができる。

(2) ここでは誰もが音楽に {狂っている / はまっている}。(→(b))

/homograph/

be moved / phr. / metaphor

to feel very emotional

感動する
かんどう

[Example]

I was deeply moved by her kind words.

僕は彼女の親切な言葉に感動した。
ぼく　かのじょ　しんせつ　ことば　かんどう

be on the front lines / phr. / metaphor

to take a leading role in s.t. significant

[Examples]

Mrs. S: Remember that incident that happened the other day? I heard the suspect and the policeman both died.

Mr. S: Yeah, I heard about that too. It must be hard for the families of people who are on the front lines of the fight against crime.

- -

(a) Underpaid teachers are always on the front lines of public education.

(b) The oncologists at this university hospital are said to be on the front lines of cancer treatment.

[Note]

Both the English and Japanese expressions were originally used to refer to the *front lines* of battle, but they have come to possess metaphorical meanings as well. Note that *front lines* and *sai-zensen* usually take the verbs *be* and *tatsu* (to stand), respectively.

be on the same wavelength (as ~) / phr. / metaphor

to think and feel the same way as s.o.

[Examples]

Saya: So Mike, how have things been going with that mean old boss of yours?

Mike: Well, things have gotten a little better than before, but we just don't seem to be on the same wavelength. The department head and I get along just fine, though.

- -

(a) My best friend and I always seem to be on the same wavelength. He always knows what I'm going to say before I even say it.

(b) I have a good friend who's on the same wavelength as I am about looking young and staying healthy.

(c) As soon as I met him, I felt like we were on the same wavelength. Now he's an important business partner of mine.

54

同形異義語

{気持ち / 考え}が動く / phr. / 隠喩

考えがかわる、その気になる
to change one's mind

例文

どんなに話し合っても、離婚すると決めた彼女の気持ちが動くことはなかった。
Even after intense discussion, her desire for divorce did not change.

最前線に立つ phr. 隠喩

何か有意義なことで指導的な役割を果たす

例文

鈴木(妻)：この間の事件、あなた覚えているでしょ？　容疑者も警官も死んだそうね。
鈴木(夫)：らしいね。犯罪と最前線に立って戦っている人々の家族は心配だろうね。

(a) 教育の最前線に立って奮闘するのは、いつも給料の安い現場の教師だ。
(b) この大学病院の医師は、癌治療の最前線に立っていると言われている。

解説

日英語とも元々は戦争の「最前線」を意味していたが、今では比喩的な意味を持つようになった。「最前線」も *front lines* も、それぞれ、動詞の「立つ」と *be* をとるのが普通である。

(〜と)波長が合う phr. 隠喩

誰かと同じように考え、感じる

関 (〜と)波長が同じだ，(〜と)馬が合う

例文

さや：マイク、その後、例のいじわる課長は、どう？
マイク：う〜ん、前よりはちょっとましになったけれど、相変わらず波長は合わないね。部長とは波長が合うんだけどなあ。

(a) 親友と僕はいつも波長が合っているみたいだ。彼は僕が何か言う前に、僕が言おうとすることがいつもわかるんだ。
(b) いつまでも若々しく健康でいたい、という点で私と波長が合っているいい友達がいます。
(c) 彼とは初対面の時から波長が合う気がしたんだけど、今では大切なビジネスのパートナーだ。

Note

This metaphor is primarily used in colloquial speech or informal writing in both English and Japanese.

REL

1. In Japanese, one may also say (~ *to*) *hachō ga onaji da*, which is almost identical to the English, but this expression is used much less frequently than (~ *to*) *hachō ga au* .

📖→関連語(**1**)

2. The Japanese has another REL, (~ *to*) *uma ga au*. This is used in colloquial speech.

📖→関連語(**2**)

be on the tip of one's tongue / phr. / metaphor

to be unable to recall s.t. but to feel that it is close to being remembered

Examples

Mrs. S: Oh, what's that person's name? It's on the tip of my tongue, but I can't remember it.

Kenta: You must be getting old.

- - - - - - - - - - - - - - - - - - - -

(a) Older people often find that they just can't remember a word even though it's on the tip of their tongue.

(b) The apology was on the tip of my tongue, but in the end I couldn't bring myself to actually tell her I was sorry.

be one step ahead / phr. / metaphor

to be ahead of {s.o./s.t.} else in terms of progress

ANT be one step behind

Examples

(a) She was one step ahead of everyone all throughout her career.

(b) When it came to improving mobile phone functionality, Japan and Korea were one step ahead of the U.S.

Note

In both the English and Japanese expressions, *one step* and *ippo* are metaphorical usages of the physical distance represented by a single step, as demonstrated in (1). 📖→解説(**1**)

ANT

The English ANT is *be one step behind,* and the Japanese ANT is *ippo okure o toru.*

📖→反意語(**1**)

56

解説

この比喩表現は日英語とも、主に、会話かくだけた書き言葉で使われる。

関連語

1. 日本語には英語と同じ「(〜と)波長が同じだ」という表現もあるが、「(〜と)波長が合う」よりはるかに使用頻度が低い。

(1) 親友と僕はいつも波長が{合っている / 同じ}みたいだ。(→(a))

2. 日本語には「(〜と)馬が合う」という表現もあり、くだけた会話で使われる。

(2) 僕と彼は、年は随分離れているんだけど、不思議と{波長が合う / 馬が合う}んだ。

He and I are not at all close in age, but strangely enough, we're on the exact same wavelength.

舌の先まで出かかっている　*phr.*　隠喩

何かを思い出せそうで思い出せない，何かを言いたいけれど言うわけにいかない

例文

鈴木(妻)：ほら、この人、なんて名前だったっけ？　ああ、舌の先まで出かかってるのに、思い出せないわ。

健太：お母さんもそろそろ年だね。

(a) 老人になると、ことばが舌の先まで出かかっているのに、出てこないということがしばしば起こる。

(b) 私の謝罪の言葉は舌の先まで出かかっていた。でも、最後まで彼女にごめんなさいと言うことはできなかった。

一歩先を行く　*phr.*　隠喩

物事の進行状況が他より進んでいる，人物の能力が他よりも優れている

反 一歩後れを取る

例文

(a) 彼女は生涯ずっとみんなの一歩先を行っていました。

(b) 日本や韓国は携帯電話の機能開発においてはアメリカより一歩先を行っていた。

解説

日英語の「一歩」と *one step* はともに(1)のように物理的な距離を表す用法からの比喩である。

(1) かつては日本人の妻は夫の一歩か二歩あとを歩いたものだ。

Japanese wives used to walk a step or two behind their husbands.

反意語

日英語には、それぞれ「一歩後れを取る」と *be one step behind* という反意表現がある。

(1) 誰もその国のバブル経済崩壊を予測していなかったし、誰もアジアの危機も予測していなかった。誰もが一歩後れを取っていたのだ。

No one predicted the bubble bursting in that country and the Asian financial crisis. Everyone was one step behind.

57

be over the hill / phr. / metaphor

to be past one's prime

Examples

(a) That boxer is over the hill, but he doesn't want to admit it.

(b) It's getting hard for him to run as fast as he used to. Guess he's over the hill.

(c) I may be over the hill, but that climb was terrific!

Note

Both the English and Japanese conjure the image of a person descending from the top of a hill. Both are based on the conceptual metaphor of life as a journey up a {hill/mountain}.

REL

Japanese has another very similar expression, *saka o {koeru/kosu}*, but its use is limited to age. 📖→関連語(1)

ANT

The Japanese has the ANT *nobori-zaka*, which means "to be on the rise." However, *uphill* cannot be used as the ANT of *over the hill* in English. 📖→反意語(1)

be rotten to the core / phr. / metaphor

for {s.o./s.t.} to be so morally corrupt that nothing can be done about it

Examples

(a) That serial killer is rotten to the core. When they arrested him, he boasted about what he'd done.

(b) Bribery, vote rigging... This government used to be rotten to the core.

(c) Bureaucracies in this country are rotten to the core.

Note

Both the English and Japanese use botanical expressions (*core*, "the central part of a fruit," and *shin*, "the central part of s.t.") as well as the related predicates *be rotten* and *kusatte iru* (to be rotten).

下り坂 / comp. n. / 隠喩

人生や能力などの頂点を越える

関 坂を {越える / 越す}

反 上り坂

例文

(a) そのボクサーは下り坂なのに、それを認めたがらない。

(b) 彼は前のように速く走るのが難しくなってきている。まあ、彼は下り坂なんだ。

(c) 僕の人生は今は下り坂だけどね。上り坂のときはすばらしかったのなんのって。

解説

日英語ともに人が丘の頂上に登りつめて、今やそこから下って来ているというイメージがある。どちらにも「人生は {丘 / 山} に登るようなものだ」という比喩的思考が潜んでいる。

関連語

日本語には、英語の表現により近い「坂を {越える / 越す}」という表現があるが、年齢に関係したことに限られる。

(1) その政治家は人生の坂を {越えて / 越して} もなお、現役で頑張っている。
That politician might be over the hill, but he's still working as hard as ever.

反意語

日本語には「上り坂」という反意表現がある。英語の *uphill* は *over the hill* の反意表現としては使えない。

(1) 彼は仕事もうまくいって、すばらしい伴侶もみつかって、まさに人生の上り坂だ。
His business is going well, and he's found his better half too. His life is really {on the rise/ ×uphill}.

芯まで腐っている / phr. / 隠喩

倫理的に腐敗していて救いようのない状況にある

例文

(a) あの連続殺人犯は本当に芯まで腐っている。逮捕されたとき、自分の犯行を自慢していたのだから。

(b) この政府は、汚職と選挙違反で芯まで腐っていた。

(c) この国の官僚組織は、芯まで腐っている。

解説

日英語とも植物的な表現「芯」と *core*(果物の中心部分)、そして「腐っている」と *be rotten* という述部から成っている。

be rusty / phr. / metaphor

to be inept and slow due to {lack of practice/old age}

REL {get/become} rusty

Examples

Kenta: Mike, I heard you're good at tennis. Let's play sometime.

Mike: I don't know. I used to play a lot, but lately I haven't, so my swing is rusty.

Kenta: Well, that probably puts you right at my level.

- -

(a) It's been a long time since I graduated from school, so my math is rusty.

(b) Membership is aimed at those who are new to golf or feeling rusty.

Notes

1. Both the English and Japanese incorporate a figurative use of *rust/sabi*, though the English uses the adjective *rusty* while the Japanese uses the compound verb *sabi-tsuku* (*sabi ga tsuku*, lit. "rust attaches itself").
2. The Japanese usually takes the stative form *sabi-tsuite iru*.

REL

In the English, the verb *be* can be replaced by *get* or *become*.

(1) My Japanese {is/has gotten/has become} rusty.
僕の日本語はさびついて {いる / きた}。

be (nothing but) skin and bones / phr. / metaphor

to be extremely thin, as if one's body consists only of skin and bones

Examples

Mrs. S: Karen, you haven't been eating very much lately. Is something the matter?

Karen: It's just that I'm on a diet right now.

Mrs. S: If you lose any more weight, you'll be nothing but skin and bones.

- -

(a) Bulimia is a potentially life-threatening psychological disorder in which the patient is reduced to skin and bones because they refuse to eat.

(b) The stray cat wasn't much to look at, being mostly skin and bones for lack of food.

Notes

1. Notice the difference in word order between the English and the Japanese. The two elements are reversed in English and Japanese. The expressions *×be bones and skin* and *×kawa to hone (bakari da)* are not used in their respective languages.
2. In Japanese, the nickname *Honekawa* (last name, lit. "bone & skin") *Sujiemon* (first name, "blood vessels") is used to refer to a really skinny person.

さびつく / comp. v. / 隠喩

老齢や練習不足のため、{何かが下手になる / 体がなまる}

例文

健太：マイク、テニスうまいんだって。今度やろうか。

マイク：う〜ん、昔はけっこうやったけど、最近は御無沙汰だから、腕がさびついちゃってるだろうな。

健太：じゃ、たぶんちょうど僕のレベルだよ。

- -

(a) 学校を出てから随分たつので、僕の数学の力はさびついています。

(b) この会員制度は、ゴルフの経験があまりない人と、ゴルフの腕がさびついている人のためのものです。

解説

1. 日英語ともに「さび」の比喩的用法であるが、日本語は「さびつく」（さびがつく）という複合動詞を、英語は *rusty*（さびた）という形容詞を使っている。

2. 日本語は例文のように、普通「さびついている」という状態表現になる。

関連語

英語の動詞 *be* は *get* あるいは *become* と置き換えられる。━📖 REL (1)

骨と皮（ばかりだ） / phr. / 隠喩

あまりにもやせていて骨と皮だけのようだ

例文

鈴木（妻）：カレンさん、最近、あまり食べないわね。どうしたの？

カレン：今、ちょっと、ダイエットをしているんです。

鈴木（妻）：それ以上やせたら、骨と皮ばかりになっちゃうわよ。

- -

(a) 拒食症は、何も食べようとせずに骨と皮ばかりになって、ついには死ぬこともあるという心の病気だ。

(b) その野良猫は食べるものがなくて、ほとんど骨と皮ばかりで見られたものじゃなかった。

解説

1. 日英語で語順が逆になっている。「×皮と骨（ばかりだ）」や ×*be bones and skin* という表現はない。

2. 日本語には本当にやせた人について、「骨皮（苗字）筋右衛門（名）」という人名もどきの表現がある。「骨皮」は骨と皮を意味し、「筋」は血管を意味する。

be starved {for/of} ~   *phr.* / metaphor

to suffer from some kind of deprivation; to lack s.t.

Examples

Mrs. S: Why do you think that young person committed such a horrible crime?

Kenta: Maybe he was starved of his parents' affection.

Mrs. S: I guess that's possible. Well, in that case, we don't have to worry about you, do we Kenta? You get plenty of love and attention from your parents.

Kenta: Yeah right!

(a) I found myself starved for books after not reading for a while.

(b) When I was in Mongolia, I was starved for news and savored every word that was sent from Tokyo.

(c) The newly created public school system was starved for money.

Notes

1. In both English and Japanese, this expression normally indicates the state of being deprived of food, but figuratively it expresses the idea of suffering from a lack of s.t. other than food.
2. In English, one can say either *starved for* or *starved of*, but *for* seems to be used more frequently than *of*.

be the bible ({for/of} ~)   *phr.* / metaphor

an indispensable book for {s.o./s.t.}

Examples

Saya: Karen, this cake you made is really delicious. How did you make it?

Karen: I used one of my grandmother's recipes. They're my bible when it comes to baking cakes!

(a) This reference book is considered the bible for students of Japanese.

(b) If you want to know where to go in Central Park, this book is your bible.

Notes

1. The Japanese is a translation of the English. There are actually two ways to translate *Bible* into Japanese: *sēsho* and *baiburu*. However, only *baiburu* is used in the phrase covered here. 📖→ 解説(1)
2. *Bible* is usually spelled with a lowercase "b" when it is used metaphorically.

（〜に）餓える　phr.　隠喩

何かが不足していて欲しくてたまらない

例文

鈴木（妻）：この子はどうしてこんな犯罪を犯したのかしら？　健太はどう思う？

健太：たぶん、親の愛情に餓えていたんじゃないの。

鈴木（妻）：そう。じゃ、健太はぜったい大丈夫ね。親の愛が満ちあふれているから。

健太：母さん、よく言うよ。

- - - - - - - - - - - - - - - - - - - -

(a) 最近はあまり読書をしていなかったから、本に飢えていた。

(b) モンゴルにいたときにはニュースに飢えていて、東京から送られてきた言葉の一語一語を味わった。

(c) 新しくできた公立学校協会は、資金不足で金に飢えていた。

解説

1. 日英語とも"食べ物以外の何かが不足して苦しんでいる"という比喩表現である。

2. 英語では be starved の後に for か of が使えるが、for のほうが of より頻度が高い。

（〜の）バイブル（だ）　phr.　隠喩

{誰か / 何か}にとって必須の本（だ）

例文

さや：カレンのケーキはほんとおいしいわね。どうやって作るの？

カレン：実はおばあちゃんのレシピがあるのよ。私のケーキ作りのバイブル！

- - - - - - - - - - - - - - - - - - - -

(a) この参考書はすべての日本語学習者のバイブルなんです。

(b) この本はセントラルパークを散歩する上でのバイブルです。

解説

1. 日本語は明らかに英語からの借用語である。Bible の訳には「聖書」と「バイブル」があるが、比喩的表現としては「バイブル」しか使えない。

(1) この参考書はすべての日本語学習者の{バイブル/*聖書}なんです。（→(a)）

2. Bible が比喩として使われる時は、大文字の Bible ではなく、小文字の bible を使うのが普通である。

be the window {of/on/to} ~   *phr.*   metaphor

s.t. through which one can understand s.t. significant

Examples

Mrs. S: Kenta, that mind of yours is up to no good again, isn't it?

Kenta: H-how did you know?

Mrs. S: The eyes are the window to the heart. One look at them and I can instantly tell what you're thinking.

- -

(a) Media is our window to the world.

(b) Architecture is a window on a city's history.

be tied up with ~   *phr.*   metaphor

to not be able to do s.t. because one is busy with s.t. else

REL   be tied hand and foot to ~; be tied down to ~

Examples

Saya: About time you got here! What took you so long?

Mike: Sorry. I got tied up with work and couldn't leave the office until nine o'clock.

Saya: Well, the important thing is that you made it. Let's forget about work and enjoy the party!

- -

(a) When I was training to become a professional pianist, I was tied up with practice every day and had no time for anything fun.

(b) He was tied up with his duties at the local theater.

(c) Lately he's been tied up with the accident investigation.

Notes

1. The English is used when one is busy with something, but the Japanese can be used not only when one is busy with something, but also when one is so restricted by someone or something that one is deprived of freedom. 📖→関連語(**1**)

2. The English also has the meaning "for {s.o./s.t.} to be {related to/involved with}{s.o./s.t.} else," as shown in (2). In this case, the Japanese has to be changed to ~ *to musubi-tsuite iru*.

(2) a. He was tied up with the mafia for over 20 years.

彼は20年以上もマフィア{と結びついて/[×]に縛られて}いた。

b. I don't know if this is tied up with the memory problems.

私はこれが記憶の問題{と結びついて/[×]に縛られて}いるかどうか知らない。

3. The Japanese can be used in the active voice as well, but the English cannot.

📖→関連語(**3**)

REL

1. Both the English and Japanese have the REL *be tied hand and foot to* ~ and *teashi o shibarareru*.

（〜の）窓（だ） /phr. /隠喩

それを通して何か重要なことがわかるもの

例文

鈴木（妻）：健太、今、なんか良くないことを考えてたでしょ。

健太：え、どうしてわかるの。

鈴木（妻）：目は心の窓ってね。あなたの目を見れば、一目瞭然よ。

(a) メディアは世界の窓だ。

(b) ある街の歴史の窓といえば、建築もその一つである。

（〜に）縛られる /phr. /隠喩

{誰か / 何か}に制限を受けて、自由な行動が取れない

関 手足を縛られる，縛りつけられる

例文

さや：あ、やっと来た！どうしてこんなに遅くなっちゃったの？

マイク：ごめん！仕事に縛られてて、9時までオフィスを出られなかったんだよ。

さや：ま、とにかく来られてよかったじゃん。さあ、仕事は忘れて、パーティを楽しもう。

(a) プロのピアニストを目指していたころは、毎日ピアノの練習に縛られて、楽しいことは何もできなかった。

(b) 彼は町の劇場での務めに縛られていた。

(c) 最近、彼は事故調査に縛られていた。

解説

1. 英語は何かで忙しいときに使うが、日本語は忙しいときだけではなく、{誰か / 何か}によって制限を受けて、自由な行動が取れないときにも使える。

(1) 日本は憲法第九条に縛られて、軍備を持つことが制限されている。
Japan is {bound by/ ×tied up with} Article 9 of its constitution, which restricts its right to possess weapons of war.

2. 英語には "{誰か/ 何か} が {誰か/ 何か} に関係がある" という比喩的意味もあるが、日本語にはそのような意味はないので、「〜と結びついている」と言わなければならない。

━━📖 Note（2）

3. 日本語は能動形でも使えるが、英語はそのようには使えない。

(3) あの親は子供を縛りすぎる。
Those parents are {too strict with/ ×tying up} their children.

関連語

1. 日英語ともに関連表現として「手足を縛られる」、*be tied hand and foot to ~* がある。

━━📖 REL（1）

(1) The Republican Party is tied hand and foot to big business.
共和党は強力な大企業に手足を縛られている。

2. Both the English and Japanese also have the REL *be tied down to* ~ and *shibari-tsukerareru*, which means "to be unable to {move/act} freely." 📖→関連語(2)

---

be tongue-tied （舌がもつれる） → {get/be} tongue-tied

---

be {under/in} the spotlight | phr. | metaphor

for {s.o./s.t.} to get a lot of public attention

REL {put/turn/focus} the spotlight on ~

Examples

Mr. S: That group "X" has really been in the spotlight lately, hasn't it?

Kenta: Yep. They're really talented performers.

- - - - - - - - - - - - - - - - - - - -

(a) Ostrich meat has been under the spotlight lately as a potential replacement for beef.

(b) Greenland is in the spotlight as a tourist spot for aurora viewing.

Notes

1. The *kō* in *kyakkō* is considered a liquid in Japanese in the figurative sense. Consequently, the verb in the Japanese version is *abiru*, the basic meaning of which is "to pour (hot) water on one's body." The English uses the verb *be* and the preposition *under* or *in*.

2. In Japanese, this expression cannot be used when something negative is implied, but in English it can be used even when something negative is implied.

(1) Mobile phone safety is in the spotlight.
携帯電話の安全性が {問題になって/[×]脚光を浴びて} いる。

REL

1. The English has three related expressions, each with a similar meaning: *{put/turn/focus} the spotlight on* ~. Note that these expressions are the active versions of *be {under/in} the spotlight*.

(1) The IT conference has {put/turned/focused} the spotlight on IT's educational applications.
IT 会議は IT の教育的使用に {スポットライト/脚光} を当てた。

2. The Japanese has two additional versions: *supotto(raito) {ga ataru/o ateru}*. Both of them are evidently translations from the English, and the former is the passive version of the latter. 📖→関連語(2)

---

be up in the air | phr. | metaphor

for s.t. to be undecided

Examples

Mike: When are you taking vacation?

Karen: It's still up in the air. I've been so busy, I haven't had time to plan.

- - - - - - - - - - - - - - - - - - - -

2. 日英語とも"{誰か/何か}が自由に動き回れない"という意味の「縛りつけられる」*be tied down to* ~ という関連表現がある。

(2) 最近まで日本の女性は家に縛りつけられて、外で自由に何かをすることは許されていなかった。
Until recently, Japanese women were tied down to the home, and they weren't allowed to go out freely and do things on their own.

{脚光 / スポット(ライト)}を浴びる　phr.　隠喩

{誰か / 何か}がプラスのイメージで世間の注目の的となる

関 スポット(ライト) {が当たる / を当てる}，脚光 {が当たる / を当てる}

例文

鈴木(夫)：最近、Xというグループ、ずいぶん脚光を浴びているね。
健太：うん、才能あふれるパフォーマー達だよね。

(a) 最近、ダチョウの肉が、牛肉に代わる食材として脚光を浴びている。
(b) グリーンランドは、オーロラが見られる旅行地として脚光を浴びている。

解説

1. 「脚光」に含まれている「光」は、比喩的に液体と考えられているので、日本語では"体に水や湯をかぶる"という基本義の動詞「浴びる」が使われている。英語では *be* という動詞と *under/in* という前置詞が使われている。
2. 日本語はマイナスイメージがある場合は使えないが、英語はマイナスイメージでも使える。
→ Note(1)

関連語

1. 英語は同じ比喩的意味を持つ三つの関連表現がある。*{put/turn/focus} the spotlight on* ~ である。これらは *be {under/in} the spotlight* の能動形であることに注意。→ REL(1)
2. 日本語には「スポット(ライト) {が当たる / を当てる}」という関連表現がある。どちらも英語の翻訳であるが、前者は自動詞、後者は他動詞である。

(2) a. 今日の会議は予算削減にスポットが当たった。
Today's meeting focused on the budget cuts.
b. 明日の会議は予算削減にスポットを当てて話し合います。
Tomorrow's meeting will focus on the budget cuts.

宙に浮いたままだ　phr.　隠喩

まだ{決定 / 実現}されていない

例文

マイク：いつ休暇を取るの？
カレン：それがまだ宙に浮いたままなの。忙しくて、ぜんぜん計画が立てられないの。

(a) Because the columnist retired, the fate of her column is up in the air.

(b) The next chapter in the UFO controversy is still up in the air.

be wrapped in ~ / phr. / metaphor

to be completely surrounded by s.t. intangible and often psychological

Examples

(a) Kennedy's death is still wrapped in mystery.

(b) Her message is wrapped in love.

(c) The affair was wrapped in secrecy.

(d) The sea of Hakodate was wrapped in night mist.

(e) When Martin Luther King Jr. was assassinated, the whole nation was wrapped in sorrow and grief.

Note

Adding the adverb *up* to the English (*be wrapped up in ~*) forms an entirely different expression with the meaning "to be absorbed in {s.o./s.t.}."

(1) All of Japan was wrapped up in the World Cup when it was hosted by Japan and Korea.
日本と韓国がワールドカップの主催者になったとき、日本全体が夢中になった。

be written all over one's face / phr. / metaphor

for one's thoughts or feelings to be obvious from one's facial expression

Examples

Karen: Don't you have some good news to share?

Saya: Wait, how'd you know?

Karen: It's written all over your face. It's practically screaming, "I'm so happy!"

Saya: Really? Wow, guess I shouldn't play poker. Anyway, since you asked...

(a) The shock was written all over his face.

(b) I could see the frustration written all over her face.

Note

The English uses the passive construction *be written*, while the Japanese uses *kaite aru*, a stative construction that is very close to a passive construction.

(a) コラムニストが定年退職したので、今後のコラムの運命は宙に浮いたままだ。

(b) UFO をめぐる論議は宙に浮いたままだ。

B

（〜に）包まれる　phr.　隠喩

実際に触れることができない心理的なものや雰囲気に完全に取り囲まれる

例文

(a) ケネディの死は、未だ謎に包まれたままだ。

(b) 彼女のメッセージは愛に包まれている。

(c) その情事は秘密に包まれていた。

(d) 函館の海は夜霧に包まれていた。

(e) マーチン・ルーサー・キング牧師が暗殺されたときは、国全体が悲しみに包まれた。

解説

英語に副詞の *up* を加えて *be wrapped up in ~* にすると"｛誰か/何か｝に夢中になっている"というまったく別の意味になる。　→📖 Note(1)

顔に書いてある　phr.　隠喩

考えや思いが表情に現れている

例文

カレン： あら、さや、何かいいことあったの？

さや： え、どうしてわかるの？

カレン： 顔に書いてあるわよ。「本当は叫びたいくらいうれしい」って。

さや： ほんと？　だめだなあ、ポーカーフェイスができなくて。実はね…。

- -

(a) 彼がショックを受けていることは顔中に書いてあった。

(b) 彼女の不満が顔に書いてあるのを読み取ることができた。

解説

英語は *be written* という受け身形で、日本語は受け身形に近い「書いてある」という状態形を取っている。

69

beanpole / comp. n. / metaphor

s.o. who is too thin

Example

After his illness, he was a beanpole.

Note

While the English uses *beanpole*, a stick used to support a bean plant, the Japanese uses *moyashi* (bean sprout).

bear fruit / phr. / metaphor

for {planning/actions/efforts} to bring about good results

Examples

Friend: I'm goinna study abroad on a Fulbright scholarship.

Saya: Congratulations! That's amazing! Guess your hard work finally bore fruit, huh?

(a) The business he started ten years ago finally bore fruit.

(b) The seed she sowed with her book idea finally bore fruit.

Note

The basic meanings of *bear* and *musubu* are "to bring forth s.t." and "to unite entities or individuals together," respectively.

beast, a / n. / metaphor

a contemptible person; a sexually aggressive person

REL animal; monster

Examples

Mr. S: Can you believe that someone would abuse their own child?

Mrs. S: He's a beast.

Mr. S: Hey, that's an insult to animals. Even an animal wouldn't do this kind of thing to their offspring.

Mrs. S: True, true.

(a) He is a beast who batters the weakest people in the family.

(b) He looks like a gentleman, but when it comes to women, he's a beast.

REL

1. English has the REL *animal*, which is a metaphor meaning "a human with an animal's physique and/or character," but *dōbutsu* cannot be used metaphorically. The difference between *animal* and *beast* is that the former simply means that someone is animal-like in some way, while the latter implies that someone is a contemptible person.

もやしのような / phr. 直喩(ちょくゆ)

とてもやせている

例文

彼(かれ)は病気(びょうき)をしてから、もやしのようにやせてしまった。

解説

日本語では「もやし」が使われているのに対して、英語では*beanpole*（豆のつるの支柱）が使われている。

実(み)を結(むす)ぶ / phr. 隠喩(いんゆ)

{計画(けいかく) / 行動(こうどう) / 努力(どりょく)}が良(よ)い結果(けっか)をもたらす

例文

友達(ともだち)：今度(こんど)、フルブライト奨学金(しょうがくきん)をもらって、留学(りゅうがく)することになったんだ。

さや：そう、おめでとう。よかったね。日頃(ひごろ)の努力(どりょく)がようやく実(み)を結(むす)んだね。

- -

(a) 彼(かれ)が10年前(ねんまえ)に始(はじ)めた事業(じぎょう)はやっと実(み)を結(むす)んだ。

(b) 彼女(かのじょ)が蒔(ま)いた本(ほん)のアイディアの種子(しゅし)がついに実(み)を結(むす)んだ。

解説

*bear*と「結ぶ」の基本義(きほんぎ)は、"何(なに)かを生(う)む"と"何(なに)か複数(ふくすう)のものを一(ひと)つにする"である。

けだもの / n. 隠喩(いんゆ)

侮蔑(ぶべつ)すべき人間(にんげん)，性的(せいてき)に攻撃的(こうげきてき)である

関 人(ひと)でなし，鬼畜(きちく)

例文

鈴木(すずき)(夫(おっと))：自分(じぶん)の子供(こども)を虐待(ぎゃくたい)するなんて考(かんが)えられないね。

鈴木(すずき)(妻(つま))：ほんと、けだもののようね。

鈴木(すずき)(夫(おっと))：そりゃ動物(どうぶつ)に悪(わる)いよ。動物(どうぶつ)だって自分(じぶん)の子(こ)にこんなひどいことしないよ。

鈴木(すずき)(妻(つま))：ほんと、そうね。

- -

(a) 彼(かれ)は家族(かぞく)の一番(いちばん)弱(よわ)い者(もの)まで痛(いた)めつけるようなけだものなんです。

(b) 彼(かれ)は紳士(しんし)に見(み)えるけれど、女(おんな)となるとけだものになる。

関連語

1. 英語では*animal*は"動物のような体型、性格を持っている人間"という比喩的な意味があるが、日本語の「動物」にはそのような意味はない。また、英語の*animal*は"動物のように非理性的な人間"を指し、*beast*は"侮蔑すべき人間"を指す。 ➡ REL(1)

2. 日本語には「人でなし」と「鬼畜」の二つの関連表現があり、前者は後者よりはるかに使用頻度が高い。

(1) You {beast/animal}!
   {けだもの/×動物}め!

2. There are two related expressions in Japanese: *hitodenashi* (non-human) and the Sino-Japanese compound *kichiku* (a person who is like a demon and animal combined). The former is used much more frequently than the latter. 📖→関連語(2)

beat ~ into s.o.'s head / phr. / metaphor
to repeatedly try to get s.o. to understand s.t.

Examples

Karen: I'm jealous that you're so good at math.

Kenta: I'm not that good! It's just that my high school teacher beat it into my head that math is fun, so I kinda like it now.

Karen: Ah, so that's it!

- -

(a) Society's beauty standards have been beaten into my head.

(b) It took me a couple of days to beat only ten kanji into my head.

Note

Both the English and Japanese can be used in the active form, as in the dialogue and (b), or the passive form, as shown in (a).

beat the drum for ~ / phr. / metaphor
to publicize or promote {s.o./s.t.}

Examples

(a) He's beating the drum for his candidacy for mayor of his hometown.

(b) I beat the drum for science as Minister of the Department of Education and Science.

(c) Previously, his company specialized in developing resources for other companies. Now it is beating the drum for its own products.

Notes

1. The English uses a particular musical instrument, the *drum*, whereas the Japanese *nari-mono* (lit. "things that ring") refers to musical instruments such as drums or flutes used in a traditional style of Japanese theater called *kabuki*.
2. The English uses the verb *beat*, while the Japanese explicitly refers to advertising with its use of *senden-suru* (to publicize/promote).

(2) それは{けだもの / 人でなし / 鬼畜}の仕業だった。
It's the work of a beast.

B

頭に叩き込む   phr.   隠喩

(自分を含めた)誰かに何かを繰り返し記憶させる

例文

カレン：健太は数学ができるからうらやましい。

健太：そんなことはないよ。ただ、高校の時の先生が「数学はおもしろいんだ」とい

うことを頭に叩き込んでくれたおかげで、とても好きになったんだ。

カレン：そうだったんだ！

────────────────────

(a) 私は、こういうのが美貌だという社会通念が頭に叩き込まれていた。

(b) たった 10 個の漢字を自分の頭に叩き込むのに、2、3 日かかった。

解説

日英語とも、会話例と(b)のように能動文でも、(a)のように受け身文でも使える。

鳴り物入りで宣伝する   phr.   隠喩

派手に騒ぎたてて宣伝をする

例文

(a) 彼は自分の町の市長になるために鳴り物入りで自己宣伝をした。

(b) 私が文部科学省の大臣だったときに、科学教育を鳴り物入りで宣伝したんです。

(c) 以前は彼の会社は他の会社のためにリソースを開発することを専門にやっていた

のだが、今は鳴り物入りで自社の製品を宣伝している。

解説

1. 日本語の「鳴り物」は歌舞伎のような古典劇で使われた楽器、例えば、鼓、笛などの楽器を
指しているが、英語は特定の楽器 *drum*(太鼓)を使っている。

2. 日本語でははっきり「宣伝する」という動詞が使われているが、英語では *beat*(叩く)だけで
ある。

73

become one with ~ / phr. / metaphor

to become {mentally/physically} inseparable from {s.o./s.t.} else

Examples

Mrs. S: I heard that you know how to ride horses. You're so athletic!

Mike: Yeah, horseback riding is great. Becoming one with a horse and racing around together is just an indescribable feeling.

- -

(a) Agriculture is an occupation in which a farmer adapts himself to nature. In a sense, he becomes one with nature.

(b) I want your life experience to be my life experience. I want to become one with you.

Notes

1. In the Japanese, the subject is usually a person.
2. The particle *to* before *naru* (to become) can be replaced by *ni* in spoken Japanese, as in the dialogue and (b).

REL

The Japanese has the REL *(~ to) hitotsu ni naru*, but the subject usually cannot be a person. 📖→関連語(1)

---

bed('s) legs (ベッドの脚) → {desk/chair/bed/table}('s) legs
あし

---

bell the cat / phr. / metaphor

to take a risk

Examples

(a) It's easy to propose impractical solutions. While I agree that it's an impressive plan, who's going to bell the cat?

(b) They are quite unhappy with American policies, but they cannot find the courage to bell the cat or risk offending the emperor by saying that he has no clothes.

Notes

1. This expression is said to be taken directly from one of Aesop's fables from the sixth century BCE. Some mice come up with the idea of hanging a bell around a cat's neck so that they will be warned of its approach. The first translation into Japanese came out in 1593. The translator is unknown.
2. The Japanese *neko no kubi ni suzu o tsukeru* means "to put a bell around the cat's neck," but *no kubi* can be omitted, resulting in the metonymic expression *neko ni suzu o tsukeru*, which is similar to the English.

（〜と）一体 {と / に} なる　phr.　隠喩

{誰か / 何か} と {心理的 / 肉体的} に離れられなくなる

関 （〜と）一つになる

例文

鈴木（妻）：マイクさんって、乗馬もできるんですって？　スポーツマンね。

マイク：ええ、乗馬はおもしろいですよ。馬と一体になって走る気持ちよさはなんとも言えませんね。

(a) 農業とは、自分自身を自然界に寄りそわせる、つまり自然と一体となる職業なのだ。

(b) あなたの人生経験を私の人生経験にしたいのです。私はあなたと一体になりたいのです。

解説

1. 日本語の「〜と一体となる」の主語は一般に人である。

2. 動詞「なる」の前の助詞「と」は、会話例と (b) のように、話し言葉では「に」も使用できる。

関連語

　日本語には関連表現として「（〜と）一つになる」があるが、主語は通常、人以外のものである。

(1) 私の心は彼女（の心）と {一つに / ×一体と} なった。

　　My heart has become one with {her heart/hers}.

猫の首に鈴をつける　phr.　隠喩

危険を承知で行動する

例文

(a) 実現不可能な解決案を提案するのは易しい。立派な計画だけれど、誰が猫の首に鈴をつけるのか。

(b) 彼らはアメリカの政策にはかなり不満なのだが、猫の首に鈴をつける勇気はないし、裸だと言って王様の気を損ねることもできないのだ。

解説

1. このことわざは西暦6世紀前のイソップの寓話の一つから引用されたようである。ねずみが身の危険をあらかじめ知ることができるように猫に鈴をつけたらどうかという妙案についての話である。最初の日本語訳は1593年に出た『伊曾保物語』である。訳者は不明。

2. 日本語は「猫の首に鈴をつける」となっているが、「の首」を省略して英語のように「猫に鈴をつける」と換喩表現にすることもできる。

belly landing / comp. n. / metaphor

when a plane's landing gear fails to deploy and it lands directly on its fuselage

[Example]

I heard that the plane's landing gear failed to deploy and it made a belly landing on the coast.

bend the rules / phr. / metaphor

to change the rules as one sees fit

[REL] {break/violate} the rules

[ANT] {obey/observe/stick to/play by} the rules

[Examples]

Mike: Could I take three weeks off this summer?

Section Chief: No, you can't take more than two weeks off.

Mike: I know, but can't you make an exception for just this summer?

Section Chief: No, I can't bend the rules just for you.

- -

(a) There will come times when common sense says you should bend the rules to accommodate the situation.

(b) If he can't win by following the rules of the game, then he's likely to bend the rules.

[Notes]

1. *[bend ~/to be bent]* has a negative connotation in both English and Japanese. The same is true of Sino-Japanese compounds with 曲 *kyoku* (bend) in them, such as 歪曲 *waikyoku* (distortion), 曲解 *kyokkai* (misinterpretation/biased interpretation), and 曲学 *kyokugaku* (bad scholarship), among others.

2. *Mageru* can take *hōritsu* (law), *jijitsu* (facts), or *jisetsu* ([one's own] view) as its direct object, but *bend* can only take the first two. 📖→解説(1)

[REL]

Break the rules and *violate the rules* correspond to *kisoku o yaburu* and *kisoku o okasu*, respectively. Note that the verbs *break/yaburu* and *violate/okasu* are also used metaphorically. 📖→関連語(1)

[ANT]

The English ANT is *{obey/observe/stick to/play by} the rules*, and the Japanese ANTs are *kisoku ni shitagau* and *kisoku o mamoru*.

(1) If you are to live in this dorm, you must {obey/observe/stick to/play by} the rules, or there will be problems.
この寮に住んでいるからには、|規則に従って/規則を守って| もらわなければ困る。

胴体着陸 / comp. n. 隠喩
飛行機が車輪を使わないで直接機体を地面にあてて着陸すること

【例文】

飛行機が故障して、海岸に胴体着陸をしたそうだ。

B

規則を曲げる / phr. 隠喩
ルールを（誰かの利益になるよう）勝手に変える

【関】規則を{破る/犯す}

【反】規則に従う，規則を守る

【例文】

マイク：この夏、休暇を３週間とってもよろしいでしょうか。

課長：いや、２週間しかとれないよ。

マイク：知っていますが、課長、今年の夏だけお願いします。

課長：いや、君だけのために規則を曲げるわけにいかないんだ。

(a) 状況に適応するために規則を曲げなければならない時が来るだろう。

(b) 試合の規則通りだと勝てない場合、彼は自分が勝つために規則を曲げるだろう。

【解説】

1. 「何かを曲げる/何かが曲げられる」は日英語ともに否定的な比喩になっている。同じことが「歪曲」「曲解」「曲学」のような漢語系複合語でも言える。

2. 日本語の「曲げる」は法律、事実、自説を直接目的語としてとれるが、英語の場合、自説には *bend* は使われない。*change (one's own) view* となる。

(1) a. 法律を曲げる

   pervert the law, bend the law

b. 事実を曲げる

   distort the facts, bend the facts

c. 自説を曲げる

   change one's views, ×bend one's views

【関連語】

break the rules と *violate the rules* はそれぞれ、「規則を破る」と「規則を犯す」に対応する。動詞 *break*「破る」も *violate*「犯す」も比喩的に使われている。

(1) a. この寮の規則を破ったら、もう住めなくなる。

   If you break the dormitory rules, you will be asked to move out.

b. 規則を犯すことは許されない。

   We cannot forgive violations of the rules.

【反意語】

日英語の反意表現は、それぞれ「規則に従う」「規則を守る」と *{obey/observe/stick to/play by} the rules* である。 → **ANT(1)**

> homograph

bet one's bottom dollar / phr. / metaphor

to be very certain about s.t.

何かについて確信している

> Example

I bet my bottom dollar that she's not interested in you at all.

彼女は絶対に君のことなんか興味ないよ。有り金全部賭けてもいいね。

between life and death / phr. / metonymy

in a situation where living and dying are equally likely

> Examples

(a) Given his condition and age, he is at a critical point between life and death.

(b) For two weeks our son wavered between life and death, but he pulled through. Now 19, he still suffers from a brain disorder.

(c) The climber who was swept away in the avalanche found himself between life and death as he desperately clung to the rope, but he managed to survive.

> Note

The English uses the spatial preposition *between*, whereas the Japanese uses the spatial noun *sakai* (border). The use of *life* and *death* is an example of metonymy, since they metaphorically represent "this world" and "the world beyond."

beyond / prep. / metaphor

for s.t. to exceed s.o.'s {imagination/means/ability}

> Examples

(a) The flu that winter was terrible beyond belief. Millions were infected and thousands died.

(b) That luxury car is definitely beyond my means.

(c) William Faulkner's novels are beyond my comprehension.

(d) These questions are far beyond my ability to answer.

> Notes

1. The English preposition *beyond* and its corresponding Japanese verb *koeru* (surpass, exceed) express the idea that something far exceeds one's mental, intellectual, creative, or economic capacity.

2. There are cases where *beyond* does not correspond to *koeru*, as in (1).

(1) a. Einstein's greatness is beyond comparison.

アインシュタインの偉大さは {比類がない/ ˣ比較を超えている}。

b. It is beyond doubt that the physical affects the mental and the other way around.

体が心に影響を与え、そしてその逆もあることは {疑いのないことである/ ˣ疑いを超えている}。

c. It is beyond dispute that society is dependent on science.

社会が科学に依存していることは {論争の余地がない/ ˣ論争を超えている}。

同形異義語

財布の底をはたく / phr. / 隠喩
　　さい ふ　そこ　　　　　　　　　　　　　　　いん ゆ

今持っているお金を全部使ってしまう
　いま も　　　　　　かね　ぜん ぶ つか
to spend all the money one has

例文

私達は財布の底をはたいて車を買った。
わたしたち　さい ふ　そこ　　　　　　くるま　か
We spent our bottom dollar on a car.

生死の境　phr.　換喩
　せい し　さかい　　　　　かん ゆ

死ぬかもしれない状況
　し　　　　　　　　　じょうきょう

例文

(a) 容態と年齢からすると、彼は今、生死の境の危ないところにいる。
　　ようだい　ねんれい　　　　　　かれ　いま　せい し　さかい　あぶ

(b) 息子は2週間も生死の境をさまよっていたが、なんとかそこから抜け出ることが
　　むすこ　　しゅうかん　せい し　さかい　　　　　　　　　　　　　　　ぬ　で
　　できた。しかし、19歳になった今も、まだ脳障害に悩まされている。
　　　　　　　　　　さい　　　　　いま　　　　のうしょうがい　なや

(c) なだれに流された登山家は、必死にロープにしがみついて生死の境を生き延びた。
　　　　　なが　　とざんか　ひっし　　　　　　　　　　　　　せい し　さかい　い　の

解説

日英語ともそれぞれ、空間名詞の「境」と、空間を表す前置詞 *between* を使っている。「生」
と「死」はこの世とあの世という空間に属しているという比喩である。

超える　v.　隠喩
　こ　　　　　　　いん ゆ

{想像 / 資産 / 能力}以上である
　そうぞう　し さん　のうりょく　い じょう

例文

(a) インフルエンザは想像を超える規模で、何百万もの人が感染して、何千人もの人
　　　　　　　　　そうぞう　こ　きぼ　　なんびゃくまん　ひと　かんせん　　　なんぜんにん　ひと
　　が亡くなった。
　　　な

(b) 高級車の値段は間違いなく僕の収入を超えているよ。
　　こうきゅうしゃ　ねだん　まちが　　　　ぼく　しゅうにゅう　こ

(c) ウィリアム・フォークナーの小説は僕の理解を超えている。
　　　　　　　　　　　　　　　しょうせつ　ぼく　りかい　こ

(d) こうした質問は私の能力をはるかに超えているので答えられません。
　　　　　しつもん　わたし　のうりょく　　　　　こ　　　　　こた

解説

1. 日本語の「超える」と英語の前置詞 *beyond*（〜の向こう側に）は、ともに精神力、知力、想像
　力、経済力が常識的な程度以上だということを表す。

2. 英語の *beyond* は、日本語には置き換えられない場合がある。→📖 **Note(1)**

The biggest fish is always the one that got away. | phr. | metaphor

{s.t./s.o.} that one failed to obtain is thought to be especially superb

Examples

Mike: Did you decline the offer to transfer to Germany?

Colleague: Yeah. I can't speak German, and besides, I wasn't that enthusiastic about the work there. But I won't necessarily be able to do what I wanna do by staying here. Now I'm thinking that I should have grabbed that chance.

Mike: The biggest fish is always the one that got away.

Colleague: Yeah, I probably should've gone.

(a) We failed to recruit a fund manager who currently works at that mutual fund. The biggest fish is always the one that got away.

(b) I thought I could buy the house I saw in the online ad, but apparently someone has already bought it. As they say, the biggest fish is always the one that got away.

big-name | comp. adj. | metaphor

a person, group, institution, product, etc., that is very well-known, especially in a specific field

Examples

Mrs. S: Don't you have a friend who's an artist, and whose father is also a famous artist? Whatever happened to him?

Mr. S: Oh, Mr. Toyama. Well, in the end he couldn't become a huge success because of his big-name father. Now he's operating an art gallery.

(a) I want to go to graduate school after leaving college, but my parents want me to work for a big-name company like Toyota.

(b) Since the writer is already such a big-name novelist, it might be hard to make a movie from his latest book. He'd want to have tight control over the script, I imagine.

Note

In Japanese, *namae ga ōkī* (lit. "the name is big") is preferable to *ōkina namae* (big-name), but English uses both.

逃がした魚は大きい　　phr.　隠喩

一度手に入れ損なったものはとりわけすばらしく思われる

例文

マイク：ドイツ転任の話、断ったんだって？

同僚：うん、ドイツ語もできないし、仕事内容もあまり気乗りしなかったからね。でも、ここにいてもしたい仕事ができるわけじゃないからね。今思うと、チャンスだったかなと思って。

マイク：逃がした魚は大きかったね。

同僚：うん、後悔してるよ。

- -

(a) 我々は、現在その投資信託で仕事をしているファンドマネージャーの引き抜きに失敗した。逃がした魚は大きい。

(b) インターネットの広告で見た家を買えると思ったが、誰かに買われてしまったらしい。逃がした魚は大きい。

名前が大きい　　phr.　隠喩

{人 / 集団 / 機関 / 製品}が特定の分野でよく知られている

例文

鈴木(妻)：あなたのお友達の画家で、お父様も有名な画家っていう人がいたじゃない。今、どうしていらっしゃるの？

鈴木(夫)：ああ、遠山のこと。う～ん、父親の名前が大きすぎて、結局大成しなかったね。今は画廊をやっているよ。

- -

(a) 私は卒業後、大学院に進みたいと思っているが、両親はトヨタのような名前の大きい会社に就職することを望んでいる。

(b) 原作者の名前が大きいだけに、彼の最近の本の映画化は難しいと思うよ。脚本に関してはすべてをコントロールしたがるだろうね。

解説

日本語では「大きな名前」より「名前が大きい」のほうを使うが、英語では *big-name* も *name is big* もよく使う。

(take a) bird's eye view of ~   phr. / metaphor

to take a broad and objective view of s.t.

Examples

(a) Let's try to take a bird's eye view of the whole situation.

(b) First, let's take a few steps back and take a bird's eye view of your job.

(c) Last weekend we went to the Tokyo Skytree and enjoyed a bird's eye view of the city.

REL

The Japanese has the REL *~ o fukan-suru* (to look down on s.t. from above). Every instance of *~ o chōkan-suru* in (a) - (c) can be replaced by *~ o fukan-suru*. However, it should be noted that, unlike the main entry, the REL is not a metaphorical expression.

関連語(1)

bite one's lip   phr. / metonymy

to keep one's mouth shut to avoid showing one's feelings, esp. to keep from crying

REL bite one's tongue

Examples

Karen: Japanese pop songs lyrics make me so angry. The women are always just biting their lip and trying not to cry. They're so passive.

Mr. S: They say that's what makes Japanese women virtuous.

Mrs. S: That's not true at all. I heard that nowadays, young men are the ones biting their lip to keep themselves from crying because they have to put up with strong-willed women.

- -

(a) Biting my lip to keep myself from crying, I simply just nodded.

(b) He bit his lip in anger and screamed "I HATE YOU!" as tears streamed down his cheeks.

Note

Bite one's lip has an almost literal meaning, but because of the temporal contiguity of the action and the emotion (frustration, anger, etc.), it could be considered a case of metonymy.

REL

The English has the REL *bite one's tongue*, meaning "for s.o. to keep {his/her} mouth shut tightly to contain {his/her} chagrin or anger." The Japanese expression *shita o kamu* literally means "s.o. bites {his/her} tongue."

(1) He bit his {lip/tongue} in anger. (→(b))

×彼は怒りで舌を噛んだ。

（〜を）鳥瞰する　phr.　隠喩

幅広い、客観的な見方をする，上から全体を見下ろす

関　（〜を）俯瞰する

例文

(a) 全体の状況を鳥瞰してみましょう。

(b) まず2、3歩後ろに下がってあなたの仕事を鳥瞰してみましょう。

(c) 先週末、私たちは東京スカイツリーに行って、東京の街を鳥瞰した。

関連語

日本語には「（〜を）鳥瞰する」と並んで“高いところから見下ろす”という意味の関連表現「（〜を）俯瞰する」がある。(a)-(c)の「〜を鳥瞰する」は、すべて「〜を俯瞰する」で置き換えられる。しかし、前者は“鳥のように上から見下ろす”という比喩だが、後者は比喩ではない。

(1) 全体の状況を{鳥瞰/俯瞰}してみましょう。（→(a)）

唇を噛む　phr.　換喩

悔しさをこらえる，泣きたいのをがまんする

例文

カレン：　日本の演歌って、聞いてられないですね。女性が唇を噛んで、泣かないでひたすら耐えるとか。

鈴木（夫）：それは日本女性の美徳なんですよ。

鈴木（妻）：あら、そんなことありませんよ。最近は若い男性が女性のわがままに唇を噛んで、涙をこらえているんですって。

(a) 私は唇を噛んで泣くのを我慢して、ただうなずいた。

(b) 彼は怒りで唇を噛み、涙をこらえながら、「君なんか大嫌いだ！」と叫んだ。

解説

「唇を噛む」というのはほとんど字義通りの解釈だが、悔しさや怒りの感情が動作にともなうので、時間的隣接から換喩の一種ではないかと考えられる。

関連語

英語には*bite one's tongue*という関連表現があり、“〜（人）が口をきっと閉じて、悔しさや怒りをおさえる”という意味で使う。日本語では「舌を噛む」は字義通りの解釈しかない。

REL（1）

83

bite the hand that feeds you / phr. / metonymy

to betray s.o. who has taken good care of you

REL return evil for good

Examples

Mike: Is it true that Sato moved to our rival company?

Colleague: Looks like it. This company taught him everything from scratch, and he even got to go abroad and earn his MBA.

Mike: I can't believe it!

Colleague: Talk about biting the hand that feeds you.

- -

(a) I taught that guy everything he knows, but he ended up transferring to a rival company. Talk about biting the hand that feeds you.

(b) When you're betrayed by an employee you treated well, it feels like they're biting the hand that fed them.

Note

The English focuses on the one receiving the benefits, whereas the Japanese focuses on the one giving the benefits.

REL

Both the English and Japanese have RELs that are very similar to the main entries: *return evil for good* and *on o ada de kaesu* (lit. "to return kindness with harm"), respectively.

(1) He lived and labored for the people, but they returned evil for good.
彼は国民のために生き、国民のために働いた。しかし、国民は恩を仇で返した。

bitter experience / n. phr. / synesthesia

unpleasant and trying experience

Examples

Saya: Mike, what's the most bitter experience of your life so far?

Mike: Let's see... A girl dumped me in high school. That was pretty rough!

- -

(a) She learned through bitter experience that he was not to be trusted.

(b) I know from bitter experience how drunk driving can wreck lives. I was 13 when my dad was hit and killed by a drunk driver.

(c) Through my own bitter experience, I am keenly aware that women's rights still lag behind those of men in Japan.

Note

This entry is an example of synesthesia because *bitter*, an adjective that describes a taste, is used as an adjective for something. one cannot taste with one's tongue.

飼い犬に手を噛まれる　/ phr. / 隠喩
かいぬにてをかまれる　　　　　　　いんゆ

世話をした人に裏切られる
せわ　　ひと　うらぎ

[関] 恩を仇で返す
　　おん　あだ　かえ

B

[例文]

マイク：佐藤君って、うちのライバル会社に転職しちゃったんだって？
　　　　さとうくん　　　　　　　　　　かいしゃ　てんしょく

同僚：らしいね。うちで一から仕事を覚えて、アメリカの大学に留学させてもらって、
どうりょう　　　　　　　いち　しごと　おぼ　　　　　　　　だいがく　りゅうがく
　　　MBA まで取らせてもらったのにね。
　　　　　　と

マイク：へえ、そうなんだ。

同僚：うん、まさに飼い犬に手を噛まれたね。
どうりょう　　　　　　かいぬ　て　か

(a) 一から技術を教えた後輩がライバル会社に転職した。飼い犬に手を噛まれるとはこ
　　いち　ぎじゅつ　おし　こうはい　　　　　　　がいしゃ　てんしょく　　かいぬ　て　か
　　のことだ。

(b) 可愛がっていた部下に裏切られるとは、まさに飼い犬に手を噛まれるようなもの
　　かわい　　　　　ぶか　うらぎ　　　　　　　　　かいぬ　て　か
　　だ。

[解説]

　　英語では、恩恵を受けた者の視点が表現されているが、日本語では恩恵を与えた者の視点が
　　表現されている。

[関連語]

　　日英語とも、「恩を仇で返す」と *return evil for good* という非常に類似した関連表現がある。

—📖 REL(1)

苦い経験　/ n. phr. / 共感覚
にが　けいけん　　　　　　　　　きょうかんかく

不愉快で辛い経験
ふゆかい　つら　けいけん

[例文]

さや：ね、マイク、今までの人生で一番苦かった経験って、どんなこと？
　　　　　　　　いま　　　じんせい　いちばんにが　けいけん

マイク：そうだなあ。高校の時に失恋したことかな。あれは、苦くて辛い経験だったね。
　　　　　　　　　こうこう　とき　しつれん　　　　　　　　　にが　つら　けいけん

(a) 彼女は苦い経験を通して、彼が信用できないことを知った。
　　かのじょ　にが　けいけん　とお　　かれ　しんよう

(b) 私は 13 歳のときに、父を飲酒運転による交通事故で亡くしました。その苦い経
　　わたし　　さい　　　　　ちち　いんしゅうんてん　　こうつうじこ　な　　　　　にが　けい
　　験から、飲酒運転で幸せな生活がめちゃくちゃになることを知っています。
　　けん　　いんしゅうんてん　しあわ　せいかつ

(c) 私は職場での自分の苦い経験を通して、日本の女性の権利がまだ男性の権利より
　　わたし　しょくば　じぶん　にが　けいけん　とお　　にほん　じょせい　けんり　　　だんせい　けんり
　　遅れていることを痛感しています。
　　おく　　　　　　つうかん

[解説]

　　この見出しは「苦い」という味覚を表す形容詞が、舌で味わえないものを形容しているので、
　　共感覚表現である。

black and white / phr. / metaphor

involving an overly simplistic outlook on s.t. based on a very clear distinction

Examples

Colleague: I'm fed up with our section chief's simplemindedness.

Mike: He has a habit of immediately viewing things in black and white.

- -

(a) Some people only see the world in black and white.

(b) People often view the complexities and ambiguities of human behavior in black and white.

(c) A close friend of mine said to me recently, after taking a course in self-development, that she never realized how she had been seeing everything in black and white; now she was being challenged to see the middle ground.

Notes

1. In the Japanese, *shiro* precedes *kuro*, so one cannot reverse the word order (*×kuro ka shiro ka*). In the English, *black* precedes *white*, so one cannot say *×white and black*. Some non-metaphorical examples include as *black-and-white film/shirokuro-ēga*, *black-and-white TV/shirokuro-terebi*, and *black-and-white photograph/shirokuro-shashin*.

2. *Black and white* can be replaced with *black or white,* which uses the same conjunction as the Japanese. However, *and* is used far more frequently than *or*.

3. In Japanese, *shiro* (white) and *kuro* (black) can mean "not guilty" and "guilty," respectively. However, this is not the case in English. Two examples of English expressions that come close to this usage are *white lie* and *blacklist*.

REL

The Japanese has two RELs: *shirokuro tsukeru* and *shirokuro (o) hakkiri saseru*. Both mean "to settle a matter in a clear-cut way." 📖→関連語(1)

(as) black as coal / phr. / simile

for s.t. to be very black

REL   as black as ink

Examples

(a) The beach was as black as coal, which I thought was rather odd because I had never seen black sand before.

(b) I ate spaghetti that was black as coal. It tasted much better than it looked, but I didn't expect my teeth to also become black as coal.

白か黒か / phr. 隠喩

いいか悪いかだけに注意を向ける単純な見方

関 白黒つける，白黒（を）はっきりさせる

例文

同僚：うちの課長は、ほんと考えが短絡的なんだから。

マイク：うん、すぐに白か黒かで判断するのは悪いくせだよね。

- (a) 世の中を白か黒かでしか見られない人もいる。
- (b) 人々はしばしば人間の行動の複雑さと曖昧さを、白か黒かで割り切ろうとする。
- (c) 自己開発の講座に出た私の親友が最近こんなことを言った。自分が今まで何についても、白か黒かでしか物事を見なかったことに気付いて、今は物事の中間を見るように努力しているのだと。

解説

1. 日本語では「白」が「黒」の前に来るため「×黒か白か」とは言えないが、英語では black が white の前に来るため ×white and black とは言えない。比喩ではないが、次のような例がある。「白黒映画」vs. black-and-white film、「白黒テレビ」vs. black-and-white TV、「白黒写真」vs. black-and-white photograph など。

2. 日英語で使われている接続詞は、「～か～か」と and で異なっている。英語の black and white は日本語の「か」と同じ接続詞 or を使った black or white で置き換えることができるが、and のほうが or より使用頻度がはるかに高い。

3. 日本語では無罪を「白」、有罪を「黒」と言えるが、英語にはそのような言い方はない。しかし、それに近い使い方としては white lie（悪意のない嘘）と blacklist（ブラックリスト）という言葉がある。

関連語

日本語には、「白黒つける」「白黒（を）はっきりさせる」という関連表現がある。どちらも"物事をはっきりさせる"という意味である。

(1) いつまでも、どっちつかずのことを言っていないで、この辺で、白黒を{つけた / はっきりさせた}ほうがいい。
Don't be so noncommittal. It's about time for you to state your position in black and white.

炭のように黒い / phr. 直喩

とても黒い

関 石炭のように黒い

例文

- (a) 砂浜の砂は炭のように黒かったんです。黒い砂など見たことがなかったので、変だと思いました。
- (b) 炭のように黒い色のスパゲッティを食べた。見た目よりおいしかったけれど、食べた後、歯も炭のように黒くなって、恥ずかしかった。

Note

> *Sumi* (charcoal) is produced by heating wood in the absence of oxygen, whereas *sekitan* (coal) is naturally fossilized carbon. Both are primarily composed of carbon, and both are used as metaphors for something black.

REL

> In English and Japanese, *ink* and *sekitan* (coal) can be used instead of *coal* and *sumi* (charcoal), respectively, but these forms are not as common.

blind spot   comp. n.   metaphor

an area s.o. cannot see or comprehend

Examples

Kenta: I wonder why I got this one wrong.

Karen: Hmm, let's see... Oh, it's because this verb is irregular.

Kenta: Ahh! This is one of my blind spots. I completely missed that.

- -

(a) Dr. Holmes declared that every man has a blind spot.

(b) Did the escaped criminal find a blind spot in the jail's defenses?

(c) At that time, he didn't realize that his employees were dissatisfied with his management policies. He later acknowledged that his ignorance was a blind spot in his company operations.

Notes

1. The English means "an area s.o. cannot see" or "an area s.o. cannot understand," but the Japanese means "s.t. one does not notice" or "s.t. one has failed to see." These semantic differences result in different interpretations of the example sentences and explain why *blind spot* and *mōten* do not work in (1) and (2), respectively. 📖→解説(1)

(2) Many people think the American media has a blind spot when it comes to Islam. That is to say, they think the press has failed to adequately to explain why Muslim terrorists might have attacked the U.S.

多くの人々が、米国のメディアはイスラムのこととなると{よくわからない点 / ×盲点} がある と思っている。すなわち、イスラム教徒のテロリストが米国を攻撃する理由について、短絡的 な説明しかできないということだ。

2. Unlike *blind spot*, *mōten* does not mean "s.t. that one cannot see." To express this idea, one must use *shikaku* (lit. "dead angle"). 📖→解説(3)

3. The Japanese is often used to mean "weak {spot/point}," but the English is not used this way. 📖→解説(4)

4. The Japanese is a loanword from Chinese.

解説

「炭」は特定の木を無酸素加熱してできるものだが、「石炭」は自然に化石化した炭素である。どちらも主成分は炭素である。しかし、黒いものの比喩としては同じように使われる。

関連語

日本語の「炭」は「石炭」(coal)に、英語の*coal*は*ink*に置き換えられるが、どちらも見出しより使用頻度が低い。

盲点 comp. n. 隠喩

人の見落としがちなところ

例文

健太：僕、この問題、どうして間違えたのかな。

カレン：え、ああ、それはこの動詞が不規則に変化するからよ。

健太：あ、そうか、それは盲点！ 気がつかなかったなあ。

(a) ホームズ博士は、人は誰でも盲点があると言い切った。

(b) この逃亡した犯罪者は、監獄の防御態勢に盲点を見つけたのだろうか。

(c) 彼はその時は従業員が彼の経営方針に不満を持っていることを知らなかった。彼はあとでそれが彼の会社運営の盲点だったことを認めた。

解説

1. 英語は"見えないところ""わからないところ"という意味だが、日本語は"気がつかないところ""見落としてしまうこと"という意味である。このような意味の違いのために異なる解釈が出てくる。(1)の英語では *blind spot* が、(2)の日本語では、「盲点」が共に使えない。

　　　　　　　　　　　　　　　　　　　　　　　　　　　　　　━📖Note(2)

(1) デジタルカメラは大変便利だが、案外盲点なのがバッテリーの消耗度。旅行には常に充電器を持っていったほうがいい。
　　Digital cameras are very convenient, but {what we fail to notice/ ×their surprising blind spot} is how quick a battery is used up. You should bring a battery charger with you when you travel.

2. 日本語の「盲点」には、英語の *blind spot* と違って"見えないところ"という意味はない。したがって、"見えないところ"を表すときには「盲点」は使えず、「死角」を使わなければならない。

(3) 車の運転手は、この {死角 / ×盲点} に入っている人や他の車は見えません。
　　The driver may not see people or other vehicles that enter these blind spots.

3. 日本語は"欠点"という意味で使われることもあるが、英語にはそのような使い方はない。

(4) どんなに完璧に見えるレポートでも、必ず盲点があるものだ。
　　No matter how perfect a student's report may look, there are always {imperfections/ ×blind spots}.

4. 日本語は中国語からの借用語である。

blood freezes　/ phr.　metaphor

to shudder at s.t. fearful or eerie

REL　{a shiver runs/shivers run} down one's spine

Examples

(a) When I heard about the terrorist attack on the evening news, my blood froze.

(b) Michiko's blood froze when she had to walk through the cemetery at night.

(c) His blood froze when he saw his own apartment engulfed in flames.

REL

1. Both the English and Japanese have RELs: *{a shiver runs/shivers run} down one's spine* and *sesuji ga samuku naru* (lit. "the line of the backbone becomes cold"), respectively.

(1) Hearing about murders here and abroad on the evening news makes {my blood freeze/ shivers run down my spine}.
晩のニュースで国内外の殺人事件が報道されると、私は {血が凍って / 背筋が寒くなって} しまう。

2. In Japanese, the REL *sesuji ga samuku naru* is used more often than *chi ga kōru*.

Blood is thicker than water.　phr.　metaphor

the relationship between people of the same family (or the same ethnic group) is stronger and more important than other relationships

Examples

(a) They say blood is thicker than water, but I think that love is thicker than blood.

(b) It's long been taken as a fundamental fact of human nature that blood is thicker than water, but whenever I think about how often parents fight with their children, I wonder if this is really true.

(c) I hadn't seen my uncle since we met when I was a small child, but after my father's death, he helped me like a parent would by paying my school tuition. This made me realize that blood really is thicker than water.

Note

This proverb expresses the idea that blood relationships are more important than other relationships.

ANT

The Japanese has one ANT: *tōku no shinseki yori chikaku no tanin* (close non-relatives are better than distant relatives). 📖→反意語(1)

血が凍る / phr. 隠喩

恐ろしさや気味悪さでぞっとする

関 背筋が寒くなる

例文

- (a) 晩のニュースでテロの報道を聞いた時、血が凍る思いがした。
- (b) 道子は夜、墓場を一人で歩いて通り抜けなければならなかったとき血が凍った。
- (c) 彼は自分のアパートが炎に包まれているのを見たとき、血が凍った。

関連語

1. 日英語の関連表現は、それぞれ「背筋が寒くなる」と *[a shiver runs/shivers run] down one's spine* である。 REL (1)
2. 日本語では、関連表現の「背筋が寒くなる」は「血が凍る」よりもよく使われる。

血は水よりも濃い / phr. 隠喩

{家族 / 血縁 / 同民族}の関係のほうが他の関係より強い

反 遠くの親戚より近くの他人

例文

- (a) 血は水よりも濃いと言われますが、愛は血よりももっと濃いと私は思います。
- (b) 「血は水よりも濃い」というのは人間性の基本的事実と考えられてきましたが、親子の葛藤を考えると本当かな、と思います。
- (c) 幼い時に会ったきりの伯父だったが、父が亡くなった後も、学費のことでは親身に助けてもらった。つくづく血は水よりも濃いと思った。

解説

このことわざは、血縁関係は、他人との関係より強いという考えを表している。

反意語

日本語には「遠くの親戚より近くの他人」という、見出しとは反対の意味のことわざがある。

(1) 火事で焼け出されたとき、近所の人達がとても助けてくれたが、親戚は誰も来てくれなかった。「遠くの親戚より、近くの他人」というが、まさにそうだ。

When our house burned down, our neighbors helped us a lot, but none of our relatives came. As the saying goes, "close non-relatives are better than distant relatives."

blood-relationship | comp. n. | metaphor

a relationship between people who are related to each other

Examples

(a) In Japan, adoption is not as common as in the States, because Japanese people place great weight on blood-relationships.

(b) We can divide property regardless of blood-relationships if someone has written a will.

(c) In all cultures, blood-relationships are the most fundamental type of human relationship.

(d) People who want to prove a blood-relationship with someone else should undergo DNA testing.

Note

Ketsuen is a compound that consists of *ketsu* (blood) and *en* (a fated relationship).

REL

In informal contexts, *chi no tsunagari* (lit. "blood connection") is used more often than *ketsuen-kankē*. In (1a), the content of the sentence is rather formal, so it is slightly unnatural to say *chi no tsunagari*, but in (1b), the content of the sentence is not so formal, so *chi no tsunagari* is perfectly fine. 📖→関連語(**1**)

blood, sweat, and tears | n. phr. | metaphor

one's great efforts to obtain s.t.

Examples

Kenta: Mom, here's a Mother's Day present for you.

Mrs. S: How sweet of you!

Kenta: It cost me almost half the money I made from my part-time job this month. I poured my blood, sweat, and tears into this gift.

Mrs. S: Well then, I'll be sure to treasure it!

- -

(a) This victory was won through our team's blood, sweat, and tears.

(b) His awe-inspiring performance was the result of blood, sweat, and tears.

Notes

1. In both English and Japanese, *blood, sweat, and tears/chi to ase to namida* is the most common ordering for the three elements.
2. The conceptual metaphor underlying both the English and Japanese is that human efforts that lead to great results are the product of blood, sweat, and tears.

血縁関係 / comp. n. / 隠喩
けつえんかんけい

親、兄弟、親戚などの同じ血統を持つ関係
おや　きょうだい　しんせき　　　　　おな　けっとう　も　　かんけい

関 血のつながり
ち

例文

(a) 日本人は欧米人より血縁関係を重んじるため、日本では養子をもらうことが欧米
にほんじん　おうべいじん　　けつえんかんけい　おも　　　　　　　にほん　　　ようし　　　　　　　　　　おうべい
ほど一般的ではない。
いっぱんてき

(b) 遺言を書けば、血縁関係に関係なく財産を分与することができる。
ゆいごん　か　　　けつえんかんけい　かんけい　　　ざいさん　ぶんよ

(c) どの文化でも血縁関係は一番基本的な人間関係だ。
ぶんか　　けつえんかんけい　いちばんきほんてき　にんげんかんけい

(d) 誰かとの血縁関係を証明したい人は、DNA のテストをするといいだろう。
だれ　　　けつえんかんけい　しょうめい　　ひと

解説

「血縁」は、「血」と"運命的に関係のある状態、事実"という意味の「縁」からなっている。

関連語

文の内容がやわらかい場合には「血縁関係」より「血のつながり」の方が使用されることが多
い。つまり、(1a)では文の内容がかたいので、「血のつながり」は多少不自然であるが、(1b)
は文の内容がやわらかいので、「血のつながり」は問題ない。

(1) a. 個人の間の{血縁関係 /? 血のつながり}は遺伝学の基本的要素である。
Blood-relationships between individuals form the foundation of the field of genetics.

b. {血縁関係 / 血のつながり}だけが親子関係ではありません。
A blood relationship alone doesn't make a parent-child relationship.

血と汗と涙 / n. phr. / 隠喩
ち　あせ　なみだ　　　　　　　　いんゆ

何かを得るための最大限の努力
なに　え　　　　　　さいだいげん　どりょく

例文

健太：お母さん、これ、母の日のプレゼント。
けんた　　かあ　　　　　　　はは　ひ

鈴木（妻）：まあ、ありがとう。
すずき　つま

健太：今月のアルバイト代の半分もしたんだ。僕の血と汗と涙の結晶だよ。
けんた　こんげつ　　　　　だい　はんぶん　　　　ぼく　ち　あせ　なみだ　けっしょう

鈴木（妻）：どうも、ありがとう。大切にするわ。
すずき　つま　　　　　　　　　　　　たいせつ

(a) この勝利はわがチームの血と汗と涙で勝ち取ったものだ。
しょうり　　　　　　　　　ち　あせ　なみだ　か　と

(b) 大勢の人々を驚かした彼のすばらしい演奏は、血と汗と涙の賜物だった。
おおぜい　ひとびと　おどろ　　　かれ　　　　　　　えんそう　　ち　あせ　なみだ　たまもの

解説

1. 日英語とも、「血と汗と涙」/blood, sweat, and tears が、三つの要素を表す最も一般的な順序
である。

2. 日英語の背後には、成果を上げるための人間の努力とは血と汗と涙の結晶であるという比喩
的な思考がある。

bloodless ~ / phr. / metaphor

to achieve change without fighting or casualties

[Example]

Mahatma Gandhi's philosophy and practice of non-violence resulted in Indian independence through a bloodless victory.

---

homograph

blow hot and cold / phr. / metaphor

to change one's mind (about something) often
すぐ気が変わる

[Example]

Jane blew hot and cold about going to college.
ジェーンは大学進学について、しょっちゅう気が変わった。

---

homograph

{blow/toot} one's own horn / phr. / metaphor

to praise oneself
自分のことを自慢する

[Example]

Though he never blows his own horn, he has written two outstanding books on economics.
彼は決して自慢をしないけれど、優れた経済学の本を2冊書いている。

---

bolt {from/out of} the blue, a / phr. / metaphor

a totally unexpected event or development

[REL] out of a clear sky; like a thunderbolt

[Examples]

Mike: I heard that Mr. Saito, the department head, is jumping ahead of five people to become company president.

Colleague: Yep. It's so out of the blue, isn't it? There weren't even any rumors.

Mike: It'll be good to shake things up a bit, don't you think?

Colleague: I hope you're right.

- - - - - - - - - - - - - - - - - - - -

(a) The news that J. F. Kennedy was assassinated came like a bolt from the blue.

(b) We had been sure that he was in Tokyo, so his sudden appearance in New York was like a bolt out of the blue.

無血(の〜) / comp. n. / 隠喩

戦いによって人が死んだり傷付いたりすることなく、何かがなされること

例文

マハトマ・ガンジーの非暴力思想と実践は、インド独立に無血の勝利をもたらした。

同形異義語

熱しやすく冷めやすい / phr. / 隠喩

すぐ夢中になって、すぐ飽きてしまう
to immediately get excited about s.t. and then get tired of it soon afterwards

例文

妹は熱しやすく冷めやすい性格で、なんでもすぐ夢中になるが、すぐに飽きてしまう。
My sister is so fickle. She'll get really excited about something and then immediately get bored.

同形異義語

ほらを吹く / phr. / 隠喩

大げさなでたらめを言う
to tell tall tales

例文

彼は大ぼら吹きだ。ほらを吹いてばかりいるので、彼の言うことは信用できない。
He's always telling tall tales. We can't trust him because he's always exaggerating things.

青天のへきれき / n. phr. / 隠喩

まったく予期していなかった出来事や展開

関 寝耳に水

例文

マイク：今度、斉藤部長が5人抜きで、新社長になるんだって。

同僚：らしいね。青天のへきれきさ。そんな噂、聞いたこともなかったから。

マイク：新しい体制になって、いいんじゃないかな。

同僚：だといいけど。

- -

(a) J.F. ケネディ暗殺のニュースは誰にとっても青天のへきれきだった。

(b) 僕達は彼がてっきり東京にいると思っていたので、突然ニューヨークに現れたのは青天のへきれきでした。

Notes

1. It should be noted that *hekireki* (bolt) cannot be used by itself as a noun.
2. *Out of the blue* can be used as an abbreviation of *bolt out of the blue*, as shown in the dialogue.

REL

The English and Japanese have the RELs {*out of a clear sky/like a thunderbolt*} and *nemimi ni mizu* (lit. "water on sleeping ears"), respectively. 📖—関連語(1)

The Japanese expression *hareta sora kara*, which is *out of a clear (blue) sky* in English, cannot be used figuratively.

bone-chilling / comp. adj. / metaphor

extremely {cold/scary}

REL chill to the bone

Examples

Kenta: Karen, where in America are you from?

Karen: Chicago.

Kenta: Chicago's pretty cold in winter, right?

Karen: Cold? More like bone-chilling, thanks to the freezing wind that blows off Lake Michigan.

- -

(a) The bone-chilling weather was apparently the biggest problem confronting the demonstrators.

(b) The cold was bone-chilling, so I put my hands in my pockets.

Notes

1. The English often appears with *weather*, as in (a), or *cold*, as in (b). By contrast, the Japanese can be used with *samusa* (coldness), as in (a), and *samui* (cold), as in (b), but it cannot be used with *tenki* (weather). 📖—解説(1)
2. The English can also mean "very scary," as in (2) or "a feeling of coldness inside/a chill," as in (3), but the Japanese cannot. Note that the Japanese literally means "a chill that seeps deeply into one's bones and body." Thus, the Japanese cannot be used to refer to chills or other sensations that arise from within the body.

(2) I loved reading *The Very Real Ghost*. It was bone-chilling!
私は「本物の幽霊」という本が気に入った。その本は読んで {背筋がぞっとする/˟骨身に沁みる} 本だった。

(3) I've had a headache since morning, and I feel bone-chillingly cold. Maybe I caught a cold.
今朝から頭が痛くて、{ぞくぞく寒気がする/˟寒さが骨身に沁みる}。風邪を引いたようだ。

3. The Japanese can be used when one is deeply affected by someone's words, but the English cannot be used this way. 📖—解説(4)

解説

1. 「へきれき」は名詞として単独には使えない。
2. 会話例のように英語では *out of the blue* という表現が、*bolt out of the blue* の省略形として使われる。

関連語

日英語にはそれぞれ、「寝耳に水」と *out of a clear sky, like a thunderbolt* という関連表現がある。

(1) しばらくとりとめもない話をした後、彼女はいきなり「実は私、誕生日に結婚するんだ」と言った。まさしく寝耳に水だった。

We were having a casual conversation when she suddenly said, "I'm getting married on my birthday." The news {came out of a clear blue sky/hit me like a bolt out of the blue/hit me like a thunderbolt}.

なお、英語の *out of a clear sky* に当たる「晴れた空から」は、日本語では比喩表現としては使えない。

骨身に沁みる / phr. 隠喩

ひどく寒い，{人の言葉 / 親切}を強く心で感じる

関 骨身にこたえる

例文

健太：カレンって、アメリカのどこ出身？

カレン：シカゴよ。

健太：シカゴって、冬、寒いんでしょ。

カレン：寒いなんてもんじゃないわよ。ミシガン湖からの風が冷たくてね。骨身に沁みる寒さって、あのことよ。

- -

(a) デモ参加者にとって、一番の問題は骨身に沁みる寒さだったようだ。

(b) 骨身に沁みるほど寒くて、僕は両手を上着のポケットに突っ込んだ。

解説

1. 英語は(a)のように *weather*、(b)のように *cold* とよく結びつく。日本語は(a)のように「寒さ」か、(b)のように「寒い」をとるが、「天気」はとれない。

(1) 骨身に沁みる{寒さ /ˣ天気}が数週間続いた後、このところ暖かくなってきている。
After weeks of bone-chilling weather, it's finally been getting warmer recently.

2. 英語は"とても怖い""寒気"という意味でも使えるが、日本語は使えない。日本語は字義通りには、"寒さが骨と体に沁み通るくらい寒い"という意味であるから、風邪の悪寒など、体内から起きる寒さには使えない。 ▶📖 Note (2) (3)

3. 日本語は、"人の言葉を強く心で感じる"という場合にも使えるが、英語では使えない。

(4) 父の励みの言葉は骨身に沁みた。
My father's encouraging words touched me deeply.
cf. ˣMy father's words chilled me to the bone.

REL

1. In Japanese, there is one REL: *honemi ni kotaeru.* The REL means "to feel terribly cold," which is the same as *honemi ni shimiru.* In addition, *honemi ni shimiru* can mean "for s.o.'s {words/deeds} to move one deeply," and *honemi ni kotaeru* can mean "to feel intense psychological pain." 📖→関連語(1)
2. The English has the REL *chill to the bone.*

(2) The cold {was bone-chilling/chilled me to the bone}, so I put my hands in my pockets. (→(b))

---

bookworm / comp. n. / metaphor

s.o. who reads a lot of books

Examples

Kenta: Dad, you're still reading? You're a real bookworm, huh?

Mr. S: If I'm a bookworm, then you're a computer worm.

- -

(a) He's a bookworm who can recall everything he reads perfectly.

(b) She was a bookworm in primary school, studied hard throughout high school, and then entered a good university.

Notes

1. The English is a nominal compound, but the Japanese is a noun phrase. It appears that there is no borrowing relationship between the two.
2. In Japanese, *~ no mushi* is frequently used to mean "a person who is crazy about s.t.," as in *shigoto no mushi* (workaholic), *benkyō no mushi* (s.o. who loves studying), *manga no mushi* (s.o. who loves reading *manga*), and so on. But in English, *worm* is not typically appended to words other than *book.*

---

bosom buddy / comp. n. / metaphor

a very close friend on whom s.o. can depend

REL bosom {friend/pal}

Examples

(a) My college roommate has become my bosom buddy.

(b) He was President Lincoln's bosom buddy.

Note

The English uses *bosom*, an archaic word for *breast*, but the Japanese version uses *fuku-shin*, a compound that consists of *fuku* (stomach) and *shin* (heart).

REL

1. The word *buddy* in *bosom buddy* can be replaced by *friend*, but this is used less frequently.

(1) He was a bosom {buddy/friend} of mine at the time.
その当時、彼は私の腹心の友だった。

2. The Japanese has the REL *kokoro no tomo*, which is used to indicate a person or pet with whom one has a strong affinity. 📖→関連語(2)

関連語

1. 日本語には「骨身にこたえる」という関連表現がある。「骨身に沁みる」と同様「寒さを強く感じる」という意味がある。また、「骨身に沁みる」は「{人の言葉 / 親切}を強く感じる」、「骨身にこたえる」は「心理的苦しみを強く感じる」という別の意味を持つ。

(1) デモ参加者にとって、一番の問題は骨身に{沁みる / こたえる}寒さだったようだ。(→(a))

2. 英語には *chill to the bone* という関連表現がある。**━📖 REL(2)**

本の虫 / n. phr. 隠喩

本をたくさん読む人

例文

健太：お父さん、また、本、読んでるの？　まったく本の虫だね。

鈴木(夫)：僕が本の虫なら、おまえはコンピュータの虫だな。

(a) 彼は本の虫で、読んだものを全部思い出す才能を持っている。

(b) 彼女は小学校のときに本の虫で、中学、高校のときはずっとよく勉強をし、そしていい大学に入った。

解説

1. 英語は複合名詞だが、日本語は名詞句である。両者に借用関係はないようである。

2. 日本語では「～の虫」は「本の虫」だけではなく、何かに熱中している人のことを言うときに「仕事の虫」「勉強の虫」「マンガの虫」などとも言う。しかし、英語では *bookworm* しかない。

腹心の友 / n. phr. 隠喩

信頼できる親しい友人

関 心の友

例文

(a) 大学時代のルームメイトは、今では私の腹心の友である。

(b) 彼はリンカーン大統領の腹心の友だった。

解説

英語では"胸"を表す *bosom* が使われているが、日本語では「腹」と「心」からなる複合名詞「腹心」が使われている。

関連語

1. 英語の *bosom buddy* の *buddy* は *friend* に置き換えることができるが、使用頻度は低い。

━📖 REL(1)

2. 日本語には同じような意味の表現「心の友」がある。強い共感を持っている人かペットを指す。

(2) 我が家の愛犬は、私たち家族の{心の友 /ˣ腹心の友}です。

Our dog is an important member of our family.

brain drain
comp. n. / metaphor/synecdoche

a phenomenon whereby talented professionals abandon their home country and go abroad to work under better conditions

Examples
- (a) The degree of brain drain from Japan to the U.S. isn't as high as it is with some other countries.
- (b) More research funding may be able to stem this country's brain drain.

Notes
1. *Drain* and *ryūshutsu* originated as verbs that mean "to gradually draw off liquid" and "to flow out," respectively.
2. Strictly speaking, the expression is a combination of metaphor and synecdoche, because *drain* and *ryūshutsu* liken human movement to the draining of liquid, and *brain* and *zunō* describe the part of a person that is the source of intelligence.

brain worker
comp. n. / metaphor

a worker who relies on mental ability rather than bodily strength; a white-collar worker

[ANT] manual laborer

Examples
- (a) Brain workers are less healthy than manual laborers because they don't move their bodies around enough.
- (b) As agriculture becomes increasingly computerized, farmers will eventually become more like brain workers than manual laborers.

[A][N][T]

The English ANT is *manual laborer* and the Japanese ANT is *nikutai-rōdōsha*. (→(a)(b))

brainwash
comp. v. / metaphor

to forcefully instill one's {ideas/ideology} into s.o. else's mind

Examples

Mike: Recently I've been getting e-mails from my grandmother back in the States.

Mrs. S: Really? From your grandmother? Wow.

Mike: Apparently her neighbor brainwashed her by going on and on about how convenient e-mail is. She even sends me photos she takes with her smartphone!

- (a) When she was 19 years old, my sister was brainwashed by a religious fanatic she met at college.
- (b) The tyrant brainwashed the citizens into worshipping him and doing his every bidding.

頭脳流出　/ comp. n.　隠喩 / 換喩
ずのうりゅうしゅつ

専門的な才能を持った{研究者 / 技術者}が、外国に行きよりよい条件で{研究 / 技術開発}
せんもんてき　さいのう　も　　けんきゅうしゃ　ぎじゅつしゃ　　　　がいこく　い　　　　　　　じょうけん　けんきゅう　ぎじゅつかいはつ
に携わり、母国に戻らないこと
たずさ　　ぼこく　もど

例文
(a) 日本からアメリカへの頭脳流出の数は、諸外国に比べてそれほど多くはない。
にほん　　　　　　　　　ずのうりゅうしゅつ　かず　　しょがいこく　くら　　　　　　　　おお
(b) 研究助成金がもっと出れば、この国の頭脳流出をせき止めることができるだろ
けんきゅうじょせいきん　　　で　　　　　　　くに　ずのうりゅうしゅつ　　と
う。

解説
1. 「流出」も drain ももともとは動詞で、基本義はそれぞれ、"液体が流れ出る"と"徐々に液体
を取り去る"である。
2. 厳密に言うとこの表現は隠喩であり、かつ換喩である。なぜなら「流出」と drain は人の移動
を液体の流れと比較しているし、「頭脳」と brain も体の一部だからである。

頭脳労働者　comp. n.　隠喩
ずのうろうどうしゃ　　　　　　　　いんゆ

体力というよりむしろ知力を使って仕事をする人
たいりょく　　　　　　　　　ちりょく　つか　　しごと　　　　ひと

反 肉体労働者
にくたいろうどうしゃ

例文
(a) 頭脳労働者は肉体労働者より不健康だ。なぜならば、彼らは十分に身体を動かさ
ずのうろうどうしゃ　にくたいろうどうしゃ　　ふけんこう　　　　　　　　　かれ　　じゅうぶん　からだ　うご
ないからだ。
(b) 農業もコンピュータ化が進むと、農民はやがては肉体労働者ではなく頭脳労働者
のうぎょう　　　　　　　か　すす　　　のうみん　　　　　　にくたいろうどうしゃ　　　　　ずのうろうどうしゃ
となるだろう。

反意語
日英語の反意表現は、それぞれ「肉体労働者」と manual laborer である。(→(a)(b))

洗脳する　comp. v.　隠喩
せんのう　　　　　　　　　　いんゆ

ほかの人の心に{考え / 思想}を入れ込む
ひと　こころ　かんが　しそう　い　こ

例文
マイク：最近、アメリカの祖母から E メールが来るんですよ。
さいきん　　　　　　　　そぼ　　　　　　　　　　く
鈴木(妻)：あら、おばあさまから？　すごいわね。
すずき　つま
マイク：近所の人に、E メールは便利だ、便利だって洗脳されちゃったらしいんです。
きんじょ　ひと　　　　　　　　べんり　　　べんり　　　せんのう
スマホで撮った写真まで送ってきますよ。
と　　しゃしん　おく

(a) 妹は 19 歳の時に、大学で出会った宗教の狂信者に洗脳された。
いもうと　さい　とき　　だいがく　であ　　しゅうきょう　きょうしんしゃ　せんのう
(b) その独裁者は市民を洗脳して、彼をあがめ、彼の命令に従うようにした。
どくさいしゃ　しみん　せんのう　　　かれ　　　　　　かれ　めいれい　したが

Notes

1. Both the English and Japanese are compounds that consist of two elements: *brain* + *wash* and *sen* (washing) + *nō* (brain), respectively. However, the order of the two elements in the English is reversed in the Japanese.
2. *Sennō* is a direct translation of *brainwashing*.

(as) brave as a lion / phr. / simile

very brave

Example

He was brave as a lion.

brazen-faced / comp. adj. / metaphor

to be very rude and disrespectful

Examples

(a) A rude, brazen-faced man suddenly forced his way into my room without my persmission.

(b) He's a shameless, brazen-faced brute who always ends up hurting people.

Notes

1. The adjective *brazen* originally came from the noun *brass*.
2. Both the English and Japanese are very close in their metaphorical meanings, but two different metals, *brass* and *tetsu* (iron), are used. Additionally, whereas the English means that "a person has a brass-like face," the Japanese means that "the skin of one's face looks like iron."

break (a bill) / phr. / metaphor

to receive a bill's value in smaller denominations

Examples

(a) Could you break this 10,000 yen bill into nine 1,000 yen bills and ten 100 yen coins?

(b) I have only large bills, so let me break them at this bank.

Note

The basic meaning of the verbs *break* and *kuzusu* are "for someone to render something unusable by destroying it" and "for someone to destroy s.t.'s original shape by smashing it," respectively.

解説

1. 日本語は「洗」+「脳」、英語は *brain*（脳）+ *wash*（洗う）で、ともに二つの要素からできている複合語である。ただし、日本語と英語では要素の順序は逆である。
2. 「洗脳」は英語の *brainwashing* の直訳である。

B

ライオンのように勇敢　*phr.*　直喩

とても勇敢

例文

彼は、ライオンのように勇敢だった。

鉄面皮 {の / な}　*comp. adj. (na)*　隠喩

とても失礼で、厚かましく図々しい

例文

(a) 非礼で鉄面皮な男が、突然許可なしに私の部屋に押し入って来た。
(b) 恥知らずで、鉄面皮の彼はいつも人の心を傷つけている。

解説

1. 英語の見出しに出ている形容詞の *brazen* は名詞の *brass* から出た形容詞である。
2. 日英語とも比喩的な意味は非常に近いが、「鉄」と *brass*（真鍮）という異なる金属が使われている。また、日本語は"顔の皮膚が鉄のようだ"という意味の表現であるのに対して、英語は"真鍮のような顔をしている"という意味の表現である。

お金を崩す　*phr.*　隠喩

単位の高いお金をもっと単位の低いお金にする

例文

(a) すみませんが、この1万円札を千円札9枚と100円玉10枚に崩していただけませんか。
(b) 大きいお金しかないから、この銀行で崩してもらいましょう。

解説

「崩す」と *break* の基本義は、それぞれ"ものの原形を砕いて壊す"と"何かを壊して使えないようにする"である。

103

break s.o.'s heart / phr. / metaphor

for {s.o./s.t.} to make s.o. else feel very sad

Examples

(a) When the dog I had loved for so many years died, it broke my heart.

(b) The news about the refugee children's deaths nearly broke my heart.

(c) What really broke her heart is when he didn't come after her.

Note

The Japanese verb *hari-sakeru* is a compound verb that consists of *haru* (to stretch) and *sakeru* (to rupture). *Sakeru* is an intransitive verb, and its transitive counterpart is *saku*. Thus, the Japanese expression means "one's heart spontaneously breaks," whereas the English expression means "the subject causes s.o.'s heart to break."

break (out) {into/in} a cold sweat / phr. / metaphor

to become frightened or nervous

Examples

Saya: What's wrong, Mike? Did something happen?

Mike: When I was crossing the intersection, a car came out of nowhere and almost hit me. I was so scared, I broke out in a cold sweat.

(a) They were trying to get me. I panicked and broke into a cold sweat before running out the back entrance.

(b) Just thinking about talking in front of so many people makes me break into a cold sweat.

Notes

1. The English and Japanese have the same figurative meaning, though they use different verbs: *break (out) {into/in}* ~ and *kaku* (to perspire), respectively.

2. The English has three main variants: *break out into a cold sweat*, *break into a cold sweat*, and *break out in a cold sweat*. *Break in a cold sweat* cannot be used.

break one's neck / phr. / metaphor

to exert oneself in order to achieve s.t.

REL break one's back

Examples

Mike: Mr. Suzuki, you really broke your neck for me. Thank you so much.

Mr. S: My pleasure. I'm glad that everything went well.

胸が張り裂ける　/ phr.　隠喩

強い悲しみや苦しみ、精神的な痛みを感じる

例文

(a) 長年かわいがってきた飼い犬が死んでしまい、私は胸が張り裂けるほど悲しかった。

(b) 難民の子供が犠牲になったニュースを見て、私は胸が張り裂けそうになった。

(c) 彼女が本当に胸が張り裂けるような思いをしたのは、彼が自分のことを追いかけてこなかった時だった。

解説

日本語の動詞の「張り裂ける」は「張る」＋「裂ける」の複合動詞である。「裂ける」は自動詞であり、対応する他動詞は「裂く」である。日英語の意味の違いは、日本語の自動詞「裂ける」は自然に「(人の)胸が裂けてしまう」という自発的な意味であるのに対して、英語の他動詞 break は文の主語が「胸を裂けさせる」という使役的な意味である点である。

冷や汗をかく　phr.　隠喩

危険や緊張した状況を経験する

例文

さや：どうしたの、マイク、そんなあせっちゃって。

マイク：いやあ、冷や汗をかいたよ。今、信号を渡っていたら突然車が走ってきて、ひかれそうになっちゃった。

(a) 彼等は僕を捕まえようとしていたのです。僕は慌てふためき、冷や汗をかき、裏口から逃げ出しました。

(b) 大勢の人の前で話すことを考えただけで冷や汗をかいてしまう。

解説

1. 日英語は比喩的な意味は同じだが、動詞が異なっている。日本語は「かく」（人が体内から汗やいびきを外に出す）で、英語は break (out) {into/in} ~（人が突然新しい状態に入る）である。

2. 英語には主に break out into a cold sweat、break into a cold sweat、break out in a cold sweat の三種類の表現がある。break in a cold sweat は使えない。

骨を折る　phr.　隠喩

何かのために苦労をする，苦心して人の世話をする

関 身を粉にする

例文

マイク：鈴木さん、今回のことではいろいろ骨を折っていただいて、どうもありがとうございました。

鈴木(夫)：いやいや、うまくいったようでよかったね。

(a) He wished his son would study harder, because he was breaking his neck to scrape up the money to keep him in college.

(b) She had to break her neck doing research in order to earn her spot at the conference in Paris.

Notes

1. The basic meaning of *oru* is "to separate a stick-like object into two or more parts" or "to bend a flat object like paper so that the parts overlap."

2. Both the English and Japanese have the literal meaning of "breaking one's {neck/bones}." The metaphorical meaning comes from the idea of "someone working so hard that {he/she} nearly breaks {his/her} {neck/bones}."

3. The Japanese cannot be used in a sentence containing a request, a question, or advice. However, the English does not have this restriction.

(1) When you enter a company, I want you to break your neck to succeed.
会社に入ったら{一生懸命働いてください/[×]骨を折ってください}。

4. In English, the subject of the expression can be anyone, but in Japanese it cannot be the first person. If it is the first person, the expression *hone o oru* has to be replaced by *kurō-suru* (to make the utmost effort to achieve s.t.), *isshō-kenmē hataraku* (to work very hard), or *ganbaru* (to do one's best). 📖➡解説(2)

REL

The English REL, *break one's back,* is used about as frequently as *break one's neck.* The Japanese REL, *mi o ko ni suru* (lit. "to make one's body into powder"), is a literary expression and used less frequently than *hone o oru.*

break new ground   phr.   metaphor

to do something that has never been done before

REL groundbreaking

Examples

(a) Star Wars broke new ground for in 1977 filmmaking with its superb special effects.

(b) The university broke new ground as one of the earliest institutions of higher education dedicated to lifelong learning.

(c) Marie Curie broke new ground in medicine.

Note

The English and Japanese have the same figurative meaning, but the verbs *break* and *kiri-hiraku* (to cut open) and the nouns *ground* and *tenchi* (heaven and earth) are different.

REL

The English has the REL *groundbreaking*, which can be used to modify a noun, but the Japanese entry has no corresponding noun modifier. *Kakkitekina* and *kakushintekina* are used instead.

(1) As science continues to advance, it is getting harder to do truly groundbreaking experiments than it was in the days of Thomas Edison.
科学の進歩とともに、一人の人間が本当に画期的な実験をするのは、エジソンの時代より難しくなっている。

（a）彼は息子を大学に入れるために骨を折って金を集めたのだ。だから、息子にもっと一生懸命勉強してほしいと思っていた。

（b）彼女は研究成果の取りまとめに骨を折った甲斐があって、パリの会議に出席することができた。

解説

1．日本語の「折る」の基本義は“棒状のものを二つかそれ以上に切り離す”、“平面状のものを曲げて重なるようにする”である。

2．日英語ともに字義通り“｛骨/首｝を折る”という解釈がある。比喩的な意味は「｛骨/首｝が折れそうになるほど何かを一生懸命する」という意味から出ている。

3．日本語は要求、質問、忠告のような文では使えない。しかし、英語にはそのような制約はない。►📖 Note（1）

4．英語では主語はどの人称でも可能だが、日本語では一人称は使えない。一人称の場合は「骨を折る」の代わりに、「苦労する」「一生懸命働く」「頑張る」などを用いる。

（2）私は｛苦労した/ˣ骨を折った｝甲斐があって、パリの会議に出席することができた。（→（b））

関連語

英語には *break one's back*（lit. 背中を折る）、日本語には「身を粉にする」という関連表現がある。*break one's back* は *break one's neck* とほぼ同じ使用頻度で使われる。日本語の「身を粉にする」は書き言葉的で、使用頻度は「骨を折る」より低い。

新天地を切り開く　phr.　隠喩

前に誰もしたことがない新しいことを始める

例文

（a）「スターウォーズ」は 1977 年に、その優れた特殊効果で映画製作の分野に新天地を切り開いた。

（b）その大学は生涯教育に尽くした最初の高等教育機関の一つとして、新天地を切り開きました。

（c）マリー・キュリーは医学の新天地を切り開いた。

解説

日英語とも比喩的な意味は同じだが、動詞の「切り開く」と *break*（壊す/切り裂く）、名詞の「天地」と *ground*（地表）は、多少意味が異なる。

関連語

英語には見出しに対応する名詞修飾語として *groundbreaking* があるが、日本語には見出しに対応する名詞修飾語はなく、「画期的な」「革新的な」などが使われる。►📖 REL（1）

break the law / phr. / metaphor

to intentionally ignore the law and do s.t. illegal

[ANT] {obey/observe} the law

Examples

Karen: Kenta, aren't you still 20? You're drinking. Aren't you breaking the law?

Kenta: Karen, in Japan you can start drinking when you're 20.

Karen: Really? In the States you have to be 21.

(a) It is a crime to break the law, no matter how bad the law may be.

(b) When children break the law, their parents must take responsibility.

Notes

1. The basic meaning of the Japanese verb *yaburu* is "for someone to damage a part of s.t. thin and flat by applying force to it."

2. In the English, *law* can be replaced by *rules, contract,* or *promise,* among others. In the Japanese, *hōritsu* can be replaced by *kisoku, kēyaku,* or *yakusoku.* See below for examples.

(1) I warned you that if you broke the {rules/contract/promise}, you would be punished.

もし {規則 / 契約 / 約束} を破ったら罰せられると警告したでしょ。

(2) I liked him, but he broke the promise he'd made me when we first started dating, so the relationship was over.

彼のことを気に入っていたけれど、はじめてデートしたときに交わした約束を彼が破ったので、二人の仲は終わってしまった。

3. There are other expressions in which *break* corresponds to *yaburu,* such as *break the silence* (*chinmoku o yaburu*), *break a record* (*kiroku o yaburu*), and so on. 📖→解説 **(3) (4)**

[ANT]

The ANTs for the English and Japanese are *{obey/observe} the law* and *hōritsu o mamoru,* respectively. 📖→反意語 **(1)**

break the mold / phr. / metaphor

to change conventional forms or methods for the better

[ANT] force s.o. into a mold

Examples

(a) Pablo Picasso broke the past mold of fine arts and invented cubism.

(b) That fashion designer had a radical fashion sense that broke the mold and immediately attracted the attention of the fashion world.

(c) That research method broke the mold and led to a new discovery.

Note

The basic meaning of *mold* is "a hollow container of a particular shape," and *kata* means "an outward form (to be followed)." For the basic meanings of *break* and *yaburu,* see the entry *break the law,* Note 1.

{法 / 法律}を破る　／ phr.　隠喩

意図的に法律を無視したり、違法なことをする

反 法律を守る

例文

カレン：健太、まだ二十歳でしょ。お酒飲んだりして法律を破ってるんじゃない？

健太：カレン、日本じゃ二十歳になったら酒を飲めるんだ。

カレン：そう？　アメリカは 21 歳からよ。

- -

（a）どんな悪法でも法律を破れば犯罪になる。

（b）子供が法律を破った場合は親の責任である。

解説

1．「破る」の基本義は "何か薄くて平たいものに力を加えてそれをだめにする" である。

2．日英語の「法律」/law は、それぞれ「規則」/ rules、「契約」/ contract、「約束」/ promise で置き換えることができる。 —📖 Note(1)(2)

3．本項目以外にも「沈黙を破る」/ break the silence、「記録を破る」/ break a record などがある。

（3）誰も口を開かない会議で、最初に沈黙を破るのには勇気がいる。
It takes courage to break the silence in a meeting where nobody speaks.

（4）世界で初めて、100 メートル 10 秒の記録を破ったのは、カール・ルイスだと言われている。
It's said that Carl Lewis was the first to break 10 seconds in the 100-meter dash.

反意語

日英語の反意表現は、それぞれ、「法律を守る」と {obey/observe} the law である。

（1）どんな悪法でも、いったん法律となったからには、それを守らなければならない。
No matter how bad a law may be, once it has been written into law, we have to {obey/observe} it.

型を破る　phr.　隠喩

決まりきった形式や方式を斬新なやり方に変える

関 型破りの

反 型にはめる

例文

（a）パブロ・ピカソはそれまでの美術の型を破ってキュービズムを創始した。

（b）そのファッションデザイナーは、それまでの型を破った過激なファッションで業界の注目を一気に浴びた。

（c）その研究方法は従来の型を破っていたので、新しい発見ができたのだ。

解説

「型」と mold の基本義は、それぞれ "（従うべき）外見上の形" と "特別の形をした中のうつろな容器" である。「破る」と break の基本義については「{法 / 法律} を破る」の解説 1 を参照。

REL

The Japanese has the REL *kata-yaburi no*, a noun phrase. 📖→関連語(1)

ANT

The ANTs for the English and Japanese are *force s.o. into a mold* and *kata ni hameru*, respectively. 📖→反意語(1)

---

breathtaking / adj. / metaphor

very exciting or surprising

Examples

(a) This property offers breathtaking views of the lake.

(b) I found this beautifully animated Japanese film to be breathtaking.

(c) India is a land with hundreds of breathtakingly beautiful monuments.

Note

Both the English and Japanese have the same figurative meaning, but while the English literally means "s.t. takes away one's breath," *iki o nomu* (lit. "swallow one's breath") means "one has momentarily stopped breathing."

---

breed / v. / metaphor

for s.t. to bring about s.t. else

Examples

(a) Eternal optimism breeds hope.

(b) Love doesn't necessarily breed respect, but respect breeds love.

(c) Fear breeds hate and hostility, and the ultimate result is violence.

Note

Breed means "to give birth to non-human offspring" or "to rear animals," but *umu* means "to give birth to human or non-human offspring."

REL

The Japanese has the REL *umi-dasu* (lit. "to give birth to s.t. and release it"), which can replace *umu* in all of the above expressions. *Umi-dasu* also means "to create s.t. new."

📖→関連語(1)

関連語

日本語には、「型破りの」という名詞を形容する句がある。

(1) そのデザイナーはいつも型破りのファッションを発表する。(→(b))

That fashion designer is always breaking the mold with her creations.

反意語

日英語にはそれぞれ「型にはめる」と *force s.o. into a mold* という反意表現がある。

(1) 日本の教育は子供たちを型にはめる教育だと言われる。

Japanese education is said to force children into a mold.

息を呑む　/ phr.　隠喩

とても感動したり、驚いたりする

例 文

(a) この土地からは息を呑むような湖の景色が見えます。

(b) 私は、この美しい日本のアニメ映画を見て息を呑んだ。

(c) インドは、息を呑むほど美しい遺跡が何百とある国です。

解 説

日英語とも同じ比喩的意味だが、日本語では"人が息を一瞬止める"という状況を表現しているのに対して、英語では"何かが息を奪う"という状況を表現している。

(〜を)生む　/ v.　隠喩

何かが他のことを引き起こす

関 生み出す

例 文

(a) この永遠の楽観主義が希望を生む。

(b) 愛がいつも尊敬の念を生むとは限りませんが、尊敬の念は愛を生むのです。

(c) 恐怖は憎悪と敵意を生み、その究極の結果は暴力である。

解 説

「生む」は"{人間/動物}の子供を出産すること"を意味するのに対して、*breed* は"動物の子供を出産すること、あるいは動物を飼うこと"を意味する。

関連語

日本語には「生み出す」という関連表現がある。これは見出しと自由に置き換えられる。また「生み出す」には、"新しい物を作る"という意味もある。

(1) 新製品を生み出すまで3年もかかった。

It took three years to {create/×breed} this new product.

111

bridge between / n. phr. / metaphor

s.t. that connects places, eras, people, etc.

Examples

Karen: What kind of person was this Umeko Tsuda?

Saya: She was the first woman to go study in America. When she returned to Japan, she founded an English language school for women.

Karen: I see. So she was the first woman to serve as a bridge between the U.S. and Japan?

Saya: That's right.

(a) Turkey is a bridge between Europe and Asia.

(b) The project is expected to become a bridge between young adults in the university and the local community.

Note

The English uses the preposition *between*, but the Japanese uses the verb *tsunagu* (to link/attach).

REL

Tsunagu can be replaced by *musubu* (to {fasten/bind/unite}). 📖➡ 関連語(1)

(as) bright as day / phr. / simile

as bright as it is during the daytime

Examples

(a) When they shot all the fireworks at once, the night sky became as bright as day, and you could see the joy on people's faces as they cheered.

(b) It might've been a night game, but the lights in the baseball stadium made it seem as bright as day.

Note

Bright and *akarui* can both be used metaphorically. *Bright* can mean "clever" or "lively," while *akarui* can mean "cheerful" or "{well-versed in/familiar with} s.t.," as shown below.
📖➡ 解説(1)(2)

(3) John was so bright that he finished college in three years.
　　ジョンは {頭がいい/ˣ明るい} ので大学を３年で卒業したんです。

bring s.t. into (sharp) relief （浮き彫りに{する / される / なる}）
→ {throw/bring} s.t. into (sharp) relief

B

（〜を）つなぐ橋　n. phr.　隠喩

{場所 / 時 / 人}などを結びつけるもの

関 （〜を）結ぶ橋

例文

カレン： この津田梅子ってどういう人？

さや： 女性で初めてアメリカに留学して、帰国してから、女性のために英語専門の学校を創った人よ。

カレン： そう。女性初の日米をつなぐ橋ってわけね。

さや： そういうこと。

- -

（a） トルコはヨーロッパとアジアをつなぐ橋である。

（b） この企画は、大学で学ぶ若者とその地域社会の人々をつなぐ橋になると期待されている。

解説

日本語は動詞の「（〜を）つなぐ」を用いるが、英語では前置詞 *between* を用いる。

関連語

日本語の動詞「つなぐ」は「結ぶ」と置き換えられる。

（1） トルコはヨーロッパとアジアを{つなぐ/結ぶ}橋である。（→(a)）

昼間のように明るい　phr.　直喩

日中のようにとても明るい

例文

（a） 花火がいっせいにあがると、あたりは一瞬昼間のように明るくなり、歓声をあげる人々の顔が照らし出された。

（b） 野球のナイターが昼間のように明るいスタジアムで行われていた。

解説

「明るい」と *bright* はどちらも比喩的に使われる。「明るい」は"性格が陽気な""あることに通じている"という意味を、*bright* は"頭がよい""活発な"という意味を持っている。

➡📖 Note (3)

（1） 彼女は性格がとても明るい。
She has such a {cheerful/bright} personality.

（2） この辺りは危険だから、土地の事情に明るい人に一緒に行ってもらったほうがいいですよ。
This neighborhood is dangerous, so it is better to ask someone who is {familiar/ ˣbright} with this area to go with you.

113

bring the curtain down on ~ / phr. metaphor

for {s.o./an organization} to put an end to s.t.

[ANT] raise the curtain on ~; the curtain opens on ~

Examples

(a) Now he has apparently chosen to bring the curtain down on his remarkble career as an actor.

(b) This company has brought the curtain down on its 45-year history as a TV manufacturer.

(c) Although he has now brought the curtain down on his competitive life, he aims to stay in the sport.

(d) They unleashed a five-minute display involving fireworks to bring the curtain down on the ceremony.

Notes

1. In both the English and Japanese, what comes to an end is often a *career*/{*kyaria/kēreki*}, as in (a), *history/rekishi*, as in (b), or *life/jinsē*, as in (c).

2. Both the English and Japanese metaphors are believed to have originated from the act of lowering the curtain at the end of a play.

[R][E][L]

The Japanese REL *maku o tojiru* (lit. "to close the curtain") is used far more frequently than *maku o orosu*. 💬→関連語(1)

[A][N][T]

1. The Japanese ANTs are *maku o akeru*, *kaimaku-suru*, and *maku ga aku*. 💬→反意語(1)

2. The English ANTs are *raise the curtain on ~* and *the curtain opens on ~*.

(2) With the fall of the Berlin Wall in 1989, the curtain opened on a new period in history.
1989年のベルリンの壁崩壊後、新しい歴史の幕が開いた。

---

broken home / comp. n. metaphor

a family that has become dysfunctional due to divorce, death, or other issues

Examples

(a) He was brought up in a broken home in an impoverished area with a high crime rate.

(b) She fled from a broken home when she was a teenager.

Note

The basic meaning of *break* and *kowareru* is "for s.t. to spontaneously crack and be rendered unusable," and both verbs can be used figuratively to mean "for s.t. to lose its original function."

(〜{に / の}）幕を下ろす　phr.　隠喩

{人 / 組織}が何かを終わりにする

関 幕を閉じる

反 幕を開ける，開幕する，幕が開く

例 文

(a) どうやら彼は俳優としてのすばらしいキャリアに幕を下ろすことにしたようだ。

(b) この会社は、テレビ生産会社としての 45 年の歴史に幕を下ろした。

(c) 彼はこれで競技人生の幕を下ろしたが、スポーツは続けていくつもりだ。

(d) 花火を 5 分間打ち上げて、儀式に幕を下ろした。

解 説

1. 日英語ともに終わりにするものは、(a)の「キャリア / 経歴」/career、(b)の「歴史」/history、(c)の「人生」/life であることが多い。

2. 日英語ともに、「劇が終わったら劇場の幕を下ろす」という状況が比喩になったと考えられる。

関連語

日本語では関連表現として「幕を閉じる」があり、「幕を下ろす」よりはるかに使用頻度が高い。

(1) まだ、議会の {幕を下ろす / 幕を閉じる} 用意がない。

We're not ready to bring the curtain down on this session of the Diet.

反意語

1. 日本語の反意表現には「幕を開ける」「開幕する」「幕が開く」がある。

(1) その年のオリンピックはアテネで {幕を開けた / 開幕した / 幕が開いた}。

They raised the curtain on that year's Olympic games in Athens.

2. 英語の反意表現には *raise the curtain on* 〜 と *the curtain opens on* 〜 がある。 ANT(2)

壊れた家庭　n. phr.　隠喩

離婚や死亡などの理由で、家族が機能しなくなった状態

例 文

(a) 彼は犯罪率の高い、経済的に落ち込んだ地域の壊れた家庭に育った。

(b) 彼女は十代のとき、壊れた家庭を飛び出した。

解 説

日本語の「壊れる」も英語の *break* も "何かが自然にめちゃめちゃになる" という基本義で、"何かの元の機能が失われる" という比喩的な意味で使える。

broken record   comp. n.   metaphor

for {s.o./s.t.} to repeat s.t. over and over again

Examples

Saya: Is it true that Mary has a crush on Mike?

Karen: Yep. Every day she goes on and on about Mike this, Mike that. She's a broken record, and I've had enough.

(a) That song played over and over again like a broken record in my head.

(b) That politician sounds like a broken record, always bringing up the same issues again and again.

Notes

1. While the English can be used as both a simile (i.e. "like a broken record") and a metaphor, the Japanese is usually used as a simile.
2. The English often goes with the verb *sound*, as in (b).
3. The English expression tends to be applied to cases in which someone, rather than something, repeats something over and over.
4. The Japanese is a translation of the English, since *record* is a borrowed English word.

bubble bursts, the   phr.   metaphor

s.t. successful fails abruptly

Examples

Mrs. S: Did Mr. Yoshimoto change jobs?

Mr. S: Yeah. Apparently his last company went bankrupt when the bubble burst. I hear he's unemployed.

Mrs. S: Really? Guess the bubble economy has claimed another victim, huh?

(a) When the bubble burst, the company had to make a drastic reduction in the numbers of workers.

(b) First the bubble economy burst, then the real estate bubble burst.

build   v.   metaphor

to systematically develop s.t. from the beginning

Examples

Mrs. S: Isn't it tough to build a career in a country like Japan where the customs are so different?

Mike: Yeah, it hasn't been easy. I had trouble building trust with my co-workers towards the beginning.

(a) Mr. Yoshida built a reputation as a leader within his party.

壊れたレコード{のよう / みたい}　　/phr./　直喩

{誰か / 何か}が同じことを何回も繰り返す

例文

さや：メアリーって、マイクに首ったけなんだって？

カレン：そうなの。壊れたレコードみたいに、マイク、マイクって毎日うるさいから、困っちゃった。

(a) その歌は頭の中で壊れたレコードのように何度も何度も繰り返し聞こえた。

(b) その政治家は、壊れたレコードのように同じ問題ばかりを何度も何度も持ち出す。

解説

1. 日本語では「のよう / みたい」を付けた直喩の形で使われることが多いが、英語は *like* を付けた直喩でも、はずした隠喩でも使われる。

2. 英語は(b)のように、*sound*（聞こえる）という動詞と一緒に使われることが多い。

3. 英語は「何か」ではなく「誰か」が「何か」を何度も繰り返すような場合に使われる傾向がある。

4. 「レコード」は英語からの借用語であるから、日本語は英語からの翻訳である。

バブルが弾ける　　/phr./　隠喩

経済的成功が急に崩壊する

例文

鈴木(妻)：吉本さんて、仕事変わったの？

鈴木(夫)：うん、前の会社、バブルが弾けて倒産したらしいよ。今、失業中だって言ってたね。

鈴木(妻)：そう。バブル崩壊の犠牲者ね。

(a) バブルが弾けたときに、その会社は大幅な人員削減に迫られた。

(b) 最初にバブル経済が弾けて、次に不動産のバブルが弾けた。

(～を)築く　　v.　隠喩

基礎から何かを体系的に作り出す

例文

鈴木(妻)：日本のような習慣の違う国でキャリアを築くのは大変でしょう？

マイク：そうですね。始めに仕事仲間と信頼関係を築くのが難しかったですね。

(a) 吉田氏は政党の指導者としての評判を築いた。

(b) Through our reliable service, we have built good relationships with our customers.

(c) Bill Gates built his Microsoft empire in a single generation.

Note

Build means "to make s.t. by putting together {materials/parts}," and *kizuku* means "to build a structure using earth and stones, etc." Figuratively, however, they both mean "to systematically develop s.t."

---

homograph

{build/light} a fire under ~ / phr. / metaphor

to urge s.o. to action
望ましい結果を実現させるために人を促す

Example

The big loss lit a fire under the whole team.
その大敗はチーム全員の士気を高めた。

---

build a plan / phr. / metaphor

to create a plan of action

REL make a plan

Examples

Kenta: Saya, have you built a plan for what you're going to do after graduation?

Saya: I'm thinking of studying abroad in the U.S. to get my MBA.

Kenta: Sounds pretty solid!

- -

(a) In order to make a success out of this project, you should write down a list of your most important collaborators and build a plan to meet with them on a regular basis.

(b) Right now we're building a plan for a trip around the world.

Note

The Japanese verb *tateru*, the transitive counterpart of *tatsu*, means "to cause {s.o./s.t.} to take an upright position." It also contains the meaning of the English word *build*.

REL

English and Japanese have the RELs *make a plan* and *kēkaku o sakusē-suru*, respectively. *Kēkaku o tateru* implies a plan that is in its beginning stages, while *kēkaku o sakusē-suru* implies a more detailed plan. 関連語(1)

(b) 信頼のおけるサービスを通して私達は顧客とのいい関係を築いてきた。

(c) ビル・ゲイツは一代でマイクロソフトの王国を築いた。

解説

日本語の「築く」と英語の *build* の基本義は、それぞれ、"土石を使って建物を建てる" と "{材料 / 部品} を使って建物を造る" という意味である。比喩的には "体系的に何かを作り出す" という意味である。

同形異義語

（〜に）火をつける　/ phr. / 隠喩

早くするように {促す / あおる}、前の状態よりさらに興奮させて攻撃的にさせる
to make s.o. work harder; to do s.t. with more energy or excitement than before

例文

メディアが二人の争いにさらに火をつけて、訴訟問題にまで発展してしまった。

The media incited the two people's dispute, and it escalated into a lawsuit.

計画を立てる　phr.　隠喩

何かを行うための方法や順序などを考える

関 計画を作成する

例文

健太：さや、卒業後はどんな計画を立ててるの？

さや：うん、アメリカへ留学して、MBA を取ろうかなって考えてるんだけど。

健太：さやは堅実だね。

- -

(a) このプロジェクトを成功させるために、まずは一番大事な相手のリストを書き出し、定期的に会う計画を立てなさい。

(b) 私達は目下、世界旅行の計画を立てているところです。

解説

日本語の「立てる」は「立つ」の他動詞で、基本義は "{誰か / 何か} を垂直にさせる" であり、英語の *build* の意味を含んでいる。

関連語

日英語にはそれぞれ、関連表現として「計画を作成する」と *make a plan* がある。見出しの「計画を立てる」は「発案する」に近く、関連表現の「作成する」はより細部にわたり具体化するという違いがある。

(1) うちの会社ではいつも社長がプロジェクトの計画を {立てて / ? 作成して}、われわれ部下がそれを具体化するための綿密な計画を {作成する / ? 立てる}。

At our company, the president {builds/makes} a plan for a project, and we subordinates {build/make} a more detailed plan.

build a wall around oneself / phr. / metaphor

to psychologically cut oneself off from others

REL there is a wall {around s.o./between ~ }

Examples

Kenta: That teacher's hard to talk to.

Saya: Yeah. It's like he's built a wall around himself.

Kenta: You can't ask him questions or even say hello.

- - - - - - - - - - - - - - - - - - - -

(a) It's important to actively interact with other people and not build a wall around yourself.

(b) She built a psychological wall around herself, focusing all her energy on her research.

Note

The verb *kizuku* (to build) can be replaced by *tsukuru* (to make). However, because the basic meanings of *kizuku* and *tsukuru* are "to construct a building using earth and stones" and "to use {materials/parts} to create s.t. with a new form," respectively, *kizuku* makes the wall sound sturdier than *tsukuru* does. 　解説(1)

REL

The English and Japanese RELs are *there is a wall {around s.o./between ~}* and *{~ no mawari/~ to ~ no aida} ni kabe ga aru*, respectively.

(1) There is a wall around him.
彼の周りには壁がある。
(2) There is a wall between you and me.
あなたと私の間には壁がある。

bull-headed / comp. adj. / metaphor

to be unreasonably stubborn

Examples

Kenta: Mike, why are you so mad?

Mike: It's my boss. He's so bull-headed. Doesn't he realize that no one's gonna listen to him if he keeps spouting that old-fashioned nonsense?

- - - - - - - - - - - - - - - - - - - -

(a) Everyone who knows him feels that he is bull-headed.

(b) My father is so bull-headed that when I told him that I wanted to leave home after entering college, he was completely against it.

Notes

1. Both the English and Japanese indicate "stubbornness," but they use *bull* and *stone* as metaphors, respectively. *Bull-headed* refers to the Minotaur from Greek mythology, a monster with a bull's head and a man's body. The Japanese is a compound that consists of *ishi* (stone) and *atama* (head) and literally means "stone-headed."

2. *Bull-headed* often goes with *stubborn*, as shown below.
(1) A bull-headed person stubbornly sticks to his opinion.
石頭の人は自分の考えをかたくなに変えようとしない。

（自分の）周りに壁を築く　／　phr.　隠喩

自分を心理的に人に近づけないようにする

関〔～の周り / ～と～の間〕に壁がある

例文

健太：あの先生って話しかけにくいね。

さや：そうだね。なんか自分の周りに壁を築いてるって感じだね。

健太：質問どころか、挨拶もできないもんね。

- (a) 自分の周りに壁を築かないで、積極的に人々と付き合うことが大切です。
- (b) 彼女は自分の周りに心理的な壁を築いて、研究に全精力を傾けた。

解説

日本語の「築く」は次の例のように「作る」で言い換えることができる。しかし、「築く」の基本義は"土石を使って建物を建てる"で、「作る」の基本義は"{材料 / 部品}に手を加えて元とは違ったものに仕上げる"である。つまり、「築く」の方が「作る」より壁がより強固な感じがする。

(1) 自分の周りに壁を〔築か / 作ら〕ないで、積極的に人々と付き合うことが大切です。（→(a)）

関連語

日英語の関連表現はそれぞれ「〔～の周り / ～と～の間〕に壁がある」、*there is a wall {around s.o./between ~}* である。📖 **REL(1)(2)**

石頭（の）　comp. n.　隠喩

考え方に融通が利かない人

例文

健太：マイク、何、そんなに怒ってるの。

マイク：課長だよ。まったく石頭なんだから。あんな古くさいこと言ってたら、誰もついていかないよ。

- (a) 彼を知っている者は誰でも、彼が石頭であると感じている。
- (b) 私の父は石頭で、大学進学と同時に家を出たいと言ったとき大反対された。

解説

1. 日英語とも"頑固"を表現しているが、それぞれ *bull*（牛）と「石」を使っている。*bull-headed* はもともとはギリシャ神話の、人身牛頭の怪物ミノタウロスからきている。日本語は「石」と「頭」からなる複合語で、英語で言えば ˣ*stone-headed* だが、英語にはこのような表現はない。

2. *bull-headed* は、*stubborn*「頑固な」と一緒に使われることが多い。📖 **Note(1)**

burst a blood vessel / phr. / metaphor

to get really angry

REL be steaming

Examples

(a) My father nearly burst a blood vessel when my sister stayed overnight without his permission.

(b) He is obviously very attached to Liz, even though he tends to burst a blood vessel whenever she refers to him in her cutesy way by calling him Leon-chan.

(c) Her father burst a blood vessel when she told him she'd dropped out of college.

Note

The English literally means "for one to become so infuriated that one bursts a blood vessel," whereas the Japanese means "for s.o. to become so angry that one can see blue blood vessels bulging from his or her forehead." Note that the Japanese explicitly uses the verb *okoru* (to get angry), but the English does not.

REL

The English REL is *be steaming*, and the Japanese REL is *yuge o tatete okoru* (lit. "be steaming and angry"). They are used to express intense anger.

(1) Even though his subordinate only made a tiny mistake, the boss {burst a blood vessel/was steaming}.

些細な間違いにも関わらず、上司は部下に{青筋を立てて / 湯気を立てて}怒った。

bury the past / phr. / metaphor

to try to forget or conceal one's past

Examples

(a) He buried his repugnant past by changing his name and having plastic surgery to alter his appearance.

(b) No matter how hard you try to bury the past, it doesn't go away.

(c) Lisa had buried her past as a criminal's daughter and settled down into a quiet life as the proprietor of an antique store.

Note

The Japanese verb *hōmuru* (to bury) can take not only the noun *kako* (past) as its direct object, but also *akkō* (evil deed), *shōko* (evidence), *akuji* (wicked deed), *hito* (person) and other nouns. Likewise, the English verb *bury* can take words such as *evil deed*, *scandal* and *evidence* as its direct object in addition to *past*. 🔲➡解説(1)(2)

青筋を立てて怒る / phr. 隠喩

激しく怒る

関 湯気を立てて怒る

例文

(a) 父は姉の無断外泊に、青筋を立てて怒った。

(b) 彼は、リズが彼のことをからかって「レオンちゃん」と呼ぶと、青筋を立てて怒るが、明らかに彼女に強い思いを寄せている。

(c) 彼女の父親は、彼女が大学をやめたと話したとき青筋を立てて怒った。

解説

日本語は"青い血管がこめかみにそって膨れ上がるほど腹を立てること"を意味するのに対して、英語は"血管が破裂するほど腹を立てること"を意味している。日本語には「怒る」という動詞が明示されているが、英語では「怒る」という動詞は使われていない。

関連語

日英語の関連表現は「湯気を立てて怒る」と *be steaming* であるが、いずれも激しく怒っていることを表している。—📖 REL(1)

過去を葬る / phr. 隠喩

かつての悪い記憶や行いをなかったことにする

例文

(a) 彼は名前を変え顔も整形して、いまわしい過去を葬った。

(b) たとえどんなに過去を葬り去ろうとしても、それは消えるものではない。

(c) リサは犯罪者の娘という過去を葬り去り、骨董屋の店主として静かな生活を送っていた。

解説

日本語では「過去」以外に「悪行」「証拠」「悪事」「人」も直接目的語として使える。同様に英語でも *evil deed*（悪行）、*scandal*（スキャンダル）、*evidence*（証拠）などを目的語として取ることができる。

(1) 悪事を闇に葬り去るために、マフィアは多くの金を使った。
The Mafia used a lot of money to {bury/cover up} their crimes.

(2) そのスキャンダルは、彼を政界から葬り去るきっかけとなった。
The scandal eventually led to him being {thrown out of/ ˣburied in} the political world.

buy time　comp. v.　metaphor

to postpone s.t. in the hope of bringing about a favorable outcome

REL　gain time; LOOK▶ Time is money.

Examples

Kenta: Mike's gonna be here soon!

Karen: Are you serious? We're still not done with the preparations. Could you take him somewhere and buy us some time?

Saya: Yeah, that'd really help us out. If he comes now, the surprise party will be ruined.

(a) If a suspicious-looking person comes in, push the button to contact the police and talk to him to buy time until they arrive.

(b) The opposition party can't win by directly confronting the majority party and forcing a vote. Their only option is to buy time using any means necessary.

Note

The Japanese verb *kasegu* (to earn) usually takes *money* as its direct object. This reveals the conceptual metaphor underlying the expression *jikan o kasegu*: "time is money."

REL

Buy is sometimes replaced by *gain*.

(1) I know this is only to {buy/gain} time.
これはただ時間を稼いでいるにすぎないとわかっている。

{by/within} a hair's breadth　phr.　metaphor

by a slim margin

REL　within a hair's breadth

Examples

Kenta: How's your new car?

Karen: The other day, I managed to avoid hitting an oncoming vehicle by a hair's breadth. Guess I'm still not used to Japanese steering wheels being on the right.

(a) The people fleeing the tsunami made it to the hill by a hair's breadth.

(b) The highway from downtown Tokyo to the airport was so congested that I ended up missing the plane by a hair's breadth.

(c) We were able to prevent a terrorist attack by a hair's breadth by discovering the leader's hideout.

Note

The Japanese originated from the idea of "a space large enough for only a single hair."

REL

1. The Japanese REL, *kiki-ippatsu de*, can be replaced by *kan-ippatsu de* only in cases where some danger has been avoided. 📖→関連語(1)

時間を稼ぐ /phr. 隠喩

自分の都合のいい状態になるまで何かをして時間を経過させる

関 **LOOK** 時は金なり

B

例文

健太：もう、マイクが来ちゃうよ。

カレン：え、ほんと？　まだ全部用意できてないのに、ちょっとどこかへ連れてって、時間稼いでてよ。

さや：うん、健太、そうして！　今マイクが来たら、サプライズパーティが台無しになっちゃう。

- -

(a) 不審者が来たときは、ボタンで通報し、警察が来るまで話しかけながら時間を稼ぐようにしてください。

(b) 数で優る与党と採決による「直接対決」を挑んでも勝ち目はありませんから、野党側はあらゆる手段を使って時間を稼ぐしかありません。

解説

日本語の動詞「稼ぐ」の目的語は「金」がくるのが通常である。したがって、時間は金であるという比喩的思考が背後にある。

関連語

英語では動詞の *buy* の代わりに *gain* を使うことができる。　**REL(1)**

間一髪で /phr. 隠喩

ほんの少しのところで

関 危機一髪で

例文

健太：どう、新車の調子は？

カレン：それが、この間、対向車とぶつかりそうになってね。間一髪で助かったけど。日本はハンドルが右だから、まだ慣れなくて。

- -

(a) 人々は津波に追われながら、間一髪で高台に逃れた。

(b) 都心からの道路が混んでいて、間一髪で飛行機に乗り遅れてしまった。

(c) 首謀者のアジトの発見により、間一髪でテロを防ぐことができた。

解説

日本語の表現はもともとは「髪の毛一本だけ入る隙間」から来ている。

関連語

1. 日本語では「間一髪で」は何か危険が避けられたときにのみ、関連表現の「危機一髪で」と置き換えられる。それ以外には置き換えることはできない。

(1) a. 1962 年のキューバ危機では、核兵器による戦争を{間／危機}一髪で免れた。

   In the 1962 Cuban Missile Crisis, the world managed to avoid nuclear war by a hair's breadth.

125

2. The English REL, *within a hair's breadth*, is used when one narrowly avoids a bad situation.

(2) The highway from downtown Tokyo to the airport was so congested that I came within a hair's breadth of missing the plane.
都心からの道路が混んでいて、もうちょっとで飛行機に遅れそうになったが、間一髪で間に合った。(→(b))

by a nose adv. phr. metaphor

by a slim margin

Examples

(a) A young female candidate won the election by a nose.

(b) It was a tough game. Our team lost by a nose.

(c) During yesterday's marathon, he was pressed really hard from behind by his rival, but he managed to outrun him to win by a nose.

Note

Originally, both the English and Japanese were used in horse racing to refer to a horse literally winning by the length of its nose, as shown in (1), but the expression eventually came to be used metaphorically to mean "to win by a slight margin."

(1) The horse won by a nose.
その馬が鼻の差で勝った。

by the sweat of one's brow adv. phr. metonymy

through hard work

Examples

Mr. S: Can you really make money by trading stocks online?

Mike: Yeah, it's possible. One of my friends told me he made tens of thousands of dollars overnight.

Mr. S: If young people hear stories like that, I'm pretty sure that they'll never want to earn money by the sweat of their brow.

Mike: Yeah, but you could just as easily lose a bunch of money, so I'm not so sure.

- -

(a) The money he earned by the sweat of his brow was stolen.

(b) In Japan, it used to be considered a virtue to make a living by the sweat of your brow, but nowadays that concept is considered old-fashioned.

Notes

1. Both the English and Japanese expressions come from the Bible (Genesis 3:19)："By the sweat of your brow you will eat your food until you return to the ground..."

2. Both the English and Japanese expressions are examples of metonymy, because the image of sweat on one's brow is closely associated with working hard.

3. In the English, *sweat* is used as a noun. But in the Japanese, *ase* is used not as a noun, but as part of the *suru*-verb *ase-suru*, which means "to sweat." However, *ase-suru* can

b. 私達は一年ほど前に｛間 /⁇ 危機｝一髪で父を心臓麻痺で失うところだった。

We came within a hair's breadth of losing our father to a heart attack about a year ago.

2．英語の関連表現 *within a hair's breadth* は、悪い状況をかろうじて回避できたときに使われる。

→📖 REL (2)

B

鼻の差で　phr.　隠喩
（はな　さ）　　　（いんゆ）

わずかな差で
（さ）

例 文

(a) この選挙では、若い女性候補者が鼻の差で勝った。
（せんきょ　わか　じょせいこうほしゃ　はな　さ　か）

(b) それはとても厳しい試合で、わがチームは鼻の差で負けてしまった。
（きび　しあい　はな　さ　ま）

(c) 昨日のマラソン大会で彼は終盤ライバルに激しく詰め寄られたが、なんとか鼻の
（きのう　たいかい　かれ　しゅうばん　はげ　つ　よ　はな）
差で逃げ切って勝利した。
（さ　に　き　しょうり）

解 説

日英語とも、もともとは(1)のように競馬で使われる表現であるが、様々な競争でも "わずか
な差で勝つ" という比喩的意味で転用されるようになった。 →📖 Note (1)

額に汗して　phr.　換喩
（ひたい　あせ）　　　（かんゆ）

一生懸命働いて
（いっしょうけんめいはたら）

関 汗水たらして
（あせみず）

例 文

鈴木（夫）：ネットトレードって、儲かるのかな？
（すずき　おっと　　　　もう）

マイク：ええ、らしいですね。僕の友達なんか、一晩で数万ドル儲けたことがあるっ
（ぼく　ともだち　ひとばん　すうまん　もう）
て言ってました。
（い）

鈴木（夫）：そんな話を聞くと、若者は額に汗して働くのがばかばかしくなるだろうね。
（すずき　おっと　はなし　き　わかもの　ひたい　あせ　はたら）

マイク：ええ、でも、大損することも多いですから何とも言えませんね。
（おおぞん　おお　なん　い）

- -

(a) 彼は額に汗して働いて得たお金を盗まれてしまった。
（かれ　ひたい　あせ　はたら　え　かね　ぬす）

(b) かつての日本では、額に汗して働くことは美徳の一つだったが、最近ではもは
（にほん　ひたい　あせ　はたら　びとく　ひと　さいきん）
やかっこいいこととは受け取られていない。
（う　と）

解 説

1．日英語ともに「あなたは額に汗してパンを食べ、ついに土に帰る…」という聖書（旧約聖書の
創世記3:19）が出典である。

2．日英語ともに、額に汗をかいて仕事をする行動は "よく働く" という意味と密接な関係があ
るので換喩用法である。

3．英語では *sweat* は名詞として使われているが、日本語の「額に汗して」の「汗」は名詞ではな

127

only be used in this particular expression. The standard Japanese expression for "to sweat" is *ase o kaku*.

REL

The Japanese expression *asemizu tarashite* (lit. "dripping one's sweat") is often used in spoken language. It can replace all the uses of *hitai ni ase-shite* in the examples.

関連語(1)

by word of mouth   adv. phr.   metonymy

for s.t. to be transmitted orally from person to person

REL   from mouth to mouth

Examples

(a) News of his death traveled by word of mouth.

(b) That story has been handed down by word of mouth from generation to generation by the Ainu people.

(c) The reputation of colleges often travels by word of mouth.

Notes

1. The English and Japanese are slightly different. The former lacks any verb, but the latter, which is a compound, includes a noun derived from the verb *tsutaeru* (to convey).

2. Both English and Japanese use the image of the mouth metonymically to represent spoken language, because language comes from the mouth.

REL

1. The English and Japanese share identical related expressions: *from mouth to mouth* and *kuchi kara kuchi e*, respectively.

(1) The most powerful advertising message is the one that is spread {by word of mouth/from mouth to mouth}.
一番有効な広告は {口伝えで / 口から口へ} 広がる広告だ。

2. In Japanese conversation, *kuchi-komi* (lit. "mouth communication") is used instead of *kuchi-zutae* when talking about something's reputation. *Komi* is a truncated form of the English word *communication*. 関連語(2)

caged bird   comp. n.   metaphor

s.o. who is deprived of freedom

REL   a bird in a cage

Examples

(a) In his e-mail newsletter, the Prime Minister admitted that he feels like a caged bird 24 hours a day.

(b) The young mother who had to stay home and take care of her small child felt as if she had become a caged bird.

く「汗する」という動詞の一部である。ただし、「汗する」はこの項目の慣用句でのみ使え、通常は「汗をかく」を使う。

関連語

日本語の関連表現「汗水たらして」は、主に話し言葉で使われる。例文の「額に汗して」はすべて置き換えられる。

(1) a. 彼は{額に汗して／汗水たらして}働いて得たお金を盗まれてしまった。(→(a))

　　b. かつての日本では、{額に汗して／汗水たらして}働くことは美徳の一つだったが、最近ではもはやかっこいいこととは受け取られていない。(→(b))

口伝えで　phr.　換喩
くちづた

人から人へ口で言い伝える
ひと　ひと　くち　い　つた

関 口から口へ，口コミで
くち　くち　くち

例文

(a) 彼の訃報は口伝えで広まった。
　　ふほう　くちづた　ひろ

(b) その物語は口伝えでアイヌの人々の世代から世代へと伝承されてきた。
　　ものがたり　くちづた　ひとびと　せだい　せだい　でんしょう

(c) 大学の評判はよく口伝えで広まる。
　　だいがく　ひょうばん　くちづた　ひろ

解説

1．日本語のほうは「伝える」から派生した名詞を含む複合語になっているのに対して、英語のほうは動詞がなく、直訳すれば「口の言葉で」になる。

2．日英語ともに、言葉は口から出てくるため、口を話し言葉として換喩的にとらえている。

関連語

1．日英語には「口から口へ」、*from mouth to mouth* という同一の関連表現がある。━📖 **REL(1)**

2．日本語では会話で物事の評判を伝える時は「口伝え」ではなく「口コミ」が使われる。これは「口」と英語の *communication* を簡略化した「コミ」が結びついたものである。

(2) {口コミ／×口伝え}でおいしいって聞いたから行ってみたけれど、実は大したことなかったよ。
I heard by word of mouth that it was good, so I went to try it. Turns out it's not that great.

かごの(中の)鳥　n. phr.　隠喩
なか　とり　いんゆ

自由を奪われている人
じゆう　うば　ひと

例文

(a) 首相はEメールのニュースレターで、自分は一日24時間かごの鳥のような感じだと率直に言っている。
しゅしょう　じぶん　いちにち　じかん　とり　かん　そっちょく　い

(b) 一日中家にいて小さな子どもの面倒を見なければならない若い母親は、かごの鳥になったような気がした。
いちにちじゅういえ　ちい　こ　めんどう　み　わか　ははおや　とり　き

(c) Nora of Ibsen's *A Doll's House* resented the fact that her husband treated her like a caged bird, and she finally left him. Her actions had a major impact on the women of the time.

Note

This expression derives its figurative meaning from the fact that a bird in a cage cannot fly or act freely.

REL

The English can be replaced by *a bird in a cage*. The Japanese can be either *kago no tori* or *kago no naka no tori*.

(1) He feels like a bird in a cage 24 hours a day.
彼は24時間かごの中の鳥のように感じている。(→(a))

call on / phr. / metaphor

to strongly ask a group or organization to do s.t. important

Examples

Mrs. S: Wow, I don't usually see you drinking carrot juice.

Kenta: They were calling on people to donate blood in front of the station today. So I did, and they gave me this.

- -

(a) The Pope called on the international community to stop the spiral of hatred and violence in the holy land of Jerusalem.

(b) The President called on the World Bank to increase its efforts to ease the difficulties being faced by poor countries.

(c) She called on educators to teach in ways that "nurture individuals not to look down upon anyone."

Note

The English and Japanese can also mean "to visit" and "to call out to s.o. in a loud voice," respectively.

calm before the storm, the / phr. / metaphor

a quiet period just before trouble or activity breaks out

REL the {quiet/silence/lull} before the storm

Examples

Kenta: Mom sure is quiet today. What's up?

Mr. S: I think she's mad about something.

Kenta: Uh oh. That means we're in the calm before the storm. I bet you she's gonna explode soon.

Mr. S: Yikes. I think I'll be going to bed now.

- -

(a) My children are at school now, but they're coming back soon. It's the calm before the storm.

(c) イプセンの『人形の家』に登場するノラは、自分の生活をかごの鳥のようだと考えて、夫の元を離れた。彼女の取った行動は当時の女性達に多大な影響を与えた。

【解説】
かごの中に閉じ込められている鳥は、自由に空を飛んだり活動したりすることができないという状況が比喩的に用いられている。

【関連語】
英語は *a bird in a cage* で置き換えることができる。日本語は「かごの鳥」とも「かごの中の鳥」とも言える。 ➡📖REL(1)

C

呼びかける / comp. v. / 隠喩

{集団 / 組織}に何か大事なことをするように{強く言う / 働きかける}

【例文】
鈴木(妻)：あら、人参のジュースなんてめずらしいの飲んでるわね。
健太：うん、今日、駅前で献血を呼びかけていて、協力したらくれたんだ。

(a) 法皇は、聖地エルサレムでの憎悪と暴力の過熱を阻止するよう国際社会に呼びかけた。

(b) 大統領は、貧しい国々が直面している困難を軽減する努力を強化するように世界銀行に呼びかけた。

(c) 彼女は教育者達に「他人を見下さないような人間を育成する」という教育を呼びかけた。

【解説】
日英語の基本義は、それぞれ"人に声をかける"と"訪ねる / 訪れる"である。

嵐の前の静けさ / phr. / 隠喩

何か大きなことが起きる前の静かなひととき

【例文】
健太：お母さん、今日はやけに静かだね。どうしたの？
鈴木(夫)：どうも何か怒っているみたいだな。
健太：え、ほんと、「嵐の前の静けさ」だね。そのうち、爆発するかな？
鈴木(夫)：恐ろしいから、僕は先に寝てしまおう。

(a) 子供は今学校に行ってるけど、もうすぐ帰って来るから、今は嵐の前の静けさなのよ。

(b) This beautiful coastal town gets brutal traffic for two months during the summer, so this is the calm before the storm.

REL

> The English can be replaced by *the {quiet/silence/lull} before the storm*, but these are used much less frequently than the main entry. Lull in particular is not very common.

calm s.o.'s nerves / phr. / metaphor

to quiet s.o.'s jittery state of mind

REL soothe s.o.'s nerves

Examples

Saya: Hey, what's aromatherapy?

Karen: Isn't that when you surround yourself with nice scents and listen to quiet music?

Saya: So it's basically a treatment for calming your nerves, huh?

- - - - - - - - - - - - - - - - - - - -

(a) A little exercise can calm your nerves and stimulate your appetite.

(b) Whether it's music or fine arts, being exposed to art calms our nerves and refreshes our minds.

REL

> The verbs *soothe* and *nadameru* (to soothe) can replace *calm* and *shizumeru* in all the examples, but *nadameru* is used quite less frequently than *shizumeru*, and *soothe* tends to be used in a literal sense more so than *calm*.

(1) Whether it's music or fine arts, being exposed to art {calms/soothes} our nerves and refreshes our minds.
音楽でも美術でも良い芸術に触れると、神経が{静まり/なだめられ}、心が清められる感じがするものだ。(→(b))

can breathe easy / phr. / metonymy

to be able to relax

REL can breathe freely

Examples

Mr. S: Hey, Mike. You're looking nice and relaxed today.

Mike: Yeah, I finally finished my project last week. Now I can breathe easy for a while.

- - - - - - - - - - - - - - - - - - - -

(a) When I'm at church, my heart is lighter and I can breathe easy.

(b) I feel great now that the presentation is over. I can finally breathe easy.

REL

1. The English REL, *can breathe freely*, can replace the main entry. However, its Japanese counterpart, *jiyū ni iki o tsukeru*, is not used very frequently.

(1) A man's true home is the place where he can breathe {easy/freely}.

(b) この美しい沿岸の町では夏の2ヵ月間は交通量が恐るべきものになりますが、今はその嵐の前の静けさです。

関連語

英語には関連表現として *the {quiet/silence/lull} before the storm* があるが、見出しより使用頻度はかなり低い。とくに、*lull* はあまり使用されていない。

神経を{静 / 鎮}める　　phr.　隠喩

いら立つ気持ちを落ち着かせる

関 神経をなだめる

例文

さや：ね、アロマセラピーって何？

カレン：いい香りに包まれて静かな音楽を聞いたりするんじゃない？

さや：神経を静める療法ってことね。

(a) 軽い運動は神経を静めるし、食欲を刺激する。

(b) 音楽でも美術でも良い芸術に触れると、神経が静まり心が清められる感じがするものだ。

関連語

日英語ともに、動詞「なだめる」と *soothe* は例文の「静める」と *calm* に置き換えられるが、「なだめる」は「静める」より使用頻度がかなり低く、*soothe* は *calm* より字義通りの意味で用いられることが多い。→📖 REL(1)

楽に息がつける　　phr.　換喩

リラックスする

関 一息つける

例文

鈴木(夫)：なんだ、マイク。今日はリラックスしているね。

マイク：ええ、先週、やっとプロジェクトが終わったんですよ。これでしばらく楽に息がつけそうです。

(a) 私は教会にいると心が軽くなり、いつもより楽に息がつける。

(b) 発表も終わり、気分がいいし、今はもっと楽に息がつけます。

関連語

1. 英語には *can breathe freely* という関連表現があり、見出しと置き換えられる。対応する日本語の表現は「自由に息をつける」であるが、あまり使われない。→📖 REL(1)

本当の自分の家というのは{楽/'自由}に息がつけるところだ。

2. The Japanese REL, *hitoiki tsukeru* (lit. "can take one breath"), is used more frequently than the main entry. But because it means "one breath," it implies that the relaxation period is relatively short. 📖→ 関連語(2)

can do s.t. with one's eyes closed / phr. / metaphor

s.o. has been doing s.t. so routinely that {he/she} can now do it very easily

REL be a piece of cake; be (as) easy as pie

Examples

Saya: I have to translate this report into English. I'm not sure I can do it.

Karen: Let me see... Oh, this? I can do this with my eyes closed. I'll do it for you.

Saya: Really? That would be a big help.

- - - - - - - - - - - - - - - - - -

(a) I know almost everything there is to know about African-American history. I can do this course with my eyes closed.

(b) It was an operation I had performed many times, so I was sure I could do it with my eyes closed.

Notes

1. The participle *closed* can be replaced by *shut*.
(1) Some people say they know their jobs so well that they can do them with their eyes shut.
自分の仕事は十分知り尽くしているので、目をつぶっていてもできるという人もいる。

2. The verb *tsuburu* (to close) can be replaced by *tsumuru*. *Tsuburu* is usually used in colloquial speech, as shown in the dialogue. The main difference between the two is the contrast between the plosive "b" sound and the nasal "m" sound, similar to the difference between, for example, *kemuru* (vi., to smoke) and *keburu*. *Tsumuru* is used much less frequently than *tsuburu*.

REL

Be a piece of cake and *be (as) easy as pie* can replace *can do s.t. with one's eyes closed* in informal speech. Likewise, *asameshi-mae da* (can be done before breakfast) can replace *me o {tsubutte/tsumutte} te mo dekiru*.

(1) She thought she could take today's test with her eyes closed./She thought today's test would be {a piece of cake/easy as pie}.
彼女は今日の試験は{目をつぶっててもできる/朝飯前だ}と思った。

can't believe one's ears / phr. / metonymy

to be unable to believe what one has just heard

Examples

Mrs. S: Did you hear? Someone asked Kenta if he would sell the Godzilla he's had since he was a kid for 100,000 yen.

Mr. S: Yeah, I could hardly believe my ears. I still can't believe someone would want to pay that much for something like that.

- - - - - - - - - - - - - - - - - -

2．日本語は「一息つける」という関連表現があり、見出しより使用頻度が高い。ただ「一息」というところから、リラックスできる時間が短いという印象を与える。

(2) この研究が終わったので、{もっと楽に息が / 一息}つけます。
　　Now that I have finished this research, I can breathe more {easily/freely}.

目を{つぶって / つむって}てもできる　/ phr.　隠喩

何かを日常的にやってきていて、とても簡単にできる

関 朝飯前だ

例文

さや：このレポート、英語にしなきゃなんないの。困ったな。

カレン：どれどれ、あ、こんなんだったら目をつぶっててもできるわ。私がやってあげる。

さや：ほんと、助かる。

(a) アフリカ系アメリカ人の歴史ならたいていなんでも知っている。だからこの科目は目をつぶっててもできる。

(b) それは私が何回となくやってきた手術だったので、目をつむっていてもできると思っていました。

解説

1．英語の動詞 closed は shut で置き換えることができる。➡📖 Note(1)

2．日本語の動詞「つぶる」は「つむる」と置き換えられる。「つぶる」は普通会話で使われる(→会話例)。[b] と [m] は同じ調音点の破裂音と鼻音の対立になっている。このような対立は他にも「煙る」{けむる / けぶる} などに見られる。「つむる」は「つぶる」よりも使用頻度ははるかに低い。

関連語

英語のくだけた話し言葉には be a piece of cake や be (as) easy as pie があり、置き換えることができる。日本語のくだけた話し言葉にも「朝飯前だ」という表現があり、置き換えることができる。➡📖 REL(1)

(自分の)耳を疑う　/ phr.　換喩

聞いたばかりのことが本当だとは思えない

例文

鈴木(妻)：あなた、聞いた？　健太が子供の時から持っているゴジラのおもちゃ、10万円で売ってくれないかって言われたんですって。

鈴木(夫)：ああ、知ってる。僕も耳を疑ったけど。あんなもの、そんな高額で買いたがる人がいるなんて信じられないね。

(a) She told me her dog was babysitting her child. I couldn't believe my ears!

(b) He suddenly told her that it would be too hard for the relationship to work. She couldn't believe her ears when he said that.

Notes

1. The English and Japanese have the same figurative meaning, but the verb is different. The Japanese uses *utagau* (to daubt), while the English uses *can't believe*. *"Doubt one's ears* is used as well, but only rarely.

2. In English, the expression is normally used in the negative form. So one cannot say *×I can believe my ears*. By contrast, the affirmative form is used in Japanese. *×Jibun no mimi o utagawanai* is never used.

can't believe one's eyes / phr. / metonymy

to be unable to believe what one has just seen

Examples

Kenta: Did you go see that magic show visiting from Las Vegas? How was it?

Karen: It was really amazing. When they made that white tiger disappear, I couldn't believe my eyes!

- -

(a) No one could believe their eyes when they saw the aftermath of the Great East Japan Earthquake.

(b) I couldn't believe my eyes. Standing in front of me was the girl who had been living on the streets just until recently. She looked so different dressed in her new warm-looking sweater.

(c) I couldn't believe my eyes when I opened my birthday present. The sapphire and diamond bracelet took my breath away.

Note

In formal written Japanese, *jibun no me o utagau* is replaced by *waga me o utagau*, as in (a).

can't see the forest for the trees / phr. / metaphor

to be unable to grasp the whole of a situation because of undue attention paid to the details

REL can't see the wood(s) for the trees

Examples

Karen: Wow, you're actually reading an English newspaper for once!

Kenta: Yeah, but the thing is, I can't understand what the article's saying even if I look up all the words.

Karen: It's like you can't see the forest for the trees, right? Why don't you try skimming the article once before you start looking up words? That way, you can just focus on the words you really need to know.

- -

(a) 彼女が自分の犬が子供の子守りをしていると言ったので、私は自分の耳を疑った。

(b) 彼は突然、二人の関係をうまく続けていくのは無理だと彼女に言った。彼の言葉を聞いた彼女は自分の耳を疑った。

【解説】

1. 日英語とも比喩的意味は同じだが動詞が異なる。日本語では「自分の耳を疑う」という表現だが、英語では、^{??}*doubt one's ears* とはまれにしか言えない。

2. 英語は否定形になるのが通常で、[×]*I can believe my ears* とは言えない。日本語は逆に肯定形が使われ、「[×]自分の耳を疑わない」とは言わない。

（自分の）目を疑う　　phr.　換喩

見たばかりのことが本当だとは思えない

【例文】

健太：ラスベガスから来たマジックショー見に行ったんだって？ どうだった？

カレン：すごかったわよ。一瞬にして白い虎が消えた時には、自分の目を疑ったわね。

(a) 東日本大震災の惨状をテレビで見たとき、誰もが我が目を疑った。

(b) 私は自分の目を疑った。私の目の前に、ついこの間まで路上生活をしていたホームレスの女の子が立っていた。彼女は暖かそうな新しいセーターを着ていて、別人のようだった。

(c) 誕生日のプレゼントを開けたとき、私は自分の目を疑った。サファイアとダイヤモンドのブレスレットに、はっと息をのんでしまった。

【解説】

(a)のように、日本語の書き言葉では「自分の目を疑う」は「我が目を疑う」に置き換えられる。

木を見て森を見ず　　phr.　隠喩

部分に注意を払いすぎて全体を把握できない

【例文】

カレン：あら、めずらしい。英語の新聞読んでんの？

健太：うん、だけど辞書で単語の意味がわかっても、文全体の意味はよくわかんないんだよね。

カレン：木を見て森を見ずってところね。単語一つ一つ調べる前に全体にざっと目を通してみたら？ そして、必要だと思う単語だけ調べてみるのよ。

(a) When you "can't see the forest for the trees," you're usually more concerned about responding to something that's right in front of you.

(b) Sometimes he can't see the forest for the trees because he's so detail-oriented.

(c) When I read his paper, I got the impression he couldn't see the forest for the trees.

Notes

1. *Mizu* is the archaic negative form of *miru*.
2. In the English, *forest* can be replaced by *wood(s)* without changing the meaning, but in the Japanese, *mori* cannot be replaced by *hayashi* (a relatively small wooded area with fewer trees than a forest).

REL

In English, *can't see the wood(s) for the trees* is a REL that has essentially the same meaning as *can't see the forest for the trees,* and it can replace the latter in all the example sentences.

(1) Sometimes he can't see the {forest/wood(s)} for the trees because he's so detail-oriented.

$(\rightarrow (b))$

---

capture s.o.'s heart   *phr.*   metaphor

for {s.o./s.t.} to cause s.o. else to have a strong interest in {him/her/it}

REL {capture/win} the hearts and minds of ~; capture s.o.'s imagination

Examples

Mike: I went to Okinawa last week. The beach and sky were so beautiful, I didn't wanna come back.

Saya: Sounds like Okinawa really captured your heart, huh?

Mike: Yeah, I totally wanna live there now.

- -

(a) Mozart's music captures my heart and transports me to another world.

(b) Indian dance has captured my heart.

Note

In English, *capture s.o.'s heart* is an active phrase, but the Japanese expression can be used in the passive form, i.e., *toraerareru,* as in (b). Generally speaking, passive constructions tend to be avoided in English, but they tend to be preferred in Japanese.

REL

1. The English REL, *{capture/win} the hearts and minds of ~,* means "to earn the {admiration/support} of a group." The Japanese REL *kokoro o tsukamu* is interchangeable with *kokoro o toraeru.*

(1) The Pope's sermon {captured/won} the hearts and minds of people around the globe.
法王の説教は世界中の人々の心を{捕らえた/つかんだ}。

2. Japanese also has the expression *kokoro o ubau.* The passive form of this expression, *kokoro {ga/o} ubawareru,* is used more often than *kokoro o toraerareta* in sentences such as (b).

(a) 「木を見て森を見ず」というときは、たいてい目前のことにとらわれている場合だ。

(b) 彼は細かいところに注意が行きすぎるから、時々「木を見て森を見ず」ということになる。

(c) 彼の論文を読むと「木を見て森を見ず」という印象を受ける。

【解説】
1. 日本語の「見ず」は「見る」の否定形の古い形である。
2. 英語の *forest* は *wood(s)* に置き換えても意味は変わらない。日本語では「森」を、「森」ほど木々に覆われていない比較的小さいところを意味する「林」に置き換えることはできない。

【関連語】
英語の関連表現の *can't see the wood(s) for the trees* は *can't see the forest for the trees* と実質的には同じで置き換えることができる。—📖 REL(1)

心を捕らえる phr. 隠喩

{誰か / 何か}に強い興味を持たせる，強く関心を引く

【関】心をつかむ，心を奪う

【例文】
マイク：先週、沖縄に行ってきたんだけど、空も海もきれいで最高だったね。帰ってきたくなかったよ。

さや：沖縄がマイクの心を捕らえたってわけね？

マイク：そう、あそこに住みたくなっちゃったよ。

- -

(a) モーツァルトの音楽は私の心を捕らえ、別世界に運んでいってくれる。

(b) 私はインドのダンスに心を捕らえられてしまった。

【解説】
英語の *capture s.o.'s heart* は能動形であるが、日本語では(b)にあるように受動形「捕らえられる」が使われることもある。一般には英語は受動形を避ける傾向にあり、日本語は好んで使う傾向がある。

【関連語】
1. 日本語の関連表現の「心をつかむ」は見出しと置き換え可能である。英語の {capture/win} the hearts and minds of ~ は "集団の {感嘆 / 支持} を得る" ことを意味する。—📖 REL(1)
2. 日本語には「心を奪う」という表現がある。この表現の受動形「心 {が / を} 奪われる」は(b)のような文では「心を捕らえられた」よりもよく使われる。

139

carpet-bomb   comp. v.   metaphor

to saturate an area with heavy bombing

Example

Due to the enemy's carpet-bombing, all of the buildings in the area were destroyed, and many people died.

carrot-{and/or}-stick   comp. adj.   metaphor

reward and punishment

Examples

(a) He had to get creative with the carrot-and-stick-approach to motivate his students.

(b) Local governments in America sometimes employ the carrot-and-stick-approach. For example, they might reward people who use public transportation by making it cheaper, while raising the gas tax on those who don't.

(c) At our home, we not only scold our child, but we also make sure to reward him when he does something good. In short, we adopt a carrot-and-stick approach.

Notes

1. Both the English and Japanese refer to food items (i.e. carrots and candy) and objects used to punish people (i.e. sticks and whips). The exact origins of the English expression remain unclear, though some posit that it came from the practice of dangling a carrot in front of a donkey in order to make it move (and resorting to the stick if that failed). The Japanese comes from Otto von Bismarck's critique of socialism, "Zuckerbrot und Peitsche," which is German for "the sweet bread and the whip."

2. The Japanese expression is used as an example of the lenient and strict techniques employed to discipline children and so on, as shown in (c).

carry {a/one's} cross   phr.   metaphor

to endure {sin/sorrow/suffering/responsibility}

REL   be one's cross to bear; have a heavy cross to bear

Examples

(a) The poor woman has to carry a heavy cross, as her family are all too ill to work.

(b) The woman took a person's life in the sudden accident, and she was made to carry a cross so heavy it was almost impossible to bear alone.

(c) Something that makes me really anxious might seem like nothing to someone else, while the cross someone else is carrying might feel abstract to me.

じゅうたん爆撃　comp. n.　隠喩

すみずみまで徹底的に爆弾で攻撃する

例文

その街は敵のじゅうたん爆撃にあい、すべての建物が破壊されて多くの人々が亡くなった。

飴と鞭　n. phr.　隠喩

報酬を与えるなどの一方で、厳しく締め付ける支配や指導の方法

例文

(a) 彼は学生を動機づけるために、工夫して飴と鞭を使い分けなければならなかった。

(b) アメリカの地方自治体は飴と鞭を使うことがある。公共の交通機関を使う人には値段を安くし、一方、それを使わない人にはガソリン税を高くするのだ。

(c) うちでは子供を叱るだけでなく何かいいことをしたとき子供をほめます。つまり飴と鞭のしつけ教育です。

解説

1. 日英語ともに食べ物(ニンジンと飴)が出てくる。人を罰するための棒や鞭も出てくることがある。語源ははっきりしないが、ロバを進ませるためにロバの前でニンジンをぶらぶらさせて、それがうまくいかないと棒を使うというところからきたという説もある。日本語は、オットー・フォン・ビスマルクの社会主義に対する批判的なドイツ語の表現 *Zuckerbrot und Peitsche*「甘いパンと鞭」からきている。

2. 日本語では(c)のように、子供のしつけなどにおいて甘やかす面と厳しくする面を併用する例えとして使われる。

十字架を背負う　phr.　隠喩

{罪 / 悲しみ / 苦難 / 責任}などを身に持ち続ける

例文

(a) かわいそうに、家族がみんな病気で働けないので、その女は重い十字架を背負っている。

(b) 突然の事故で人の命を奪ってしまった女は、一人では支えきれないほどの重い十字架を背負うことになった。

(c) 僕にとっては真剣な悩みであっても、他の人にとっては何でもないことだったりするし、人にとっては十字架を背負うような事でも、僕にとっては真実味がなかったりする。

Note

The English is taken from the New Testament of the Bible (Luke 9:23), when Christ asks each of his disciples to "take up his cross and follow me." But this expression originally came from the Roman custom of forcing criminals to carry crosses on their backs to their place of execution. The Japanese is a translation of the English.

REL

The English has two RELs: *be one's cross to bear* and *have a heavy cross to bear*.
(1) a. I have to always strive to be creative. That is my cross to bear.
　　私は創造的なことをしなければならない。それは私が背負う十字架だ。
　b. You have a heavy cross to bear, and I feel heartsick for the situation you're in.
　　あなたは重い十字架を背負っている。私はあなたが置かれている状況を思い、心が強く痛む。

---

cast a shadow over ~　/ **phr.**　**metaphor**

for {an event/situation} to cause a negative emotional state

Examples

(a) Homelessness has not gone away, but rather continues to cast a shadow over the lives of many of our nation's people.

(b) The war caused enormous damage to the country's infrastructure and cast a big shadow over its economic future.

(c) If the birthrate continues to decrease and the population continues to age, these problems will cast a dark shadow over our country's future.

Notes

1. Both the English and Japanese are used in formal writing.
2. In the English, *shadow* can be modified by adjectives such as *big, long, dark,* and *deep*. In the Japanese, *kage* (shadow) can be modified by *kurai* (dark) and *ōkina* (big). In both the English and Japanese, these adjectives emphasize the resultant negative state.
(1) Homelessness has not gone away, but rather continues to cast a long shadow over the lives of many of our nation's people. (→(a))
　　ホームレスの問題は消えず、わが国の多くの人々の生活に{大きな/ˣ長い}影を落としている。
(2) The war caused enormous damage to the country's infrastructure and cast a deep shadow over its economic future. (→(b))
　　戦争はその国のインフラに多大な被害を与え、経済に{大きな/暗い}影を落とした。

REL

The Japanese REL, *kage o nage-kakeru*, can replace *kage o otosu*, but the latter is used far more frequently. 📖→関連語(1)

---

cast a spell {on/over} ~　/ **phr.**　**metaphor**

for {s.o./s.t.} to capture s.o.'s heart

Examples

(a) The first time I saw a classic ballet performance, it cast a spell over me.

(b) My wife is constantly talking to our cat. It's like it cast a spell on her.

解説

英語は、聖書(新約聖書)の福音書のルカ伝(9:23)でキリストが弟子に「自分の十字架を背負って私についてきなさい」と言っているところから来ている。しかし、もともとは、ローマ時代に罪人が処刑場まで自分で十字架を背負っていった風習からきたものである。日本語は英語の翻訳である。

関連語

英語には関連表現 *be one's cross to bear* と *have a heavy cross to bear* がある。—📖 **REL(1)**

C

(〜に)影を落とす *phr.* 隠喩

ある状況から不安や心配事が出てくる

関 影を投げかける

例文

(a) ホームレスの問題は消えず、わが国の多くの人々の生活に影を落としている。

(b) 戦争はその国のインフラに多大な被害を与え、経済に大きな影を落とした。

(c) このまま少子高齢化が続くと、我が国の将来に暗い影を落とすことになる。

解説

1. 日英語ともにかたい書き言葉で使われる。

2. 日本語では「影」は「暗い/大きな」を修飾語として使える。英語では *shadow*(影)は *big, long, dark, deep* といった形容詞をつけることができる。日英語とも否定的な状況を強調する形容詞を用いる。—📖 **Note(1)(2)**

関連語

日本語には「影を投げかける」という関連表現があり、「影を落とす」と言い替えることができるが、頻度は「影を落とす」よりはるかに低い。

(1) 戦争はその国のインフラに多大な被害を与え、国家の経済に大きな影を{落とした/投げかけた}。(→(b))

(〜に)魔法をかける *phr.* 隠喩

{人/何か}が誰かの心を捕らえる

関 **LOOK**▶心を捕らえる

例文

(a) 初めてクラシックバレエのステージを観た時、私は魔法をかけられてしまった。

(b) 妻は猫に魔法をかけられたのか、いつでも猫と話している。

143

(c) Not only can he play music, but he also has the magical ability to cast a spell on strangers that makes them befriend each other.

Note

The English and Japanese use different verbs of motion, i.e., *cast* vs. *kakeru* (to hang).

cast (one's) pearls before swine   phr.   metaphor

to give s.t. valuable to s.o. who cannot appreciate its value

Examples

Mr. S: I'm thinking I might hand this Leica camera down to Kenta.

Mrs. S: You'll just be casting your pearls before swine. His mobile phone camera's enough for him.

- -

(a) He tried to explain the beauty of the music to his students, but it was just like casting pearls before swine.

(b) I decided that treating her to such high-quality wine would be like casting pearls before swine.

Notes

1. The English comes from the Bible (New Testament, Matthew [7:6]), "Do not give dogs what is holy; and do not throw your pearls before swine, lest they trample them under foot and turn to attack you." The Japanese is a translation of this biblical quote.
2. The English includes the verb *cast*, but in the Japanese, the verb (such as *nageru* [to throw] or *yaru* [to give]) is implied.

REL

The Japanese has three RELs: *uma no mimi ni nenbutsu* (lit. "a Buddhist sutra for a horse's ears"), *neko ni koban* (lit. "money for a cat"), and *inu ni rongo* (lit. "The Analects of Confucius for a dog"). *Neko ni koban* has a meaning similar to that of the main entry, but *uma no mimi ni nenbutsu* and *inu ni rongo* are different. They mean "it is useless to tell s.t. valuable to s.o. who can't understand."

castle(s) in the air, (a)   n. phr.   metaphor

a plan or dream that is not likely to become reality; a fictitious entity

REL **LOOK** pie in the sky, (a)

Examples

(a) The plan I made to become an architect when I was young was definitely not a castle in the air.

(b) Getting an education was a castle in the air for me and my six brothers. When we were young, we barely had food to eat or clothes to wear.

(c) Without the necessary financial resources, our ideas are just castles in the air.

Note

The Japanese *kūchū-rōkaku* comes from the Chinese book *Muke Hitsudan* (1086) by Shen Kuo.

(c) 彼は音楽を奏でるだけでなく、知らない人同士をすぐ友達にしてしまうという「魔法」をかける名人なのです。

解説

日英語とも動きを表す動詞だが、「かける」と *cast*（投げる）のように意味が少し異なる。

豚に真珠　*phr.*　隠喩
ぶた　しんじゅ　　　　　　いんゆ

真価を理解できない者に価値あるものを与えても無駄だ
しんか　りかい　　　　　もの　かち　　　あた　　　　む だ

関 馬の耳に念仏，猫に小判，犬に論語
うま　みみ　ねんぶつ　ねこ　こばん　いぬ　ろんご

例文

鈴木（夫）：このライカのカメラ、そろそろ健太にゆずろうかな。
すずき　おっと　　　　　　　　　　　　　　けんた

鈴木（妻）：そんなことしたら、豚に真珠もいいとこよ。健太には携帯電話のカメラで
すずき　つま　　　　　　　　　ぶた　しんじゅ　　　　　けんた　けいたいでんわ
十分。
じゅうぶん

- -

(a) 彼は音楽の美しさを学生に説明しようとしたけれど、まさに豚に真珠のようなものだった。
かれ　おんがく　うつく　　　がくせい　せつめい　　　　　　　　　　ぶた　しんじゅ

(b) こんなに高級なワインは彼女には豚に真珠なので、ふるまわないことにした。
こうきゅう　　　　かのじょ　　ぶた　しんじゅ

解説

1. 英語は聖書（新訳聖書マタイ伝(7:6)）の「聖なるものを犬にやるな。また真珠を豚に投げてやるな。恐らく彼らはそれらを足で踏みつけ、向きなおってあなたがたにかみついてくるであろう」からきている。日本語はその翻訳である。
2. 英語には動詞の *cast*（投げる）が含まれているが、日本語は「投げる」、あるいは「やる」が省かれている。

関連語

日本語の関連表現には、「馬の耳に念仏」「猫に小判」「犬に論語」がある。「猫に小判」は見出しと同じ意味だが、「馬の耳に念仏」と「犬に論語」は、「価値のあることをわからない人に聞かせても無駄だ」という意味である。

空中楼閣　*comp. n.*　隠喩
くうちゅうろうかく　　　　　　　　いんゆ

実現しそうにない計画や夢，架空のものごと
じつげん　　　　　けいかく　ゆめ　かくう

関 砂上の楼閣，**LOOK▶**絵に描いた餅
さじょう　ろうかく　　　　え　か　もち

例文

(a) 若いころ建築家になろうとしたことは決して空中楼閣なんかではなかった。
わか　　　けんちくか　　　　　　　けっ　　くうちゅうろうかく

(b) 若いときに衣食さえままにならなかった私と６人の兄弟にとっては、学校教育を受けるなど空中楼閣だった。
わか　　　いしょく　　　　　　　　わたし　にん　きょうだい　　　　がっこうきょういく　　　　　　くうちゅうろうかく

(c) 必要な財源がなければ、われわれのアイディアは空中楼閣だ。
ひつよう　ざいげん　　　　　　　　　　　　　　　　くうちゅうろうかく

解説

日本語の「空中楼閣」の出典は中国の沈括の『夢渓筆談』（1086）であると言われている。
しんかつ

ⓇⒺⓁ

The English REL is *(a) pie in the sky*, and the Japanese RELs are *sajō no rōkaku* (lit. "castle on the sand") and *e ni kaita mochi* (a picture of rice cake), both of which are conceptually similar to the English REL.

chain reaction   comp. n. / metaphor

a phenomenon in which one reaction causes a series of reactions

Examples

Mrs. S: The rise in American stocks caused a chain reaction that made Japanese stocks rise, too.

Mr. S: Yeah. Here's hoping that continues.

- -

(a) It was such a boring class. One student yawned and started a chain reaction that made the other students yawn one after another.

(b) If you leave your bad teeth untreated, your other teeth will get worse too, like a chain reaction.

(c) When shares on the New York Stock Exchange took a hit, it set off a chain reaction that lowered stocks across the globe.

Note

Both the English and Japanese are metaphors based on the series of metal links in a chain.

chair('s) legs （椅子の脚）→ **{desk/chair/bed/table}('s) legs**

---

homograph

chicken / n. / metaphor

a coward
弱虫，臆病者

Example

I don't like to say this about my own son, but he's a chicken.
自分の息子について言いたくないんですが、うちの息子は弱虫なんです。

---

chicken and egg problem, {a/the}   / n. phr. / metaphor

to be unable to tell which is the cause and which is the effect

ⓇⒺⓁ a chicken and egg situation

Examples

(a) Blood pressure and anxiety are intricately related. But does one's blood pressure increase because one is anxious, or does one become anxious because one's blood pressure increases? This is a chicken and egg problem.

関連語

英語には *(a) pie in the sky* という関連表現があるが、日本語にはそれと発想が似ている「絵に描いた餅」と「砂上の楼閣」がある。

連鎖反応 comp. n. 隠喩

一つの反応がもう一つの反応を引き起こし、それが繰り返し続いていく現象

例 文

鈴木(妻)：アメリカの株が上がって、その連鎖反応で日本の株も上がったようね。

鈴木(夫)：そうだね。続けばいいけどね。

（a）それは退屈な授業だった。一人があくびをすると、連鎖反応で他の学生達も次々とあくびを始めた。

（b）悪い歯を治療しないでおくと、連鎖反応的に他の歯もどんどん悪くなっていく。

（c）ニューヨークの株価が突然下がると、連鎖反応で次々と世界各国の株が下がった。

解 説

日英語とも、連結した「鎖」(*chain*) に基づいた比喩表現である。

同形異義語

ひよこ / n. / 隠喩

未熟者
a greenhorn

例 文

こんな社会常識も知らないなんて、大学で何を勉強しているか知らないけれど、まだまだひよこだね。

He doesn't have any common sense. I don't know what he's been studying at college, but he's still just a greenhorn.

鶏が先か卵が先か(の問題) phr. 隠喩

二つのことのどちらが原因で、どちらが結果なのかがわからない

例 文

（a）血圧と心配の関係は密接だ。心配するから血圧が高くなるのか、血圧が高いから心配なのか、鶏が先か卵が先かの問題だ。

147

(b) It's a chicken and egg problem—because there's no public interest, there's no media coverage, but without media coverage, public interest can't be generated.

Note

The Japanese specifically references the sequence of events by using the phrase *X ga saki*, which means "X is earlier," but the English does this implicitly.

R(E)L

A *chicken and egg situation* can replace the main entry, but it is used less frequently.

(1) Does a gloomy personality cause illness, or does illness cause a gloomy personality? It's a chicken and egg {problem/situation}.

chill runs down one's spine, a phr. metaphor

to feel great fear or excitement

REL send (a) chill(s) down one's spine; spine-chilling

Examples

Mike: I heard you went to a Yo-Yo Ma concert.

Saya: Yep! The performance was so good, a chill ran down my spine.

Mike: Wow, I wish I could've gone too.

- - - - - - - - - - - - - - - - - - - -

(a) A chill ran down my spine when I learned that a murder had taken place in my town.

(b) I still remember a chill running down my spine the first time I saw the aurora.

(c) He lowered his voice and said something that made a chill run down my spine: "Every person who sets foot in this house gets murdered."

Notes

1. *Run* means "for s.o. to move quickly on foot," and *zokuzoku suru* means "to feel very cold."

2. Both the English and Japanese can be used not only when one feels afraid, as shown in (a) and (c), but also when one feels excited, as shown in the dialogue and (b).

R(E)L

1. The English can be replaced by *send (a) chill(s) down one's spine* whether it is used to mean "to feel afraid" or "to feel excited," but the subject must be something that causes fear or excitement.

(1) a. His ominous words sent a chill down my spine. (→(c))

   b. Seeing the aurora for the first time sent a chill down my spine. (→(b))

2. When the Japanese is used to mean "to feel afraid," it can be replaced by *sesuji ga samuku naru* (lit. "the line of the backbone gets cold") or *sesuji ga kōru*. 関連語(2)

3. *Spine-chilling* can replace the English when it means "to feel afraid."

(3) His ominous words were spine-chilling. (→(c))

148

（b）大衆の興味がないからメディアで扱われないが、メディアで扱われないと大衆の興味も出てこない、という 鶏 が先か卵 が先かの問題なのです。

解説

日本語は「Xが先」という句で時間の先か後かが明示されているが、英語では明示されていない。

関連語

英語では見出しは *a chicken and egg situation* と置き換えられるが、使用頻度ははるかに低い。

📖 REL（1）

背筋がぞくぞくする ／ phr. ／ 隠喩

恐怖を感じる，興奮する

関 背筋が{寒くなる／凍る}

例文

マイク： ヨーヨーマのコンサートに行ったんだって？

さや： そうなの、本当にすばらしい演奏で、背筋がぞくぞくしちゃったわ。

マイク： いいなあ、僕も行きたかったなあ。

（a）殺人がわれわれの町で起きたのを知ったとき、背筋がぞくぞくした。

（b）オーロラをはじめて見たときのことをまだ覚えています。興奮で背筋がぞくぞくしたんです。

（c）彼は声を低めて「この家に足を踏み入れた者はみんな誰かに殺されるんだ」とつぶやいた。私はおそろしさに背筋がぞくぞくした。

解説

1．「ぞくぞくする」と *run* の基本義は、それぞれ“〜（人）がとても寒く感じる”と“〜（{人／生き物}）が足で早く動く”である。

2．日英語ともに（a）（c）のように「怖い」ときだけではなく、会話例や（b）のように「興奮した」ときにも使える。

関連語

1．英語は“怖い”と“興奮する”のどちらの意味の場合も、*send (a) chill(s) down one's spine* に置き換えることができる。ただし、主語は怖さ、興奮を引き起こすものでなければならない。

📖 REL（1）

2．日本語は“怖さを感じる”という意味のときは「背筋が寒くなる」と「背筋が凍る」によって置き換えることができる。

（2）殺人がわれわれの町で起きたのを知ったとき、背筋が{ぞくぞくした／寒くなった／凍った}。

（→（a））

3．英語の *spine-chilling* は文の意味が“恐怖を感じる”ときにのみ置き換えることができる。

📖 REL（3）

circumstances permitting   phr. / personification

if a given circumstance allows a certain action; if the situation allows

Examples

Section Chief: Mike, would you mind interpreting for tomorrow's conference?

Mike: Tomorrow? I've got another conference tomorrow, but circumstances permitting, I'll do it.

Section Chief: I'd appreciate if you could arrange it somehow.

(a) Time and circumstances permitting, the president said he would be pleased to discuss any issues raised in the meeting.

(b) Since I have to attend an academic conference in Geneva, Switzerland next year, I might try to visit Italy as well, circumstances permitting.

Notes

1. *Yuruseba* is the conditional form of *yurusu* (to permit).
2. Since both *permit* and *yurusu* usually take a human subject, *circumstances permitting* and *jōkyō ga yuruseba* are examples of personification.
3. *Weather permitting/tenkō ga yuruseba* and *time permitting/jikan ga yuruseba* are other examples of personification in which *permitting* and *yuruseba* are used.

(1) a. Weather permitting, the lifting of the wrecked Russian nuclear submarine from the seabed is due to take place tomorrow.
天候が許せば、沈没したロシアの原子力潜水艦を海底から引き上げる作業は明日行われる予定である。

   b. Time permitting, I shall discuss particle dynamics and describe the three conservation laws.
時間が許せば、分子力学を論じ、3つの分子の基本法則について述べたい。

---

clear one's head (of) （頭を {空 / 空っぽ} にする） → {empty/clear} one's head (of)

---

clear {a/the} hurdle(s)   phr. / metaphor

to overcome an obstacle

Examples

(a) We have successfully cleared the legislative hurdle.

(b) Most women in middle management have not yet cleared the hurdles standing between them and a promotion.

(c) By the end of the semester, successful students will have cleared the hurdles to confident public speaking.

Note

The Japanese is likely a direct translation of the English, which is based on the hurdles event from track and field.

REL

1. The verb *koeru* (to clear) in the Japanese can be replaced by *kuria-suru* (vt.), but this is

状況が許せば　/ phr.　擬人化

その時の状況がある行動をするのに可能な状態であれば

例文

課長：マイク、明日の会議だけど、通訳をしてくれないかな。

マイク：明日ですか。明日は別の会議が一つ入っているんですけど、状況が許せばできるかもしれません。

課長：なんとか、アレンジしてくれないかな。

- -

(a) 時間と状況が許せば、社長は会議で出た問題点について喜んで話し合うそうです。

(b) 来年は学会出席のためスイスのジュネーブに行かなければならないが、状況が許せば、イタリアも訪ねてみたい。

解説

1. 「許せば」は「許す」の条件法の形である。

2. 「許す」も *permit* も通常は人間を主語にとるので「状況が許せば」も *circumstances permitting* も擬人化の例になる。

3. 「天候が許せば」と *weather permitting*、「時間が許せば」と *time permitting* も、「許せば」と *permitting* を使った他の擬人化の例である。➡📖 Note (1)

ハードルを越える　phr.　隠喩

困難な {問題 / 状況} の解決に成功する

関 ハードルをクリアする，ハードルを {置く / 設定する}

例文

(a) われわれはその立法化のハードルをうまく越えた。

(b) 中間管理職の女性の大半は、上級管理職へのハードルを越えていない。

(c) 今学期の終わりまでには、学生は「人前で話す恐怖」というハードルを越えているでしょう。

解説

日本語は、陸上競技の障害走で使用されるハードルを比喩化した英語の直訳と考えられる。

関連語

1. 日本語の動詞「越える」は「クリアする」で置き換えることができるが、使用頻度は低い。

151

used infrequently. 📖→関連語 (1)

2. The Japanese also has the REL *hādoru o {oku/settē-suru}*, which means "to set high goals." 📖→関連語 (2)

---

clear {a/the} path for ~ / phr. metaphor

to make it easier for {s.t./s.o.} to follow

REL {clear/pave} the way for ~

Examples

(a) Martha Graham is a pioneer of modern dance who cleared a new path for dancers who were disillusioned with classical ballet.

(b) He cleared a new path for NASA and for other aspiring astronauts, showing that it was, in fact, possible for humans to live and work in space.

(c) The use of atomic power for generating electricity cleared a path for countries to become less dependent on fossil fuels, but it also created hazards for people living in the areas surrounding the facilities.

Note

Clear and *kiri-hiraku* do not mean exactly the same thing. *Clear* means "to free s.t. from undesirable elements," and *kiri-hiraku* means "to cultivate the wilderness and make it habitable, etc."

REL

The REL *{clear/pave} the way for ~* can be used interchangeably with *clear {a/the} path for ~*.

(1) Martha Graham is a pioneer of modern dance who {cleared/paved} the way for dancers who were disillusioned with classical ballet. (→ (a))

(as) clear as crystal / phr. simile

highly transparent

REL crystal clear

Example

The water in this lake is as clear as crystal.

REL

The English has the REL *crystal clear*, which can mean both "very clear" (when used to describe an image or object) and "very easy to understand."

(1) This river is crystal clear. You can even see the bottom.
この川は水が透き通っていて、川底まで見える。

(2) Professor Wilson's lectures are crystal clear.
ウィルソン教授の講義はとてもわかりやすい。

(1) われわれはその立法化のハードルをうまく{越えた/クリアした}。(→(a))

2. 日本語には、目標を高く設定するという意味の「ハードルを{置く/設定する}」という関連表現がある。

(2) 新社長は、自分にも部下にも高いハードルを設定することで、倒産の危機を乗り越えた。
By setting high goals for both himself and his workers, the new president was able to avert his company's bankruptcy.

道を切り開く　phr.　隠喩

新しい領域を開拓する

例文

(a) マーサ・グラハムは、従来のクラシックバレエの分野に幻滅を感じていたダンサーたちのために新しい道を切り開いたモダンダンスの先駆者である。

(b) 彼は人間が宇宙に住んでそこで仕事ができることを示し、NASAと宇宙飛行士志望者たちに宇宙生活への新しい道を切り開いた。

(c) 発電における原子力使用は、化石燃料の依存低減への道を切り開いたものの、施設周辺の住民への危険も生んだ。

解説

日本語の「切り開く」と英語の *clear* は同じ意味ではない。「切り開く」は"森や山などを崩して道をつくる"という意味であり、*clear* は"望ましくないものをなくす"という意味である。

関連語

英語の *{clear/pave} the way for ~* は *clear {a/the} path for ~* の関連表現で、これらは自由に置き換えられる。■ REL(1)

水晶のように透き通っている　phr.　直喩

透明度が高い

例文

この湖は水晶のように透き通っている。

関連語

英語には関連表現として *crystal clear* があり、その意味の一つは「(映像や物の記述で)とてもきれいに透き通っている」で、もう一つは「とてもわかりやすい」という意味である。

■ REL(1)(2)

153

climb the ladder of success / phr. / metaphor

to succeed in life

Examples

Mike: I'm gonna have someone working under me soon.

Mr. S: Wow! Sounds like you've started climbing the ladder of success.

Mike: Well, not really. It's just because another American's gonna be joining us.

- -

(a) The only way to climb the ladder of success is to get to know the right people in the right places.

(b) The founders of McDonald's and Wendy's understood that you cannot climb the ladder of success without first getting on the ladder.

Note

While *ladder* and *kaidan* (stairs) have different meanings, they are both objects one climbs step by step (or rung by rung).

(1) He tried to climb the {ladder/ ×stairs} of success.
彼は出世の{階段/ ×はしご}を上がろうとした。

cling to power / phr. / metaphor

to hold fast to one's power

Examples

Mr. S: This politician's never going to step down, is he?

Mrs. S: Probably not, even though he really should step aside and give young people a chance instead of clinging to power.

- -

(a) The leaders of that country are clinging to power when they should be out of power.

(b) He's a crafty, stubborn guy. My guess is that he'll cling to power for longer than people think.

(c) As long as politicians keep clinging to power, there's little hope the Japanese economy will make a full recovery.

Note

The basic meaning of *power* is "the capacity or authority to do s.t.," while *kenryoku* means "the power to dominate s.o. and make {him/her} obey." Both *cling to ~* and *~ ni shigami-tsuku* mean "to hold on tightly to ~," but the subject for the Japanese is restricted to {s.o./s.a.}.

(1) There's an odor clinging to the cup.
においがコップに{しみついて/ ×しがみついて}いる。

{出世 / 成功}の階段を上がる / **phr.** 隠喩

出世する

例文

マイク：今度、僕にも部下がつくことになったんですよ。

鈴木（夫）：おっ、いよいよマイクも出世の階段を上がり始めたな？

マイク：いえ、そんなことはないんですが、アメリカ人がもう一人、入るんですよ。

- -

(a) 出世の階段を上がる唯一の方法は、然るべき所で然るべき人と知りあうことだ。

(b) マクドナルドやウェンディーズの創業者は、成功の階段を上がるためには、まず
その一段目に足をかけなければならないということを心得ていた。

解説

英語の *ladder*（はしご）と日本語の「階段」は、意味は異なるが、両者とも一歩一歩上がるという点では共通している。━ Note（1）

権力にしがみつく / **phr.** 隠喩

自分の権力を持ち続けようとする

例文

鈴木（夫）：この政治家はいつまでもやめないね。

鈴木（妻）：そうね。いつまでも権力にしがみついていないで、早く若い人たちに道を
譲ったらいいのにね。

- -

(a) その国の指導者は、権力の座を去るべきときに権力にしがみついている。

(b) 彼は陰険で頑固者だ。私の推測では、彼は大方が思っているよりも長い期間権
力にしがみついているだろう。

(c) 政治家が権力にしがみついているかぎり、日本の経済が根本的な回復を遂げる希
望はほとんどない。

解説

日英語の名詞の「権力」と *power* の基本義は、それぞれ、"他人を支配して従わせる力"と"何
かを行う{能力 / 権威}"である。動詞の「〜にしがみつく」と *cling to 〜* はいずれも"〜にくっ
つく"という意味であるが、日本語の場合は主語が人か生き物でなければならない。

━ Note（1）

clip s.o.'s wings / phr. / metaphor

to restrict s.o.'s ability to {move/act} freely

Examples

(a) If my car were to break down on the highway in California, I'd feel as if my wings had been clipped.

(b) That violinist said that when someone took away his violin, which he had been playing for the past thirty years, he felt as if his wings had been clipped.

(c) When illness kept me from my design work for two years, I felt as if my wings had been clipped.

Notes

1. An important distinction between the English and Japanese is that the English is used as a metaphor in both the active and passive voice, whereas the Japanese is most naturally used as a simile in the passive voice. The sentences below cannot be rendered naturally in Japanese.

(1) He's become too aggressive. We have to clip his wings.
   彼はあまりにも攻撃的だから、{おとなしくさせ/×羽をもが}なければならない。

2. In Japanese, both *hane o mogareru* and the compound verb *hane o mogi-torareru* can be used, as shown in (a)/(c) and (b), respectively. Both mean "to pluck and take," but the latter is more vivid in its description.

close at hand / phr. / metonymy

to be near in {proximity/time}

Examples

Kenta: Mom, what's this?

Mrs. S: It's a new kind of fire extinguisher.

Kenta: Wow, it's so small it hardly takes up any space. Perfect for keeping close at hand.

Mrs. S: Not to mention it's lightweight and easy to use. It can put out small fires in no time.

- -

(a) You should always keep *A Dictionary of Japanese and English Metaphors* close at hand. Use it often and your vocabulary will grow by leaps and bounds.

(b) You should keep your mobile phone close at hand whether at work or play.

(c) I love chocolate, so I always keep some close at hand.

Notes

1. In English, *close at hand* can be used for both spatial and temporal expressions. In Japanese, *majika ni* (soon) is used for temporal expressions.

2. The Japanese is used to refer to something small and/or convenient that is situated very close to the speaker, but the English can refer to anything that is situated close to the speaker.

(1) I was just lucky that my father was close at hand.

羽を{もがれる / もぎ取られる}ようだ / phr. | 直喩

自由に動けないように感じる

例文

(a) もしカリフォルニアのハイウェイで車が故障したら、羽をもがれたような気がするだろう。

(b) そのバイオリニストは、30年間も使ってきたバイオリンを盗まれた時、羽をもぎ取られたように感じたそうだ。

(c) 病気で2年間もデザインの仕事ができなかった時は、羽をもがれたように感じましたね。

解説

1. 日英語の間には重要な違いがある。日本語は例文に見られるように受動形で、「ような」を伴う直喩が自然であるのに対し、英語では受動形でも(1)のような能動形でも使える。日本語は(1)のように言うことはできない。 📖 Note(1)

2. 日本語の(a)と(c)では「羽をもがれる」が使われ、(b)では複合動詞の「羽をもぎ取られる」が使われている。どちらも何かをねじり取るという意味だが、後者は前者より描写的である。

手近に | comp. adv. | 換喩

何かが簡単に手が届く範囲にある

関 間近に，身近に

例文

健太：お母さん、これ何？

鈴木(妻)：新型の消火器。

健太：へえ、小さくて場所を取らないから、手近に置けていいね。

鈴木(妻)：それに軽くて使いやすいしね。ちょっとした出火ならすぐ消せるんだって。

- -

(a) メタファー辞典はいつも手近に置いて活用するとよい。語彙が格段に増えるはずだ。

(b) 携帯電話は仕事をしているときも遊んでいるときも、手近に持っているほうがいいですよ。

(c) 僕はチョコレートが大好きだから、チョコレートはいつも手近にあるんだ。

解説

1. 英語の *close at hand* は空間的表現を表す他に時間的表現としても使われる。日本語で時間的表現を表す場合は「間近に」を使う。

2. 日本語は話し手の近くにある「何か小さい、あるいは小さくて便利なもの」を指すのに対して、英語は話し手の近くにあるものなら何でも指すことができる。 📖 Note(1)

関連語

日本語の「身近に」は「手近に」と似ているが、前者は親しい、心理的に近い関係にあることを指すのに対して、後者はそのような関係を指すことはできない。

私は父が｛そば/近く/˟手近｝にいたので運がよかった。

REL

> The Japanese REL *mijika ni* (lit. "body-close; near oneself") can be used to refer to a psychologically close relationship with {s.o./s.t.}. However, *tejika ni* cannot be used in this manner. 📖→関連語(1)

close one's eyes to ~　*phr.*　metaphor

to refuse to acknowledge s.t.

REL shut one's eyes to ~; turn a blind eye to ~

Examples

(a) Today the nations of the free world prefer to close their eyes to the reality of the Middle East as a whole.

(b) The securities company went bankrupt because it closed its eyes to the illegal dealings of one of its employees, eventually leading to the whole company getting involved in a cover-up.

(c) People tend to close their eyes to the wrongdoings of people they agree with.

Notes

1. The English and Japanese expressions are very close metaphorically, but the Japanese verb *tsuburu* is not as general as the English verb *close*, because the direct object of *tsuburu* is limited to *eyes*. It is possible to say *me o tojiru* (to shut one's eyes), but this expression does not have any metaphorical meaning. In addition, *shimeru*, the verb most commonly used to say "to close" in Japanese, cannot take *eyes* as its direct object.

📖→解説(1)

2. *Tsuburu* can be changed to *tsumuru* by replacing the bilabial stop "bu" with the bilabial nasal "mu." But the latter is used much less frequently. 📖→解説(2)

REL

> The English RELs, *shut one's eyes to ~* and *turn a blind eye to ~*, have the same meaning as the main entry, though *shut one's eyes to ~* is not used as frequently as the other two.

(1) Today the nations of the free world prefer to {{close/shut} their eyes/turn a blind eye} to the reality of the Middle East as a whole. (→(a))

close to ~　*phr.*　metaphor

for s.o.'s idea to be similar to s.o. else's

ANT 📖 distant

Examples

Saya: Hey Karen, are you reading that person's essays again?

Karen: Yeah, her way of thinking is close to mine, so it really resonates with me.

(a) My idea is close to his, but slightly different.

(b) Berlusconi's governing style was close to that of the late Margaret Thatcher, for whom he has boundless admiration.

(1) あなたの{身近/[×]手近}にもアニメ好きな外国人がいますか。
Do you know any foreigners who like anime?

(〜に)目をつぶる　phr.　隠喩

{知って/見て}いるが{知らない/見ない}ふりをしてとがめない

例文

(a) 今日、自由世界の国家は中東全般に関する真実に目をつぶりたがっている。
(b) その証券会社の倒産は、一社員の不正取り引きに目をつぶり続け、あげくの果てにそれを会社ぐるみで隠蔽しようとした結果である。
(c) 人々は、自分と意見の同じ人の犯罪には目をつぶる傾向がある。

解説

1. 日英語の比喩的意味は非常に近いが、日本語の「つぶる」という動詞の目的語は「目」に限られているから、英語の close よりはるかに限定的である。日本語でも「目を閉じる」とは言えるが、これには比喩的な意味は一切ない。日本語で最も一般的に使われている close の意味の「閉める」は直接目的語として「目」をとることができない。
(1) 私は{ドア/[×]目}を閉めた。
I closed {the door/my eyes}.
2. 日本語の「つぶる」は、「つむる」のように「ぶ」を両唇鼻音の「む」に代えられるが、「つむる」の使用頻度ははるかに低い。
(2) 人々は、自分と意見の同じ人の犯罪には目を{つぶる/つむる}傾向がある。(→(c))

関連語

英語の二つの関連表現 shut one's eyes to ~ と turn a blind eye to ~ は、どちらも見出しと置き換えられる。しかし、shut one's eyes to ~ は他の二つの表現ほど使用頻度は高くない。

→📖 REL (1)

{〜に/と}近い　phr. adj. (i)　隠喩

誰かの考えが他の人の考えとだいたい同じである

反 LOOK 遠い

例文

さや：あら、カレン、また、その人のエッセイ読んでるの？

カレン：うん、彼女の考え方、私に近いところがあって、共感できるのよ。

(a) 私の考えは彼のと近いですが、でもちょっと違います。
(b) ベルルスコーニの政治は、彼が尊敬してやまないマーガレット・サッチャーのそれと近かった。

159

(c) Everyone has different opinions on that subject, but I think my views are close to yours.

Notes

1. In the case of both the English and Japanese expressions, the original spatial expression has been transformed metaphorically to mean "a similarity of ideas."
2. Both the English and Japanese expressions can be used as temporal expressions, as shown in (1).

(1) The interview is scheduled close to noon.
インタビューは正午近くに予定されている。

---

cold / adj. / synesthesia

not {affectionate/cordial}; lacking kindness

REL LOOK▶ (as) cold as ice

ANT LOOK▶ warm

Examples

Mr. S: Kenta, my computer just froze. Do you think you could take a look at it?

Kenta: I'm on my way to the gym now.

Mrs. S: How can you be so cold to your father? Who do you think bought you your computer?

Kenta: All right, all right, I'll fix it.

- -

(a) That child's so cold and selfish. No wonder the other children don't like him.

(b) She had no idea why his expression suddenly turned so cold.

REL

1. *Cold* corresponds to *tsumetai* and *samui* in Japanese, but note that *samui*, which is used to indicate cold weather, cannot be replaced by *tsumetai*. 📖→関連語(1)
2. The *on*-reading of 寒 is *kan*. There are several compounds in which *kan* possesses a metaphorical meaning. 📖→関連語(2)
3. The English expression *(as) cold as ice* is *kōri no yō ni tsumetai* in Japanese. Both are used as similes.

(3) Her eyes were as cold as ice.
彼女は氷のように冷たい目をしていた。

(as) cold as ice / phr. / simile

cold-hearted

Example

She may be beautiful, but her personality is as cold as ice.

(c) みんなはその話題について色々と違った意見を持っていますが、私の意見はあなたのに近いと思います。

解説

1. *close to ~* も「{～に / と} 近い」も、元の空間的な表現で考え方の近似性を比喩的に表現したものである。

2. 日英語とも時間表現にも使える。━━📖 Note(1)

C

冷たい｜adj. (i)｜共感覚
つめ｜｜きょうかんかく

思いやりがない，失礼な，やさしさに欠けている

関 寒い，**LOOK** 氷のように冷たい

反 **LOOK** 温(暖)かい / 温(暖)かな

例文

鈴木(夫)：健太、ちょっとコンピュータがフリーズしちゃったんだ。見てくれないかな。

健太：僕、これからジムに行くんだけどなあ。

鈴木(妻)：健太、どうしてそんな冷たいことが言えるの？ いったい誰があなたのコンピュータ、買ってくれたと思ってるの。

健太：わかった、じゃ、今、直すよ。

(a) あの子はとても冷たくて、わがままなので、他の子供達から嫌われている。

(b) どうして彼が急に冷たい表情を見せたのか、彼女には分からなかった。

関連語

1. 英語の *cold* は日本語の「冷たい」と「寒い」に対応するが、「寒い」は大気の気温が低いことを表すため、「冷たい」に置き換えられないので、注意する。

(1) a. あの先生は{冷たい/×寒い}。
   That teacher is cold.

   b. {冷たい/×寒い}返事が返ってきた。
   I received a cold reply.

2. 「寒」の音読みは「カン」であるが、その音読みの複合語の比喩例がいくつかある。

(2) a. 寒色 *kan-shoku* (cold color)

   b. 寒村 *kan-son* (poor village)

3. 英語の関連表現 *(as) cold as ice* は、日本語では「氷のように冷たい」になる。日英語とも直喩として使われる。━━📖 REL(3)

氷のように冷たい｜phr.｜直喩
こおり｜つめ｜｜ちょくゆ

心がとても冷たい

例文

彼女は美人かもしれないけど、心は氷のように冷たい。

cold-blooded / comp. adj. / metaphor

cruel

REL in cold blood

Examples

(a) He's a cold-blooded guy who doesn't even care if his kids are in danger.

(b) It is said that the fifth emperor of the Roman Empire, Nero, was a cold-blooded tyrant.

R E L

The English has the REL *in cold blood*.

(1) The criminal killed the taxi driver with a gun in cold blood and ran away with the money.
犯人は残酷にもタクシーの運転手を銃で殺し、金を持って逃げた。

cold war / comp. n. / metaphor

a nonviolent conflict

Examples

(a) During the Cold War between the U.S. and the Soviet Union, there were not many acts of terror.

(b) Even though they used to be so close, now they don't even talk. It's like there's a cold war between them.

(c) The cause of the cold war among the local residents was deciding where the waste treatment plant should be located.

come back to life / phr. / metaphor

to regain {strength/vitality}

Examples

Karen: Phew, thank goodness we're outside. It feels like I just came back to life!

Saya: It was so stuffy in that shop. The cigarette smoke was awful, and the music was way too loud!

Karen: Seriously, it was horrible. I felt like I was gonna suffocate!

- -

(a) Drinking the cold beer made me feel like I'd come back to life.

(b) Due to depopulation, the city fell into decline for a while before coming back to life with the arrival of a new factory.

(c) After forgetting to water the withered plants in my room for a while, I watered them, and they had come back to life by this morning.

冷血（な） / comp. adj. (na) 隠喩

非情な

例文

(a) あの男は冷血な男で、自分の子供が危険にさらされていても何とも思わない。

(b) ローマ帝国の第5代皇帝ネロは冷血な暴君だったと言われている。

関連語

英語には *in cold blood* という関連表現がある。 ▶📖 REL(1)

冷戦 / n. 隠喩

武力は用いないが、戦争を思わせるような激しい対立

例文

(a) かつての米国とソ連の冷戦構造の中では、テロはあまりなかった。

(b) 彼らはあんなに仲がよかったのに、今は冷戦状態で、口もきかない。

(c) 地域住民の間の冷戦の原因は、ゴミ処理場の設置場所をどこにするかだった。

生き返る / comp. v. 隠喩

元気や活力を取り戻す

例文

カレン： はああ、外に出てやっと生き返ったね。

さや： ほんと、空気悪い店だったね。たばこの煙がひどいし、音楽はうるさいし。

カレン： ほんと、最悪。息ができなくて、死にそうだったわ。

(a) 冷たいビールを飲んだら生き返った気がしました。

(b) 過疎化によってしばらく沈滞していた町は、新工場の誘致とともに生き返った。

(c) しばらく水やりを忘れて枯れしぼんでいた部屋の観葉植物に水をやったら、今朝生き返っていた。

come out of one's shell / phr. / metaphor

to become more outgoing

[REL] break out of one's shell

[ANT] {go/withdraw/retreat} into one's shell

Examples

Saya: How was your high school English class, Karen?

Karen: Everyone was really quiet. I wish they'd come out of their shells and talk more.

Saya: They're probably just not used to talking with foreigners.

Karen: I hope that's all it is.

- -

(a) Thanks to his friend's constructive advice, Michael gradually came out of his shell and started socializing with people.

(b) She's really come out of her shell these past few months. She even started playing outside with other kids from the neighborhood.

Note

The nouns *shell* and *kara* are very similar, but the verbs *come out* and *yaburu* (to break) reveal the difference in focus between the English and Japanese expressions. Whereas the English focuses on "coming out of the shell," the Japanese focuses on "breaking the shell." Neither expression explicitly states the idea of "breaking through the shell and emerging from it."

[REL]

In English, there is the REL *break out of one's shell*, which is closer to the Japanese expression than *come out of one's shell*. However, the former is used much less frequently than the latter.

(1) Thanks to his friend's constructive advice, Michael gradually {came/broke} out of his shell and started socializing with people. (→(a))

[ANT]

The English ANT is *{go/withdraw/retreat} into one's shell*, and the Japanese ANT is *kara ni toji-komoru*. 📖→反意語(1)

{reach/come to} s.o.'s ears (耳に {入る / 届く}) → **{reach/come to} s.o.'s ears**

---

come to light / phr. / metaphor

for a secret to become known

Examples

(a) One of the most serious spy scandals in U.S. history came to light in 1994.

(b) The scandal came to light in June after the company declared bankruptcy.

(c) He was rearrested last May when new evidence came to light.

(d) It came to light that there had been cases where patients were not admitted to the hospital despite there being beds available.

Notes

1. Both the English and Japanese use intransitive verbs (*come* and *deru*) and express the

殻を破る / phr. / 隠喩

それまでの内向きの{人間関係 / 態度 / 考え方}を思い切って外向きに転換して行動する

反 殻に閉じこもる

例文

さや：どう、カレン、高校の英語のクラスは？

カレン：うん、みんな静かなのよ。もっとみんな自分の殻を破って話してくれるといいんだけど。

さや：外国人と話すことに慣れていないんじゃないかな。

カレン：そうだといいんだけど。

- - - - - - - - - - - - - - - - - - - -

(a) マイケルは友人の前向きな助言のおかげで、自分の殻を破って人と付き合えるようになった。

(b) この数か月、少女は本当に自分の殻を破りました。外で近所の子供達と遊び始めたのです。

解説

「殻」と *shell* の意味は非常に近いが、「破る」と *come out* (出てくる)とでは焦点が異なる。つまり、英語は「殻から出てくる」ところに、日本語は「殻を破る」ところに焦点がおいてあり、どちらもはっきり「殻を破って出てくる」とは表現していない。

関連語

英語には関連表現として *come out of one's shell* よりも日本語の見出しに近い *break out of one's shell* があるが、見出しよりも使用頻度がはるかに低い。 →📖 REL(1)

反意語

日英語それぞれの反意表現は「殻に閉じこもる」と *{go/withdraw/retreat} into one's shell* である。

(1) 息子に女友達との関係について聞いたら、自分の殻に閉じこもってしまい、私と口を聞かなくなった。
When I asked my son about his relationship with his girlfriend, he {went/withdrew/retreated} into his shell and stopped talking to me.

明るみに出る / phr. / 隠喩

隠れていた否定的なことが世間に知られる

例文

(a) アメリカの歴史上一番深刻なスパイ事件の一つが、1994 年に明るみに出た。

(b) そのスキャンダルは会社が倒産宣言をした後、6 月に明るみに出た。

(c) 彼は去年の 5 月に、新しい証拠が明るみに出たときに再逮捕された。

(d) 病院にベッドが空いていたにも関わらず患者が入院できなかったケースが審査中に明るみに出た。

解説

1. 日英語ともに自動詞の「出る」と *come* が使われ、何かが自然に発見されることを意味している。似た意味で対応する他動詞表現として、それぞれ「明るみに出す」と *bring to light* がある。

idea of something being spontaneously discovered. Likewise, they both have transitive counterparts (*bring to light* and *akarumi ni dasu*). 📖➡解説(**1**)

2. While the English can be used when anything hidden becomes known, the Japanese means "for s.t. negative to become public." As a result, it cannot be used in (2) below. It must be replaced by the verb *hakken-suru* (to discover) in (2a) and *hi no me o miru* (lit. "see the sun's eye") in (2b).

(2) a. As the search progressed, more items came to light: a camera, which proved to be the victim's, and a water canteen.
捜査をしていくうちに被害者の所持品と考えられるカメラや水筒のような物品が {発見された/ [×]明るみに出た} 。

b. The buried treasure came to light.
埋もれていた宝物が {陽の目を見た/ [×]明るみに出た} 。

3. While the underlying meaning of the English and Japanese expressions is the same, the English literally means "for s.t. to appear in a bright place."

common ground / comp. n. / metaphor

basic {ideas/objectives} shared by two or more parties

Examples

(a) We have to build common ground that transcends opposing ideologies and immediate interests.

(b) Regarding the notion of intellectual property, we have to try to find common ground between cultures.

(c) When attempting to stand on common ground and share ideas, it helps to have experiences in common.

REL

Kiban means "s.t. that provides the basis for s.t.'s success." *Kiban* can be replaced by *jiban* and *dojō*, which mean "a basis for growth and development." 📖➡関連語(**1**)

connect / v. / metaphor

to establish a relationship between {people/things}

REL tie together

Examples

(a) The clues the criminal left behind should help us connect the two cases.

(b) Japanese bullet trains are an important part of the transportation system that connects northern and southern Japan.

(c) Inazo Nitobe wanted to become a bridge connecting Japan and the U.S.

(d) I tried calling my husband after I got into the accident, but the company operator wouldn't connect me to him, so I got frustrated.

Note

Connect and *tsunagu* both mean "to use s.t. to put two separate things together."

（1）首相のスキャンダルが週刊誌で明るみに出された。
The prime minister's scandals were brought to light by a weekly magazine.

2. 英語は"何でも隠れていたものが知られるようになる"を意味するが、日本語は"何か悪い{もの / こと}が人の目に触れるようになる"を意味する。したがって、Note (2) のような文では日本語は使えない。(2a) では動詞「発見する」に、(2b) では「陽の目を見る」に、それぞれ置き換えなければならない。 📖 **Note (2)**

3. 日英語は基本的に同義であるが、英語のほうは字義通りには「光に来る」、つまり"光の当たるところに出てくる"という意味である。

共通の基盤　／ n. phr.　隠喩
きょうつう　きばん　　　　　　　いんゆ

共有されている基本的な考えや目的
きょうゆう　　　　　きほんてき　　かんが　　もくてき

関　共通の {地盤 / 土壌}
きょうつう　　じばん　どじょう

例文

（a）私達はイデオロギーや目前の利害の対立を超えた共通の基盤を築かなければならない。
わたしたち　　　　　　　もくぜん　りがい　たいりつ　こ　　きょうつう　きばん　きず

（b）知的財産の考え方に関して、異文化間の共通の基盤を見い出す努力をすべきだ。
ちてきざいさん　かんが　かた　かん　　いぶんかかん　きょうつう　きばん　みだ　どりょく

（c）共通の基盤に立って考えを共有しようとする時に、似たような経験は役に立つ。
きょうつう　きばん　た　　かんが　きょうゆう　　　　とき　に　　けいけん　やく　た

関連語

日本語の「基盤」は"何かが成り立つ基礎になるもの"を表す。「基盤」は、"何かが {生成 / 発展} する基盤"を表す関連表現の「地盤 / 土壌」と置き換えることができる。

（1）地球温暖化の問題に関して、共通の {基盤 / 地盤 / 土壌} に立って話し合う必要がある。
We must seek common ground in our discussion of global warming.

つなぐ　／ v.　隠喩
いんゆ

何かと何か、誰かと誰かを関係づける
なに　なに　だれ　だれ　かんけい

関　結ぶ
むす

例文

（a）この犯人の遺留品は、二つの事件をつなぐ手がかりとなるにちがいない。
はんにん　いりゅうひん　　ふた　じけん

（b）新幹線は、北から南まで日本の大都市をつなぐ大切な輸送機関だ。
しんかんせん　きた　みなみ　にほん　だいとし　　　たいせつ　ゆそうきかん

（c）新渡戸稲造は日米をつなぐ橋になりたいと言った。
にとべいなぞう　にちべい　　　はし　　　　　い

（d）事故にあって夫に電話をしたとき、会社の交換手がすぐに私の電話をつないでくれなかったので、いらいらした。
じこ　　　おっと　でんわ　　　　　かいしゃ　こうかんしゅ　　　わたし　でんわ

解説

「つなぐ」と connect の基本義は、ともに"二つの離れたものを何かを使ってくっつける"である。

167

REL

1. The RELs *tie together* and *musubu* mean "to put two things together, or to bind loose objects together using string or a string-like object."
2. In (a)-(c), *connect* and *tsunagu* can be replaced by *tie together* and *musubu*, respectively, but in (d), *tie together* and *musubu* cannot be used due to the idiomatic nature of the expression.

(1) I tried calling my husband after I got into the accident, but the company operator wouldn't {connect/ ×tie together} me to him, so I got frustrated.
事故にあって夫に電話をしたとき、会社の交換手がすぐに私の電話を {つないで/ ×結んで} くれなかったので、いらいらした。(→(d))

---

construct a theory / phr. / metaphor

to create a systematic theory

Examples

Saya: Karen, you're giving a presentation at the next conference, right?

Karen: Yeah, but the other day when I had the professor look at a draft of my paper, he told me that I need to reconstruct my theory.

- -

(a) Our intention is to construct a theory of international relations.

(b) Astronomers have constructed a theory of stellar motion consistent with the laws of physics.

Note

Construct means "to build a physical structure," and *kumi-tateru* means "to create s.t. out of assembled materials."

REL

Kumi-tateru can be replaced by *kōchiku-suru* in written Japanese. 📖 関連語(1)

---

constructive criticism / comp. n. / metaphor

positive and useful advice

Example

Don't just criticize. Offer constructive criticism.

(the) conversation jumps / phr. / metaphor

for the topic of conversation to change abruptly from one thing to another

Examples

(a) Whenever she talks to someone, the conversation jumps from topic to topic without any logical connections.

(b) Too often, especially during meetings, the conversation jumps to something completely unrelated and nothing gets done.

関連語

1. 日英語の関連表現は、それぞれ「結ぶ」と *tie together* である。どちらも基本義は"紐か紐のようなものを使って二つのものを一つにする、あるいは、ばらばらになっている複数のものを一つに束ねる"である。

2. (a)-(c)では「つなぐ」と *connect* は「結ぶ」と *tie together* で置き換えることができるが、(d)は慣用句なので、「つなぐ」と *connect* しか使えない。→ REL**(1)**

理論を組み立てる   *phr.*   隠喩
りろん　　く　　た　　　　　　　　　　いんゆ

体系的な理論を造りあげる
たいけいてき　りろん　　つく

関 理論を構築する
　　りろん　こうちく

例 文

さや：カレン、今度、学会で発表するんでしょ。
　　　　　　　　こんど　がっかい　はっぴょう

カレン：そうなんだけど、この間、教授に論文の草稿を見てもらったら、もう一度、
　　　　　　　　　　　　　　あいだ　きょうじゅ　ろんぶん　そうこう　み　　　　　　いちど
理論を組み立て直したほうがいいって言われちゃった。
りろん　く　　た　　なお　　　　　　　　　　　　い

(a) 私達の意図は、国際関係の理論を組み立てることです。
　　わたしたち　いと　　こくさいかんけい　りろん　く　た

(b) 天文学者たちは、物理学の法則に合った星の運行の理論を組み立てた。
　　てんもんがくしゃ　　　　ぶつりがく　ほうそく　あ　　　ほし　うんこう　りろん　く　た

解 説

「組み立てる」と *construct* の基本義は、それぞれ"材料を組み合わせて何かを作る"と"物理的な構造物を建てる"である。

関連語

日本語の「組み立てる」は、書き言葉では「構築する」で置き換えることができる。

(1) 私達の意図は、国際関係の理論を{組み立てる / 構築する}ことです。(→(a))

建設的な意見   *n. phr.*   隠喩
けんせつてき　　いけん　　　　　　　　　　いんゆ

前向きで役に立つ意見
まえむ　　やく　た　　いけん

例 文

批判するばかりではなく、もっと建設的な意見を述べてください。
ひはん　　　　　　　　　　　　けんせつてき　いけん　の

話が飛ぶ   *phr.*   隠喩
はなし　と　　　　　　　　　いんゆ

話の話題があることから急に他のことに変わる
はなし　わだい　　　　　　　きゅう　ほか　　　　か

例 文

(a) 彼女の話はよく飛んで、話題と話題の論理的なつながりがない。
　　かのじょ　はなし　　と　　　わだい　わだい　ろんりてき

(b) 特に会議などでは、話が一つの話から他のほうに飛んでしまい、何の成果も得
　　とく　かいぎ　　　　　はなし　ひと　はなし　ほか　　　と　　　　　　なん　せいか　え

169

(c) During the business luncheon, the conversation jumped from business to politics to culture.

Note

Jump means "for {s.o./s.t.} to move quickly and suddenly away from a surface through use of the legs," and *tobu* means "for {s.o./s.t.} to move through the air." However, they can be used figuratively to express the idea of a conversation changing quickly and suddenly from one topic to another.

crawl into a hole and die / phr. / metaphor

to feel so {ashamed/embarrassed} that one wants to die

Examples

Kenta: Whoa, how'd you get hurt?

Saya: I fell down the stairs at the station. The worst part was I was wearing a miniskirt. I just wanted to crawl into a hole and die.

Kenta: Bet the embarrassment came before the pain, huh?

(a) I accidentally handed him a tube of hemorrhoid cream instead of the toothpaste. I wanted to crawl into a hole and die.

(b) When Julie fell during her dance solo, she wanted to crawl into a hole and die.

Note

The Japanese expresses a feeling of shame, but the English can also be used to express either general feelings or intense negative emotions, as shown in the examples. The Japanese expression merely describes wanting to crawl into a hole if one is available, without any mention of death.

(1) a. I'm tired, I'm sick, and I hate school. I just wanna crawl into a hole and die.
俺は疲れていて、気分が悪いんだ。学校なんて大嫌いだ。{死にたいぐらいだ/[×]穴があったら入りたい}。

b. No matter what I do, everyone hates me. I want to crawl into a hole and die.
何をしてもみんなから憎まれるんだ。{死にたい気持ちだ/[×]穴があったら入りたい}。

homograph

crooked / adj. / metaphor

dishonest; immoral
不正直な，不道徳な

Example

No one trusts him because he has a crooked personality.
彼は不正直なので、誰にも信頼されていない。

ずに終わってしまうことが非常によくある。

(c) ビジネスランチの間、話はビジネスのことから政治に飛び、さらに文化のことに飛んだ。

解説

「飛ぶ」とjumpは、それぞれ"｛誰か/何か｝が空中を動く"と"｛誰か/何か｝が足を使って地面から素早く体を離す"というのが基本義であるが、その比喩的な意味は"会話の話題があることから別のことへ急に素早く変わる"である。

穴があったら入りたい　　phr.　隠喩

とても恥ずかしくて身を隠したい

例文

健太：どうしたの、その怪我？

さや：駅の階段で上から転げ落ちちゃったのよ。それもミニスカートはいて。まったく、穴があったら入りたい心境だったわ。

健太：痛さより恥ずかしさのほうが先だったんだ。

(a) 私は歯磨き粉のチューブの代わりに間違って痔の軟膏を彼に渡してしまい、穴があったら入りたいと思いました。

(b) ジュリーは、ソロで踊っているときにころんでしまって、穴があったら入りたいくらいだった。

解説

日本語の見出しは、恥ずかしいという気持ちを表現するのに対し、英語の見出しは恥ずかしいに加え、例文にあるように、一般的、あるいはより強烈で否定的な心理を表す。日本語はただ穴があったらその中に入りたいと言っているだけで、死にたいという意味は含まない。

→📖Note⑴

同形異義語

曲がっている　/ v. / 隠喩

｛心 / 性格 / 考え｝がひねくれている
for one's {mind/personality/thoughts} to be twisted

例文

子供の頃から、彼女の性格は曲がっている。
She has had a twisted personality since she was young.

cross (over) {a/the} line / phr. / metaphor

to behave in a way that people consider unacceptable

REL (step) out of line

Examples

Karen: Did you hear? Someone managed to clone a child.

Saya: Really? That's unbelievable.

Karen: They've cloned animals, so I guess technology-wise it's possible to clone humans, too.

Saya: I feel like that's crossing a line.

Karen: I agree.

- -

(a) It's important for parents to be strict with their children. But physical punishment is crossing the line, I think.

(b) Certain individual rights are sacrosanct—that is, there is a line that cannot, must not, be crossed.

Notes

1. The Japanese expression literally means "to go beyond a line," but the underlying concept is the same as in the English.
2. In Japanese, *issen o koeru* can specifically mean "to have sexual relationship," but the English expression does not have this specific meaning. 📖→解説(1)

REL

The REL *(step) out of line* means "deviating from demanded or acceptable behavior." It is typically used when one disobeys specific orders or rules as opposed to societal norms.

(1) Physical punishment is {crossing the line/out of line}. (→(a))

cross one's mind / phr. / metaphor

to think about s.t. suddenly or momentarily

Examples

(a) The idea of discussing this subject has occasionally crossed my mind.

(b) I couldn't get in touch with her. The possibility that she'd been involved in some incident or accident crossed my mind.

(c) It had never crossed his mind that such a dream was within reach until today.

Notes

1. In the English, the subject of *cross* is usually an idea or thought, but in the Japanese, it is an emotion such as longing, anxiety, emptiness, loneliness, fear, and so on. 📖→解説(1)
2. The Japanese is used only in written Japanese, but the English can be used in both spoken and written English. In spoken Japanese, the speaker uses expressions such as *futo omou* (to suddenly think s.t.). 📖→ 解説(2)

一線を越える / phr. 隠喩

一般に認められないような{行動 / 行為}をする

例文

カレン： 人間のクローンの子供が生まれたんですってね。

さや： ほんと、信じられないね。

カレン： クローン動物も生まれてるから、人間も技術的には OK なのかもしれないけど。

さや： でも、越えてはいけない一線てあるよね。

カレン： ほんと。

- - - - - - - - - - - - - - - - -

(a) 親が子供を厳しくしつけることは大切だ。しかし、お仕置に体罰を用いるのは、一線を越えていると思う。

(b) 個人の権利の中には神聖で犯すことのできないものがある。つまり越えてはいけない一線というものがあるのだ。

解説

1. 日本語を英訳すると *go beyond a line* で *cross (over) {a/the} line* とは違うが、基本的には同じだと考えられる。

2. 日本語の「一線を越える」は性的関係を持つことにも使えるが、英語では使えない。

(1) この二人、一線を越えちゃったね。
These two {did s.t. they were not supposed to do/ ×crossed over the line}.

関連語

英語の関連表現 *(step) out of line* は、"すべきこと、または受け入れ可能な行動から外れること"を意味する。社会的な規則や義務に従わない時によく使用される。—📖 REL(1)

心をよぎる / phr. 隠喩

{急に / 瞬間的に}あることを思う

例文

(a) その懸案について討議したいという思いが、折に触れて私の心をよぎった。

(b) 彼女と連絡が取れない。事件や事故に巻き込まれたのではないかという不安が心をよぎった。

(c) 今日まで、このような夢が実現できるなどという思いは彼の心をよぎったことはなかった。

解説

1. 英語では心をよぎるものはまず第一に *idea/thought*（考え）だが、日本語では「思い」「不安」「空しさ」「寂しさ」「恐怖」といった心理系の言葉である。

(1) {不安 / 空しさ}が心をよぎった。
I suddenly felt {anxious/empty}.

2. 日本語は主に書き言葉で使われるが、英語は話し言葉でも書き言葉でも使える。日本語の話し言葉では「ふと思う」などが使われる。

(2) ほかのキャリアを試そうかと、ふと思ったんだ。
The idea of trying another career crossed my mind.

| homograph |

cross swords with ~ / phr. / metaphor

to argue or fight
議論する，戦う
ぎ ろん　　　たたか

Example

When I was in high school, I was a member of the debate team and had to cross swords with rival teams.
高校の時、僕はディベート・チームに参加して、相手チームと議論を戦わせた。
こうこう　とき　ぼく　　　　　　　　　　　　　　　さん か　　　あい て　　　　　　ぎ ろん　たたか

crossfire / comp. n. / metaphor

an attack from all sides

Example

The district soon fell after being caught in a crossfire from above and below.

crow's-feet / comp. n. / metaphor

the wrinkles at the edges of the eyes showing one's age

Example

My crow's feet have gotten worse recently. It's gotten to the point where I'm afraid to laugh.

cry wolf / comp. v. / metaphor

to ask for help when no help is needed; to raise a false alarm

Examples

(a) Kazuo always cries wolf, so nobody believes him anymore.

(b) Even though the child was telling the truth, no one believed him because he'd cried wolf so many times.

(c) He keeps claiming that he's going to study abroad, but I've never seen him study. Talk about crying wolf.

Notes

1. The metaphor originated from one of Aesop's fables, *The Boy Who Cried Wolf*, in which a shepherd boy twice fools the villagers into thinking a wolf is attacking. As a result, when the wolf actually shows up, no one believes him.
2. *Cry wolf* is a combination of a noun and a verb, but the Japanese is a compound noun.

同形異義語

剣を交える / phr. / 隠喩
（けん　まじ）　　　　　　（いんゆ）

剣を使って戦う
（けん　つか　たたか）
to fight with a sword

例文

日本の伝説の剣士、宮本武蔵と佐々木小次郎は巌流島で剣を交えたという。
（にほん　でんせつ　けんし　みやもとむさし　ささきこじろう　がんりゅうじま　けん　まじ）
Legendary Japanese swordsmen Musashi Miyamoto and Kojirō Sasaki crossed swords on Ganryū Island.

十字砲火 / comp. n. / 隠喩
（じゅうじほうか）　　　　　　（いんゆ）

四方八方から集中攻撃を受ける
（しほうはっぽう　　　しゅうちゅうこうげき　う）

例文

その街は、空から地上から十字砲火を浴びて、ついに陥落した。
（まち　そら　　ちじょう　　じゅうじほうか　あ　　　　　　　かんらく）

からすの足跡 / n. phr. / 隠喩
（あしあと）　　　　　　（いんゆ）

年を取ると現れる目尻のしわ
（とし　と　　あらわ　めじり）

例文

最近、目尻にからすの足跡が増えてきた。笑うのがちょっとこわい。
（さいきん　めじり　　　あしあと　ふ　　　　　わら）

狼少年 / comp. n. / 隠喩
（おおかみしょうねん）　　　　　（いんゆ）

常習的なうそつきなので本当のことを言っても信じてもらえない人
（じょうしゅうてき　　　　　　　ほんとう　　　　　　い　　　しん　　　　　　ひと）

例文

(a) 一男は狼少年だ。だから、今では彼を信じる者は誰もいない。
（かずお　おおかみしょうねん　　　　　　いま　　かれ　しん　もの　だれ）

(b) その子は本当のことを言ったにもかかわらず、普段から嘘ばかりついていたので、
（こ　　ほんとう　　　　　　い　　　　　　　　　　　　ふだん　　うそ）
狼少年扱いされて信じてもらえなかった。
（おおかみしょうねんあつか　　　　　　しん）

(c) 彼はいつも、もうすぐ留学する、留学すると騒いでいるが、勉強をしていると
（かれ　　　　　　　　　　　りゅうがく　　りゅうがく　　さわ　　　　　　べんきょう）
ころを見たことがない。まったく狼少年だ。
（み　　　　　　　　　　　　おおかみしょうねん）

解説

1. この比喩表現は、狼がいないのに、羊飼いの少年が「狼だ、狼だ」と村で２回も叫んで歩いたので、狼が本当に出てきたときに信じてもらえなかったというイソップ物語の『羊飼いの少年』という話が出典である。

2. 英語の *cry wolf* は動詞＋名詞であるが、日本語は複合名詞である。

cut / v. / metaphor

to {shorten/reduce} s.t.

Examples

Mike: How was the meeting?

Colleague: Well, they cut the budget again. Don't they realize we're in bad shape?

Mike: Yeah, apparently they've been trying to cut expenses.

Colleague: Geez, they should cut our overtime too while they're at it!

- -

(a) If you have high blood pressure, you should cut some salt from your diet.

(b) The company decided to cut employee salaries because of poor performance.

(c) We decided to cut violent scenes from the movie in order to make it suitable for children.

Note

The Japanese clearly comes from the English verb *cut*. The Japanese verb *kiru* has the same basic meaning as *cut*, but its metaphorical meanings are very different from those of *cut*, as exemplified by expressions such as *kotoba o kiru* (to stop talking), *sēkai o kiru* (to sharply criticize the political world), *te o kiru* (to sever a relationship), and so on.

cut one's own throat / phr. / metaphor

to bring about one's own destruction

REL LOOK dig one's own grave

Examples

Mrs. S: Kenta, what does *own goal* mean in soccer?

Kenta: That's when a player puts the ball into their own goal by mistake. It's called *jisatsu-ten* (suicide point) in Japanese. You'd be surprised how often players cut their own throats like that.

Mrs. S: Wow, I had no idea.

- -

(a) I ended up cutting my own throat by putting off a complicated task until later.

(b) The residents are opposed to this law, but defeating it will lead to lower land prices. They don't realize that they're cutting their own throats.

Note

The English and Japanese expressions are slightly different. Whereas the English literally means "to cut one's own throat," the Japanese means "to strangle one's own neck." However, both expressions reference similar body parts, i.e., *throat* and *kubi* (neck).

カットする / v. 隠喩

何かを短くする，量などを減らす

例文

マイク：会議、どうだった？

同僚：また、予算、カットされちゃったよ。うちも苦しいからね。

マイク：経費カットが続いているよね。

同僚：まったく、超過勤務もカットしてほしいよ。

(a) 血圧が高いんだったら、もっと塩分をカットした食事をしたほうがいいよ。

(b) その会社は、業績の悪化から、社員の賃金をカットすることにした。

(c) 子供が見ることも考慮して、その映画の暴力シーンの一部をカットすることにした。

解説

日本語の「カットする」は明らかに英語の cut から来ている。日本語の「切る」の基本義は英語の cut に対応するが、比喩的な慣用句として「言葉を切る」(話すのを止める)、「政界を切る」(鋭く批判する)、「手を切る」(関係を絶つ)のように使われ、英語の cut と対応していない。

(自分で)自分の首をしめる / phr. 隠喩

自分で自分を苦しい状況に置く

関 LOOK▶墓穴を掘る

例文

鈴木(妻)：サッカーのオウンゴールって、どういう意味？

健太：間違って自分のゴールにボールを入れてしまうことだよ。日本語では自殺点ていうかな。自分で自分の首をしめるようなへぼなミスだけど、わりとよくあるんだ。

鈴木(妻)：へえ、そうなの。

(a) 面倒なことを先送りにした結果、自分で自分の首をしめるようなことになってしまった。

(b) 住民はこの法律に反対しているが、それは地価を下げることになり、結局、自分で自分の首をしめるということに気がついていない。

解説

日英語で多少の表現上の違いがある。日本語の「(自分で)自分の首をしめる」に対して、英語は文字通りには "自分ののどを切る" を意味する。しかし、日英で非常に近い体の部分、すなわち「首」と首の前側である throat が使われているという類似点がある。

dance to s.o.'s tune / phr. / metaphor

to unquestioningly do whatever s.o. tells one to do

Examples

Karen: These dishes are nice.

Mrs. S: You think so? The salesperson had me dancing to his tune, so I bought them. But they were expensive, so I kind of regret it.

Karen: So that's what happened. Still, they're really nice.

- -

(a) He's always telling you to do this and that. You're just dancing to his tune.

(b) He was good at manipulating people's minds, and they were all dancing to his tune.

Note

> The English uses the active voice, but as shown in the dialogue and Examples (a) and (b), the Japanese uses the passive voice.

dark / adj. / metaphor

gloomy; evil; having limited knowledge

ANT bright

Examples

Saya: Kenta, what happened? Why the dark expression?

Kenta: I didn't pass my economics final, so I might fail the course.

Saya: That's what happens when you don't study. Whatever, let's forget about all that and focus on something positive. Like, say, a ski trip or something.

Kenta: I'll try, but I don't think there's much that can cheer me up right now.

- -

(a) Before I met her, I'd spent years wandering alone from one dark day to the next.

(b) Everyone has a dark side hidden behind their friendly smile.

(c) She had a dark past that she tried to hide from herself and others.

(d) While there is a dark history between the two countries, young people have been overcoming it with music.

Notes

> 1. In both the English and Japanese, the original visual meaning of the adjectives *dark* and *kurai* is applied to psychological or ethical concepts gloomy/evil.
> 2. Both the English and Japanese can also mean "to be ignorant of ~," but the Japanese can be used only when someone does not have general knowledge about {s.o./s.t.}, whereas the English can be used only when someone does not have knowledge about {s.o./s.t.} specific. 📖→解説(1)

178

（～の）言葉に踊らされる / phr. 隠喩

他の人の言いなりになる

例文

カレン： この食器、いいですね。

鈴木（妻）： そう？　セールスの言葉に踊らされて買っちゃったんだけど、高くて、ちょっと後悔してたのよ。

カレン： そうですか。でも、すごくいいですよ。

- -

（a）あなたはいつも彼にこうしろ、ああしろと言われているようだね。彼の言葉に踊らされているんだよ。

（b）彼は人の心をあやつるのがうまく、みんなは彼の言葉に踊らされていたのだ。

解説

英語は能動形をとるが、日本語は会話例や(a)(b)でわかるように、受動形をとる。

暗い / adj. (i) 隠喩

ゆううつなこと，知識のないこと

反 明るい

例文

さや：健太、どうしたの、そんな暗い顔して。

健太：うん、経済学の期末試験ができなかったから、赤点取るかもしれないんだ。

さや：そう、勉強してなかったもんね。ま、嫌なことは忘れて、明るいことも考えましょう。たとえば、スキー旅行とか。

健太：うん、でも、あまり、明るい気持ちになれそうにないけど。

- -

（a）彼女に出会うまで、私は長年、暗い日々を一人でさまよっていた。

（b）親しげな微笑でうまく隠してはいても、どの人間も暗い面を持っているものだ。

（c）彼女には人にも自分にも隠したい暗い過去があった。

（d）両国の間には暗い歴史が横たわっているが、若者達は音楽でそれを乗り越えつつある。

解説

1. 日英語とも、もともとは視覚的な意味を持っている「暗い」と *dark* が、心理的、倫理的な意味に移行している。

2. 日英語とも "詳しくない" という意味もある。日本語は誰かが｛誰か/何か｝について一般的知識を持っていない場合に使われるのに対して、英語は誰かが特定の｛誰か/何か｝について一般的な知識を持っていない場合に使われる。

（1）a. 僕は彼のこと｛は詳しく知らない/˟に暗い｝。
　　When it comes to him, I'm in the dark.

　　b. 私は文学専攻だったから経済のこと｛に暗い/ をよく知らない｝。
　　I majored in literature, so I {don't know much/ ˟am in the dark} about economics.

3. *Dark days* in (2a) and *dark outlook* in (2b) can be replaced by *black days* and *black outlook*, respectively, though these alternatives are used much less frequently. The Japanese adjective *kurai*, however, can never be replaced by *kuroi* (black). This is because *kuroi* can be used metaphorically to describe the heinous nature of a person or people involved in something, and "days" and "outlook" cannot be described as such.

(2) a. Those were the {darkest/blackest} days of my life.

それは私の人生で一番{暗い/×黒い}日々であった。

b. This year opened with a very {dark/black} outlook for real progress on global warming.

地球温暖化問題に関して実のある進歩があるかどうか。今年は大変{暗い/×黒い}見通しで始まった。

[A][N][T]

1. The English ANT is *bright*, and the Japanese ANT is *akarui*.

(1) a. The dark days are done and the bright days are near.

暗い日々は終わり、明るい日々が近づいている。

b. She has a bright personality.

彼女は明るい性格だ。

c. This town has a bright future ahead of it.

この町の将来は明るい。

2. In Japanese, *akarui* is used to mean that someone knows something very well, but *bright* does not have this meaning. 📖➡反意語(2)

---

dark clouds ~ (on the horizon)　/ phr. / metaphor

s.t. bad is very likely to occur

(Examples)

(a) Due to the slump in our stock, dark clouds began to loom over our new business.

(b) Dark clouds loom on the horizon for that country. Economists warn that the pace of its economic growth could be halved by a global recession.

(c) The country is doing a good job of being fiscally responsible, yet dark clouds are on the horizon.

(Notes)

1. The English can be used as a noun phrase, as in (a), but it often includes verbs such as *are* (Example [c]), *loom* (Example [b]), *gather*, *form*, and so on.
2. The Japanese contains the verb *tadayou* (to drift, to float), but this can be replaced by *tare-komeru* or *tachi-komeru* (to hang over), both of which make the meaning slightly more ominous. Note that the Japanese, unlike the English, cannot be used with *chihēsen ni* (on the horizon); rather, it co-occurs with variants of "in the future" such as ~ *no zento ni* (Example [a]), ~ *no shōrai ni* (Example [b]), or ~ *no yukusue ni* (Example [c]).

---

dawn of ~, the　/ n. phr. / metaphor

the beginning of s.t. new and historical

(Examples)

(a) Baron Pierre de Coubertin brought about the dawn of the modern Olympics.

3. 英語の(2a) *dark days* と(2b) *dark outlook* はそれぞれ *black days* と *black outlook* で置き換えることができるが、使用頻度はずっと低い。日本語の形容詞の「暗い」は「黒い」と置き換えることができない。その理由は、「黒い」が隠喩として使われる場合は何かの背後に関わっている人間が極悪だという意味を持ち、(2a)と(2b)の「日々」や「見通し」は、それ自体が極悪ではないからである。━📖 Note(2)

反意語

1. 日英語の反意表現はそれぞれ、「明るい」と *bright* である。━📖 ANT(1)
2. 日本語では「何かをよく知っている」という意味で「明るい」が使われるが、英語では言えない。
(2) 彼はこの地域に明るいので、いいレストランを知っている。
He is familiar with the area, so he knows good restaurants.

D

暗雲が漂う /phr. 隠喩
あんうん　　　ただよ　　　　　　　　　　いんゆ

何か悪いことが起こりそうだ
なに　わる　　　　　　　　お

例文

(a) 株価の暴落で、新事業の前途に暗雲が漂い始めた。
かぶか　ぼうらく　　しんじぎょう　ぜんと　　あんうん　ただよ　はじ

(b) その国の将来には暗雲が漂っている。経済学者は、世界的不況のためにその経
くに　しょうらい　　あんうん　ただよ　　　けいざいがくしゃ　　せかいてきふきょう　　　けい
済の発展速度は半減するだろうと警告している。
ざい　はってんそくど　はんげん　　　　　　　けいこく

(c) この国はしっかりと財政上の責任を取ってはいるが、それでも、その行く末には
くに　　　　　　　　ざいせいじょう　せきにん　と　　　　　　　　　　　　　　　ゆ　すえ
暗雲が漂っている。
あんうん　ただよ

解説

1. 英語は(a)では名詞句であるが、(c)のように *are*、(b)のように *loom*(見える)、*gather*(集まる)、*form*(でき上がる)などといった動詞が使われる。
2. 日本語の動詞は「漂う」(to drift, to float)であるが、やや不吉さを強める「垂れ込める」(to hang over)、「立ち込める」(to hang over)という動詞を使うこともできる。英語と違って、日本語は「地平線に」とは一緒に用いられない。むしろ、(a)「～の前途に」、(b)「～の将来に」、(c)「～の行く末に」などと共に使う。

(～の)夜明け /n. phr. 隠喩
よ　あ　　　　　　　　　　　　いんゆ

歴史的にきわだって新しいことの始まり
れきしてき　　　　　　　　　　あたら　　　　　　はじ

例文

(a) 近代オリンピックの夜明けは、クーベルタン男爵によってもたらされた。
きんだい　　　　　　　　　よあ　　　　　　　　　　　　だんしゃく

181

(b) The publication of Einstein's paper at that time was epoch-making in the field of theoretical physics and brought with it the dawn of atomic energy.

(c) Impressionism, which began in the latter half of the 19th century, signaled the dawn of modern art.

Note

> *Yo-ake* is a compound originating from *yo ga akeru* (lit. "the night opens").

---

homograph

day after the fair, a / n. phr. / metaphor

to do s.t. even though it's too late
遅すぎるけれど、してみる

Example

Last Saturday was an outdoor party for the children of the town. We thought it was a day after the fair, but it was all the same to the little ones.
土曜日は町の子供たちの屋外パーティーだった。遅すぎたのではないかと思ったが、子供たちにとってはそんなことはかまわなかった。

---

day of reckoning, the / n. phr. / metaphor

the time when one must deal with the results of one's {efforts/transgressions}

Examples

(a) As the competition approached, we rehearsed more and more frequently. When the day of reckoning came, we headed to the concert hall and prepared for the finals.

(b) We have spent five years working on this project. Tomorrow is the day of reckoning—we have to report to the company executives.

(c) That election was the day of reckoning for postwar politics. It was a general election that would serve as a public referendum on the direction of Japanese politics.

Note

> Both the English and Japanese reference a "final calculation" of sorts, but the English can refer to facing the results of either one's efforts (as shown in the examples) or one's transgressions (as shown below in [1]). The Japanese, on the other hand, can only refer to facing the results of one's efforts. The Japanese expressions that correspond to the idea of "dealing with the results of one's transgressions" are *nengu o osameru* (lit. "to pay the land tax") and, more colloquially, *tsuke o harau* (lit. "to pay a bill").

(1) At last his day of reckoning arrived, and he was forced to pay for his arrogance and disloyalty.
彼は傲慢で義理を欠いていたために、ついに{年貢を納める/つけを払う/×総決算の}時が来た。

(b) 当時発表されたアインシュタインの論文は、理論物理学の分野では画期的なもの
で、原子力に夜明けをもたらしたと言える。

(c) 19世紀後半から展開された印象派の近代絵画改革運動は、まさに近代芸術の夜
明けを告げるものだった。

解説

日本語の「夜明け」は「夜が明ける」、つまり「夜が明るくなってくる」から来た複合語である。

同形異義語

後の祭り / n. phr. / 隠喩

後悔しても遅い
it's too late to feel regret

例文

今さら泣いたって、後の祭りさ。あのとき、もっと一生懸命、勉強しておけばよかっ
たんだ。
There's no use crying now. You should have studied hard when you had the
chance.

総決算の時 / n. phr. / 隠喩

何か継続してきた努力を最後に締めくくる時

例文

(a) コンクールが近づくにつれリハーサルの頻度は増えました。ついに総決算の時が来
て、私達は最終選考のためにコンサートホールに向かいました。

(b) 私達は5年間このプロジェクトに費やし、明日はいよいよ総決算の時です。会社
の重役に報告をしなければなりません。

(c) その時の選挙は、戦後政治の総決算の時だった。日本の政治の将来について、民
意を問う選挙だった。

解説

日英語とも最後の計算という概念が入っているが、比喩的意味の記述と例文に示されている
ように、英語は"誰かの過去から継続してきた努力の総決算"という意味と"過去から継続し
てきた悪い{行動/行為}のつけを払う"という二つの比喩的意味がある。しかし、日本語の
比喩的意味は"誰かの過去から継続してきた努力の総決算"という意味しかない。英語の二
番目の意味に対応する日本語は「年貢を納める」か、口語的な表現の「つけを払う」である。

📖 Note(1)

deep / adj. / metaphor

reaching the bottom or innermost part of s.t.; strong or intense {color/meaning/silence/reason/connection/knowledge/impression/understanding/emotion/sleep}

(ANT) (LOOK) shallow

Examples

(a) Japanese *kimono* go through a complex dying process, resulting in colors that are deep and rich in tone.

(b) Japanese *tanka* and *haiku* are made up of very few words, but they are often deep in meaning.

(c) When he began to speak, a deep silence fell over the participants.

(d) She wrote in one of her books that she feels a deep personal bond with Japanese culture.

(e) That researcher has deep knowledge about science in general, even topics beyond his specialty.

(f) There were some deep reasons behind why I left the company.

(g) The movie that won the Academy Award for Best Picture this year left a deep impression on me.

(h) I hope that more and more foreigners come to have a deep understanding of Japanese culture.

(i) She fell into a deep depression when the pet she had kept for years died.

(j) If you want to taste a rich, deep-flavored bouillabaisse, why don't you go to that restaurant?

(k) When Juliet awoke from her deep sleep, Romeo had already killed himself.

Note

> The spatial, non-metaphorical meaning of *deep* and *fukai* is "extending far downward from the surface or far toward the back from the front."

deep-rooted / comp. adj. / metaphor

deeply embedded

(REL) deep-seated

Examples

(a) The cause of their religious differences is deep-rooted and cannot be easily resolved.

(b) It is important to understand the characteristics of deep-rooted conflicts in divided societies.

(c) A new report claiming that deep-rooted animal cruelty exists in British society alarmed animal lovers across the country.

Notes

1. *Ne-bukai* is a compound that comes from *ne ga fukai* (lit. "the roots are deep"), though *ne ga fukai* itself is also used quite often. In this case, *ne* can be replaced by *nekko* in spoken Japanese. 📖→ 解説(1)

深い / adj. (i) / 隠喩

何かが{底 / 奥}に達するほどである，{色 / 意味 / 沈黙 / 理由 / 関係 / 知識 / 印象 / 理解 / 感情 / 眠り}などの{度合い / 程度}が{大きい / 強い}

反 **LOOK** 浅い

例文

(a) 日本の着物は染めの工程が複雑なだけに、深い色合いがあって、味わい深い。

(b) 日本の短歌や俳句は、言葉数は少ないが、深い意味が込められている。

(c) 彼が話し始めると、参加者の間に深い沈黙が生まれた。

(d) 彼女は著書で、日本文化に深い個人的な縁を感じると述べている。

(e) その研究者は科学のことなら専門分野以外にも深い知識を持っている。

(f) 私があの会社をやめたのには、実は深い訳があるんです。

(g) 今年アカデミー賞をとった映画は深く印象に残る作品だ。

(h) 日本の文化に深い理解を示す外国人が増えることを願っています。

(i) 長年飼っていたペットが死んで、彼女は深い悲しみに沈んでいる。

(j) もし、豊かで味わい深いフランス風魚貝スープを試したかったら、そのレストランに行ってみたら？

(k) ジュリエットが深い眠りから目覚めたとき、ロミオはすでに自害して果てていた。

解説

「深い」と *deep* の基本義は "表面から下のほうに伸びること、あるいは、前から奥のほうに伸びること" である。

根深い / comp. adj. (i) / 隠喩

何かよくない事の原因が長い間取り除きにくい状況下にある

例文

(a) 彼らの宗教的対立の原因は根深く、簡単に解決できるものではない。

(b) 分裂した社会における根深い紛争の性格を理解することは大切だ。

(c) 新しい報告で、英国社会にも根深い動物虐待があることを指摘されたために、英国の動物愛護者は驚いている。

解説

1. 日本語の「根深い」は「根が深い」から来ている複合語だが、「根が深い」もそのままよく使う。その場合、会話では「根」は「根っこ」としてもよい。

(1) 彼らの宗教的対立の原因は{根深く / 根が深く / 根っこが深く}、簡単に解決できるものではない。（→(a)）

2. Whereas *ne-bukai* is only used to describe something negative, *deep-rooted* has no such restriction, as shown in the example below.

(2) To understand the deep-rooted relationship between man and cow, we must review its history.

人間と牛の〈深い/[×]根深い〉関係を理解するためにはその歴史を振り返らなければならない。

REL

The REL *deep-seated* can replace *deep-rooted* in most cases, though *deep-seated* is more frequently used with nouns such as *emotion*, *conviction*, and *prejudice*, whereas *deep-rooted* tends to be used with nouns such as *cause* and *tradition*.

(1) In that region, deep-seated racial prejudice is one of the causes of conflict.

その地方では、人種間の偏見が根深く、それが争いの原因の一つとなっている。

{desk/chair/bed/table}('s) legs / comp. n. / personification

a supporting part that resembles a leg in form or function

Example

I secured the table legs in preparation for earthquakes.

diamond in the rough, a / n. phr. / metaphor

s.o. who possesses exceptional potential but lacks refinement

REL a rough diamond

Examples

(a) When the coach observed the new player, he said that the player was definitely a diamond in the rough.

(b) The future of our company depends on our ability to recruit good talent. I wonder how we should go about finding those diamonds in the rough?

(c) Despite being only five years old, she managed to beat an adult at a chess tournament. She may be a diamond in the rough.

Note

A diamond in the rough means "unpolished diamond," and *genseki* means "raw stone."

REL

The English REL, *a rough diamond*, is identical in meaning to *a diamond in the rough*, but used much less often.

die in one's bed / phr. / synecdoche

to die a natural death at home

Examples

Mr. S: When I die, I want to die peacefully in my bed, not in some accident or natural disaster.

Mrs. S: Definitely. No one wants to die while traveling.

2．日本語の「根深い」はよくないことに関してのみ使われるのに対して、英語の *deep-rooted* は中立的なことにも使える。➡️📖 **Note（2）**

関連語

英語には *deep-seated* という関連表現があり、ほとんどすべての場合 *deep-rooted* と置き換えられる。しかし、*deep-seated* は *emotion*（感情）、*conviction*（確信）、*prejudice*（偏見）などの名詞と使われることが多く、*deep-rooted* のほうは *cause*（原因）、*tradition*（伝統）などの名詞と使われることが多い。➡️📖 **REL（1）**

D

{机 / 椅子 / ベッド / テーブル}の脚　　n. phr.　擬人化

机や椅子を支える部分

例 文

地震に備えて、テーブルの脚をしっかり固定した。

ダイヤの原石　　n. phr.　隠喩

まだ磨きがかかっていないけれど才能を秘めている人

例 文

（a）入団したばかりの選手を見たコーチは、その選手はダイヤの原石に違いないと言った。

（b）我が社の将来は新人採用の手腕に掛かっている。ダイヤの原石のような逸材を見つけるにはどうしたらいいのだろうか。

（c）彼女はまだ５歳なのにチェスの対戦で大人を打ち負かした。ダイヤの原石かもしれない。

解 説

「原石」と *a diamond in the rough* の基本義は、それぞれ、"もとのままの石"、"磨かれていないダイヤモンド"である。

関連語

英語の関連表現の *a rough diamond* は *a diamond in the rough* と同義語だが、使用頻度がはるかに低い。

畳の上で死ぬ　　phr.　提喩

家（自宅）で穏やかに死ぬ

例 文

鈴木（夫）：死ぬときは、事故や災害なんかじゃなくて、畳の上で静かに死にたいね。

鈴木（妻）：ほんとうに。旅行中に死ぬんてのも、嫌ですね。

(a) He died in his bed, not on the field of battle.

(b) After a long career as a politician, he died in his bed surrounded by his family in 1978.

Notes

1. The English and Japanese mention different locations, but both are in the home. Both the English and Japanese versions mean that someone dies not in an unexpected accident, but rather peacefully at home. The place of death is *bed* in English and *tatami mat* in Japanese.

2. The superordinate concept of *home* is expressed by the nouns *bed* and *tatami*, so this is an example of synecdoche.

The die is cast.　phr.　metaphor

s.t. that has been started cannot be stopped

REL　cross the Rubicon

Examples

(a) It's too late to change our minds about the war we started. The die is cast.

(b) Now that the die has been cast, there is no going back.

(c) The die is now cast; I have crossed the Rubicon. Sink or swim, live or die, survive or perish with my country—such is my unalterable determination.

Note

The proverb comes from the quote "alea jacta est," which was said by Julius Caesar in 49 BCE when, after some hesitation, he crossed the Rubicon to march against Pompey in defiance of the senate's orders. It is said that Caesar was quoting the Greek playwright Menander when he said this.

REL

As explained above, Caesar supposedly quoted Menander when he crossed the Rubicon river, so *cross the Rubicon* can be be used in the same sense as *the die is cast*. However, the corresponding Japanese expression, *rubikon-gawa o wataru*, cannot be used as a proverb.

die like a dog　phr.　simile

to die in a degrading manner; to die for no reason

Examples

(a) If only we had more ammunition, he wouldn't have died like a dog!

(b) Charlie Brown scoffed at Snoopy. "I don't want to die like a dog!"

(c) I'm not sending my son off to war just so he can die like a dog.

(a) 彼は戦場では死なず、畳の上で死んだ。

(b) 彼は政治家としての長いキャリアのあと、1978年に家族に囲まれ畳の上で静かに死んだ。

解説

1. 日英語で、自然死をする場所が「畳」と *bed* で違うが、家で死ぬという点では同じである。日英語ともに、事故などで予期せずに死ぬのではなく、自宅で穏やかに死ぬことを意味している。英語はベッド、日本語は畳で死の場所を示している。

2. 「畳」/*bed* で上位概念の「家」/*home* を表しているので提喩である。

D

賽は投げられた　phr.　隠喩

何か大事なことが始められたので最後までやり通すよりほかにない

例文

(a) 我々が始めた戦争について考えを変えるのには遅すぎる。賽は投げられたのだ。

(b) 賽が投げられた以上、もう引き返すわけにはいかない。

(c) 今や賽は投げられた。もうルビコン川を渡ってしまったのだ。泳ぐにしろ沈むにしろ、生きるにせよ死ぬにせよ、我が祖国と生き残るにせよ滅び去るにせよ、私はその決意を変えることはできない。

解説

このことわざは、ジュリアス・シーザー（＝カエサル）が少し躊躇したあと、元老院の命令を無視してポンペイウスに兵を向けるためにルビコン川を渡った紀元前49年に言った言葉、*Ālea jacta est* から来ている。もともとはシーザーがギリシャの戯曲家メナンドロスの劇の台詞を引いたものだと言われている。

関連語

解説に記述してあるようにカエサルはルビコン川を渡るときにメナンドロスの言葉を引用したので、英語では *cross the Rubicon*（ルビコン川を渡る）も *the die is cast* と同じ意味のことわざとして使われるが、日本語では「ルビコン川を渡る」はことわざとしては使えない。

犬死する　comp. v.　隠喩

{無駄な/屈辱的な}死に方をする

例文

(a) 弾薬が十分に補給されていたら、彼は犬死しなかっただろうに。

(b) チャーリー・ブラウンはスヌーピーに「犬死はしたくないなあ」と失礼なことを言いました。

(c) 私は息子を犬死させるために戦場に送るつもりはない。

dig one's own grave / phr. / metaphor

to do s.t. that will lead to one's own death or downfall

REL LOOK▶ cut one's own throat

Examples

(a) If you get pulled over for a traffic violation, you shouldn't resist. You'll dig your own grave by making up poor excuses.

(b) Okamoto was so overconfident that he ended up digging his own grave.

(c) You shouldn't speak badly about your boss no matter what. You'll just end up digging your own grave.

REL

The Japanese REL, *(jibun de) jibun no kubi o shimeru* (lit. "strangle one's own neck"), is very similar to *boketsu o horu.* 📖▶関連語(1)

direction / n. / metaphor

the course upon which s.t. is progressing

Examples

Kenta: So Karen, you really look up to your grandmother, huh?

Karen: I do. Whenever I'm lost, she always gives me direction. As long as I listen to her, I'm sure I'll never stray from the right path.

- -

(a) Japanese politicians must think about taking politics in a new direction.

(b) This war is getting out of hand. It's starting to head in a dangerous direction.

(c) He lost his direction in life and became a criminal.

dirty one's hands / phr. / metaphor

to do s.t. shameful

REL soil one's hands; get one's hands dirty

Examples

(a) The Mafia boss didn't dirty his own hands; he left the killing to his underlings.

(b) That professor dirtied his own hands and tampered with medical data in order to make a profit off the medicine.

(c) They were getting what they wanted without dirtying their own hands.

Note

In Japanese, both *yogosu* and *kegasu* mean "to dirty s.t." and are written with the same kanji (汚す). However, the latter is used metaphorically, as in *na o kegasu* (lit. "dirty one's {name/reputation}"), *shokumu o kegasu* (betray one's duty), and so on.

190

墓穴を掘る（ぼけつをほる） /phr. 隠喩（いんゆ）

自分で自分を破滅させるような原因を作る（じぶんでじぶんをはめつさせるようなげんいんをつくる）

関 **LOOK▶**（自分で）自分の首をしめる（じぶんで じぶんのくびをしめる）

例文

(a) 交通違反でつかまったときは、あまり逆らわないほうがいい。へたに言い訳をするとかえって墓穴を掘ることになる。（こうつういはん／さか／いわけ／ぼけつ／ほ）

(b) 岡本は自信満々のせいで何でも手を出し、自ら墓穴を掘ることになった。（おかもと／じしんまんまん／なん／て／だ／みずか／ぼけつ／は）

(c) どんなに嫌な上司でも、悪口は言わない方がいいよ。墓穴を掘ることになるから。（いや／じょうし／わるぐち／い／ほう／ぼけつ／ほ）

関連語

日本語の関連表現「（自分で）自分の首をしめる」は「墓穴を掘る」とほぼ同義である。

(1) 環境を破壊し続けることは、人間が{墓穴を掘る／自分で自分の首をしめる}のと同じだ。
By continuing to destroy the environment, humanity is basically sealing its own fate.

方向（ほうこう） /n. 隠喩（いんゆ）

何か抽象的なものが向かっているところ（なに／ちゅうしょうてき／む）

例文

健太（けんた）：カレンって、おばあさんのことをとても尊敬しているんだって？（そんけい）

カレン：そうよ。迷ったときには、いつも人生の方向を示してくれるの。祖母の言うことを参考にしていれば、あまり間違った方向に行くことはないわね。（まよ／じんせい／ほうこう／しめ／そば／い／さんこう／まちが／ほうこう／い）

(a) 日本の政治家は新しい政治の方向を考えなければならない。（にほん／せいじか／あたら／せいじ／ほうこう／かんが）

(b) この戦争はなかなか収拾がつかず、ますます危険な方向に向かっている。（せんそう／しゅうしゅう／きけん／ほうこう／む）

(c) 彼は人生の方向を見失って、犯罪者になってしまった。（かれ／じんせい／ほうこう／みうしな／はんざいしゃ）

手を汚す（てをよごす） /phr. 隠喩（いんゆ）

自ら恥ずべき事をする（みずか／は／こと）

例文

(a) そのマフィアのボスは自分では手を汚さないで、手下に人殺しを命じた。（じぶん／て／よご／てした／ひとごろ／めい）

(b) その教授は薬の利益を得るために、自ら手を汚して医学データを改ざんした。（きょうじゅ／くすり／りえき／え／みずか／て／よご／いがく／かい）

(c) 彼らは自分の手を汚さないで欲しいものを手に入れていた。（かれ／じぶん／て／よご／ほ／て／い）

解説

日本語には「よごす」と並んで「けがす」という動詞もある。二つとも表記は「汚す」であるが、「手をけがす」とはふつう言わない。「けがす」は「名を汚す」や「職務を汚す」のように何かを比喩的に汚すという意味しかない。

191

REL

The English RELs *soil one's hands* and *get one's hands dirty* can replace *dirty one's hands*. Because *soil* literally means "to stain (with dirt)," *soil one's hands* sounds more descriptive than *get one's hands dirty*.

(1) That professor {{dirtied/soiled} his hands/got his hands dirty} and tampered with medical data in order to make a profit off the medicine. (→(b))

distance oneself from ~ / phr. metaphor

to stay away from {s.o./s.t.}; to avoid becoming emotionally involved with s.o.

REL keep s.o. at arm's length; put some distance between oneself and ~

Examples

(a) The composer Handel distanced himself somewhat from the monarch.

(b) Following her friend Kaori's advice, Tomoe began to distance herself from Takuya, whom she'd been dating for a long time.

(c) The prime ministers distanced themselves from environmental activist groups such as Greenpeace.

Notes

1. The English and Japanese are very similar, because *distance* means both physical and psychological distance in both languages. The only difference is that they use slightly different verbs, i.e., *keep* and *oku* (to put).

2. The English can only be used with the preposition *from*, but the Japanese can be used with three different particles. *Kara*, which indicates distance, is the most frequently used, followed by *to*, which indicates a relationship, and *ni*, which indicates contact.

📖—解説(1)

3. The noun that precedes the particle (in the case of the Japanese) or follows the preposition (in the case of the English) can be either animate, as in (a) and (b), or inanimate, as in (c).

REL

1. *Keep s.o. at arm's length* is another way of saying *distance oneself from* ~ in English. The corresponding Japanese expression is ~ *ni chikazukanai* (to not come close to ~).

(1) She seems like a nice, friendly person. But it's wise to {distance yourself from her/keep her at arm's length}.
彼女は親切でやさしい人のようですが、彼女{と距離を置いた / に近付かない}方がかしこいですよ。

2. The RELs *put some distance between oneself and* ~ and *keep s.o. at arm's length* indicate a more active effort to avoid involvement with someone or something.

(2) I think you should {put some distance between yourself and him/keep him at arm's length} and consider whether breaking up is really what you want to do.
彼からはちょっと距離を置いて、本当に彼と別れたいのか考えたほうがいいと思うよ。

関連語

英語の見出し *dirty one's hands* は、関連表現の *soil one's hands* と *get one's hands dirty* に置き換えることができる。*soil one's hands* は字義通りには「土で汚す」という表現のため、*get one's hands dirty* より描写的である。━📖 REL (1)

～ {から / と / に} 距離を置く   phr.   隠喩

他の人との関係で心理的に引き込まれるのを避ける

関 ～に近付かない，距離を取る

例 文

(a) 作曲家ヘンデルは、君主からは適当に距離を置いていた。

(b) 友恵は友人の香織のアドバイスで、長く付き合っていた卓也から距離を置き始めた。

(c) 各国の首相は、グリーンピースのような環境問題活動家のグループとは距離を置いた。

解 説

1. 「距離」も *distance* も物理的な距離だけでなく心理的な距離も表すので、この日英語表現は大変近い。ただ一つのわずかな違いは動詞「置く」と *keep* (保つ) の違いである。

2. 英語の前置詞は *from* だけであるが、日本語の前に来る三つの助詞は距離を表す助詞の「から」の使用頻度が高く、関係を表す「と」が次で、接触を表す「に」の使用頻度が一番低い。

(1) 作曲家ヘンデルは君主 {から / と / に} は距離を置いていた。(→ (a))

3. 日本語では助詞の前に来る名詞、英語では前置詞の後にくる名詞は、(a) (b) のように生物か、(c) のように無生物でもかまわない。

関連語

1. 英語には *keep s.o. at arm's length* という関連表現があるが、これに意味的に対応する日本語の表現は「～に近付かない」である。この関連表現は見出しと置き換えることができる。

━📖 REL (1)

2. 英語には *put some distance between oneself and ～*、*keep s.o. at arm's length* という関連表現もあり、"誰かが他の人との関係で心理的に引き込まれないように、積極的に努める" という意味を持っている。━📖 REL (2)

distant   adj.   metaphor

to be far away temporally, psychologically, or genealogically

REL   far; remote

ANT   **LOOK▶** close to ~; **LOOK▶** near

(Examples)

Karen: Who is this person sitting next to you in the picture?

Saya: She's my distant cousin.

Karen: Oh, but she really looks like you. I thought she was your older sister.

Saya: Yeah, lots of people say that. I guess distant relatives can look alike.

(a) The galaxies are now seen as they were in the distant past.

(b) After that incident, my relationship with him became distant.

(c) The country town I grew up in has turned into a bustling city. I used to run around chasing frogs and dragonflies, but that's all a distant memory now.

(Note)

Just like other space-related expressions, both *distant* and *tōi* can be used to describe time, as in (a). They can also describe remote human relationships, as in the dialogue and (b), and psychological distance, as in (c).

R E L

1. The Japanese REL, *soen'na*, can only be used in the figurative sense of "a distant human relationship." The ANT is *shin'mitsuna* (adj. [na]).
2. The English RELs are *far* and *remote*. Like *distant*, both can be used to describe something that is far away temporally, psychologically, or genealogically.

(1) We will probably establish bases on several planets in the {distant/far/remote} future.
私達は 遠い未来には幾つかの惑星に宇宙基地を建設することになるだろう。

---

do a 180(-degree turn) （180度転換する） → **{take/do} a 180(-degree turn)**

---

dog eat dog/dog-eat-dog   phr./comp. adj.   metaphor

characterized by ruthless, selfish competition

(Examples)

(a) The large number of department stores around this terminal station makes for a pretty dog-eat-dog situation.

(b) It's dog eat dog for the conservative candidates in this election.

(c) The entertainment industry is a harsh, unwelcoming, dog-eat-dog world.

(Note)

Both the English and Japanese conjure the image of a bunch of animals of the same type (dogs in the English) fighting and eating one another to survive.

遠い / adj. (i) / 隠喩

{時間的 / 心理的}にかけ離れている，血縁関係が離れている

関 疎遠な

反 LOOK {〜に / と} 近い

例文

カレン： このさやの隣に写っている人、誰？

さや： 遠いいとこ。

カレン： そう、でも顔、よく似てるね。お姉さんかと思った。

さや： うん、よく言われる。遠い親戚でも似ることあるんだね。

(a) 今見えている銀河は遠い過去のものだ。

(b) あの出来事以来、私と彼の関係は遠くなってしまった。

(c) 子供の頃遊んだ田舎も、今はにぎやかな町になってしまった。カエルやトンボを追いかけて遊んだなんて、もう遠い思い出だ。

解説

他の空間表現と同じように、「遠い」*distant* は(a)のように時間にも使えるし、会話例と(b)のように疎遠な人間関係にも、(c)のように心理的な距離にも使える。

関連語

1. 日本語の「疎遠な」は「親密な」の反意表現であり、"人間関係が遠い"という意味でしか使えない。

2. 英語の関連表現には *far* と *remote* がある。どちらも何かが一時的、心理的に距離がある、あるいは、血縁関係が離れている時に使われる。 — REL(1)

共食い(の〜) / n. phr. / 隠喩

同業者や同種の者が互いに利益を奪い合う

例文

(a) このターミナル駅周辺にはデパートがたくさんあって、共食い状態になっている。

(b) 今回の選挙は保守派候補者同士の共食いになった。

(c) 娯楽産業は苛酷かつ冷酷な世界で、そこは共食いの状況だ。

解説

日英語とも同類の動物(英語では「犬」と特定している)が激しく争って、互いを食べ合うことによって生き残るというイメージである。

dog paddle / comp. n. / metaphor

a type of swimming stroke that mimics the way dogs swim

Example

I'm a really bad swimmer. I can only swim about 20 meters using the dog paddle.

domino effect, {a/the} / comp. n. / metaphor

a process in which one negative {event/action} causes a sequence of other {events/actions}

REL the domino theory

Examples

(a) The domino effect of democratic movements in the Near and Middle East influenced the countries of Asia and Africa as well.

(b) The company's bankruptcy and falling stock prices created a domino effect that caused the stocks of almost all listed companies to slump.

(c) The initial layoff caused a domino effect that resulted in as many as 22 additional people losing their jobs.

Notes

1. The Japanese is a translation of the English.
2. The expression *domino effect* comes from the pastime of lining dominos up and toppling them.
(1) A single delay affected the entire schedule, like dominos toppling one after another.
一日遅れたことがドミノ倒しのようになって、ほかのすべての日程を変えることになった。
3. In Japan, there is a similar pastime called *shōgi-daoshi* (Japanese chess piece toppling), but this expression is used figuratively to describe people falling down in a chain reaction.

📖→解説(2)

REL

The domino theory refers to the American policy of containing the spread of Communism during the Cold War era of the 1950s. The policy was based on the assumption that if one country were to become communist, neighboring countries would follow suit.

A doomed mouse will bite a cat if he has no choice. phr. metaphor

The weak will defend themselves when left with no choice

Example

I wouldn't push him too far. You don't know what he might do. You can't be too careful. They say even a doomed mouse will bite a cat if he has no choice.

犬かき　／ comp. n.　隠喩

犬が泳ぐような泳ぎ方の一種

例文

私は泳ぎが下手だ。犬かきで20メートルぐらいしか泳げない。

ドミノ現象　／ comp. n.　隠喩

一つの悪い{出来事 / 行動}が連続して他の悪い{出来事 / 行動}を引き起こすこと

関 ドミノ理論

例文

(a) 中近東での民主化運動のドミノ現象は、アジアやアフリカ諸国にも影響を与えた。

(b) その会社の倒産と株価下落がドミノ現象を起こし、上場企業のほとんどの株が暴落した。

(c) 最初の解雇がドミノ現象を起こし、さらに22人もの多くの人が仕事を失った。

解説

1. 日本語は英語の翻訳である。

2. 「ドミノ現象」は「ドミノ倒し」というゲームから来ている。📖Note(1)

3. 日本にも「将棋倒し」というゲームから来た表現があるが、これは群衆が連鎖的に倒れるときに比喩として使われる。

(2) エスカレータの最上段で人が倒れ、下にいる人達が次々と将棋倒しになった。
 A person fell down at the top of the escalator, and the people below him fell down like *shogi* pieces toppling.

関連語

「ドミノ理論」は、元は、一国の共産主義化が起きれば隣国も次々に共産化が起こるという前提で、アメリカが1950年代の冷戦時代にとった共産主義封じ込め政策のことである。

窮鼠猫を噛む　／ phr.　隠喩

窮地に追い詰められれば、弱い者も強い者に反撃することがある

例文

あいつは追いつめられたら何するかわからないぞ。気をつけるに越したことはない。「窮鼠猫を噛む」ってこともあるからな。

double-edged sword / comp. n. / metaphor

possessing both positive and negative aspects

Examples

Mike: Things like atomic energy research and genetic engineering are double-edged swords.

Saya: Yeah. One small mistake can turn a useful tool into a disaster.

(a) Every medication is a double-edged sword with both good and bad effects.

(b) Advances in medicine are a double-edged sword. The sophistication of modern surgical techniques has allowed us to do things that a few short years ago we merely dreamed of. However, with this increasing power to alter human lives come certain ethical and philosophical questions.

Note

The first recorded literal use of the Japanese appears in the *Man'yōshū*, an anthology of traditional poetry written in the 8th century. The first recorded metaphorical use is in *jōruri*, a form of puppet theater that originated in the Edo period (1603-1867).

REL

The Japanese expression *ryōba no {ken/tsurugi}* has the same meaning as *moroha no {ken/tsurugi}*. 📖→ 関連語 **(1)**

---

homograph

double-minded / comp. adj. / metaphor

to be undecided
決めかねている

Example

The government is double-minded about how to deal with the threat of terrorism.
政府はこのテロリズムをどう扱っていいか決めかねている。

---

dove / n. / metaphor

s.o. who supports diplomacy and peaceful solutions as opposed to military action

ANT hawk

Examples

(a) He was a dove who had to work and survive among the hawks in the administration.

(b) That politician used to be a hawk when he was young, but towards the end of his life he apparently became a dove.

諸刃の剣 / n. phr. / 隠喩

何事にもプラス面とマイナス面があり、どう扱うかに注意が要る

【関】両刃の剣

例文

マイク：原子力の研究とか、遺伝子操作の研究って、諸刃の剣だよね。

さや：そうね。一歩間違うと、人類に役に立つことが、大変な害を及ぼすことにもなるもんね。

- (a) どんな薬も諸刃の剣だ。いい面と悪い面がある。
- (b) 医学の進歩は諸刃の剣である。現代の外科技術が洗練されてきて数年前には想像もできなかったことができるようになっている。しかしながら、人間の生活を変える力が増すにつれて倫理的、哲学的な問題が生じてくる。

解説

日本語で字義通りに使用されたのは、8世紀の『万葉集』で、その比喩的用法は江戸時代(1603-1867)の浄瑠璃（文楽）に出てくる。

関連語

日本語には「両刃の剣」という同じ意味の表現がある。

(1) どんな薬も{諸刃 / 両刃}の剣だ。いい面と悪い面がある。(→(a))

D

同形異義語

二心 / comp. n. / 隠喩

裏切りの心
disloyal

例文

その侍は飢えと貧しさに堪えかねて、主君に対して二心を抱くようになった。
The samurai couldn't stand his hunger and poverty and began to harbor treacherous thoughts against his lord.

ハト派 / comp. n. / 隠喩

強硬手段を取らず、穏健に事を収めようという立場を取る{人々 / 人}

【反】タカ派

例文

- (a) 彼はハト派でありながら、現政権のタカ派の中で仕事をして、生き残らなければならなかった。
- (b) その政治家は若い頃はタカ派でならしたそうだが、晩年はハト派に変わったらしい。

199

(c) It is difficult for a diplomat to realize diplomatic solutions without being at least somewhat of a dove.

Note

The dove, a symbol of peace, is used figuratively to represent a certain political tendency. Doves are speculated to have been used as a symbol of peace since before biblical times, because they keep the same mate year after year and often gathered in flocks at holy temples. The first mention of a dove in the Bible is in the Old Testament (Genesis 8: 8-11), when Noah sends out a dove twice to see if the floodwaters have receded. When it returns the second time, it is carrying an olive branch in its beak, and Noah knows then that the waters have receded.

ANT

The English and Japanese ANTs are *hawk* and *taka-ha*, respectively. Both utilize the powerful image of the hawk as a bird of prey to describe someone who prefers using military force to achieve their goals. ($\rightarrow$(a) (b))

drag into / phr. / metaphor

to involve s.o. in a situation against {his/her} will

Examples

Kenta: Saya, do you want to go see a soccer game with me next Friday afternoon?

Saya: Next Friday? What about our econ seminar?

Kenta: We'd skip it, of course.

Saya: No way! I don't know about you, but I'm a serious student, you know. Don't drag me into your scheme!

- - - - - - - - - - - - - - - - - - - -

(a) Hey, that's between you and your girlfriend. Don't drag me into it.

(b) People are worried about their country unwittingly being dragged into the war.

Note

The *komu* in *hikizuri-komu* is a suffix used in compound verbs to emphasize the main verb. Other examples include *hairi-komu* (lit. "to enter deeply into s.t.") and *kangae-komu* (to go deeply into thought).

draw {a/the} line (between ~ and ~) / phr. / metaphor

to establish a boundary

Examples

Kenta: Mom, can you lend me some money? I'm going on a trip.

Mrs. S: Absolutely not. Your father and I are drawing a line between school expenses and money for recreation.

- - - - - - - - - - - - - - - - - - - -

(a) After being betrayed by someone I trusted, I was forced to draw a line in our interactions.

（c）外交官はある程度ハト派でないと、外交交渉をまとめることが難しくなる。

解説

鳩が持つ平和のイメージを政治的傾向を比喩として表すために用いた。平和のシンボルとしての鳩は、聖書時代よりも以前からあったとされている。それは鳩の雌雄が相手を何年も替えないことと、初期の聖なる寺院に群れをなして住みついていたことからきているらしい。聖書では旧約聖書（創世記8:8-11）にはじめて出てくる。そこでは、ノアが洪水の水が引いたかどうかを確かめるために鳩を2度送り出して2度目には「くちばしには、オリーブの若葉があった」ので、ノアは洪水が引いたことを知ったとなっている。

反意語

日英語の反意表現は、それぞれ「タカ派」と *hawk* で、猛禽類であるタカが強い力をイメージさせ、自分の理念を貫くためには、武力をも辞さないという政治的傾向を持つ人々を指す。

（→（a）（b））

引きずり込む　/ comp. v.　隠喩

ある状況に巻き込む

例文

健太：さや、来週の金曜日の午後、サッカー、見に行かない？

さや：来週の金曜日って、経済学のゼミはどうするの？

健太：もちろん、サボりさ。

さや：いやよ。私はまじめに学生生活やってるんだから、悪の道に引きずり込まないでちょうだい。

（a）おい、それは君と彼女の間の問題だよ。僕を引きずり込まないでくれ。

（b）国民は、国が間違って今回の戦争に引きずり込まれることを心配している。

解説

日本語の「引きずり込む」の「込む」は複合動詞の接尾辞で、「入り込む」「考え込む」など、"動詞の意味することを深く行う"という意味である。

（一）線を引く　phr.　隠喩

区別をする，限界を設定する

関 一線を画す

例文

健太：お母さん、ちょっとお金貸してくれないかなあ。旅行に行くんだけど。

鈴木（妻）：だめよ。うちは学校の必要経費と、あなたの個人的な遊びのお金は、しっかりと線を引いてありますからね。

（a）信じていた人に裏切られて、彼とは一線を引いてつきあうようになった。

(b) Because the Internet is widely available, more people are using computers for personal use during business hours. I think we ought to draw a line between business and private use.

(c) It is probably just a matter of time before animal cloning becomes widespread to supplement the food supply, but from an ethical standpoint, we have to seriously discuss where to draw the line.

Note

Issen o hiku is used when the speaker/writer is convinced on a moral or ethical basis that people should distinguish between two things, as shown in (b). To distinguish between two things on an objective basis, *sen o hiku* is used, as shown in the other examples.

REL

Issen o kakusu has the same meaning as *issen o hiku*. 📖➡ 関連語(1)

draw s.o.'s attention / phr / metaphor

to get s.o. to notice the existence or characteristics of {s.o./s.t.}

REL   catch s.o.'s {eye/attention}

Examples

Karen: Kenta, what happened to your foot?

Kenta: I sprained it when I went skiing.

Karen: I bet you were trying to draw people's attention by showing off, right?

Kenta: Bingo! But I messed up.

Karen: Well, you still managed to draw people's attention.

- - - - - - - - - - - - - - - - - - - -

(a) Traffic signs often use red or yellow to draw people's attention.

(b) His plain appearance drew nobody's attention.

Note

Draw s.o.'s attention can also be used, as shown below in (1), but in Japanese, *hiku* (to draw) is replaced by *mukeru* (to direct) to express the same idea. 📖➡解説(1)

REL

The English REL, *catch s.o.'s {eye/attention}*, shares the same figurative meaning as *draw s.o.'s attention*, and they are interchageable.

(1) Traffic signs often use red or yellow to {draw people's attention/catch people's {eye/attention}}. (→(a))

draw s.o.'s interest / phr. / metaphor

to cause s.o. to become interested in s.t.

Examples

Saya: I wonder what aspects of American culture draw Japanese children's interest.

Karen: Well, it's probably movies and music. When I talk about them during my English class, my students get really interested.

- - - - - - - - - - - - - - - - - - - -

(b) インターネットが普及してから、仕事中に私的にコンピュータを使う人が増えているが、仕事と私的な使用には一線を引くべきだと思う。

(c) 食料確保のため、やがて動物のクローンが一般化されるであろうが、どこで線を引くかはしっかり議論されなければならない。

[解説]

日本語では、「一線を引く」は(b)のように{話し手/書き手}が道義上、倫理上、そうすべきだと強く感じているときに使い、二つのものの客観的な区別を問題にするときは、その他の例のように「線を引く」を使う傾向にある。

[関連語]

日本語には「一線を画す」という同じ意味の表現がある。

(1) 仕事と私的な使用には{一線を引く/一線を画す}べきだと思う。(→(b))

注意を引く phr. 隠喩

誰かの注目や関心を得る

[例文]

カレン：健太、その足、どうしたの？

健太：ああ、スキーで捻挫しちゃったんだ。

カレン：どうせ、みんなの注意を引こうと思って、何かやって見せたんでしょ。

健太：あたり！ でも、みごとに失敗。

カレン：それなら、ねらい通り十分注意を引いたわよ。

(a) 交通標識は人々の注意を引きやすいように、赤や黄色を使ってあることが多い。

(b) 彼の地味な風采は誰の注意も引かなかった。

[解説]

英語は、注意を促す場合にも *draw s.o.'s attention* という形で使われることが多いが、日本語では注意を促す場合には、「引く」を「向ける」に変える。

(1) 興味があると思われる情報に、注意を向けていただきたいと思います。
Let me draw your attention to some information that may be of interest to you.

[関連語]

英語の関連表現の *catch s.o.'s {eye/attention}* の意味は *draw s.o.'s attention* と同じで置き換えができる。━📖REL(1)

興味を引く phr. 隠喩

興味を起こさせる

[例文]

さや：日本の子供達って、アメリカのどんなところに興味を引かれるのかなあ。

カレン：う〜ん、やっぱり映画と音楽かしらね。英語を教えるときに、その話題を出すと、とっても興味を示すわ。

(a) Among things Japanese, anime draws the strongest interest from American college students.

(b) I don't know why, but Haruki Murakami's novels draw my interest.

(c) Maybe it's because I like following trends, but I've been taking pictures of beautiful things, interesting things—whatever draws my interest.

Note

Both *draw* and *hiku* (to pull) are basic action verbs that treat interest as an entity that can be "pulled into" something. In English, the subject is the entity actively drawing someone's interest, but in Japanese, the one showing interest can be the subject of a passive construction, as demonstrated in the dialogue and Example (b).

draw {s.o.'s/s.t.'s} teeth *phr.* **metaphor**

to weaken {s.o./s.t.} dangerous

REL pull teeth

Examples

(a) The best way to draw gangsters' teeth is cutting off their fraudulent financial sources.

(b) We need to cut off the terrorist organization's funding in order to draw its teeth.

Note

Interestingly, the English uses *teeth* while the Japanese uses *kiba* (fang), a word reserved for animals.

REL

The English REL, *pull teeth*, is a figurative expression meaning "to do something undesirable, such as pulling teeth, that requires a large amount of effort."

dream of ~ *phr.* **metaphor**

to desire to {do s.t./become s.t.} in the future

REL have a dream (of ~)

Examples

Saya: Kenta, what do you want to be in the future?

Kenta: Hmm... I dream of becoming an international lawyer.

Saya: Impressive. Think you can actually make that a reality?

Kenta: Hey, anyone can dream.

- - - - - - - - - - - - - - - - - - - -

(a) I dream of becoming a professional baseball player.

(b) I dream of creating a program for statistical analysis.

REL

The English REL, *have a dream (of~)*, is used less frequently than the main entry. The Japanese REL, *yume o motsu* and *(~ o) yume-miru*, is used as frequently as the main entry.

(a) 日本のものの中で、アメリカの大学生の興味を一番強く引くものはアニメだ。

(b) 私はどうしてかわからないけれど村上春樹の小説に興味を引かれた。

(c) もともとミーハーだからか、キレイなもの、面白いもの、興味を引かれたものは、何でも写真に撮っています。

解説

英語の動詞は draw で日本語の意味は「〜を引く」、日本語の動詞は「引く」で英語の意味は pull である。どちらも動作を表す動詞であり、人を興味の対象に引きつけるという比喩的表現である。英語では、興味を引くものが主語になるが、日本語では会話例と (b) のように興味を示す人が受け身文の主語になることがある。

牙を抜く / phr. 隠喩

危険な {誰か / 何か} を弱体化させる

例文

(a) 暴力団の牙を抜くための最良の方法は、不正な資金源を断つことである。

(b) テロ組織の牙を抜くには、資金源を断つことが必要だ。

解説

日本語の「牙」は動物にしか使えない点で、英語の teeth と面白い対照をなしている。

関連語

英語には pull teeth（lit. 歯を抜く）という関連表現がある。「歯を抜くように好ましくないことをする」という比喩である。

夢がある / phr. 隠喩

将来 {何かをしたい / 何かになりたい} という願望がある

関 夢を持つ，(〜を)夢見る

例文

さや：健太は将来何になりたいの？

健太：そうだな、できれば国際弁護士とか。

さや：へぇ、すごい夢があるんだね。実現できるの？

健太：誰だって、夢を持つのは自由だろ。

(a) 僕にはプロ野球の選手になる夢がある。

(b) 私は統計分析のプログラムを作成するという夢がある。

関連語

日本語の関連表現「夢を持つ」と「(〜を)夢見る」は、見出しの「夢がある」と同じくらいの使用頻度である。英語の have a dream (of 〜) は、見出しの dream of 〜 より使用頻度が低い。

REL (1)

(1) "I have a dream that my four little children will one day live in a nation where they will not be judged by the color of their skin, but by the content of their character." - Martin Luther King Jr.
「私には夢があります。いつの日か、私の4人の子供たちが肌の色ではなく、その人格によって判断される国に住める日が来るという夢が。」マーチン・ルーサー・キング牧師

one's {dream is/dreams are} shattered / phr. / metaphor

for a dream to fail to become a reality

REL broken dreams

Examples

Saya: Kenta, what's wrong? You look really bummed out.

Kenta: Yeah, I just got my TOEFL score, and it wasn't very good. I guess I won't be studying abroad after all. My dreams have been completely shattered.

Saya: Come on now, you're not gonna give up that easily, are you? Hold onto your dream and work hard to make it come true.

Kenta: Yeah, you're right. I'll give it another shot.

- -

(a) After the accident, his dream of becoming a football player was shattered. Now he's studying to become a doctor.

(b) Since she was unable to improve her record, her dream of participating in the Olympics was shattered.

Note

The English REL is *broken dreams*, and the Japanese RELs are *yume ga kudakeru* and *yume ga kowareru*. *Broken dreams* can replace the main entry, but it is used less frequently. The Japanese can be replaced by either REL, though *yume ga kudakeru* implies a higher degree of destruction than the other two expressions. 関連語(1)

drink (from) {a/the} bitter cup (of ~) / phr. / metonymy

to have a heartbreaking experience; to be defeated

REL swallow a bitter pill; taste the bitter cup (of ~)

Examples

(a) The women's team seized victory, but the men's team drank from the bitter cup of defeat.

(b) There are many cases where powerful people are forced to drink from a bitter cup.

(c) If invaders try to start a war in this country, they are bound to taste the bitter cup of defeat.

夢が破れる　/ phr.　隠喩
（ゆめ　やぶ）　　　　　　　　（いん ゆ）

夢が現実になり損なう
（ゆめ　げんじつ　　　　　そこ）

関 夢が{砕ける / 壊れる}
（ゆめ　くだ　　こわ）

D

例文

さや：健太、どうしたの、元気ないじゃない。
　　　（けんた）

健太：うん、この間受けた TOEFL の結果が出たんだけど、点数があまりよくなく
（けんた）　　　（あいだう）　　　　　　　　　　（けっか　で）　　　　（てんすう）
　　　て…。やっぱり、留学は無理みたい。夢が破れちゃったなあ。
　　　　　　　　　　（りゅうがく　むり）　　（ゆめ　やぶ）

さや：そんな、もうあきらめちゃうの？　もっと、夢を持ち続けて、努力しなさいよ。
　　　　　　　　　　　　　　　　　　　　　（ゆめ　も　つづ）　　（どりょく）

健太：うん、もう少し、がんばってみるか。
（けんた）　　（すこ）

- -

（a）彼は事故にあって、フットボール選手になる夢が破れたので、今は医者になるた
　　（かれ　じこ）　　　　　　　　　（せんしゅ　　ゆめ　やぶ）　　　（いま　いしゃ）
　　めの勉強をしている。
　　　　（べんきょう）

（b）彼女は記録を伸ばすことができなかったので、オリンピックへの夢が破れてし
　　（かのじょ　きろく　の）　　　　　　　　　　　　　　　　　　　　（ゆめ　やぶ）
　　まった。

関連語

日本語には「夢が砕ける」と「夢が壊れる」という関連表現があり、「夢が破れる」と置き換え
ることができる。「夢が砕ける」はほかの二つより夢の破壊度が高い感じがある。英語には
broken dreams という関連表現があり、見出しと置き換えができるが、使用頻度数は見出し
より低い。

（1）医者に1年しかもたないと言われた晩、私の夢は{破れた / 砕けた / 壊れた}。
　　My dreams were {shattered/broken} the night the doctors told me I only had a year left to
　　live.

苦杯をなめる　/ phr.　換喩
（く はい）　　　　　　　　　　（かん ゆ）

つらい経験をする，負ける
（けいけん）　　　（ま）

例文

（a）女性チームは勝利をもぎ取ったが、男性チームは敗北という苦杯をなめた。
　　（じょせい　　　　しょうり　と　　　　だんせい　　　　はいぼく　　く はい）
（b）普段の実力者が本番で苦杯をなめる例はいくらでもある。
　　（ふだん　じつりょくしゃ　ほんばん　く はい　れい）
（c）この国で侵略者が戦争に火をつければ、敗北の苦杯をなめることは必至だ。
　　（くに　しんりゃくしゃ　せんそう　ひ　　　　　はいぼく　く はい　　　　　　ひっし）

解説

1．英語では *drink (from) {a/the} bitter cup*（苦杯を飲む）と表現しているのに対して、日本語は「苦
　　杯をなめる」となっており、多少ニュアンスが違う。

2．「苦杯をなめる」と *drink (from) {a/the} bitter cup (of ~)* は換喩の例である。なぜなら、実際に
　　カップそのものを飲んだり舐めたりすることはないからである。

Notes

1. The English and Japanese are slightly different in that the former says *drink (from) {a/ the} bitter cup*, whereas the latter literally means "lick a bitter cup."
2. *Drink (from) {a/the} bitter cup (of ~)* and *kuhai o nameru* are examples of metonymy, because one does not literally drink from or lick the cup.

REL

The English REL *taste the bitter cup (of ~)* has the same meaning as the main entry, but uses a different verb.

(1) The women's team seized victory, but the men's team had to {drink/taste} the bitter cup of defeat. (→(a))

drop a bomb(shell)　phr.　metaphor

to suddenly make a upsetting statement

REL explode a bomb(shell)

Examples

(a) He dropped a bombshell by stating that he has evidence of the mayor receiving a bribe in connection with civil engineering work.

(b) The children were surprised when their parents, who had had a good relationship for many years, suddenly dropped a bombshell by saying that they were getting a divorce.

Note

Bakudan o otosu is used occasionally, but it sounds unnatural.

REL

Drop can be replaced by *explode*, but the latter is not used as frequently.

(1) The parents suddenly {dropped/exploded} a bombshell by saying that they were getting a divorce. (→(b))

drop one's eyes (to ~)　phr.　metaphor

to direct one's eyes downwards toward s.t.

Examples

(a) She couldn't bear to look at her mother's concerned expression, so she dropped her eyes and looked at the floor.

(b) Ron fell silent. He dropped his eyes to the book for a moment, then looked back up.

(c) She dropped her eyes to the immense bouquet of roses on her knee. Her white-gloved fingertips touched the flowers softly.

関連語

英語の関連表現 *taste the bitter cup (of ~)* は見出しと同じ意味であるが、動詞が異なる。

—📖 REL(1)

D

爆弾発言をする　/phr.　隠喩
ばくだんはつげん　　　　　　　　いんゆ

突然衝撃的なことを伝えて周囲を混乱させる
とつぜんしょうげきてき　　つた　　しゅうい　こんらん

例文

(a) 彼は、市長が土木工事に関連して賄賂を受け取った証拠を持っていると爆弾発言
かれ　しちょう　どぼくこうじ　かんれん　　わいろ　う　と　しょうこ　も　　　　　ばくだんはつげん
をした。

(b) 長年仲のよかった両親が突然離婚を決めたという爆弾発言をして、子供達は驚いた。
ながねんなか　　　　りょうしん　とつぜんりこん　き　　　　　ばくだんはつげん　　　こどもたち　おどろ

解説

日本語でも「爆弾を落とす」と言えないことはないが、あまり自然な言い方ではない。

関連語

英語の動詞 *drop* は *explode* と置き換えることができるが、*explode* の使用頻度は *drop* よりも
はるかに低い。—📖 REL(1)

(～に)目を落とす　/phr.　隠喩
め　お　　　　　　　　　いんゆ

目を下のほうの何かに向ける
め　した　　　　なに　む

例文

(a) 彼女は母親の心配そうな顔を見ることができなかったので、床に目を落とした。
かのじょ　ははおや　しんぱい　　かお　み　　　　　　　　　　　ゆか　め　お

(b) ロンは黙ってしまい、ちらっと本に目を落として、それからまた、目を上げた。
だま　　　　　　　ほん　め　お　　　　　　　　　　　め　あ

(c) 彼女は膝の上にあるバラの大きな花束に目を落とした。白い手袋をはめた指先が
かのじょ　ひざ　うえ　　　　　おお　はなたば　め　お　　　　しろ　てぶくろ　　　ゆびさき
花に軽く触れた。
はな　かる　ふ

209

drop in the bucket, a / phr. / metaphor

a portion so small that it doesn't affect anything

REL a drop in the ocean

Examples

(a) The portion of the budget allocated to social services is just a drop in the bucket compared to the total budget for the year.

(b) Our current knowledge of the human brain is merely a drop in the bucket when you consider all there is to know.

(c) The reason for low voter turnout is probably that voters believe that a single vote is just a drop in the bucket.

Notes

1. The Japanese is quite hyperbolic when compared to the English, since *ocean* is used instead of *bucket*.

2. The English and Japanese usually take the adverbs *just/merely* and ~ *ni suginai/~ de shika nai* (only, just, merely), respectively.

REL

1. The English has the REL *a drop in the ocean*, which is identical to the Japanese, but this is used less frequently than *a drop in the bucket*.

2. The Japanese has two RELs: *kyūgyū no ichimō* (lit. "one hair out of nine cows") and *yakeishi ni mizu* (lit. "water on heated stones"). The former illustrates how miniscule an amount is by comparing a single hair to the massive number of hairs nine cows collectively possess. The latter expresses the idea of futility through the image of attempting to cool heated stones with only a small amount of water. The former expression can be substituted for the main entry in all of the Japanese examples, but the latter cannot unless it is meant to imply futility. 関連語(1)(2)

drop one's shoulders / phr. / metonymy

a gesture that indicates lack of spirits due to disappointment

Examples

Saya: Mike, what happened? You look depressed.

Mike: Is it that obvious?

Saya: When you're dropping your shoulders that much, yeah. What happened?

(a) When the girl he liked turned down his request for a date, he sighed and dropped his shoulders.

(b) When he saw his take-home pay, he sighed and dropped his shoulders.

(c) "Strike three. You're out!" shouted the umpire. Seiichi dropped his shoulders as he walked back to the bench, dragging the bat behind him.

大海の一滴 / n. phr. | 隠喩

あまりにも大きい量の中で少量すぎて、なんの影響も及ぼさない

関 九牛の一毛，焼け石に水

例文

(a) 社会福祉に割り当てられる予算は、今年度の予算総額からすると大海の一滴にすぎない。

(b) 人間の脳に関して現在わかっていることは、わかっていないことに比べたら大海の一滴でしかない。

(c) 選挙の投票率が低いのは、一票を投じたとしても、それは大海の一滴に過ぎないと考えるからではないだろうか。

解説

1. 日本語では一滴の容器が「大海」で、英語の*bucket*（バケツ）に比べると誇張した表現である。

2. 通常、日英語ともに、それぞれ「～に過ぎない」「～でしかない」、*just/merely* といった副詞をとる。

関連語

1. 英語の関連表現には日本語と同一の *a drop in the ocean* という表現がある。ただし、*a drop in the bucket* より使用頻度は低い。

2. 日本語には「九牛の一毛」（lit. 九頭の牛の中の一本の毛）と「焼け石に水」（lit. 熱く焼けた石に水をかける）という二つの関連表現がある。前者の意味は"多くの中の極めて少ない一部分"で、後者の意味は"火に焼けた石に多少の水をかけても冷ますことはできない"である。後者は何か無意味なことをするときにしか使えないが、前者はすべての場合に用いることができる。

(1) 膨大な赤字補填には、このビルの売却など｛大海の一滴でしかない / 焼け石に水だ｝。
Compared to the massive deficit, selling off this building is like a drop in the {bucket/ocean}.

(2) この大自然にくらべたら、私の写生は｛九牛の一毛 / ˣ焼け石に水｝にすぎません。
Compared to Mother Nature, my sketches are nothing.

肩を落とす phr. | 換喩

がっかりして力がなくなったときの仕草

例文

さや：マイク、どうしたの。元気ないわね。

マイク：わかる？

さや：わかるわよ。そんなに肩を落としちゃって。どうしたの？

- -

(a) 彼は好きな女の子にデートを申し込んで断られ、肩を落とした。

(b) 彼は給料の手取りを見て、ため息をついて肩を落とした。

(c) 「ストライク、アウト！」とアンパイアは叫んだ。成一はバットを引きずりながら肩を落としてベンチに戻った。

Note

When one is despondent, one spontaneously bends forward, causing one's shoulders to be lowered. Because the psychological state of despondence coincides with the physical action of dropping one's shoulders, this can be considered a case of metonymy based on temporal proximity.

A drowning man will clutch at a straw. phr. metaphor

when desperate, you will look for anything that might help you, even if it's useless

REL grasp at straws; cling to the last straw

Examples

Kenta: Hey Saya, can you give me the answer to this problem?

Saya: Wow, are you actually asking for my help?

Kenta: The test's tomorrow. You know what they say: a drowning man will clutch at a straw.

Saya: Hey, who're you calling straw?!

- -

(a) The parents brought their severely ill daughter to a famous fortune-teller. They felt like a drowning man clutching at a straw.

(b) One of the team members got injured before the soccer game, so I asked my sister to play as his replacement since she likes soccer. A drowning man will clutch at a straw, after all. But she actually did an amazing job!

Notes

1. The Japanese is a translation of the English.
2. *O mo* consists of the direct object marker *o* and the marker of {addition/emphasis} *mo*. This combination is rarely used in modern Japanese except in archaic idiomatic phrases.

REL

The English RELs are *grasp at straws* and *cling to the last straw*, both of which are similar to the main entry. The Japanese REL is *(oboreru mono wa) wara ni mo sugaru*. A common collocation is *wara ni mo sugaru omoi {da/de}* (to feel like one is clinging to a straw). 📖➡関連語(1)

dull / adj. / metaphor

mentally sluggish; lacking sharpness; {light/pain/sound} lacking in intensity; uninteresting

ANT LOOK▶ sharp

Examples

Mrs. S: Doctor, I've been suffering from headaches lately, and I haven't been able to sleep.

Doctor: What sort of a pain is it? Is it a sharp pain?

Mrs. S: No, it's a dull pain most of the time, but sometimes it can become very intense.

解説

人は落胆した時は自然に前屈みになるため、肩の位置も下がる。これは落胆の心理と同時に起きる動作で、時間的な近接を表すから、換喩と考えられる。

（溺れる者は）わらをもつかむ　/ phr. / 隠喩

{緊急 / 危急}のときは、まったく頼りにならないものにでも必死に頼ろうとする

関 （溺れる者は）わらにもすがる

例 文

健太：ねえ、さや、この問題の解き方、教えてくれないかな。

さや：あら、珍しい。健太が私に質問するなんて。

健太：明日、テストなんだ。溺れる者はわらをもつかむだよ。

さや：ま、私はわら程度なの、失礼ね。

(a) 両親はわらをもつかむ思いで難病の娘を占い師のもとに連れて行った。

(b) サッカーの試合前にメンバーが怪我をしたので、溺れるものはわらをもつかむ思いで、サッカー好きの妹にピンチヒッターを頼んだところ、驚きの大活躍だった。

解説

1. 日本語は英語からの翻訳である。

2. 日本語の「をも」は目的格の「を」に追加、強調の意味の助詞「も」がついた古い形で、現代語では古い慣用表現でしか使われない。

関連語

日本語の関連表現には「（溺れる者は）わらにもすがる」があり、「わらにもすがる思い{だ/で}」として使われることが多い。英語の関連表現には見出しと近い意味 *grasp at straws* と *cling to the last straw* という表現がある。

(1) 両親は{わらをもつかむ / わらにもすがる}思いで難病の娘を占い師のもとに連れて行った。
(→(a))

The parents brought their severely ill daughter to a famous fortune-teller. They felt like {a drowning man clutching at a straw/they were grasping at straws/they were clinging to the last straw}.

鈍い　/ adj. (i) / 隠喩

{動き / 頭の働き}が普通よりおそい，刃物の切れ方が普通より劣る，{光 / 痛み / 音 / 聴覚}が普通より弱い

反 **LOOK▶** 鋭い

例 文

鈴木(妻)：先生、最近、頭が痛くて、よく寝られないんですが。

医師：どんな痛みですか。鋭い痛みですか。

鈴木(妻)：いえ、どちらかというと鈍い痛みですが、時々強く痛むこともあります。

213

(a) The dull winter sunlight is streaming in through the window.

(b) He's so dull. No matter how hard I try to explain it, he just doesn't get it.

(c) I heard a dull squishing sound come from under my shoe. I must've stepped on something.

(d) As he grew older, his sense of hearing grew duller.

(e) This knife is dull.

Note

As becomes evident upon comparing the English and Japanese definitions, *nibui* can be used to describe movements or actions, but *dull* cannot be used in this sense. However, *dull* can be used to mean "boring," whereas *nibui* cannot. □📖→解説(1)(2)

ANT

The ANTs of *dull* and *nibui* are *sharp* and *surudoi*, respectively.

---

dump   v.   metaphor

to part with s.o. such as a {family member/sweetheart/friend with whom one used to have a close relationship} in a one-sided way

Examples

Saya: What happened? You look depressed.

Friend: I dumped my boyfriend. He just made me so angry.

Saya: Wow, you make it sound like he was just a cat or something.

Friend: Well, he would've dumped me if I hadn't dumped him first. We were gonna break up eventually anyway.

(a) The woman dumped her boyfriend after they'd been constantly fighting.

(b) Jose's father apparently dumped his family and left Mexico to seek refugee status in the U.S.

---

earn points (with ~)   phr.   metaphor

to do favors for s.o. to gain an advantage

Examples

Kenta: Mom, show me how to cook this dish.

Mrs. S: Huh? Since when do you want to cook?

Kenta: Well, I just met this girl and...

Mrs. S: Ahh, so that's it. You want to make her something and earn points with her, right?

（a）窓から冬の鈍い光がさしこんでいる。

（b）あの人は頭が鈍いのか、いくら説明してもわからないようだ。

（c）足下でぐしゃっと鈍い音がした。何かを踏んだようだ。

（d）年を取って聴覚が鈍くなった。

（e）切れ味の鈍いナイフだ。

解説

日英語の定義を比べるとわかるように、日本語では動きや行動にも「鈍い」が使えるが、英語では動きや行動に *dull* は使えない。逆に、英語では何かが面白くないときに *dull* が使えるが、日本語では使えない。

（1）太ると行動が鈍くなる。
Gaining weight causes your movements to {slow down/ ×become dull}.

（2）その教授の講義は{つまらない/ ×鈍い}。
That professor gives dull lectures.

反意語

「鈍い」、*dull* の反意表現は、それぞれ、「鋭い」、*sharp* である。

（〜を）捨てる　/ v.　隠喩

親密だった{家族 / 恋人 / 友人}と一方的に別れる

例文

さや：どうしたの、元気ないね。

友達：うん、彼と別れたんだ。あんまり腹が立ったから捨ててやったの。

さや：そんな、猫の子捨てるみたいに。

友達：うん、でも、捨てられる前にこっちから先手を打ったのよ。いつかは別れることになったから。

- - - - - - - - - -

（a）女は争いを重ねた末、恋人を捨ててしまった。

（b）ホセの父親は家族を捨ててメキシコを出て、アメリカで難民の資格を取ろうとしたらしい。

（〜の）点数を稼ぐ　/ phr.　隠喩

自分にとって有利になると思う人に気に入られるようにする

例文

健太：お母さん、この料理の作り方、教えて。

鈴木（妻）：あら、めずらしい。どうしたの。

健太：うん、ちょっと知り合った女の子がいて…。

鈴木（妻）：ああ、そうなんだ。何か料理を作って彼女の点数を稼ごうっていう魂胆ね。

215

(a) He earned points by giving the CEO seasonal gifts in midsummer and the end of the year, and he ended up being promoted much more quickly than his peers.

(b) The candidate earned points with farmers when he made deliberate stops in rural areas during his campaign.

Note

The Japanese fits the construction *A ga B no tensū o kasegu*, in which A is the subject of the sentence and B is the possessor of the points A gains. For example, in (b), A would be "the candidate" and B would be "farmers."

emperor's (new) clothes, the   / n. phr.   metaphor

s.t. that is accepted as true or worthy of praise even though it is not

Examples

Mike: Ever since the boss praised the intern's plan, no one has had the courage to point out its obvious flaws.

Colleague: Sounds like a clear case of the emperor's new clothes. Someone ought to speak up and clearly point out the problems.

- - - - - - - - - - - - - - - - - - - -

(a) The former star was wearing the emperor's new clothes. Nobody dared to talk to him about his problems, and his acting ability just kept getting worse.

(b) Higher-ups who surround themselves with yes-men will end up wearing the emperor's new clothes.

Notes

1. *The emperor's (new) clothes* is different from the more straightforward *hadaka no ōsama* (the naked king). However, both are based on Hans Christian Andersen's famous fairy tale in which no one, including the emperor himself, is willing to admit that the emperor is naked until a small child innocently declares, "The emperor has no clothes."
2. The subject of *hadaka no ōsama* must be a person, but the subject of *the emperor's (new) clothes* can be anything that is regarded as true despite being untrue.

(1) Room after room of junk. This is not art. This is the Emperor's New Clothes, a con game played for fun and profit by artists, art dealers, and collectors.
どの部屋も駄作の陳列だ。これは芸術じゃない。これは {まやかしもの/ˣ裸の王様} だ。芸術家、画商、コレクターたちが楽しみと金もうけのためにやっている詐欺行為だ。

empire, {an/the}   / n.   metaphor

a powerful organization

REL kingdom

Examples

Mrs. S: Bill Gates may be young, but he's really something, isn't he?

Mr. S: No kidding. He did create the Microsoft empire, after all.

- - - - - - - - - - - - - - - - - - - -

(a) 彼は毎年社長にお中元・お歳暮を贈って点数を稼ぎ、同年輩の社員よりずっと昇進が早かった。

(b) 候補者は選挙遊説中、農村地帯をまめに回って農民の点数を稼いだ。

解説

日本語は「AがBの点数を稼ぐ」という構文の中で使われて、Aは文の主語でBは点数の所有者である。例えば(b)では、Aは「候補者」でBは「農民」である。

裸の王様 / n. phr. / 隠喩

馬鹿なことをしているのに下の者があえて批判しないでいる高い地位の人

例文

マイク：課長、自分の企画に自信満々だね。誰もその企画、明らかに問題があるって言えないんだ。

同僚：まさに裸の王様っていったところだね。誰かが立ち上がって、はっきり問題点を指摘するべきだね。

(a) その往年のスターは裸の王様だった。誰も彼の問題を進言しようとせず、演技力は衰えるばかりだった。

(b) 周囲にイエスマンばかり置くトップは、結局、裸の王様になってしまう。

解説

1. 英語は「王様の(新しい)服」となっているが、日本語はより直接的に「裸の王様」と表現している。しかし、どちらも小さい子供が無邪気に「王様は何も着ていない」と言い切るまでは、王様を含めて誰も王様が裸だという事実を認めなかった、というアンデルセンの有名な童話から来ている。

2. 日本語では「裸の王様」の主語は人に限られているが、英語 *the emperor's (new) clothes* の主語は、本物ではないのに本物と見なされている物だったら何でもかまわない。 ▶📖 **Note(1)**

帝国 / comp. n. / 隠喩

強大な力を持った組織

関 王国

例文

鈴木(妻)：ビル・ゲイツって、若いのにすごいわね。

鈴木(夫)：うん、一代にしてマイクロソフトを一大帝国に築きあげたね。

217

(a) Certain countries have used funds from organized crime to create a criminal empire.

(b) She used how-to books, magazines, and television shows to create a mass media empire. But she quickly lost influence due to an insider trading scandal.

Note

Empire and *tēkoku* can be used metaphorically to refer to influential organizations that bring to mind historical empires ruled by powerful emperors.

REL

Kingdom and *ōkoku* can be used to describe an area where something is dominant.

(1) a. Japan is the {kingdom/ ^{??}empire} of electronics.
日本はエレクトロニクス{王国 / ^{??} 帝国} だ。

b. Vienna is the kingdom of music.
ウイーンは音楽{王国 / ^{??} 帝国} だ。

{empty/clear} one's head (of) / phr. / metaphor

to try not to think

REL s.o.'s head is empty

Examples

Mike: I'm dead tired. I'm just so busy.

Saya: Why don't you go to a hot spring resort and take it easy for a few days?

Mike: That's a great idea! I just wanna empty my head and relax for a bit.

(a) One of the benefits of sports is that they can clear your head.

(b) He tried to empty his head of thoughts about the women he broke up with.

(c) It is important to clear your head before a big game or exam.

REL

Both the English and Japanese main entries have a positive connotation, but the RELs *s.o.'s head is empty* and *atama ga karappo da* almost always carry the negative connotation of stupidity.

(1) His head is as empty as a balloon.
彼の頭は風船のように空っぽだ。

empty promise / comp. n. / metaphor

a promise one has no intention of keeping; a promise that has not been kept

Examples

(a) The things politicians say publicly before an election always end up being nothing more than empty promises.

(b) The scholarship that the foundation decided to support has become an empty promise due to its financial problems.

(c) The constitutional guarantee of equal rights for men and women all too often ends up being an empty promise.

(a) 某国は、マフィアの資金を元に犯罪者の帝国を築いている。

(b) 彼女はハウツー本や、雑誌、テレビショーなどを手がけ、マスメディアの一大帝国を築いたが、株取引のスキャンダルで急速に影響力を失った。

解説

日英語とも「帝国」と *empire* の比喩的意味は、"強い皇帝が君臨した歴史上の帝国を思い起こすくらい、強大な力を持った組織のこと"である。

関連語

何かが勢力を張っている地域を指す場合は「王国」と *kingdom* が使われる。 📖 REL (1)

E

頭を{空 / 空っぽ}にする　　phr.　隠喩

何も考えないようにする

関　頭が空っぽだ

例文

マイク: ああ、疲れた。このところ、忙しくて。

さや: ちょっと温泉でも行って、少し休んだら?

マイク: いいね。ちょっと頭を空っぽにして、リラックスしたいよ。

- -

(a) スポーツの良さは、頭を空っぽにできることだ。

(b) 彼は頭を空っぽにして、縁を切った女性たちのことを忘れようとした。

(c) 大きな試合や試験の前は、いったん、頭を空にしてのぞむことが大切だ。

関連語

日英語とも見出しは肯定的な意味合いを持つが、関連表現の「頭が空っぽだ」 /s.o.'s head is empty は、ほとんど "愚かだ" という否定的な意味しか持たない。 📖 REL (1)

空約束　　comp. n.　隠喩

実現する気のない約束, 実現しなかった約束

例文

(a) 政治家は選挙の前に多くの公約をするが、それはいつもただの空約束になってしまう。

(b) その財団が支給を決めた奨学金は、財政難から空約束となってしまった。

(c) 憲法による男女均等法の保証は、しばしば空約束になってしまう。

Note

While *empty promise* is a noun phrase, *kara-yakusoku* is a nominal compound, similar to *karate* (lit. "empty hand") and *karaoke* (lit. "empty orchestra"). However, both are used as individual nouns.

empty stomach, (on) an *phr.* metaphor

the state of not having eaten anything

Example

I haven't eaten anything since this morning. I feel like I'm about to collapse from an empty stomach.

Even a bad shot hits the mark given enough tries. *phr.* metaphor

even s.o. who is not good at s.t. can succeed with enough tries

Examples

(a) Let's just submit a plan—any plan. Even a bad shot hits the mark given enough tries.

(b) I've tried all sorts of methods to find a job. I figure even a bad shot hits the mark given enough tries.

Notes

1. While this proverb is used to indicate that one can succeed by chance given enough tries, it can also be used as an example of a poor approach to problem-solving, as shown in (1). 📖→解説(**1**)

2. The English proverb is not used often nowadays.

eye for an eye, an *phr.* metaphor

the idea that a criminal should suffer the same crime {he/she} committed

Examples

Colleague: When is the next soccer game? I'll be there to support your team.

Mike: Thanks. We lost the last game because the other team played dirty, so this time we can't lose.

Colleague: Yeah, if they play dirty this time around, you should do the same thing to them. Eye for an eye.

- - - - - - - - - - - - - - - - - - - -

(a) As Gandhi sagely observed, "an eye for an eye" would leave the whole world blind.

220

解 説

英語の *empty promise* は名詞句だが、日本語の「空約束」は「空手」とか「カラオケ」と同じように、複合名詞である。しかし、いずれも一つの独立した名詞として通用している。

空腹 （くうふく） / comp. n. 隠喩（いんゆ）

お腹がすいている状態（なか・じょうたい）

例 文

今朝から何も食べていないので、空腹で倒れそうだ。
（けさ・なに・た・くうふく・たお）

下手な鉄砲も数撃{てば / ちゃ}当たる （へた・てっぽう・かず・あ） / phr. 隠喩（いんゆ）

（下手でも）何度もやれば（まぐれで）うまくいくこともある（へた・なんど）

例 文

(a) 何でもいいからとにかく企画を出そう。下手な鉄砲も数撃てば当たるさ。
（なん・きかく・だ・へた・てっぽう・かずう・あ）

(b) 下手な鉄砲も数撃てば当たると思って、色々と仕事を探しているんです。
（へた・てっぽう・かずう・あ・おも・いろいろ・しごと・さが）

解 説

1. このことわざは、"あきらめないで何度もやればまぐれでうまくいくこともある"という意味に使われるが、(1)のように、"そんな考えの浅い、しかも無駄なことをしてはいけない"という意味で使われることもある。

(1) 問題を解決するのに「下手な鉄砲も数撃てば当たる」という安易な気持ちでやってはいけない。理詰めでやりなさい。

"Even a bad shot hits the mark given enough tries" is not a good philosophy for solving problems. Use logical reasoning instead.

2. 英語のことわざは一般的にはあまり使われていない。

目には目を （め・め） / phr. 隠喩（いんゆ）

被害者が加害者から受けたのと同じ害を加害者に与える（ひがいしゃ・かがいしゃ・う・おな・がい・かがいしゃ・あた）

例 文

同僚：次のサッカーの試合、いつ？　また、応援に行くよ。
（どうりょう・つぎ・しあい・おうえん・い）

マイク：ありがと。この間の試合、相手のきたないプレーで負けたから、今度はぜったいに負けるわけにはいかないんだ。
（あいだ・しあい・あいて・ま・こんど・ま）

同僚：そうだよ。もし、今度も同じことされたら、こっちも仕返ししてやればいいんだ。「目には目を」だよ。
（どうりょう・こんど・おな・しかえ・め・め）

- -

(a) ガンジーがいみじくも言ったように、「目には目を」の論理でいけば、世界は盲人でいっぱいになってしまう。
（い・め・め・ろんり・せかい・もうじん）

221

(b) I used to live by the "an eye for an eye" philosophy. If someone provoked me, my first instinct was to do the same thing to them. But I've discarded that way of thinking.

Note

Both the English and Japanese are a translation of an excerpt from the Hebrew Old Testament (Exodus 21:22-25) that explains the laws of retaliation: "[22] If men who are fighting hit a pregnant woman and she gives birth prematurely but there is no serious injury, the offender must be fined whatever the woman's husband demands and the court allows. [23] But if there is serious injury, you are to take life for life, [24] eye for eye, tooth for tooth, hand for hand, foot for foot, [25] burn for burn, wound for wound, bruise for bruise." In the New Testament (Luke 6:29), however, Christ offers a radically different ethical code that condemns reciprocal violence: "If someone strikes you on one cheek, turn to him the other also. If someone takes your cloak, do not stop him from taking your tunic."

eye of a needle / n. phr. / personification

the hole in a needle through which one passes the thread

Example

My eyes have grown weaker with age, and it has gotten harder to pass thread through the eye of a needle.

(in the) eye of the {storm/hurricane} / n. phr. / personification

the center of a chaotic situation; a temporary respite before more trouble arrives

Examples

Kenta: Wait, is that lady coming to my cousin's wedding too?

Mrs. S: I hope nothing happens.

Kenta: Yeah, she's always in the eye of some storm. I hope she doesn't stir up trouble.

(a) When her parents got divorced, poor Sarah felt like she was in the eye of the hurricane.

(b) When the politician's scandal came to light, the members of his staff found themselves in the eye of the storm.

Note

Both the English and Japanese mean "being involved in a confusing situation." However, the English can mean "a quiet period before the occurrence of trouble or confusion," as in (2), and the Japanese can mean "a person or thing that causes trouble or confusion," as in (1). 📖→解説(1)

(2) Don't get to comfortable—we're just in the eye of the storm. Things're gonna get busy very soon.
リラックスしすぎちゃダメだよ。今はちょっと嵐がおさまっているだけなんだ。もうすぐまたすごく忙しくなるから。

（b）以前は「目には目を」という考え方をしていました。誰かが僕に腹の立つようなことをすれば、まずはやり返していました。でも今はそんな考え方は捨てました。

解説

日英語とも、仕返しの律法である旧約聖書(出エジプト記21：22-25)の原語であるヘブライ語からの翻訳である。「22. もし人が互いに争って身ごもった女たちを撃ち、これに流産させるならば、ほかの害がなくとも、彼は必ずその女の夫の求める罰金を課せられ、裁判人の定めるとおりに支払わなければならない。23. しかし、ほかの害がある時は、命には命、24. 目には目、歯には歯、手には手、足には足、25. 焼き傷には焼き傷、傷には傷、打ち傷には打ち傷をもって償わなければならない」。一方、新約聖書(ルカ伝6：29)では「あなたの頬を打つ者にはほかの頬をも向けてやり、あなたの上着を奪い取る者には下着をも拒むな」となっており、キリストが仕返しの律法を仕返しのないまったく正反対の倫理に切り替えている。

E

針の目　　n. phr.　擬人化

糸が通る針の穴

例文

年を取ったせいか、針の目が見えにくくなって、すんなりと針に糸を通すことができなくなった。

台風の目（の中にいる）　　n. phr.　擬人化

混乱した状況の中にいる，混乱の原因となる{人 / 身近な人 / 物}

例文

健太：え、あのおばさんも、いとこの結婚式に出るの？

鈴木(妻)：そ、まずいことにならないといいけどね。

健太：そうだよね。なんせ、いつも台風の目だからね。また、問題起こさなきゃいいけど。

（a）両親が離婚した時、かわいそうなサラは自分が台風の目の真ん中にいると感じた。

（b）その政治家のスキャンダルが明るみに出た時、彼のスタッフ達は、自分たちも台風の目に巻き込まれてしまったことを知った。

解説

日英語とも、「混乱した状況に巻き込まれた状態」という意味を持つが、日本語には他に「トラブルや混乱の原因となる {人 / 身近な人 / 物}」という意味があり(1)、英語には「トラブルや混乱が起こる直前の冷静期間」(2)を表す意味がある。 📖 Note (2)

(1) 彼女は我々グループの台風の目だ。来るたびにみんなを混乱に巻き込んでしまう。

She is the troublemaker of our group. Each time she visits, she throws all of us into confusion.

223

eye-catcher / comp. n. / metaphor

s.t. that attracts s.o.'s attention

Example

The half-price dresses are the real eye-catcher of today's sale.

eyes pop out of one's head / phr. / metonymy

to be completely surprised by s.t.

REL eyeballs pop out of one's head; heart leaps into one's mouth

LOOK fall {off/out of} one's chair; **LOOK** one's jaw drops

Examples

Kenta: What surprised you the most when you came to Japan for the first time?

Mike: Hmm, probably the price of melons. When I found out a single luxury melon costs 10,000 yen, my eyes popped out of my head.

(a) The curry dish I ate the other day at an Indian restaurant was so spicy that I thought my eyes would pop out of my head.

(b) I hadn't seen my niece since she was a child, so when she visited town the other day, my eyes popped out of my head. She's grown into a very beautiful young lady.

Note

There are two common variants for the English expression: *eyes pop out of one's head* and *eyes pop out of one's sockets*. The Japanese tends to be used metaphorically, as in the expression *me ga tobi-deru kurai odoroku* (to be so surprised that one's eyes pop out).

REL

Eyes and *me* (eye) can be replaced by *eyeballs* and *{me no tama/me-dama}*, respectively.

📖─関連語(1)

one's face clouds (over) / phr. / metaphor

one's face looks worried or uneasy

REL one's eyes cloud (over)

Examples

(a) When he found out that he failed the exam, his face instantly clouded over.

(b) After my father died, my mother never let her face cloud over in front of her children, no matter how tough the situation was.

(c) The newscaster's face clouded over as she reported on the disaster.

目玉商品 （めだましょうひん） / comp. n. 隠喩（いんゆ）

誰かの注意を引く品物（だれかのちゅういをひくしなもの）

例文

本日（ほんじつ）のセールの目玉商品（めだましょうひん）は、半額（はんがく）の婦人物（ふじんもの）ドレスです。

目が飛び出る（めがとびでる）{ほど / くらい / ぐらい} phr. 換喩（かんゆ）

何かにひどく驚く（なにかにひどくおどろく）

関 {目の玉（めのたま） / 目玉（めだま）} が飛び出る（とびでる）{ほど / くらい / ぐらい}, 心臓（しんぞう）が飛び出す（とびだす）{ほど / くらい / ぐらい}

LOOK▶ 椅子（いす）から（転（ころ）げ）落ちる（おちる）{ほど / くらい / ぐらい}, **LOOK▶** あごがはずれる {ほど / くらい / ぐらい}

例文

健太（けんた）：マイク、日本（にほん）に初（はじ）めて来（き）た時（とき）は、何（なに）に一番（いちばん）驚（おどろ）いた？

マイク：そうだねえ。高級（こうきゅう）メロンの値段（ねだん）かな。一個（いっこ）1万円（まんえん）もするなんて、目の玉（めのたま）が飛（と）び出（で）たよ。

- -

(a) この間（あいだ）インド料理（りょうり）のレストランで食（た）べたカレー料理（りょうり）は、目（め）が飛（と）び出（で）るほど辛（から）かった。

(b) 私（わたし）は姪（めい）には子供（こども）のときから会（あ）っていなかったもんですから、この間（あいだまち）町に来（き）たときには目（め）が飛（と）び出（で）るくらい驚（おどろ）きました。とってもきれいな女性（じょせい）に成長（せいちょう）していたんです。

解説

日本語（にほんご）は「目が飛び出るくらい驚く」という表現（ひょうげん）で隠喩的（いんゆてき）に使（つか）われることが多（おお）い。英語（えいご）では *eyes pop out of one's head*（lit. 目が頭から飛び出る）や *eyes pop out of one's sockets*（lit. 目が本来収まっているくぼみから飛び出す）という表現を使う。

関連語

「目」と *eyes* は、それぞれ、「目の玉 / 目玉」と *eyeballs* で置（お）き換（か）えられる。

(1) 日本（にほん）に行（い）ったとき、メロンの値段（ねだん）が {目（め） / 目の玉（めのたま） / 目玉（めだま）} が飛び出るほど高（たか）くて驚（おどろ）いた。

When I went to Japan and saw how expensive the melons were, my eyeballs popped out of my head.

顔が曇る（かおがくもる） / 顔を曇らせる（かおをくもらせる） phr. 隠喩（いんゆ）

{心配（しんぱい） / 困惑（こんわく）}の表情（ひょうじょう）になる

関 涙で目が曇る（なみだでめがくもる）

例文

(a) 試験（しけん）で不合格（ふごうかく）になったことを知（し）ると、彼（かれ）の顔（かお）はみるみる曇（くも）っていった。

(b) 父（ちち）が亡（な）くなった後（あと）、どんなに大変（たいへん）な時（とき）も、母（はは）は子供達（こどもたち）の前（まえ）では、決（けっ）して顔（かお）を曇（くも）らせることはなかった。

(c) アナウンサーは顔（かお）を曇（くも）らせながら、その緊急（きんきゅう）ニュースを読（よ）み上（あ）げた。

225

Note

Kao ga kumoru implies that someone's face clouds over spontaneously, whereas *kao o kumoraseru*, the causative form, sounds less spontaneous. The fact that the adverb *wazato* (intentionally) can be used in (1a) but not (1b) emphasizes this. 📖→ 解説(1)

REL

The English REL is *one's eyes cloud (over)*, but one cannot say {×*me ga kumoru*/×*me o kumoraseru*} in Japanese unless *namida de* (with tears) is included.

(1) Shinobu's eyes were wide with fear. They clouded over with tears that soon trickled down her cheeks.

しのぶの目は恐怖で見開かれていた。両の目は涙で曇り、やがてその涙が頬を伝って流れ落ちた。

face turns white / phr. / metonymy

to be so shocked or frightened that one's face turns pale

REL be (as) white as {chalk/a sheet}

Examples

(a) His face turned white with fear.

(b) "It would perhaps be better for you to read the account for yourself." He placed the newspaper in her hands. When she read the first few lines, her face turned white.

(c) When Takeo heard the news that his close friend Yoshio had been killed in a car accident, his face turned white.

Notes

1. Both the English and Japanese expressions have the same meaning: "for s.o.'s face to turn pale due to shock or fright."
2. The Chinese compound *sōhaku* correspond to *ao-jiroi* (pale), which is used in spoken language.

REL

1. The English REL, *be (as) white as {chalk/a sheet}*, can replace the main entry.

(1) When Takeo heard the news that his close friend Yoshio had been killed in a car accident, his face was as white as {chalk/a sheet}. (→(c))

2. Both *ganmen-sōhaku {ni naru/da}* and *massao {ni naru/da}* can be used in both spoken and written Japanese. 📖→ 関連語(2)

(as) faithful as a dog / phr. / simile

very faithful

Examples

Karen: Kenta, I saw you with a girl! Is she your new girlfriend?

Kenta: What are you talking about?

226

解説

日本語の見出しには「顔が曇る」と「顔を曇らせる」の二種類の表現がある。違いは「顔が曇る」は顔が自然に曇ることを意味するが、「顔を曇らせる」は使役文のため自発性が低いという点である。「わざと」という副詞が(1a)では使えるが、(1b)では使えないことからもわかる。

(1)a. 彼はわざと顔を曇らせた。
　　　He made a grim expression.
　 b. ˣ彼の顔はわざと曇った。
　　　ˣHis face clouded over intentionally.

関連語

英語には *one's face clouds (over)* と並んで *one's eyes cloud (over)* という関連表現があるが、日本語にはそれに対応する「ˣ目が曇る」「ˣ目を曇らせる」は存在しない。しかし、「涙で」がつくと、英語と同じように使える。➡📖 REL(1)

F

顔面蒼白{になる/だ}　comp. n.　換喩

気が動転して顔が青くなる

関 真っ青{になる/だ}

例文

(a) 彼は恐怖で顔面蒼白になった。
(b) 「その説明は自分で読んだほうが多分いいと思うよ。」と、彼は新聞を彼女に手渡した。最初の2、3行を読むと彼女は顔面蒼白となった。
(c) 武雄は親友の良雄が自動車事故で死んだという知らせを聞いたとき、顔面蒼白になった。

解説

1. 日英語とも、"何かショックや恐怖で気が動転して顔が青くなる"という意味である。
2. 漢語系複合語の「蒼白」は話し言葉の「青白い」に当たる。

関連語

1. 英語の関連表現の *be (as) white as {chalk/a sheet}* は見出しの *face turns white* と置き換えられる。

➡📖 REL(1)

2. 見出しの「顔面蒼白{になる/だ}」も関連表現の「真っ青{になる/だ}」も話し言葉でも書き言葉でも使える。
(2) 彼は恐怖で{顔面蒼白だった/顔色が真っ青になった}。(→(a))

犬のように忠実　phr.　直喩

とても忠実な

例文

カレン：健太、この間、見ちゃった。あれ、新しいガールフレンド？

健太：えっ、なんのこと？

227

Karen: Don't play dumb. I saw you walking with this cute girl at the department store. You were following her around faithful as a dog, carrying all her bags for her and everything.

Kenta: Oh, *that* girl? She's not my girlfriend. She's one of the upperclassmen from the tennis club. She likes making the underclassmen do her every bidding.

Karen: You didn't seem to mind at all.

(a) The soldiers followed the captain as faithfully as dogs.

fall asleep / phr. / metaphor
to go to sleep

Examples

(a) She fell asleep thinking of her ailing mother.

(b) Last night I fell asleep with wet hair. When I woke up this morning, my hair was sticking straight up like a mushroom.

Note

Fall asleep can be used in both spoken and written English, but *nemuri ni ochiru* is usually used in written Japanese. 📖→解説(1)

fall ill / phr. / metaphor
to become sick

Examples

Saya: Karen, I heard that you're going back to America. Is that true?

Karen: Yeah, my mother fell ill, and I'm a bit worried, so I want to see her.

(a) Many people fall ill due to lack of exercise and an unhealthy lifestyle.

(b) Last weekend, about 5% of the residents fell ill one after another from an unknown cause.

Note

Because not everyone literally falls down when they are ill, the use of *fall ill* and *byōki de taoreru* is metaphorical.

REL

1. In written Japanese, *byōki de taoreru* is replaced by *yamai ni taoreru*. 📖→関連語(1)
2. In ordinary Japanese conversation, *byōki ni naru* (to become ill) is typically used.

カレン：とぼけちゃって。デパートでかわいい女の子に犬のように忠実に従ってた
じゃない。荷物いっぱい持たされて。

健太：あ、あれ、ガールフレンドじゃないよ。テニスクラブの先輩。人使い荒いんだ。

カレン：そう？　けっこう、うれしそうに見えたけど。

(a) 兵士達は、犬のように忠実に隊長に従った。

眠りに落ちる　/ phr.　隠喩

眠ってしまう

例文

(a) 彼女は病んでいる母親のことを思いながら、眠りに落ちた。

(b) 昨夜は濡れた髪のまま眠りに落ちた。今朝起きると髪の毛はつんつん突っ立っていて、まるできのこのようだった。

解説

英語の *fall asleep* は話し言葉でも書き言葉でも使えるが、日本語の「眠りに落ちる」は書き言葉で使われることが多い。

(1) 僕はね、昨日の晩は11時ごろ{寝た/×眠りに落ちた}んだよ。
I fell asleep around 11:00 p.m. last night.

病気で倒れる　/ phr.　隠喩

重い病気になる

関 病に倒れる

例文

さや：カレン、アメリカに帰るんだって？

カレン：そうなの。母が病気で倒れたから、ちょっと心配で。様子を見てこようと思って。

(a) 運動不足と不規則な生活のために病気で倒れる人が多い。

(b) 先週末、住民の5%ぐらいが、次から次へと原因不明の病気で倒れた。

解説

病気になれば患者がみんな文字通り倒れるわけではないので、「病気で倒れる」 *fall ill* は比喩になる。

関連語

1. 日本語の「病気で倒れる」は書き言葉では「病に倒れる」となる。

(1) モーツァルトの母親は、彼の「パリ交響曲」初演の直後に{病気で/病に}倒れ、亡くなっている。
Mozart's mother fell ill right after the premiere of his Paris Symphony and passed away.

2. 日常会話では普通は「病気になる」が使われる。

fall in love with ~ / phr. / metaphor

to become extremely fond of s.o.

Examples

(a) Romeo and Juliet fell in love with each other at first sight.

(b) It is said that in the Heian period, people often fell in love with someone simply after reading a love poem, even without ever having met the author.

Note

Fall in love with ~ can be used in both spoken and written English, but *koi ni ochiru* is used almost exclusively in written Japanese. In spoken Japanese, *~ o (dai-)suki ni naru* (to become fond of ~) should be used. ⊞—解説(1)

fall into {a/the} trap / phr. / metaphor

to be tricked into {doing/thinking} s.t.

REL | fall into {a/the} snare

ANT | set a trap for ~

Examples

(a) The mother fell into the trap of believing it was her son asking for money when it was actually a case of bank transfer fraud. She ended up transferring five million yen into the thief's bank account.

(b) She fell into the trap of believing an advertisement for a quick weight loss product and wasted a huge amount of money on it, but she didn't lose any weight at all.

(c) The drug smuggler fell into the undercover operation's trap and was captured with ease.

Note

Both *trap* and *wana* are devices used to capture animals. It is believed that the oldest example of *wana* (snare) being used in the sense of "s.t. that deceives s.o." appears in *Chinsetsu Yumiharizuki* (1801). It is very unlikely that the Japanese was adopted from English during this time. Likewise, since *wana* is a *kun*-reading, the Japanese was probably not borrowed from Chinese, either. Humans all over the world have been using snares to capture animals since time immemorial, so it is likely that metaphorical usage of the word developed independently through universal semantic expansion. In other words, there is a good chance that trap and *wana* developed their metaphorical meanings independently of one another.

R E L

1. *Wana ni ochiru* is similar to *fall into {a/the} trap*, but *wana ni kakaru* is used more frequently. The two expressions are interchangeable.

2. The Japanese RELs use two different verbs: *kakaru* (to be trapped) and *hamaru* (lit. "to get into"). These can be used metaphorically in the same manner as *ochiru* (lit. "to fall"). Likewise, in English, *snare* can be used metaphorically in the same manner as *trap*.

⊞—関連語(1)

恋に落ちる　/ phr.　隠喩

誰かのことを一瞬で好きになる

例文

(a) ロミオとジュリエットは会った瞬間、一目で恋に落ちてしまった。

(b) 平安時代は、作者に会わなくても、送られてきた恋の歌を読んだだけで、恋に落ちることがあったらしい。

解説

英語の *fall in love with* ~ は話し言葉としても書き言葉としても使えるが、日本語の「恋に落ちる」のほうはほとんど書き言葉でしか使えない。話し言葉では「~を(大)好きになる」が使われる。

(1) ちょっと、ちょっと、治が由利{を好きになった/? と恋に落ちた}みたいよ。
Guess what? Osamu's in love with Yuri!

F

罠に落ちる　/ phr.　隠喩

だまされて相手の思う通りになってしまう

関 罠にかかる，罠にはまる

反 ~に罠を(仕)掛ける

例文

(a) 母親は「振り込め詐欺」の罠に落ち、息子だと思い込んで、500万円も相手の口座に振り込んでしまった。

(b) 彼女は短期間でやせることができるという広告の罠に落ちて、多額の金を使ったが、少しもやせなかった。

(c) 麻薬の密輸入者は、おとり捜査の罠に落ちて簡単に警察に捕まった。

解説

「罠」も *trap* も動物などを捕獲する器具である。「罠」を「人をだますもの」という比喩で使用された一番古い例は1801年の「椿説弓張月」だとされる。この時代に英語から日本語に入ったとは考えにくい。また、「わな」は訓読みなので、中国語から入ったとも考えられない。人類にはどの文化にも太古から罠というものが存在したので、そこから独立して比喩的使用が生まれ、普遍的な意味拡張があったと考えられる。従って、この比喩用法は日英語で独立に出てきた可能性が高い。

関連語

1. 見出しの「罠に落ちる」は英語の *fall into {a/the} trap* に近いが、「罠にかかる」の方が「罠に落ちる」より使用頻度が高い。この二つは自由に入れ替えられる。

2. 日本語には「落ちる」とともに「かかる」「はまる」が同じように比喩的に使われる。英語では *trap* とともに *snare* が同じように使われる。

(1) 可哀想なことに、リズはその詐欺師の仕掛けた罠に何度も{落ちた / かかった / はまった}。
Poor Liz kept falling into the swindler's {traps/snares}.

231

[A][N][T]

Both the English and Japanese have transitive equivalents: *set a trap for* ~ and ~ *ni wana o (shi)kakeru*, respectively. 📖→反意語(1)

fall into the hands of ~　/ phr.　metonymy

for s.t. {dangerous/secret} to become the possession of s.o. who will use it in a harmful manner

[REL]　get into the wrong hands

Examples

Saya: Research on biological weapons and poison gas sure is scary, huh?

Karen: It sure is. If it ever fell into the hands of terrorists, we'd be in big trouble.

- -

(a) The FBI claimed that no classified information or details about national security plans have fallen into the hands of the enemy.

(b) It's possible the gun may have fallen into the hands of the criminal.

Notes

1. In the English, *wrong* can always be used, but in the Japanese, the corresponding word, *machigatta*, is rarely used. Instead, modifiers such as *terorisuto no* (terrorists') or *teki-gawa no* (enemies') must be used.

2. In English, *the wrong hands* is often used, but in Japanese, *machigatta te* is extremely low in frequency. 📖→解説(1)

[R][E][L]

1. *Fall into the hands of* ~ can be replaced by *get into the wrong hands*.

(1) If my credit card ever {fell into the hands of some criminal/got into the wrong hands}, I'd probably be stuck paying the bill for the crime.
クレジットカードが犯罪者の手に落ちたら、不法な支払い請求の分を払わなければならないはめになるだろう。

2. *Ochiru* can be replaced by *wataru* (to cross). *Wataru* is used more frequently than *ochiru*.

📖→関連語(2)

fall {off/out of} one's chair　/ phr.　metonymy

to be extremely surprised; to find s.t. extremely funny

[REL]　heart leaps into one's mouth;

[LOOK] eyes pop out of one's head; [LOOK] one's jaw drops

Examples

(a) I nearly fell out of my chair laughing while watching a Charlie Chaplin DVD.

(b) When I discovered I'd won $150,000, I nearly fell off my chair!

(c) I asked what the cost would be for a first-class seat on a flight to Japan. I almost fell off my chair when I was told it would be over ¥1,000,000!

反意語

日英語とも他動詞表現の「〜に罠を(仕)掛ける」と *set a trap for ~* がある。
(1) チャンは殺人者に罠を(仕)掛けることにした。
　　 Chan decided to set a trap for the killer.

（〜の）手に落ちる　　phr.　隠喩

{危険なもの / 秘密のこと}が、それを悪用して他人に危害を与える人間のものになる

関 （〜の）手に渡る

例文

さや：生物兵器や毒ガスの研究ってこわいわね。
カレン：うん、万一、テロリストの手に落ちたら、大変なことになるからね。

- -

(a) FBI は、極秘情報も国家の機密計画情報も敵側の手には落ちていないと主張した。
(b) 銃が犯罪者の手に落ちた可能性がある。

解説

1. 英語ではいつも *wrong* が使えるが、日本語では対応する「間違った」がかなり使いにくいので、場合場合で「テロリストの」とか「敵側の」という修飾語が必要である。
2. 英語では *the wrong hands* はよく使われるが、日本語では「間違った手」の頻度は非常に低い。
(1) [?]銃が間違った手に落ちた可能性がある。
　　 It is possible that the guns may have fallen into the wrong hands.

関連語

1. 英語の *fall into the hands of ~* は *get into the wrong hands* で置き換えることができる。— 📖 REL (1)
2. 日本語の「落ちる」は「渡る」で置き換えることができ、「渡る」の方が使用頻度が高い。
(2) 生物兵器や毒ガスの研究がテロリストの手に {落ちたら / 渡ったら}、大変なことになる。

（→会話例）

　　 If research on biological weapons and poison gas ever fell into the hands of terrorists, we'd be in big trouble.

椅子から（転げ）落ちる {ほど / くらい / ぐらい}　　phr.　換喩

何かにひどく驚く、何かをとてもおかしく思う

関 心臓が飛び出す {ほど / くらい / ぐらい}
　　 LOOK 目が飛び出る {ほど / くらい / ぐらい}, **LOOK** あごがはずれる {ほど / くらい / ぐらい}

例文

(a) チャーリー・チャップリンの DVD を見ていて、もうちょっとで椅子から転げ落ちるほど笑いこけた。
(b) 15 万ドル当たったことがわかったとき、私はすんでのところで椅子から転げ落ちそうになった。
(c) ファーストクラスで日本まで飛ぶといくらぐらいかと聞いてみた。100 万円以上

233

Note

Both the English and Japanese expressions are used when one is very surprised or amused. The English often takes adverbs such as *nearly* ([a] and [b]) and *almost* ([c]), while the Japanese is often used with *sunde no tokoro de* ([b]) and *mō chotto de* ([a], and [c]).

fall (squarely) on s.o.'s shoulders　*phr.*　metaphor

to become the main responsibility of s.o.

REL　shoulder s.t.

Examples

(a) Responsibility for the new project fell on his shoulders.

(b) When my parents died, the burden of raising my siblings fell squarely on my shoulders.

(c) I'm exhausted. I want to step down from a position like this where so much responsibility falls on my shoulders.

Note

The body parts used in the English and Japanese are *shoulder* and *kata* (shoulder), respectively. In addition, both expressions are passive in meaning.

REL

Both the English and Japanese have RELs that use transitive verbs: *shoulder s.t.* and ~ *o (se)ou*, respectively.

(1) He shouldered responsibility for the new project.
彼は新しいプロジェクトの責任を(背)負っている。(→(a))

fall prey to ~　*phr.*　metaphor

to be harmed by {s.o./s.t.}

REL　become a sacrifice to ~; fall victim to ~

Examples

Mrs. S: Why do such talented young people fall for such corrupt religious fanatics?

Mr. S: The more serious and impressionable a person is, the more likely they are to fall prey to these new religions. One minute they're searching for something in life, and the next thing you know, they're hooked.

(a) During recessions, subcontractors can fall prey to the strategies of big business enterprises and be forced out of business.

(b) If you try to make a move in the jungle at night, you'll fall prey to guerillas.

Note

The nouns *prey* and *ejiki* share the same meaning: "an animal taken by a predator."

だと言われたときには、もうちょっとで椅子から転げ落ちるところだった。

解説

日英語ともに、驚いたときとか笑いこけるときに使われる。日本語は「すんでのところで」(b)、「もうちょっとで」(a)(c)、英語は*nearly*(a)(b)、*almost*(c)といった副詞と一緒に使われることが多い。

肩に（のし）かかる　phr.　隠喩

{責任 / 重圧 / 期待}などの負担がかかる

関　〜を（背）負う

反　LOOK▶肩の荷が下りる

例文

(a) 新しいプロジェクトの責任が彼の肩にかかっている。

(b) 両親が亡くなって以来、弟や妹を育てるという重荷が私の肩にのしかかってきた。

(c) 私は大層疲れました。このように重圧のかかる地位から降りたいのです。

解説

日英語とも、体の部分は「肩」と*shoulder*で同じである。さらに、日英語とも受動的な表現である点も共通している。

関連語

日英語とも他動詞表現の*shoulder s.t.*と「〜を（背）負う」という関連表現がある。

→📖REL (1)

（〜の）餌食 {に / と}なる　phr.　隠喩

誰かに利用され、犠牲になる

関　（〜の）犠牲になる

例文

鈴木（妻）：どうして、こんな若くて優秀な人達が、こんな詐欺のような宗教に入信するのかしら。

鈴木（夫）：純粋でまじめな人ほど、新興宗教の餌食になりやすいんだよ。真剣に何かを求めているうちにはまってしまうんだろうね。

(a) 不景気のときには、下請け企業が大企業の経営戦略の餌食となって潰されてしまう。

(b) ジャングルでは、夜間に行動しようとするとゲリラのかっこうの餌食となる。

解説

名詞の「餌食」/*prey*は"天敵に食べられる生物"という日英共通の意味を持っている。

235

REL

The English RELs are *become a sacrifice to ~* and *fall victim to ~*, and the Japanese REL is *(~ no) gisē ni naru*. Etymologically, both *become a sacrifice to ~* and *(~ no) gisē ni naru* were originally used to refer to a sacrifice offered to a god. Compared to these two expressions, *fall prey to ~*, *(~ no) ejiki {ni/to} naru*, and *fall victim to ~* can be considered more direct and emotive.

(1) Millions of people fell victim to the war, which lasted more than 30 years.
何百万という人々が、30年以上続いた戦争の犠牲になった。

feast one's eyes on ~   *phr.*   metonymy
to greatly enjoy looking at {s.t./s.o.} beautiful

Examples

(a) I feasted my eyes on the actress's beauty.

(b) I feasted my eyes on the green mountain range as I sat in the outdoor spa.

Note

In the English, the one having the experience becomes the subject, and the person or thing that follows the preposition *on* becomes the object of admiration. By contrast, in the Japanese, the one having the experience seldom appears in the sentence; rather, the person or thing being admired becomes the subject. The double particle *~ ni wa* is used to indicate the one having the experience. 📖➡解説(1)

feel one's age   *phr.*   metaphor
to realize that one is no longer young

Examples

Mrs. S: Recently, my shoulders have been feeling stiff and I've been getting more forgetful.

Mr. S: I know what you mean. It's rough feeling your age, isn't it?

- -

(a) Not to brag, but I don't feel my age at all. I have no trouble keeping up with the younger guys.

(b) I feel my age whenever I take the elevator instead of the stairs.

Note

Both the English and Japanese are figurative because the verbs *feel* and *kanjiru* literally mean "to discover s.t. by touching."

関連語

日本語の関連表現には「(〜の)犠牲になる」があり、英語の関連表現には *become a sacrifice to ~* と *fall victim to ~* がある。「(〜の)犠牲になる」と *become a sacrifice to ~* は、どちらも語源的には "神の生贄" という意味がある。これらの表現と比べ、見出しの「(〜の)餌食 {に / と} なる」/*fall prey to ~* と関連表現の *fall victim to ~* はより直接的で感情的な表現である。

→📖 REL (1)

目の保養　/ n. phr.　隠喩
め　ほよう　　　　　　　いんゆ

{景色 / 物 / 人}など美しいものを見てとても楽しむこと

例文

(a) その女優の美しさは目の保養になった。

(b) 露天風呂から眺めた緑の山並みは目の保養になった。

解説

英語では体験者が主語となり、前置詞 *on* の後に来る {物 / 人} が鑑賞の対象物となる。それに対して、日本語では体験者は文章上に表れることは稀で、美しい {物 / 人} が主語となる。体験者を表す場合には、「〜には」を用いる。

(1) 僕には、その女優の美しさは目の保養になった。(→(a))

年を感じる　/ phr.　隠喩
とし　かん　　　　　　いんゆ

もう若くはないことに気づく

例文

鈴木(妻)：最近、肩も凝るし、物忘れも多くなったわ。

鈴木(夫)：そうだね。いやでも年を感じるね。

- -

(a) 自慢じゃないけど、私は年を感じませんね。問題なく若い連中について行けます。

(b) このごろ階段を上らず、エレベーターに乗ってしまうとき、年を感じます。

解説

日英語ともに、動詞「感じる」と *feel* の基本義は、いずれも "触れることで何かを見つける" であるから、比喩だと考えられる。

feel small / phr. / metaphor

to feel insignificant

ANT feel big

Examples

(a) When I stand before the majesty of nature, I feel so small.

(b) When I heard that my colleague who entered the company at the same time had already been promoted to department chief, I felt small since I'm still just a section head.

Note

Both the English and Japanese are figurative because the verbs *feel* and *kanjiru* literally mean "to discover s.t. by touching." In addition, the adjectives *small* and *chīsai* normally refer to physical size, but in this case they do not.

ANT

While one can say *feel big* in English, *(jibun o) ōkiku kanjiru* cannot be used in Japanese, as shown in (1). The expression *kimochi ga ōkiku natta yō ni omoeru* (to feel as if one's feelings have become big) can be used to express an idea similar to that of *feel big*.

(1) This was Sarah's first day at school. She felt like she was part of something big. And she herself felt big as well.
この日はサラの初登校日でした。サラは何か大きなものの一部になったような気がしました。そして{気持ちが大きくなったように思えました/ ⁇ 自分を大きく感じました}。

fight like cats and dogs / phr. / simile

to fight bitterly with each other

Examples

Mrs. S: Dad's sisters will be coming over for New Year's.

Kenta: Seriously? Those two fight like cats and dogs. You're gonna have a hard time dealing with them.

Mrs. S: I know. I can already feel the headache coming on!

- -

(a) Those two have been fighting like cats and dogs for years, but they aren't divorced yet.

(b) Neighboring countries occasionally fight like cats and dogs over territory.

Notes

1. The English expression uses dogs and cats to describe people fighting, but the Japanese uses dogs and monkeys.

2. The English often uses verbs such as *fight* and *argue*, but the Japanese simply states that the relationship is like that between dogs and monkeys.

（自分を）小さく感じる　/ phr.　隠喩

自分のことを取るに足らない人間だと思う

例文

(a) 大自然の前に立つと自分をとても小さく感じる。

(b) 会社の同期が早々と部長に昇進したと聞き、未だ係長の自分を小さく感じた。

解説

日英語ともに、動詞「感じる」と feel の基本義は"触れることで何かを見つける"であり、さらに形容詞「小さい」と small は物理的な大きさを指しているのではないので、比喩である。

反意語

英語には feel big という反意表現があるが、日本語には「（自分を）大きく感じる」という反意表現はない。その場合は、「気持ちが大きくなったように思える」を使う。**ANT(1)

F

犬猿の仲だ　/ phr.　隠喩

互いに憎み合っている

例文

鈴木（妻）：今度のお正月は、お父さんのお姉さんも妹も来るんですって。

健太：え、ほんと？　あの二人、犬猿の仲じゃなかったっけ。お母さん、おばさん達の間に入って大変だよ。

鈴木（妻）：そうなの。今から、頭が痛いわ。

- -

(a) あの夫婦は長年犬猿の仲だけれど、まだ離婚していない。

(b) 隣り合った国は領土問題が原因で犬猿の仲になることがある。

解説

1. 日本語では犬と猿が仲の悪い例として挙げられているが、英語では犬と猫が挙げられている。

2. 英語では動詞の fight と argue が一緒に用いられやすいが、日本語では「犬猿の仲だ」とだけ言う。

239

fill (s.t. with) / v. / metonymy

to satisfy or complete {s.o./s.t.}

REL LOOK full of ~; ~ is full

Examples

(a) Ichiro makes it a rule to fill his spare time with music and reading.

(b) My heart was filled with satisfaction when I finally finished the project.

(c) When I stepped through the school gates on the first day of school, I was filled with excitement and curiosity.

(d) Nature is being destroyed in order to fill the needs of human beings.

Notes

1. When the English and Japanese expressions are used with nouns such as *kokoro* (heart) and *jikan* (time), they are likening these nouns to containers. The Japanese can also be used with nouns such as *yokkyū* (desire) and *jōken* (conditions), and both the English and Japanese can be used with *yōkyū* (demand).

2. In most cases, the English and Japanese share the same figurative meaning, but there are cases where *mitasu* can be used figuratively while *fill* cannot. 📖→解説(1)

3. *Mitasu* (to {fill/satisfy}) has the non-metaphorical meaning of "to fill a container with liquid or grain-like objects."

REL

The English and Japanese RELs are *full of ~/~ is full* and *~ {ga/de} ippai*, respectively. Both the English and Japanese RELs can replace their respective main entries when the metaphorical container is one's heart. 📖→関連語(1)

fill {a/the} hole(s) / phr. / metaphor

to fill in an area where s.t. is missing

Examples

Saya: That part-time job sure is keeping you busy, isn't it?

Friend: Yeah. Moving was really expensive—it cost me everything I had set aside for rent. So I'm trying to fill the hole in my wallet by working everyday.

Saya: That's tough. Hang in there.

- -

(a) European airlines are moving quickly to fill some of the holes in the transatlantic business travel market created by the bankrupt American airline's cutbacks.

(b) As Alumni Coordinator, Mr. Yoshida will be working to fill some of the holes in our alumni database.

（〜を）満たす　v. 換喩

人間の{心理 / 欲求 / 感情}を満足させる

関 LOOK {〜が / で} いっぱい

例 文

(a) 一郎は暇な時間を音楽と読書で満たすことにしている。

(b) やっとプロジェクトが完成したときには、心は満足感で満たされた。

(c) 始業の日に校門をくぐり抜けたとき、私は興奮と好奇心に満たされた。

(d) 人間の欲望を満たすために、多くの自然が破壊されている。

解 説

1. 日英語とも、例文に見られるように「心」や「時間」のような名詞を容器に見立てている。日英語とも「要求」などの名詞、日本語ではさらに「欲求」「条件」などの名詞が使われる。

2. 日英語の動詞はたいていの場合、比喩的意味を共有しているが、日本語の「満たす」は使えるのに英語の *fill* が使えない場合もある。

(1) a. 目前の欲望を満たすだけでは人生の展望がなくなる。
　　　We'll be sacrificing our future prospects if we only {satisfy/ ×fill} our short-term desires.
　　b. あなたのすべての希望条件を満たしてくれる会社は非常に少ないようだ。
　　　It's likely that very few companies will be able to {satisfy/ ×fill} all of your conditions.
　　c. 今年度は何とか利潤の目標額を満たすことができた。
　　　This year we were somehow able to {achieve/?satisfy/ ×fill} our profit goals.

3. 日本語の動詞「満たす」の基本義は"容器を液体か粒状のものでいっぱいにする"という意味である。

関連語

日本語には「{〜が / で} いっぱい」、英語には *full of* 〜 と〜 *is full* という関連表現がある。日英語共に、心を比喩的に容器とみなした場合に、見出しと置き換えられる。

(1) a. やっとプロジェクトが完成したときには、心は満足感でいっぱいだった。(→(b))
　　b. 始業の日に校門をくぐり抜けたとき、私は興奮と好奇心でいっぱいだった。(→(c))

穴を埋める　phr. 隠喩

足りないところを補う

例 文

さや：アルバイト、忙しそうね。

友達：うん、引っ越したらお金かかっちゃって。家賃分も使っちゃったの。それで、その穴を埋めるんで、毎日働いているってわけ。

さや：大変だね。がんばって。

- - - - - - - - - - -

(a) ヨーロッパの航空会社が、アメリカの破産した航空会社の運航削減で生じた大西洋横断ビジネス旅行の市場の穴を埋めるべく、すばやい動きを見せている。

(b) 校友会のコーディネーターの吉田さんは、校友会名簿のデータベースの穴を埋めようとしています。

> **Note**
>
> Using *hole/ana* to figuratively express the idea of something being missing is common to both English and Japanese.

homograph

{fire licks/flames lick} at ~ / phr. / personification

for flames to slightly touch s.t.
炎が何かを少しかすめる

> **Example**
>
> The flames licked at him as he tried to escape the burning building.
> 彼が燃えているビルから逃げ出そうとした時、炎が彼の身体をかすめた。

> **Notes**
>
> 1. Both the English and Japanese personify *{fire/flames}* by using the verbs *lick* and *nameru*, respectively, which are usually used to describe the movements a tongue makes.
> 2. The Japanese sounds more natural if the predicate is *name-tsukusu*, which means "to lick s.t. thoroughly," as opposed to just *nameru* (to lick).

firebrand / comp. n. / metaphor

s.o. who stirs up unrest

> **Examples**
>
> Mike: They're arguing about this year's financial report, aren't they?
>
> Colleague: Yeah. Who's the firebrand that started this whole mess?
>
> Mike: It's Mr. Yamada from sales, apparently, but I don't know the whole story.
>
> -
>
> (a) The firebrands in the mass media are the ones who caused this mess.
>
> (b) This huge protest was started by young firebrands dissatisfied with the government.

> **Notes**
>
> 1. The basic meaning of *firebrand* is "a piece of burning wood," while *hitsuke-yaku* means "s.o. in charge of creating a fire."
> 2. The English can only refer to people who cause some kind of trouble or unrest, but the Japanese can also be used to refer to people or entities that cause trends, developments, and so on. 📖→解説(**1**)

解説

何か欠けているものを表すために「穴」を比喩的に使うのは日英語とも共通である。

同形異義語

炎が（〜を）なめ尽くす / phr. / 擬人化

炎が何かを全部燃やしてしまう
for flames to consume s.t.

例文

強風にあおられた炎が集落の農家を次から次へとなめ尽くした。
Fanned by strong winds, the fire engulfed the farmhouses one after another.

解説

1. 日英語とも「火」を擬人化して、おいしいものをなめる時の舌の動きに喩えている。
2. 日本語は述部を「なめる」ではなくて、「なめ尽くす」としたほうが自然に聞こえる。

F

火付け役 / comp. n. / 隠喩

{議論 / 事件 / 改革 / 開発}などのきっかけをつくる{もの / 人}

例文

マイク： 今年度の収支決算報告、もめてるね。

同僚：うん、誰が論争の火付け役なの？

マイク： 営業の山田らしいけど、本当のところはわからないね。

(a) マスメディアが、この混乱の火付け役だ。

(b) 今この大規模なデモの火付け役は、政府に不満を持っている若者達だった。

解説

1. 「火付け役」と*firebrand*の基本義は、それぞれ、"火をつける人"と"燃えている材木"である。
2. 英語は、扇動的なことを始める人についてしか使えないのに対して、日本語は流行や開発などのきっかけになった人や物にも使える。

(1) 母の日にカーネーションを贈る習慣が、インターネットショッピングを普及させる火付け役になった。
The practice of sending carnations on Mother's Day helped popularize internet shopping.

243

first step, the / n. phr. / metaphor

the first action s.o. takes as part of a longer process

Examples

Kenta: Karen, you speak Japanese so well. How were you able to get so good?

Karen: Well, I've still got a long way to go, but I think the first step to getting better at a foreign language is to just keep speaking without being afraid of making mistakes. Thanks for being such a great conversation partner!

(a) The first step is always the most difficult.

(b) Egypt took the first step towards peace under that President.

(c) When it comes to making a successful website, the design is the first step.

flame / v. / metaphor

to post hostile electronic messages, especially as online comments

Example

The politician was flamed for making a controversial statement on his blog.

flame(s) of passion / n. phr. / metaphor

intense romantic sentiment

REL flame(s) of {love/anger/jealousy/hate}

Examples

Saya: Kenta, did you ever have a chance to go out with that girl again?

Kenta: Things didn't really work out. The flames of passion made me act without thinking.

Saya: You sound like a pop song. Basically, she dumped you, right?

Kenta: I'm afraid so.

(a) If you want to learn the secret to igniting the flames of passion in your lover, read this book.

Notes

1. The Japanese can also take the form *jōnetsu o moyasu* (to burn with passion), which omits *honō* (flame). 📖→ 解説(1)
2. While the English can only be used to describe intense romantic sentiment, the Japanese can be used to express a passion for anything.

R E L

The expressions *flame(s) of ~* and *~ no honō* can be used to describe intense emotions, as in *flame(s) of love/ai no honō, flame(s) of anger/ikari no honō, flame(s) of jealousy/shitto no honō, flame(s) of hate/zōo no honō*, and so on. However, these expressions are only used in written language. 📖→関連語(1)

244

第一歩 / n. phr. 隠喩

長い過程の中で最初にとる行動

例文

健太：カレンは日本語うまいね。どうしたらそんなうまくなれるの？

カレン： う〜ん、まだまだだけど。でもとにかく間違ってもなんでも話すことが語学

上達の第一歩かな。健太はいい練習相手で、感謝してるわ。

- (a) 何事も第一歩が一番難しい。
- (b) エジプトはその大統領のもとで平和への第一歩を踏み出した。
- (c) ウェブサイトの成功を決める第一歩はそのデザインだ。

炎上する / v. 隠喩

問題発言、失言などで、ネットやSNS上で強く非難され、収拾がつかなくなる

例文

あの政治家のブログが、問題発言でまた炎上した。

情熱（の炎） / n. phr. 隠喩

何かに対するとても強い気持ち

関 {愛 / 怒り / 嫉妬 / 憎悪} の炎

例文

さや：健太、例の彼女、その後、デートのチャンスはあったの？

健太：それが、情熱の炎を燃やして突進したんだけど、うまくいかなかったんだ。

さや：なに歌謡曲みたいなこと言ってるのよ。結局、振られちゃったんでしょ。

健太：残念ながら、そういうこと。

- (a) 恋人に対する情熱の炎を燃やす秘訣を学びたいのなら、この本を読むといい。

解説

1. 日本語には「炎」を省略した「情熱を燃やす」という言い方もある。

(1) 恋人に対する {情熱 / 情熱の炎} を燃やす秘訣を学びたいのなら、この本を読むといい。
   If you want to learn the secret to igniting the flames of passion in your lover, read this book.
   (→ (a))

2. 日本語の見出しは恋愛対象以外でもそのまま使用できるが、英語の場合は熱烈な恋愛感情に
   しか使用できない。

関連語

日英語とも、とても強い感情なら何でも「〜の炎」と *flame(s) of ~* となり得る。例えば、「愛
の炎」と *flame(s) of love*、「怒りの炎」と *flame(s) of anger*、「嫉妬の炎」と *flame(s) of jealousy*、
「憎悪の炎」と *flame(s) of hate* などがある。しかし、これはすべて書き言葉でしか使えない。

245

flames lick at ~ （炎が（〜を）なめ尽くす） → **{fire licks/flames lick} at ~**

flavor / n. / synesthesia

a predominant characteristic

Examples

Kenta: Saya, have you ever read this comic?

Saya: No. Is it any good?

Kenta: Yeah. It might be a comic, but it has a literary flavor.

- -

(a) This movie has an artistic flavor.

(b) The gardens were designed to take on the historical flavor of 19th-century France.

Notes

1. This is a case of synesthesia, because both *flavor* and *aji* refer to the sense of taste, yet here they are used to refer to something that one cannot taste.

2. In addition to the examples provided here, there are many other figurative uses of *flavor* and *aji*, such as *Western flavor/sēyō-tekina aji*, *Oriental flavor/tōyō-tekina aji*, *European flavor/yōroppa-tekina aji*, *Japanese flavor/nihon-tekina aji*, *Chinese flavor/chūgoku-tekina aji*, and so on.

REL

The Japanese expression *~ tekina ajiwai* can be replaced by *~ tekina aji*, but the main entry is used more frequently. 📖→ 関連語(1)

float on air / phr. / metaphor

to be full of joy

REL {walk/tread} on air

Examples

(a) When Michiko took a picture with the famous movie star, she was floating on air.

(b) When I learned that I would be awarded a scholarship by the university, I was floating on air.

Note

Uchōten is a Buddhist term that refers to "the highest point among the nine heavens," and *float on air* means "floating at the highest point possible." Both figuratively evoke the idea of "feeling uplifted and full of joy."

(1) a. 二人の愛の炎は燃え上がり、誰にも消すことはできなかった。
   No one could extinguish the flame of their love.
   b. 彼女は、嫉妬の炎にかられて、復讐を企てた。
   Burning with the flames of jealousy, she plotted her revenge.

～的な味わい　　n. phr.　共感覚

何か深みのあるものを思い起こさせるような特徴

関 ～的な味

例文

健太：さや、このマンガ読んだことある？

さや：ないけど、おもしろいの？

健太：うん、マンガなんだけど、けっこう、文学的な味わいがあるんだ。

(a) この映画には芸術的な味わいがある。

(b) 庭園はフランスの 19 世紀の歴史的な味わいを出すように設計された。

解説

1. 「味」も*flavor* も味覚に属しているが、ここでは味覚を超えたものに転移しているから、共感覚に当たる。

2. 例文に挙げられている以外にも、「味」/*flavor* を使っている比喩的用例はたくさんある。「西洋的な味」/*Western flavor*、「東洋的な味」/*Oriental flavor*、「ヨーロッパ的な味」/*European flavor*、「日本的な味」/*Japanese flavor*、「中国的な味」/*Chinese flavor* などがある。

関連語

日本語の「～的な味わい」は「～的な味」と言い替えることができる。しかし、見出しの方がよく使われる。

(1) 彼女の絵には文学的な {味わい / 味} がある。
   Her paintings have a literary flavor.

有頂天 {だ / になる}　　phr.　隠喩

とてもうれしい

関 天にも昇る {心地 / 気持ち} である

例文

(a) 有名な映画スターと一緒に写真を撮って、みちこは有頂天だった。

(b) 大学から奨学金をもらえるとわかり、私は有頂天になった。

解説

日本語の「有頂天」は仏教語では九つある天のなかで最も高い所を指し、英語の*float on air* は "空の上"(on air)、つまり「「最も高い所」に浮かんでいる"(to float) という意味で、どちらも「喜びに満ちて気持ちが高揚する」ことを意味する隠喩である。

REL

The English and Japanese RELs are *{walk/tread} on air* and *ten ni mo noboru {kokochi/ kimochi} de aru*, respectively. Both can replace the main entries, though the Japanese RELs are used in written language. 📖➡ 関連語(1)

flood of ~, a / n. phr. / metaphor

an extremely large {number/quantity} of s.t.

Examples

Saya: I hear this film that's playing now is really good.

Karen: Yeah, it's amazing. The final scene made me cry a flood of tears. My handkerchief was completely soaked.

Saya: Really? I think I'll go see it this weekend.

- -

(a) A flood of cars is headed toward the beach.

(b) These days, the Tanzawa Mountains are suffering from a flood of people who want to enjoy themselves in the lush mountain environment.

(c) The flood of information available is causing more and more people to have trouble deciding which information to choose.

Note

In both English and Japanese, virtually anything quantifiable can be likened to a *flood/ kōzui*. Some examples of nouns used in Japanese include *kuruma*, *hito*, *jōhō*, and *sōon*, while in English, *lawsuits*, *questions*, *complaints*, and *emotions* can also be used.

flow / n. / metaphor

continuous, liquid-like movement

REL stream; current

Examples

Karen: The flow of traffic today is so smooth, I can hardly believe it.

Kenta: Well, it is Sunday, after all.

- -

(a) The flow of people entering the shop showed no signs of stopping.

(b) Time itself is the same for everyone, but how one perceives the flow of time differs from person to person.

Note

The basic meaning of *flow* and *nagare* is "a steady, unidirectional movement of liquid." The following are examples of the metaphorical uses of *flow*, *stream*, and *current*, which correspond to *nagare* in Japanese. 📖➡解説(1)

関連語

日本語には書き言葉で「天にも昇る{心地/気持ち}である」という関連表現、英語には *{walk/tread} on air* という関連表現がある。どちらも見出しと置き換えられる。

(1) 大学から奨学金をもらえるとわかり、私は{有頂天/天にも昇る{心地/気持ち}}でした。

$(\rightarrow(b))$

When I learned that I would be awarded a scholarship by the university, I was {floating/walking/trodding} on air.

(〜の)洪水 こうずい / n. phr. 隠喩 いんゆ

何かの数量が非常に多い

例文

さや：今やってる映画、とってもいいんだって？

カレン：うん、最高。最後のシーンなんか、大感激で涙の洪水。ハンカチがぐちゃぐちゃになっちゃった。

さや：ほんと？　今週末、見に行こうっと。

- - - - - - - - - - - - - - -

(a) 車の洪水がビーチに向かって押し寄せている。

(b) このごろの丹沢は、緑の山に行楽を求める人々の洪水に悩まされている。

(c) 情報の洪水によって、適切な情報の選択に迷う人々が多くなっている。

解説

日英語とも、数量に関わるものならほとんど何でも「洪水」/*flood* にたとえられる。主な例では、日本語では車、人、情報、騒音、英語ではそれらに加えて訴訟、問題、不平、感情なども洪水にたとえられる。

流れ なが / n. 隠喩 いんゆ

液体でないものが、まるで液体のごとく動き続ける

例文

カレン：今日は車の流れが信じられないくらいスムーズね。

健太：そうだね。日曜だからね。

- - - - - - - - - - - - - - -

(a) 店に入ってくる人々の流れは、とどまるところを知らなかった。

(b) 時間の長さそのものは誰にとっても平等だが、時間の流れの感じ方は人によって違う。

解説

「流れ」も *flow* も、液体の連続的な一方向への動きを表す。(1a)-(1e)は日本語の「流れ」に対応する英語の {*flow/stream/current*} がどのように比喩的に使われているかを示す。

(1) a. 人の流れ　{*flow/stream/current*} of people

　　b. 意識の流れ　{*flow/stream/* ×*current*} of consciousness

249

In Japanese, the Sino-Japanese compounds formed with ~*ryū* can be used in addition to *nagare*, as shown in (2). In English, there are some cases where only *stream* can be used.

📖➡解説(2)(3)

R̲E̲L̲

As shown in the above examples, there are two RELs: *stream* and *current*. The basic meaning of *stream* is "a continuous unidirectional movement of {liquid/gas/light}," while *current* means "a continuous unidirectional movement of {water/air/electricity}."

📖➡解説(1)(2)(3)

flower of ~, the / n. phr. / personification

s.o. who is the center of attention; s.o. on whom others place the hopes of the group

R̲E̲L̲ ~ star

【Examples】

(a) Beautiful and smart, she has always been the flower of society.

(b) In our acting troupe, she's the flower of the flock. But she can be a bit selfish sometimes.

R̲E̲L̲

The English has the REL ~ *star*. Like the main entry, this can be translated as ~ *no hana(gata)*.

(1) Babe Ruth was an American baseball star.

ベーブ・ルースは、アメリカ野球界の花形選手だった。

follow / v. / metaphor

to understand s.t.

【Examples】

Colleague: I can never seem to follow our department chief's train of thought. I wonder what's going on inside his head?

Mike: He always acts on instinct. He simply doesn't think.

- - - - - - - - - - - - - - - - - - -

(a) I couldn't follow my Japanese teacher's grammar explanation.

(b) I couldn't follow his talk very well because I knew nothing about Japanese history.

【Notes】

1. Both the English and Japanese are usually used in the negative form, as shown in the examples.

2. When *follow* is used to mean "obey," the corresponding Japanese verb is not *tsuite-iku*, but *shitagau*. 📖➡解説(1)

250

c. 光の流れ　{flow/stream/[×]current} of light

d. 時代の流れ　{flow/current/[×]stream} of the times

e. 歩行者の流れ　{flow/stream/[×]current} of pedestrians

ただし、(2)のように和語の「流れ」も、漢語の「〜流」も使える場合がある。また、英語には(3)のように stream 以外は使えない場合もある。

(2) 電気の流れ，電流　flow of electricity（electric current ともいう）

(3) 車の流れ　a {stream/[×]flow/[×]current} of cars

関連語

英語の見出し flow の関連表現は二つある。一つは stream で、基本義は"液体、ガス、光の連続的な一方向性の動き"、もう一つは current で、基本義は"水、空気、電気の連続的な一方向性の動き"である。📖➡解説(1)(2)(3)

〜の花（形）　n. phr.　擬人化
はな　がた　　　　　　　　　ぎじんか

あるグループの中で華やかで目立つ{人 / もの}
なか　　はな　　　め　だ　ひと

例 文

(a) 彼女は美しく、頭もよく、いつも社交界の花形だ。
かのじょ　うつく　　あたま　　　　　　　　しゃこうかい　はながた

(b) 彼女は、私達劇団の花形的存在だが、ちょっとわがままなので困る。
かのじょ　わたしたちげきだん　はながたてきそんざい　　　　　　　　　　こま

関連語

英語には ~ star という関連表現がある。その場合も日本語では「〜の花（形）」と言える。

➡📖 REL(1)

（〜に）ついていく　phr.　隠喩
だれ　　　　　　　　　　　　いんゆ

誰かの考えや説明を理解して受け入れる
だれ　　かんが　　せつめい　りかい　　う　い

例 文

同僚：まったく、うちの課長にはついていけないよ。何考えてんだろう。
どうりょう　　　　　　　かちょう　　　　　　　　　　　　なにかんが

マイク：いつも本能に従って行動してるんだよ。考えるなんてしてないさ。
ほんのう　したが　こうどう　　　　　　かんが

(a) 僕は日本語の先生の文法の説明についていけなかった。
ぼく　にほんご　せんせい　ぶんぽう　せつめい

(b) 日本の歴史を全然知らないので、彼の講演についていけなかった。
にほん　れきし　ぜんぜんし　　　　　　　かれ　こうえん

解 説

1. 日英語とも例文のように、普通は否定形で使われる。

2. follow が"従う"という意味のときは、日本語では「ついていく」ではなく「従う」を使う。

(1) a. 私は父の忠告に{従わない/[×]ついていかない}で、小説家になった。
　　I didn't follow my father's advice. I became a novelist.

　 b. 彼はキリストの教えに{従っている/[×]ついていく}クリスチャンだ。
　　He is a Christian who follows the teachings of Christ.

251

follow one's heart / phr. / metaphor

to act according to one's true feelings

Examples

(a) If she had followed her heart for once instead of her head, maybe none of this would have happened.

(b) In 1994, he followed his heart and traveled to London after being accepted into the Royal Academy of Dramatic Art.

(c) Though many of my friends did not understand my decision to pass up a career in golf, I knew I was following my heart.

Notes

1. The Japanese specifically refers to *kokoro no koe* (voice inside one's heart), unlike the English. However, English does have the expression *listen to the voice inside one's heart*.

(1) I often wonder whether to listen to the voice inside my heart or the voices of others. I choose the voice inside my heart every time.
私はよく心の声を聞くべきか、周りの声を聞くべきか迷いますが、いつも正解は心の声です。

2. The Japanese is used almost exclusively in written Japanese, but the English can be used in both spoken and written language.

{follow/walk} the same path as ~ / phr. / metaphor

to choose the same way of life as s.o. else

REL follow in s.o.'s footsteps

Examples

(a) Takuya walked the same path as his father, a mathematician.

(b) Those born into the families of *kabuki* or *noh* actors tend to follow the same path as their fathers and grandfathers.

Note

Path and *michi* (path) share the same metaphorical meaning of "one's course in life."

REL

The English REL, *follow in s.o.'s footsteps*, has the same metaphorical meaning as *{follow/walk} the same path as ~* and is used more frequently.

(1) I followed in my father's footsteps and went to Princeton.
私は父と同じ道を歩んでプリンストン大学に入った。

forbidden fruit / comp. n. / metaphor

{s.t./s.o.} pleasurable that is regarded as {immoral/dangerous}

Examples

(a) Her close friend's boyfriend is forbidden fruit.

(b) Because he suffers from gout, beer is a forbidden fruit for him.

心の声に従う / phr. / 隠喩

自分の気持ちに従って、正直に行動する

例文

(a) 彼女がもし自分の頭ではなく、一度だけでも自分の心の声に従っていたら、おそらくこのようなことは何一つ起きなかっただろう。

(b) 1994年に王立演劇アカデミーに受け入れられたとき、彼は心の声に従ってロンドンへ行ったのであった。

(c) 友人の多くは僕がゴルフの道を捨てる決心をしたことを理解できなかったが、僕としては自分の心に従ったまでだ。

解説

1. 日本語は「心の声」とはっきり言っているが、英語はただ *heart*(心)と言っている。ただし、英語でも *listen to the voice inside one's heart* と言うことは可能である。 → Note(1)

2. 日本語はほとんど書き言葉に限られているが、英語は話し言葉、書き言葉の両方で使える。

F

(〜と)同じ道を歩む / phr. / 隠喩

誰かと同じ生き方を選ぶ

例文

(a) 卓也は数学者だった父親と同じ道を歩んだ。

(b) 歌舞伎や能などの伝統芸能の家庭に生まれた人たちは、たいてい父親や祖父と同じ道を歩むものだ。

解説

英語の名詞 *path* と日本語の名詞「道」はどちらも"人生の進む道"という比喩を共有している。

関連語

英語は {follow/walk} the same path as 〜 と同じ比喩の意味を持っている *follow in s.o.'s footsteps* という、より使用頻度の高い関連表現がある。 → REL(1)

禁断の果実 / n. phr. / 隠喩

固く禁じられているが、非常に{魅力的/誘惑的}な{もの/人}

関 禁断の木の実

例文

(a) 彼女にとって親友の彼氏は禁断の果実だ。

(b) 痛風持ちの彼にとって、ビールはまさに禁断の果実だ。

253

Note

Both the English and Japanese come from the Bible (Old Testament, Genesis 2:16-17): "You may eat the fruit of any tree in the garden, except the tree that gives knowledge of what is good and what is bad. You must not eat the fruit of that tree; if you do, you will die the same day." This expression is used much more commonly in English than in Japanese.

REL

In Japanese, *kindan no konomi* is used in addition to *kindan no kajitsu*. But the latter is used much more frequently than the former.

(as) free as a bird   /phr.   /simile
able to do as one pleases

Examples

(a) Whenever I race down the ski slope, I feel as free as a bird.

(b) I spent last month traveling around the world. It was amazing! I felt free as a bird.

from head to toe   /phr.   /synecdoche
the entire body

REL from head to {foot/heel}; from top to toe

Examples

(a) I heard that Kashmiri women must be covered from head to toe.

(b) Her whole body quivered with excitement from head to toe.

Note

Both the English and Japanese can be considered examples of synecdoche in that they describe the entire body by referring to the top and bottom parts only. However, given that the expressions can be interpreted almost literally, they are not very figurative.

REL

The RELs *from head to {foot/heel}* and *from top to toe* can replace the more common *from head to toe*.

(1) She was dressed in purple from {head to {foot/heel} /top to toe}.

from the bottom of one's heart   /phr.   /metaphor
with genuine feeling

Examples

Saya: Kenta, these are the lecture notes from the class you skipped.

Kenta: Thanks, you're a lifesaver! I owe you one.

Saya: Really? Do you mean that from the bottom of your heart?

Kenta: Of course!

解説

日英語ともに聖書(旧約聖書の創世記2：16-17)が出典である。「あなたは園のどの木からでも心のままに取って食べてよろしい。しかし、善悪を知る木からは取って食べてはならない。それを取って食べるときっと死ぬだろう。」英語で使われる使用頻度のほうが日本語よりはるかに高い。

関連語

日本語では見出しのほかに、「禁断の木の実」という関連表現もある。しかし、前者の方が使用頻度ははるかに高い。

鳥のように自由
とり　　　　　じゆう
phr.　直喩
ちょくゆ

自分の思うままに行動できる
じ ぶん　おも　　　　　こうどう

例文

(a) スキー場で競いながらすいすいと滑降していくときは、いつでも鳥のように自由
　　じょう　きそ　　　　　　　　　　　かっこう　　　　　　　　　　　とり　　　　じ ゆう
　　な気分です。
　　　き ぶん

(b) 先月は世界一周旅行に出かけた。すばらしかった。鳥のように自由な気持ちだった。
　　せんげつ　せ かいいっしゅうりょこう　で　　　　　　　　　　　　　　とり　　　じ ゆう　 き も

頭のてっぺんから爪先まで
あたま　　　　　　　　つまさき
phr.　提喩
ていゆ

全身
ぜんしん

例文

(a) カシミールの女性は、頭のてっぺんから爪先まで布で覆っていなければならない
　　　　　　　　じょせい　あたま　　　　　　　つまさき　ぬの　おお
　　そうだ。

(b) 彼女は体全体、頭のてっぺんから爪先まで、興奮で震えた。
　　かのじょ　からだぜんたい　あたま　　　　　　　つまさき　こうふん　ふる

解説

日英語とも体の両端を使って体全体を表す提喩の一種だと思われるが、ほとんど字義通りの解釈に近いので、比喩性は低い。

関連語

英語の関連表現は *from head to {foot/heel}* と *from top to toe* であり、見出しの *from head to toe* と置き換えることができるが、見出しが一番、使用頻度が高い。　📖**REL(1)**

心の底から
こころ　そこ
phr.　隠喩
いんゆ

真実の気持ちで
しんじつ　き も

関　心底
しんそこ

例文

さや：健太、これ、この間、あなたが休んだときの講義ノート。
　　　けん た　　　　　　あいだ　　　　　　やす　　　　　　こうぎ

健太：お、サンキュ！　助かるなあ。恩に着るよ。
けん た　　　　　　　　　たす　　　　　おん　き

さや：ほんとかな。心の底からそう思ってる？
　　　　　　　　　こころ そこ　　　　　おも

健太：思ってるよ。
けん た　おも

255

(a) My mother thanked the man from the bottom of her heart for saving her cat's life.

(b) I would like to take this opportunity to express my appreciation from the bottom of my heart.

RELL

Japanese has the expression *shin-soko* in addition to *kokoro no soko kara*. 📖→解説(1)

full of ~; ~ is full phr. / metonomy

to be filled with ~

REL LOOK fill (s.t. with)

Examples

Kenta: Huh? Is that all you're gonna eat? Are you full?

Saya: No, my heart's full, 'cause I finally met the man of my dreams.

Kenta: Really?! Who? Who?!

Saya: It's a secret.

(a) After I heard the news, I was full of joy.

(b) You're full of energy. Your eyes and face are shining.

(c) This summer I'm going to Japan for the first time. My mind is full of anticipation.

Note

Onaka/stomach, *mune/heart*, *jinsē/life*, *shintai/body*, and so on can be considered containers in a figurative sense. This expression describes these "containers" as being full of something.

RELL

The English REL, *fill (s.t. with)*, is the causative form of *full of ~/~ is full*.

(1) We filled the vase with beautiful roses.

私達は花びんにきれいなバラをいっぱい差した。

future {looks/is} black / phr. / metaphor

the prospects for the future are predicted to become worse

REL future {looks/is} {bleak/dark}

Examples

(a) The future looked black for Bill after he dropped out of school.

(b) The company's financial future looks black, so new employees could be fired at any time.

Note

The Japanese adjective *kurai* means "dark," not "black," although they share the same stem, *kur-*. *Kuroi* (black) cannot replace *kurai*, but *dark* (*kurai*) can replace *black*.

(a) 母は、猫の命を救ってくれた男性に心の底からお礼を言った。

(b) この機会に心の底からお礼を申し上げたいと存じます。

関連語

日本語には「心の底から」と並んで、「心底」という関連表現もある。

(1) その作家は妻の後を追って自殺したそうだ。{心の底から/心底}妻を愛していたのだろう。
They say that the writer killed himself just after his wife died. He must have loved her from the bottom of his heart.

{〜が/で}いっぱい　phr.　換喩

{〜が/で}満たされている

例 文

健太：あれ、もう食べないの。お腹、いっぱい？

さや：ううん、胸がいっぱいなの。ついにあこがれの人に会えたから。

健太：へえ、誰、誰？

さや：内緒。

(a) そのニュースを聞いて、喜びでいっぱいになった。

(b) 君は元気いっぱいだ。目も顔も輝いている。

(c) この夏ははじめて日本に行くので期待でいっぱいです。

解 説

「おなか」/ stomach、「胸」/ heart、「人生」/ life、「身体」/ body などは、比喩的な容器とみなされていて、その中に何かがたくさん詰まっている状態を示す。

関連語

英語には fill (s.t. with)(lit. 何かでいっぱいにする)という見出しの使役形がある。

→📖 REL (1)

(将来の)見通しが暗い　phr.　隠喩

将来に向かって状態が悪化すると予測される

例 文

(a) 学校を中退してから、ビルの将来の見通しは暗かった。

(b) 会社の業績見通しが暗いため、新入社員はいつ首を切られるかわからない。

解 説

日本語の「暗い」は「黒い」と語幹の kur- を共有しているが、英語の black には対応していない。日本語では「黒い」は使えないが、英語では dark が black の代わりに使える。

Ⓡ Ⓔ Ⓛ

Black in the English can be replaced by *bleak* or *dark*. *Bleak* is most frequently used.

(1) Due to the decreasing birthrate and the aging population, that country's future {looks/is} {black/bleak/dark}.

少子高齢化のために、その国の将来は暗くなってきている。

future {looks/is} bright / phr. / metaphor

to have high potential to success in the future

Examples

(a) He's smart, got into a good university, is a great speaker, and gets along well with people. His future is very bright.

(b) I would say that the future of their country looks bright, because the college students I teach have great potential and strong pride in their country.

(c) The economy has been improving, and the employment rate has improved as well. The future is looking bright.

gather dust / phr. / metaphor

for s.t. to be left alone for an extended period of time without being used

Examples

(a) In one of the rooms of that bankrupt firm, there are a bunch of old documents just gathering dust.

(b) I haven't been playing tennis recently, so my racket's just been gathering dust.

Notes

1. While both the English and Japanese can be interpreted literally, the focus is on the fact that something has not been used for a long time.

2. *Kaburu* means "to cover one's head with s.t.," but figuratively it can also mean "for {s.o./ s.t.} to be completely covered by {water/dust/flour/etc.}." By contrast, *gather* means "to bring {s.o./s.t.} together in a single place."

Ⓡ Ⓔ Ⓛ

The Japanese REL, *okura-iri*, means "for s.t. to be placed in storage." The crucial difference is that *hokori o kaburu* implies something visible remaining unused for a long time, whereas *okura-iri* indicates that something has been intentionally shelved by someone and placed out of sight. Therefore, *hokori o kaburu* cannot be replaced by *okura-iri* in any of the above examples. 📖→ 関連語(1)

Likewise, *okura-iri* cannot be replaced by *hokori o kaburu*. 📖→ 関連語(2)

関連語

英語の *black* は *bleak*（きびしい）か *dark*（暗い）で置き換えられるが、*bleak* の使用頻度が一番高い。

将来が明るい　／ phr.　隠喩

将来成功する可能性が高い

例文

(a) 彼は頭がいいし、いい大学に入ったし、弁が立つし、人との付き合いもいいし、彼の将来はとても明るいね。

(b) 彼らの国の将来は明るいと思う。なぜなら、僕が教えている学生たちはすばらしい可能性を持っているし、自分たちの国に誇りを持っているから。

(c) 経済が上向きになって、就職率もよくなった。将来の見通しも明るくなってきた。

ほこりをかぶる　／ phr.　隠喩

長い間使われていない

関 お蔵入り

例文

(a) 倒産した企業の一室には、今も、当時の書類がほこりをかぶったまま放置されている。

(b) 最近、テニスから遠ざかって、ラケットはすっかりほこりをかぶったままだ。

解説

1. どの例文も字義通りの解釈もできるが、意味の焦点は「長い間何かが使われていない」というところにある。

2. 英語で使われている動詞の *gather* は "{誰か / 何か} を同じところに {持ってくる / 連れてくる}" という意味であるのに対して、日本語の「かぶる」はもともとは "頭を覆うものをつける" という意味から "{水 / ほこり / 粉} などを頭から浴びる" という比喩的な意味になっている。

関連語

日本語には「お蔵入り」という関連表現がある。大きな違いは、「ほこりをかぶる」は使わなくなったものがたいてい見える状態で、字義通りほこりをかぶっているのに対して、「お蔵入り」は使わなくなったものが蔵という別の建物に意図的に入れられ、人目につかない状態であるという点である。したがって、「ほこりをかぶる」は「お蔵入り」で置き換えることはできない。

(1) 今は音楽も映像もデジタル配信が普通だよ。どうしてこんな CD や DVD を持っているんだい？{ほこりをかぶっている/ ×お蔵入り} じゃないか。

You know that digital distribution for music and movies is the norm now, right? Why do you have so many CDs and DVDs? They're just gathering dust.

一方、「お蔵入り」も「ほこりをかぶる」では置き換えられない。

259

homograph

get burned (by s.o.) / phr. / metaphor

to be scammed by s.o.
だまされる

Example

I got burned by the car salesman and ended up with a hunk of junk.
セールスマンに騙されて、ひどい車をつかまされた。

get egg all over one's face / phr. / metaphor

to be embarrassed

Examples

(a) He decided to shoplift on the spur of the moment and got caught by the police. Thanks to him, his parents have gotten egg all over their face.

(b) My colleague spread a false rumor about my divorce. Now I've gotten egg all over my face.

(c) His political opponents eviscerated his reputation. He's really got egg on his face!

Notes

1. The English and Japanese expressions are very close figuratively, but the difference between the two is that, while the English is used in the passive voice, the Japanese can also be used in the active voice. 📖➡解説(1)

2. The English has the person getting *(raw) egg* smeared all over his/her face, whereas the Japanese uses *doro* (mud).

get one's foot in the door / phr. / metaphor

to gain access to an organization or field

Examples

Mr. S: Saya, congratulations on the job offer. It's great that you got hired by the company you wanted to work at most.

Saya: Thank you.

Mr. S: Now that you've graduated, you can finally get your foot in the door of a new world. Do your best.

(2) せっかく準備したプロジェクトも、上司の独断で{お蔵入りになって/*ほこりをかぶって}しまった。

The project we spent so much time preparing was shelved because of an arbitrary decision by our boss.

同形異義語

やけどする / phr. / 隠喩（いんゆ）

何（なに）か失敗（しっぱい）をして、ひどい目にあう
to fail at s.t. and get into trouble

例文

ギャンブルに手（て）を出（だ）して、大（おお）やけどをしてしまった。今日（きょう）から、一文無（いちもんな）しだ。
I started gambling and got myself into big trouble. Now I don't have a penny to my name.

G

顔（かお）に泥（どろ）を塗（ぬ）る / phr. / 隠喩（いんゆ）

恥（はじ）をかかせる

関 **LOOK** {自尊心（じそんしん）/ プライド} を傷（きず）つける

例文

(a) 彼（かれ）はつい出来心（できごころ）で万引（まんび）きをして警察（けいさつ）に捕（つか）まり、両親（りょうしん）の顔（かお）に泥（どろ）を塗（ぬ）ってしまった。
(b) 同僚（どうりょう）が僕（ぼく）の離婚（りこん）について虚偽（きょぎ）の噂（うわさ）を広（ひろ）めた。僕（ぼく）は顔（かお）に泥（どろ）を塗（ぬ）られてしまった。
(c) 政敵（せいてき）たちは彼（かれ）の性格（せいかく）をあくどく攻撃（こうげき）した。彼（かれ）は顔（かお）に泥（どろ）を塗（ぬ）られたのだ！

解説

1. 日英語（にちえいご）とも比喩（ひゆ）の意味（いみ）は大変（たいへん）近（ちか）いが、英語（えいご）は受（う）け身文的（みぶんてき）な意味（いみ）で使（つか）われ、日本語（にほんご）は能動文（のうどうぶん）でも使（つか）える点（てん）が違（ちが）っている。
(1) あいつ、俺（おれ）の顔（かお）に泥（どろ）を塗（ぬ）りやがって。(lit. *That guy put mud all over my face!)
2. 「塗（ぬ）る」ものが日本語（にほんご）では「泥（どろ）」で、英語（えいご）では「たまご（生卵）（なまたまご）」である。

足（あし）を踏（ふ）み入（い）れる / phr. / 隠喩（いんゆ）

新（あたら）しい{世界（せかい）/ 分野（ぶんや）}に入（はい）り込（こ）む

例文

鈴木（夫）（すずき おっと）：さやさん、就職（しゅうしょく）おめでとう。思（おも）い通（どお）りの会社（かいしゃ）に入（はい）れてよかったね。
さや：はい、ありがとうございます。

鈴木（夫）（すずき おっと）：学生（がくせい）を卒業（そつぎょう）して、これから、新（あたら）しい世界（せかい）に足（あし）を踏（ふ）み入（い）れるんだね。がんばってください。

261

(a) The wine party I attended the other day helped me get my foot in the door of an exclusive wine-tasting club.

(b) Ever since she got her foot in the door of the show business world at the age of 18, she has been one of its most prominent stars.

Notes

1. The English is specific about the location of one's foot (i.e. in the door), but the Japanese is not.

2. The Japanese can be used in both negative and positive situations, but the English phrase can only be used in positive situations, as shown in the example sentences.

(1) He {entered/ˣgot his foot in the door of} the evil world of gambling.
彼はギャンブルのような悪の世界に{足を踏み入れた/入った}。

get one's hands on ~　/ phr.　metonymy

to gain possession of s.t.

Examples

Mike: Whoa, this car is amazing!

Colleague: I really had to save up to get my hands on this.

Mike: The next order of business is getting your hands on a girlfriend.

Colleague: Exactly.

- - - - - - - - - - - - - - - - - - -

(a) I got my hands on a brand-new computer, but I can't figure out how to use the new features at all.

(b) I love watch design, and I've read every watch-related publication I can get my hands on.

Note

Both the English and Japanese share the same figurative meaning. However, the English means "to put one's hands on s.t.," while the Japanese means "to put s.t. into one's hands." The manner in which one obtains the object is different.

get on s.o.'s nerves　/ phr.　metaphor

to irritate s.o.

REL　get under s.o.'s skin

Examples

Mrs. S: You look really upset, Mike. What happened?

Mike: I had a run-in with Mr. Tanaka again. The way he talks really gets on my nerves.

- - - - - - - - - - - - - - - - - - -

(a) The sound of pieces of glass being scraped against each other really gets on people's nerves.

(b) Has it ever occurred to you that the way you do things sometimes gets on his nerves?

(a) この間出たワイン・パーティのおかげで、私は特別なワイン・テースティングの
クラブに足を踏み入れた。

(b) 彼女は18歳のとき芸能界に足を踏み入れてから、ずっと第一線を走っている。

解説

1. 英語は「足を踏み入れる」場所を *door*(ドア)と特定しているが、日本語では特定していない。

2. 日本語は肯定的な場所だけではなく、否定的な場所に入る場合も使えるが、英語は肯定的な場所に入る場合に限られる。 ━📖 Note(1)

(〜を)手に入れる　*phr.*　換喩

何かを自分の持ち物にする

例文

マイク： すごい車に乗ってるね。

同僚：飲まず食わずで手に入れたんだ。

マイク： じゃ、次はガールフレンドを手に入れるんだね。

同僚：そういうこと。

- -

(a) 新しいコンピュータを手に入れたんだけど、最新の機能の使い方がどうもわからない。

(b) 時計のデザインが大好きで、時計関係の出版物はすべて手に入れて読んでいます。

解説

日英語ともに比喩的意味は同じであるが、日本語は"物を手の中に入れる"という動作を表し、英語は日本語と違って"物の上に手を置く"という仕方で持ち物にする点が異なる。

神経に障る　*phr.*　隠喩

何かがひどく気持ちをいら立たせる

関 神経を逆なでする

例文

鈴木(妻)：マイク、なんだか、ずいぶん腹を立ててるようじゃない。

マイク： ええ、今日、また田中課長とやっちゃったんですけどね。彼の物の言い方、本当に神経に障るんですよ。

- -

(a) ガラスの破片をこすり合わせるような音は、神経に障って気持ちが悪いものだ。

(b) お前のやり方が彼の神経に障るなんてこと、考えたことあるのか。

(c) He just wasn't my type. Even the way he used his utensils got on my nerves.

Note

The English and Japanese use different verbs. The English uses the verb phrase *get on*, while the Japanese uses *sawaru* (to touch). Note that the *kanji* used for *sawaru* is 障る (to {hinder/interfere}), which in this context means "for s.t. to touch s.t. else and result in s.t. bad."

REL

The figuratively vivid descriptive *get under s.o.'s skin* can replace *get on s.o.'s nerves*, as shown below. Likewise, the Japanese REL, *shinkē o sakanade-suru* (lit. "rub the nerves in the wrong direction"), can replace *shinkē ni sawaru*, but the former has a more negative meaning.

(1) The sound of pieces of glass being scraped against each other really gets {on people's nerves/under people's skin}. (→(a))
ガラスの破片をこすり合わせるような音は、神経{に障る/を逆なでする}。(→(a))

get on the bandwagon / phr. / metaphor

to {follow/support} s.t. popular or successful

REL {hop/climb} on the bandwagon

Examples

(a) Countries all over the world have gotten on the outsourcing bandwagon and are seeking countries with low wages.

(b) That company has adopted the latest accounting system and gotten on the technology bandwagon.

(c) Those who thought they could succeed by getting on the dot-com bandwagon lost a lot of money when the bubble burst.

Note

The English has another meaning: "to join an influential movement," as shown in (1). This meaning is missing in the Japanese.

(1) In the aftermath of the indiscriminate terrorist attack, a lot of people got on the "war on terror" bandwagon.
その無差別テロ攻撃以来、大勢の人々が反テロの戦いという{運動に加わろう/ˣ勝ち馬に乗ろう}とした。

REL

Get can be replaced by verbs such as *hop* and *climb*, though *climb* is not used as often as the others.

get out of hand / phr. / metaphor

to become very hard to control; to be able to do nothing about a given situation

Examples

Saya: I have to babysit my sister's children today. I hate looking after them.

Karen: But why? They're your nephews!

Saya: They get so out of hand because they have no discipline. It's like they're not even my own nephews.

(c) 彼って私の好きなタイプじゃなかったの。箸の上げ下ろしさえ、神経に障ってさ。

解説

日英語で動詞が違う。日本語は「さわる」（漢字表記は「障る」）で、基本義は"何かが何かにさわって悪いことが起きる"である。英語の *get on* は"上に乗る"という意味である。

関連語

英語には *get under s.o.'s skin*（lit. 皮膚の下に入る）という、より描写的な比喩表現があり、*get on s.o.'s nerves* の代わりに使える。日本語では関連表現として「神経を逆なでする」がある。「神経に障る」より否定的な意味が強いが、見出しと置き換えられる。 📖REL(1)

勝ち馬に乗る /phr. 隠喩

調子がいいもの、うまくいっているものの側について、自分も利を得る

例文

(a) 世界の国々はより賃金の低い国を求めて、アウトソーシングという勝ち馬に乗ろうとしている。

(b) あの企業は最新の会計システムを取り入れ、テクノロジーという勝ち馬に乗った。

(c) ネットビジネスという勝ち馬に乗ったつもりだった人々は、ネット関連株の暴落で、多くの資産を失った。

解説

英語は日本語にはない「強力な運動に加わる」というもう一つの意味を持っている。

📖Note(1)

関連語

英語の動詞 *get* は *hop* や *climb* に置き換えができる。しかし、*climb* はほかの動詞ほど使用頻度が高くない。

手に負えない /phr. 隠喩

コントロールをすることが難しい，今の状況に関して自分の力では何もできない

関 手に余る

例文

さや：今日は姉の子供達のベビーシッターをしなくちゃ。いやだな。

カレン：あら、どうして、甥っ子でしょ。

さや：すっごくしつけが悪くて手に負えないのよ。わたしの甥とは思えないわ。

265

(a) Lately his pranks have gotten out of hand.

(b) Apparently the radiation leaks caused by the nuclear meltdown are getting out of hand.

Note

Whereas the English expresses a lack of control by stating that "one's hand cannot control the situation any longer," the Japanese does so by saying "one's hand cannot carry s.t." Nevertheless, both express the same metaphorical concept.

REL

The Japanese REL, *te ni amaru* (lit. "s.t. is more than a hand can handle"), can replace the main entry when the speaker is adversely affected by a situation. Therefore, this substitution is possible in Example (a) since the speaker himself is affected by his heavy drinking, but not in Example (b). 関連語 **(1)(2)**

---

get the (whole) picture phr. metaphor

to understand the most important facts about s.t.

Examples

(a) After reading her thesis, I got the whole picture of what she was trying to say.

(b) In just two days, we got the whole picture of what marketing is about.

Note

Zentai-zō is a Sino-Japanese compound that consists of *zentai* (whole) and *zō* (icon). Note the difference between *zō* and *picture*.

{get/put} one's thoughts together phr. metaphor

to organize one's thoughts

REL {gather/collect} one's thoughts

Examples

Friend: Have you started writing your thesis?

Saya: Not yet. I know I have to get started, but it takes a long time for me to put my thoughts together.

- -

(a) I asked him to leave me alone for a few minutes so that I could get my thoughts together.

(b) We're trying to get our thoughts together for a paper related to our project.

Note

Both *{get/put} s.t. together* and *matomeru* mean "to gather together discrete objects."

REL

Gather one's thoughts is similar in meaning to the main entry. *Collect one's thoughts*, on the other hand, implies regaining one's composure after a period of turbulence or distress.

(1) It's taken me a while to {{get/put} my thoughts together/{gather/collect} my thoughts}

(a) 彼の悪ふざけはこのごろ手に負えなくなってきた。

(b) 原発事故による放射能漏れは手に負えなくなっているようだ。

解説

英語は"手がもはや状況を制御できない"という意味、つまり"制御不能"ということを意味するのに対して、日本語は"手で何かを運べない"ということを意味する。日英語とも"制御できない"ということを表現している点で同じ比喩である。

関連語

日本語の「手に余る」は、話し手が直接被害にあっている場合に、「手に負えない」の代わりに使える。したがって、(a)は話し手が被害者だから置き換えることができるが、(b)では話し手が被害者ではないから置き換えることができない。

(1) 彼の悪ふざけはこのごろ手に{負えなく / 余るように}なってきた。(→(a))

(2) 原発事故による放射能漏れは手に{負えなく /×余るように}なっているようだ。(→(b))

全体像をつかむ / phr. 隠喩

全体を理解する

例文

(a) 彼女の論文を読んで、彼女が言わんとすることの全体像をつかんだ。

(b) 私達は、たった二日でマーケティングの全体像をつかむことができた。

解説

日本語の「全体像」は「全体」+「像」の漢語系複合名詞であり、「像」は英語の *icon* に当たるので、英語の *picture* と多少異なる。

考えをまとめる / phr. 隠喩

いろいろな意見や考えを一つにする

例文

友達：卒論、もう手をつけた？

さや：ううん、まだ。もう、始めなきゃいけないんだけど、考えをまとめるのに時間がかかって。

(a) 考えをまとめるまで2、3分ほっといてくれるように彼に頼んだのよ。

(b) われわれはプロジェクトに関する論文のために考えをまとめようと努めています。

解説

日本語の「まとめる」も英語の *{get/put} s.t. together* も"個々のものを一つにくくる"という意味である。

関連語

英語の *gather one's thoughts* は見出しと意味が同じで置き換えることができる。*collect one's thoughts* は、"混乱、苦悩があった後落ち着きを取り戻す"という意味がある。 📖 REL(1)

regarding this problem.
この質問に関する考えをまとめるのにしばらく時間がかかった。

get to the core of ~   phr.   metaphor

to reach the most important point

REL   reach the core of ~

ANT   LOOK scratch the surface

Examples

(a) The detectives' step-by-step investigation is getting them close to the core of the case.

(b) His book introduces research that gets to the core of what Van Gogh's paintings are about.

(c) We need to get to the core of what this bill is about.

Note

There is some semantic difference between *get to* and *semaru* (to approach), but the metaphorical meanings are the same.

REL

The English REL, *reach the core of ~*, is more formal than *get to the core of ~*. The Japanese REL is *kakushin o tsuku*. It should be noted that the verb *tsuku* (to reach) is much more forceful in meaning than *semaru* (to draw near). 📖 関連語(1)

{get/be} tongue-tied   phr.   metonymy

to be unable to speak due to {stress/confusion}

Examples

(a) I get nervous and tongue-tied whenever I'm in front of people.

(b) When I got into a traffic accident and called the police, I was tongue-tied and couldn't explain the situation well.

(c) After he suffered a stroke, he would often get tongue-tied when trying to speak.

Note

Just as non-verbal gestures and actions often indicate a state of mind, a tongue-tied state indicates that one cannot speak well. Such simultaneity between the physical and the psychological is an example of metonymy.

（〜の）核心に迫る / **phr.** 隠喩

最も重要な部分に近づく

関 核心を突く

反 **LOOK▶** 表面をなぞる

例文
(a) 刑事達の地道な捜査が、事件の核心に迫ろうとしている。
(b) 彼の本はゴッホ絵画の核心に迫る研究を紹介している。
(c) 今度の法案については、もっと核心に迫る論議をする必要がある。

解説
「迫る」と *get to*（着く）の意味は多少異なるが、比喩的意味は同じである。

関連語
英語には *reach the core of* ~ という関連表現があり、*get to the core of* ~ よりフォーマルである。「核心を突く」は日本語の「核心に迫る」の関連表現であるが、「突く」という動詞は見出しの動詞「迫る」より意味が強い。

(1) 彼の言葉は人生の核心{に迫って / を突いて}いる。
His words {get to/reach} the core of human existence.

舌がもつれる / **phr.** 換喩

{緊張 / 動揺 / 病気}などのためにうまく話せない

例文
(a) 人前に出ると、緊張して舌がもつれてうまく話せない。
(b) 交通事故に遭って警察に電話した時、舌がもつれてしまって、ちゃんと状況を説明できなかった。
(c) 彼は脳卒中になってから舌がもつれるようになった。

解説
通常、身振りや動作が心理状態を示すように、舌がもつれる状態はよく話せないことを示す。このような肉体と心理の間の同時性は換喩の例になる。

269

homograph

{get/have} cold feet / phr. / metaphor

to lose the courage to do s.t.
躊躇する, ためらう, たじろぐ
_{ちゅうちょ}

Example

Mary was supposed to give a speech to her entire class, but she got cold feet and couldn't do it.
メアリーはクラス全体にスピーチをするはずだったのだが、おじけづいてしまって、できなかった。
_{ぜんたい}

{get/have} goose bumps / phr. / metonymy

to be so {afraid/cold} that one's skin feels bumpy

Examples

Karen: I got so scared when that car bumped into us.

Saya: Yeah, I got goose bumps all over my body and I couldn't stop shaking. I'm so glad neither of us got injured!

(a) I got goose bumps when I saw a big snake in my backyard.

(b) This book was spine-tingling. I got so immersed in the story that I literally had goose bumps right up until the last page.

Note

The Japanese is normally used only when someone is terrified, but the English can be used when someone is terrified, as in Example (a), or excited, as demonstrated below.

(1) The night we won the baseball tournament, I got goose bumps and couldn't sleep.
野球大会で優勝した夜、{すっかり興奮して/*鳥肌が立って}、なかなか眠れなかった。
Recently, however, the Japanese has also begun to be used to indicate excitement as well. 📖→ 解説(2)

give s.o. a hand ((～に)手を貸す) → {lend (s.o.)/give s.o.} a hand
_て _か

give s.t. to {s.o./s.t.} / phr. / metaphor

for {s.o./s.t.} to provide s.t. that impacts {s.o./s.t.} else

Examples

(a) The American professor is popular with her students because she gives them many opportunities to ask her questions.

(b) He likes to give advice to everybody.

(c) The doctor gave him permission to travel.

(d) Knowing something about the author gives depth to their works.

同形異義語

足が凍りつく / phr. / 隠喩

こわくて先に進めない
to get too scared to do s.t.

例文

バンジージャンプに挑戦しようとしたが、下を見たら足が凍りついて、飛び下りることができなかった。

I tried to go bungie jumping, but when I looked down, I got too scared to jump.

鳥肌が立つ / phr. / 換喩

あまりに{怖くて / 寒くて}肌に(実際に)ぶつぶつができるような感じだ

例文

カレン：突然、車がぶつかってきたときは、ほんとびっくりしたね。

さや：うん、全身鳥肌が立って、しばらく震えがとまらなかったよね。二人とも怪我がなくて、ほんとによかったね。

- -

(a) 裏庭で大きな蛇を見たときには、鳥肌が立った。

(b) この本を読んで背筋がぞっとした。話にはまってしまって、最終章を読み終わるまでに文字通り鳥肌が立ちっぱなしだった。

解説

日本語では主に恐怖を感じたときに使われるが、英語では(a)のように誰かが怖いときにも、(1)のようにいい意味で興奮したときにも使える。📖 Note(1)

しかし、日本語でも英語と同じように興奮したときにも使われるようになってきた。

(2) 最後の独唱は魂を揺さぶられるすさまじい熱唱で、感動で鳥肌が立った。

The last solo was so soul-stirring and intense that it gave me goose bumps.

(〜に〜を)与える / phr. / 隠喩

上の人が下の人に何かの所有権を移す，影響を及ぼしたり課題を課す

例文

(a) そのアメリカ人の教授は学生によく質問する機会を与えるので、学生達から好かれている。

(b) 彼は誰にでもアドバイスを与えるのが好きだ。

(c) 医者は彼に旅行の許可を与えた。

(d) 作者について何か知っていることは、小説の理解に深みを与える。

(e) The daughter gave the home a cheerful atmosphere that had been missing ever since her father's death.

Notes

1. The semantic range of *ataeru* is narrower than that of *give*. *Ataeru* means "a person of higher status provides a person of lower status with commodities, benefits, advice, a warning, permission, or an examination, or causes them to suffer from damage or loss, among other things." On the other hand, *give* covers the semantic range of *ataeru* in addition to that of *ageru* and *kureru*.

2. *Ataeru* is often used instead of *ageru* in formal situations and writing. 📖➡解説(1)

3. *Give* is also used in idiomatic expressions, but Japanese *ataeru* cannot be used there in such cases.
   (2) a. John gave his name to his guest.
      ジョンは客に名前を{教えた/[×]与えた}。
   b. Scarlet gave birth to a baby girl.
      スカーレットは女児{を出産した/[×]に誕生を与えた}。
   c. He gave his life for his country.
      彼は祖国のために自分の命を{捧げた/[×]与えた}。

4. There are cases where *give* cannot be used in the English even though *ataeru* can be used in the Japanese. 📖➡関連語(3)(4)(5)

---

go {around/round} in circles / phr. / metaphor

for discussion to keep coming back to the original point without making any progress

Examples

Saya: So you still haven't decided where you're going for vacation?

Kenta: Nope. We just keep going round in circles. Everyone wants to do something different.

Saya: It's hard being the organizer, isn't it?

- -

(a) Manami and I went around in circles trying to decide how, when, and where we would have our wedding.

(b) The more I agonized over it, the more I kept going around in circles. Nothing was getting resolved.

Note

The original meaning of the Japanese is "to circle a Buddhist temple while praying."

(e) 父親が亡くなってからずっと沈欝だった家に、娘が明るさを与えた。

解説

1. 日本語の「与える」の意味領域は英語の *give* より狭く、「上の人が下の人に物品、恩恵、忠告、注意、許可を授けたり、試験を受けさせたり、被害、損害を被らせる」などという意味である。他方、英語の *give* は日本語の「与える」という意味のほかに、日本語の「あげる」、「くれる」の意味もある。

2. 「与える」はフォーマルな場面や文章では「あげる」の代わりに用いられることが多い。

(1) 動物に食べ物を{ 与え / あげ }ないでください。
   Please do not feed the animals.

3. 英語の *give* は慣用句の中でも使われる。その場合日本語の「与える」は使えない。

→ 📖 Note (2)

4. 日本語には「与える」が使えるが、英語では *give* が使えない例がある。

(3) 台風はその島に多大な被害を与えた。
   The typhoon inflicted enormous damage on the island.

(4) 体罰は子供の身体だけでなく、精神にも苦痛を与える。
   Corporal punishment causes not only physical pain, but psychological pain as well.

(5) 彼の行動はクラスメートに悪い影響を与えた。
   His actions had a bad influence on his classmates.

G

堂々巡りをする / phr. / 隠喩

話し合いが絶えず元に戻ってしまい、先へ進まない

例文

さや：旅行先、まだ決まらないの？

健太：そうなんだよ。さっきから堂々巡りばっかり。みんないろいろ注文つけるからさ。

さや：幹事さんは、大変ね。

(a) 真奈美と僕は結婚式を、いつ、どこで、どうやってするかということを決めようとして堂々巡りをしていた。

(b) 悩めば悩むほど堂々巡りをしてしまい、結局、何もできなかった。

解説

日本語の「堂々巡りをする」の基本義は"祈願のため仏堂のまわりを回る"ことである。

273

go back to the basics /phr. metaphor

to return to the fundamental elements

Examples

(a) You have to go back to the basics to remember and relearn what is important in life.

(b) My students have a weak understanding of Japanese grammar, so I told them to go back to the basics.

Notes

1. The basic meaning of the English and the Japanese is "to return to the original {place/ state}."

2. *Go back* and *tachi-kaeru* in the Japanese can be replaced by *return* and *modoru*, respectively.

---

go beyond a joke（冗談が過ぎる）→ {be/go} beyond a joke

---

go in one ear and out the other /phr. metaphor

heard but quickly forgotten

Examples

Mrs. S: Kenta, are you listening to me? I swear, whatever I say just goes in one ear and out the other.

Kenta: That's not true. I'm listening.

Mrs. S: Sure you are!

- - - - - - - - - - - - - - - - - - - -

(a) I told Naomi that it was foolish to marry that old man, but it seems that my advice went in one ear and out the other.

(b) All I got from school was a bunch of useless information that went in one ear and out the other.

Note

The difference between the English and Japanese expressions is that the Japanese specifies which ears serve as the entrance and exit.

REL

The Japanese has two RELs. The first is *bajitōfū* (lit. "horse ears, east wind"), which was originally used by Li Bo, a Chinese poet (701-762), and which means "for s.o. not to listen to s.o. else's advice or criticism." The second is *uma no mimi ni nenbutsu* (lit. "a Buddhist sutra for a horse's ears"), which means "for s.o. not to listen to s.o. else's advice carefully, or for s.o. to be unable to understand sophisticated subjects." Both can replace the main entry when used to mean "s.o. who ignores another's advice."

基本に立ち返る　phr.　隠喩

基本的なことに戻る

例文

(a) 人生で大事なことが何かを思い出し、学び直すためには、基本に立ち返る必要がある。

(b) 学生の日本語文法の理解が弱いので、私は彼らに基本に立ち返るように言った。

解説

1. 日英語とも基本義は"元の {場所 / 状態} に戻る"である。

2. 日本語の動詞「立ち返る」と英語の動詞 *go back* は、それぞれ、「戻る」と *return* で置き換えられる。

G

右の耳から（入って）左の耳に（抜ける）　phr.　隠喩

聞いたことが頭に残らない，相手の言うことをよく聞かない

関 馬耳東風, 馬の耳に念仏

例文

鈴木（妻）：健太、ちゃんと聞いてる？　どうせ、私の言うことなんか、右の耳から入って左の耳に抜けてるんでしょ。

健太：そんなことないよ。ちゃんと聞いてますよ。

鈴木（妻）：嘘ばっかり！

(a) ナオミに「あんな老人と結婚するのはバカげている」と言ったのに、私の言葉は右の耳から入って、左の耳に抜けてしまったようだ。

(b) 学校で習ったことは全部役に立たない情報で、みんな右の耳から入って、左の耳に抜けてしまった。

解説

日英語の違いは、日本語ではどちらの耳から入ってどちらの耳から出るのかを特定しているが、英語では特定していないという点だけである。

関連語

日本語の関連表現は二つある。「馬耳東風」の出典は李白(701-762)の詩で、"人の忠告、批判を注意深く聞こうとしない"という意味である。「馬の耳に念仏」は"人の忠告を注意深く聞かない、あるいは、高尚なことがわからない"である。どちらも"聞いたことが頭に残らない"という意味では「右の耳から（入って）左の耳に（抜ける）」と置き換えられる。

go over s.o.'s head / phr. metaphor

to approach s.o.'s boss without consulting them first

Examples

Karen: So I've been working part time, and yesterday someone called my workplace asking for English lessons, so I decided to handle it myself and tell my boss afterwards, but he got angry at me.

Mike: Oh wow. Guess you shouldn't have gone over his head like that.

Karen: Yeah, I guess not.

- -

(a) Kate was so anxious to change her work hours that she went over her supervisor's head and asked the manager.

(b) Not having any luck with your car dealer? Go over his head and right to the top to get satisfaction.

Note

> The English is a verb phrase, but the Japanese is an adverbial phrase that consists of *atama + goshi ni*.

go over s.o.'s head / phr. metaphor

for s.t. to be beyond s.o.'s comprehension

REL LOOK go in one ear and out the other

Examples

Mike: Well, look at you. Studying Japanese?

Karen: Yeah. I haven't really been studying lately, so whenever I listen to the news, I barely understand it. It just goes right over my head. I can't get by with just daily conversation—I've actually gotta read and learn the language.

Mike: You and me both.

- -

(a) Complicated political discussions go right over my head.

(b) I couldn't make heads or tails of the movie I saw yesterday. Everything the characters said went over my head, and I ended up falling asleep.

Notes

> 1. In English, this expression is used only when something is so complicated that one can't understand it. But the Japanese is free from such restrictions. 📖→解説 (**1**)
> 2. While the English uses the verb *go*, the Japanese does not use *iku* (to go), but rather *tōri-sugiru* (to pass through).

REL

> *Migi no mimi kara (haitte) hidari no mimi ni (nukeru)* (*go in one ear and out the other*) is similar to *atama no ue o tōri-sugiru* (*go over s.o.'s head*). However, the former is used when someone is not listening to what someone else is saying, whereas the latter is used when something is difficult to understand or is not stored in one's memory. 📖→関連語 (**1**)

頭越しに / adv. phr. / 隠喩

直属の上司を越えて、さらに上の地位の人と重要なことを話し合い、決定する

例文

カレン：今、バイトしているんだけど、昨日、英語のレッスン依頼の電話がかかって
きたから、直接請けちゃって事後報告したら、上司に怒られちゃった。

マイク：そうか。頭越しに仕事の話を進めたのはよくなかったかもね。

カレン：うん、ちょっと、まずかったかもね。

─────

（a）ケイトは労働時間を変えたくてしかたがなかったので、監督者の頭越しに支配人
のところへ行った。

（b）車のディーラーの担当者とうまくいかないのなら、頭越しにトップのところに行
けば満足が得られます。

解説

英語は動詞句であるが、日本語は「頭」+「越しに」の複合副詞句である。

G

頭の上を通り過ぎる / phr. / 隠喩

何かを聞いたり読んだりしても、{よく理解できない／記憶に残らない／よくわからない}

関 LOOK 右の耳から（入って）左の耳に（抜ける）

例文

マイク：あれ、めずらしいね。日本語の勉強？

カレン：そうなの。最近、ちゃんと勉強していないから、ニュースを聞いていても、
よくわかんなくて、頭の上を通り過ぎちゃうのよ。日常会話だけじゃだめね。ちゃ
んと読んで勉強しないと。

マイク：そうだね。

─────

（a）難しい政治の話は、頭の上を通り過ぎてしまう。

（b）昨日見た映画はまったくわけがわからなかった。登場人物の会話がみんな頭の上
を通り過ぎて、気がついたら寝てしまっていた。

解説

1. 英語はとても複雑で理解不可能な場合に使われるが、日本語はそのような制限はなく、もっ
と自由に用いられる。

（1）あんまり疲れていたので、入浴をせかす妻の声も頭の上を通り過ぎてしまった。
I was so tired that when my wife told me to go take a bath, I didn't notice at all.

2. 英語の動詞は *go* で、日本語の動詞は「行く」ではなく「通り過ぎる」である。

関連語

「右の耳から（入って）左の耳に（抜ける）」と英語の *go in one ear and out the other* は見出しの「頭
の上を通り過ぎる」と *go over s.o.'s head* に似ているが、前者は相手が自分の話をよく聞いてい
ないときに使い、後者は何かが自分に難しくてわからないし、記憶に残らないときに使う。

277

go through fire and water (for ~) *phr.* metaphor

to do anything, even s.t. unpleasant or dangerous, for s.o.

Examples

(a) The mayor was ready to go through fire and water for the sake of his citizens.

(b) I would go through fire and water to protect my family.

Notes

1. The English comes from the an excerpt from the Old Testament (Psalm 66:12) written by King David: "We went through fire and water, but you brought us to a place of abundance." It should be noted that this expression is quite old-fashioned and rarely used nowadays. The Japanese appears to have developed independently of this biblical excerpt.

2. The Japanese literally means "one does not refuse even water and fire." *Jisanai* (does not refuse) is the negative form of *{jisu/jisuru}*.

go up in smoke *phr.* metaphor

for s.t. important to be {ruined/lost}

REL go (straight) down the drain

Examples

(a) Hundreds of milions of investment dollars went up in smoke when the market bubble burst in March 2000.

(b) I failed the medical school entrance exam, and my dream of becoming a doctor went up in smoke.

(c) I was devastated when my computer suddenly crashed and all the data that I had been collecting for years went up in smoke.

Note

The English and Japanese have the same figurative meaning, but use different verbs: *go up* and *kieru* (to disappear), respectively.

REL

1. The English REL is *go (straight) down the drain*, which means "for s.t. (esp. one's {efforts/plans}) to go to waste." This metaphor is based on the image of something important literally being washed down the drain. 📖→関連語(1)

2. The Japanese has two RELs: *mizu no awa to naru* (lit. "s.t. becomes bubbles"), and *suihō ni kisuru* (lit. "s.t. is reduced to bubbles"). These two expressions are often used when someone's efforts are in vain. 📖→関連語(1)

(1) 私の言うことなんか、{右の耳から入って左の耳に抜ける / ?頭の上を通り過ぎる}んでしょ？

I swear, whatever I say just goes in one ear and out the other.

（〜のために）水火も辞さない　phr.　隠喩

（人のために）多大の危険を冒す

例文

(a) 市長は市民のためなら水火も辞さない覚悟だった。
(b) 家族を守るためなら、私は水火も辞さない。

解説

1. 英語の出典は旧約聖書の詩編(66：12)のダビデの「われらは火の中、水の中を通った。しかしあなたはわれらを広いところに導き出された」という句である。大変古く、今日ではめったに使われないことに注意。日本語は聖書の出典とは無関係のようである。
2. 日本語の基本義は"水も火も拒まない"という意味である。「辞さない」は「辞す / 辞する」の否定形である。

煙と消える　phr.　隠喩

何か大事なものが急になくなる，大事なことが実現できずに終わる

関 水の泡となる，水泡に帰する

例文

(a) 2000年3月に市場のバブルがはじけたときに、何億ドルという投資が煙と消えた。
(b) 医学部受験に失敗して、医者になる夢が煙と消えた。
(c) コンピュータが突然故障して、長年集めたデータがすべて煙と消えた。がっくりきてしまった。

解説

比喩的意味は日英語ともに同じであるが、動詞は「消える」と go up（上る）で異なっている。

関連語

1. 英語にはくだけた表現の go (straight) down the drain という関連表現がある。"何か、特に努力や計画が無駄になる"という意味である。これは何かが下水溝に流れ去るイメージが土台になっている比喩である。📖→ 関連語(1)
2. 日本語には二つの関連表現がある。一つは「水の泡となる」とその漢語表現の「水泡に帰する」である。どちらも、特に誰かの努力が無駄になったときに使われる。

(1) プロジェクトの突然の中止で、成功に向けて費やしてきたあなたの労力がすべて{煙と消えた / 水の泡となった / 水泡に帰した}。

When the project was suddenly canceled, all the effort we had put into making it a success {went up in smoke/went down the drain}.

golden age / comp. n. / metaphor
a period of great {success/prosperity}

Examples

Saya: Wow, is this a picture of you as a child? You were so cute!

Kenta: I sure was. I had girlfriends all over the neighborhood. I guess you could say it was my golden age.

- - - - - - - - - - - - - - - - - - - -

(a) Some people claim that the bubble economy in the latter half of the 20th century was a golden age for the Japanese economy.

(b) Many people say the 1930s and 40s were the golden age of jazz.

Note

This phrase originated from the Greek method of classifying the ages (Golden Age, Silver Age, Copper Age, Iron Age). Among these, the Golden Age is said to have been a period of peace and prosperity. The Japanese is very likely a translation of the English.

(goose that lays the) golden egg, the / n. phr. / metaphor
s.t. that produces profit

Examples

Kenta: Doesn't this new computer have such an awesome design?

Mike: Yeah, they really laid a golden egg with this one. I bet it's gonna sell really well.

- - - - - - - - - - - - - - - - - - - -

(a) Wherever you go in the world, tourism is the goose that lays the golden egg.

(b) Knowledge is the golden egg, and an educated population is the goose.

Notes

1. This expression comes from one of Aesop's fables in which the owner of a goose that lays one golden egg a day kills it, believing he will be able to receive all of the golden eggs at once. In fact, this story also gave rise to the expression *kill the goose that lays the golden egg*, which means "to destroy s.t. profitable."
2. The English only refers to something that produces profit, but the Japanese can also refer to someone who has a great future ahead of him/her. 📖→解説(1)

(as) graceful as a swan / phr. / simile
to have very elegant gestures and movements

Example

The audience was drawn to the ballerina's elegant dancing. She was as graceful as a swan.

黄金時代（おうごんじだい） / comp. n. / 隠喩（いんゆ）

最も繁栄していた時代（もっともはんえいしていたじだい）

例文

さや：へえ、この写真、健太の子供の時なの。可愛かったんだね。

健太：そうなんだよ。近所にガールフレンドもいっぱいいたんだ。まさに僕の黄金時代だったね。

(a) 20世紀後半のバブル期が日本の黄金時代だったと唱える人もいる。

(b) 多くの人が1930年代と1940年代はジャズの黄金時代だったと言う。

解説

この表現は古代ギリシャの金、銀、銅、鉄の時代という時代区分に由来する。その中で、金の時代が平和で豊かな生活ができたという神話に基づく。日本語は英語の翻訳の可能性が高い。

G

金の卵（きんのたまご） / n. phr. / 隠喩（いんゆ）

利益を生むもの，将来性のある人材（りえきをうむもの，しょうらいせいのあるじんざい）

例文

健太：この新しいコンピュータ、デザインがすごくいいね。

マイク：うん、この会社は金の卵を生み出したね。これは売れると思うよ。

(a) 世界中どこへ行っても観光は金の卵である。

(b) 知識は金の卵で、教育を受けた大衆は金の卵を産むガチョウだ。

解説

1. この名詞句は、毎日金の卵を一つ産むガチョウの持ち主が、金の卵を一度に全部取ろうとしてガチョウを殺すというイソップ物語からきている。英語ではこの話から"利益になるものをだめにしてしまう"という意味の慣用句 *kill the goose that lays the golden egg*「金の卵を産むガチョウを殺す」が出ている。

2. 英語は利益を生むものという意味しかないが、日本語は将来性のある人材という意味もある。

(1) 君は将来性のある金の卵だ。

You are a promising {young man/[×]golden egg}.

白鳥のように{優美 / 優雅}（はくちょうのように{ゆうび / ゆうが}） / phr. / 直喩（ちょくゆ）

動きや仕種がとても優美だ（うごきやしぐさがとてもゆうびだ）

例文

聴衆はバレリーナの優雅なダンスに魅了された。白鳥のように優美だった。

grasp / v./n. / metaphor

to understand the meaning of s.t.

REL seize

Examples

Mike: *Kanji* are such a pain!

Karen: Really? I think *kanji* are useful because it's possible to grasp an entire concept by reading just one or two characters.

- -

(a) When you speed read, the goal is to grasp the main points without spending too much time on the details.

(b) By taking this course, you should gain a firm grasp of the basic principles of physics. You should not expect to delve into more advanced material.

(c) I was finally able to grasp the whole picture of that incident after hearing explanation on the news.

Note

Grasp and *tsukamu* have the same non-metaphorical meaning, which is "to hold {s.o./s.t.} tightly with the fingers and not let go."

REL

The basic meaning of the English REL *seize* is "to take hold of {s.t./s.o.} suddenly and quickly," whereas the basic meaning of the Japanese REL *(~ o) toraeru* is "to prevent {s.t./s.o.} from escaping."

(1) a. The writer should write in such a way that the reader can {grasp/??seize} his/her meaning without having to expend a large amount of effort.
書き手は、読者がそれほどの努力をしなくても意味が{つかめる/捉えられる}ように書くべきです。

b. In America, he {seized/??grasped} an opportunity and became a big success.
彼はアメリカで機会を{つかんで/捉えて}大成功をした。

c. The plots of that author's mystery novels are so interesting that they have {seized/??grasped} the imaginations of many readers.
その作家のミステリー小説は筋がとても面白いので、読者の心を{つかんだ/捉えた}。

The grass is (always) greener (on the other side of the fence).
/ phr. / metaphor

s.o. else seems to be in a better situation than you

REL The apples on the other side of the wall are the sweetest.

Examples

Kenta: I think I wanna use the money from my part-time job to buy a new car.

Mrs. S: What's wrong with the one you have now?

Kenta: My friend is driving this awesome new car, so I wanna get the same one.

Mrs. S: The grass is always greener, you know. Your car used to be your father's, so it's not too shabby itself.

- -

（〜を）つかむ　/ v. /　隠喩

{意味 / 要点}などを理解する

関 （〜を）捉える

例文

マイク：漢字ってほんと面倒だね。

カレン：そう？ たった１字か２字で全体の意味をつかむことができるから、とっても便利だと思うけど。

(a) 文を速く読む時には、細かいところに時間をとられないで、要点を速くつかむことが大切だ。

(b) この講義を取れば、物理の理論の基礎がつかめるようになるはずですが、それ以上深いところに入れるとは期待しないでください。

(c) ニュース解説を聞いてはじめて、その事件の全体像がつかめた。

解説

日英語の動詞「つかむ」と grasp の基本義は共通で"人や物を放さないように手の指で硬く握る"という意味である。

関連語

日本語の関連表現「（〜を）捉える」の基本義は"{何か / 誰か} が逃げないようにする"で、英語の関連表現 seize の基本義は"{何か / 誰か} を突然すばやくつかむ"である。 📖REL（1）

G

隣の芝生は{青い / 青く見える}　/ phr. /　隠喩

他人が自分よりいいものを持っているという羨望の心理

関 隣の花は赤い

例文

健太：今度、バイト代で、新しい車買おうと思うんだ。

鈴木(妻)：あら、あなたの車、まだ動くでしょ。

健太：友達が乗ってる新車、すごくいいから、僕もあれが欲しいんだけど。

鈴木(妻)：隣の芝生は青く見えるのよ。あなたの車だって、お父さんの車だったんだから、なかなかいいものなのよ。

283

(a) My wife left me for another man. She was convinced the grass was greener on the other side of the fence.

(b) For those parents, the grass was always greener on the other side of the fence, and the only way for their children to obtain what their neighbors had was education.

Notes

1. The Japanese is very likely a translation of the English.
2. *Green* in the English expression corresponds not to *midori* (green) but to *aoi*, which is the color used to describe fresh {grass/leaves}.

REL

The apples on the other side of the wall are the sweetest and *tonari no hana wa akai* (the neighbor's flowers are redder) are similar in meaning to the main expressions. However, they are not used nearly as frequently.

(1) My wife thought that {the grass was greener on the other side of the fence/the apples on the other side of the wall were the sweetest}.
隣の芝生は青い/隣の花は赤い と、妻は思い込んだんですよ。(→(a))

grass roots; grassroots ~ / comp. n./comp. adj. / metaphor

the basic level of {society/an organization}

Examples

(a) They mobilized the grass roots to secure black voting rights.

(b) For many years, this prefecture has been assisting grassroots-level international exchange.

(c) Let's promote fitness at the grassroots level.

(d) The consumer movement was a success because of the nationwide grassroots efforts of people like you.

Notes

1. The Japanese is very likely a direct translation of the English.
2. In both English and Japanese, the main entry is often used as the first element of the compound. The second element is most frequently *movement*/*undō*, as shown in (a) and (d).

gray area / comp. n. / metaphor

an area that cannot be categorized in a clear-cut way

REL gray zone

Examples

(a) People who download music for free off the Internet are taking advantage of a legal gray area created by technological innovation.

(b) In school, we learned that in science, there is always a right and a wrong; gray areas are almost unheard of. However, when it comes to real-world applications, we knew that most of science is a gray area.

(a) 妻は他の男と出ていってしまった。隣の芝生は青いと、妻は思い込んだんですよ。

(b) 両親にとって隣の芝生は青く見えました。子供たちが隣の芝生に入っていける方法は教育だけだったんです。

解説

1. 日本語は英語からの翻訳の可能性が高い。

2. 英語の *green* は日本語では「緑」ではなくて、「青い」で対応している。「青」は、新しく生えてきた草や葉の色を指す時にも使う。

関連語

「隣の花は赤い」は、「隣の芝生は {青い / 青く見える}」よりはるかに頻度が低いが、類似のことわざとして使われている。英語には *The apples on the other side of the wall are the sweetest.* (塀の向こうのリンゴが一番甘い) という類似のことわざがあるが、見出しのことわざほどには使われていない。━📖 REL(1)

G

草の根 (の〜) / n. phr. 隠喩

名もない {一般大衆 / 一般市民}

例文

(a) 彼らは黒人の投票権を獲得するために草の根運動を組織した。

(b) この県はもう何年も草の根レベルの国際交流を支援している。

(c) 草の根レベルで健康づくり運動を広めていこう。

(d) この消費者運動が成功したのは、全国の、あなたのような人々の草の根運動のおかげなのです。

解説

1. 日本語は英語からの翻訳の可能性が高い。

2. (a)(d)のように日英語とも複合語の第1要素として使われ、第2要素として一番よく使われるのは「運動」/ *movement* である。

灰色の部分 / n. phr. 隠喩

はっきり {分類 / 区別} できない部分

関 グレーゾーン, グレーエリア

例文

(a) インターネットから無料で音楽をダウンロードする人達は、技術開発によってもたらされた法律上の灰色の部分をうまく利用しているのだ。

(b) 科学はいつも間違っているか正しいかのどちらかで、灰色の部分はめったにないと学校では習ったが、現実の世界では、科学の大半は灰色の部分ということがわかった。

285

(c) The current system of determining what defines cheating and how it should be punished is shaky. The new policy should eliminate the gray areas.

REL

1. The English REL, *gray zone*, can replace *gray area* in all the examples, but it is used less frequently.
2. The related Japanese expressions are translations of *gray zone* and *gray area*, and they can replace *hai-iro no bubun* in all the example sentences. Unlike its English equivalent, *gurē-zōn* is used with much higher frequency than *gurē-eria*. 📖→関連語(1)

green   n.   synecdoche

green vegetation; money

Examples

(a) The mayor said that the town needs more green.

(b) This area is close to the center of the city, but it's quiet and there's a lot of green.

(c) For me, green and water are symbols of life.

Notes

1. The color *green* is an important component of plants. Since it is used to represent the whole plant, this is an example of synecdoche.
2. In the USA, *green* can also be used to mean "money"—specifically paper money, since the ink color of American bill is green.

(1) If you don't show me the green, we don't have a deal.
現金を見せてくれなければ、取り引きはしません。

greenhorn   comp. n.   metaphor

s.o. who is inexperienced

Examples

Mr. S: I heard that your baseball team's going to be playing Company B.

Mike: That's right. We can't afford to lose to those greenhorns, so we're practicing really hard.

Mr. S: That's the spirit!

- -

(a) That guy sure talks big for a greenhorn just out of college.

(b) A greenhorn who doesn't know anything about the world wants to be in charge of a civic organization.

(c) カンニングとは何か、どのようにそれは罰せられるべきかは今の体制ではおぼつかない。新しい方法で灰色の部分を取り除くべきだ。

関連語

1. 英語の関連表現 *gray zone* は例文中のすべての *gray area* と置き換えることができるが、*gray area* のほうがはるかに使用頻度は高い。

2. 日本語の関連表現「グレーゾーン」と「グレーエリア」は、英語の *gray zone* と *gray area* の音訳で、例文中の「灰色の部分」と置き換えることができる。ただし、英語とは逆に「グレーゾーン」のほうが「グレーエリア」より使用頻度がはるかに高い。

(1) 科学はいつも間違っているか正しいかのどちらかで、{灰色の部分 / グレーゾーン / グレーエリア} はめったにない。(→(b))
Science is always either right or wrong, and gray {areas/zones} seldom exist.

緑 / n. / 提喩
みどり　　　　　ていゆ

木々や草花などの植物
きぎ　くさばな　　しょくぶつ

例文

(a) 市長は町にもっと緑が必要だと言った。

(b) この辺りは、都心に近いのに緑が多くて、静かな所だ。

(c) 僕にとって緑と水は命のシンボルだ。

解説

1. 緑の色は植物の大事な色彩要素の一部である。つまり、全体の一部である緑色が全体を表すために使われているから、その用法は提喩である。

2. アメリカでは *green* には「お金」、特に「紙幣」の意味がある。理由は米ドル紙幣が緑色のインクを使っているためである。📖 **Note(1)**

青二才 / comp. n. / 隠喩
あおにさい　　　　　　いんゆ

若くて経験の浅い男性を馬鹿にしたことば
わか　けいけん　あさ　だんせい　ばか

関 くちばしが黄色い
きいろ

例文

鈴木(夫)：マイクの野球チーム、今度、B 社と試合なんだって。
すずき おっと

マイク：そうなんですよ。あんな青二才達に負けるわけにはいかないんで、みんな猛
あおにさいたち　ま　　　　　　　　　　　　　　もう
練習ですよ。
れんしゅう

鈴木(夫)：おお、それはまた、随分、必死だね。
すずき おっと　　　　　　　　　ずいぶん　ひっし

(a) あいつは大学を出たばかりの青二才のくせに、大きいことばかり言っている。
だいがく　で　　　　　あおにさい

(b) 世間のことを何も知らない青二才が、市民団体のトップになりたがっている。
せけん　　なに　し　　あおにさい　しみんだんたい

287

Note

The English comes from the idea of an animal with greenish, newly grown horns. The Japanese appears to have originated from the practice of referring to young mullets (a type of fish) as *nisai* (two years old), and from the fact that the fish has a greenish-blue hue.

R E L

In Japanese, there is another REL: *kuchibashi ga kīroi* (lit. "beak is yellow"). This expression refers to the yellowish beaks of young birds. Whereas *ao-nisai* is used only in reference to men, *kuchibashi ga kīroi* can be used for both sexes. 📖→関連語(1)

In addition, *ao-nisai* is used much more frequently than *kuchibashi ga kīroi*.

grit one's teeth / phr. / metonymy

to be determined to deal with a difficult situation

Examples

(a) He closed his eyes and gritted his teeth in a futile attempt to stave off a headache.

(b) The survivors of that disaster gritted their teeth and lived through the hardship.

(c) The children took the loss hard, but they gritted their teeth and fought back their tears.

Note

Both the English and Japanese expressions describe the act of dealing with a difficult situation in a patient or determined manner. As the nonverbal action coincides with the psychological state, this can be considered a case of metonymy in a borad sense.

grope in the dark / phr. / metaphor

to search aimlessly for a solution

Examples

Saya: Karen, how's your latest paper coming?

Karen: I'm still groping in the dark. It's gonna take me a while.

(a) They're all groping in the dark and haven't found the first step toward a solution.

(b) Police continued to grope in the dark, making no headway on the difficult murder case.

Note

The English can be used both literally and figuratively, but the Japanese can only be used figuratively. To express the literal meaning, *kurayami no naka de* is used. 📖→解説(1)

解説

英語は動物の緑っぽい出たばかりの角が語源だが、日本語はボラの稚魚を二才と呼び、青っぽい色をしていることから来ているらしい。

関連語

日本語の関連表現「くちばしが黄色い」はひな鳥のくちばしが黄色いことからきている。「青二才」は男性にしか使わないが、「くちばしが黄色い」は男女ともに使う。

(1) ローラは高校を出たばかりの{くちばしが黄色い/˟青二才の}、田舎者の少女だった。
Laura was a greenhorn from the country who had just graduated from high shcool.
また、「青二才」のほうが「くちばしが黄色い」よりもはるかに使用頻度が高い。

歯を食いしばる　/ phr.　換喩

我慢する、こらえる

例文

(a) 無駄だとわかっているのに、彼は頭痛を食い止めようと、目を閉じ、歯を食いしばった。

(b) その災害の被災者たちは、歯を食いしばって生きてきた。

(c) 子供達は、試合に負けて悔しかったけれど、歯を食いしばって泣くのを我慢した。

解説

日英語ともに、"よく{我慢する/勇気を出す/頑張る}"という意味を持っている。非言語行為と心理が同時に起きることから、これは広い意味での換喩と考えられる。

暗中模索（する）　/ phr.　隠喩

やり方がわからないまま、いろいろなことを試みる

例文

さや：カレン、今度の新しい論文はどう？

カレン：うん、まだ暗中模索の状態で、先は遠いわね。

- -

(a) 彼らはみな暗中模索しているのだが、問題解決の糸口が見えていない。

(b) 警察はいまだ暗中模索を続けていて、その殺人事件の捜査は前進していない。

解説

英語は文字通りにも比喩的にも使えるが、日本語では比喩的にしか使われない。文字通りの意味を表す場合は「暗闇の中で」を使う。

(1) 台風で停電になってしまい、私は{暗闇の中で/˟暗中模索して}ろうそくを探した。
The power outage caused by the typhoon left me groping in the dark for a candle.

one's hair stands on end phr. metaphor

one is terrified

REL LOOK▸ blood freezes

Examples

(a) My hair stood on end when I watched a certain scene in the movie "Silence of the Lambs."

(b) When I took a glimpse into the horrifying valley, my hair stood on end, my teeth chattered, and my limbs trembled.

(c) Testing our bravery, a friend and I visited a cemetery in the middle of the night. It was so scary it made our hair stand on end, but we had fun.

Note

On end means "standing straight up," but *yodatsu* means "(for hair) to stand up."

R E L

The Japanese RELs are *ke ga sakadatsu* (hair stands upside down) and *sōke-datsu* (all hairs stand up), and they are interchangeable with *mi no ke ga yodatsu*. *Sōke-datsu* is used more frequently than *mi no ke ga yodatsu*, but *ke ga sakadatsu* is used less frequently. ▱▸ 関連語(1)

hand n. metonymy

the cards dealt to players in a card game

Examples

Kenta: Man, why do I always get such bad hands? I'll never win.

Karen: You really think you can beat me at poker? Maybe in ten years.

Kenta: How are you always getting such good hands?

Karen: Um, rude! It's not that I get good hands—I'm just that good.

- -

(a) When I was playing cards yesterday, I got so many good hands that I just kept winning.

(b) If you have a good hand, play aggressively; if you have a bad hand, study your opponents carefully.

Note

Note that the basic meanings of *hand* and *te* are slightly different, because *te* can mean *arm* as well. But the metaphorical usages are based on the same definition: "the movable part of a person's arm from the wrist down."

身の毛がよだつ / phr. / 隠喩

得体の知れないものに対して強い恐怖を感じる

関 総毛立つ，毛が逆立つ **LOOK▶**血が凍る

例文

(a) 映画「羊たちの沈黙」のあるシーンを見たときは、身の毛がよだつほど怖かった。

(b) 恐ろしい谷を見下ろしたときに、身の毛がよだち、歯はガチガチと音をたて、手足が震えた。

(c) 肝試しで、友達と夜中にお墓に行った。身の毛がよだつくらい怖かったけど、おもしろかった。

解説

On end は "何かがまっすぐに立つ" という意味であるが、「よだつ」は "からだの毛が立つ" という意味である。

関連語

例文中の「身の毛がよだつ」は、「毛が逆立つ」「総毛立つ」に置き換えることができる。「総毛立つ」は「身の毛がよだつ」より高い頻度で使われるが、「毛が逆立つ」は、あまり使われない。

(1) 「羊たちの沈黙」という映画を見たときは、{身の毛がよだった / 総毛立った / 毛が逆立った}。
(→(b))

My hair stood on end when I watched a movie called "Silence of the Lambs."

手 / n. / 換喩

カードゲームの競技者に配られるカード

例文

健太：ちぇっ、今度も悪い手ばかりだな。とても勝てそうにないや。

カレン：あら、ポーカーで私に勝とうなんて、10年早いわよ。

健太：カレンの手って、どうしていつもそんなにいいのかな。

カレン：失礼な。手がいいんじゃなくて、腕がいいのよ。

(a) 昨日トランプのゲームをしたら、いい手がたくさん来て、大勝ちしてしまった。

(b) いい手だったら積極的にゲームをやり、悪い手だったら相手をよく見ることだ。

解説

「手」は「腕」の意味にもなるから「手」と *hand* の基本義は異なる。しかし、比喩用法は "手首から下の動く部分" という意味から派生している。

291

handful of ~, a   n. phr.   metaphor

very few

Examples

Kenta: This Japanese baseball player is awesome.

Mike: I know, right? There are only a handful of Major League players like him.

- -

(a) Only a handful of countries are not members of the UN.

(b) The grandparents spoke Spanish and knew only a handful of English words.

(c) Our country's auto industry is controlled by only a handful of companies.

Notes

1. The basic meaning of the main entries is "the amount one can grasp with one hand."
2. Both the English and Japanese can often be followed by abstract words such as *yūki* (courage) and *shiawase* (happiness). 📖→解説(1)
3. The English and Japanese usually take *only* or *hon'no*, respectively.

hang {on/upon} ~   phr.   metaphor

for s.t. (esp. {success/the future/progress}) to depend on s.t. else

REL   hinge {on/upon} ~

Examples

Section Chief: The success or failure of tomorrow's meeting completely hangs on your interpreting skills. I'm counting on you, Mike.

Mike: I'll do my best.

- -

(a) The future of our children hangs on education.

(b) Success or failure as a businessman hangs upon one's ability to find customers.

(c) Whether or not I can get a job at this company hangs on today's interview.

Notes

1. The Japanese *(~ ni) kakatte iru* is the stative form of *(~ ni) kakaru*.
2. *Hang* means "for s.t. to be fixed at the top without support for the lower part." *Kakaru* means "for s.t. to extend toward and come in contact with {s.t. else/s.o. else}."

REL

The English REL, *hinge {on/upon} ~*, is used more frequently than *hang {on/upon} ~*. There is no corresponding metaphor in Japanese.

(1) Success or failure as a businessman {hangs/hinges} upon one's ability to find customers.

(→(b))

一握り（の〜） / n. phr. / 隠喩

わずか（の〜）

例文

健太：この日本人野球選手ってすごいね。

マイク：ほんと、アメリカ大リーグでも、彼ほどの選手はほんの一握りだろうね。

- (a) 国連に加盟していない国は、ほんの一握りだ。
- (b) 祖父母はスペイン語を話して、英語はほんの一握りの単語を知っているだけだった。
- (c) ほんの一握りの会社が、わが国の自動車産業を支配している。

解説

1．日英語とも基本義は"手でつかめるだけの量"である。

2．日英語とも「一握りの勇気」とか「一握りの幸せ」という抽象語彙も使われる。

(1) 神様でも仏様でも誰でもいいですから、僕に勇気をください。一握りの勇気をください。
God or Buddha or whoever, please give me courage, just a handful of courage.

3．日英語とも、それぞれ「ほんの」、*only* と一緒に使われるのが普通である。

H

（〜に）かかっている / phr. / 隠喩

重要なこと（特に{成功 / 進歩 / 勝利}）が何かと強く関わっている

例文

課長：明日の会議が成功するかどうかは、ひとえにマイクの通訳にかかっているから
ね。頼りにしてるよ。

マイク：はい、がんばります。

- (a) われわれの子供たちの将来は教育にかかっている。
- (b) ビジネスマンとして成功するか失敗するかは、顧客を見つける腕にかかっている。
- (c) この会社に就職できるかどうかは、今日の面接にかかっている。

解説

1．「（〜に）かかっている」は「（〜に）かかる」の状態表現である。

2．*hang* と「かかる」の基本義は、それぞれ、"何かが上のほうで留められて下のほうが自由に
なっている"と"何かが{何か/ 人}まで伸びて接触している"である。

関連語

英語には *hang {on/upon}* 〜 よりはるかによく使われる比喩表現 *hinge {on/upon}* 〜 があるが、
日本語にはこれに対応する比喩表現はない。→ 📖 REL(1)

293

(as) hard as (a) rock / phr. / simile

very hard

ANT (as) soft as down

Examples

Mrs. S: Kenta, I can't cut this pumpkin at all. Give me a hand, would you?

Kenta: Sure, leave it to me! ... Whoa! This thing's as hard as a rock!

- -

(a) The ground here is as hard as rock, so plowing is impossible.

(b) Cutting-edge technology has made it possible to make ceramics as hard as rock.

ANT

Both the English and Japanese have multiple ANTs, but *(as) soft as down* and *umō no yō ni yawarakai* are the only ones that correspond to one another. Some language-specific examples include *(as) soft as {butter/clay}* in English and *tōfu no yō ni yawarakai* ([as] soft as *tōfu*) in Japanese.

(1) This luxury towel is as soft as down.
この高級タオルは羽毛のように柔らかい。

(as) hard as steel / phr. / simile

very hard

Example

This wrestler's chest and abs are as hard as steel.

harden s.o.'s attitude / phr. / metaphor

to cause s.o.'s attitude toward s.t. to become inflexible and stern

ANT soften s.o.'s attitude

Examples

(a) The attacks on Sept. 11, 2001 hardened Americans' attitudes toward immigrants.

(b) Negotiations between the union and the company are continuing, but it has not been easy because the company has hardened some union members' attitudes toward it.

(c) He should try to talk more normally. I think his blunt way of speaking is hardening his listeners' attitudes toward him.

Note

The English and Japanese verbs are both transitive. *Kōka-saseru* is the causative form of *kōka-suru*. The verbs in the examples can all be replaced with their intransitive versions.

📖→解説(1)

ANT

The English ANT is *soften s.o.'s attitude*, and the Japanese ANT is *taido o nanka saseru*.

294

石のように固い / phr. 直喩

とても固い

反 羽毛のように柔らかい

例文

鈴木（妻）：健太、このかぼちゃ、ぜんぜん切れないの。ちょっと切ってくれない？

健太：どれどれ、う～ん、ぜんぜんだめだね。石のように固いよ。

(a) この土地は石のように固いから、耕すことができない。

(b) 最新の技術では、セラミックスを石のように固くすることができる。

反意語

日英語ともに複数の反意表現があるが、共通の表現は「羽毛のように柔らかい」と *(as) soft as down* だけである。日本語特有の表現は「豆腐のように柔らかい」で、英語特有の表現は *(as) soft as butter*（バターのように柔らかい）、*(as) soft as clay*（粘土のように柔らかい）がある。

→ ANT (1)

H

{鋼鉄 / 鋼}のように硬い / phr. 直喩

とても硬い

例文

そのレスラーの胸部や腹部は鋼鉄のように硬い。

態度を硬化させる / phr. 隠喩

{誰か / 何か}に対して前よりも頑な態度に出る

反 態度を軟化させる

例文

(a) 2001 年 9 月 11 日の攻撃は、アメリカ人の移民に対する態度を硬化させた。

(b) 労働組合と会社側の交渉は続いているが、一部の労働組合が会社側に対して態度を硬化させているために、交渉は難航している。

(c) あの人はもうちょっと普通に話せばいいのに。あの無愛想な話し方が聞き手の態度を硬化させていると思う。

解説

日英語とも見出しの動詞は他動詞である。日本語の「硬化させる」は「硬化する」の使役形である。例文(a)-(c)は全て自動詞で書き換えることができる。

(1) 2001 年 9 月 11 日の攻撃以降、アメリカ人の移民に対する態度が硬化した。（→(a)）

American's attitudes toward immigrants have hardened since the attacks on Sept.11, 2001.

反意語

日英語とも、「態度を軟化させる」、*soften s.o.'s attitude* という反意表現がある。→ ANT (1)

295

(1) It was in the best interest of both parties to reach an agreement, so they somehow managed to soften their attitudes and come together.

双方のグループの利害が合意に達するのが最大の関心事だった。それで、とにかくお互いの態度を軟化させて歩み寄ったのだ。

one's hat is off to ~ / phr. / metaphor

for s.o.(= the speaker) to give {praise/respect} to s.o. else

REL I take my hat off to ~; my hat goes off to ~

Examples

Mr. S: Last week after work, we all went out for karaoke. My hat goes off to the boss for his singing ability.

Mrs. S: Really? He's that good?

Mr. S: Yeah. We asked him about it, and apparently he used to want to be a singer and took voice lessons.

- - - - - - - - - - - - - - - - - - - -

(a) My hat's off to whomever came up with this wonderful idea.

(b) My hat's off to the poet for his insight into human life.

(c) My hat's off to the players and coaches. They did a good job preparing for the game.

Notes

1. The English is used when the speaker is the subject. However, the Japanese does not have this restriction. 📖— 解説 (1)

2. *Datsubō* is a Sino-Japanese compound that consists of *datsu* (to take off) and *bō* (hat).

REL

1. The main English expression can be replaced by *I take my hat off to ~* or *my hat goes off to ~* without changing the meaning.

(1) {My hat's off to/I take my hat off to/My hat goes off to} whomever came up with this wonderful idea. (→(a))

2. Japanese has the expression *shappo o nugu*, but it is old-fashioned and rarely used in modern Japanese. Note that *shappo* comes from the French word *chapeau* (hat).

📖— 関連語 (2)

have / v. / metaphor

to possess s.t. intangible

REL possess; own

Examples

(a) I still had confidence in myself. I knew that I could still do something good.

(b) One who is aware of the existence of various cultures has pride in his/her own cultural heritage.

(c) We have information on all the airlines that fly to Japan.

(d) I have experience teaching English as a foreign language.

（〜に）脱帽する　phr.　隠喩

誰かのすばらしさ{をほめる / に敬意を表す}

関 シャッポを脱ぐ

例文

鈴木（夫）：先週、会社の後、みんなでカラオケに行ったけれど、部長の歌のうまさには脱帽したよ。

鈴木（妻）：へえ、そんなにうまいの。

鈴木（夫）：うん、聞けば、昔は歌手を目指して勉強したこともあるらしいね。

(a) このすばらしいアイディアを思いついた人には、それが誰であれ脱帽します。

(b) その詩人の人生への洞察力に脱帽する。

(c) 試合の準備を見事に成し遂げてくれた選手やコーチには脱帽だ。

解説

1．英語では、脱帽する人が話者の場合に使われるが、日本語にはそのような制約はない。

(1) {私 / 彼}は彼女の数学的才能に脱帽した。

[×]His hat was off to her mathematical talents.

2．日本語の「脱帽する」の「脱帽」は「脱ぐ」＋「帽子」の複合語である。

関連語

1．英語では *my hat is off to ~* は *I take my hat off to ~* か *my hat goes off to ~* で意味を変えずに置き換えることができる。 📖 REL(1)

2．日本語では少し古い表現として「シャッポを脱ぐ」があるが、現在の日本語ではまれにしか使われない。「シャッポ」はフランス語の *chapeau*（帽子）からきている。

(2) このすばらしいアイディアを思いついた人には、それが誰であれ{脱帽します / シャッポを脱ぎます}。（→(a)）

（〜を）{持つ / 持っている}　phr.　隠喩

{手で捕らえられないようなもの / 目に見えないもの}を所有{する / している}

関 〜は〜がある

例文

(a) 僕はまだ自信を持っていた。何かいいことができるってわかっていたんだ。

(b) 色々な文化の存在に気づいている人は自国の文化遺産に誇りを持っている。

(c) 私どもでは日本に行くすべての航空会社の情報を持っております。

(d) 私は英語を外国語として教えた経験を持っています。

(e) We have wonderful memories of our trip to Paris.

(f) That physicist has a talent for linking theory and application.

(g) I have doubts about this city's commitment to education.

(h) I have an opinion that is supported by a very large supply of facts.

(i) He has a congenital heart condition.

Notes

1. The basic non-metaphorical meaning of *have* is "for {s.o./s.t} to possess s.t.," and the meaning of *motte iru* is "for s.o. to be in the state of holding {s.t./s.o.}." Note that the possessor is usually an animate noun in Japanese, but it can also be an inanimate object in English, as shown below.

(1) a. When your computer has problems, it can disrupt your whole business.
コンピューター {に問題がある／ˣが問題を持っている} と、仕事全体に支障が起きる。

   b. The dress has a pretty color.
そのドレスは {色がきれいだ／ˣきれいな色を持っている}。

   c. This flower has a nice smell.
この花は {においがいい／ˣいいにおいを持っている}。

2. As shown in (2a), the English and Japanese differ when used non-metaphorically. In the case of body parts such as eyes, one can use *have*, but not *motte iru*. *Kirē na me o motte iru* means that someone is holding eyes taken from someone's face. Instead, in Japanese, one can combine an adjective with a body part or the noun "personality," or alternatively, one can use *~ o shite iru*. 📖→解説(2)

3. In Japanese, *(~ o) motte iru* is the stative form of *(~ o) motsu*. The latter is used in general statements such as (3). 📖→解説(3)

REL

1. Japanese has the possessive expression *~ wa ~ ga aru* (s.t. exists somewhere), which is derived from an expression that indicates existence. All the uses of *(~ o) {motsu/motte iru}* in the examples can be replaced by *~ wa ~ ga aru*. 📖→関連語(1)

2. Even when *(~ o) {motsu/motte iru}* is used to describe something intangible, it retains the aura of physical possession, whereas *~ wa ~ ga aru* does not. For this reason, (2a) gives the impression that the person has a tighter grip on the information than (2b) does.

📖→関連語(2)

3. Two other verbs that indicate possession in English are *possess* and *own*. Both mean "for s.o. to have s.t. as property." *Possess* can be used figuratively, but *own* can only be used literally. *Possess* can take nouns such as *confidence*, *pride*, *memory*, and *talent* as its direct object, but *own* cannot. *Own* is usually not used with *information*, though it can be in rare cases where information is valuable or being sold.

(3) a. We {have/possess/ˣown} information on all the airlines that fly to Japan. (→(c))
日本に行くすべての航空会社の情報 {があります／持っています／ˣを所有しています}。

   b. I {have/ˣpossess/ˣown} an opinion that is supported by a very large supply of facts.
(→(h))
私は数多くの事実に基づいた意見 {を持っている／⁇がある／ˣを所有している}。

   c. The spy {has/possesses/owns} top-secret information about that country, and he can sell it to its enemies at an enormous price.
スパイはその国の極秘情報 {があり／を持っていて／を所有していて}、敵国に莫大な金で売ることができる。

4. *Mochi*, the stem of the verb *motsu* (to have), can be used as the second element in compounds, such as in *kare wa {yōtsū/zutsū/zensoku}-mochi da* (he is prone to {backaches/headaches/asthma attacks}). This sounds more natural than saying *kare wa {yōtsū/ˀzutsū/zensoku} o motte iru* (he has {a backache/a headache/asthma}).

298

(e) 私達はパリ旅行のすばらしい思い出を持っている。

(f) その物理学者は理論と応用を結びつける才能を持っている。

(g) 私はこの市の教育へのコミットメントに関して疑いを持っています。

(h) 私は数多くの事実に基づいた意見を持っている。

(i) 彼は先天的に心臓に欠陥を持っている。

解 説

1. 日英語の基本義は、それぞれ、"人が{物/人}を手に持つ"、"人が物を所有する"である。日本語では所有者は通例人を含む生物だが、英語では無生物も所有者になり得る。

━━ 📖 Note (1)

2. (2a)のように非比喩的な用法の場合は日英語で異なる。「目」のようにある物がその所有者の身体の一部分である場合、英語では *have* が使えるが、日本語では「持っている」とは言えない。日本語で「持っている」と言えば、誰かの顔から取り出された目を手に持っているという意味になる。日本語では(2a)(2b)(2c)のように「{体の部分の名称/性格}＋形容詞」あるいは「～をしている」を使うことができる。

(2) a. メアリーは{目がきれいだ/きれいな目をしている/×きれいな目を持っている}。
   Mary has beautiful eyes.
   b. ジョンは{髪の毛が黒い/黒い髪の毛をしている/×黒い髪の毛を持っている}。
   John has black hair.
   c. デービットは{性格がすばらしい/すばらしい性格をしている/×すばらしい性格を持っている}。
   David has a great personality.

3. 日本語の「(～を)持っている」は「(～を)持つ」の状態形であるが、後者は(3)のような一般論を言う時に使われる。

(3) 常に新しいことに挑む精神を持つことは大事だ。
   It is very important to have the spirit to try new things.

関連語

1. 日本語には「～は～がある」という存在表現から出てきた所有表現もある。例文の「(～を){持つ/持っている}」のすべての用法は「～は～がある」によって置き換えることができる。

(1) a. 僕は自信{を持っていた/があった}。(→(a))
   b. 英語を教えた経験{を持っています/があります}。(→(d))
   c. 市の教育へのコミットメントに関して疑い{を持っている/がある}。(→(g))
   d. 彼は先天的に心臓に欠陥{を持っている/がある}。(→(i))

2. 「(～を){持つ/持っている}」はたとえ触れることができないものであっても、何か手元に個体として存在している感じがするのに対して、「～は～がある」にはそのような感じがない。例えば、(2a)は(2b)より情報の掌握の程度が高い。

(2) a. 僕はその情報を持っているよ。
   I have the information.
   b. 僕はその情報があるよ。
   I have the information.

3. 英語では *possess* と *own* という動詞も使える。両方とも "何かを所有物とする" という意味である。*possess* は比喩的に使えるが、*own* は字義通りにしか使えない。*possess* は *confidence*（自信）、*pride*（誇り）、*memory*（思い出）、*talent*（才能）を直接目的語としてとれるが、*own* はとれない。また、*own* は通例 *information*（情報）では使えないが、情報が価値があり、売ることができる場合には使える。━━ 📖 REL (3)

4. 日本語では「持つ」の語幹の「持ち」が複合の第2要素として使われると「彼は{腰痛/頭痛/ぜんそく}持ちだ」のように表現する。「彼は{腰痛/?頭痛/ぜんそく}を持っている」より

299

homograph

have a big mouth / phr. / metaphor

to reveal secrets
秘密をばらす

Example

She has a really big mouth. She simply can't keep a secret.
彼女は本当になんでも言ってしまう。まったく秘密を守ることができない。

have a nose for ~ / phr. / metaphor

to have an instinctive ability to {find/recognize} s.t.

Examples

Mike: Wait, Kimura's not here yet?

Collegue: I bet he'll be here soon. He has a nose for a party, so there's no way he'll miss one like this with so many VIPs in attendence.

(a) The police academy grads have a nose for bomb detection.

(b) If you have a nose for news, how about joining the staff of the college's daily newspaper?

(c) I don't have a nose for money-making ideas. That's why I'm still a renter even though I'm this old.

Note

Kiku means "(for one's nose) to work effectively."

homograph

have a screw loose / phr. / metaphor

to be {eccentric/crazy}
ちょっとおかしくなる

Example

Sam's had a screw loose ever since he lost his mother.
サムは母親を亡くしてからちょっとおかしくなった。

300

も自然な表現になる。

同形異義語

大口をたたく / phr. / 隠喩

偉そうなこと、大げさなことを言う
to brag or exaggerate

例文

彼はいつも大口をたたくが、何もしない。
He always brags, but he never acts.

鼻が利く / phr. / 隠喩

何かを{見つける / 認める}本能的な能力を持っている

例文

マイク：あれ、木村君、まだ来ていないの？

同僚：もうすぐ、現れるんじゃないかな。彼は鼻が利くから、こんなに VIP が集まる
パーティに来ないわけがないよ。

- (a) 警察学校の卒業生は、爆弾探知に鼻が利く。
- (b) ニュースに対して鼻が利くのなら、学生新聞の編集部に加わりませんか。
- (c) 私はもうけ話にはまったく鼻が利きません。おかげでこの年になっても借家住
まいです。

解説

日本語の「利く」は"(鼻の)働きが十分発揮される"という意味である。

同形異義語

ねじがゆるんでいる / phr. / 隠喩

緊張感がなくて、だれている
to run out of energy

例文

大学に入ってから、弟はねじがゆるんでしまった。勉強もせず、遊んでばかりいる。
After entering college, my younger brother ran out of energy for studying and
ended up just fooling around all the time.

H

301

have a weakness for ~ / phr. metaphor

to love {s.t./s.o.} so much that one cannot resist {it/that person}

REL have a {weak/soft} spot for ~

Examples

Saya: Hey, Mrs. Suzuki.

Mrs. S: Oh, Saya, what a good timing! I was just about to have tea and cake.

Saya: More like bad timing. I just started a diet yesterday, and this is the worst temptation possible. You know I have a weakness for sweets.

- -

(a) I have a huge weakness for science fiction, especially when it speaks to the human condition.

(b) Since graduating from college, Sally has only dated policemen and military officers. Apparently she has a real weakness for men in uniform.

Notes

1. The basic meaning of both *weakness* and *yowai* is "having little strength."
2. In addition to the meaning "to love," *(~ ni) yowai* can also mean "to be unable to handle ~." The expression *(~ ni) tsuyoi* can be used in the opposite sense of "to be good at ~." 📖💬—解説(**1**)(**2**)

REL

The English REL, *have a {weak/soft} spot for ~*, is similar to the main entry in that it describes a strong affinity, but *have a weakness for ~* tends to have a romantic connotation when used to describe one's feelings toward another person, whereas *have a {weak/soft} spot for ~* often denotes platonic affection.

have an eye for ~ / phr. metaphor

to be very good at {noticing/assessing} the value of s.t.

REL have a sharp eye for ~

Examples

Mrs. S: Did Mr. Goto really quit the company and open a store?

Mr. S: Yes, apparently he started up an antique shop. He's always had an eye for china.

- -

(a) My friend George has an eye for sculptures.

(b) I probably don't have an eye for people, considering how often I get tricked.

Note

In Japanese, one cannot say *me ga aru* (to have an eye); rather, one must say *miru me ga aru* (lit. "to have an eye that sees").

REL

The English REL, *have a sharp eye for ~*, can replace the main entry; in fact, the adjective *sharp* is implied even when it is not used. The Japanese RELs *(~ni) me ga kiku* (one's

（〜に）弱い　/ phr. adj. (i)　隠喩

{何か / 誰か}が大好きで、その魅力に逆らえない

例文

さや：こんにちは。

鈴木(妻)：あら、さやさん、グッドタイミング！　これからお茶とケーキにするところよ。

さや：いいえ、バッドタイミングですよ。昨日からダイエット始めたのに、すごい誘惑。私、甘いものに弱いんですよね。

(a) 私はとりわけ SF に弱いんだ。特に人間の置かれた状況を扱っている場合はね。

(b) 大学を卒業して以来、サリーは警察官や軍人とばかりデートをしている。明らかに制服を着た男性に弱いようだ。

解説

1. 「弱い」と weakness の共通の基本義は、"{人 / 何か}が肉体に力がない状態"である。

2. 日本語の「(〜に)弱い」には "好きだ" という意味の他に "(〜が)苦手だ" という意味がある。その反意表現として「(〜に)強い」という表現があり、"(〜が)得意だ" という意味である。

(1) 私は数学{に弱い/ が苦手だ}。
I'm not good at math. (lit. "I'm weak at math.")

(2) 私は数学{に強い/ が得意だ}。
I'm good at math. (lit. "I'm strong at math.")

関連語

英語の関連表現に have a {weak/soft} spot for ~（〜に弱いところがある）がある。見出しの have a weakness for ~ が相手に対する恋愛的な気持ちを表す時に用いられる傾向があるのに対し、have a {weak/soft} spot for ~ は精神的な愛情を表す時に使用される。

見る目がある　/ phr.　隠喩

何かを評価することに秀でている

関　(〜に)目が利く，(〜については)目利きだ

例文

鈴木(妻)：後藤さんって、会社をやめて何かお店を始めたの？

鈴木(夫)：うん、骨董店を始めたらしいよ。彼は昔から焼き物を見る目があったからね。

(a) 友人のジョージは彫刻を見る目がある。

(b) 私は人を見る目がないのか、よく人にだまされる。

解説

日本語は英語のようにただ「目がある」とは言えない。「見る目がある」と言わなければならない。

関連語

日本語の関連表現の「(〜に)目が利く」と「(〜については)目利きだ」は「見る目がある」と

eyes function well with regards to ~) and *(~ ni tsuite wa) me-kiki da* (to have a sharp eye with regards to ~) can replace *miru me ga aru*. The verb *kiku* means "for s.t.'s {function/effect} to manifest itself." 📖→関連語(1)

have {an/one's} eye on ~ / phr. / metaphor

to show strong interest in or pay careful attention to {s.t./s.o.}

Examples

Mrs. S: What's a niche business?

Mr. S: It's a business that has its eye on an area very few people deal with.

Mrs. S: So if you can figure out what people want, you can earn a lot of money.

Mr. S: Yeah, it's possible.

(a) To revitalize his prefecture's economy, the governor has his eye on high-tech enterprises and tourism.

(b) I've had my eye on Michiya since freshmen year. He's super cute, funny, and sooo smart.

---

have cold feet → **{get/have} cold feet**

---

have eyes in the back of one's head / phr. / metaphor

to be very alert and notice everything, even things that others are trying to conceal

Examples

Mrs. S: Kenta! Don't eat your snack with those dirty hands!

Kenta: Wait, how'd you see me when you're looking the other way?

Mrs. S: Don't you know I've got eyes in the back of my head?

(a) My father always knew when I was up to no good. I was convinced he had eyes in the back of his head.

(b) They say that pitcher has eyes in the back of his head. A base never gets stolen on his watch.

Note

The basic meaning of *have* is "to be in possession of s.t.," and the meaning of *tsuite iru* is "for {s.t./s.o.} to be attached to {s.t. else/s.o. else}."

同じ意味で使われる。「利く」は"作用や効果が現れる"という意味である。英語の関連表現は見出しに形容詞の *sharp*（鋭い）が加わっただけである。

(1) 祖父は骨董品 {を見る目がある / に目が利く / については目利きだ}。
My grandfather has {an eye/a sharp eye} for antiques.

（〜に）目をつける　　phr.　隠喩

強い関心を示す，よく注意する

例文

鈴木(妻)：ねえ、ニッチビジネスって何？

鈴木(夫)：需要はあるけれど特殊なので、あまり人が手を出さないところに目をつけたビジネスだよ。

鈴木(妻)：じゃ、目のつけどころがよかったら、大成功もあり得るわけね。

鈴木(夫)：まあ、そうだね。

(a) 知事は県の経済復興のためにハイテクと観光に目をつけている。

(b) 私、大学1年のときから道也に目をつけてきたのよね。彼ってとってもかわいいし、おもしろいし、とっても頭がいいのよ。

H

頭の後ろに（も）目がついている　　phr.　隠喩

見てもいないのに何が起きているかがわかる

例文

鈴木(妻)：こら、健太、そんな汚い手で、つまみぐいするんじゃないの。

健太：え、お母さん、向こうむいてたのに、どうしてわかるの。

鈴木(妻)：あら、私は頭の後ろにも目がついているのよ。知らなかった？

(a) 父は僕が何か悪さをしようとしていると、いつでもわかっていたんです。だから私は父の頭の後ろに目がついているとばかり思っていました。

(b) そのピッチャーは頭の後ろに目がついていると言われる。彼がマウンドにいるときは、盗塁はぜったいに不可能だ。

解説

「ついている」と *have* の基本義は、それぞれ、"{誰か / 何か}につながっている"と"何かを所有している"である。

305

have one's feet on the ground /phr. / metaphor

for s.o.'s {behavior/feelings} to be sensible and realistic

Examples

Mr. S: How's Kenta doing these days?

Mrs. S: Just working part-time and messing around as usual. He doesn't have his feet on the ground. I wish he'd study harder.

- -

(a) He is a good family man who has his feet on the ground.

(b) My boss has his feet on the ground and doesn't rush into any decision.

Note

The affirmative form is more frequently used in English, while the negative form is more frequent in Japanese.

---

have goose bumps (鳥肌が立つ) → {get/have} goose bumps
とりはだ　　　た

---

have one's hands full (with ~) /phr. / metaphor

to be so busy doing s.t. that one cannot do anything else

Examples

Section Chief: Mike, would you mind translating this letter for me?

Mike: Actually, I have my hands full with something else right now.

Section Chief: Oh, okay. I'll have you do it later, then.

- -

(a) When my children were small, I had my hands full taking care of them and doing housework.

(b) American college students have their hands full with their studies and extra-curricular activities, so they have no time to watch the news.

Notes

1. *Have one's hands full (with ~)* and *(~de) te (ga) ippai* both mean "to be unable to carry anymore because one's hands are full of s.t."
2. In Japanese, *ippai* (full) is the colloquial version of *takusan*, but *ˣte ga takusan* cannot replace *te ga ippai*.

REL

The Japanese REL, *te ga fusagatte iru*, means "one cannot use one's hands due to s.t. occupying them." It can replace *(~ de) te (ga) ippai.* 📖→関連語(1)

306

足が地に着いている　/phr.　隠喩

{行動 / 気持ち}が常識的、現実的でしっかりしている

例文

鈴木(夫)：最近、健太はどうなの？

鈴木(妻)：相変わらずバイトと遊びばかりで足が地に着いていないのよ。もっとしっかり勉強してほしいんだけど。

- -

(a) 彼はいい家庭人で、足が地に着いた生活をしている。

(b) 私の上司は足が地に着いている人で、性急に結論を出さない。

解説

日本語では否定形が、英語では肯定形が、それぞれ使用頻度が高い。

(〜で)手(が)いっぱい　/phr.　隠喩

とても忙しくて他のことをする余裕がない

関 手がふさがっている

例文

課長：マイク、この手紙の翻訳をしてくれないかなあ。

マイク：すみません、今、ちょっと他の仕事で手がいっぱいなので。

課長：ああ、じゃ、後で頼むよ。

- -

(a) 子供が小さかった頃は、子育てや家事で手がいっぱいだった。

(b) アメリカの大学生は、勉強や宿題や論文やクラブ活動で手がいっぱいで、ニュースを見る時間もないそうだ。

解説

1. 「(〜で)手(が)いっぱい」と *have one's hands full (with 〜)* は、どちらも"手に何かがたくさんあって、それ以上は持てない"という意味である。

2. 「いっぱい」は「たくさん」の会話体であるが、「手(が)いっぱい」の代わりに「*手(が)たくさん」とは言えない。

関連語

日本語には関連表現として「手がふさがっている」があり、見出しの「(〜で)手(が)いっぱい」と置き換えることができる。

(1) 母親は{手(が)いっぱいだった / 手がふさがっていた}ので、幸恵は下の兄弟たちの世話をしなければならなかった。

Her mother had her hands full, so Yukie often had to care for her younger siblings.

have no {backbone/spine} / phr. / metaphor

to lack courage

REL spineless

Examples

(a) He has no backbone, so he can't hold out against pressure.

(b) He doesn't have a backbone or any real convictions, so they call him "the weathervane."

(c) People say she has no backbone, that she gets too emotional when faced with adversity.

Notes

1. The English and Japanese are different only in that the former uses *backbone* while the latter uses *hone* (bone).
2. *Nashi* is an archaic form of *(~ ga) nai* (s.t. does not exist).
3. In Japanese, one can also say *hone-nashi no* (*noun*), which means "a boneless (noun)."

R E L

1. *Hone-nashi* is typically used in casual speech. In writing or formal speech, the Sino-Japanese *kikotsu ga nai* can be used. 📖→関連語(1)
2. The English REL, *spineless*, is an adjective with the same meaning as the main entry.

(2) He {has no backbone/is spineless}. (→(a))

A N T

The Japanese has two ANTs: *hone ga aru* (to have bones) and *kikotsu ga aru* (lit. "to have a soul and bones"). The latter is more formal than the former. 📖→反意語(1)

have (s.t.) on hand / phr. / metaphor

for s.t. to be readily accessible

REL keep (s.t.) on hand

Examples

Saya: Karen, this dictionary is pretty good.

Karen: Let me see. Hmm, *A Bilingual Dictionary of English and Japanese Metaphors*, huh...

Saya: It's really useful having something like this on hand. You should buy a copy.

- -

(a) The following is crucial data you need to have on hand.

(b) You should have the following items on hand in case of a storm.

(c) I always make sure to have a credit card on hand in case of an emergency.

Note

The English verb is simply *have*, but in Japanese, the verb can be *motte iru* (to possess), as in (a); *aru* (to exist), as shown in the dialogue; or *sonaeru* (to prepare), as shown in (b).

R E L

Te-moto is a compound noun that indicates the area closest to one's hands. It can be replaced by the compound *tejika*, which means "s.t. close enough to the hands to be

骨無し / comp. n. 隠喩
性格がしっかりしていない

関 気骨が無い

反 骨がある，気骨がある

例文

(a) 彼は骨無しで、プレッシャーに弱い。

(b) 彼は骨無しで、自分の信念がないから風見鶏と言われている。

(c) 彼女は苦境に立つと感情的になり過ぎて、骨無しになるそうだ。

解説

1. 日英語は、日本語がただの「骨」に対して、英語は*backbone*（背骨）という点で異なっている。

2. 日本語の「無し」は「（～が）無い」の古い形である。

3. 「骨無し」は「骨無しの＋名詞」のように修飾語としても使える。

関連語

1. 日本語の「骨無し」はどちらかというと話し言葉だが、書き言葉か改まった会話では、漢語の「気骨が無い」という表現が使われる。

(1) 彼は｛骨無しで／気骨が無くて｝、プレッシャーに弱い。（→(a)）

2. 英語には、見出しと同じ意味の形容詞 *spineless* という関連表現がある。━📖REL(2)

反意語

日本語には反意表現として「骨がある」と「気骨がある」があり、後者は前者より堅い表現である。

(1) 彼は｛骨／気骨｝があり、プレッシャーに強い。

He has {a firm character/ ×bones} and can hold out against pressure.

H

手元に {ある /（おいて）おく / 持っている} phr. 隠喩
何かがそばにある

関 手近に {ある /（おいて）おく / 持っている}

例文

さや：カレン、この辞書、なかなかいいよ。

カレン：どれどれ、『日英共通メタファー辞典』…。

さや：こんな辞書が手元にあると、とても便利。カレンも買ったら。

(a) 手元に持っているべき重要なデータは次の通りです。

(b) 暴風が来る前に次のようなものを手元に備えておくべきです。

(c) 緊急時に備えて、私は常にクレジットカードを手元におくことにしている。

解説

英語の動詞は*have*だけであるが、日本語では(a)のように「持っている」や、会話例のように「ある」や、(b)のように「備える」などが使える。

関連語

日本語の「手元」は複合名詞で、手のごく近くの空間を表す。これは"何かが近くにあって便利だ"という意味の複合語の「手近」で置き換えることができる。

conveniently within reach." 📖📄→関連語(1)

have one foot in the grave / phr. / metaphor

to be likely to die soon

Examples

Kenta: Grandpa's so energetic.

Mrs. S: I know. He might be in his 90s, and he says that he has one foot in the grave, but he still works out in the fields.

(a) I battled cancer for six years, and I felt like I had one foot in the grave the whole time.

Note

Both the English and Japanese refer to death euphemistically.

have some nerve / phr. / metaphor

to speak and behave shamelessly without paying attention to other people's feelings

REL thoughtless; inconsiderate; shameless; shame on you

Examples

Mr. S: When I told the girl at the reception desk that she'd put on some weight, she just glared at me.

Mrs. S: Of course she did! You have some nerve!

(a) The teacher had some nerve saying such a thing to my sister. Now she's even stopped going to school!

(b) Scott told me that when he went to Japan, he felt the people had a lot of nerve for staring at him and making him uncomfortable.

Note

Mu-shinkē (*mu* [nothing] + *shinkē* [nerves]) is a Sino-Japanese compound that means "to have no nerves," but the latter cannot be used metaphorically.

REL

1. In English, there are some adjectives related to the main entry, such as *thoughtless*, *inconsiderate*, and *shameless*, among others. In the dialogue, *You have got some nerve!* can be replaced by *Shame on you!* Likewise, (a) and (b) can be rephrased using *thoughtless* or *inconsiderate*.
2. In Japanese, there are two RELs. One is *kokoro-nai* (lit. "the heart does not exist"), which means "to have an inconsiderate character or do s.t. people dislike." This is used in written Japanese. The other expression is *derikashī ga nai* (lit. "delicacy is missing"), which borrows the word *delicacy* from English. This phrase means "to lack delicacy in one's words and actions or waver in one's beliefs and principles." 📖→ 関連語(1)

310

(1) 研究論文を書くときに、どんな参考文献を{手近/手元}に持っていたらいいでしょうか。
What kinds of reference materials should you have on hand when writing a research paper?

棺桶に片足を突っ込む　phr.　隠喩

死が近いこと

例文

健太：おじいちゃんて、ほんと元気だね。

鈴木(妻)：そうね。もう90を過ぎて、棺桶に片足を突っ込んでるなんて言いながら、まだまだ元気に畑仕事をしているんだもんね。

(a) 6年以上、私は癌と闘ってきた。本当に棺桶に片足を突っ込んだ感じだった。

解説

日英語共に、死というものを直接表現することを避けた婉曲話法である。

無神経(な)　adj. (na)　隠喩

他人の気持ちや自分の恥、外聞を気にしない言動を取ること

関 心ない, デリカシーがない

例文

鈴木(夫)：会社の受け付けの女の子に、「君、最近、ちょっとぽっちゃりしてきたね」って言ったら、すごい目でにらまれちゃった。

鈴木(妻)：当たり前よ。あなたって無神経ね。

(a) 先生に無神経なことを言われたせいで、妹は学校に行くのをやめてしまった。

(b) 日本に行ったとき、人々にじろじろ無神経に見られて、不愉快な気分にさせられたとスコットが言っていた。

解説

日本語の「無神経」は漢語系複合語で、字義通りには"神経が無い"という意味である。「神経が無い」は英語に対応するが、これは比喩としては使われない。

関連語

1. 英語には関連表現として、*thoughtless*(思いやりがない)、*inconsiderate*(思いやりがない)、*shameless*(恥を知らない)、*shame on you!*(恥を知れ！)などがある。会話例の*You have some nerve!* は *Shame on you!* に言い換えることができる。(a)(b)の同じ表現も *thoughtless* か *inconsiderate* で言い換えることができる。

2. 日本語には関連表現が二つある。一つは「心ない」で、"人への思いやりがない"あるいは"人が嫌がることをする"性格を意味する。もう一つは英語の *delicacy* を「デリカシー」として借用して、人を思いやる繊細さがない、あるいは節操がないことを「デリカシーがない」という。

(1) あなたって{無神経/心ない人/デリカシーがない}ね。(→会話例)
You have some nerve!/Shame on you!/How {thoughtless/inconsiderate} of you!

have strings attached (to ~) / phr. / metaphor

for {help/an offer} to come with conditions

Examples

(a) It should be emphasized that future American aid will have strings attached.

(b) The school superintendent said some grants have strings attached to them.

(c) If they insist on attaching strings to the money, then we don't need it.

Note

The negative version of the English expression, i.e., *have no strings attached*, is quite common, especially as an adverbial phrase. However, the negative version of the Japanese expression, i.e., *himo tsuki {de wa nai/ja nai}*, is very seldom used.

(1) I thought the grant I received would have no strings attached, but then I found out that my research would have to be in line with what the foundation thought was appropriate.
私が受け取った奨学金はひも付きではないと思っていたが、私の研究は基金が適当だと考えるような線に添わなければならないことがわかった。

have the last laugh / phr. / metaphor

to win or succeed in the end in spite of difficulties

Examples

Mrs. S: Kenta, how's the studying for your entrance exams coming along?

Kenta: I'll be fine. It'll work out somehow.

Mrs. S: "It'll work out somehow?" Remember: He who works hard has the last laugh! Don't get too complacent!

- -

(a) Everyone said that there was nothing good in store for us. But it looks like we had the last laugh!

(b) They beat us every time except in the Championships last year, so you could say we had the last laugh.

Notes

1. *Laugh* is used as a noun, but *warau* is a verb.
2. The Japanese usually appears within a dependent clause. 📖→解説(1)

ひも付きの〜　/ n. phr. /　隠喩

条件付きの{援助 / 申し出}

例文

(a) 今後のアメリカの援助は、ひも付きになるだろうということを強調しておく必要がある。

(b) 教育長は、助成金の中にはひも付きのものがあると言った。

(c) 援助金をひも付きにしなければならないというのなら、そんな金は要らない。

解説

英語の否定形は特に *have no strings attached* という副詞句の形でよく使われているが、日本語の否定形の「ひも付き{ではない / じゃない}」は、言うことはあるが使用頻度は低い。

→📖Note(1)

最後に笑う　/ phr. /　隠喩

H

困難な状況にもかかわらず最終的に{成功する / 勝つ}

例文

鈴木(妻)：健太、留学試験のほう、どうなってるの？

健太：大丈夫だよ、お母さん。なんとかなるよ。

鈴木(妻)：何言ってるの。最後に笑うことができるのは、努力をし続けた者だけなんですからね。油断してたら、だめよ。

(a) みんなが僕達にはいいことはないなんて言っていたけど、最後に笑ったのは誰だと思っているんだ？　僕たちじゃないか。

(b) 優勝決定戦以外は、ずっと彼らにしてやられたが、結局、最後に笑ったのはわれわれだったと言える。

解説

1. 日本語では「笑う」は動詞であるが、英語の *laugh* は名詞である。

2. 日本語は従属節内で使われることに注意。

(1) a. 最後に笑ったのは彼だった。

　　　It was he who had the last laugh.

　　b. ×彼は最後に笑った。

　　　(lit. "He laughed last."/"He had the last laugh.")

313

have (a) wide knowledge of ~ / phr. / metaphor
to know a lot of things about s.t.

Examples

(a) He has a wide knowledge of computer technology.

(b) She has a wide knowledge of art, literature, and music.

(c) In order to obtain a doctorate, one is expected to have a wide knowledge of one's particular field.

Notes

1. *Wide* means "containing a large area between two sides," and *hiroi* means "extensive in terms of two-dimensional space." So *hiroi* can be used not only in reference to something of great width, but also when the space in general is large. 📖→解説(1)(2)
2. When something has a large width, *haba-hiroi* can be used in addition to *hiroi*. One cannot use *haba-hiroi* in (2), since a room is a space, but one can say, for example, *kono tsukue wa haba (ga) hiroi* (this desk is wide).

REL

The Japanese REL is *hiroi chishiki ga aru*. 📖→関連語(1)

head count / comp. n. / metonymy
the number of {people/animals}

Examples

Karen: Mike, you're coming to the party next week, right?

Mike: Yeah, I'm going. I'm thinking of bringing drinks. Can you give me an approximate head count?

Karen: Let's see... I think it's around 30. Thanks so much.

- -

(a) Reducing the employee head count during an economic downturn isn't exactly the best strategy.

(b) The head count for the course dropped, so one of the sections was canceled.

Notes

1. If the Japanese is read *atamakazu* (the *kun* reading), then it refers to the number of people, but if it is read *tōsū* (the *on* reading), it refers to the number of animals.
2. Since the entire body is being represented by the head, this is a case of metonymy.
3. *Head count* can be used for both people and animals, but *atamakazu* can be used only to count people.

知識が（幅）広い　/ phr.　隠喩

あることについていろいろなことを知っている

関 広い知識がある

例 文

(a) 彼はコンピュータテクノロジーについて知識が広い。

(b) 彼女は芸術、文学、音楽の知識が広い。

(c) 博士号を取るには、専門分野についてかなり広い知識が要求される。

解 説

1. 日英語の「広い」と wide は、それぞれ、"二次元の空間が大きい"と"一つの側からもう一つ
の側までの空間が大きい"という意味を持っている。したがって、日本語の形容詞「広い」は
幅が大きい場合だけではなく、空間が大きい場合にも使う。

(1) この道は広い。
This street is wide.

(2) この部屋は{広い/×幅広い}。
This room is {large/×wide}.

2. 幅が大きい場合は、日本語の「広い」は「幅広い」とも言う。(2)のような場合、部屋は空間
なので「×この部屋は幅広い」とは言えないが、「この机は幅(が)広い」とは言える。

関連語

日本語の関連表現は「広い知識がある」である。

(1) 彼女は芸術、文学、音楽について広い知識がある。(→(b))

頭数　comp. n.　換喩

人の数

例 文

カレン：マイクも来週のパーティ、来るでしょ。

マイク：うん、行くよ。何か飲み物持って行こうと思うけど、参加者の頭数、だいた
いどのぐらいかな。

カレン：う～ん、30 人ぐらいかな。よろしくね。

- -

(a) 不況のときに従業員の頭数を減らすのが一番いいやり方だとは言えない。

(b) 学生の頭数が減ったので、クラスが一つキャンセルになった。

解 説

1. 日本語では、「頭数」を「あたまかず」と訓読みにすれば人の数だが、「とうすう」と音読みに
すれば動物の数になる。

2. 体の一部の頭で全体を表しているので換喩である。

3. 英語では、人でも動物でも数をかぞえるときに head count を使えるが、日本語の「あたまか
ず」は人を数えるときにしか使えない。

H

315

head of ~ / n. phr. / personification

the upper part of s.t.

Examples

(a) When I drove the nail into the board, I hit my finger instead because the head of the nail was so small. It really hurt!

(b) You know those greetings you use at the head of each e-mail? You should make templates.

(c) Hey, that guy just skipped to the head of the line!

Note

When a person or a thing is at the top of a category, *head of* ~ can be used, but *atama* cannot be used in this manner. 📖→解説(1)

heads {will/are going to} roll / phr. / metaphor

people will be {severely punished/dismissed}

REL get fired

Examples

Colleague: Apparently heads are, going to roll after that screwup the other day.

Mike: Talk about harsh. Our company hasn't exactly been doing great, so I can't afford to give them an excuse to fire me.

- -

(a) Heads are rolling in upper management, and there've been rumors about more employee layoffs on the horizon.

(b) Eventually it was revealed that the company's senior management had been involved in widespread fraud, so many heads will end up rolling.

Note

Heads {will/are going to} roll can also be used in tenses other than the future tense, such as the present progressive and past tenses. Likewise, *(~ no) kubi ga tobu* can be used in the future, present progressive, and past tenses.

REL

The English REL is *get fired* and the Japanese REL is *kubi ni naru* (lit. "to become a head"). 📖→関連語(1)

It should be noted, however, that *heads will roll* does not necessarily refer to losing one's job.

(2) If the teacher finds out the students cheated, heads will roll.
先生が学生のカンニングに気がついたら、その学生は退学をさせられる。

316

～の頭 n. phr. 擬人化

何かの{上 / はじめ}の部分

例文

(a) 板に打ちつけるとき、くぎの頭が小さかったので自分の指をたたいてしまった。とても痛かった。

(b) メールの頭でよく使う挨拶文がありますよね。登録しておくといいですよ。

(c) おい、あいつが行列の頭に割り込んだぞ。

解説

人や物がある範疇でトップの時に英語では *head of ~* が使えるが、日本語では(1)で示すように「頭」は使えない。

(1) メアリーはずば抜けて優秀だ。クラスで { 一番 / ˣ頭 } だそうだ。
Mary is super smart. I heard she's at the {head/top} of her class.

(～の)首が飛ぶ phr. 隠喩

解雇される，罷免される

関 首になる

例文

同僚：あいつら、この間の仕事のミスで、みんな首が飛ぶぞ。

マイク：そんなに厳しいのか。うちも不景気だから、首になる口実を与えないようにしないとね。

(a) 上級管理職の首が飛んで、事務職の一時解雇も増えるといううわさが流れている。

(b) 最後には会社の上層部が絡んだ詐欺事件がすべて明るみに出たから、多くの首が飛ぶだろう。

解説

英語の見出し *heads {will/are going to} roll* は未来形だが、現在進行形でも過去形でも自由に使える。また、日本語の見出し「(～)の首が飛ぶ」は現在形だが、未来形でも現在進行形でも過去形でもよい。

関連語

日英語の関連表現には、それぞれ、「首になる」と *get fired* がある。

(1) あの男 {の首が飛ぶ / は首になる} だろう。
His head's gonna roll./He's gonna get fired.
ただし、*heads will roll* は、「厳罰に処する」という意味もあり、必ずしも「首になる」という意味とは限らないことに注意。　📖 REL(2)

317

healthy /adj. / metaphor

for s.t. to be conducive to one's health

[ANT] unhealthy; sick

Examples

Mr. S: What's your hometown like?

Mike: It's a country town in Wisconsin surrounded by forest and lakes. The air's clean and it's a very healthy environment.

- - - - - - - - - - - - - - - - - - - -

(a) If you keep eating healthy food, you will become healthy.

(b) As a mother, it's important to exemplify a healthy lifestyle.

(c) We know that healthy habits are good for our well-being. But that's not all: they're good for our society, too!

Notes

1. The non-metaphorical meaning of *healthy* and *kenkō(-teki)na* is "for {s.o./s.t.} to be in good health," but when used figuratively they mean "for s.t. to be likely to produce good health."

2. Both *kenkōna* and *kenkō-tekina* can be used, but *kenkōna* is used more often when followed by the nouns *shakai* (society), *sēkatsu* (life), or *kokoro* (heart). *Kenkō-tekina* is used more often when followed by the nouns *kankyō* (environment), *imēji* (image), *shokuji* (food), or *shūkan* (custom).

[R][E][L]

Kenkōna means "having a strong body," but *kenzenna* means "well-balanced in both mind and body." 📖— 関連語(**1**)

[A][N][T]

The English ANTs are *unhealthy* and *sick*, and the Japanese ANTs are *fukenkōna* and *byōki (no)*.

(1) He often gets sick because he has a very unhealthy lifestyle. He's out sick today, too.
彼は非常に不健康な生活をしているので、よく病気になる。今日も病気で会社に来ていない。

one's heart aches for s.o. /phr. / metaphor

one feels sympathy for s.o. who is in an unfortunate situation

Examples

Karen: Look at these kids. They're nothing but skin and bones! They must be starving.

Saya: Yeah. My heart aches for them whenever I see photos like this.

- - - - - - - - - - - - - - - - - - - -

(a) The pain of being abandoned must've been too much to bear. My heart aches for her.

(b) You've lost a pet you were close to as well. Please know that my heart aches for you.

健康(的)な adj. (na) 隠喩

健康そうに見える，健康のためになる（健康にいい）

関 健全な

反 不健康な，病気(の)

例文

鈴木(夫)：マイクの郷里はどんなところなの。

マイク：ウィスコンシンの田舎ですよ。緑や湖に囲まれて、空気もきれいでとても健康的な環境です。

- (a) 健康的な食事を続ければ、健康になる。
- (b) 母親として健康的なイメージのお手本を実際に示すことは、大変大事だと思います。
- (c) 健康的な習慣はわれわれの幸福のためにいいことはわかっているが、それだけではない。われわれの社会にもいいのだ。

解説

1. 「健康(的)な」も *healthy* も、その基本義は "{誰か/何か} が元気だ" という意味であるが、その比喩的意味は "何かが健康を生みやすい" という意味である。

2. 日本語の「健康な」と「健康的な」はどちらも使えるが、次に来る名詞が「社会」「生活」「心」では「健康な」が、「環境」「イメージ」「食事」「習慣」では「健康的な」のほうが多く使われている。

関連語

「健康な」は "人の体が丈夫だ" という意味であるが、「健全な」は "心身ともにうまくバランスがとれている" という意味である。

(1) {健全 /×健康} な精神は {健康 / 健全} な身体に宿る。
   Strong body, strong mind.

反意語

日本語には反意表現として「不健康な」「病気(の)」があり、英語には *unhealthy*、*sick* がある。

→📖 ANT(1)

心が痛む phr. 隠喩

誰かの状況にとても同情して苦しくなる

例文

カレン：この子達、こんなにやせちゃって、ろくに食べていないんでしょうね。

さや：そうね。こんな写真を見ると心が痛むわね。

- (a) 彼女にとって捨てられたことはあまりにも大きな出来事だったにちがいない。彼女の気持ちを思うと、私は心が痛む。
- (b) あなたも可愛がっていたペットをなくしたのね。他人事でなく、私も心が痛みます。

Note

Since *ache* is typically used to refer to body parts, its usage with the emotional *heart* is figurative.

---

one's heart sinks / **phr.** / **metaphor**

to feel extremely disappointed or dismayed; to lose hope

ANT one's heart leaps

Examples

Saya: Did you hear that the Giants lost?

Karen: Yeah. When I heard the news, my heart sank. They were so close to winning the series!

- - - - - - - - - - - - - - - - - - -

(a) When my family learned that our dog, which we'd had for 18 years, couldn't be saved due to his old age, our hearts sank.

(b) My heart sank when I thought of my troubles with the department chief.

Notes

1. The English can be used to express shock in addition to dejection, but the Japanese can only be used to express dejection.

(1) I was just about finished with the main part of my paper when the power suddenly went out. My heart sank when I realized I hadn't saved it.
僕は論文の主な部分をもうちょっとで書き終えるところだったのに停電になっちゃって、{がっくりきた/⁺気分が沈んだ}ね。論文を保存しておかなかったんだ。

2. Both the English and Japanese use verbs that describe being submerged in water, i.e., *sink* and *shizumu*. It is probably not a coincidence that both languages use this kind of verb to express feelings of depression.

REL

The Japanese RELs are *ki ga shizumu* (lit. "one's soul sinks") and *kokoro ga shizumu* (lit. "one's heart sinks"). Both can replace *{kimochi/kibun} ga shizumu*, but *kibun ga shizumu* is the most commonly used form, whereas *kokoro ga shizumu* is the least common, as it is used in written Japanese. 📖➡関連語⑴

ANT

The English ANT is *one's heart leaps*, and the Japanese ANT is *kokoro ga {odoru/hazumu}* (lit. "one's heart {dances/bounds}").

(1) When I found out he was coming here, my heart leapt with joy.
彼がここに来ると知ったとき、喜びのあまり心が{躍った/弾んだ}。

解説

普通は痛むのは体の一部であるから、「心」と *heart* が痛むのは比喩表現である。

{気持ち / 気分} が沈む　　phr.　隠喩

{憂鬱 / 落ち込んだ気持ち} になる

関 気が沈む，心が沈む

反 心が {躍る / 弾む}

例文

さや：ねえ、ジャイアンツが負けたって聞いた？

カレン：うん、そのニュースを聞いて、気分が沈んじゃった。ほとんどシリーズ優勝すると思っていたのに。

(a) 18年も飼っていた犬が老衰でもう助からないと聞いて、家族はみんな気分が沈んでしまった。

(b) 部長とのもめ事のことを考えると気持ちが沈んだ。

解説

1. 英語は沈んだ感情ばかりではなく、心理的なショックを表現するのにも使えるが、日本語は沈んだ気持ちだけを表す。━📖 Note(1)

2. 日英語とも水中に下降する運動を表す同じ動詞「沈む」と *sink* を使っている。沈んだ気持ちがこのような動詞で表現されるのは偶然ではないだろう。

関連語

日本語には「気が沈む」と「心が沈む」という関連表現がある。どちらも「{気持ち / 気分} が沈む」と置き換えられるが、「気分が沈む」が一番よく使われ、書き言葉の「心が沈む」が一番使用頻度が低い。

(1) 崩壊していく建物からもくもくと上がってくる煙を見つつ、ひどく {気分 / 気 / 心} が沈んだのを思い出した。

I remembered how my heart sank as I watched the smoke billowing up from the collapsing buildings.

反意語

日英語とも、「心が {躍る / 弾む}」と *one's heart leaps*(lit. 心が飛び跳ねる)という反意表現がある。━📖 ANT(1)

H

one's heart stops | phr. | metaphor

one experiences such strong emotions that one's heart (figuratively) stops beating

REL   one's heart stands still; one's heart skips a beat; one's heart freezes

Examples

Kenta: Boo!

Saya: Eek! Geez, you scared me! You really shouldn't sneak up on people like that! You almost made my heart stop!

Kenta: Sorry.

- -

(a) My heart stopped when the truck on the highway almost hit our car.

(b) When a young handsome man smiled at me, my heart stopped.

Note

The English and Japanese expressions are metaphors that are quite close to their literal meanings.

REL

The English RELs *one's heart stands still* and *one's heart skips a beat* can freely replace the main entry. *One's heart freezes* can also replace the main entry, but it is usually used to indicate shock as opposed to positive emotions such as joy and love.

(1) a. When a young handsome man smiled at me, my heart {stopped/stood still/skipped a beat}. (→ (b))

b. My heart {stopped/froze} when the truck on the highway almost hit our car. (→ (a))

heartburn | comp. n. | metaphor

a hot, uncomfortable feeling in one's chest

Examples

Saya: Ugh, I feel sick.

Kenta: What's wrong?

Saya: I've got heartburn from eating too many sweet potatoes.

- -

(a) You should limit or avoid consumption of foods that cause heartburn.

(b) You're more likely to get heartburn if you're overweight.

Notes

1. The nouns *burn* and *yake* are derived from the verbs *burn* and *yakeru* (vi., to burn), respectively.

2. The nouns used in the metaphors, i.e., *heart* and *mune* (chest), are similar, but not exactly the same.

心臓が{止まる / 止まりそうになる}　/ phr. / 換喩

嬉しさや驚きを瞬間的に非常に強く感じる

例文

健太：ワッ！

さや：キャッ！　ああ、びっくりした。驚かさないでよ、そんな後ろから。心臓が止まるかと思っちゃった。

健太：ごめん。

(a) 高速道路でトラックにぶつけられそうになったときには、私は心臓が止まりそうになった。

(b) 若いイケメンの男に微笑みかけられて、私は心臓が止まりそうになった。

解説

日英語は字義通りの解釈にかなり近い比喩である。

関連語

英語の関連表現 one's heart stands still と one's heart skips a beat は、見出しと自由に置き換えることができる。one's heart freezes は、喜びや愛などの好ましい情感とは逆に、何かよくないことで衝撃を受けた気持ちを表す場合に使われる。▶ REL(1)

H

胸焼け　/ comp. n. / 隠喩

胸の内側に感じる熱い不快感

例文

さや：あ、何か気持ち悪い。

健太：どうしたの？

さや：お芋食べ過ぎたら、胸焼けしちゃって。

(a) 胸焼けの原因になるような食べ物は制限するか、食べないようにしなさい。

(b) 太り過ぎだと胸焼けになりやすい。

解説

1. 日英語に使われている名詞の「焼け」と burn は、それぞれ動詞の「焼ける」と burn から来ている。

2. この比喩表現の名詞は「胸」と heart（心臓）で、近いが、同じではない。

323

heartwarming   comp. adj.   metaphor

resulting in feelings of happiness or satisfaction

Examples

Karen: Saya, have you seen this movie?

Saya: Yeah, it was amazing. Really heartwarming. I recommend it.

- -

(a) I expected the volunteer work to be really difficult, but it turned out to be a fun, heartwarming experience.

(b) I always find Mozart's Requierm to be heartwarming whenever I hear it, even during tough times.

(c) Thank you very much for taking the time to write this heartwarming letter.

Note

Both the English and Japanese can be used either before a noun, as in the dialogue, (a), and (c), or in a predicate, as in (b).

heat wave   comp. n.   metaphor

a period of abnormally hot weather

ANT cold wave

Examples

Saya: You look awful today! What's wrong?

Mike: Well, it's been so hot because of the heat wave that I couldn't sleep.

Saya: I heard it's gonna be like that tonight too. It's supposed to go over 90 ℉.

Mike: I'm doomed.

- -

(a) A heat wave occurs when the temperature stays at over 29 ℃ (85 ℉).

(b) Sixty years ago, the most terrible heat wave ever recorded fell upon the city.

Notes

1. *Neppa* is a Chinese compound that consists of *netsu* (heat) and *ha* (wave).
2. Both *wave* and *{ha/pa}* are often used metaphorically. The Japanese is likely to be a direct translation of the English. 📖→解説(1)
3. In Japanese weather forecasts, *neppa* is used far less frequently than *heat wave*, but *kanpa*, like *cold wave*, is used frequently.

ANT

The ANTs of *heat wave* and *neppa* are *cold wave* and *kanpa*, respectively. 📖→反意語(1)

心（が）温まる　/ phr. / 隠喩
（こころ）（あたた）　　　　　（いん ゆ）

穏やかな気持ちになる
（おだ）　　（き も）

例 文

カレン： ねえ、さや、この映画、もう見た？
　　　　　　　　　　（えい が）　　（み）

さや： うん、すごく良かったよ。とっても心温まる映画。お勧めよ。
　　　　　　　（よ）　　　　　　　　　　（こころあたた）（えい が）　　（すす）

(a) 奉仕活動は大変かなと思っていましたが、やってみて楽しい、心温まる体験で
　　（ほう し かつどう）（たいへん）　　　（おも）　　　　　　　　　（たの）　　（こころあたた）（たいけん）
　　した。

(b) モーツァルトのレクイエムを聴くと、どんなに苦しい時でもいつも心が温まる。
　　　　　　　　　　　　　　（き）　　　　　（くる）（とき）　　　　　（こころ）（あたた）

(c) 時間をかけて、この心温まる手紙を書いてくださって、どうもありがとうござい
　　（じ かん）　　　　　（こころあたた）（て がみ）（か）
　　ます。

解 説

日英語とも会話例や(a)(c)のように名詞の前でも、(b)のように述部としても使える。

熱波　/ comp. n. / 隠喩
（ねっ ぱ）　　　　　　　　　（いん ゆ）

H

温度が非常に高い大気の塊が波のように押しよせる現象
（おん ど）（ひ じょう）（たか）（たい き）（かたまり）（なみ）　　　（お）　　　　（げんしょう）

反 寒波
（かん ぱ）

例 文

さや： あら、今日はひどい顔してるじゃない。
　　　　　　（きょう）　　　　　（かお）

マイク： うん、熱波のせいで、暑くてぜんぜん寝られなかったんだ。
　　　　　　　（ねっ ぱ）　　　　（あつ）　　　　　（ね）

さや： 今夜も熱波は続くそうよ。夜になっても30度以上ですって。
　　　　（こん や）（ねっ ぱ）（つづ）　　　（よる）　　　　（ど い じょう）

マイク： 参ったなあ。
　　　　　（まい）

(a) 熱波は気温が摂氏29度（華氏85度）以上が続くときに起こる。
　　（ねっ ぱ）（き おん）（せっ し）（ど）（か し）（ど い じょう）（つづ）　　（お）

(b) 60年前に史上最悪の熱波がその町を襲った。
　　（ねんまえ）（し じょうさいあく）（ねっ ぱ）　　（まち）（おそ）

解 説

1．「熱波」は「熱」+「波」からできている漢字系複合名詞である。

2．「波」も *wave* もよく比喩的に使われる。日本語は英語からの翻訳の可能性が高い。

(1) 音波（おんぱ）/sound wave, 電波（でんぱ）/radio wave
　　短波（たんぱ）/short wave, 長波（ちょうは）/long wave

3．天気予報などでは日本語の「熱波」は英語の *heat wave* よりはるかに使用頻度が低い。しかし、「寒波」は *cold wave* と同じように天気予報でよく使われる。

反意語

日英語の反意表現は、それぞれ「寒波」と *cold wave* である。

(1) ひどい寒波がその町を襲った。
A terrible cold wave hit the city.

325

hide one's feelings / phr. / metaphor

to avoid revealing one's true feelings

Examples

Saya: How's your relationship with him been lately?

Friend: We're still just friends.

Saya: If you keep hiding your feelings like that, someone else may snatch him up.

Friend: I know, but I just don't have the courage.

- -

(a) In most societies, young men tend to hide their feelings for fear of being considered weak.

(b) In Japan, so much emphasis is placed on outward appearances that one often has to hide one's feelings.

Note

Hide one's feelings and (jibun no) kimochi o kakusu are figurative, because in this case, hide and kakusu are being used in reference to something invisible, despite the fact that both mean "to keep {s.o./s.t.} visible out of sight."

high / adj. / metaphor

{a voice/a level/a cost/a temperature/quality/an IQ/etc.} considered above average in degree by general or individual standards

ANT low

Examples

Saya: Kenta, do you want to go to karaoke? Michiko says she's coming too.

Kenta: I'm not going if she goes. When she sings in that tinny, high-pitched voice of hers, I get a headache.

Saya: You're so mean! I'm telling her you said that.

- -

(a) John has attained a high level of proficiency in Japanese.

(b) Oil prices are high because of tensions in the Middle East.

(c) The boy has the flu and is running a high temperature.

(d) This hotel is famous for providing high quality service.

(e) Chimpanzees and dolphins are known for their high IQ.

(f) The company had high profits, so it gave its employees a good bonus.

(g) The student had high aspirations and studied diligently.

(h) Whisky has a much higher alcohol content than beer.

Notes

1. For the most part, the spatial adjectives high and takai share many of the same metaphorical usages, as shown in the examples. But there are some usages that are exclusive

（自分の）気持ちを隠す　/ phr. /　隠喩 /

自分の本当の気持ちを表現しない

【例　文】

さや：例の彼とはその後、どうなの。

友達：相変わらず、友達関係……。

さや：そんないつまでも本当の気持ち隠してると、そのうち他の人に取られちゃうよ。

友達：そうだね。でも、なかなか勇気がなくって。

(a) たいていの社会では、青年は自分が弱いと思われたくないので自分の気持ちを隠す傾向がある。

(b) 日本では、建て前を重んじるあまり、本当の気持ちを隠さなければならないことが多い。

【解　説】

「（自分の）気持ちを隠す」と *hide one's feelings* の基本義は、どちらも "見える{人 / 何か}を見えないようにする" であり、見出しの場合、人の気持ちのように見えないものに「隠す」と *hide* を使っていることから、比喩表現といえる。

H

高い　/ adj. (i) /　隠喩 /

{声 / レベル / 値段 / 温度 / 質 / 知能} など、何かの程度が一般的、あるいは個人的基準に照らして、平均より上に位置する

【反】低い

【例　文】

さや：健太、カラオケ、行かない？　みちこも行くって。

健太：みちこが行くんならやめとくよ。あの高い声で、きんきん歌われると、頭が痛くなるんだ。

さや：ひどい。みちこに言ってやろう。

(a) ジョンの日本語は高いレベルに達している。

(b) 石油の値段は中東の緊張状態のために高くなっている。

(c) 男の子が流感にかかって、高い熱を出している。

(d) このホテルは質の高いサービスを提供することで有名だ。

(e) チンパンジーやイルカは知能が高い動物として知られている。

(f) その会社は、高い収益をあげたので、社員にボーナスをはずんだ。

(g) その学生は常に高い志を持って、勤勉に学んだ。

(h) ウイスキーはビールよりもアルコール度が高い。

【解　説】

1. 日英語は、例文でわかるように、「高い」と *high* という空間関係の形容詞の比喩的な用法を

327

to one language. (1a) - (1e) illustrate cases in which *high* can be used but *takai* cannot. (2a) and (2b) illustrate cases in which *takai* can be used but *high* cannot. 📖 解説(2)

(1) a. The high point of the film is without a doubt the ending.

その映画の{山場/×高い点}は間違いなくラストシーンだ。

b. The former prisoner of war, a young lady who is only 19 years old, is in high spirits.

捕虜だったその19歳の女性は{元気/×高い精神}だった。

c. High winds uprooted a lot of trees around town.

{強風/×高い風}で町の木が何本も根こそぎ倒れた。

d. This meat contains a high amount of fat.

この肉は脂肪の量が{多い/×高い}。

e. In high summer, the temperature often climbs to around 35 ℃.

{真夏/×高い夏}には気温はよく摂氏35度ぐらいまで上がります。

2. There are many Sino-Japanese compounds that use *kō-* (high). 📖 解説(3)

[A][N][T]

Low and *hikui* can be used as ANTs in all of the example sentences. For examples of instances in which *hikui* cannot replace *takai*, see (1a) and (1b). 📖 反意語(1)

hit {a/the} wall　　/ phr. / metaphor

to encounter a non-physical obstacle and be at a loss for what to do about it

[REL] {bump/run} into a wall

Examples

Section Chief: Mike, have you finished the draft for the next project?

Mike: Actually, would you mind waiting just a little longer? We've hit a wall.

- -

(a) When studying a foreign language, everyone hits a wall at some point.

(b) The development of the new game software hit a wall because of financial difficulties, so all progress came to a halt.

(c) As she tried to break out of the role of docile wife, she hit the wall called society.

[R][E][L]

The verbs *hit* and *butsukaru* (to bump into) can be replaced by *{bump/run} into* and *tsuki-ataru* (to run into), respectively. However, these tend to be used less frequently than the main entries.

(1) As she tried to break out of the role of docile wife, she {hit/bumped/ran} into the wall called society. (→(c))

彼女は従順な妻の役割を捨てようとしたとき、世間の壁に{ぶつかった/突き当たった}。

(→(c))

ほとんどすべて共有している。しかし、それぞれの言語固有の使い方もある。(1a)-(1e)は英語では使えるが日本語では使えない例を、(2a)(2b)は日本語では使えるが英語では使えない例を指している。 ➡📖 **Note(1)**

(2) a. この百合は香りが高い。
This lily, {is fragrant/ˣsmells high}.
b. あの人はお高い人だと思っていましたが、実はいい人でした。
I thought he was {a snob/ˣhigh}, but he actually turned out to be nice.

2. 日本語の漢語表現では音読みの複合語がたくさんある。

(3) 高度、高額、高齢、高学年、高品質、高価、高血圧、高気圧、高級、高熱、高温、高音、高低、高等、高速など

kō-do (high degree), *kō-gaku* (high price), *kō-rē* (old age), *kō-gakunen* (upper grades [of elementary school]), *kō-hinshitsu* (high-quality), *kō-ka* (high price), *kō-ketsuatsu* (high blood pressure), *kō-kiatsu* (high atmospheric pressure), *kō-kyū* (high-class), *kō-netsu* (high fever), *kō-on* (high temperature), *kō-on* (high tone/pitch), *kō-tē* (fluctuating), *kō-tō* (advanced), *kō-soku* (high speed), etc.

反意語
反意表現の「低い」と *low* は、例文のほとんどの「高い」と *high* を逆の意味で置き換えることができる。日本語で「高い」が使えるが「低い」が使えないのは次のような場合である。

(1) a. この百合は香りが{高い/ˣ低い}。(→解説(2a))
b. あの人はお{高い/ˣ低い}人だと思っていましたが、実はいい人でした。(→解説(2b))
cf. 腰が{ˣ高い/低い}。(lit. "one's lower back is {high/low}./s.o. is {haughty/humble}.")

H

壁にぶつかる 　phr.　隠喩

何か障害があって、それ以上先に行けない状態

関 壁に突き当たる

例文
課長：マイク、今度のプロジェクトの草稿、できたかな？
マイク：あ、課長。もうちょっと、待っていただけませんか。ちょっと、壁にぶつかっているんですよ。

- -

(a) 外国語を勉強するとき、誰でもどこかで必ず壁にぶつかることがある。

(b) 新しいゲームソフトの開発は、資金難の壁にぶつかって、前に進めなくなってしまった。

(c) 彼女は従順な妻の役割を捨てようとしたとき、世間の壁にぶつかった。

関連語
日英語の動詞「ぶつかる」と *hit* は、それぞれ「突き当たる」と *{bump/run} into* で置き換えることができるが、使用頻度ははるかに低い。➡📖 **REL(1)**

hit the mark / phr. / metaphor

for s.t. to be {precise/valid}

REL be on target

Examples

(a) Your plan hit the mark. We couldn't have achieved our goals without it.

(b) His observations always hit the mark.

(c) Her advice always hits the mark. She taught me to examine myself first if I want to improve my relationships.

Note

The Japanese verb *iru* (to shoot) is often replaced by *eru* (to obtain), although this is incorrect from an etymological perspective. 📖➞解説(1)

[R][E][L]

The English entry can be replaced by *be on target*.

(1) His observations {always hit the mark/are always on target}. (→(b))

[A][N][T]

The Japanese has the ANT *mato ga hazureru.* 📖➞反意語(1)

hold (all) the cards / phr. / metaphor

to have a strong advantage; to be in control

REL {have/hold} a trump card; have an ace up one's sleeve

Examples

(a) When it comes to oil prices, the Middle East now appears to hold all the cards.

(b) The leaders of that country believe that they can hold the cards of diplomacy as long as they obtain a nuclear weapon.

(c) Our team held all the cards throughout the game.

Note

Since this expression comes from card games, the Japanese is likely a translation of the English.

[R][E][L]

1. The English RELs *{have/hold} a trump card* and *have an ace up one's sleeve* are similar to the main entry, though they refer to a specific advantage rather than a general advantage.

2. Likewise, in *kirifuda o motte iru* (to be holding a trump card), *kirifuda* refers to the strongest card in a card game. This expression can replace all instances of *kādo o nigitte iru* in the example sentences. 📖➞ 関連語(1)

的を射る / phr. / 隠喩

物事の肝心な点を確実にとらえる

反 的がはずれる

例文

(a) あなたの計画案はまさに的を射ていた。あなたの案がなかったら私達は目標を達成できなかっただろう。

(b) 彼の意見は、いつも的を射ている。

(c) 彼女のアドバイスはいつも的を射ています。人間関係を改善したいのなら、まず自分を顧みるようにと私に教えてくれました。

解説

語源的には正しくないが、日本語の動詞「射る」はしばしば「得る」で置き換えられる。

(1) あなたの計画案は的を{射/得}ていたから、私達の目標達成に役立った。(→(a))
We were able to meet our goals thanks to your presentation hitting the mark.

関連語

英語の見出しは関連表現の be on target に置き換えられる。►📖 REL(1)

反意語

日本語の反意表現は、「的がはずれる」である。

(1) 彼の意見は、いつも的がはずれている。
His comments always miss the mark.

カードを握る / phr. / 隠喩

何か大事なことに関して、他の人より強い{決定権/発言権}を持っている

関 切り札を持っている

例文

(a) オイルの値段は、現在、中東がカードを握っているように見える。

(b) その国の指導者達は、とりあえず核兵器を持っておけば外交上のカードを握ることができると考えている。

(c) そのゲームの勝敗のカードを握るのは、我がチームだ。

解説

この表現はカードゲームから来たもので、日本語は英語の翻訳の可能性が高い。

関連語

1. 英語の関連表現には見出しに似た {have/hold} a trump card と have an ace up one's sleeve がある。ただし、関連表現の意味する利点は、一般的な利点ではなく特定の利点である。

2. 日本語には「切り札を持っている」という関連表現がある。「切り札」は勝負で最強のカードのことである。例文の「カードを握っている」はすべて「切り札を持っている」と置き換えられる。

(1) オイルの値段は、現在、中東が{カードを握っている/切り札を持っている}ように見える
(→(a))

H

hold the key (to ~) / phr. / metaphor

to provide an important clue that helps to {explain/identify} s.t.

REL be the key to ~

Examples

(a) I believe the witness holds the key to this case's solution.

(b) The one who holds the key to the success of the environmental project is Mr. Sato.

(c) Traditionally, the New Hampshire primary is said to hold the key to a candidate's success in the general election for president.

(d) Since the city's earliest days, tourism has held the key to our region's prosperity.

Note

The verbs used in the English and Japanese expressions differ slightly. *Hold* means "to take and {keep/support}{s.t./s.o.} in one's {hands/arms}," whereas *nigiru* means "to bend the fingers inward tightly or take and {keep/support} s.t. in one's hand(s)."

REL

Both the English and Japanese have similar metaphorical expressions, i.e., *be the key to ~* and *(~ no) kagi da.*

(1) The witness's statement is the key to solving the case.
目撃者の証言が事件解決の鍵だ。

hold the purse strings / phr. / metaphor

to have control over financial matters

REL {control/tighten} the purse strings; loosen the purse strings

Examples

Kenta: Dad, don't you think it's time we bought a new car?

Mr. S: Yes, but you're talking to the wrong person. You know your mother holds the purse strings in this family. You'd better ask her.

Kenta: You know how tightly she holds those strings. There's basically no hope.

- -

(a) As consumers, we hold the purse strings. If we don't buy a product, the company will cease to make a profit and will have to change.

(b) The legislature holds the purse strings, so it needs an honest accounting of where taxpayer money is going.

Notes

1. This expression can be used in reference to both individuals and public institutions, as shown in (b).

2. For the basic meanings of *hold* and *nigiru*, see the Notes section of the *hold the key (to ~)/ (~ no) kagi o nigiru* entry.

REL

1. *Tighten* and *shimeru* can replace *hold* and *nigiru*, respectively. In this case, the expressions take on the meaning of "to reduce expenses." Likewise, replacing them with *loosen* and *yurumeru*, respectively, gives the expression the meaning of "to increase expenses." 📖→関連語(1)(2)

（〜の）鍵を握る / phr. 隠喩

重要な手がかりを持っている

関 （〜の）鍵だ

例文

(a) この事件は、目撃者が事件解決の鍵を握っていると思う。

(b) 環境プロジェクトで成功の鍵を握っているのは佐藤氏だ。

(c) 伝統的に、ニューハンプシャー州の予備選挙に勝つかどうかが、その後のアメリカ大統領指名選挙の鍵を握っている。

(d) この町では昔から観光がその地域一帯の繁栄の鍵を握ってきた。

解説

日英語の動詞「握る」と *hold* の基本義は、それぞれ "自分の指を内側に固く曲げる、あるいは何かを手に取って離さない" と "{物 / 人} を自分の {手 / 腕} に {保持して / 支えて} おく" で、多少異なっている。

関連語

日英語には似たような比喩表現として「（〜の）鍵だ」と *be the key to ~* がある。 📖 **REL（1）**

H

財布のひもを握る / phr. 隠喩

金銭のことを管理する権限をもつ

関 財布のひもを締める，財布のひもが固い，財布のひもを緩める

例文

健太：お父さん、車、新しく買い替えようか。

鈴木（夫）：そうだなあ。でも、健太、聞く相手を間違えてるよ。我が家の財布のひもはお母さんが握っているからね。お母さんに頼んだほうがいいよ。

健太：お母さん、財布のひも固いからな。望み薄だな。

(a) 財布のひもを握っているのは、われわれ消費者なのです。われわれが製品を買わなければその会社は収益が止まるのですから、その会社は変わらざるを得ないのです。

(b) 立法府は国の財布のひもを握っているのだから、納税者の税金の使い道を正直に説明する必要がある。

解説

1. この表現は(b)のように日英語とも個人だけではなく、公の機関にも使える。

2. 「握る」と *hold* の基本義については、*hold the key (to ~)*「（〜の）鍵を握る」の解説を参照。

関連語

1. 日英語とも「握る」と *hold* を、それぞれ「締める」と *tighten* で置き換えると、"支出を抑える" という意味になり、「緩める」と *loosen* に置き換えると "支出を緩くする" という意味になる。

333

2. The English can be replaced by *control the purse strings* without changing the meaning.

(3) As long as the wife {holds/controls} the purse strings, the husband has to take her wishes into account.
妻が財布のひもを握っているかぎり、夫は妻の意向を気にせざるを得ない。

3. The Japanese REL *saifu no himo ga katai* (lit. "the purse strings are tight") refers to the state that results from someone tightening the purse strings, whereas *saifu no himo o shimeru* refers to the act of tightening the strings itself. (→ dialogue)

hold water / comp. v. / metaphor

for {a theory/an argument} to stand up under criticism or analysis

REL airtight

Examples

(a) I was pretty sure that his theory held water.

(b) She earned high praise for presenting a plan that held water during the meeting.

(c) I admit that the argument held water, though the choice of terms was sometimes inaccurate.

Notes

1. The verb in the English phrase can be used either in the affirmative, as shown in the examples, or in the negative, as demonstrated below in (1). By contrast, in Japanese, the verb in *mizu mo morasanai* (lit. "does not leak water") must be in the negative form, as shown in the examples. The affirmative form cannot be used metaphorically.

(1) At the meeting she presented a perfect plan that {holds water/does not hold water}.
(→(b))

彼女は会議で{水も漏らさない/ ×水を漏らす}完璧な計画を発表した。(→(b))

2. The Japanese is a prenominal adjectival phrase, as demonstrated in all the example sentences. *Mizu mo morasanu* is often used in written Japanese, as shown in (a).

3. The Japanese can also be used in reference to security that is perfectly maintained.

📖→解説(2)

REL

The English REL is *airtight*.

(1) Your reasoning {holds water/is airtight}, so I think you must have come to the correct conclusion.
あなたの理由付けは完璧ですから、正しい結論に行き着くと思いますよ。

holy war / comp. n. / metaphor

a war fought for religious purposes

Example

Leaders of terrorist organizations are urging people to wage holy war by carrying out suicide bombings.

(1) 会社の景気が悪くてボーナスが出ないので、我が家は財布のひもを締めなくてはならない。
The company isn't doing so well, and we're not receiving a bonus, so my family needs to tighten its purse strings.

(2) 観光旅行中はつい財布のひもを緩めてしまいます。
Whenever we go sightseeing, we end up loosening our purse strings.

2. 英語の見出しの *hold the purse strings* は意味を変えずに *control the purse strings* によって置き換えられる。 ➡📖 REL (3)

3. 日本語には「財布のひもが固い」という類似表現がある。「財布のひもを締める」は誰かが財布のひもを締めるという行動を示すが、「財布のひもが固い」という表現は誰かが締めた結果、今そういう状態にあるということを示す。(→会話例)

水も漏らさない phr. 隠喩
みず　も　　　　　　　　　　　　　　いんゆ

{理論 / 議論 / 規則 / 法則 / 計画 / 警備}が緻密で完璧である
　りろん　ぎろん　きそく　ほうそく　けいかく　けいび　　ちみつ　かんぺき

例 文

(a) 私は、彼の理論は水も漏らさぬ理論だと確信していた。
　　わたし　　かれ　りろん　みず　も　　　りろん　　かくしん

(b) 彼女は会議で水も漏らさない完璧な計画を発表して高く評価された。
　　かのじょ　かいぎ　みず　も　　　　　かんぺき　けいかく　はっぴょう　たか　ひょうか

(c) 水も漏らさない議論だったことを認めるが、用語の選択が時々不正確だった。
　　みず　も　　　　ぎろん　　　　　　みと　　　　ようご　せんたく　ときどきふせいかく

解 説

1. 英語の動詞は例文のように肯定形で使うことも、Note (1) のように否定形で使うこともできる。対して、日本語「水も漏らさない」の動詞は例文のように否定形でしか使えない。肯定形は比喩としては使えない。 ➡📖 Note (1)

2. 日本語は、すべての例文でわかるように、名詞を修飾する表現である。書き言葉では (a) のように「水も漏らさぬ」となる。

3. 日本語は警備の安全性にすきのないときにも使える。

(2) ワシントン D.C. の警備は、水も漏らさない体制である。
The security in Washington D.C. {is airtight/ [??]holds water}.

関連語

英語には関連表現として *airtight* という形容詞がある。 ➡📖 REL (1)

聖戦 n. 隠喩
せいせん　　　　いんゆ

宗教など神聖な{大義 / 目的}のための戦い
しゅうきょう　しんせい　たいぎ　もくてき　　　　たたか

例 文

テロリストのリーダーたちは、聖戦という名の下に、自爆を奨励している。
　　　　　　　　　　　　　せいせん　　　な　もと　　じばく　しょうれい

335

honeymoon (period/phase), {a / the}   comp. n.   metaphor

a period of unusual harmony, especially following the establishment of a new relationship

REL   honeymoon era

Examples

Mrs. S: Mike, you don't look so good.

Mike: Yeah, my girlfriend and I aren't getting along. The honeymoon is over.

Mrs. S: This is where your relationship really begins. Good luck!

- -

(a) The American people give every new president a gift in the form of the "honeymoon phase," a period during which they are receptive to his/her policies.

(b) It has only been two months since he became the conductor, so everyone should still be in the honeymoon phase, but he has already stirred up trouble with members of the orchestra.

Notes

The Japanese expression is a direct translation of the English. 📖➡解説(1)

REL

The English and Japanese RELs are *honeymoon era* and *mitsugetsu-jidai*, respectively. Both *mitsugetsu-jidai* and *mitsugetsu-kikan* are used. 📖➡関連語(2)

horse face   comp. n.   metaphor

a very long face that resembles a horse's

Example

Karen: Saya, you actually like this actor?

Saya: Yeah. He's got a bit of a horse face, but he's a great actor.

Notes

1. Both the English and the Japanese expressions are derived from similes, i.e., *a face like a horse's* and *uma no yōna kao*, respectively. However, [×]*uma-gao* cannot be used.

2. The *zura* in *uma-zura* is the slang version of *kao*. *Uma-zura* has a negative connotation because a human face is being compared to that of an animal. The neutral, non-metaphorical version of the expression is *omo-naga*. 📖➡解説(1)

336

蜜月期間 / comp. n. 隠喩

とてもいい関係の期間

関 蜜月時代

例文

鈴木（妻）：マイク、元気ないわね。

マイク：ええ、彼女とうまくいっていないんですよ。蜜月期間は終わりです。

鈴木（妻）：これから本物の関係を作っていくのよ。がんばってね。

(a) アメリカ国民は新しい大統領に「蜜月期間」をプレゼントして、その間、政策を温かく見守る。

(b) 彼はまだ指揮者になって2か月で、まだ蜜月期間中のはずなのに、もうメンバーといざこざを起こしている。

解説

日本語は英語からの翻訳である。

(1) 最近の両国の関係を考えると、蜜月 {期間 / 時代} は終わったような印象だ。

Judging from recent problems between the two countries, it would be appear that the honeymoon {period/phase} has come to an end.

関連語

日本語には「蜜月時代」、英語には *honeymoon era* という関連表現がある。日本語では「蜜月時代」も「蜜月期間」も用いられる。

(2) 蜜月 {期間 / 時代} は終わりです。（→会話例）

The {honeymoon/honeymoon era} is over.

H

馬面 / comp. n. 隠喩

馬のような長い顔

例文

カレン：あら、さや、この俳優、好きなの？

さや：うん、ちょっと馬面だけどね。演技がうまいから。

解説

1. 日英語の表現ともに直喩の名詞句、すなわち、「馬のような顔」と *a face like a horse's* から出てきている。ただし「×馬顔」とは言えない。

2. 「馬面」の「面」は「顔」の俗語である。「馬面」は人の顔を動物に例えているので、否定的なイメージがある。中立的に言う場合は「面長」という比喩ではない表現を使う。

(1) あの女性は {面長 / ×馬面} の美人です。

She is a beautiful lady with a {long/ ×horse} face.

337

hothouse; hothouse flower   *comp. n.*   metaphor

used to describe s.o. who is overprotected

Example

> She was raised in a hothouse and never developed the strength to overcome difficulties.

hurt s.o.'s feelings   *phr.*   metaphor

to cause emotional pain or anguish; to offend

Examples

> Karen: Kenta, you and Saya haven't been seeing each other much lately, have you?
>
> Kenta: Afraid not. I said something mean and apparently hurt her feelings. I wonder if she's still mad?
>
> Karen: Why don't you give her a call?

> (a) I want to move out, but I don't want to hurt my dad's feelings.
>
> (b) Kazuko's always calling my clothes ugly. She hurts my feelings.

Note

> Both the English and Japanese can be used in the passive voice, as demonstrated in (1). In addition, the Japanese has an intransitive form, i.e., *(~no kimochi) ga kizu-tsuku.*
>
> 解説(1)

hurt s.o.'s pride   *phr.*   metaphor

to {do/say} s.t. that will damage s.o.'s pride

REL   (make s.o.) lose face

Examples

> (a) My teacher hurt my pride when he scolded me in front of my classmates.
>
> (b) Ever since my husband had a stroke, he hasn't been able to care for himself or do the things he used to. How can I take care of him without hurting his pride?

Notes

> 1. The basic meaning of both *hurt* and *kizu-tsukeru* is "to cause physical pain." This meaning is employed metaphorically to express the psychological pain of one's pride being damaged.
> 2. The Japanese can use either *jisonshin* or the loanword *puraido* (pride).

REL

> 1. The intransitive version of *hurt (s.o.'s) pride* is *(s.o.'s) pride gets hurt.* 関連語(1)
> 2. The Japanese RELs are *menboku o tsubusu* (to break s.o.'s pride) and *~ no kao ni doro o nuru* (lit. "to smear s.o.'s face with mud"). English has the expression *(make s.o.) lose face*, which corresponds to *menboku o tsubusu.* 関連語(2)

温室育ち / n. phr. 隠喩

甘やかされて大事に育てられた人

例文

彼女は温室育ちで、困難を乗り越える力がない。

(～の気持ち)を傷つける phr. 隠喩

心理的な苦痛を与える

例文

カレン：健太、この頃、さやと会っていないでしょ。

健太：そうなんだ。ちょっと、ひどいこと言って、さやを傷つけちゃったみたいで。
まだ、傷ついているかなあ。

カレン：電話して聞いてみたら。

(a) 家を出たいんですが、父の気持ちを傷つけたくないんです。

(b) 和子ったら、私の着ているものが醜いとか言って私の気持ちを傷つけるのよ。

解説

日英語ともに受け身形が可能だが、日本語はそのほかに「(～の気持ち)が傷つく」という自
動詞形にもなる。

(1) つまらない噂で私の気持ちは深く {傷つけられた / 傷ついた}。
My feelings were really hurt by the baseless rumors.

{自尊心 / プライド}を傷つける phr. 隠喩

誰かの自信を失わせるようなことを {する / 言う}

関 面目をつぶす, LOOK 顔に泥を塗る

例文

(a) 僕は同級生の前で先生に叱られ、自尊心を傷つけられた。

(b) 夫は脳卒中になってからは身の回りのことができないし、前にできたこともでき
なくなった。夫のプライドを傷つけずにどうやって世話をしたらいいだろうか。

解説

1. 日英語の動詞「傷つける」と hurt の基本義はともに"誰かを肉体的に苦しめる"であり、そこ
から自尊心を傷つけるような心理的苦痛に比喩的転移をしたのである。

2. 日本語は「自尊心」も外来語の「プライド」も使える。

関連語

1. 「{自尊心 / プライド}を傷つける」の自動詞版は「{自尊心 / プライド}が傷つく」である。

(1) 僕は同級生の前で先生に叱られ、自尊心 {を傷つけられた / が傷ついた}。(→(a))
My pride got hurt because my teacher scolded me in front of my classmates. (→(a))

2. 日本語には「{自尊心 / プライド}を傷つける」という意味の「面目をつぶす」や「～の顔に泥

339

hush money comp. n. metaphor

money paid to keep s.o. silent about a secret

Example

If you want to keep it a secret, you should pay him some hush money.

ice age comp. n. metaphor

a period of unbearably harsh conditions

Example

Saya: It's March already, but I hear that no seniors have gotten jobs yet.

Karen: We're in a depression—an ice age for employment—so things are looking tough.

Ignorance is bliss. phr. metaphor

the idea that s.o. may be happier not knowing about a problem or an unpleasant fact

Examples

Saya: Kenta hasn't arrived yet, and we're already out of meat for the sukiyaki.

Mike: I think I still have some in the freezer that I bought a month ago. The flavor may not be quite as good, though.

Saya: Kenta's not picky, so he probably won't even notice. Still, let's not mention it to him. As they say, ignorance is bliss.

- -

(a) I wish that the teacher hadn't told us about all the bacteria that's in the food we eat. I guess it's true that ignorance is bliss.

(b) I learned from the blood test that the boy is not my real son. Ignorance was bliss for all those years. But after raising him all this time, I've come to love him like my own son. I can't part with him.

Notes

1. The English and Japanese proverbs employ different nouns: *bliss* and *hotoke* (Buddha), respectively. The former simply means "complete happiness," while the latter means "a mind as peaceful as the Buddha's." Note that in English, one cannot say "*×Ignorance is God*," since God is considered to be an omnipotent and omniscient entity.
2. *Shiranu ga* is an archaic form of *shiranai no ga* (not knowing s.t.).
3. Both the English and Japanese expressions can be used to mean "s.o. who is being ridi-

340

を塗る」などがある。英語には「面目をつぶす」に当たる *(make s.o.) lose face* がある。

(2) 私は彼女に{自尊心を傷つけられ／面目をつぶされ／顔に泥を塗られ}た。
She {hurt my pride/made me lose face}.

口止め料　/ n. phr.　隠喩

何かを秘密にしてもらうために払うお金

例文

そのことを秘密にしておきたかったら、彼に口止め料を払ったほうがいい。

氷河期　/ n.　隠喩

辛く困難な状況が続く時期

例文

さや：もう3月なのに、先輩達、誰も就職決まっていないそうよ。

カレン：この不況で就職氷河期だから、難しいかもね。

知らぬが仏　/ phr.　隠喩

悪いことを知らなくて幸いだ

例文

さや：まだ健太が来てないのに、もうすきやきのお肉がなくなっちゃったよ。

マイク：あ、冷凍庫に1か月前に買ったのがまだあったと思うよ。味はちょっと落ちるかもしれないけど。

さや：健太は味わかんないから、大丈夫。でも、彼に言っちゃだめよ。知らぬが仏なんだから。

- - - - - - - - - - - - - - - - - - - -

(a) 先生が、私達が食べている食べ物の中に菌がうようよいるなんて言わなきゃよかったのに。知らぬが仏だったのにな。

(b) 血液検査をしたら、息子が自分の子供でないことがわかってしまった。今まで、知らぬが仏だったが、何年も育ててきたので息子はかわいい。手離すことはできない。

解説

1. 日英語のことわざは、それぞれ「仏」と *bliss* を使っている。「仏」は "仏様のような平和な心"、*bliss* は "完全な幸せ" という意味である。英語では神様は全智全能であるから、˟*Ignorance is God* とは言えない。

2. 「知らぬが」は「知らないのが」の古い形である。

3. 日英語ともに「知らないので平然としていられるのは本人だけだと、陰であざ笑う」という意味がある。

culed behind {his/her} back but remains ignorant of this fact." 📖➡ 解説(1)

(all) in a {fog/haze}　*phr.*　metaphor

to be in a state of confusion or bewilderment

Examples

(a) It was my first time going to Japan, so when I got off the plane at Narita, I was in a haze. I was tired and completely overwhelmed.

(b) All of us employees were in a fog, because we couldn't understand what the company president was thinking at all.

(c) When we began our project, we were all in a fog, but after a few months of intensive work, we finally gained our bearings.

Notes

1. The English can express a state of mental confusion, but the Japanese cannot.
(1) When I woke up from the surgery, I was all in a fog.
手術から目が覚めたとき、私は状況がつかめず{混乱していた/ˣ五里霧中だった}。

2. The Japanese comes from *Hou Han Shu* (a.k.a. *Gokansho/Book of the Later Han*), a Chinese historical text completed ca. 432 CE that tells the story of 張楷 (Kai Zhang), who had the ability to summon a fog for 2.4 square miles whenever he did not wish to have visitors.

in a world of one's own　*phr.*　metaphor

to be in a state of mental detachment from other people

REL　in one's own (little) world

Examples

Karen: Oh, Saya, I didn't see you there.

Saya: Yeah, you were in a world of your own! I've been calling your name this whole time and you didn't even notice.

Karen: Really? I had no idea.

- -

(a) While the other children play together during recess, Alex sometimes becomes absorbed in a world of his own.

(b) Dr. Arai had become something of a recluse, living in a world of his own dominated by his biochemical research.

(c) Amy rents an apartment in the middle of the city, but she lives in a world of her own, delighting in the simple pleasures of reading books and taking care of her cats.

Note

The English co-occurs with verbs such as *absorb* ([a]), *live* ([b] and [c]), and *be* (dialogue).

342

(1) あいつは弁がたつと思い込んでいるけれど、知らぬが仏、実はみんな陰では彼の話しぶりをあざけっている。

He thinks he's such a good speaker, but ignorance is bliss. Behind his back, everybody laughs at the way he talks.

五里霧中 ／ comp. n. 隠喩

現在の状態も、これから先どう{なる / したらいい}かもわからない

例文

(a) 日本に行くのは初めてだった。それで、成田で飛行機を降りたときには、まったく五里霧中だった。疲れていたし、途方に暮れてしまった。

(b) 社長の考えていることがわれわれ社員には全くわからず、五里霧中だった。

(c) プロジェクトを始めたときは五里霧中だったが、数か月の集中作業のあと、どちらへ行くべきかその方向が見えてきた。

解説

1. 英語ではなんらかの精神的混乱も表現できるが、日本語はそのような混乱は表現できない。

—📖 Note (1)

2. 日本語の出典は中国の『後漢書』(432年ごろ完成)という歴史書である。張楷(チョウ・カイ)という人がいて、人に会いたくないときに五里四方に霧を起こすことができたという故事からきている。

自分だけの世界に ／ phr. 隠喩

まわりが見えず、自分(のこと)だけに{興味 / 関心}がある

例文

カレン： あら、さや、いたの？

さや： 何、自分だけの世界に浸ってるのよ。さっきから呼んでるのにぜんぜん気がつかないんだから。

カレン： ほんと？　ぜんぜん知らなかった。

(a) ほかの子供達が休み時間に一緒に遊んでいるのに、アレックスはときどき自分だけの世界に浸っていることがある。

(b) 新井博士は生化学の研究に没頭して、何か世捨て人のようになり、自分だけの世界に生きていた。

(c) エイミーは街のまん中にアパートを借りているのに、読書とか猫の世話といった単純なことに喜びを見い出しながら、自分だけの世界に生きている。

解説

日本語で一緒に使われる動詞は会話例と(a)の「浸る」、(b)(c)の「生きる」、である。英語で一緒に使われる動詞は(a)の absorb、(b)(c)の live、会話例の be である。ただし、英語の

The Japanese co-occurs with *hitaru* (to be absorbed), *ikiru* (to live; [b] and [c]), and *iru* (to be; dialogue). In English, however, *absorb* is used with much less frequency than the other verbs.

R E L

The English REL, *in one's own (little) world*, can replace the main entry.
(1) Alex sometimes becomes absorbed in {a world of his own/his own world}. (→(a))

in light of ~ / phr. / metaphor

in consideration of the knowledge now possessed

Examples

(a) In light of this new research, there is no doubt that child abuse is a major factor in juvenile delinquency.

(b) In light of this new linguistic theory, it may be time to reexamine how children acquire language.

(c) In light of concerns about cultural imperialism, it may be useful to think carefully about the relationship between globalization and the media.

in one breath / adv. phr. / metaphor

(spoken) very quickly

REL in one gulp

Examples

(a) The nervous young man delivered his whole speech in one breath and immediately left the stage.

(b) He read a long poem in one breath.

Notes

1. Both *in one breath* and *hitoiki de* can be used literally, as shown in (1).
(1) That guy can blow out a hundred candles in one breath.
   彼は一息でろうそく100本でも吹き消すことができる。
2. If *ato (mō)* (a little more) is used before *hitoiki de*, the expression's meaning becomes "if you make a little more effort, ~." ☐☐← 解説(2)

R E L

1. The Japanese REL is *ikki ni*. ☐☐← 関連語(1)
2. The English REL is *in one gulp*. Whereas *in one breath* describes the action of speaking, *in one gulp* describes the action of eating or drinking.
(2) He drank the big mug of beer in one gulp.
   彼は大きなジョッキのビールを{一息で/一気に}飲み干した。

344

absorb は使用頻度が非常に低い。

関連語

英語の見出しは、*in one's own (little) world* と置き換えられる。→📖 REL(1)

(〜に) 照らして{みる / 考える}　phr.　隠喩

ある視点から何かを{見る / 考える}

例文

(a) 子供への虐待が少年非行の大きな原因となっていることは、この新しい調査に照らしてみても、疑いのない事実です。

(b) この新しい言語学理論に照らして考えれば、子供の言語習得について再調査すべき時期に来ているかもしれない。

(c) 文化帝国主義に関する問題に照らして考えれば、グローバル化とメディアの関係について注意深く考えることは有益かもしれない。

一息で　adv.　隠喩

短い間で

関 一気に

例文

(a) 神経質そうな若者は一息でスピーチをして、壇上をすぐ離れた。

(b) 彼は長い詩を一息で読み上げた。

解説

1. 「一息で」も *in one breath* も、字義通りの解釈でも使われる。→📖 Note(1)

2. 日本語の「一息で」の前に「あと(もう)」をつけると、「あともう少しの努力で」という意味になる。

(2) a. あともう一息で、この作品も完成だ。
   One more push and this work will be complete.

   b. あと一息で、私の絵は入選するところだったのに、残念だった。
   A little more effort and my painting would have been selected. Too bad!

関連語

1. 日本語の「一気に」は「一息で」と同義に使える。

(1) 私はその本を{一息で / 一気に}読み、とても気に入った。
   I read the book in one sitting and really enjoyed it.

2. 英語の関連表現は *in one gulp* である。*in one breath* が話す動作に用いられるのに対し、*in one gulp* は飲んだり食べたりする動作にも用いられる。→📖 REL(2)

in the blink of an eye *adv. phr.* **metaphor**

very quickly; in an instant

REL in the twinkling of an eye

Examples

Karen: Saya, you're soaked!

Saya: I know. I thought I heard thunder, and then, in the blink of an eye, it started to pour. I didn't even have time to take cover.

- -

(a) In the blink of an eye, the girl was gone.

(b) Firefighters like to say that fires can start in the blink of an eye.

(c) Fiber-optic technology should allow you to transmit information in the blink of an eye.

Note

Matataku is a combination of *ma* (eye) and *tataku* (to hit) and means "to blink." In the English, *blink* is used as a noun, but the basic meaning of the expression is the same as that of the Japanese.

REL

The English can be replaced by *in the twinkling of an eye*, though this is not as common as the main entry. The Japanese REL is *atto iu ma ni* (lit. "while one says 'a!'"), which is more colloquial than the main expression.

(1) {In the blink of an eye/In the twinkling of an eye} the girl was gone. (→(a))
{瞬く間に/あっと言う間に} 女の子は行ってしまった。(→(a))

invasion *n.* **personification**

the entry of s.t. hurtful

Examples

(a) All the data disappeared after the virus invasion.

(b) Internet security systems protect businesses and individual Internet users from outside invasion by hackers.

(c) This room has double-paned windows in order to protect against the invasion of outside noise.

(d) The invasion of Internet porn into households must be controlled more strictly.

Notes

1. Because the subject of *invasion* is usually an animate being (including humans), all of the above sentences are examples of personification.

2. The English and Japanese often use the verbs *invade* and *shin'nyū-suru* instead.

解説(1)

瞬く間に　/ adv./phr.　隠喩

何かがとても速い速度で起こる様子

関 あっと言う間に

例文

カレン：まあ、さや、ずぶ濡れじゃない。

さや：そう、雷が鳴り出したかと思ったら、瞬く間にどしゃぶり。雨宿りする間もなかったわ。

(a) 瞬く間に女の子は行ってしまった。

(b) 消防士たちの口癖は、火事は瞬く間に起こり得るということだ。

(c) 光ファイバーを使えば情報を文字通り瞬く間に伝達できるはずです。

解説

日本語は「ま(＝目)」＋「叩く」からできていて、意味は英語の動詞 *blink*(まばたきする)と同じである。英語では *blink* が名詞として使われているが、基本義は日英語とも同じである。

関連語

英語は *in the twinkling of an eye* という関連表現があるが、見出しほど一般的ではない。日本語には「あっと言う間に」という関連表現があり、見出しよりも会話的である。 REL(1)

侵入　/ n.　擬人化

何かよくないものがどこかへ入り込む

例文

(a) ウイルスの侵入後、情報は全部消えてしまった。

(b) インターネット安全装置を使うと、企業や個人は外部からのハッカーの侵入を防ぐことができます。

(c) この部屋は外から騒音が侵入するのを防ぐため、窓が二重になっている。

(d) インターネットポルノの家庭への侵入をもっときびしく規制する必要がある。

解説

1. 侵入するのは普通は(人間を含む)生き物だから、例文はすべて擬人化の例である。

2. 本項目は名詞だが、日英語とも動詞「侵入する」と *invade* もよく使われる。

(1) ウイルスが侵入したあと、情報は全部消えてしまった。(→(a))
All the data disappeared after the virus invaded. (→(a))

invite / v. / personification

to increase the likelihood of s.t. happening

Examples

(a) As the phrase "Lucky Seven" shows, seven is believed to be a number that invites luck.

(b) Porcelain statues of beckoning cats are sometimes displayed in store entrances because they are a symbol that is believed to invite luck.

(c) The group's spirit and superb teamwork invited success.

(d) He doesn't mean any harm, but his lack of manners invites misunderstandings.

(e) Using smartphones while driving invites a risk of accidents.

(f) The military leader's careless actions invited the deaths of many of his own soldiers.

Notes

1. The English and Japanese can be used to describe both good things, as shown in (a) – (c), and bad things, as shown in (d) – (f).
2. Both the English and Japanese are typically used either in writing or formal speech.

iron will / comp. n. / metaphor

a very strong will

Examples

Karen: Mike's planning to compete in a triathlon.

Kenta: Wow, that's impressive. I'm sure he can do it. That guy has an iron will.

- - - - - - - - - - - - - - - - - - - -

(a) Margaret Thatcher, former prime minister of Britain, was a lady with an iron will.

(b) Do you have an iron will? Can you handle extreme pressure?

(c) There are few misfortunes in this world that you cannot turn into personal triumphs if you have an iron will and the necessary skills.

Note

The compound *iron will* can be replaced by the phrase *will of iron*.

ivory tower / comp. n. / metaphor

a place removed from everyday affairs

Examples

(a) Universities were once called "ivory towers" and quite removed from the rest of society, but recently this hasn't been the case.

(b) Our colleagues in the law and medical schools have descended from their ivory towers to actually make contact with the real world.

（〜を）招く / v. 擬人化

何かが起こる可能性を高める

例文

(a) ラッキーセブンというように、7は幸運を招く数字だと思われています。

(b) 招きネコは金運を招く印として、店頭に飾られることもある。

(c) みんなの頑張りと、抜群のチームワークが好結果を招いた。

(d) 彼に悪気はないのだが、礼儀をわきまえない言動はいつも誤解を招く。

(e) 運転中のスマホの使用は事故の危険を招く。

(f) 隊長の軽率な行動が、多くの兵士の死を招いた。

解説

1. この見出しは日英語ともに、(a)-(c)のようにいい事にも、(d)-(f)のように悪い事にも使われる。

2. 日英語ともに書き言葉か、硬い話し言葉で使用されることが多い。

鉄の意志 / n. phr. 隠喩

とても固い意志

例文

カレン：マイクはトライアスロンに出ようと計画しているよ。

健太：わぁ、すごいな。彼はやるだろうね。鉄の意志の持ち主だからね。

- -

(a) イギリスの元首相マーガレット・サッチャーは鉄の意志の女性だった。

(b) あなたは鉄の意志を持っていますか。容赦のないプレッシャーに耐えられますか。

(c) この世の中には、鉄の意志と必要な能力さえあれば個人で打ち勝てない不幸はほとんどないのです。

解説

英語の見出し、複合語の *iron will* は *will of iron* という名詞句で置き換えることができる。

象牙の塔 / n. phr. 隠喩

世俗的で現実的な事柄から隔離されているところ

例文

(a) かつて大学は象牙の塔と呼ばれ、社会とはかけ離れた存在だったが、最近そうでもなくなってきた。

(b) 法学部と医学部の同僚は象牙の塔から降りて実社会と実際に接触している。

349

Note

Both the English and Japanese expressions are direct translations of the French term *tour d'ivoire*, which was used by famed literary critic Charles Augustin Sainte-Beuve (1804-1869) when he criticized the poetry of Alfred de Vigny (1797-1863) as being too unrealistic. There is also a reference to this expression in the Song of Solomon (7:4) in the Old Testament: "Thy neck is as a tower of ivory." This line refers to the beauty of Solomon's companion, and it is possible that ivory's white color is used to suggest purity, innocence, and freedom from the corrupting influence of worldly affairs. However, it is not clear why ivory was chosen for this purpose.

one's jaw drops   phr. / metaphor

to be very surprised

REL LOOK eyes pop out of one's head; LOOK fall {off/out of} one's chair

Examples

Saya: Kenta, weren't you on TV the other day?

Kenta: Oh, you saw that?

Saya: Yeah, you were talking so confidently. I was so surprised my jaw dropped.

Kenta: Guess that means I'm famous now, huh?

Saya: What're you talking about? You just happened to get interviewed when you walked by!

(a) I asked him how much he wanted for the table and chairs. I was thinking it would be somewhere in the $400 - $500 range, so when he said $65 for the whole set, my jaw dropped.

(b) My jaw dropped when the criminal was acquitted of murder due to lack of evidence.

Notes

1. The English uses the verb *drop*, which means "for s.t. to fall down suddenly." The Japanese uses the verb *hazureru*, which means "for s.t. fixed to come apart."

2. As shown in the Japanese examples, the verb *odoroku* (to be surprised) is used most frequently, but verbs such as *warau* can be used as well. In this context, *warau* means "to laugh loudly." 解説(1)

   Japanese Example (2) provides an example of the expression being used literally.

   解説(2)

   When the verb *ochiru* (vi., to drop) is used, it is often paired with *oishī* (delicious).

   解説(3)

350

解 説

日英語ともフランス語の*tour d'ivoire*から来ている。これは著名な批評家のサント・ブーヴ (Charles Augustin Sainte-Beuve 1804-1869)が、アルフレッド・ド・ヴィニー(Alfred de Vigny 1797-1863)の詩を現実離れしていると評して使った言葉である。西暦前まで遡ると旧約聖書(ソロモンの雅歌(7：4))にもソロモンの恋人の美しさに言及している箇所に「汝の首は象牙の塔のようだ」とある。おそらく象牙の白い色が純粋さ、純真無垢、さらには世俗のことにさらされていないということを暗示しているのであろうが、どうして「象牙」なのかということは誰もはっきりわかっていないようである。

あごがはずれる{ほど / くらい / ぐらい}　/ phr. / 隠喩

とても驚く

関 **LOOK▶** 目が飛び出る{ほど / くらい / ぐらい}，
LOOK▶ 椅子から(転げ)落ちる{ほど / くらい / ぐらい}

例 文

さや：健太、この間、テレビに出てたでしょ。

健太：あ、あれ、見た？

さや：見たわよ。得意そうにしゃべってて、あごがはずれるくらい驚いたわよ。

健太：僕もすっかり有名人だね。

さや：何言ってるの。通りすがりにインタビューされただけでしょ。

(a) テーブルと椅子はいくらだと聞いたんだよ。僕は 400 ドルから 500 ドルぐらいを考えていたんだけどね、セットで 65 ドルだと言われたときには、あごがはずれるぐらい驚いたね。

(b) 殺人犯が証拠不十分で釈放された時は、あごがはずれるほど驚いた。

解 説

1．日本語の動詞は「はずれる」で、基本義は "何か固定されていたものが離れる" である。英語の動詞は*drop*で、基本義は "何かが急に上から下へ移動する" である。

2．日本語は例文に示したように動詞は「驚く」がよく使われるが、ほかにも「笑う」も「大笑いをする」という意味で使われる。

(1) あまりに面白い話で、あごがはずれるぐらい笑った。
The story was so funny that we burst out laughing.
比喩でない使い方としては次のような例がある。

(2) 顔をひどく殴られて、あごがはずれてしまった。
Someone hit my face so hard that my jaw dropped.
なお、見出しの「はずれる」を「落ちる」とすると、「食べ物がとてもおいしい」という意味になる。

(3) このすしはあごが落ちるほどおいしい。
This sushi is super delicious!（lit. "This sushi is so good that my jaw drops."）

J

351

join hands phr. / metonymy

to cooperate with s.o. to do s.t.

Examples

Mike: Wait, this bank's merging with an American bank?

Colleague: Apparently. I think they're joining hands to address the management crisis.

- -

(a) Ever since the game studio and movie studio joined hands, they've been stronger than ever. Their games are selling well, and lots of people are seeing their movies. Their success is pretty much guaranteed.

(b) If the Arab states and Israel were to join hands, that would be a big step forward for world peace.

(c) Someday the world will join hands across social and national boundaries.

Notes

1. The English and Japanese have the same figurative meaning, though the meanings of the constituent elements are slightly different.

2. The English is typically not used in personal situations, but the Japanese does not have this restriction. 📖→ 解説(1)

joking aside phr. / metaphor

an expression used when one wants to address s.t. seriously

Examples

Mike: If this project proposal gets rejected, I'm going back to the States.

Colleague: Wait, are you serious?

Mike: I'm just kidding. But joking aside, I'll be really disappointed if this isn't approved.

- -

(a) When I eat buckwheat noodles (*soba*) with you by my side (*soba*), even plain ol' buckwheat noodles taste amazing! But joking aside, I wonder if buckwheat noodles are good for you.

Notes

1. *Joking* means "{saying/doing} s.t. that makes people laugh," and *jōdan* means "s.t. said or done to make people laugh."

2. *Sateoki* consists of *sate* (leaving s.t. as it is) and *oki*, the progressive form of *oku* (to put). It can be used figuratively with intangible objects, such as jokes, and has the overall meaning of "setting s.t. aside as it is." See (1a) - (1c) for more examples. 📖→ 解説(1)

352

手をつなぐ /phr. 換喩

協力して何かを行う

例文

マイク: え、この銀行、アメリカの銀行と合併するの？

同僚: らしいね。お互いに手をつないで、経営危機に当たるんじゃないかな。

- -

(a) ゲーム製作会社と映画会社が手をつないだんだから、強いよ。ゲームは売れるし、たくさんの人が映画を見るし。成功間違いなしだね。

(b) アラブとイスラエルが手をつなぐようなことがあれば、世界平和は大きく前進するだろう。

(c) いつの日か、私達は社会の階層と国境を越えて、手をつなぐようになるだろう。

解説

1. 日英語それぞれの言葉の要素の意味は多少異なるが、比喩的意味は同じである。

2. 英語は個人的な状況では使いにくいが、日本語はそのような制約がない。

(1) あの老夫婦は長年、共に手をつないで生きてきた。もう、2人とも80を超えているそうだ。
??That old couple joined hands and have been living together for a long time. I heard they're over 80 years old.

冗談はさておき /phr. 隠喩

話を本題に戻すときの表現

関 冗談はおいといて

例文

マイク: このプロジェクトが通らなかったら、僕はアメリカに帰ろうと思う。

同僚: え、うそだろ！

マイク: とまあ、冗談はさておき、もしこれが認められなかったら、本当にがっかりだよ。

- -

(a) あなたのおそばでおそばを食べると、ただのおそばもめっちゃおいしい。とまあ、冗談はさておき、そばって体にいいのかな。

解説

1. 「冗談」と joking の基本義は、それぞれ、"人を笑わせることを言うこと"と"人を笑わせることを |言う／する| こと"である。

2. 日本語の「さておき」の「さて」は「そのまま」という意味で、「おき」は「置く」で、それがもの以外の事（「冗談」など）に比喩として使われている。全体としては「～をそのまま脇に置いて」という意味である。ほかの用例として次のような例がある。

(1)a. ここのお寿司は、値段はさておき、味は最高です。
Setting the price aside, the sushi here tastes amazing.

 b. 前置きはさておき、本論に入りたいと思います。
Let me get straight to the main issues.

353

REL

In colloquial speech, *jōdan wa sateoki* can be replaced by *jōdan wa oitoite*.

(→Japanese dialogue)

jump at ~ / phr. / metaphor

to (hastily) take advantage of an opportunity

Examples

Kenta: Have you ever thought about trying to get a job with Company A?

Friend: Are you kidding? I'd jump at the chance to work at that company. But they'd never hire someone as inexperienced as I am.

(a) When I was offered the role of the Director of the Research Institute of Sociology, I jumped at the opportunity.

(b) When an offer sounds too good to be true, you shouldn't jump at it right away. Give it some thought first.

Notes

1. Note that *tobu* can mean both "to fly" and "to jump." 📖► 解説(1)
2. *Tobi-tsuku* is a compound verb that consists of *tobu* (to jump / fly) and *tsuku* (to cling to). The original meaning is "{s.o./s.t.} literally jumps at s.t. and clings to it." See (2a) - (2c) for other examples in which the [verb] + [*tsuku*] construction is used. 📖► 解説(2)

keep a cool head / phr. / metaphor

to {be/become} calm in a stressful situation

REL cool off; chill out

Examples

Kenta: Oh, man, that was rough.

Saya: What happened?

Kenta: I was so nervous that I could barely write anything. And I studied so hard, too...

c. 何はさておき、ビールで乾杯しましょう。
Before anything else (lit. "Setting everything else aside"), I would like to make a toast.

関連語

日本語の会話では「冗談はさておき」は「冗談はおいといて」と置き換えられる。

（〜に）飛びつく　phr.　隠喩

（性急に）何か（の機会）を自分のものにしようとする

例文

健太：A社に勤めてみようなんて、考えたことある？

友達：冗談だろ。あそこで働けるチャンスがあるんなら、飛びつきたいよ。でも、A社は僕のような経験のない者の採用はぜったいにしないんだ。

(a) 私は社会学研究所の所長になる話が持ち上がったとき、そのまたとない機会に飛びついた。

(b) あまりにうまい話はすぐに飛びつかないで、よく考えてからにしたほうがいい。

解説

1. 日本語の「飛ぶ」には、英語の *fly* "（空中を）跳ぶ" と *jump* "（足を使って）跳ぶ、跳び上がる" の2つの意味があるので注意。

(1) a. 飛行機が飛んでいる。
   The plane is flying.
   b. 彼は向こう岸まで跳んだ。
   He jumped to the opposite riverbank.

2. 「飛びつく」は「飛ぶ」+「つく」の複合動詞で、元の意味は "|人／何か| が何かに向かって飛び上がり、それにしがみつく" という意味である。「動詞」+「つく」のほかの例には以下のようなものがある。

(2) a. 犬が子供に噛みついた。
   A dog bit the child.
   b. 池は凍りついていた。
   The pond was frozen.
   c. 女は男にすがりついた。
   The woman clung to the man.

頭を冷やす　phr.　隠喩

興奮状態から冷静さを取り戻す

例文

健太：まったくもう、本当に大変だったよ。

さや：どうしたの？

健太：経済の試験の最中に緊張しすぎて、ほとんどなんにも書けなかった。あんなに一生懸命勉強したのに。

Saya: That's happened to me before. It's tough keeping a cool head during exams.

(a) During the soccer game, the goalkeeper urged his agitated teammate to try to keep a cool head.

(b) It was shocking to see an accident happen right before my eyes, but I had to go to work, so I bought a coffee at the convenience store and tried to keep a cool head.

Notes

1. The English is usually used in the sense of "maintaining one's composure."

(1) It's important to keep a cool head when you're negotiating with someone.
誰かと交渉事に臨むときは{冷静さを保つ/ ×頭を冷やす}ことが大切だ。

2. The Japanese expression *rēsē da* (to be cool-headed) can be used when someone is calm in a stressful situation. 📖→解説(2)

REL

English RELs are *cool off* and *chill out*. The former is typically used when calming down from anger, and the latter is typically used when calming down from anger or panic.

(1) During the soccer game, the goalkeeper urged his agitated teammate to try to {keep a cool head/cool off/chill out}. (→(a))

---

keep a lid on ~ / phr. / metaphor

to control a situation so that secret or private information does not become known; to confine, limit, or suppress s.t.

REL 👀 put a lid on ~

Examples

(a) They kept a lid on the scandal until the very end.

(b) Pat keeps a lid on her infamous past.

(c) We've managed to keep a lid on the rash of complaints and returns from shoppers so far. But we've started to worry that this could eventually put us out of business.

Notes

1. The English can be used to mean "to suppress s.t.," as in (1) below, but the Japanese cannot be used in this manner.

(1) She kept a lid on the rage boiling within her.
彼女は自分の中で煮えたぎっている怒り{を抑えた/ ×に蓋をした}。

2. Japanese has the idiomatic expression *kusai mono ni futa o suru* (lit. "to keep a lid on s.t. that smells"), which means "to take temporary measures to keep s.t. bad from getting out." The equivalent English expression is *sweep s.t. under the rug*. 📖→解説(2)

356

さや：私も前にそんなことがあった。試験を受けてる最中に頭を冷やすのって難しいんだよね。

(a) サッカーの試合で興奮した選手に、味方のゴールキーパーが頭を冷やすように注意した。

(b) 目の前で事故を見てショックを受けたけれど、会社に行かなければならないので、コンビニでコーヒーを買って飲み、頭を冷やした。

解説

1．英語の見出しは通常"冷静な状態を維持する"という意味で使われる。 ➡📖 Note(1)

2．日本語は"ストレスの多い状況で冷静にしている"という意味のときは「冷静だ」を使う。

(2) ボクサーは試合前の記者会見でも{冷静だった / ˣ頭を冷やした}。
The boxer kept a cool head throughout the pre-fight press conferences.

関連語

英語には *cool off* と *chill out* という関連表現がある。前者は怒りを鎮める時に使われ、後者は怒りやパニック状態から落ち着く時に使われる。 ➡📖 REL(1)

（～に）蓋をする   phr.   隠喩

状況をコントロールすることで、秘密や知られては困ることが外に出ないようにする

例文

(a) 彼らはそのスキャンダルに最後まで蓋をしておいた。

(b) パットは自分の不名誉な過去に蓋をしている。

(c) 今までのところ、われわれは買い物客の不満や返品が続出している事実に蓋をしてきた。しかし、このままだと会社がつぶれるのではないかという懸念が出始めている。

解説

1．英語では、(1)のように、"何かを抑える"という意味でも使うが、日本語ではそのような使い方はしない。 ➡📖 Note(1)

2．日本語には"悪いことが外に漏れないように一時しのぎの手段をとる"という意味の「臭いものに蓋をする」という慣用句がある。英語にはそれに対応する *sweep s.t. under the rug* (lit. 何かを敷物の下に押し入れる)という表現がある。

(2) 彼はこのスキャンダルに正面から取り組むのを嫌い、臭いものに蓋をしてしまった。
Because he did not want to face the scandal, he swept it under the rug.

keep a secret / phr. / metaphor

to not tell a secret to anyone

Examples

Kenta: Saya, you seem awfully cheerful today.

Saya: So you noticed!

Kenta: Come on, what is it? I won't tell anyone.

Saya: Can you keep a secret?

Kenta: Of course!

(a) The servant kept his master's secret until his own death.

(b) Attorneys are obligated to keep their clients' secrets.

Note

> The basic meanings of *keep* and *mamoru* are "to cause {s.t./s.o.} to continue in a particular state" and "to cause {s.t./s.o.} not to be {harmed/injured/violated}, respectively."

keep a tight {rein/leash} on ~ / phr. / metaphor

to strictly control s.t. or s.o.'s behavior

REL keep s.o. on a {short/tight} leash

ANT {loosen/slacken} the reins (on ~)

Examples

Mrs. S: Kenta's been spending so much time at his part-time job lately that he barely studies.

Mr. S: We need to start keeping a tight rein on him. I'll talk to him tonight.

Mrs. S: Thanks.

(a) At the summer camp, I plan to keep a tight rein on the children while still respecting their creativity.

(b) After our father's death, there was no one to keep a tight rein on my brother, and he got more and more out of control.

(c) After a series of wins, the coach began to keep a tight rein on his players so that they wouldn't start thinking they could take it easy.

Notes

1. The English and Japanese are figurative expressions that originated from *rein* and *tazuna* (a strap used to control an animal, esp. a horse), respectively. It is very likely that they developed independently of each other.

2. While the English can be used when talking about monetary matters, this is not the case with the Japanese.

(1) Japanese wives usually keep a tight {rein/leash} on the family finances.
日本の主婦は家計の {財布のひも /?? 手綱} を締める。

秘密を守る / phr. 隠喩

誰にも秘密を話さない

例文

健太：さや、ずいぶんうれしそうだね。

さや：え、わかる？

健太：言いなよ。誰にも言わないからさ。

さや：ちゃんと秘密守る？

健太：もちろんさ。

(a) その召し使いは、死ぬまで主人の秘密を守り続けた。

(b) 弁護士には、クライアントの秘密を守る義務がある。

解説

「守る」の基本義は、"{何か／誰か}に{危害／被害}が加わらないようにする"で、*keep* の基本義は、"{誰か／何か}の置かれている状態を続行させる"である。

手綱を締める / phr. 隠喩

誰かの行動を強く制御する

関 手綱を取る

反 手綱を緩める

例文

鈴木(妻)：最近、健太はバイトばかりしていて、ろくに勉強していないんですよ。

鈴木(夫)：このへんで手綱を締めないといけないね。今夜ちょっと話してみるか。

鈴木(妻)：お願いします。

(a) 合宿では、子供の発想を大切にしながらも、手綱を締めるところはしっかり締めていこうと思っています。

(b) 父が亡くなって、弟の手綱を締める人がいなくなってから、彼の暴走はますますひどくなった。

(c) 勝ちが続いているので、選手達がいい気になって油断しないよう、監督は手綱を締めにかかった。

解説

1. 日英語の比喩表現は動物、特に馬を制御するための「手綱」と *rein* から出てきている。両者は独自に生まれた可能性が高い。

2. 英語は金銭上のコントロールについても使えるが、日本語は使えない。 📖 **Note(1)**

関連語

英語には関連表現として *keep s.o. on a {short/tight} leash*（誰かの行動を制限する）がある。この言い回しは、"犬のような動物をひもで制御する"という意味が基本にある。 📖 **REL(1)**

359

REL

The REL *keep s.o. on a {short/tight} leash* means "to restrain s.o.'s behavior." This comes from the idea of restraining an animal such as a dog with a leash.

(1) My father kept {a tight rein on me/me on a short leash} when I was in high school. He didn't even allow me to go to the movies alone.

私は高校の時、父に手綱を締められていて、一人で映画にも行けなかったんです。

ANT

The English and Japanese ANTs are *{loosen/slacken} the reins (on ~)* and *tazuna o yurumeru*, respectively. 📖→反意語(1)

---

keep s.t. on hand　/ phr.　metaphor

to make sure that s.t. is always available

REL LOOK have (s.t.) on hand

Examples

Kenta: Mom, what's this box for?

Mrs. S: There's a flashlight, medicine, and some other stuff inside. These are things you should always keep on hand in case of an earthquake or other emergency.

Kenta: Wow, you're really prepared.

- -

(a) Locate your computer manual and keep it on hand.

(b) We ate the same thing for four to five days in a row because our family kept only a few different kinds of ingredients on hand.

Notes

1. The verb *keep* in the English can be replaced by *have* without changing the figurative meaning.
2. The Japanese verb *oku* is very close to *put*. *Temoto ni* means "close to one's hand."

---

kill time　/ comp. v.　metaphor

to do s.t. to pass the time

Examples

Karen: Hey Saya, the meeting's dragging on and I don't think I'll be able to make it by 6.

Saya: Got it. I'll kill some time at a bookstore in front of the station. Take your time.

Karen: Sorry! See you soon!

- -

反意語

日英語の反意表現はそれぞれ「手綱を緩める」と *{loosen/slacken} the reins (on ~)* である。

(1) 教師はいつ学生の手綱を締め、いつ緩めるかを知っているべきだ。

A teacher should know when to keep a tight rein on his/her students and when to loosen the reins.

手元に置く phr. 隠喩

大切な{人 / もの}を自分の近くに置く

関 LOOK 手元に {ある /(おいて)おく / 持っている}

例文

健太：お母さん、この箱、何？

鈴木(妻)：懐中電灯や薬なんかよ。地震や災害に備えて、いつも手元に置いておく箱。

健太：へえ、用心がいいんだね。

(a) コンピュータのマニュアルを見つけて、手元に置いておきなさい。

(b) 手元に2、3種類の食べ物しか置いていなかったから、私達は4、5日続けて同じものを食べた。

解説

1. 英語の動詞 *keep* は *have* と置き換えることができる。

2. 日本語の動詞「置く」は英語の *put* にとても近い。日本語の「手元に」は"手の近くに"という意味である。

K

時間をつぶす phr. 隠喩

空いている時間をほかのことに使う

関 暇をつぶす

例文

カレン：もしもし、さや、会議が長引いちゃって、ちょっと6時に間に合いそうにないわ。

さや：わかった。じゃ、駅前の本屋で時間つぶしてるわ。急がなくていいからね。

カレン：悪いわね。ごめん。じゃ、また、後で。

(a) After hearing about the traffic jam on the car radio and realizing he wouldn't be able to make it back right away, he went shopping to kill some time.

(b) We arrived at the movie theater an hour early, so we killed time by playing *pachinko*.

Note

Kill and *tsubusu* (to crush/smash) share the meaning of "making {s.t./s.o.} nonfunctional."

R E L

Jikan (time) in the Japanese can be replaced by *hima* (free time) without changing the meaning. 関連語(1)

Japanese also has the noun compounds *jikan-tsubushi* and *hima-tsubushi*, both of which mean "killing time." 関連語(2)

kill two birds with one stone / phr. / metaphor
to achieve two things through a single action

Examples

Karen: Would you be interested in working part-time as a tour guide during the upcoming break?

Kenta: What sort of work is it?

Karen: My friends are coming here from the States. I'd like someone to take them around Tokyo.

Kenta: Sure, I'll do it. I'll be making money and practicing my English at the same time. It'll be like killing two birds with one stone.

(a) Swimming is good, not just as exercise for the body, but also as a form of mental relaxation. You kill two birds with one stone.

(b) A homestay experience allows you to practice a living language and to observe the culture from within. It's like killing two birds with one stone.

Notes

1. The Japanese is a transliteration that comes from English, not Chinese. The Japanese expression subsequently spread to China and is now used there as well.

2. Unlike the English expression, the Japanese expression lacks a verb. A more faithful rendering would be *isseki de ni-chō o uchi-otosu* (to shoot down two birds with one stone).

R E L

The Japanese REL is *ikkyo ryōtoku* (lit. "one action, two profits"). 関連語(1)

A N T

The Japanese ANTs are *ni-to o ou mono wa, itto o mo ezu* (if you run after two hares, you will catch neither), and *abu hachi torazu* (you can't get both horseflies and bees).

反意語(1)

362

(a) 車のラジオで交通渋滞のニュースを聞いたので、すぐには帰らずに、少し買い物を
　　して時間をつぶした。
(b) 映画館には1時間早く着いたので、パチンコをして時間をつぶしました。

解説

日本語の動詞は「つぶす」で、英語の動詞は*kill*（殺す）を使っているが、"何らかの機能を壊す"
という意味は共有している。

関連語

日本語の「時間」は「暇」と意味を変えずに置き換えることができる。

(1) 車のラジオで交通渋滞のニュースを聞いたので、すぐには帰らずに、少し買い物をして｛時間
　　/ 暇｝をつぶした。（→(a)）
　　さらに、日本語には「時間つぶし」や「暇つぶし」という複合名詞がある。

(2) 映画館には1時間早く着いたので、｛時間つぶし / 暇つぶし｝にパチンコをしました。（→(b)）

一石二鳥　／ n. phr. ／ 隠喩

1つの行為で2つのことをうまくやり遂げる

関　一挙両得

反　二兎を追う者は一兎をも得ず，あぶ蜂取らず

例文

カレン：今度の休み、観光ガイドのアルバイトしない？

健太：え、それ、どんな仕事？

カレン：うん、アメリカから友達が来るから、東京を案内してほしいんだけど。

健太：やる、やる。バイト代と英語の練習なんて、一石二鳥だもん。

- -

(a) 水泳は体の運動としてばかりでなく、精神のリラックス法としてもいい。一石二鳥
　　なのである。

(b) ホームステイは、生きた言葉の練習ができると同時に、文化を内側から観察できる
　　という一石二鳥の経験ができる。

解説

1. 日本語は中国語から来たものではなく、英語の字訳である。日本語が中国に渡り、中国でも使
　　われるようになった。

2. 日本語は英語と異なり動詞がないが、それを補った文は「一石で二鳥を打ち落とす」であろう。

関連語

日本語には「一石二鳥」と同じ意味の関連表現「一挙両得」がある。「一挙」は"1つの行為"、
「両得」は"2つの利益"を意味する。

(1) 水泳は体の運動としてばかりでなく、精神のリラックス法としてもいい。｛一石二鳥 / 一挙
　　両得｝なのである。（→(a)）

反意語

日本語には「二兎を追う者は一兎をも得ず」「あぶ蜂取らず」という反意表現がある。

(1) 彼は美人と恋に落ちたがガールフレンドも愛していた。彼のガールフレンドはその美人のこ
　　とを知って、彼と別れてしまった。その同じ日に美人は金持ちのボーイフレンドを見つけた
　　からと言って彼と別れた。「二兎を追う者は一兎をも得ず」なのだ。

363

king / n. / metaphor

{s.o./s.t.} that is superior to its competitors

Examples

Karen: Mike, are you eating cup noodles again?

Mike: You bet. It's the king of the instant foods, after all. It tastes amazing!

Karen: I'm a big fan myself, but I'm careful not to eat it too often because it's not good for you.

- - - - - - - - - - - - - - - - - - -

(a) During his baseball career, he was a home run king.

(b) The lion is the king of beasts.

Note

In the dialogue and (b), the English and Japanese are phrasal, but they are used as nominal compounds in (a). The Japanese phrasal usage takes the pattern ~ *no ōsama* or ~ *no ōja*. Some more examples of phrasal usage are *bīru no ōsama* (*king of beers*), *kawa no ōsama* (*king of the river*), and *kuruma no ōsama* (*king of cars*).

homograph

king of the hill / n. phr. / metaphor

the most powerful or successful person in a group
集団の中の一番力がある、あるいは成功している人
しゅうだん　なか　いちばんちから　　　　　　　せいこう　　　　　　ひと

Example

Robert is king of the hill around the office. Every decision requires his approval.
ロバートはこのオフィスで一番力を持っている。あらゆる決定に彼の承認が必要だ。
　　　　　　　　　　　いちばんちから　も　　　　　　　　けってい　かれ　しょうにん　ひつよう

know ~ inside (and) out / phr. / metaphor

to be very familiar with {s.o./s.t.}

Examples

Saya: Kenta, I'm going to Okinawa. Do you know any good tourist attractions?

Kenta: If you're going to Okinawa, You should talk to Kimura. Apparently he goes there every year for scuba diving, so he knows the area inside out. He brags that it's like his own backyard.

- - - - - - - - - - - - - - - - - - -

He fell in love with a beautiful woman, but he loved his girlfriend as well. His girlfriend found out about the beautiful woman and broke up with him, and on the same day the beautiful woman said goodbye to him, saying that she'd found a rich boyfriend. Remember: If you try to have it both ways, you'll end up with nothing.

～王 / comp. n. / 隠喩

競争者の中で最高の地位を持っている{誰か/何か}

例文

カレン：マイク、またカップラーメン食べてるの？

マイク：うん、カップラーメンはインスタント食品の王様だね。ほんと、うまい！

カレン：私も大好き。体によくないからあまり食べないようにしてるけどね。

(a) 彼は野球選手の現役時代、ホームラン王として活躍した。

(b) ライオンは百獣の王だ。

解説

会話例と(b)では日英語共に句(フレーズ)になっているが、(a)では複合名詞になっている。日本語では句用法の場合は「～の王様」とか「～の王者」となる。句の他の例として、ほかに「ビールの王様」「川の王様」「車の王様」などが挙げられる。

K

同形異義語

お山の大将 / n. phr. / 隠喩

自分の周りしか知らず、その中で自分が一番だと得意になっている人
s.o. who thinks {he/she} is more powerful than {he/she} actually is

例文

課長はお山の大将だ。大して実力もないのに、課内ではいつも偉そうにいばっている。
The section chief thinks he's king. He acts big even though he doesn't actually have any real power.

裏も表も{知っている/知る} / phr. / 隠喩

{誰か/何か}を知り尽くしている

例文

さや：健太、今度沖縄に行くんだけど、観光スポット教えてくれない？

健太：沖縄のことなら、木村に聞くといいよ。毎年ダイビングに行ってるから、裏も表も知り尽くしてる、自分ちの庭のようなものだって、豪語してたよ。

365

(a) Kobayashi knows the banking business inside and out.

(b) My husband's a perfectionist. When he gets into something, he dissects it until he knows it inside out.

Note

The spatial terms used in the English and Japanese are slightly different. *Ura* and *omote* mean "reverse side" and "surface/front side," respectively. The terms used in the English correspond more closely to *uchi* (inside) and *soto* (outside), but one cannot say ×*uchi mo soto mo shitte iru*.

label ~ (as) / phr. / metaphor

to judge {s.o./s.t.} as having a certain attribute

Examples

Saya: Karen, why're you so mad?

Karen: Look, don't label foreign women as being unwilling to serve tea. It depends on the situation. I'm more than happy to serve coffee or whatever when the situation calls for it.

(a) Don't label me as a gangster just because I have tattoos.

(b) The world labeled him an insensitive racist, and his reputation was immeasurably damaged.

Notes

1. The English uses *label* as a verb, while the Japanese uses *retteru o haru*, which literally means "to attach a label." *Retteru* comes from the Dutch word *letter*.

2. The English expression can be used in a positive sense as well, as shown in (1), but the Japanese can only be used in a negative sense.

(1) The greatest compliment I have ever received came from my readers, who labeled me "a woman's woman."
私の読者からいただいた一番の賛辞は「女性の中の女性」{と呼ばれた / ×というレッテルを貼られた} ことだ。

landslide (victory) / comp. n. / metaphor

a win by a very large margin

Example

The party that prevailed in the election won by a landslide.

late bloomer / comp. n. / metaphor

a person who achieves success later than average

Examples

Saya: Have you ever heard of the pianist Fujiko Heming?

(a) 小林は金融事業の裏も表も知っている。

(b) 夫は完璧主義者です。何かを始めるとその裏も表も知るまで分析するんです。

解説

日英語で使われている空間を表す言葉が互いに少し異なる。英語のほうは *inside*（内）と *out*（外）であるが、日本語のほうは「裏」と「表」であり、「*内も外も知っている」という表現はない。

（〜という）レッテルを貼る　/ phr.　隠喩

誰かを根拠もなく一方的に判断して評価をつける

例文

さや：カレン、何をそんなに怒ってんのよ。

カレン：まったく、外国人の女はお茶汲みは絶対しない、なんてレッテルは貼らないでほしいわ。ケースバイケースよ。必要な時には、コーヒーだって何だって入れますよ。

(a) 入れ墨をしているからって、俺にパンクというレッテルを貼るのはやめてくれ。

(b) 彼は世間から、「思いやりのない人種偏見者」というレッテルを貼られて、計り知れないほど評判に傷をつけられた。

解説

1. 日本語は「〜にレッテルを張る」を使うが、英語では *label* は動詞である。なお「レッテル」はオランダ語の *letter* から来ている。

2. 英語では、レッテルは否定的なものでも肯定的なものでもかまわないが、日本語の「レッテル」は、常に否定的である。　▶📖 Note (1)

L

地滑り的勝利　/ comp. n.　隠喩

選挙で圧倒的に勝つこと

例文

選挙では主流派が地滑り的勝利を収めた。

遅咲き（の花）　/ comp. n.　隠喩

平均よりはるかに時間がかかるが、最後には成功する人

関 大器晩成

例文

さや：フジコ・ヘミングっていうピアニスト、聞いたことありますか？

367

Mrs. S: Isn't she the one who became successful when she was over seventy years old? She seems pretty popular.

Saya: Yeah, they say she's a wonderful performer. I hear it's pretty hard to get a ticket to one of her concerts.

Mrs. S: She's a real late bloomer, isn't she?

(a) Takagi was a late bloomer in the business world, not because he was slow, but because he started late.

(b) People think he's a late bloomer as a novelist, but he was a remarkably active playwright when he was young.

Note

Both the English and Japanese liken human success to the blooming of flowers. Incidentally, *{bloom/blossom} into* ~ and *kaika-suru* are botanical metaphors for human success. 📖← 関連語(**1**)

REL

The Japanese REL is *taiki-bansē* (great talents mature late). 📖← 関連語(**1**)

laughing drunk   comp. n.   metaphor

s.o. who laughs a lot when drunk

REL   a crying drunk

Example

I'm a laughing drunk, but he's a crying drunk, so whenever we drink there's always a mixture of laughing and crying.

Note

The Japanese can also mean "a person who laughs easily," as shown in the example.

📖← 解説(**1**)

lay (down) {one's / s.o.'s} bones   phr.   metonymy

to die in a specific place; to bury s.o.

REL   lay to rest

Examples

Mrs. S: The Kawamuras apparently gave up their U.S. citizenship and came back to Japan.

Mr. S: Right, and they lived there for 30 years, too.

Mrs. S: That's right. I heard that now that they're getting old, they want to lay their bones in their homeland.

鈴木(妻)：70歳を過ぎてから売れ出したっていう人でしょ。すごい人気らしいわね。

さや：ええ、素晴らしい演奏だそうですよ。チケットもなかなか手に入らないって。

鈴木(妻)：まさに遅咲きの花ね。

- -

(a) 高木は実業界では遅咲きだが、それは彼がのろまだったからではなく、始めたのが遅かったからだ。

(b) 彼は遅咲きの小説家と思われているが、実は若い頃は劇作家として活躍していたのだ。

解説

日英語ともに人間の成功を開花にたとえている。ちなみに、「開花する」と *{bloom/blossom} into ~* はどちらも人間を植物化した比喩表現である。

(1) 彼は開花して、偉大な叙情詩人となった。

He {bloomed/blossomed} into a great lyrical poet.

関連語

日本語には「大器晩成」という同じ意味の関連表現がある。

(1) 高木は実業界では {遅咲き / 大器晩成} だが、それは彼がのろまだったからではなく、始めたのが遅かったからだ。(→(a))

笑い上戸　comp. n.　隠喩

お酒を飲むとよく笑う(人)，何かにつけてすぐに笑う(人)

関 泣き上戸

例文

私は笑い上戸だけれど、彼は泣き上戸で、お酒を飲むといつも泣き笑いになってしまう。

解説

日本語には下の例のように「何かにつけてすぐ笑う(人)」という意味があるが、英語にはない。

(1) 笑い上戸の人は明るくて人付き合いもよく、そばにいるとこちらも楽しくなる。

A person who laughs easily is cheerful, easy to get along with, and enjoyable to be around.

(〜に)骨を埋める　phr.　換喩

ある場所で死ぬ

例文

鈴木(妻)：川村さん御夫妻、一度とったアメリカ国籍を捨てて帰国なさったらしいわよ。

鈴木(夫)：うん、30年も住んでいたのにね。

鈴木(妻)：ええ、年をとって、生まれた国に骨を埋めたくなったんですって。

- -

(a) He eventually returned to lay his bones to rest in China.

(b) From the moment he arrived in Ireland as a missionary till he laid his bones in its soil, not a day did he absent himself from the country.

Notes

1. Both the English and Japanese expressions focus on the specific place (esp. a country) where someone dies.

2. The English can mean either "s.o.'s death" or "s.o.'s burial," but the Japanese can only mean "s.o.'s death."

(1) We laid his bones in the casket.
私達は棺に骨を{入れた/ ˣ埋めた}。

3. The verbs used in the English and Japanese expressions are *lay* and *uzumeru* (to bury), respectively.

4. The Japanese expression has an additional reading, 骨を埋める（うめる）, but this can only be used literally. 📖➡ 解説(2)

REL

The English has the REL *lay to rest* (to bury the dead).

(1) My father told us before he died that he would like to be laid to rest under the old oak tree.
父は死ぬ前に、古い樫の木の下に葬ってほしいと私達に言った。

lay down one's arms　　/ phr. / metonymy

for {s.o./some group} to stop fighting or to surrender

ANT take up (one's) arms

Examples

(a) The war will continue until both sides agree to lay down their arms.

(b) Both parties should have laid down their arms for a moment and talked things through before the dispute became so serious.

(c) The terrorists finally laid down their arms and surrendered.

ANT

The ANTs for the English and Japanese are *take up (one's) arms* and *buki o toru*, respectively.

(1) Joan of Ark was just 19 years old, but she took up arms and fought for her people.
ジャンヌ・ダルクはたった19歳だったけれど、武器をとって民衆のために戦った。

leak (out)　/ v. / metaphor

for s.t. secret to become known with unwelcome consequences

Examples

Section Chief: Mike, you're making sure to protect the information about the new software we're developing, right?

Mike: Yes, sir. The password is being protected as welll so that nothing leaks out.

Section Chief: Good. Make absolutely sure there aren't any leaks.

Mike: Yes, sir. I'll be careful.

(a) 彼は最後には中国に戻ってそこに骨を埋めた。

(b) 彼は宣教師としてアイルランドに着いたその瞬間からその土地に骨を埋めるまで、その国から1日たりとも出ることはなかった。

解 説

1. 日英語とも、人が死ぬ、ある特定の場所(特に国)に焦点が当たっている。

2. 英語は "誰かの死" か "誰かの埋葬" を意味するが、日本語は "誰かの死" の意味しかない。

➡📖 Note (1)

3. 動詞は日本語では「埋める」(bury)、英語では lay (置く)である。

4. 日本語には同じ漢字を使って読み方が違う「骨を埋める(うめる)」があるが、これは字義通りの意味でしか使われない。

(2) 弟は、死んだ犬の骨を、犬が好きだった木の根元に埋めた。
My younger brother buried his dog at the base of the tree that it liked.

関連語

英語には関連表現として lay to rest (lit. 休ませる)がある。➡📖 REL (1)

武器を置く / phr.　換喩

戦いをやめる, 降伏する

反 武器をとる

例 文

(a) その戦いは、どちらかが武器を置くまで続くだろう。

(b) 争いがそこまで深刻になる前に、双方が一旦武器を置いて、話し合うべきだった。

(c) テロリストたちはついに武器を置いて投降してきた。

反意語

日英語の反意表現は、それぞれ、「武器をとる」と take up (one's) arms である。➡📖 ANT (1)

漏れる / v.　隠喩

秘密の事柄が知られてしまう

例 文

課長 :マイク、今度の新しいソフトウエアの開発情報は極秘扱いにしてあるね。

マイク: はい、課長。情報が漏れないように、パスワードもガードされています。

課長 :そう、くれぐれも外部に漏れないようにしてくださいよ。

マイク: はい、気をつけます。

371

(a) The news leaked despite his efforts to keep it secret.

(b) I heard that the university had to create a new exam when the questions leaked before the exam date.

(c) News of their secret relationship didn't leak until the woman died and her diary was published.

Notes

1. *Leak* and *moreru* have the same basic meaning: "for {liquid/gas/sound/light} to accidentally escape through a small opening." Underlying both the English and Japanese expressions is the conceptual metaphor of human speech as a liquid. The expressions *conversation flow* and *kaiwa no nagare* are examples of this concept. (**LOOK** flow)

2. The transitive counterparts of the intransitive verbs *leak (out)* and *moreru* are *leak* and *morasu*, respectively. 📖➝ 解説(1)

---

lean toward(s) ~   phr.   metaphor

for s.o.'s {views/feelings/tastes} to be drawn in a particular direction

Examples

Mr. S: Does Kenta still want to study abroad?

Mrs. S: He doesn't seem to be studying English very much these days, so it seems like maybe he's leaning toward not going.

Mr. S: That's a shame! How can he give up so easily? Maybe I should talk to him.

- -

(a) Recently, international opinion has leaned towards the elimination of commercial whaling.

(b) For a while during the postwar period, intellectual opinion tended to lean toward the left.

(c) Faced with political instability and a lagging economy, the government began leaning toward socialism.

Notes

1. The basic meanings of *lean* and *katamuku* are "for {s.o./s.t.} to bend from a vertical position (and rest one's body against {s.o./s.t.})" and "for {s.o./s.t.} to bend from a vertical position," respectively. So in the context of (1), *katamuku* cannot be used.

(1) She leaned toward him and took his hand.
   彼女は彼に{もたれかかって / ˣ傾いて}彼の手を取った。

2. While the English can mean "for s.o.'s tastes to be drawn in a particular direction," the Japanese cannot.

(2) He leans toward songs that have a message or some kind of meaning.
   彼はメッセージか意味のある歌{のほうが好きだ / ˣに傾いている}。

(a) そのニュースは彼が秘密にしておいたのにもかかわらず漏れてしまった。

(b) 試験前に入学試験問題が漏れてしまったので、大学は新しい問題をもう一度作らなければならなかったそうだ。

(c) 彼女が死んで日記が明らかになるまで、二人の秘密の関係が漏れることはなかった。

解説

1. 「漏れる」と *leak* の基本義は全く同じで、"{液体 / 気体 / 音 / 光}が小さい開口部から偶然外に出る"である。日英語はその根底に「言葉は液体である」という深層の比喩的思考がある。「会話の流れ」*conversation flow* などという表現もこの思考から来ている。(**LOOK** flow)

2. 自動詞「漏れる」と *leak (out)* に対応する他動詞は、それぞれ「漏らす」と *leak* である。

(1) 誰かが入試問題を漏らした。(→(b))
Someone leaked the entrance examination questions. (→(b))

(〜に)傾く / **phr.** 隠喩

誰かの{見解 / 気持ち}が特定の方向に引かれている

例文

鈴木(夫)：健太はまだ留学したがってるの？

鈴木(妻)：最近、英語の勉強もあまりしてないみたいだし、かなり、やめる方向に傾いているようよ。

鈴木(夫)：情けないやつだなあ。どうしてそんなに早くあきらめてしまうんだ？ちょっと話してみるか。

(a) 最近の国際世論は、商業捕鯨を廃止する方に傾いてきている。

(b) 戦後しばらくの間、知識人の思想が左に傾いた時期があった。

(c) 不安定な政情と未改善の経済という重圧に押されて、その国の政府は社会主義に傾いた。

解説

1. 「傾く」と *lean* の基本義は、それぞれ"{誰か / 何か}が垂直の状態を曲げる"と"{誰か / 何か}が垂直の状態を({誰か / 何か}にもたれかかるために)曲げる"である。したがって「傾く」が英語に対応して使えない場合がある。 **Note(1)**

2. 日英語の比喩的意味の違いは、英語は"誰かの趣味がある特定の方向に向いている"という意味があるのに対して、日本語にはそれがない点である。 **Note(2)**

373

leave a bad taste (in one's mouth) / phr. / synesthesia

for an experience to cause unpleasant emotions

Examples

Karen: Saya, what's wrong? You seem a little down.

Saya: Yeah, my friend and I had a fight. Kinda leaves a bad taste in your mouth, you know?

Karen: Oh, do I ever.

- - - - - - - - - - - - - - - - - - - -

(a) Things were awkward between my friend and me, which left a bad taste in my mouth.

(b) The main reason why the novel left such a bad taste in my mouth is probably because there were so many cruel descriptions overall.

Note

> The figurative use of *bad taste* and *atoaji* is an example of synesthesia, because it combines a physical sensation (taste) with a psychological state.

leave this {life/world} / phr. / metaphor

to die

REL shuffle off this mortal coil

Examples

(a) When I was four years old, my father left this world.

(b) Yesterday a film icon, Katherine Hepburn, left this world.

(c) With an entire drawerful of nearly completed manuscripts in his desk, the great author left this world.

Notes

1. The basic meanings of *leave* and *saru* are the same, but the Japanese is used only in written or formal speech.

2. Euphemisms such as *leave this world* and *kono yo o saru* are very similar in nature to metaphors in that both types of expressions are analogical and indirect in their construction and are not subject to literal interpretation. Referring to death directly is considered taboo in many cultures. Below is a list of English and Japanese euphemisms for death. Note that these expressions are also RELs.

   · be gone → *itte shimau* (lit. "to end up going")
   · breathe one's last (breath) → *iki o hikitoru*
   · depart this {life/world} → *ano yo ni iku* (lit. "to go to that world"), *takai-suru* (to go to the other world)
   · expire → *iki o hikitoru* (to breathe one's last breath)
   · give up one's breath → *iki o hikitoru*
   · give up the ghost → *shōten-suru* (to go up to heaven)
   · go to heaven → *tengoku ni iku*
   · go to one's long rest → *ēmin-suru* (to sleep forever)
   · lose one's life → *inochi o {nakusu/otosu/ushinau}* (to lose one's life), *inochi ga hateru*

374

後味が悪い / phr. 共感覚

何かをした後に悪い感じが残る

例文

カレン： あら、さや、どうしたの？ 元気ないわね。

さや： うん、友達とけんかしちゃったの。けんかした後って、後味悪いね。

カレン： そうだね。

- -

(a) 友人とぎくしゃくしてしまい、後味が悪い。

(b) その小説を読んだあと後味が悪かった主な理由は、全体的に残酷な描写が多かったからだろう。

解説

「後味」と *bad taste* の比喩的使用は共感覚である。なぜなら、それは肉体的な感覚（味覚）と心理的な状態を同時に含んでいるからである。

この世を去る / phr. 隠喩

死ぬ

例文

(a) 私が4歳のとき、父はこの世を去った。

(b) 昨日、米映画界のシンボル、キャサリン・ヘップバーンがこの世を去った。

(c) 完成寸前の原稿で机の引き出しをいっぱいにして、偉大な作家がこの世を去った。

解説

1. 「去る」と *leave* の基本義は同じだが、日本語のほうは書き言葉か、硬い話し言葉でしか使わない。

2. 「この世を去る」 *leave this world* といった婉曲話法は比喩表現と性格が似ている。なぜなら、婉曲話法も比喩表現も類推と間接性を土台に作られていて字義通りの解釈ができないからである。「死」を直接的に言うことはどの文化でもタブーである。以下、日英語の死に関する婉曲話法を挙げる。これらの婉曲話法は関連表現でもあることに注意。

   - あの世に行く（lit. "to go to that world"） → *depart this {life/world}*
   - あの世の人となる（lit. "to become a person of that world"）
   - 息を引き取る（lit. "to take breath away"） → *give up one's breath, breathe one's last (breath)*
   - 行ってしまう（lit. "to end up going"） → *be gone*
   - 命が果てる（to finish one's life） → *lose one's life*
   - 命を{なくす / 落とす / 失う}（lit. "to lose one's life"） → *lose one's life,*
   - 永眠する（to sleep forever） → *rest in the grave, sleep the final sleep, take one's last sleep, go to one's long rest*
   - 御陀仏だ（Buddha!）
   - お迎えが来た（s.o. has come to take you）
   - 帰らぬ人となる（lit. "to become a person who does not return"）
   - 昇天する（to go up to heaven） → *go to heaven, give up the ghost*

(to finish one's life)

- pass away → *o-nakunari ni naru* (lit. "to become non-existent")
- rest in the grave → *ēmin-suru*
- return to Mother Earth → *tsuchi ni kaeru* (lit. "to go back to the earth"), *tsuchi ni naru* (lit. "to become earth")
- sleep the final sleep → *ēmin-suru*
- take one's last sleep → *ēmin-suru*

[R][E][L]

English has the REL *shuffle off this mortal coil*, a poetic expression that originated in Shakespeare's *Hamlet*. Though the archaic usage of *shuffle* (to rid) and *coil* (troubles) may lend the expression an air of formality, it can also be used in casual contexts, often in a lighthearted manner.

left wing/left-wing   comp. n./comp. adj   metonymy

the more liberal or radical section of a political {party/group/body}

[REL] left; left-leaning

[ANT] 🔍 right wing/right-wing

Examples

(a) It seems every country has left-wingers, right-wingers, and centrists.

(b) A well-known left-wing Indian journalist and publisher was arrested in Delhi.

(c) Berlin policemen struggled with left-wing protesters during a demonstration against a far-right Neo-Nazi march.

Note

In the French Parliament (post-Revolution), the progressive party used to sit to the left from the perspective of the president. Thus, *left wing* came to serve as metonymy for progressives.

[R][E][L]

1. *Left-wing* and *sayoku* can be replaced by *left-leaning* and *hidari-yori*, respectively.
(1) This newspaper is rather left-leaning.
    この新聞はどちらかというと左寄りだ。
2. In Japanese, sometimes the terms *hidari* (left) is used in place of *sayoku* (left wing).

📖→ 関連語(2)

3. The Japanese has another REL, *sa-ha* (the left-leaning faction of a party), which is the opposite of *u-ha* (the right-leaning faction of a party). 📖→ 関連語(3)

[A][N][T]

The ANTs for *left wing* and *sayoku* are *right wing* and *uyoku*, respectively.

(1) Yukio Mishima became absorbed in right-wing ideology later on in life, and he even organized his own army.
    三島由紀夫は、晩年右翼的な思想に傾倒し、自分の軍隊まで組織した。

- 他界する（to go to the other world）　→ *leave this world, depart this {life/world}*
- 冷たくなる（lit. "to become cold"）
- 土に帰る（lit. "to return to the earth"）　→ *return to Mother Earth*
- 土になる（lit. "to become earth"）　→ *return to Mother Earth*
- 天国に行く（to go up to heaven）　→ *go to heaven*
- （お）亡く（なりに）なる（lit. "to become nonexistent"）　→ *be gone, pass away*
- 灰になる（lit. "to become ashes"）
- 星になる（lit. "to become a star"）
- 仏（様）になる（lit. "to become Buddha"）

関連語

英語には、シェークスピアの『ハムレット』で最初に使われた *shuffle off this mortal coil* という関連表現がある。"この世の煩わしさを捨て去る"、つまり"死ぬ"という意味の詩的表現である。*shuffle*（捨て去る）と *coil*（煩わしさ）という古い使い方のために形式ばって聞こえるが、形式ばらない脈絡でも気楽に使うことができる。

左翼（さよく）　／ comp. n. ／ 換喩（かんゆ）

政治的に{社会主義 / 共産主義}的な思想を持った{人 / 政治家 / 政党}

関 左（ひだり）, 左寄り（ひだりよ）, 左派（さは）

反 右（みぎ）, 右寄り（みぎよ）, 右派（うは）　**LOOK▶** 右翼（うよく）

例文

(a) どこの国にも左翼（さよく）と右翼（うよく）、そして中道派（ちゅうどうは）がいるようだ。

(b) 著名（ちょめい）な左翼（さよく）のインドのジャーナリスト兼出版者（けんしゅっぱんしゃ）がデリーで逮捕（たいほ）された。

(c) ベルリンの警官（けいかん）は、極右（きょくう）のネオナチの行進（こうしん）を阻止（そし）しようとした左翼（さよく）の抗議（こうぎ）のデモ隊（たい）ともみ合（あ）った。

解説

もともとは革命後のフランスの国会の議長の席から見て左側に革新党が座っていたので、そこから「左翼」は革新的な人を示す換喩となった。

関連語

1. 「左翼」と *left-wing* は、それぞれ、「左寄り」、*left-leaning* ともいう。 **📖REL（1）**

2. 日本語では「左翼」と言わずに「左」と言うこともある。

(2) あの政治家は{左翼 / 左}だ。
   That politician is a {left-winger/leftist}.

3. 日本語にはもう一つ、「左派」（cf.「右派」）という関連表現がある。これは党の中の左寄りの人々を指す。

(3) どんな政党にも多かれ少なかれ、内部には左派も右派も存在するものだ。
   Every political party has a left and right faction.

反意語

「左翼」と *left wing* の反意表現は、それぞれ「右翼」と *right wing* である。 **📖ANT（1）**

377

{lend (s.o.)/give s.o.} a hand   *phr.* *metonymy*
to help s.o. do s.t.

Examples

Kenta: I'm home!

Mrs. S: Kenta, you're just in time. Lend me a hand with this box, will you? It's too heavy for me.

Kenta: Sure.

(a) In the past 14 years, she has lent a hand in some way to almost every local charity.

(b) He was arrested on the suspicion of lending a hand to the criminal in his escape abroad.

Notes

1. This is one of very few cases in which the English and Japanese expressions match perfectly without either one borrowing from the other.

2. The English occasionally ends with the preposition *to* in order to emphasize the direction in which assistance is given, but it can also end with the preposition *with* to emphasize the matter that necessitates the assistance, as shown in the dialogue.

lend {s.o. an ear/an ear to s.o.}   *phr.* *metaphor*
to listen to s.o. or s.t.

Examples

Mrs. S: My friend came over again today to ask me for advice.

Mr. S: Really? It's nice of you to lend her your ear so often.

(a) He often lends an ear to other's complaints about the workplace.

(b) He's seven years older than me, but he's been kind enough to always lend me an ear whenever I need his advice.

(c) My friend lent me an ear on many occasions when I needed someone to talk to about my various problems.

REL

Japanese has another expression similar to the main entry: *mimi o katamukeru* (to bend an ear to). It means "to listen to s.o. earnestly, regardless of position." *Mimi o katamukeru* implies more attentiveness on the part of the listener than *mimi o kasu*.

関連語(1)(2)

（〜に）手を貸す　/ phr. / 隠喩

誰かが何かをするのを助ける

例文

健太：ただいま。

鈴木（妻）：あ、健太、いいところへ帰ってきたわ。ちょっと、手を貸して。この箱、重くて。

健太：いいよ。

- -

(a) 過去14年間、彼女はほとんどすべての地域の慈善事業に何らかの手を貸してきた。

(b) 彼はあの事件の犯人の国外逃亡に手を貸した容疑で逮捕された。

解説

1. この項目は日英語が完全に一致しているが、お互いからの借用関係のない稀なケースである。

2. 英語では援助を誰に与えるかをはっきりさせるために、時々前置詞の *to* をこのフレーズの終わりにつけることがある。しかし、会話例のように援助を必要とする事柄を強調する時には前置詞の *with* も使える。

（〜に）耳を貸す　/ phr. / 隠喩

同等か下の人の言うことを聞く

関 耳を傾ける

例文

鈴木（妻）：お友達が、また今日も私にアドバイスを求めてきたの。

鈴木（夫）：ほんと？　そんなにたびたび耳を貸してなんて、親切だね。

- -

(a) 彼は職場で他人の不平不満によく耳を貸す。

(b) 彼は僕より七つも年上だけれど、親切な人で、相談事があるときはいつでも耳を貸してくれる。

(c) 私がいろいろな問題について誰か話し相手が欲しいときに、友人は何回となく耳を貸してくれました。

関連語

日本語には「耳を貸す」以外に「耳を傾ける」という表現がある。後者は「目上、目下に関わらず、真剣に相手の言うことを聞く」という意味がある。「耳を傾ける」の方が「耳を貸す」よりも真剣さの度合いが高い。

(1) 彼は相手の地位の上下に関係なく、誰の言うことにも耳を｛貸す / 傾ける｝人だ。

He is the type of a person who lends an ear to everybody regardless of his or her status.

(2) 色々アドバイスをもらいたかったのに彼は1、2分ぐらいしか耳を｛貸して / ?傾けて｝くれなかった。

I wanted to get as much advice from him as possible, but he only lent me his ear for a couple of minutes.

Let sleeping dogs lie.　/ phr.　metaphor

avoid stirring up trouble

Example

> I think my parents know that I dropped out of college, but they haven't said anything yet. I guess it's best to just let sleeping dogs lie.

homograph

leverage　/ n./v.　/ metaphor

the power to achieve a desired effect, often by influencing others
ねらった効果を達成する力。多くの場合は、その効果を達成するために人に影響を与えることになる

Example

> The businessman used his contacts as leverage to secure the deal.
> ビジネスマンは交渉を有利に運ぶために知り合いのコネを使った。

Note

> While *lever* has the literal meaning of "s.t. sturdy that is used to move or dislodge s.t. heavy," it can also be used metaphorically to mean "a tool used to achieve a desired outcome."
> 英語の *lever* の字義通りの意味として、"何か重量のあるものを移動したり除去したりするもの"という意味があるが、比喩的には"希望する結果を生むために使う手段"を意味する。

{lick/smack} one's lips　phr.　metonymy

to anticipate with pleasure

REL　lick one's chops

Examples

(a) The wolf smacked his lips as he waited for the bunny to emerge from the burrow.

(b) When my favorite steak was served, I inadvertently licked my lips.

REL

1. Both English and Japanese also have metaphorical usages for the word *saliva*.

📖→関連語(1)

2. The English REL is *lick one's chops*. It can be used instead of *lick one's lips*.

(1) When my favorite steak was served, I inadvertently licked my {lips/chops}. (→(b))

380

寝た子を起こすな / phr. / 隠喩

せっかく収まっている問題を思い出させるようなことはしないほうがいい

例文

両親は僕が大学を中退してしまったことを知っていると思うんだ。でも、まだ何も言ってこないけど。ま、たぶん、寝た子は起こさないようにしておいたほうがいいよね。

同形異義語

てこ / n. / 隠喩

何かを行うための有効な手段
an effective method for achieving s.t.

例文

彼女は父親の政治力をてこにして、希望していた会社に職を得た。
She used her father's political influence to get a job at the company she wanted to work at.

舌なめずりをする / phr. / 換喩

獲物や大好物の食べ物を待ち構える

関 よだれが出る, よだれをたらす

例文

(a) 狼は子ウサギが穴の中から出てくるのを、舌なめずりをして待っていた。
(b) 大好物のステーキが出てきたので、思わず舌なめずりをした。

関連語

1. 日英語には「よだれ」*saliva* の入った次のような比喩表現がある。
(1) 友達からおいしい神戸牛を食べた話を聞いて、僕は{よだれが出た/よだれをたらした}。
   When my friend talked about the delicious Kobe beef he ate, I salivated (lit. "saliva {came out/dripped out}).
2. 英語には *lick one's chops* という関連表現があり、見出しと置き換えることができる。

→ REL (1)

lick one's wounds / phr. / metaphor

to recover from a disappointing situation

Example

> When you've experienced defeat, just sitting around licking each other's wounds won't help you move forward.

lift a finger / phr. / metonymy

to {help/do one's share}

Examples

> Mrs. S: Honey, if you're just reading the newspaper, could you give me a hand? Our guests will be here any minute now.
>
> Mr. S: Oh, uh, sure.
>
> Mrs. S: Sitting there without lifting a finger—I can't stand it.

- -

(a) We cleaned the garage out this weekend, and Jim didn't even lift a finger to help us.

(b) I consider Michiko a friend, but she doesn't lift a finger when I need help.

(c) Someday robots will be able to do anything, and we humans will be able to live our lives without lifting a finger.

Note

> While *lift* and *ugokasu* (to cause {s.t./s.o.} to move) are different, they both have to do with "movement."

---

light a fire under ~ （（～に）火をつける　） → **{build/light} a fire under ~**

(as) light as a feather / phr. / simile

very light

ANT as heavy as lead

Examples

(a) The ad said the tennis shoes were "as light as a feather," so I went ahead and bought a pair. I'm really glad I did—they're the most comfortable shoes I own.

(b) The ballet dancer lifted his partner so effortlessly that she looked as light as a feather.

ANT

> The ANTs for *as light as a feather* and *hane no yō ni karui* are *as heavy as lead* and *namari no yō ni omoi*, respectively.

(1) When I got up this morning, my legs felt as heavy as lead.
朝起きると両足が鉛のように重かった。

傷口をなめる / phr. 隠喩

精神的痛手を癒そうとする

例文

失敗してもお互いに傷口をなめあっているばかりでは、前には進まない。

指一本動かさない / phr. 隠喩

何も{手伝おう/しよう}としない

例文

鈴木(妻)：あなた、新聞読んでるんだったら、ちょっと手伝ってくださいよ。もうすぐ、お客さんがお着きになるのよ。

鈴木(夫)：え、あ、う〜ん。

鈴木(妻)：もう。座ったまま指一本動かそうとしないんだから。いやになっちゃう。

(a) 今週末、みんなでガレージを掃除したけど、ジムは指一本動かそうとしなかった。

(b) 僕はみちこのことを友達だと思っているが、彼女は僕が助けが必要なときに、指一本動かそうとしない。

(c) いつかロボットが何でもできるようになり、人間は指一本動かさなくても、生活できるようになるだろう。

解説

日英語の動詞は「動かす」と *lift*(上げる)で、異なる動詞だが、"動き"を表すという意味で同じである。

L

羽のように軽い / phr. 直喩

とても軽い

反 鉛のように重い

例文

(a) 「羽のように軽いテニスシューズ」という宣伝文句につられて買ったけれど、実際、このシューズは履き心地がいい。

(b) バレーダンサーはパートナーを何の苦もなく持ち上げたので、彼女は羽のように軽く見えた。

反意語

日英語のそれぞれの反意表現は、「鉛のように重い」と *as heavy as lead* である。 📖 ANT(1)

light at the end of the tunnel / phr. / metaphor

to be hopeful that a difficult situation will soon come to an end

Examples

(a) Just as we began to see the light at the end of the tunnel, we ran into an insurmountable problem.

(b) The recession has continued for a long time, but the economy has been improving recently, and we're beginning to see a light at the end of the tunnel with the employment situation.

(c) With the advent of the new medicine, there was finally some light at the end of the tunnel for patients with chronic pain.

Notes

1. The English can be used with verbs other than *see*. In the Japanese, *mieru* is a non-volitional verb that means to visually identify something; the volitional verb *miru* is not used.

2. In the Japanese, *ton'neru no saki ni* (at the end of the tunnel) is optional, but in English, *see the light at the end of the tunnel* and *see the light* are two different expressions. The latter means "to come to understand s.t. that one could not understand before," as shown in (1).

(1) I used to think that that TV series was overrated, but when I tried watching it again, I finally saw the light.
以前はそのテレビ番組のシリーズは過大評価されていると思ったものだ。しかし、もう一度見直してみて、ついにそのよさがわかった。

3. Note that the expression *ton'neru no saki ni* is borrowed from English.

light purse / comp. n. / metaphor

the state of not having

Example

A light purse makes a heavy heart.

homograph

like a bullet out of a gun / phr. / simile

very quickly
素早く
すばや

Example

After coming home from school, the students picked up the soccer ball and were off again like bullets out of a gun.

学校から家に帰ると、学生たちはサッカーのボールを拾い上げるや否や、また素早く
がっこう　　いえ　かえ　　　　　がくせい　　　　　　　　　　　　　　　　ひろ　あ　　　　　いな　　　　　すばや
家を飛び出した。
いえ　と　だ

384

（トンネルの先に）明かりが見える　／ phr.　隠喩

否定的な事柄がようやく{終わって／改善して}希望が出てくる

例文

(a) トンネルの先に明かりが見え始めたちょうどそのとき、私たちは乗り越えられないような問題にぶつかった。

(b) 長らく不況が続いていたが、最近多少景気が上向いてきて、雇用状況にも明かりが見えつつある。

(c) 長年続いてきた患者達の苦しみも、今や新薬の出現によって、真っ暗なトンネルの先に明かりが見えてきた。

解説

1. 日本語の「見える」は自発的に視覚で認知するという意味の無意志動詞で、有意志動詞の「見る」は使わない。英語は *see* 以外の動詞も使用できる。

2. 日本語では「トンネルの先に」はあってもなくてもいいが、英語では *at the end of the tunnel* がつかないと"今までわからなかったものがわかるようになる"という意味に変わってくるので注意。→ Note (1)

3. 「トンネルの先に」は、英語からの借用語であることに注意。

財布が軽い　／ phr.　隠喩

お金を持っていない

例文

財布が軽けりゃ、心は重い。

同形異義語

鉄砲玉のように　／ phr.　／ 直喩

行ったきり帰ってこない
to leave and not come back

例文

娘はどこかに遊びに出かけると、鉄砲玉のように帰ってこない。
Once my daughter goes out, she doesn't come home, like a bullet fired from a gun.

(sound) like a fairy tale / phr. / simile

to be unrealistic

REL like s.t. right out of a fairy tale

Examples

Karen: Do you know this singer? I heard she recently married the president of a record company. He discovered her when she was waitressing and working her way through music school.

Saya: Wow, first a waitress and now a CEO's wife. It's like a modern-day fairy tale!

Karen: You can say that again.

- - - - - - - - - - - - - - - - - - - -

(a) The prince getting married to a commoner was like a fairy tale.

(b) Last week, I met the woman of my dreams at a party. As soon as I laid eyes on her, I knew she would be my wife. Bet this sounds like a fairy tale, huh? Well, it gets better.

Note

The English and Japanese expressions can both be used as metaphors as well.

(1) Our wedding ceremony was truly beautiful. It was a fairy tale come true.
私達の結婚式は実にすばらしかったんです。おとぎ話の世界そのものでした。

REL

1. The English and Japanese RELs, *like s.t. right out of a fairy tale* and *otogi-banashi kara tobidashite kita yōna*, are very similar to one another. 📖 関連語(1)

2. The Japanese REL *yume no yōna hanashi da* has a much wider application than *otogi-banashi no yō da*, because whereas the latter describes something similar to a fairy tale, the former can be anything that reminds one of a dream. 📖 関連語(2)

like a fish out of water / phr. / simile

the state of being unaccustomed to or uncomfortable in a certain situation

Examples

(a) At the time, I felt like a fish out of water during the Skype meetings because I didn't know much about computers.

(b) He worked at Company M for many years, but he never got used to the corporate climate or the cool, rainy weather of the Northwest. He always said he felt like a fish out of water.

(c) As she is a teacher, she felt like a fish out of water among those distinguished lawyers.

Note

There is a minor difference between the English and Japanese. In the former, it is a *fish* that is out of water, but in the latter, it is a mysterious creature called a *kappa*. This is an imaginary, river-dwelling animal that is about the size of a small child and has a face

おとぎ話（のような） *phr.* 直喩

話が非現実的だ

関 おとぎ話から飛び出してきたような，夢のような話

例文

カレン： この歌手、知ってる？　最近、レコード会社のオーナーと結婚したそうよ。その社長って、彼女がウエイトレスしながら歌の勉強していたときに、彼女を見つけたんだって。

さや： へえ、ウエイトレスが今は社長夫人か。現代のおとぎ話のようね。

カレン： ほんと。

- -

(a) 庶民階級出身の女性と王子の結婚は、まるでおとぎ話のようだった。

(b) 僕は先週パーティで理想の女性と出会ったんだ。一目で自分の妻に出会ったのだとわかった。おとぎ話のようだろう。ま、それから先がもっといいんだ。

解説

日英語ともに直喩になっているが、隠喩としても使える。 ─📖 Note (1)

関連語

1. 日英語ともそれぞれ「おとぎ話から飛び出してきたような」と *like s.t. right out of a fairy tale* というお互いに同じ発想の関連表現がある。

(1) 庶民階級出身の女性と王子の結婚は、おとぎ話から飛び出してきたようだった。（→(a)）
The prince getting married to a commoner {sounded/seemed} like something right out of a fairy tale. （→(a)）

2. 日本語の関連表現に「夢のような話」があるが、「おとぎ話」に限られている見出しと異なり、この関連表現は夢のようなものなら何でもいいので、使い方の幅がずっと広い。

(2) オックスフォード大学に入れるなんて {夢のような話 / ˣおとぎ話のよう} だ。
Getting into Oxford University would be like a dream.

L

陸に上がった河童 {のよう / みたい} な *phr.* 直喩

勝手が違ってどうにもならないこと

反 水を得た魚 {のよう / みたい} に

例文

(a) 当時、私はコンピュータのことはほとんど知らなかったから、スカイプ会議では陸に上がった河童のように感じた。

(b) 彼は長年 M 社に勤めてきたが、会社の風土とアメリカ北西部の肌寒い、雨の多い気候に未だに慣れていない。彼いわく、いつも陸に上がった河童のように感じているそうだ。

(c) 彼女は教師なので、立派な弁護士の中では陸に上がった河童のような気持ちだった。

解説

日本語では伝説上の架空の生き物である「河童」、英語では *fish* が使われているというわずかな違いがある。河童は 4〜5 歳ぐらいの子供の大きさと体型をした想像上の水陸両生動物で、

387

like a tiger with a snout, as well as a saucer-like depression on top of its head that contains water. It is said that if a *kappa* comes ashore, the water on its head will evaporate and it will lose its powers.

[A][N][T]

The ANT for the Japanese is *mizu o eta uo {no yō/mitai} ni* (like a fish that has found water). 📖— 反意語(1)

(to be caught) like a rat in a trap   /phr. simile

to be unable to escape from s.t.

Examples

Mr. S: Today was rough. It took me an hour to get home because of all the police checkpoints.

Mrs. S: That sounds terrible!

Mr. S: With that kind of surveillance, a drunk driver would be like a rat in a trap.

(a) He was walking through town alone when he was surrounded by three guys and couldn't escape. He was like a rat in a trap.

(b) This house is structured in such a way that even if a burglar were to get in, he'd be caught like a rat in a trap and unable to escape.

Notes

1. The English uses *a rat in a trap*, but the Japanese uses *fukuro no nezumi* (a rat in a bag).
2. The Japanese is usually used as a metaphor, but can also be used as a simile like the English. (→ (a)(b))

like a ship without a rudder   /phr. simile

for {s.o./s.t.} to not have a clearly defined direction or purpose

Examples

Mrs. S: Ever since the coach got sick and a new coach took over, this team has been on a losing streak. They were doing so well before, too.

Mr. S: Yeah, they have no idea what they're doing. They're like a ship without a rudder.

(a) Without his wife, he would be like a ship without a rudder.

(b) A company without a strategic plan is like a ship without a rudder.

くちばしがとがっていて、虎のような顔をして、頭上に凹みの皿があり、そこに水が入っている。河童が陸に上がると、その水が干上がって河童は無力になると言われている。

反意語

日本語の反意表現に「水を得た魚{のよう/みたい}に」 *like a fish in water* (lit. "like a fish that has found water")がある。

(1) あの子は国語のクラスでは怖じ気づいて一言も話さないが、数学のクラスでは水を得た魚のように生き生きとして、どんな質問にも答える。

That child is so nervous in Japanese class that he won't utter a single word, but in math class he's like a fish that has found water and will answer any question.

袋のねずみ　　*n. phr.*　隠喩

どこにも逃げられない状態

例文

鈴木(夫)：はあ、参ったよ。交通取り締まりのおかげで、帰りの道、1時間もかかったよ。

鈴木(妻)：そんなにすごかったの。

鈴木(夫)：うん、あれじゃ、飲酒運転なんか、袋のねずみだね。

(a) 彼は町を一人で歩いていたら3人の男らに囲まれて逃げようがなかった。まるで袋のねずみみたいだった。

(b) この家は、万が一泥棒が侵入してもどこからも逃げることができない構造になっている。侵入者はまるで袋のねずみだ。

解説

1. 英語は「わな」のねずみだが、日本語は「わな」とは言わず、「袋」のねずみと言っている。

2. 日本語は普通は隠喩として使われるが、英語のように直喩としても使える。(→(a)(b))

L

舵のない船{のよう/みたい}な　　*phr.*　直喩

{人/機関/国}がどちらの方向に行くべきか、何をすべきかわからない状態

例文

鈴木(妻)：このチーム、監督が急病で変わってから、ほんと負けっぱなしね。前はあんなに調子よかったのに。

鈴木(夫)：うん、舵のない船とは、まさにこのことだね。

(a) 妻がいなかったら、彼は舵のない船のようになるだろう。

(b) 戦略上の計画のない会社は、舵のない船のようだ。

like (a) Rip Van Winkle / phr. / simile

describes the feeling of disorientation one feels when s.t. one is accustomed to suddenly changes

Examples

Mr. S: Coming back to Japan after living in a foreign country for twenty years made me feel like Rip Van Winkle.

Mrs. S: Really? But didn't you come back once a year?

Mr. S: True, but two- or three-day business trips don't really count.

- -

(a) When I came back to Japan after staying overseas for 15 years, the clothing, food, and lifestyle had changed so much that I felt like a Rip Van Winkle.

(b) When I came back to the company after working at a subsidiary for three years, everyone had changed departments. I felt like Rip Van Winkle.

Note

The English is based on Washington Irving's *Rip Van Winkle* from *The Sketch Book* (1820), and the Japanese is based on the folk legend *Urashima Taro*. The following is a short summary of each story:

<*Rip Van Winkle*> A man named Rip Van Winkle drank liquor in the mountains with a mysterious group of people and ended up falling asleep for 20 years. But when he woke up and went home, his village had completely changed, and no one recognized him.

<*Urashima Taro*> Taro Urashima was a kind fisherman who saved a turtle that was being tormented by children. The turtle invited him to the Dragon Palace under the sea, where he enjoyed himself for what seemed to be several days. But when he returned to his village, it had completely changed, and no one recognized him.

like the wind / phr. / simile

for {s.o./some action} to be very quick

Examples

(a) John is always busy. He shows up, and then suddenly he's gone like the wind.

(b) I ran after her, but she ran like the wind.

Note

The verbs used most frequently in this expression are *go* (*iku*) and *run* (*hashiru*).

like two peas in a pod / phr. / simile

very similar to one another

Example

Those two brothers might be years apart, but they're still like two peas in a pod.

浦島太郎{のよう/みたい}な   phr.   直喩

自分がずっと知っていたものが突然変化して戸惑う気持ちを表す

例文

鈴木(夫)：20年も外国に住んでから日本に戻ってきたので、浦島太郎のような感じがしたよ。

鈴木(妻)：あら、あなたは1年に一度は日本に帰ってきていたじゃない？

鈴木(夫)：それはそうだけど、仕事で2、3日ということが多かったからね。

(a) 15年ぶりに海外から日本に戻ったときは、日本の衣食住が変わってしまっていて浦島太郎になったような気持ちだった。

(b) 3年間子会社に出向して古巣に戻ってきたら、社員がみな部署が替わっていて浦島太郎みたいだった。

解説

日英語はそれぞれ『浦島太郎』という説話と『リップ・ヴァン・ウインクル』というワシントン・アーヴィングの『スケッチブック』(1820)に載っている物語が出典である。2つの話の要約は次の通りである。

『浦島太郎』は、子供にいじめられた亀を救った漁師が海底の竜宮城に招かれ、大いに楽しい生活をして、数日だと思って村に戻ったら、村はすっかり様変わりして、自分を知っている者はひとりもいなかった、という話である。

『リップ・ヴァン・ウインクル』は山中で出会った奇妙な群れの人達と酒を飲んでいる間に20年間も眠ってしまい、目が覚めて自分の村に戻ったら、村はすっかり変わってしまっていて、誰も彼のことを知っている者はいなくなっていた、という話である。

L

風{のよう/みたい}に   phr.   直喩

とても速く

例文

(a) ジョンはいつも忙しいので、風のように現れて、風のように去っていく。

(b) 僕は彼女を走って追いかけたが、彼女は風のように行ってしまった。

解説

日英語とも一緒に使われる動詞は「行く」*go* と「走る」*run* が多い。

瓜二つ   n. phr.   隠喩

よく似ている,そっくりである

例文

あの二人は年が離れた兄弟だが、瓜二つでまるで双子のようだ。

391

Note

When referring to things that resemble each other, English uses *peas* and Japanese uses *uri* (*oriental melon*).

like water off a duck's back / phr. simile

for s.t. unpleasant, such as criticism, to have no effect on the person involved

Examples

Mike: Did you tell the section chief about the issue?

Colleague: Of course I did, but it was like water off a duck's back. He simply doesn't care.

(a) He let the criticism roll off him, like water off a duck's back.

(b) I've learned to let insults roll off me like water off a duck's back.

Notes

1. Both ducks and frogs can live both on land and in water, so getting water on their back or face does not bother them. This fact can be employed to figuratively describe a person who is not affected by a negative situation.

2. The English expression is a simile, but the Japanese is a metaphor. The English expression comes from the fact that water rolls off a duck's back because its feathers are oily. The Japanese expression is apparently based on the assumption that frogs are not disturbed by water because they are amphibians.

3. The English expression frequently occurs with the verb *roll off*, as shown in (a) and (b).

4. *Mizu* can be replaced by *shōben* (urine) in casual speech.

5. The English cannot be used in the case of constructive criticism, as in (1).

(1) I keep telling my friend that he's stupid to waste all his money on gambling, but {he just doesn't listen/ ×it's like water off a duck's back} .

私は友人に給料の全部を博打に賭けるなんて馬鹿だと言い続けているのに、蛙の面に小便だ。

REL

1. The Japanese has the REL *uma no mimi ni nenbutsu* (lit. "Buddhist chants in a horse's ear"). 🔖→ 関連語(1)

However, *uma no mimi ni nenbutsu* has another meaning: "to not understand the meaning or value of s.t." When used in this sense, *uma no mimi ni nenbutsu* cannot be replaced by *kaeru no tsura ni mizu*. 🔖→ 関連語(2)

2. The Japanese has another REL, *baji tōfū* (lit. "a horse's ears and eastern wind"), which means that, while humans can feel the spring wind blowing from the east, horses do not feel anything. This expression originated with Chinese poet Li Bao (701-762), who compared people's inability to appreciate his poems with horses' inability to appreciate the eastern wind blowing in spring. It is now used to refer to a person who pays no attention to what others are saying.

解説

お互いに似ているものに対して英語では*pea*(エンドウ)を使うが、日本語では「瓜」(oriental melon)を使う。

蛙の面に{水 / 小便}　　**n. phr.**　　隠喩
かえる　つら　みず　しょうべん　　　　　　　　　　　　　　　いんゆ

否定的な状況(特に人に批判されること)が当人に全然影響を与えない
ひていてき　じょうきょう　とく　ひと　ひはん　　　　　　　　　　とうにん　ぜんぜんえいきょう　あた

関 馬の耳に念仏, 馬耳東風
うま　みみ　ねんぶつ　ばじとうふう

例文

マイク: 課長に例の件について、言ってみた?
　　　　かちょう　れい　けん　　　　　い

同僚: もちろん言ったよ。でも、蛙の面に水。なんとも思っちゃいないね。
どうりょう　　　　い　　　　　　　　かえる　つら　みず　　　　　　おも

(a) 彼は批判を蛙の面に水のようにかわした。
かれ　ひはん　かえる　つら　みず

(b) 人からの侮辱を蛙の面に水みたいにかわす方法を覚えたんだ。
ひと　　　ぶじょく　かえる　つら　みず　　　　　　ほうほう　おぼ

解説

1. 蛙もアヒルも水陸で生息しているから水などが顔や背中についていても全くかまわない。このことから否定的な状況が当人に全然影響を与えないという比喩が出てくる。

2. 英語は直喩で日本語は隠喩である。英語はアヒルの羽の油のせいで背中から水がはじけ落ちることから、日本語は蛙は両生類なので水をかけても平気な顔をしていることから出てきた。

3. 英語は(a)と(b)のように、動詞の*roll off*(転げ落ちる)と一緒に使われることが多い。

4. 「水」は、日本語のくだけた表現では「小便」になる。

5. 英語は、批判が建設的な場合には使えない。 —📖**Note(1)**

関連語

1. 日本語には「馬の耳に念仏」という関連表現がある。

(1) 私は友人に給料の全部を博打に賭けるなんて馬鹿だと言い続けているのに、{蛙の面に小便 / 馬の耳に念仏}なんだ。 —📖**Note(1)**
　しかし、「馬の耳に念仏」は「意味、価値を理解しない」という別の意味があり、この場合は見出しに置き換えることができない。

(2) 先生のすばらしい話もその学生には{馬の耳に念仏 / ×蛙の面に水}だった。
The teacher gave the students a wonderful lecture, but it was like casting pearls before swine.

2. 日本語には関連表現として「馬耳東風」という言葉もある。意味は東風が吹いて、人は春を感じるが、馬の耳は何も感じないということで、中国の唐代の詩人李白(701-762)が詩の中で、自分の詩を理解してくれないのを馬が春風を感じないことにひっかけたのが始まりである。比喩として使うときは、人の話をいい加減に聞いている人のことを言う。

L

limp as a (wet) rag / phr. / simile

to feel exhausted

Examples

Mike: What's wrong? You look really tired.

Karen: Yeah, I'm limp as a wet rag. I've been busy since this morning and I didn't even have time to eat lunch.

(a) I just joined the tennis club, and they worked me until I was as limp as a rag.

line / n. / metaphor

a course of action or thought

Examples

Kenta: I want a new mobile phone, but I'm not sure what I should get.

Mr. S: The cheaper the fees the better, right? If you're thinking along those lines, it might be best to go with Company A's phones.

Kenta: But their phones' app selection is limited, so I don't know.

(a) The suspect that line of investigation led to has been investigated before for a similar crime.

(b) Then let's discuss the matter along those lines.

Notes

1. The basic meaning of *line* and *sen* is "a long, narrow mark on a surface," but both can be used metaphorically, as in *line of investigation* and *along those lines*.

2. Interestingly, *deadline* and *shisen* (life-or-death crisis) have completely different meanings. 📖→解説(1)

3. In Japanese, *kokunai-sen* and *kokusai-sen* are used, but ˣ*domestic line* and ˣ*international line* should be replaced by *domestic flight* and *international flight*, respectively. However, when referring to a train line, such as Tokyo's Yamanote Line or Marunouchi Line, both *sen* and *line* can be used, perhaps because the linear nature of train tracks makes the metaphorical usage of *sen* and *line* more appropriate.

REL

In Japanese, *rain* (line) is used in borrowed words such as *sutāto-rain* (start line), *sēsan-rain* (production line), *paipu-rain* (pipeline), and *sukai-rain* (skyline). However, in these examples, *rain* cannot be replaced by *sen*.

ぼろ雑巾のよう（になる） phr. 直喩

とても疲れて、へとへとになる

例文

マイク： どうしたの。疲れた顔してるね。

カレン： うん、もうぼろ雑巾のようにくたくたよ。今日は朝からめちゃくちゃ忙しくて、昼ご飯を食べる間もなかったの。

（a） 新しく入ったテニス部で、ぼろ雑巾のようになるまで、しごかれた。

線 n. 隠喩

方向, コース, 計画, 交通組織

関 ライン

例文

健太： 携帯電話、買い替えたいけど、どれがいいかなあ。

鈴木（夫）： 通信料が安いほうがいいね。その線で考えると、Ａ社のかな。

健太： でも、あれはアプリの数が少ないから、ちょっとね。

（a） 捜査線上に現れた容疑者は、以前にも似たような事件で取り調べを受けたことがあった。

（b） では、その線に沿って話を進めてください。

解説

1. 日英語ともその基本義は"平面上の長い細い印"であるが、そこから「捜査線」line of investigation、「〜の線で」「〜の線に沿って」「〜の線で」along those lines のような比喩的用法が出てくる。

2. 面白いことに「死線」（生死の境）と deadline（締め切り）は全然意味が違う。

(1)a. 友達がひどい交通事故にあって死線をさまよっていたが、一命だけは取り留めた。
   My friend was involved in a bad traffic accident and hovered between life and death.

 b. 今日中にこの論文を書いて送らないと、〈締め切り / ×死線〉に間に合わない。
   If I don't finish writing this paper and send it in today, I won't make the deadline.

3. 日本語では「国内線」と「国際線」が使われるが、対応する英語の×domestic line と×international line は使えない。しかし、東京の「山の手線」「丸の内線」のように電車の場合は「線状」の比喩が分かりやすいためか、英語でも Yamanote Line、Marunouchi Line となる。

関連語

日本語では、「ライン」は「スタートライン」「生産ライン」「パイプライン」「スカイライン」のような借用語の中で使われる。これらのラインを「線」で置き換えることはできない。

L

literally / adv. / metaphor

used to emphasize that a statement is true; an exaggerated way of emphasizing s.t.

Example

(a) Our dog literally jumps for joy when our father comes home.

(b) If I eat any more, I will literally explode.

live under the same roof / phr. / metaphor

to live together

REL eat at the same table

Examples

Saya: Your cat died?

Karen: Yeah. I'm really depressed. I've been living with him for 18 years under the same roof, you know.

Saya: 18 years?!

Karen: You heard that right. He'd been with me since I was a kid, and I even brought him with me to Japan.

- - - - - - - - - - - - - - - - - - - -

(a) We lived under the same roof when we were young, you know.

(b) Three generations of the Kimura family are living under the same roof. They seem to be a lively, happy bunch.

Notes

1. *Kurasu* (to lead one's daily life) can be replaced by *sumu* (to reside in a certain place), but the latter is not used as frequently.

2. This expression is typically used to describe an unusual combination of people living together. The Japanese expression can also be used to describe pets whom one has lived with for a long time.

R E L

The Japanese REL is *onaji kama no meshi o kū* (to eat rice from the same pot), while the English equivalent is *eat at the same table*. 📖→ 関連語(1)

{load/weight} off one's shoulders, a / n. phr. / metonymy

describes the feeling of relaxation one feels after some burden has been lifted

REL LOOK take a load off one's mind; LOOK {load/weight} off one's shoulders, a

Examples

Mr. S: Kenta finishes college next year. Time sure flies!

Mrs. S: It sure does. That'll be a load off our shoulders.

- - - - - - - - - - - - - - - - - - - -

文字通り（に） / adv. / 隠喩 /

文字に書かれている状況がそのままである，何かを強調するために誇張して表現する

例 文

(a) 我が家の犬は父が帰ってくると、文字通り飛び上がって喜ぶ。

(b) これ以上食べたら、文字通りお腹が破裂してしまいそうだ。

同じ屋根の下で暮らす / phr. / 隠喩 /

一緒に住む

関 同じ釜の飯を食う

例 文

さや：ネコちゃん、死んじゃったんだって？

カレン：そうなの。もう悲しくて。18年も同じ屋根の下で暮らした仲なんだもの。

さや：18年も！

カレン：そう、子供の時から一緒で、日本にも連れてきたからね。

- -

(a) 僕たちは若い頃、同じ屋根の下で暮らした仲なんだ。

(b) 木村家は、親子三代が同じ屋根の下で暮らしていて、とてもにぎやかで楽しそうだ。

解 説

1. 日本語の動詞「暮らす」は「住む」に置き換えることができるが、「暮らす」に比べると使用頻度は低い。

2. この比喩は、本来は一緒に住む必要がない組み合わせの人達が一緒に住むとか、日本語ではペットが特別長く生きて一緒に住んだような場合にも使われる。

関連語

日本語には「同じ釜の飯を食う」という関連表現がある。これにほぼ対応するのが英語の *eat at the same table* であろう。

(1) われわれは同じ釜の飯を食った仲だ。（lit. "We ate at same rice out of the same pot.)

L

肩の荷が下りる / phr. / 換喩 /

何か大事なことが終わってほっとする

関 LOOK▶ 心の重荷が取れる

例 文

鈴木(夫)：健太は来年は大学卒業か。早いなあ。

鈴木(妻)：そうね。ようやく、親として肩の荷が下りるわね。

(a) Our son was finally released from the hospital after a long stay. It was quite a load off our shoulders.

(b) Publishing my first book was a time-consuming process. I felt like a load had been lifted from my shoulders when it finally came out.

REL

1. The English and Japanese have the RELs *a load off one's mind* and *kokoro no omoni ga toreru*. Both can be used instead of the main entry. 📖→ 関連語(1)

2. English also has the REL *a {load/weight} (is lifted) {off/from} one's shoulders*, which is interchangeable with the main entry.

(2) I felt like a {load/weight} was lifted {off/from} my shoulders when my first book finally came out. (→(b))

lock horns (with ~)　phr.　metaphor

to get into a dispute with s.o.; to compete with s.o.

Examples

Karen: Are you two still arguing? I wish you'd stop locking horns and make up already.

Saya: Sure, but only if I get an apology.

Kenta: That's my line!

- -

(a) I thought that Greece and Turkey were on friendly terms, but they're actually hostile toward one another and routinely lock horns over issues surrounding Cyprus.

(b) The representatives from developed countries locked horns with their counterparts from developing countries over the tricky issue of drafting trade rules.

Note

In English, this expression can be applied to any two parties who compete with one another or get involved in a dispute, but the Japanese expression can only be used in cases where two parties are in a bad relationship.

(1)a. The Red Socks locked horns with their rivals, the Yankees.

レッドソックスはライバルのヤンキースと{戦った/ $^{??}$ 角を突き合わせた}。

b. The professor and his student locked horns with each other over a new academic theory.

教授と教え子は、新しい学説について、激しく{議論した/ $^{??}$ 角を突き合わせた}。

(a) 長い間入院していた息子がやっと退院して、肩の荷が下りた。

(b) 処女出版は大変時間のかかる仕事でした。本が出たときには肩の荷が下りる思いでした。

関連語

1. 日英語には関連表現として「心の重荷がとれる」a load off one's mind がある。「肩の荷が下りる」と同じように使える。

(1) 長い間入院していた息子がやっと退院して {肩の荷が下りた / 心の重荷が取れた}。(→(a))

Our son was finally released from the hospital after a long stay. It was quite a load off our {shoulders/mind}. (→(a))

2. 英語には a {load/weight} (is lifted) {off/from} one's shoulders という関連表現もあり、見出しと置き換えることができる。━📖 REL(2)

角(を)突き合わせる　phr.　隠喩

人や国などが相手方と悪い関係にある

例文

カレン：なんだ、まだ二人はけんかしてるの？　そんなにいつまでも角突き合わせてないで、いいかげん、仲直りしなさいよ。

さや：健太が謝ってくれるんならね。

健太：それはこっちのせりふだよ。

(a) ギリシャとトルコは隣国で仲がいいと思っていたが、実際はキプロス問題で角突き合わせる敵国同士だそうだ。

(b) 貿易ルールの草案作りという微妙な問題で、先進国の代表は、発展途上国の代表と角を突き合わせた。

解説

日本語は二者が悪い関係にあるときにしか使えないが、英語は二者がスポーツで競う場合とか議論し合う場合にも使える。━📖 Note(1)

L

399

lone wolf / comp. n. / metaphor

s.o. who prefers to be alone

Examples

Mrs. S: I heard that my friend Sato quit the police force and started his own detective agency.

Mrs. S: So he's a lone wolf now, huh? Maybe that suits him better than being a part of the system.

- -

(a) He's social in his private life, but he's a lone wolf at the workplace.

(b) That artist is a lone wolf who is afraid of losing his individuality by working with other artists.

look back on ~ / phr. / metaphor

to reflect on s.t. from the past

Examples

Mr. S: We'll be having our silver anniversary soon.

Mrs. S: We certainly will. Looking back on everything, it's been a long journey. But it seems like it all happened in the blink of an eye, don't you think?

- -

(a) Looking back on this year, there were quite a few natural disasters.

(b) When I look back on our school days, it seems as if they were a century ago.

Note

In both English and Japanese, the act of looking back is a metaphor for reflecting on something from the past.

look down {on / upon} ~ / phr. / metaphor

to think that {s.o./s.t.} is inferior and hold {him/her/it} in contempt

ANT look up to ~

Examples

Colleague: He's always looking down on us. What a rude guy.

Mike: He just thinks he's a big shot. He wants everyone to say that he's great and look up to him.

Colleague: If he really wants to be respected, he should change his attitude.

- -

(a) Rich people sometimes look down upon those who don't have much money.

(b) Elisa likes classical music, but she looks down on rock music because she considers it too noisy.

一匹狼 いっぴきおおかみ / comp. n. 隠喩いんゆ

人と交わったり回りの影響を受けたりせず、独りで自分の生き方を通す人

例文

鈴木（夫）：友達の佐藤、警察を辞めて、探偵事務所を始めたそうだよ。

鈴木（妻）：あら、一匹狼になっちゃったのね。でも、あの人は組織の中にいるより、そのほうが合うかもね。

(a) 彼はプライベートでは社交的だが、職場では一匹狼で周囲と話をしようとしない。

(b) あの人は一匹狼の芸術家で、他の芸術家と一緒に仕事をして自分を失うことを恐れている。

振り返ってみる ふ かえ / phr. 隠喩いんゆ

過去のことに思いを向ける

例文

鈴木（夫）：われわれも、もうすぐ銀婚式だね。

鈴木（妻）：そうですね。振り返ってみると、長いようで、あっという間でしたね。

(a) 今年1年を振り返ってみると、自然災害の多い年でした。

(b) 学校時代を振り返ってみると、まるで1世紀も前のような気がする。

解説

日英語で「振り返ってみる」という行動が過去のことへの思いの隠喩になっている。

L

（〜を）見下す みくだ / comp.v. 隠喩いんゆ

｛誰か／何か｝のことを、価値がなく劣っていると思ってばかにする

関	（〜を）見下げる，（〜を）下に見る
反	（〜を）見上げる

例文

同僚：彼はいつも人を見下した態度を取って、本当に失礼だよ。

マイク：偉そうにしたいだけさ。みんなからあの人はすごいって、見上げてもらいたいんだよ。

同僚：本当に尊敬されたいんなら、態度を改めないといけないね。

(a) 金持ちの人は時々お金のない人々を見下すことがあります。

(b) エリサはクラシックは好きですが、ロックはうるさいと言って見下しています。

401

Note

Mi-kudasu used to have a non-metaphoric meaning of "to look down on s.t.," but it no longer has this meaning. The same is true of the REL *mi-sageru*. 📖➡ 関連語(1)

REL

The Japanese REL *mi-sageru* is usually used to modify a noun, such as in *mi-sageta yatsu*. 📖➡ 関連語(1)

ANT

The ANTs in English and Japanese are *look up to ~* and *(~ o) mi-ageru*, respectively.

(1) All the students look up to the erudite professor.
学生たちはその博学の教授を尊敬の念で見上げている。

---

look like a drowned rat / phr. / simile

to be soaking wet

Examples

Kenta: I'm home! I got caught in a shower on my way back.

Mrs. S: You're back. Wow, you look like a drowned rat! Hurry up and change before you catch a cold!

- - - - - - - - - - - - - - - - - - - -

(a) My hair looked as if I had just gotten out of the shower, and my shirt was completely soaked. I looked like a drowned rat.

Note

The Japanese is usually used as a metaphor, but it can also be used as a simile like the English. 📖➡ 解説(1)

---

look on the bright side (of ~) / phr. / metaphor

to look at a situation positively (even though the situation looks bad)

REL wear rose-colored glasses

Examples

Saya: How did your interview at Company X go?

Friend: Well, the last part didn't go so well.

Saya: Don't be discouraged—look on the bright side. I hear that company's not performing well and that it's actually in the midst of restructuring.

Friend: True. It would be terrible to start working there only to get fired and end up worse off than before.

- - - - - - - - - - - - - - - - - - - -

(a) When life doesn't go as planned, it's tempting to view everything in a negative light, but that's precisely when you should look on the bright side of life.

解説
日英語の「見下す」はかつては "下のものを見る" という字義通りの意味があったが、現代語ではその意味はない。関連表現の「見下げる」も同じである。

関連語
日本語には「見下げる」という表現があるが、これは普通「見下げた奴」のように名詞の前にくる修飾語としてしか使えない。

(1) あいつは老人をだましては金をまきあげる見下げた男だ。

He is a despicable guy who has repeatedly chiseled money out of older people.

反意語
日英語の反意表現は、それぞれ、「(～を)見上げる」と *look up to ~* である。 ━━ ANT(1)

濡れねずみ　/ comp. n.　隠喩

服を着たまま体中が濡れていて見苦しい

例文

健太：ただいま。途中ですっごい夕立ちにあっちゃった。

鈴木(妻)：お帰りなさい。あら、まあ、濡れねずみじゃない。早く着替えないと、風邪引くわよ。

(a) あたしの髪の毛はまるでシャワーから出てきたばかりのように見えた。シャツはぐっしょりで、濡れねずみった。

解説
日本語は普通は隠喩として使われるが、英語のように直喩としても使える。

(1) 彼は濡れねずみ{のよう / みたい}に見えた。

He looked like a drowned rat.

明るい面を見る　/ phr.　隠喩

物事の(悪いところを見ないで)いいところを見る

反 暗い面を見る

例文

さや：X 社の面接、うまくいった?

友達：うん、それが、最終で落っこっちゃったんだ。

さや：そう。でも、そんなにがっかりしていないで、もっと明るい面を見てみたら。あそこは、業績が落ちてリストラしているって聞いたよ。

友達：そうだね。入ってもすぐ辞めさせられたら、仕事が見つからないよりもっと大変だもんね。

(a) 人生がうまくいかないと、何事も暗い面を見てしまいがちだが、その時がまさに人生の明るい面を見なければならない時なのだ。

(b) When the economy is as bleak as it is now, it is hard to look on the bright side of society.

Note

The preposition *on* can be replaced by *at*, but this is fairly uncommon.

REL

The English REL is *wear rose-colored glasses*. Unlike the main entry, this expression has negative connotations.

(1) People often tell me I'm naïve—that I'm wearing rose-colored glasses and not facing reality. 僕はよく人に無知だとか、{物事を楽観的に見過ぎる / ''物事の明るい面を見る} とか、現実を直視していないなどと言われる。

ANT

The English and Japanese ANTs are *the dark side (of s.o./s.t.)* and *kurai men o miru*, respectively. ▢▤ 反意語(1)

It should be noted that the English ANT is used to refer to a negative aspect of someone or something that is ordinarily hidden from view.

---

look through ~ / phr. metaphor

to examine s.t.

Examples

(a) You should look through the questionnaire before deciding whether or not to fill it out.

(b) Before you take medicine, look through not only the directions but also the explanation of the side effects.

(c) Every morning my dad looks through two newspapers while eating breakfast. Then he leaves for work.

---

lose ~ / v. metaphor

to no longer have {s.t./s.o.} as a result of s.t.

Examples

(a) I lost a good friend because we had a huge argument.

(b) I haven't had a pet since I lost the dog I had in elementary school.

(c) I lost all of my possessions in a fire, so I returned to my hometown.

(d) Companies selling products often lose customers to competitors who undercut them.

(e) Every year, many people lose their lives in auto accidents.

Note

The Japanese entry is not often used with concrete objects. In such cases, *nakusu* is used instead of *ushinau*. ▢▤ 解説(1)

(b) 今のように経済状況が悪いと、社会の明るい面を見るのが難しい。

【解説】
英語では *on* は *at* で置き換えることができるが、*at* のほうが *on* より使用頻度がはるかに低い。

【関連語】
英語には *wear rose-colored glasses*（lit. バラ色の眼鏡をかける）という関連表現がある。比喩としては「根拠なく楽観的になる」という意味である。この比喩表現はたいてい否定的な意味合いがあるが、見出しにはそのような意味合いはない。 ▶📖 REL(1)

【反意語】
日本語には「明るい」を「暗い」に変えた「暗い面を見る」という反意表現がある。ただし、英語では *bright* を *dark* に変えただけの ˣ*look on the dark side (of s.o./s.t.)* とは言えないことに注意。
(1) 物事の暗い面を見る人より、明るい面を見る人のほうが幸せだ。
People who looks on the bright side of things are happier than those who {focus on the negative/ˣlook on the dark side}.
英語の反意表現の場合、普通は外から見えない何かや誰かの否定的な側面を指摘する時に使われる。

（〜に）目を通す　phr.　隠喩

全体をざっと読む

【例文】
(a) 全部の質問に目を通してから、アンケートに答えるかどうか決めたほうがいい。
(b) 薬を飲む前に、飲み方だけでなく、副作用の説明についても目を通してくださいね。
(c) 父は毎朝、朝食をとりながら新聞二紙に目を通す。それから、会社に出かける。

L

（〜を）失う　v.　隠喩

今まで存在した{何か/誰か}が何かの理由で存在しなくなる

【例文】
(a) 大げんかをして、大切な友達を失ってしまった。
(b) 小学生の時に愛する犬を失って以来、動物は何も飼ったことがありません。
(c) 火事ですべての財産を失ったので、故郷に帰ることにした。
(d) 商品を提供する企業は、競争相手がより安い値段で売るために客を失うことが多い。
(e) 毎年、交通事故で多くの人が命を失う。

【解説】
日本語の見出しは具体的な物にはあまり使用されない。物がなくなった時には、「失う」ではなくて「失くす」を使う。
(1) 電車の中で財布を{失くした/ˣ失った}。
I lost my wallet on the train.

405

lose confidence (in ~) / **phr.** **metaphor**

to become unable to believe in one's abilities or worth

[ANT] gain confidence

Examples

Mike: Man, I've lost confidence in myself.

Kenta: Why? What happened?

Mike: Well, it's just that I've been making mistakes at work.

Kenta: Heck, I'm always losing confidence in myself. All of my tests are disasters.

(a) What do I do when I lose confidence in myself during a game?

(b) I am mentally and physically exhausted and have lost confidence in my ability to do my job.

Notes

1. In English, one can *lose confidence in* anything, including entities such as banks, the market, schools, governments, etc. *Jishin o nakusu*, however, cannot be used that way. *Shinyō shinaku naru* (to not trust s.o. any longer) has to be used instead, as shown in (1). The Japanese can only be applied to someone's ability, academic studies, etc., as illustrated in the dialogue and the examples. 📖➡ 解説(**1**)

2. In Japanese, the verb *nakusu* can be replaced by *ushinau* in formal speech or writing.

   📖➡ 解説(**2**)

3. When used non-metaphorically, both *lose* and *ushinau* mean "to no longer have s.t. tangible," but when used metaphorically, they can take all sorts of intangible objects as their direct object, such as *opportunity*, *dream*, *energy*, *interest*, *life*, *position*, *reason*, *time*, *trust*, and *meaning*, among others.

(3) a. Because of the war, many young people lost their dreams for the future.
   戦争によって、多くの若者が将来の夢を失った。

   b. In a debate, the one who loses control is the one who loses.
   討論は理性を失った方が負けだ。

   c. He may lose his current position because of a scandal involving a woman.
   彼は女性スキャンダルで、今の地位を失うかもしれない。

[REL]

Japanese has the REL *jishin o sōshitsu-suru* (lose confidence), which is a Sino-Japanese nominal compound. 📖➡ 関連語(**1**)

[ANT]

The ANTs for *lose confidence* and *jishin o nakusu* are *gain confidence* and *jishin o tsukeru*, respectively. 📖➡ 反意語(**1**)

（〜に）自信をなくす　/ phr. / 隠喩

自分の{能力 / 価値 / 行動}が正しいと思えなくなる

関 自信を喪失する，**LOOK**（〜を）失う

反 自信をつける

例文

マイク： あ〜あ、自信をなくしたな。

健太： 何かあったの？

マイク： いや、仕事でちょっと失敗しちゃって。

健太： 僕なんか、いつも自信喪失の連続。試験で失敗ばかりしているもんね。

(a) 試合中に自信をなくしたらどうしたらいいでしょうか。

(b) 私は心身ともに疲れ果てて、仕事をやる能力に自信をなくしてしまいました。

解説

1. 英語では銀行、市場、学校、政府などの組織に関しても *lose confidence in ~* が使えるが、日本語の「自信をなくす」はそのようには使えない。その場合は、「信用しなくなる」と言わなければならない。「自信をなくす」ものは人と密接な関係のある能力とか、勉強とかに限られている。

(1) 人々が銀行{を信用しなくなる / ˣに自信をなくす}と、銀行にどんなにお金があってもつぶれることがあり得る。
   Banks can fail when people lose confidence in them, even if they are financially sound.

2. 日本語の「なくす」は書き言葉か硬い話し言葉では「失う」で置き換えることができる。

(2) 私は小説を書く自信を{なくした / 失った}。
   I've lost confidence in my ability to write a novel.

3. 非比喩的に使われる場合、動詞「失う」と *lose* は"何か触れるものをもはや持っていない"という意味であるが、比喩的に使う場合は、「機会」「夢」「元気」「興味」「命」「地位」「理性」「時間」「信用」「意味」など、さまざまな触れないものを直接目的語としてとれる。▶📖 **Note (3)**

関連語

日本語には「自信を喪失する」という表現もある。

(1) 仕事で失敗して自信を{なくした / 喪失した}。
   I made a mistake at work and lost confidence in myself.

反意語

日英語の反意表現は、それぞれ、「自信をつける」と *gain confidence* である。

(1) 自己主張をして相手の間違いを立証しようと思ったら、まずはあなたが自信をつけなければいけません。
   You need to gain confidence in order to assert yourself and prove them wrong.

L

lose one's cool / phr. / metaphor

to become emotional

[ANT] keep one's cool

Examples

(a) He lost his cool and began shouting, throwing his arms up in anger and causing quite a scene.

(b) He lost his cool when the referee made a call that wasn't favorable to him.

(c) That store clerk keeps smiling and never loses her cool no matter how terribly the customers treat her.

Note

Lose one's cool can be used in both spoken and written English, but the Japanese is only used in written Japanese. The spoken versions are *katto naru* (to anger) and *kanjōteki ni naru* (to become emotional). 📖➡ 関連語(1)

[REL]

The Japanese RELs are *katto naru* and *kanjōteki ni naru*. 📖➡ 関連語(1)

[ANT]

The English and Japanese ANTs are *keep one's cool* and *rēsēsa o tamotsu*, respectively.

(1) The golfer lost his ball but kept his cool.
そのゴルファーはボールを見失ったのに冷静さを保っていた。

lose face / comp. v. / metaphor

for s.o.'s reputation to suffer due to an {error/failure}

[ANT] restore one's reputation

Examples

Colleague: The department head was proud of his English, but when you corrected him during the meeting you made him completely lose face.

Mike: Yeah, I just felt such major mistakes couldn't be ignored. Do you think I did the wrong thing?

Colleague: No, not at all. He needed that.

- -

(a) It took an understanding friend to get him to play the piano. He was known as a perfectionist and never wanted to lose face.

(b) Even though that athlete was considered a shoe-in for the gold medal, he was eliminated and lost face.

Note

The basic meaning of *face* is evident, but *{menmoku/menboku}* come from *men* (face) and *moku* (eye).

[REL]

The Japanese REL, *mentsu o ushinau*, is more formal and used much less frequently than *{menmoku/menboku} o ushinau*. 📖➡ 関連語(1)

冷静さを失う /phr. 隠喩

感情的になる

関 カッとなる，感情的になる，**LOOK▶**（〜を）失う

反 冷静さを保つ

例文

(a) 彼は冷静さを失い、叫び出し、怒りに手を上げ、騒ぎ立て始めた。

(b) 気に入らない判定を審判がしたときに、彼は冷静さを失った。

(c) あの店員は客にどんなに悪態をつかれても冷静さを失わず笑顔で対応している。

解説

英語は話し言葉でも書き言葉でも使えるが、日本語は書き言葉で使われる。話し言葉では「カッとなる」や「感情的になる」などが使われる。📖━関連語(1)

関連語

日本語には「カッとなる」「感情的になる」という関連表現がある。

(1) 彼は新しいプロジェクトが期待通りにはかどっていなかったので{冷静さを失った / カットなった / 感情的になった}。
When the new project didn't go as well as he expected, he {lost his cool/got angry/ became angry}.

反意語

日英語の反意表現は、それぞれ、「冷静さを保つ」と *keep one's cool* である。━📖 ANT(1)

面目を失う /phr. 隠喩

{間違い / 失敗}のために信用を失う

関 面子を失う，**LOOK▶**（〜を）失う

反 面目を施す

例文

同僚：英語が得意なのを鼻にかけていた部長、会議でマイクに言い直されて、まったく、面目を失ってたね。

マイク：ひどく違うこと言ってたから、まずいと思ったんだよ。悪いことしたかな？

同僚：ぜんぜん。いい薬だよ。

(a) ピアノを彼に弾いてもらうのには理解のある友人の説得が必要だった。完璧主義者として知られている彼は絶対に面目を失いたくなかったのだ。

(b) その選手は金メダルを確実視されていたのに、予選で落ちて面目を失った。

解説

英語の *face* の基本義は明らかであるが、日本語の「面目」は「面」（face）＋「目」（eye）からなる複合語である。

関連語

日本語には、使用頻度は「面目を失う」より低いが、書き言葉的な関連表現「面子を失う」がある。

(1) その選手は金メダルを確実視されていたのに、予選で落ちて{面目 / 面子}を失った。（→(b)）

409

[A][N][T]

The ANTs are *restore one's reputation* and *{menmoku/menboku} o hodokosu*. Note that
^×*mentsu o hodokosu* does not exist. 📖→ 反意語(1)

lose sight of ~ / phr. / metaphor

to no longer be able to see s.t.; to forget about s.t. important

[Examples]

Kenta: All right, our car will be in front, so stay close and make sure not to lose
sight of us.

Mike: Got it. But Tokyo Highway is crowded, so I might lose sight of your car. If
I do, I'll give you a call.

Kenta: Sounds good.

- -

(a) A country's prime minister shouldn't lose sight of the big picture no matter
how hard he or she has been criticized.

(b) No matter how busy my life might be, I don't ever want to lose sight of
myself.

[Note]

The Japanese is a compound verb formed from *mi* (to see) and *ushinau* (to lose). The
English is also a compound verb formed from *lose* and *sight of*, where *sight* is a noun.
They share the same figurative meaning.

Love is blind. phr. metaphor

One cannot see the faults in the person one loves

[REL] Love sees no faults

[Examples]

Mrs. S: I thought Keiko preferred good-looking men. I wonder why she
married a guy like Matsumoto?

Mr. S: As they say, "love is blind."

- -

(a) Do you know why she is able to love such a mean guy? Easy. Love is blind.
That's why.

[Note]

Love is blind was first used in *The Merchant's Tale*, one of the stories included in *The
Canterbury Tales* (ca. 1387-1400) written by Chaucer (1340-1400). It appears in the
sentence "For loue is blynd alday and may not see." The expression became widespread
after Shakespeare (1564-1616) started to use it in several of his plays, including *Romeo
and Juliet*.

反意語

日英語の反意表現は、それぞれ、「面目を施す」と *restore one's reputation* である。ただし、「[×]面子を施す」という表現はない。

(1) サッカーの試合で、ゴールキーパーは相手チームのシュートを全て阻んで{面目/[×]面子}を施した。
At the soccer game, the goalkeeper blocked all the other team's shots and restored his reputation.

（〜を）見失う　/ comp. v.　隠喩

見えなくなる，わからなくなる

例文

健太：じゃ、僕達の車が先に行くから、ちゃんと見失わないでついて来てよ。

マイク：わかった。でも、首都高は交通量が激しいから、健太の車、見失っちゃうかもね。そうなったら、電話するよ。

健太：わかった。

- -

(a) 一国の首相は、たとえどんなにたたかれても、大局を見失うようなことがあってはならない。

(b) 毎日多忙な生活の中でも、自分を見失わないように生きていきたい。

解説

英語は *lose + sight + of* という複合動詞になっていて、*sight* は "見ること" という意味の名詞である。日本語も「見 + 失う」という複合動詞で、「見」は動詞の語幹である。しかし、両者の比喩的意味は共通である。

恋は盲目　/ phr.　隠喩

恋をしている人は理性を失う

関 あばたもえくぼ

例文

鈴木(妻)：けい子さん、あんなに面食いだったのに、どうして松本さんと結婚することにしたのかしら。

鈴木(夫)：要するに、恋は盲目っていうことだろうね。

(a) 彼女がどうしてあんないやらしい男と結婚したかわかるかい？　簡単なのさ。恋は盲目なんだ。

解説

「恋は盲目」という表現を最初に使ったのはチョーサー(1340-1400)で、『カンタベリー物語』(1387-1400頃)に含まれている「商人の物語」で使った「恋は終日盲目で(恋人達は)目が見えない」である。この表現が一般的に普及したのは、シェクスピア(1564-1616)の『ロミオとジュリエット』ほか数作品で使われてからだと言われている。

411

REL

The Japanese REL, *abata mo ekubo* (lit. "even pockmarks on the face are dimples") uses more descriptive imagery and is more general than the English REL, *Love sees no faults.*

love nest / comp. n. / metaphor

a place where two lovers meet (often illicitly)

Examples

(a) He fell in love with a waitress and the two set up a love nest in Paris.

(b) Legend has it that Queen Margot had a love nest on this site. Today, each of the twenty rooms feels like a love nest.

Notes

1. Both the English and Japanese expressions are based on the idea of a literal nest occupied by two birds in love, but the Japanese is likely a direct translation of the English.

2. The English expression often refers to a place where people engaged in cheating/adultery meet, but the Japanese expression is also used for married couples and lovers and does not necessarily imply an illicit relationship.

love triangle / comp. n. / metaphor

a romantic relationship involving three people

Example

Both Taro and Jiro are in love with Hanako, and all three are tired of the love triangle they're in.

make a clean sweep of ~ / phr. / metaphor

to completely eliminate s.t. unwanted; to secure an overwhelming victory

Examples

(a) Making a clean sweep of the terrorists in this area won't be easy.

(b) We would like the new prime minister to institute a new policy that will make a clean sweep of all the corrupt elements in politics.

(c) The new CEO made a clean sweep of the company's disreputable accounting practices by hiring an outside auditing firm.

Note

The English expression can also be used to mean "to secure an overwhelming victory."

(1) The politician made a clean sweep of all the counties in the election.
その政治家は選挙ですべての地域の圧倒的な勝利を確実なものとした。

関連語

日本語の「あばたもえくぼ」は、英語の *Love sees no faults*（lit. 愛は欠点を見ない）よりも描写的で、かつ一般的である。

愛の巣
あいす **n. phr.** 隠喩 いんゆ

愛し合っている者同士の住まい
あいあ ものどうし す

例文

(a) 彼はウェイトレスと恋に落ち、パリで愛の巣をかまえた。
かれ こいお あいす

(b) 伝説によると、マルゴ女王はこの地に愛の巣をかまえたそうだ。今でも、20の部屋
でんせつ じょおう ち あいす いま へや
の一部屋、一部屋が愛の巣のような感じがする。
ひとへや ひとへや あいす かん

解説

1. 日英語ともに"鳥の居心地よい愛の巣"という字義通りの解釈に基づいているが、日本語は英語からの直訳の可能性が高い。

2. 英語の表現は普通浮気や不倫の出会いの場所に使われることが多いが、日本語の表現は夫婦、恋人同士などの場合にも用いられ、必ずしも不倫関係だけとは限らない

三角関係
さんかくかんけい **comp. n.** 隠喩 いんゆ

3人の間の複雑な恋愛関係
にん あいだ ふくざつ れんあいかんけい

例文

太郎と次郎はともに花子を愛していて、3人は三角関係に疲れ果てていた。
たろう じろう はなこ あい にん さんかくかんけい つか は

（〜を）一掃する
いっそう **comp. v.** 隠喩 いんゆ

古く悪いものをすべて取り除く
ふる わる とのぞ

例文

(a) この地域のテロ組織を一掃するのは容易ではない。
ちいき そしき いっそう ようい

(b) 新しい首相には、政治腐敗を一掃するような斬新な政策を打ち出してほしい。
あたら しゅしょう せいじふはい いっそう ざんしん せいさく うだ

(c) 新しいCEOは、外部の監査会社を雇い入れることで、評判の悪い会計監査の慣例を
あたら がいぶ かんさがいしゃ やといい ひょうばん わる かいけいかんさ かんれい
一掃した。
いっそう

解説

英語の見出しには「圧倒的な勝利を確実にする」という意味もある。 ▶ Note（1）

413

make {a friend/friends} / phr. / metaphor

to intentionally become friends with s.o.

REL make friends with ~

Examples

Kenta: I wonder if there's any way to become proficient in English quickly.

Karen: Well, how about making friends with someone who speaks English?

Kenta: But wait, we're friends, right? This friendship hasn't helped me improve at all.

Karen: It's helped me get good at Japanese, though. Thanks!

- -

(a) I've made a lot of friends online and through social networks.

(b) How about joining our club and making some new friends? We can go camping and skiing together.

Note

The verbs *make* and *tsukuru* mean "to cause s.t. concrete to come into existence," and their use in these expressions is a metaphorical extension of this basic meaning.

REL

1. The English REL is *make friends with ~*, which means "to become friends with ~."

(1) I realized that Yukio was going to be very lonely by himself and decided to make friends with him.
幸夫はひとりぼっちでとても淋しくなるだろうということが分かったので、友達になってやることにしたんです。

2. The Japanese REL is *~ to tomodachi ni naru* (to become friends). It is the intransitive version of *tomodachi o tsukuru* (to make a friend). Note that *make a friend* cannot be followed by *with*. 📖► 関連語(2)

3. The Japanese has another REL, *tomodachi ga dekiru*, which indicates a friendship that forms spontaneously. 📖► 関連語(3)

---

homograph

make a hole in ~ / phr. / metaphor

to use up a large amount of money
お金をたくさん使う

Example

This trip is going to make a huge hole in my savings.
今度の旅行は私の貯金をたくさん使うことになるだろう。

友達を作る / phr. / 隠喩

誰かと友達になる

関 友達ができる

例文

健太：何か手っ取り早く英語が上手になる方法ってないかな？

カレン：それはもう、英語を話す友達を作ることよ。

健太：あれ、カレンって僕の友達じゃなかったっけ？　でも、効果ないな。

カレン：あら、あったわよ。おかげで、私は日本語が上手になったわ。ありがとう。

- (a) 私は、インターネットやSNSを通して、たくさん友達を作った。
- (b) 私たちのサークルに入って、友達をたくさん作りませんか。一緒にキャンプをしたり、スキーをしたりしましょう。

解説

「作る」と *make* の基本義は"何か具体的なものをゼロから創造する"であるから、見出しの用法はそこから出た隠喩である。

関連語

1. 英語には *make friends with ~*（〜と友達になる）という関連表現がある。 ◆📖 **REL(1)**
2. 日本語の「〜と友達になる」は「友達を作る」の自動詞形である。*make a friend* はそのあとに with を取れないことに注意。
- (2) 今日娘はエリサという小学校1年の同級生と友達になりました。コンピュータゲームをしたり、塗り絵をしたりしていました。
  Today my daughter made {friends/ˣa friend} with another first grade girl, Elisa. They played computer games and colored together.
3. 日本語のもう一つの関連表現は「友達ができる」で、友情関係が自発的にできる場合に使う。
- (3) 自分が変わってしまうような一生の友達{ができた /⁇を作った}。
  I made a lifelong friend who has changed who I am.

同形異義語

（〜に）穴をあける / phr. / 隠喩

何かが欠けている状態にする
to cause a loss of some sort

例文

ひどい風邪を引いて会社を休み、仕事に穴をあけてしまった。
I caught a bad cold and had to take time off work, so I fell behind on my tasks.

homograph

make s.o.'s blood boil / phr. / metaphor

for s.t. to make s.o. angry
誰かを怒らせる

Example

The politician's provocative speech made the opposition's blood boil.

その政治家の挑発的な演説は、反対派を激怒させた。

---

make one's eyes spin / phr. / metaphor

for s.t. to make s.o. dizzy

Examples

(a) Standing for so long under the blazing sun made my eyes spin.

(b) The jumble of letters and punctuation in his e-mails always makes my eyes spin.

Note

In addition to meaning "to feel dizzy," the Japanese main entry can also mean "to be very busy." 📖→ 解説(1)

---

homograph

make s.o.'s head spin / phr. / metaphor

to confuse s.o.
頭がくらくらする

Example

He wrecked the house, yelling all the while. The whole thing made my head spin.

彼はわめきながら、家の中をめちゃくちゃにしてしまった。私は頭がくらくらしました。

同形異義語

血を沸き立たせる / phr. / 隠喩

何かが人をいい意味で興奮させる
for s.t. to excite s.o. positively

例文

彼は聴衆の血を沸き立たせる演説で有名な政治家だ。
That politician is known for giving speeches that get his audience all fired up.

目が回る / phr. / 隠喩

何かでめまいがする

例文

(a) 長い間炎天下に立っていたので、目が回って倒れてしまった。
(b) 彼から来るメールは、いつも文字がぎっしり詰まっていて、ごちゃごちゃしている。それを見るたびに目が回る。

解説

日本語には「めまいがする」という意味の他に、「とても忙しい」という意味もある。

(1) 企画会議が近づいてきて、プレゼンの準備と配布資料の作成に追われて目が回るほど忙しい。
The planning meeting is almost here, and between preparing for the presentation and making all the materials, things are very hectic.

同形異義語

目が回る / phr. / 隠喩

とても忙しい
very busy

例文

子供が生まれてから、仕事と子育ての両立で忙しくて目が回る。夫にもう少し手伝ってほしい。

Ever since my baby was born, I've been so busy juggling work and parenting. I wish my husband would help a bit more.

homograph

make noise (about ~) / phr. / metaphor

to draw attention to s.t. significant
強い言葉で注意を引きつける

Example

The Administrator of NASA made noise about the closing of three NASA Centers and the massive delay this caused in plans for the Space Station.

NASA の長官は 3 つの NASA センターを閉じることについて、それは宇宙ステーション計画をひどく遅らせることになると強調した。

make waves / comp. v. / metaphor

to cause a {disturbance/sensation} with s.t. new or unusual

Examples

Mr. S: What do you think of our new prime minister?

Mrs. S: Well, they say he's really making waves in Nagatacho with his radical ideas about changing the system of government.

- -

(a) This historian has written a controversial book that is making waves in his field.

(b) They don't like the idea of making waves and disrupting parliamentary proceedings, but unless they do so, it seems unlikely that they'll be able to pursue reforms.

Notes

1. The direct object in the English is simply *waves*, but in the Japanese, both *nami* and *kaze* (waves and wind) are used.
2. The English cannot be used when the direct object is a relationship, but the Japanese can.

解説(1)

{man/woman} of the hour, the / n. phr. / metaphor

a person who is currently the object of attention

Examples

Mrs. S: The performance of this Japanese player in the Major Leagues is impressive.

Kenta: Yeah, he's the man of the hour.

- -

(a) Winning the new client made Rebecca the woman of the hour at work.

Note

The basic definition of *man/woman* and *hito* is "an individual human; a person other than oneself."

M

同形異義語

（〜と言って）騒ぐ　/ phr. / 隠喩

つまらないことを大げさに言う
to make a fuss about s.t. trivial

例文

夫はめがねがなくなったと言って騒いでいる。
My husband is making a fuss about not being able to find his glasses.

波風を立てる　/ phr. / 隠喩

普通と変わった{行動 / 考え}によって{動揺 / センセーション}を起こす

例文

鈴木（妻）：今度の首相についてどう思う？

鈴木（夫）：うん、政府組織改革について急進的な考えを持っているから、永田町に波風を立てることになるだろうね。

(a) この歴史家は、自分の専門分野に波風を立てるような本を著した。

(b) 彼らは、とにかく議会の運営に波風を立てることを嫌うが、それでは、何も改善はされないだろう。

解説

1. 英語は*wave*（波）だけが目的語であるが、日本語は「波と風」が目的語になっている。

2. 日本語は人間関係を荒立たせるような場合にも使えるが、英語は使えないことに注意。

(1) 彼女の出現は、信頼し合ってきた夫婦の関係に波風を立てることになった。
The woman's appearance eventually {disturbed/×made waves in} the trust our marriage was built on.

時の人　/ n. phr. / 隠喩

社会で話題になっている人

例文

鈴木（妻）：この日本人野球選手の大リーグでの活躍はすごいわね。

健太： うん、今やすっかり時の人だね。

(a) 新規顧客獲得競走で優勝したことは、レベッカを社内で「時の人」にした。

解説

「人」と*man/woman*の基本義は、"人間、あるいは自分以外の人間の総称"である。

419

manna from heaven　/ n. phr. / metaphor

unexpected assistance that arrives in a time of need

Examples

Saya: We finally got some decent rain last week, huh?

Karen: No kidding. The days were so hot that the dam nearly ran dry. Talk about manna from heaven!

(a) A poor widow was struggling to pay for a small house which she lived with her four children. That money was like manna from heaven to her.

(b) For music buffs, the album is manna from heaven. Few albums pack such quality into each song.

(c) I was out of a job at the time, so when my friend told me that his dad's company was looking for someone, it was manna from heaven.

Notes

1. The English originated in the Old Testament of the Bible (Exodus 16), which tells the story of how God bestowed bread upon the Israelites being led out of Egypt by Moses as they were starving in the Arabian wilderness. Exodus 16:31 reads: "The people of Israel called the bread manna. It was white like coriander seed and tasted like wafers made with honey." The Japanese simply means "heaven's {blessing/kindness}" and has no relation to the Bible.
2. The Japanese can also mean "the rich blessings of Mother Nature." 📖➡解説(1)
3. The English is a metaphor, but the Japanese is a case of personification.

REL

The Japanese has the RELs *jigoku de hotoke* and *jigoku ni hotoke*, which mean "seeing Buddha in Hell" or "Buddha in Hell," respectively. Both are used as metaphors that mean "to receive assistance during a time of distress." 📖➡関連語(1)

A man's home is his castle.　/ phr. / metaphor

one can behave as one pleases in one's home

Example

Mr. S: This feels great!

Mrs. S: What're you doing walking around the house in your underwear?!

Mr. S: Hey, I can do what I want! A man's home is his castle, after all!

420

天の恵み　／ n. phr.　擬人化

何かが欠乏して困難な状況にある人に、奇跡的に与えられる助け

関 地獄で仏

例 文

さや：先週は久しぶりにまとまった雨が降ったわね。

カレン：本当ね。毎日かんかん照りでダムの水も底を突きかけていたから、まさに天の恵みね！

- -

(a) 貧しい未亡人は4人の子供と住んでいる小さな家の家賃を支払うのに四苦八苦していた。その金は彼女にとって天の恵みとして届いたのだった。

(b) 音楽狂にはそのアルバムは天の恵みだ。他のアルバムで全曲そんなに質の高いものは少ない。

(c) その頃僕は失職中だったから、友人からおやじさんの会社で人を探していると聞いた時には天の恵みだと思った。

解 説

1. 英語は聖書（旧約聖書）の出エジプト記16章から出ている。イスラエル人がモーゼに率いられてエジプトから出て、アラビアの荒野で餓死寸前のところに神がパンを天から降らせた、という箇所である。出エジプト記16：31には「イスラエルの民はそのパンをマナと呼んだ。それはコリアンダーの実のように白く、その味は蜜を入れたウエハースのような味であった」とある。日本語は聖書とは無関係である。

2. 日本語には、英語にない"自然の豊かな恩恵"という意味がある。

(1) 天の恵みが造り出した極上の純米酒。
The best *sake* made from pure rice created from the rich blessings of Mother Nature.

3. 日本語は擬人化であり、英語は隠喩である。

関連語

日本語には「地獄で仏」あるいは「地獄に仏」という関連表現がある。これはそれぞれ「地獄で仏に会ったようだ」「地獄に仏がいるようだ」の縮まった形であり、"苦しい状況にいたときに思いがけず人に助けられる"という意味である。

(1) 私が卒論で苦しんでいるときに、院生がいいアドバイスをしてくれて、地獄｛で / に｝仏だった。
When I was struggling to write my senior thesis, a grad student gave me good advice. It was manna from heaven.

我が家は我が城　phr.　隠喩

家では自分が好きなようにふるまえる

例 文

鈴木（夫）：リラックスできるなあ。

鈴木（妻）：あなた、家中を下着姿で歩き回って何してるの？

鈴木（夫）：やりたいようにやるさ。「我が家は我が城」なんだから！

Note

The Japanese is evidently a translation of a famous British proverb, which is actually a legal doctrine that describes people's right to be secure in their own homes.

mecca {for/of} ~, {a/the}　/ n. phr.　metaphor

a place considered the center of an activity

REL　a/the ~ mecca

Examples

(a) The Motown recording studio in Detroit was once considered the mecca of soul music.

(b) That island is a mecca for bird watchers.

(c) Hollywood is the mecca of movies.

Notes

1. Mecca is the holy city of Islam located in Saudi Arabia where Muhammad, the founder of Islam, was born. Mecca is spelled with the capital "M" when referring to the Islamic holy site and with a lowercase "m" when being used as a metaphor.
2. The Japanese expression was likely borrowed from English.

REL

The English can also appear in the form *a/the ~ mecca*.

(1) Hollywood is the {mecca of movies/movie mecca}. (→(c))

meet with opposition (from ~)　/ phr.　metaphor

to encounter resistance to one's views or efforts

Examples

Colleague: Hey Mike, did we have to redo that project we finished recently?

Mike: Yeah. Apparently it met with opposition at the meeting held by the section and department chiefs.

Colleague: Really? I hope we can get it approved, even if we have to partially modify it.

- -

(a) The building plan met with opposition from some residents near the proposed site.

(b) The proposal met with opposition from the American public, businesses, and foreign governments, and eventually failed.

Note

The English and Japanese verbs both have the basic meaning "to see s.o.," but when used figuratively, they obtain the more passive meaning of "to encounter." In fact, in English, it is possible to say *encounter opposition from ~*.

422

解説

日本語は英語（イギリス）の有名なことわざの翻訳である。英語は実は、"人は自分の家では安全である権利を持つ"という法学説なのである。

（～の）メッカ　　n. phr.　　隠喩（いんゆ）

何か（なに）の中心地（ちゅうしんち）

例文

(a) デトロイトのモータウンスタジオは、ソウルミュージックのメッカと言（い）われている。

(b) その島（しま）はバードウォッチャーのメッカです。

(c) 映画（えいが）のメッカといえばハリウッドだ。

解説

1. メッカはサウジアラビアにあるイスラム教の開祖モハメッド生誕の地で、イスラム教の聖地。地名を表す場合は *Mecca* と大文字で書くが、比喩として使われる場合は *mecca* のように小文字で書く。

2. 日本語は英語からの直訳の可能性が高い。

関連語

英語では *a/the ~ mecca* という言い方をすることもある。━━📖REL(1)

（～の）反対（はんたい）にあう　　phr.　　隠喩（いんゆ）

意見（いけん）、努力（どりょく）、結果（けっか）を受け入（い）れてもらえない

例文

同僚（どうりょう）：マイク、この間（あいだ）のプロジェクト、やり直（なお）しだって？

マイク：うん、部課長会議（ぶかちょうかいぎ）で反対（はんたい）にあったらしいよ。

同僚（どうりょう）：そうか。一部変更（いちぶへんこう）してでもなんとか通（とお）したいね。

(a) その建設計画（けんせつけいかく）は建設予定地（けんせつよていち）の一部（いちぶ）の住民（じゅうみん）の反対（はんたい）にあった。

(b) その提案（ていあん）はアメリカの国民（こくみん）、ビジネス関係者（かんけいしゃ）と外国政府（がいこくせいふ）の反対（はんたい）にあい、結局失敗（けっきょくしっぱい）した。

解説

日英語とも動詞は"誰か{に / と}会う"という基本義だが、比喩に転化すると受け身的な"遭遇する"という意味になる。事実、英語では *encounter opposition from ~*（lit. 反対に遭遇する）とも言える。

meshes of the law, the / n. phr. / metaphor

a carefully prepared network of laws for arresting criminals

Examples

(a) He made frantic efforts to escape the meshes of the law.

(b) That politician is always trying to find ways to slip through the meshes of the law.

(c) When one of that influential figure's relatives got in trouble with the law, he used his money and connections to ingratiate himself with executives and politicians and slip through the meshes of the law.

Notes

1. *Mesh* means "an opening in a net," which directly corresponds to *ami no me* (lit. "the eye of a net") in Japanese. In Japanese, however, *hōritsu no ami no me* is used much less frequently than *hōritsu no ami*.

2. The English and Japanese expressions use the same verbs: *escape/nogareru*, as shown in (a); *slip through/kuguri-nukeru*, as shown in (b); and *slip through/kaikuguru*, as shown in (c).

one's mind goes blank / phr. / metaphor

one cannot remember anything

Example

When I went onstage, my mind went blank and I forgot all my lines.

Note

The Japanese can also be used to express one's inability to think due to anxiety, surprise, shock, and so on. 📖→解説(1)

Money talks. / phr. / personification

money has great influence

Examples

(a) After becoming a lawyer, I learned that money talks when you want to persuade people.

(b) In that country, if you give a generous tip when you arrive at your hotel, you can receive better room service. After all, money talks.

Note

Since money cannot actually talk, this proverb is an example of personification.

REL

Japanese has the proverb *Jigoku no sata mo kane shidai* (even hell runs on money), which is similar to *kane ga mono o iu*. This proverb originated from the idea that if one has money,

M

法（律）の網 / n. phr. 隠喩
（ほう　りつ　あみ）　　　　　（いんゆ）

犯罪者を捕らえるために綿密に準備された法律
（はんざいしゃ　と　　　　　めんみつ　じゅんび　　　ほうりつ）

例文

(a) 彼は法の網を逃れようと必死にもがいた。
（かれ　ほう　あみ　のが　　　　　　ひっし）

(b) その政治家はいつも法律の網を潜り抜ける方法を見つけようとする。
（せいじか　　　　　ほうりつ　あみ　くぐ　ぬ　　　ほうほう　み）

(c) その有力者は、家族が違法なことをしたとき、カネとコネを駆使して役人や政治家
（ゆうりょくしゃ　かぞく　いほう　　　　　　　　　　くし　　　やくにん　せいじか）
に取り入り、法律の網をかいくぐろうと画策した。
（と　い　　ほうりつ　あみ　　　　　　　　かくさく）

解説

1. 英語の *mesh* は"網の目"を意味するから、日本語の「網の目」に符合しているが、日本語では「法律の網の目」は「法の網」より使用頻度がはるかに低い。

2. 日英語ともに、一緒に使われる動詞が(a)の「逃れる」*escape*、(b)の「潜り抜ける」*slip through*、(c)の「かいくぐる」*slip through* で、全く同じである。

頭が真っ白になる / phr. 隠喩
（あたま　ま　しろ）　　　　　　　（いんゆ）

何も思い出せなくなる，何も考えられなくなる
（なに　おも　だ　　　　　　　なに　かんが）

例文

舞台に立ったとき、頭が真っ白になって、台詞を全部忘れてしまった。
（ぶたい　た　　　　　あたま　ま　しろ　　　　　せりふ　ぜんぶわす）

解説

日本語には緊張、驚き、ショックなどで何も考えられなくなるという意味もある。

(1) 司法試験に落ちたことを知った時は、頭が真っ白になってしまった。長い間必死に勉強してきたのに。
When I found out I failed my bar examination, my mind froze. And I studied so hard for so long, too...

金が物を言う / phr. 擬人化
（かね　もの　い）　　　　　　（ぎじんか）

お金は何事においても大きな影響力がある
（かね　なにごと　　　　　　　おお　えいきょうりょく）

関 地獄の沙汰も金次第
（じごく　さた　　かねしだい）

例文

(a) 私が弁護士になって学んだことは、人を動かすには金が一番物を言うということだ。
（わたし　べんごし　　　　まな　　　　　ひと　うご　　　　　かね　いちばんもの　い）

(b) その国では、ホテルに着いたら最初にチップをはずむとルームサービスがよくなるよ。金は物を言うってね。
（くに　　　　　　　　　　　さいしょ　　　　　　　　　　　　　　　　　　　　　　かね　もの　い）

解説

金は物を言わないのだから、このことわざは擬人化表現になる。
（かね　もの　い）

関連語

日本語には「地獄の沙汰も金次第」という「金が物を言う」に近いことわざがある。これは生前

425

one will be treated leniently upon arriving in hell after leading a life full of wrongdoing. The implication is that money allows one to act as one pleases. In Christianity, Archbishop Albrecht of Mainz, Germany began selling indulgences to his flock of believers in 1517. These indulgences would supposedly lighten the punishment for people's souls when they entered purgatory. While this idea is similar, there is no proverb that involves indulgences.

Monkey see, monkey do. / phr. metaphor

describes s.o. who thoughtlessly mimics another's actions

REL copycat

Examples

(a) Monkey see, monkey do! Our four-year old daughter followed her brother up the tree, but then she couldn't get back down!

(b) When the leading company in an industry comes out with a new product, all the other companies try to develop something similar. Monkey see, monkey do. But copying others doesn't guarantee success.

Note

The English expression is a rhythmic compound sentence without any number agreement that sounds like a proverb. By contrast, the Japanese expression is simply composed of the nominal compound *saru-mane* (monkey-copy), and it does not sound like a proverb.

REL

The English has the REL *copycat*, which means "s.o. who thoughtlessly imitates s.o. else's behavior."

(1) Your friends' bad habits are rubbing off on you. {Monkey see, monkey do/You're such a copycat}!
君は友達から悪い習慣を受け継いでいるんだ。猿真似なんだ！

monolithic / adj. metaphor

characterized by uniformity

Examples

(a) That company's employees worked together in monolithic fashion to overcome the bankruptcy crisis.

(b) When a natural disaster occurs, it is essential for the local government and residents to work together in monolithic fashion.

(c) The Japanese market isn't monolithic. Some industries are more receptive than others.

Note

Splitting the English adjective into *mono* (single) and *lithic* (of a stone) reveals the metaphorical nature of the compound. The Japanese expression is simply composed of *ichi-mai* (one flat object) and *iwa* (rock).

悪いことをした人が地獄に落ちても、金があればえんま様に裁かれるとき手加減をしてもらえるという考え方で、何事も金さえあれば思い通りのことができるという意味である。キリスト教ではドイツのマインツ大司教であったアルブレヒトが1517年に煉獄の霊魂の罪の償いが軽くなるという免罪符を信徒に売り始めた。考え方は似ているが、免罪符は比喩的なことわざには入っていない。

猿真似 （さるまね） comp. n. 隠喩（いんゆ）

考えなしに何でもそのまま真似をする

【例文】

(a) まさに猿真似。うちの4歳になる娘はお兄ちゃんのあとを追って木に登ったまではよかったんだけど、下りられなくなったんです。

(b) 最先端を行く製造業の会社が一度新しい製品を開発すると、他の会社もみな似たような製品を作ろうとする。でも、猿真似では成功しないのだ。

【解説】

英語は数の一致もないリズミカルな重文で、ことわざ風になっているのに対して、日本語は「猿真似」という複合語で、ことわざの響きはない。

【関連語】

copycat は"誰かの行動を盲目的に真似をする人間"という意味で、*Monkey see, monkey do.* の関連表現である。→📖 REL（1）

一枚岩 （いちまいいわ） comp. n. 隠喩（いんゆ）

組織やグループが強くまとまっていること

【関】一枚板（いちまいいた）

【例文】

(a) その会社は全社員が一枚岩となって、倒産の危機を乗り越えた。

(b) 災害に際しては、地方自治体と地域住民が一枚岩で協力しあうことが大切だ。

(c) キリスト教は決して一枚岩ではない。社会変化に対応するために何世紀もの間に様々に変化してきた。

【解説】

英語の不透明な形容詞 *monolithic* を *mono*（一つ）と *lithic*（石の）に分解するとその比喩性がわかる。日本語は簡単に「一枚」と「岩」に分解できる。

427

homograph

monster / n. / metaphor

an unusually {ugly/wicked} person
ひどく醜く、悪の権化のような人

Example

You might think he's a monster, but he's actually a sweet guy who works his tail off for his family.

あなたは彼のことを極悪非道の奴と頭に描いているかもしれませんが、彼は実は家族のために身を粉にして働くような、気の優しい奴なのです。

mother tongue   comp. n.   metaphor

the first language one acquires

REL mother language

Examples

Mrs. S: I hear that you speak five languages, but which one is your mother tongue?

Anna: Polish. But my husband's American, so I'm a near-native English speaker as well.

Mrs. S: Wow, that's amazing.

- -

(a) While Chinese is his mother tongue, he also speaks and works in English.

(b) Students are not permitted to take a course in their mother tongue to satisfy the foreign language requirement.

REL

The main entry can be replaced by *mother language*, but this is used much less frequently and is not as metaphorical. While *language* is derived from the Latin word *lingua* (tongue), most people are not aware of this fact.

motherland / comp. n. / metaphor

one's native country; the country where s.t. originated

REL fatherland; homeland

Examples

Mrs. S: Mr. Chen, where were you born?

Mr. Chen: I was born in China, but I moved to Singapore when I was small.

Mr. S: Oh, really? Which country do you consider your motherland?

Mr. Chen: I would say Singapore.

- -

M

〔同形異義語〕

怪物 / n. / 隠喩
かいぶつ　　　　　いんゆ

能力や体力が飛び抜けている人
のうりょく　たいりょく　と　ぬ　　　　　ひと
a person with exceptional (physical) ability

〔例 文〕

前の晩、全然寝ないでトライアスロンを完走するなんて、それも優勝するなんて、まっ
まえ　ばん　ぜんぜん ね　　　　　　　　　　　　　　　かんそう　　　　　　　　　　ゆうしょう
たく、あいつは怪物だよ。
かいぶつ
He finished the triathlon without any sleep and won. What monstrous talent.

母語 | comp. n. | 隠喩
ぼ ご　　　　　　　　　　　　　いんゆ

人が生まれて最初に習得する言語
ひと　う　　　　さいしょ　しゅうとく　げんご

〔例 文〕

鈴木(妻)：アナさんは、5か国語も話せるって聞いたけど、母語は何語なの？
すずき つま　　　　　　　　　こくご　はな　　　　　き　　　　　ぼご　なにご

アナ：ポーランド語よ。でも、夫がアメリカ人だから、英語ももう母語のようなものね。
おっと　　　　　じん　　　えいご　　　ぼご

鈴木(妻)：すごいわね。
すずき つま

(a) 彼の母語は中国語だが、英語も使って仕事をしている。
かれ ぼご ちゅうごくご　えいご つか しごと

(b) 学生は母語を必修外国語として履修することはできません。
がくせい ぼご ひっしゅうがいこくご　りしゅう

〔関連語〕

英語には関連表現として *mother language* があるが、見出しのほうが「母」＋「舌」という組み
合わせのため比喩性が高い。もっとも、*language* もラテン語の *lingua* (舌)から来てはいるが、
普通、そのような語源は意識されていない。

母国 / comp. n. / 隠喩
ぼ こく　　　　　　　　　　　いんゆ

生まれ育った国
う　そだ　　　くに

〔例 文〕

鈴木(夫)：チェンさんは、どこで生まれたの？
すずき おっと　　　　　　　　　　う

チェン：生まれたのは中国ですが、幼いときにシンガポールに移りました。
う　　　　　ちゅうごく　　おさな　　　　　　　　　　うつ

鈴木(夫)：そう、じゃ、どっちが母国という感じかな？
すずき おっと　　　　　　　　　　ぼこく　　　　かん

チェン：シンガポールですね。

429

(a) Poland is the motherland of many famous individuals, such as Chopin, John Paul II, and Walesa, among others.

(b) After finishing his PhD, he intends to go back to his motherland and use what he has learned for the sake of his country.

Notes

1. While the Japanese consists of *bo* (mother) and *koku* (country), the English compound is formed from *mother* and *land*, so it can be used to refer to an area within a country where someone is born.

(1) Rostov is the motherland of such famous writers as Chekhov and Sholokhov.
ロストフはチェーホフやショーロフのような有名な作家の{生誕の地 / ×母国} です。

2. As indicated in the definition, the English expression can be used to refer to something that started in a certain place, but the Japanese cannot be used in this manner.

(2) Europe is the motherland of soccer.
ヨーロッパはサッカーの{発祥の地 / ×母国} だ。

REL

The RELs *fatherland* and *homeland* mean "one's native {land/country}."

(1) ポーランドはショパンの{母国 / 祖国} である。
Poland is the {motherland/fatherland/homeland} of Chopin. (→ (a))
Note that there is no such expression as ×*fu-koku* (lit. "father country") in Japanese. *Sokoku* (lit. "ancestor country") must be used instead, as shown directly above in (1).

mountain of ~, a / n. phr. / metaphor

a large amount of s.t.

Examples

Karen: Saya, you look so busy.

Saya: Yeah, I've got a mountain of homework plus my part-time job. I don't know how I'm gonna survive.

- -

(a) I have a mountain of DVDs piled around my television.

(b) There is a mountain of biographical information on this man.

(c) If I look at a mountain of work, I think, "I can't possibly get all of this done."

Notes

1. *Yama no yō ni* in (a) and (b) is the adverbial form of *yama no yōna*.

2. The English expression can refer to psychological matters such as *emotions, feelings, love, expectations, hate*, and so on, but the Japanese cannot be used in this manner.

(1)a. A mountain of feelings of love and hatred undulated within the seven-year-old girl's little heart.
{あふれんばかりの / ×山のような} 愛と憎しみの感情が、7 つの女の子の小さな心の中で波打った。

　 b. Groomed as a child prodigy, he has had to live with a mountain of expectations.
神童として仕込まれた彼は {計り知れない / ×山のような} 期待感と同居しなければならなかった。

REL

Yama no yō ni can be replaced by *yama hodo*. 📖→ 関連語(1)

（a）ポーランドは、ショパン、ジョンパウロ2世、ワレサなどの著名な人の母国である。

（b）彼は博士課程を修了したら、母国に帰って、国のために学んだことを役立てるつもりだ。

解説

1. 英語は *mother*（母）+ *land*（土地）となっていて、日本語のように「母」+「国」ではないので、国の一部が{誰か / 何か}の生誕地であることを示す場合にも使える。➡️📖 **Note（1）**

2. 定義にあるように、英語は何かの発祥の地にも使えるが、日本語では使えない。➡️📖 **Note（2）**

関連語

英語には関連表現として *fatherland*（「父」+「土地」）と *homeland* がある。いずれも"誰かが生まれ育った国、土地か、父親か祖先の生まれ育った{国 / 土地}"を指す。➡️📖 **REL（1）**
日本語には「×父国」のような複合語はない。「祖国」を使わなければならない。

山のような　**phr.**　直喩

たくさんの

関 山ほど

例文

カレン：忙しそうね、さや。

さや：うん、宿題が山のようにあって、アルバイトもあるから、死にそう。

- -

（a）テレビのまわりにはDVDが山のように積んである。

（b）この人物については、伝記的な情報が山のようにある。

（c）山のような仕事を見ると、こんな全部はできっこないと思う。

解説

1. 日本語の会話例と（a）（b）は「山のような」の副詞形である。

2. 英語は *emotions*（感情）、*feelings*（気持ち）、*love*（愛）、*expectations*（期待）、*hate*（憎しみ）といった心理的な事柄にも使えるが、日本語にはそのような使い方はない。➡️📖 **Note（1）**

関連語

日本語の「山のように」は「山ほど」で置き換えることができる。

（1）宿題が山{のように / ほど}ある。（→会話例）

431

move / v./n. / metaphor

for s.t. to change (s.t.); a change

Examples

(a) Due to the premier's visit to the U.S., the stagnant stock market suddenly started to move.

(b) The videos that were posted online moved people to action.

(c) There was a move to strengthen anti-terror measures after 9/11.

Note

The basic meaning of *move* and *ugoku* is "to change location," but when used figuratively, they mean "for s.t. to change."

myth / n. / metaphor

an unfounded notion

Examples

Mrs. S: Banks went bankrupt one after another at the end of the 20th century, right?

Mr. S: Yeah. That's when the myth that Japanese banks are completely safe was shattered.

- - - - - - - - - - - - - - - - - - - -

(a) The claim that church and state are kept completely separate in Christian countries is nothing but a myth.

(b) It is a myth that women in today's society are liberated.

Notes

1. The Japanese expression may sound slightly unnatural because it is usually used when one is referring to mythical success stories, as demonstrated by the dialogue. But in contemporary written Japanese, one can find the usages demonstrated in (a) and (b).

2. *Shinwa* is a translation of the English word *mythology,* which originated from the Greek word *mythos* (story).

homograph

nail down / phr. / metaphor

to establish s.t. definitively
確実にする, はっきりさせる, 落着させる

Example

The investigator nailed down the truth and dispelled the rumors by checking all the facts.

検査官は事実をすべて洗って、その噂に根拠がないことを証明した。

動く（動き） / v.(n.) / 隠喩

変化する（変化）

例文

(a) 膠着していた株式市場が、首相の訪米で急に動き出した。

(b) ネット上に投稿された映像が人々を行動へと動かした。

(c) 9.11 テロの後、テロ対策を強化する動きが起こった。

解説

「動く」move の基本義は"移動により場所が変わる"であるが、比喩的には何かの変化を意味する。

神話 / comp. n. / 隠喩

根拠がないのに真実だと信じられている事柄

例文

鈴木（妻）：20世紀の終わり頃、銀行の倒産が連続して起きたわね。

鈴木（夫）：うん、日本の銀行は絶対安全だという神話はあのとき崩れたね。

(a) キリスト教国家で教会と国家が完全に分離されているという考えは、神話に過ぎない。

(b) 今日の社会で、女性が解放されているというのは神話である。

解説

1. 日本語の(a)(b)はやや不自然かもしれない。それは日本語は会話例のように、何か神話的な成功物語の場合によく使われるからである。しかし、現在の書き言葉では(a)(b)のような例もある。

2. 「神話」は古典ギリシャ語の物語を表す *mythos* から英語に入った *mythology* の翻訳である。

同形異義語

釘付けになる / phr. / 隠喩

{何かに魅了されて / 恐怖で} 身動きのできない状態になる
to cause {s.t./s.o.} to be unable to move

例文

その絵の前に来たとき、私の目は釘付けになってしまった。

When I stopped in front of that painting, I couldn't tear my eyes away from it.

naked eye(s), {the/one's} / phr. / metaphor

sight unaided by a device

Examples

Karen: If you keep playing computer games so much, your eyesight will get worse.

Kenta: I'm guessing your eyesight's pretty good, huh?

Karen: Yep. I have better than 20/20 vision with my naked eyes.

Kenta: Wow!

- -

(a) When I was five, I lost the ability to read small letters with my naked eyes. I've been wearing glasses ever since.

(b) I saw a comet last night for the first time with my naked eyes.

(c) A microscope is a device that enables us to see things that we cannot see with the naked eye.

Notes

1. The English corresponds both to *nikugan* (eyes unassisted by instruments such as a telescope or microscope) and to *ragan* (eyes unassisted by glasses or contact lenses).
2. Both the English and Japanese are a metaphorical expression of the idea of "naked eyes that aren't wearing anything." However, *nikugan* means "the eyes belonging to the body one is born with," and its figurative impact is rather weak.
3. The Japanese expressions are of Chinese origin and consist of *ra* (naked)/*niku* (flesh/body) and *gan* (eye).

narrow / adj. / metaphor

for s.o.'s {viewpoint/idea/action/mind/field of study} to be highly limited

[ANT] broad; wide; open

Examples

Kenta: A lot of wars seem to have to do with religion.

Mr. S: True. When it comes to religion, one small misstep can lead to a narrow outlook on things.

- -

(a) Reading material that falls within a narrow scope leads to narrow thinking.

(b) He's narrow-minded and has an aversion to anything new.

(c) If one's field of research is too narrow, one won't produce great results.

Note

The English and Japanese have non-metaphorical basic meanings that are spatial in nature. Both share the metaphorical meaning "for s.o.'s {viewpoint/idea/action/mind/field of study} to be limited."

裸眼 / 肉眼　comp. n.　隠喩

裸眼：眼鏡やコンタクトレンズを使わない目，肉眼：顕微鏡や望遠鏡を使わない目

例文

カレン：健太、そんなにコンピュータゲームばかりやってると、ますます眼が悪くなるわよ。

健太：カレンは、眼がいいからね。

カレン：そうよ。私の視力は裸眼でも2.0以上あるのよ。

健太：すごいな。

(a) 私は5つのときから裸眼で細かい字を読むことができなくなりました。それからはいつも眼鏡をかけています。

(b) きのうの晩、僕は初めて肉眼で彗星を見た。

(c) 顕微鏡は肉眼で見られないものを見られるようにしてくれる器具です。

解説

1. 英語には2つの意味がある。その一つは日本語の"望遠鏡とか顕微鏡のような器具を使わない目"という意味の「肉眼」に、もう一つは"眼鏡やコンタクトレンズを使わない目"という意味の「裸眼」に対応する。

2. 日英語とも「何もつけていない裸の目」という比喩表現から出ている。ただし、「肉眼」は"生来の肉体の一部としての目"という意味で比喩性は低い。

3. 日本語の「裸眼」と「肉眼」はともに中国語からの借用である。

狭い　adj.(i)　隠喩

誰かの{見方 / 考え / 行動 / 心 / 研究分野}が非常に限られている

反 (〜が)(幅)広い

例文

健太：戦争の原因って、結構、宗教に関係したことが多いね。

鈴木(夫)：そうだね。宗教は一歩間違うと、物の見方を狭くしてしまうこともあるからね。

(a) 狭い読書経験は狭い思想につながる。

(b) 彼は考えが狭く、新しいことにはいっさい手を出さない。

(c) ただ狭い研究分野を研究していても成果は小さい。

解説

日英語の基本義はどちらも空間的である。両者には共通の比喩的意味、すなわち、"誰かの{見方 / 考え / 行動 / 心 / 研究分野}が非常に限られている"がある。

ANT

The ANTs for the English and Japanese are *broad* and *hiroi*, respectively.

(1) a. Reading widely leads to broad thinking.
(幅)広い読書は(幅)広い思想に繋がる。

b. He is analytical and broad in his thinking.
彼はものの見方が分析的で、考えが広い。

narrow-minded / comp. adj. / metaphor

lacking tolerance and unwilling to accept or consider another's views

REL closed-minded

ANT broad-minded

Examples

Kenta: I think one of my professors is biased against certain groups. Some of his comments during lecture sounded pretty narrow-minded.

Karen: Wow. I guess being educated doesn't mean you can't be narrow-minded, huh?

- - - - - - - - - - - - - - - - - - - -

(a) Isn't it narrow-minded for you to think that you're right and everyone else is wrong?

(b) Some claim that men are the only gender capable of leading the world, but this is a narrow-minded viewpoint.

REL

1. *Closed-minded* is a REL for *narrow-minded*, and the two expressions can be used interchangeably.

(1) I have read your column on several occasions and am amazed at how foolish and {narrow-minded/closed-minded} you are.
あなたのコラムを繰り返し読んできましたが、あなたの{心の狭い/偏狭な}愚かさには唖然としています。

2. The Japanese REL *henkyōna* is preferable to *kokoro ga semai* in formal contexts, such as in Japanese examples. (2) and (3). There is also the REL *doryō ga {semai/chīsai}* (lit. "generosity is narrow"). 📖➡ 関連語 **(2) (3)**

ANT

Broad-minded and *open-minded* are the ANTs for *narrow-minded* and *closed-minded*, respectively. *Kokoro ga hiroi* and *doryō ga {hiroi/ōki}* are the ANTs for *kokoro ga semai* and *doryō ga {semai/chīsai}*, respectively. 📖➡ 反意語 **(1)**

反意語

日英語の反意表現は、それぞれ、「(幅)広い」broad である。 ➡📖 ANT（1）

N

心が狭い　phr.　隠喩
（こころ　せま）　　　　（いん　ゆ）

{物の見方 / 考え方}にゆとりがない
（もの　み　かた　かんが　かた）

関 偏狭な，度量が {狭い / 小さい}
（へんきょう　どりょう　せま　ちい）

反 心が広い，度量が {大きい / 広い}
（こころ　ひろ　どりょう　おお　ひろ）

例 文

健太：僕は、教授の一人はある特定の集団に対して、偏見を持っていると思うな。講
（けん　た　ぼく　きょうじゅ　ひとり　とくてい　しゅうだん　たい　へんけん　も　おも　こう）
　　　義の時のコメントを聞いていると、ひどく心が狭い感じがするんだ。
（ぎ　とき　こころ　せま　かん）

カレン：そお！　いくら教育を受けていても、了見が狭いってことはあるんだよね。
（きょういく　う　りょうけん　せま）

- -

(a) 自分は正しくて他の人はみんな間違っていると考えるのは、心が狭いと思いません
（じぶん　ただ　ほか　ひと　まちが　かんが　こころ　せま　おも）
　　か。

(b) 世界を統率できるのは男性だけだと主張している人もいるが、これは心の狭い見方
（せかい　とうそつ　だんせい　しゅちょう　ひと　こころ　せま　みかた）
　　である。

関連語

1．英語の関連表現 closed-minded (lit. 閉ざされた心) は、narrow-minded と交換できる。

➡📖 REL（1）

2．日本語には関連表現として「偏狭な」がある。これは次の(2)と(3)のような硬い文脈では「心が
　狭い」よりも適切である。その他の関連表現として「度量が{狭い / 小さい}」という表現もある。

(2) 世界を統率できるのは男性だけだと主張している人もいるが、これは{?心の狭い / 偏狭な}
　　見方である。(→(b))

(3) 自分は正しくて他の人はみんな間違っていると考えるのは、{?心が狭い / 度量が狭い / 度量
　　が小さい}と思いませんか。(→(a))

反意語

日本語では、「心が広い」「度量が{広い / 大きい}」がそれぞれ「心が狭い」「度量が{狭い / 小
さい}」の反意表現である。英語では broad-minded と open-minded がそれぞれ narrow-minded
と closed-minded の反意表現である。

(1) 僕は、{心が広くて / 度量が広くて / 度量が大きくて}、リラックスしていて、笑うのが好きで、
　　カジュアルな着こなしの女性を見つけたい。
　　I would like to find a woman who is {broad-minded/open-minded}, laid back, likes to
　　laugh, and is a casual dresser.

near / adj. / metaphor

{physically/temporally/psychologically/genetically} close

REL close

ANT LOOK distant

Examples

Mrs. S: How much should we give my nephew for his wedding?

Mr. S: Hmm. I wonder what the standard rate is nowadays when the recipient is your near relative?

- - - - - - - - - - - - - - - - - - - -

(a) If they continue to manage the company so recklessly, it's bound to go bankrupt in the near future.

(b) Near the end of the year, New York City's buildings are decorated with illuminations, creating an enchanting sight.

(c) The election's almost here, but I'm having trouble deciding which political party's platform is nearest to my beliefs.

Note

As with other spatial expressions, both *near* and *chikai* can be used in a temporal sense, as in (a) and (b). They can also indicate a genetic link, as in the dialogue.

REL

The English REL, *close,* has the same basic meaning as *near*, "within a short distance." However, while *close* can be used figuratively to mean "intimate," *near* cannot. Note that with the Japanese, when a relationship is personal, *chikai* has to be changed to *chikashī*, the emotive *-shī* form. 関連語(1)

neck of a bottle / n. phr. / personification

the part of a bottle that looks like a human neck

REL bottleneck

Example

There was a cute ribbon attached to the neck of the bottle of wine we received yesterday.

REL

The REL *bottleneck* means "the area or part of a process that slows down otherwise speedy progress."

(1) There is always a traffic jam around the tollgate on the highway; it's a bottleneck they should fix.
高速道路の出口付近では渋滞がしょっちゅう起こる。こんなボトルネックはなくすべきだ。

近い / **adj.(i)** / 隠喩
ちか いんゆ

{物理的 / 時間的 / 心理的 / 血縁関係上}距離が短い
ぶつりてき　じかんてき　しんりてき　けつえんかんけいじょう　きょり　みじか

関 近しい
ちか

反 **LOOK** 遠い
とお

例 文

鈴木(妻)：甥っ子の結婚祝い、いくら包んだらいいかしら？
すずき つま　おい こ　けっこんいわ　　つつ

鈴木(夫)：そうだね。近い親戚の場合、最近は、いくらぐらいが相場だろうね。
すずき おっと　　　　　ちか しんせき ばあい さいきん　　　　　　　　そうば

(a) あんな無理な経営を続けていけば、近い将来、あの会社が倒産するのは間違いない
むり けいえい つづ　　　ちか しょうらい　　かいしゃ とうさん　　　　まちが
だろう。

(b) ニューヨークでは、年末近くになると、どこのビルもイルミネーションで飾られ、と
ねんまつちか　　　　　　　　　　　　　　　　　　　　　　かざ
てもきれいだ。

(c) 選挙を前にして、自分の考えに近い政党はどれか今も決めかねています。
せんきょ まえ　　じぶん かんが ちか せいとう　　　いま き

解 説

他の空間表現と同じように「近い」near は(a)と(b)のように時間を表現できるし、さらに、会
話例のように近親関係も表現できる。

関連語

英語の唯一の関連表現 close は near と同じく "何かとの間に空間がほとんどない" という基
本義を共有しているが、前者は比喩的に "親密な" という意味があるのに対して、near にはそ
のような意味がない。関係が個人的な場合は普通の形容詞の「近い」は情意的な「～しい」形
容詞の「近しい」に変わることに注意。

(1)a. マミは僕の{近しい / ˣ近い}友達だ。
Mami is a {close/ˣnear} friend of mine.

b. われわれの会社はその会社と近い関係にある。
Our company has a {close/ˣnear} relationship with that company.

びんの首 **n. phr.** 擬人化
くび　　　　　　　　ぎじんか

びんの一部でくびれているところ
いちぶ

例 文

昨日もらったワインのびんの首のところに、かわいいリボンが結んであった。
きのう　　　　　　　　　　くび　　　　　　　　　　　　むす

関連語

英語の関連表現は bottleneck であり、その意味は "普通は迅速に進むのに渋滞する所、あるい
はその過程" である。—📖 **REL(1)**

need a hand / phr. / metaphor

to need help from one or more people

[REL] [LOOK] {lend (s.o.)/give s.o.} a hand

Examples

Mike: Kenta, are you free next Sunday?

Kenta: Sure. Why?

Mike: I'm moving out and I need a hand. Could you help me?

Kenta: Sure!

- -

(a) For the event next month, we're going to need a hand from a lot of volunteers. Try to gather about 20 people.

(b) Apparently factories nowadays let robots handle most of the work, but they still need a hand from humans in the end.

Note

Need a hand and te ga iru are very close in form and meaning. Iru can be replaced by hitsuyō da. 📖 解説(1)

new blood / comp. n. / metonymy

new people that revitalize a system

Examples

Mike: Another foreigner's gonna be joining our department soon. Someone was saying that he's Singaporean.

Mr. S: Oh, that's good to hear. New blood changes relationship dynamics, so maybe you'll start getting along better with your section chief.

- -

(a) As long as that university doesn't inject some new blood into its ranks, its classes will continue to revolve around the professors as they always have.

(b) New blood needs to be added to the executive ranks to encourage a transfer of power.

Notes

1. Atarashī chi is likely a direct translation of new blood.

2. Ketsueki is the Sino-Japanese version of chi. It is rarely used figuratively. 📖 解説(1)

[REL]

The Japanese has the REL shinpū (o fukikomu) (lit. "to blow new wind into ~"; "to usher a new phase into ~"). Unlike atarashī chi, the REL does not refer to people, but to a new method or era. 📖 関連語(1)

手が要る / phr. / 隠喩

人の助けを必要とする

関 **LOOK▶** (〜に)手を貸す

例文

マイク：健太、今度の日曜、暇？

健太：うん、時間あるよ。どうして？

マイク：引っ越しするんで、ちょっと手が要るんだ。手伝ってくれないかな？

健太：いいよ。

- -

(a) 来月のイベントには多くのボランティアの手が要ります。20人くらい集めてください。

(b) 最近の工場はほとんどロボットが仕事をするそうだが、最後の段階だけは人間の手が要るらしい。

解説

「手が要る」と *need a hand* は形も意味もとても近い。日本語では「要る」を「必要だ」に置き換えることができる。

(1)〈手 / 人手〉が〈要る / 必要〉なら、そう言ってください。
　If you need a hand, just let me know.

新しい血 / n. phr. / 換喩

組織に活力を与える新しい人々

関 新風(を吹き込む)

例文

マイク：今度、僕の課に、もう一人、外国人が入ってくるんですよ。シンガポールの人らしいんですけどね。

鈴木(夫)：あ、そう、それはよかったね。新しい血が入ると、人間関係も変わるから、マイクと課長の関係もよくなるかもしれないよ。

- -

(a) 大学が新しい血を入れない限り、昔からの教師中心の授業の仕方は変わらない。

(b) 権力を移行させるためには、執行部に新しい血を入れる必要がある。

解説

1．日本語の「新しい血」は英語の *new blood* の直訳の可能性が高い。

2．「血液」は「血」に対する漢語であるが、比喩的に使用される頻度は非常に少ない。

(1) 組織に新しい〈血 / 血液〉を注入することが組織の活性化につながるものと思われる。
　It seems to me that injecting new blood into the system would revitalize it.

関連語

日本語の関連表現として「新風(を吹き込む)」がある。「新しい血」は人を指すのに対して、「新風」は新しい手法、風潮を指す。

(1) 彼は日本の映画界に新風を吹き込んだ。
　He ushered in a new era of Japanese film.

nine (times) out of ten　n. phr.　metaphor

most of the time; usually

Example

It used to be that if you got cancer, nine times out of ten you couldn't survive.

nip ~ in the bud　phr.　metaphor

to eliminate s.t. before it becomes a problem

Examples

(a) The number one priority for the new prime minister was to nip long-standing political corruption in the bud.

(b) At the first sign of a youngster going wrong, you've got to nip it in the bud.

(c) The flu spreads like wildfire, so it's important to diagnose it early and nip it in the bud.

Note

The English and Japanese metaphors are very similar, as are the verbs they use. The basic meanings of *nip* and *tsumu* are "to sever s.t. by pinching sharply" and "to remove a {bud/leaf} with one's fingers before it grows," respectively.

nose around　phr.　metaphor

to snoop around in an effort to find s.t.

REL　nose about

Examples

Kenta: Mom, did you call my friend and ask him where I was?

Mrs. S: Yes, because I needed to get in touch with you about something urgent.

Kenta: Would you stop nosing around in my business?

Mrs. S: I'm not "nosing around" anything. Don't talk to your mother like that!

- -

(a) That police officer's been nosing around because of the incident the other day.

(b) I don't like when telemarketers call and start asking me all kinds of questions. It makes me nervous to have a stranger nosing around like that.

Note

The English uses *nose* as a verb meaning "to sniff," while the Japanese uses the verb *kagu* (to sniff) as the first element of the compound.

REL

The English entry can be replaced by *nose about*.

(1) That police officer's been nosing {around/about} because of the incident the other day.

$(\rightarrow (a))$

N

十中八九 （じゅっちゅうはっく） / comp. n. 隠喩（いんゆ）

大方（おおかた），ほとんど，大部分（だいぶぶん）

例 文

昔（むかし）は癌（がん）になったら、十中八九（じゅっちゅうはっく）、助（たす）からなかった。

（〜の）芽（め）を摘（つ）む / phr. 隠喩（いんゆ）

問題（もんだい）が小（ちい）さいうちに取（と）り除（のぞ）く

例 文

(a) 新（あたら）しい首相（しゅしょう）の第一（だいいち）の課題（かだい）は、長年続（ながねんつづ）いてきた政治家達（せいじかたち）の汚職（おしょく）の芽（め）を摘（つ）むことだった。

(b) 青少年（せいしょうねん）が非行（ひこう）に走（はし）りそうな気配（けはい）が見（み）えたら、すぐにその芽（め）を摘（つ）まなければならない。

(c) インフルエンザはまたたく間（ま）に流行（りゅうこう）する。だから、早期（そうき）に診断（しんだん）し、その芽（め）を摘（つ）むことが肝心（かんじん）です。

解 説

日英語（にちえいご）の比喩（ひゆ）はとても似（に）ているし、使（つか）われている動詞（どうし）の意味（いみ）も近（ちか）い。「摘（つ）む」と nip の基本義（きほんぎ）はそれぞれ"指（ゆび）で{芽／葉}が大（おお）きくならないうちに取（と）ってしまう"と"何（なに）かを摘（つ）んで取（と）ってしまう"である。

嗅（か）ぎ回（まわ）る / comp.v. 隠喩（いんゆ）

何（なに）か隠（かく）れたものを探（さが）し回（まわ）る

例 文

健太（けんた）：お母（かあ）さん、昨日（きのう）、僕（ぼく）の友達（ともだち）に電話（でんわ）して、僕（ぼく）がどこにいるか聞（き）いた？

鈴木（すずき）（妻（つま））：ええ、急用（きゅうよう）があったから、連絡（れんらく）がとりたかったのよ。

健太（けんた）：そんないろいろと嗅（か）ぎ回（まわ）らないでくれないかな。

鈴木（すずき）（妻（つま））：嗅（か）ぎ回（まわ）っちゃいないわよ。親（おや）に向（む）かってそんな口（くち）の利（き）き方（かた）するの、やめなさい！

- - - - - - - - - - - - - - - - - -

(a) 警官（けいかん）がこの前（まえ）の事件（じけん）についてあちこち嗅（か）ぎ回（まわ）っている。

(b) 私（わたし）、セールスの電話（でんわ）でいろいろ質問（しつもん）されるの好（す）きじゃないわ。知（し）らない人（ひと）に何（なに）か嗅（か）ぎ回（まわ）られているようで、気（き）になるのよ。

解 説

日本語（にほんご）では動詞（どうし）の「かぐ」を複合語（ふくごうご）の第1要素（だいいちようそ）として使（つか）い、英語（えいご）では「かぐ」という意味（いみ）で nose を動詞（どうし）として使（つか）っている。

関連語

英語（えいご）の見出（みだ）しは nose about と置（お）き換（か）えられる。▶📖 REL（1）

443

not worth a dime *phr.* metaphor

for s.t. to be worthless

Examples

Kenta: You sure look busy.

Mrs. S: Well, I just found out that some of your dad's business associates are coming over.

Kenta: You're a good wife, Mom. Dad should thank you.

Mrs. S: That's nice of you to say. But praise isn't worth a dime. How about giving me a hand to show your appreciation?

- -

(a) Knowledge is not worth a dime unless you put it to work.

(b) You know what they say about insurance: it's not worth a dime until you really need it.

Note

The basic meanings of *dime* and *sen* are "a U.S. coin worth one tenth of a dollar" and "one hundredth of a yen," respectively. The *dime* is still used as currency in the U.S., but the *sen* is no longer used in Japan.

oil and water *n. phr.* simile/metaphor

two people or things that are so different as to be incompatible with each other

Examples

Saya: Karen, did you live in an apartment when you were a student?

Karen: Nope, I lived in a dorm. The first year, I didn't get along with my roommate. We were oil and water, and we had a terrible relationship. But eventually we sort of became friends.

Saya: That's interesting.

- -

(a) Literature and science may seem like oil and water, but they are deeply connected under the surface.

(b) Muraki and Kimura have such divergent political views, you'd think they'd be like oil and water. But put them together and they actually get along really well.

Notes

1. This expression can be used as a metaphor in both English and Japanese, as shown in the dialogue, but it can also be used as a simile, as shown in (a) and (b).
2. Note the reversal of the word order of *oil* (*abura*) and *water* (*mizu*) in the English and Japanese.

一銭の価値もない / **phr.** 隠喩

まったく値打ちがない

例文

健太：お母さん、忙しそうだね。

鈴木（妻）：急にお父さんのお客様が来ることになったのよ。

健太：お母さんはいい奥さんだよ。おやじは感謝すべきだね。

鈴木（妻）：どうもありがと。でも、そんなほめ言葉、一銭の価値にもならないわ。それより手伝ってくれるほうが、よっぽどありがたいんだけど。

- -

(a) 知識は正しく使わなければ、一銭の価値もない。

(b) 保険のことを人が何と言っているか知っているだろう。必要になるまでは一銭の価値もないんだよ。

解説

「銭」と *dime* の基義は、それぞれ"1円の100分の1"と"アメリカの10セント"である。アメリカの *dime* はまだ使われているが、日本の「銭」はもはや使われていない。

水と油 **n. phr.** 直喩 / 隠喩

{人 / もの}がお互いにあまりにも違いすぎて相容れないこと

例文

さや：カレンって、大学時代もアパートに住んでたの？

カレン：ううん、寮よ。初めの年はルームメートと合わなくてね。水と油！ 最悪だったけど、そのうち、なんだか仲良くなっちゃった。

さや：へえ、おもしろいね。

- -

(a) 文学と科学は水と油のように見えるが、実は深くつながっている。

(b) 村木と木村は政治的見解がとても違うから、一見水と油のように見えるだろ。でも、一緒にいると実はとても仲がいいんだよ。

解説

1. 英語も日本語も会話例のように隠喩としても使えるが、(a)と(b)のように、「水と油のようだ」 *like oil and water* のように直喩として使われることが多い。

2. 「水」（water）と「油」（oil）の語順が日英語で逆になっていることに注意。

old wound(s)   comp. n. / metaphor

past mistakes and bad experiences

Example

> Steve's divorce is an old wound. He doesn't like talking about it and never mentions his previous wife.

---

homograph

on paper / adv. phr. / metaphor

theoretically
理論上は
りろんじょう

Example

The plan looks fine on paper, but I'm not sure it will actually work.
その計画は理論上は問題ないようだけれど、本当にうまくいくかは心もとない。
けいかく　りろんじょう　もんだい　　　　　　　　　　　　　ほんとう　　　　　　　　　　こころ

---

on the rocks / phr. / metaphor

on the verge of failure

Examples

(a) The Japanese economy looked like it was on the rocks due to the sudden appreciation of the yen.

(b) This was 1933, the height of the Great Depression. My grandfather's business was on the rocks.

(c) The two were deeply in love, but their parents fiercely opposed the idea of marriage, which left their union on the rocks.

Notes

1. Both the English and Japanese expressions refer to the idea of a boat getting stranded on rocks, which metaphorically suggests "getting stuck due to bad circumstances." Underlying these expressions is the conceptual metaphor of human life as a voyage.

2. The verbs used in the English and Japanese expressions are *be* and *noriageru* (to run aground), and the nouns used are *rocks* and *anshō* (rocks hidden under the sea), respectively.

3. The English expression can also be used to mean "served with ice cubes" when referring to alcoholic drinks. Because ice cubes are not literally rocks, the expression is figurative. The Japanese equivalent is the transliteration *on za rokku*.

(1) He had whiskey on the rocks.
彼はウイスキーをオン ザ ロックで飲んだ。

446

古傷 （ふるきず） / comp. n. / 隠喩（いんゆ）

思（おも）い出（だ）したくない、かつての記憶（きおく）や思（おも）い出（で）

例文

スティーブは離婚（りこん）の古傷（ふるきず）に触（ふ）れられるのを嫌（きら）って、先妻（せんさい）の話（はなし）は一切（いっさい）しなかった。

同形異義語

紙上（しじょう）で / phr. / 隠喩（いんゆ）

新聞（しんぶん）や雑誌（ざっし）で
in a paper or magazine

例文

この問題（もんだい）は、紙上（しじょう）やインターネットでたびたび話題（わだい）になっているのに、テレビなどのメディアは全然取（ぜんぜんと）り上（あ）げない。何（なに）か規制（きせい）が入（はい）っているのだろうか。
This issue is often a topic of debate in the papers and online, but it doesn't show up on television and the like at all. I wonder if there's some sort of regulation going on.

暗礁（あんしょう）に乗（の）り上（あ）げる / phr. / 隠喩（いんゆ）

{事業（じぎょう） / 交渉（こうしょう） / 結婚（けっこん）}などがうまく進（すす）まず止（と）まってしまう

例文

(a) 急激（きゅうげき）な円高（えんだか）で日本（にほん）の経済（けいざい）は暗礁（あんしょう）に乗（の）り上（あ）げた。

(b) これはちょうど世界恐慌（せかいきょうこう）のピークの1933年（ねん）のことで、祖父（そふ）の事業（じぎょう）は暗礁（あんしょう）に乗（の）り上（あ）げていました。

(c) 二人（ふたり）は相思相愛（そうしそうあい）だったが、結婚話（けっこんばなし）はそれぞれの両親（りょうしん）から猛反対（もうはんたい）されて暗礁（あんしょう）に乗（の）り上（あ）げてしまった。

解説

1. 日英語（にちえいご）とも"立（た）ち往生（おうじょう）して進（すす）めない、船（ふね）が暗礁（あんしょう）に乗（の）り上（あ）げる"という基本義（きほんぎ）で、そこから"悪状況（あくじょうきょう）のためににっちもさっちも動（うご）きがとれなくなる"という比喩表現（ひゆひょうげん）になる。この表現（ひょうげん）の底（そこ）には"人生（じんせい）は航海（こうかい）のようだ"という比喩思考（ひゆしこう）がある。

2. 日英語（にちえいご）の動詞（どうし）は、それぞれ「乗（の）り上（あ）げる」と be で、名詞（めいし）は、それぞれ「暗礁（あんしょう）」と rocks（岩（いわ））である。

3. 同（おな）じ英語表現（えいごひょうげん）が"氷（こおり）だけを入（い）れてアルコール類（るい）を飲（の）む"という意味（いみ）でも使（つか）われる。氷（こおり）は岩（いわ）ではないのだから、これも比喩表現（ひゆひょうげん）である。日本語（にほんご）は英語（えいご）の発音通（はつおんどお）り「オンザロック」という。

📖 Note（1）

447

on the surface / phr. / metaphor

in terms of outward appearances

Examples

Mike: The slump in business should have the president worried, but on the surface he looks fine, doesn't he?

Colleague: Yeah, I don't know why he's always smiling.

- -

(a) On the surface, composing *haiku* seems simple, but it is actually very challenging.

(b) On the surface, it looks like they're doing the right thing, but they're actually doing the exact opposite.

Note

The figurative meaning of the English and Japanese expressions comes from the spatial terms *surface* and *hyōmen*.

REL

Uwabe-jō and *gaiken-jō* are similar to *hyōmen-jō*. *Uwabe-jō* is a native Japanese word very close to *hyōmen-jō* in meaning, but *gaiken-jō*, which means "the way s.t. looks from the outside" is different from the other two in that it is used often in objective statements, whereas the other two are mostly used in subjective statements, as shown in (1). 📖→ 関連語(1)

(tread) on thin ice / phr. / metaphor

to be in a precarious situation

REL {skate/walk} on thin ice

Examples

(a) Our company is in such bad shape financially that every day is like treading on thin ice.

(b) For journalists on the battlefield, every day is like treading on thin ice, never knowing when their lives will be put in danger.

(c) Turkey is treading on thin ice by engaging in peace negotiations with the Chechen rebels.

Notes

1. The English has two meanings: "to be in a precarious situation" and "to be engaged in some provocative or dangerous activity (and headed for big trouble)." The first meaning is sometimes expressed in the form of a simile, as shown in (a) and (b). However, the Japanese expression only has the first meaning and cannot be used to express the second meaning. Thus, the following sentence sounds strange in Japanese.

(1) He doesn't want to tread on thin ice, even though the latest poll shows him leading by 15 points.
   彼は最近の世論調査では15ポイントも勝っているのに {冒険をし / [×]薄氷を踏み} たがらない。

448

表面上 / phr. / 隠喩
ひょうめんじょう

目に見える情報から判断すれば
め み じょうほう はんだん

関 うわべ上，外見上
じょう がいけんじょう

例文

マイク：経営不振で悩んでいるはずなのに、社長、表面上はなんでもないような顔を
けいえい ふ しん なや しゃちょう ひょうめんじょう かお
しているね。

同僚：そうだね。なんでいつもにこにこしているのか分からないな。
どうりょう わ

- -

(a) 俳句を作るのは、表面上は簡単に見えますが、実はとても複雑なのです。
はいく つく ひょうめんじょう かんたん み じつ ふくざつ

(b) 表面上、彼らは正しいことをやっているように見えるが、実際には間違ったことを
ひょうめんじょう かれ ただ み じっさい まちが
やっているのだ。

解説

日英語とも比喩的意味は空間表現としての「表面」と *surface* から出ている。

関連語

日本語には「表面上」の類似表現として「うわべ上」と「外見上」がある。前者は「表面上」に対
応する和語で、意味は「表面上」にとても近い。後者は「外から見た様子」という意味であるが、
(1)が示すように客観的な叙述によく使われる。「表面上」と「うわべ上」は主観性が強く、客
観的な叙述では普通使われない。

(1) この二つのきのこは{外見/[×]表面/[×]うわべ}上は似ているが、一つは毒きのこで、もう一つは
食用きのこである。
Those two mushrooms resemble each other, but one is poisonous and the other is edible.

薄氷を踏む / phr. / 隠喩
はくひょう ふ いんゆ

危ないと思いながら非常に危険な状況にのぞむ
あぶ おも ひじょう きけん じょうきょう

関 危ない橋を渡る
あぶ はし わた

例文

(a) うちの会社は経営状態がひどくて、毎日が薄氷を踏むような状態だ。
かいしゃ けいえいじょうたい まいにち はくひょう ふ じょうたい

(b) 戦場にいるジャーナリストは、毎日が薄氷を踏むような思いだろう。だって、自
せんじょう まいにち はくひょう ふ おも じ
分たちの生命がいつ危機にさらされるか、わからないのだから。
ぶん いのち きき

(c) トルコはチェチェンの反乱軍と和平交渉をして、薄氷を踏む思いをしている。
はんらんぐん わへいこうしょう はくひょう ふ おも

解説

1. 英語には"ひやひやしながら非常に危険な状況にのぞむ"という意味と、"何か危険なこと、刺
激的なことを積極的にやってみる(その結果、大きな問題を引き起こすかもしれない)"という
意味がある。前者の意味のときは(a)(b)にあるように、ときどき直喩で表現されることがあ
る。しかし、日本語は前者の意味しかなく、後者の意味はない。 Note(1)

2. The Japanese is often used in the expression *hakuhyō o fumu omoi de* (to feel as if one is treading on thin ice). 📖➡解説(2)

3. *Hakuhyō* (thin ice) is the Chinese *on*-reading. When it is read using the *kun*-reading, *usu-gōri*, it does not have any metaphorical meaning.

4. The Japanese comes from the oldest Chinese poetic anthology, the Shijing (詩経). Originally, *fumu* was represented by the Chinese character 履(む), but it is now represented by 踏(む).

R E L

1. The English RELs, *skate on thin ice* and *walk on thin ice*, have essentially the same meaning as the main entry.

(1) I've {walked/skated} on thin ice on many assignments and have somehow managed to get away with it this whole time.
仕事でずいぶん薄氷を踏むようなことをやってきたが、今までのところ、どうにか無事だ。

2. *Abunai hashi o wataru* (to cross a dangerous bridge) is a metaphor very close in meaning to *hakuhyō o fumu*. However, while the former means "to intentionally get involved in s.t. risky," the latter means "to find oneself in a risky situation." Thus, *abunai hashi o wataru* is closer in meaning to the English than the main entry is. 📖➡関連語(2)

---

on top of that / phr. / metaphor

in addition to what has been {said/done}

R E L to top it all off

Examples

Saya: Mika is getting married soon.

Karen: Oh, really? Who is she going to marry?

Saya: I heard that he's a really handsome athlete. On top of that, he's super rich.

Karen: Wow, sounds like she found the perfect guy.

- -

(a) There are many advantages to doing a homestay. First, you can practice using the country's language every day and get an inside look at its culture. On top of that, you can enjoy homecooked meals.

(b) Mozart is a great composer. He composed symphonies, sonatas, operas, and on top of that, pieces for children.

(c) Reading and writing Japanese is difficult. You have to learn *kanji* in addition to *hiragana* and *katakana*. On top of that, *kanji* usually have both Sino-Japanese and Japanese readings.

Note

The English and Japanese both use spatial nouns—*top* and *ue*, respectively—to indicate the additional information.

R E L

The English REL, *to top it all off*, can be used instead of the main entry when describing a series of good or bad events.

(1) Yesterday I burned my finger, my camera broke, and {on top of that/to top it all off}, I lost my house key.
昨日は、指はやけどするわ、カメラは壊れるわ、その上、家の鍵はなくなるわで最悪だった。

450

2．日本語は「薄氷を踏む思いで」という句としてもよく使われる。

(2) 戦場にいるジャーナリストは、毎日薄氷を踏む思いで、取材を続けているだろう。(→(b))
For journalists on the battlefield, gathering news every day must feel like treading on thin ice.

3．日本語の「薄氷」は音読み「ハクヒョウ」で、訓読みの「うすごおり」のときは、比喩的な意味はない。

4．日本語は中国最古の詩集『詩経』の「如履薄氷」から来ている。元の「履む」は日本語では「踏む」で表記するのが普通である。

関連語

1．英語には *[skate/walk] on thin ice* という関連表現がある。 📖REL(1)

2．日本語の関連表現「危ない橋を渡る」は見出しの「薄氷を踏む」に近い比喩であるが、"やむをえず危ない状況に立つ"という意味はなく、"敢えて危険な道を選ぶ"といった積極的な意味がある。「危ない橋を渡る」のほうが英語の見出しに近い。

(2) アメリカ人は{危ない橋を渡る/??薄氷を踏む}のが好きなようだ。一方、日本人はそれが嫌いなようだ。
Americans seem to enjoy treading on thin ice, whereas Japanese people don't.

その上（に）　*phr.*　隠喩

既に{述べられた/なされた}ことに加えて

例文

さや：今度、美香が結婚するのよ。

カレン：へえ、相手はどんな人？

さや：すっごいハンサムでスポーツマン、その上、超お金持ちなんですって。

カレン：へえ、いい人見つけたね。

- -

(a) ホームステイには、いろいろ良い点がある。毎日その国の言葉で話すことができるし、文化を内側から見ることができる。その上、食事も作ってもらえるので助かる。

(b) モーツァルトは偉大な作曲家だ。交響曲からソナタ、オペラ、その上、子供のための楽曲まで作っている。

(c) 日本語を読んだり書いたりするのは大変だ。ひらがな、カタカナに漢字を覚えなくてはいけないし、その上、その漢字にはたいてい音読みと訓読みがあるときている。

解説

日英語とも「上」と *top* という空間名詞が情報の追加を意味している。

関連語

英語には *to top it all off* という関連表現があり、何かいいこと、あるいは悪いことが続けて起こる時には、見出しの代わりに使うことができる。 📖REL(1)

one more push / phr. / metaphor

a final effort needed to gain success

Examples

Kenta: Aren't you going on a silver anniversary trip with Dad?

Mrs. S: It looks like we can't because he's too busy. He was initially pretty excited about it, though.

Kenta: Give him one more push! This is a once-in-a-lifetime event that you'll never forget, you know.

(a) I thought we would win the soccer match with just one more push, but we ended up losing.

(b) One more push is needed to gain full funding for the project.

Note

The English is often used in a nearly literal manner during childbirth, but the Japanese cannot be used in the same situation.

(1) The doctor said, "Just one more push and you'll have yourself a newborn baby!"
「{あと一踏ん張り/ ×もう一押し}で赤ちゃんが生まれますよ」とお医者さんが言った。

REL

1. The Japanese REL *hito funbari (suru)* (to brace one's legs) means "to persevere." This is quite different from *hito oshi (suru)*, which means "to put pressure on others to achieve one's goal." 📖➡ **Note(1)**

2. The " 一 " in " 一押し " can also be read as *ichi-oshi*. This reading is used when one is giving one's best recommendation. 📖➡ 関連語(1)

---

one step ahead (of ~) / phr. / metaphor

to be at an advantage in terms of preparation or knowledge

ANT   one step behind ~

Examples

Kenta: Saya, have you read this part yet?

Saya: Of course I have. That's next week's homework!

Kenta: You're always one step ahead of me. My hat goes off to you.

Saya: Actually, you're just one step behind me.

(a) She was one step ahead of her classmates in math.

(b) We have to change our philosophy if we want to stay one step ahead of the competition.

Notes

1. The verbs that can precede *one step ahead (of ~)* include *be*, as in the dialogue and (a), *stay*, as in (b), *keep*, and *remain*.

2. The English expression can also be used to mean "to do s.t. before one is told about it," but the Japanese does not have this meaning.

{もう / あと}一押し　phr.　隠喩

あともう少しの{努力 / 圧力}

関 一踏ん張り(する)，一押し

例文

健太：お母さん、お父さんと銀婚式の旅行、行かないの？

鈴木(妻)：仕事が忙しいから、無理みたい。初めは乗り気だったんだけど。

健太：もう一押ししてみたら。一生に一度しかないんだから。いい思い出になるよ。

(a) そのサッカーの試合は、もう一押しで勝てると思ったのに負けてしまった。

(b) そのプロジェクトのための資金を全額得るためには、あと一押しが必要だ。

解説

ほとんど字義通りの用法であり、英語では出産の場面でよく使われる。しかし、日本語はそのような場面では使えない。▶📖 Note(1)

関連語

1. 日本語には"頑張る"という意味の「一踏ん張り(する)」という関連表現がある。「一押し(する)」は普通"自分以外の人にプレッシャーをかける"という意味があるのに対して、「一踏ん張り(する)」にはそういう意味はない。▶📖 Note(1)

2. 日本語には漢字の「一」を「ひと」ではなく「いち」と読む「一(いち)押し」という表現がある。何かを一番に推薦する時によく使われる口語的な表現である。

(1) 京都で泊まるなら、X ホテルが一押し！　安くてきれいだし、駅に近くて便利だよ。
   If you're staying in Kyoto, Hotel X is my No.1 recommendation.

一歩先を行く　phr.　隠喩

技術や知識、準備の点で{誰か / 何か}よりも有利な地点にいる

反 一歩遅れる

例文

健太：さや、ここの部分、もう読んだ？

さや：もちろんよ。来週の課題じゃない。

健太：さやはいつも僕の一歩先を行ってるね。えらい！

さや：健太が一歩遅れてるのよ。

(a) 彼女は数学ではクラスメートより一歩先を行っていた。

(b) 戦いにおいて常に一歩先を行くには、われわれの考え方を変えなければならない。

解説

1. 英語の one step ahead の前に来る動詞は、会話例と(a)のように be、(b)のように stay、そして keep、remain などである。

2. 英語は"言われる前からやっている"という意味でも使えるが、日本語にはそのような使い方はない。▶📖 Note(1)

(1) I'm one step ahead of you—I already packed snacks for the trip, so don't worry about it.
{君がいいたいことは分かってる/*僕は君より一歩先を行ってる} よ。旅行用のおやつなら、もう入れたから心配しなくていいよ。

ANT

The English and Japanese ANTs are *one step behind* ~ and *ippo okureru*, respectively.
📖→反意語(1)

one-sided love   / comp. n. / metaphor

when only one person is in love but not the other

Example

She seems to have feelings for a man three years older than she, but it's a one-sided love.

open one's eyes to ~   / phr. / metaphor

to realize s.t. significant for the first time

Examples

(a) Star Wars was the film that opened my eyes to sci-fi.

(b) His college education opened his eyes to several new aspects of various people's cultures.

(c) Many children's eyes were opened to the wonders of nature through Fabre's books on insects.

Note

While the English expression takes a nonhuman subject in (a) through (c), it can also take a human subject. The Japanese uses *(~ ni) me ga hirakareru*, a passive construction, when the subject is nonhuman, and *(~ ni) me o hiraku*, an active construction, when the subject is human.

REL

The Japanese REL is *(~ ni) kaigan suru*, which is more formal than *(~ ni) me {ga hirakareru/o hiraku}*. 📖→関連語(1)

open one's heart (to ~)   / phr. / metaphor

to share one's true feelings; to show empathy or understanding

REL LOOK open one's mind (to ~); open-minded

Examples

(a) The mayor opened his heart to the homeless people in the city.

(b) At college, students are encouraged to open their hearts and minds to new ideas.

反意語

日英語の反意表現は、それぞれ、「一歩遅れる」、*one step behind* ~ である。

(1) 僕は時代から一歩遅れている。

I am one step behind the times.

0

片思い　comp. n.　隠喩

一方的に恋い慕うこと

例文

彼女は今、三つ上の男性に片思いしているらしい。

(～に) 目 {が開かれる / を開く}　phr.　隠喩

ある経験などをきっかけとして、初めて大事なこと {に気がつく / をさとる}

関 (～に) 開眼する

例文

(a) 私は「スターウォーズ」という映画によって SF に目が開かれた。

(b) 彼は大学の教育のおかげで、人間の文化のより幅の広い見方に目が開かれた。

(c) ファーブルの昆虫記を通して、子供達は自然の世界へと目を開いた。

解説

日本語の「目が開かれる」は (a) (b) のように受け身型で、「目を開く」は (c) のように能動型で使用される。一方、英語の *open one's eyes to* ~ の (a) (b) は能動型、(c) は受け身型が使用されている。

関連語

日本語では見出しと並んで「(～に) 開眼する」が同じような意味で使われるが見出しよりフォーマルである。

(1) まだまだ下手ではあるが、最近ゴルフの面白さに {目が開かれた / 開眼した}。

I'm still a novice, but my eyes were recently opened to golf's appeal.

(～に) 心を開く　phr.　隠喩

本当の気持ちを人に示す

例文

(a) 市長はその町のホームレスの人々に心を開いた。

(b) 大学では、学生達は新しい考え方に心を開くように導かれる。

455

Note

The English can take a nonhuman object, but the Japanese cannot.

(1) He opened his heart to Buddhism.
  ?? 彼は仏教に心を開いた。

REL

1. The English has the REL *open one's mind (to ~)*. It differs from *open one's heart (to ~)* in that the former usually means "to show intellectual involvement with s.o. or s.t.," whereas the latter implies an emotional connection. In (1b), the corresponding Japanese is *(~ ni) kokoro o hiraku*, while in (1a) it is *(~ ni) me o hiraku* (to open one's eyes to ~).

(1) a. Taking Math 101 opened his mind to mathematics.
     彼は数学入門のコースを取ったとき、数学に{目を開いた/目が開かれた}。

   b. The teacher kept an open mind in dealing with his rebellious student.
     先生は心を開いて反抗的な学生に接した。

---

open one's mind (to ~) / phr. / metaphor

to be receptive to others' ideas and opinions

REL **LOOK** open one's heart (to ~); open-minded; (keep an) open mind

ANT close one's mind; closed-minded

Examples

(a) Under Annie Sullivan's guidance, Helen Keller opened her mind to communicating with others through language for the first time.

(b) You'd better open your mind and listen to what the doctor has to say. That's the only way you're going to get better.

(c) It's important to open your mind to people of different backgrounds and political views.

Notes

1. As indicated by the definition, the figurative meaning of *kokoro o hiraku* is ambiguous; it can mean both *open one's heart* and *open one's mind*.

2. The English can be used to mean "to open one's own mind" or "to open s.o. else's mind." But the Japanese can only be used to mean the former, as shown in (1) below.

(1) He tried to open her mind to music, but failed to do so.
  ×彼は彼女の心を音楽に開こうとしたが失敗した。

REL

1. *Open-minded* and *hirakareta kokoro no ~* are the adjectival forms of *open one's mind (to ~)* and *kokoro o hiraku*, respectively.

(1) He's open-minded, so everyone feels comfortable talking to him.
  彼は開かれた心の持ち主なので、誰もが話しやすい。

2. *Open mind* is the nominal form, and it is often used with the verb *keep*.

(2) You'd better {open your mind/keep an open mind} and listen to what the doctor has to say.

  (→(b))

ANT

The ANTs for *open one's mind* and *kokoro o hiraku* are *close one's mind* and *kokoro o tozasu*, respectively. Note that the Japanese ANT is used with both interpretations of the expression, *open one's mind* and *open one's heart*. 📖 反意語(1)

解説
　英語は人だけでなく事柄への共感も示すことができるが、日本語はできない。▶📖 **Note(1)**

関連語
　英語は *open one's mind (to ~)* という関連表現がある。それは情意的な共感を示す *open one's heart (to ~)* とは違って、誰か、あるいは、何かに知的な関わりを持つことを意味する。(1b)に対応する日本語は「(~に)心を開く」だが、(1a)に対応する日本語は「(~に)目を開く」である。
▶📖 **REL(1)**

0

（～に）心を開く　/ phr.　隠喩

第三者からの{情報 / 忠告}などを受け入れる，誰かを信頼して自分の気持ちを正直に話す

関 開かれた心の～

反 心を閉ざす

例文

(a) サリバン女史の指導のもとで、ヘレン・ケラーは初めて心を開き、言葉で他の人と意思疎通をしたのだった。

(b) 医師には心を開いて、言うことを聞いたほうがいいよ。それが唯一快復する方法さ。

(c) 異なった背景や政治的見解を持つ人々にも心を開くことが大切です。

解説

1. 日本語は、比喩的意味の記述にあるように2つの意味があり曖昧である。一つは英語の *open one's heart* の"誰かを信頼して自分の気持ちを正直に話す"という意味で、もう一つは *open one's mind* の"第三者からの{情報 / 影響 / 忠告}などを受け入れる"という意味である。

2. 英語版は「自分で自然に心を開く」、あるいは「何かに対して誰かの心を開かせる」という意味で用いることができる。しかし、日本語の場合は(1)に見られるように「自分で自然に心を開く」という意味でしか使えない。▶📖 **Note(1)**

関連語

1. 「開かれた心の～」と *open-minded* は、それぞれ「心を開く」と *open one's mind (to ~)* の形容詞的用法である。▶📖 **REL(1)**

2. 英語の関連表現 *open mind* は名詞句で、しばしば動詞 *keep* と共に用いられる。▶📖 **REL(2)**

反意語

　日英語の反意表現は、それぞれ、「心を閉ざす」と *close one's mind* であるが、日本語のほうは *open one's heart* と *open one's mind* の二つの意味の反意表現である。

(1)a. あの人は心を閉ざして、本音を言わない。
　　　He closes his heart and doesn't share his true feelings.

　 b. あの人は外国の文化に心を閉ざしている。
　　　His mind is closed to foreign cultures.

open one's mouth / phr. / metonymy

to speak

Examples

In class Bob seldom opens his mouth because he is afraid of saying something wrong.

open (a) Pandora's box / phr. / metaphor

to {release/reveal} a plethora of hidden problems

Examples

(a) Investigating the wrongdoings of that industry would be akin to opening Pandora's box.

(b) I couldn't ask about his past misdemeanors. That was a Pandora's box I didn't want to open.

(c) Debate on constitutional reform has been lively, but we should be careful how we respond lest we end up opening a Pandora's box.

Note

This expression comes from Greek mythology and refers to the box which Zeus asked Pandora to carry to the human world. She had been told not to open it, but she did, releasing a swarm of evils. In the end, only hope remained. The Japanese is most likely a direct translation of the English.

open the door {to/for} ~ / phr. / metaphor

to create new opportunities or possibilities

REL open doors

ANT {shut/close} the door on ~

Examples

(a) Her novels opened the door for postmodern literature.

(b) It was an astounding breakthrough, and it opened the door to an understanding of biology at the molecular level.

(c) The discoveries in the 1930s and 1940s that opened the door to both nuclear weapons and nuclear power were made by scientists from several nations.

R E L

1. The Japanese REL *(~ ni) monko o {hiraku/kaihō-suru}* means "to provide an opportunity {for/to} ~." 📖➡関連語(1)

2. The English REL, *open doors*, has the same meaning as the main entry, but it typically takes a person as its direct object.

(2) The success of the TV show opened new doors for the minor actress.
　そのテレビ番組の成功は、端役の女優にも新しい扉を開いた。

口を開く / phr. / 換喩
くち ひら かんゆ

話す
はな

例文
ボブは何か間違ったことを言うのを恐れて、授業中に滅多に口を開かない。
なに まちが い おそ じゅぎょうちゅう めった くち ひら

パンドラの箱を開ける / phr. / 隠喩
はこ あ いんゆ

非常に望ましくない事態を招く
ひじょう のぞ じたい まね

例文
(a) その業界の不正を追求することは、パンドラの箱を開けるに等しい。
ぎょうかい ふせい ついきゅう はこ あ ひと

(b) 僕は彼の過去の悪事を聞き出すことはできなかった。それは開けたくないパンドラ
ぼく かれ かこ あくじ き だ あ
の箱だからだ。
はこ

(c) 憲法改正論議が盛んだが、慎重に対応すべきだ。なぜならそれはパンドラの箱を
けんぽうかいせいろんぎ さか しんちょう たいおう はこ
開けることになりかねないからだ。
あ

解説
この見出しはギリシャ神話から来ている。ゼウスの神がパンドラに人間の世界に持って行くよ
うにと言った箱を指している。彼女はそれを開けないように言われていたが開けてしまい、次々
と不幸が飛び出し、最後に希望だけが残ったという。日本語は英語からの直訳の可能性が高い。

(〜(へ)の)扉を開く / phr. / 隠喩
とびら ひら いんゆ

新しくて大事な{事柄 / 領域}を知るきっかけを{与える / 作る}
あたら だいじ ことがら りょういき し あた つく

関 (〜に)門戸を{開く / 開放する}
もんこ ひら かいほう

反 (〜に(対して)){扉 / 門戸}を閉ざす
たい とびら もんこ と

例文
(a) 彼女の小説はポストモダン文学への扉を開いた。
かのじょ しょうせつ ぶんがく とびら ひら

(b) それは驚くべき突破口になった。そのために生物学の分子レベルの理解への扉が
おどろ とっぱこう せいぶつがく ぶんし りかい とびら
開かれたのだ。
ひら

(c) 核戦争と原子力への扉を開いた1930年代と1940年代の発見は、4、5か国の科学
かくせんそう げんしりょく とびら ひら ねんだい ねんだい はっけん こく かがく
者によってなされた。
しゃ

関連語
1. 日本語の関連表現には「(〜に)門戸を{開く / 開放する}」があり、"機会を与える"という意味
で使われる。
(1) 去年この病院はボランティアワーカーに門戸を{開いた / 開放した}。
Last year, this hospital opened its doors to volunteer workers.
2. 英語の関連表現 open doors は見出しと同じ意味だが、一般的に直接目的語として人物を取る。

REL(2)

[A][N][T]

The English and Japanese ANTs are *{shut/close} the door on* ~ and *~ni (taishite) {tobira/ monko} o tozasu*, respectively. *Tobira* (door) in (1a) and *monko* (lit. "gate and door") in (1b) mean "opportunity."

(1) a. His stubbornness has essentially {shut/closed} the door on an amicable resolution.

彼が頑固なせいで、実質的に円満解決への{扉 / ?門戸}を閉ざすことになってしまった。

b. Some European countries have tried to {shut/close} the door on Turkey's membership in the European Union.

ヨーロッパはトルコに対してEU加入の{門戸 / ?扉}を閉ざしている。

open the way {to/for} ~ / phr. / metaphor

to make s.t. possible

[REL] pave the way for ~

[Examples]

(a) She opened the way for other women to enter astronomy.

(b) He was the first Japanese player to enter the Major Leagues, and he opened the way for many other players to follow him.

(c) Her hard work in high school earned her a scholarship and opened the way for her to attend college.

[R][E][L]

Pave, which means "to cover with material that creates a solid, even surface," can replace *open* in *open the way for* ~. In fact, *pave the way for* ~ is used much more frequently than *open the way for* ~. However, *pave* emphasizes the preparatory aspect of the action more strongly than *open* does. In Japanese, *michi o hosō-suru* (to pave the way) cannot be used in a metaphorical sense.

(1) Sidney Poitier {opened/paved} the way for other black actors to succeed in Hollywood.

シドニー・ポワティエは黒人俳優がハリウッドで成功するための道を切り開いた。

out of the question / phr. / metaphor

not allowed; not possible

[Examples]

Kenta: I've decided not to study abroad after all.

Saya: Why not?

Kenta: My English teacher told me that with such a low TOEFL score, getting into an American university would be out of the question.

- - - - - - - - - - - - - - - - - - - -

(a) Going to a job interview with a red shirt on is out of the question.

(b) I had no money, so going to Paris for vacation was out of the question.

反意語

日英語とも反意表現として、「〜に（対して）｛扉／門戸｝を閉ざす」{shut/close} the door on ~ がある。(1a)の「扉」、(1b)の「門戸」ともに"機会"という意味である。━📖 ANT(1)

〜｛の／に｝道を（切り）開く　phr.　隠喩

顕著な目標を初めて達成し、後に続く人が同じ目標を達成できるようにする

例 文

(a) 彼女は他の女性達が天文学に進むための道を切り開いた。

(b) 彼は日本人で初めて野球選手として大リーグで活躍し、その後の日本人の野球選手が大リーグに行くための道を開いた。

(c) 彼女は高校で勤勉だった。それが大学での奨学金獲得のための道を開いたのだ。

関連語

英語の関連表現の動詞 pave（舗装する）は、open the way for ~ の動詞 open と置き換えることができる。実は pave the way for ~ のほうが open the way for ~ よりはるかに使用頻度が高い。ただし、pave を使うと"先鞭をつける"ことが open より強く表現される。日本語では「道を舗装する」は比喩にならない。━📖 REL(1)

問題外　comp. n.　隠喩
もんだいがい

議論する余地もない
ぎろん　　　　　　よち

関 論外
　　ろんがい

例 文

健太：僕、結局、留学するのあきらめたよ。

さや：どうして？

健太：英語の先生に「TOEFL の成績がそんなに悪くては、アメリカの大学に入るなんて、問題外です」って、言われちゃったんだ。

- - - - - - - - - - - - - - -

(a) 就職の面接のとき赤いシャツを着て行くなんて問題外だ。

(b) お金がなかったから、休暇でパリに行くなんて問題外だった。

Notes

1. The word *question* has two primary meanings: "an expression that seeks an answer" and "an issue or problem." In *out of the question*, it is being used in the latter sense.
2. This expression is considered a metaphor because neither *out of* nor *-gai* is used to express its original spatial meaning.

REL

In Japanese, *ron-gai da* can replace *mondai-gai da*. *Out of the question* corresponds to both expressions. 関連語(1)(2)

---

one's own flesh and blood / n. phr. / synecdoche

one's close relative

REL blood relative; close relative

Examples

Mr. S: Mike, you'll be getting your bonus soon, right?

Mike: That's right. I plan to give my bonus to my little brother, because apparently he's having trouble paying his tuition.

Mr. S: That's awfully kind of you!

Mike: If you don't help your own flesh and blood, who will?

- -

(a) We're brothers. We're each other's flesh and blood. We'll get through our parent's death together.

(b) Marie is my own flesh and blood, but she chose another path and turned her back on me.

Notes

1. Both the English and Japanese expressions use essential parts of the human body to represent an entire {body/person}, which makes them examples of synecdoche.
2. The English is a noun phrase, but the Japanese is a modifier that takes nouns such as *kyōdai* (brother), as shown in the dialogue and (a); *kodomo* (child), as shown in (b); *musume* (daughter), *musuko* (son), and *mono* (person).

REL

The English RELs are *blood relative* and *close relative*, and the Japanese REL is *nikushin* (lit. "flesh-body"). However, these lack the imagery of the main entries.

---

pack a punch / phr. / metaphor

to have a powerful effect

REL pack a wallop

Examples

(a) She's from Southern India, so she makes delicious curry, but be careful—it really packs a punch!

解説

1. 英語の *question* には「質問」と「問題」の二つの意味があり、*out of the question* では「問題」という意味で使われている。
2. この項目が比喩とみなされる理由は *out of* も「〜外」もここでは空間概念を表していないからである。

関連語

見出しの「問題外」は関連表現の「論外」で言い換えができる。英語では両方とも *out of the question* である。

(1) 就職の面接のとき赤いシャツを着て行くなんて{問題外 / 論外}だ。(→(a))
(2) お金がなかったから、休暇でパリに行くなんて{問題外 / 論外}だった。(→(b))

血肉を分けた〜 / phr. 提喩

血のつながった(親族)

関 肉親, 近い親戚

例文

鈴木(夫):マイク、そろそろボーナスの季節だね。

マイク: ええ、今度のボーナスは弟に送るつもりなんです。学費に困ってるようだから。

鈴木(夫):それは、えらいね。

マイク: お金のことは、血肉を分けた兄弟が助け合わなかったら、誰も助けてくれませんからね。

- - - - - - - - - - - - - - - - - - - -

(a) 血肉を分けた兄弟同士、親の死を乗り越えて力を合わせて頑張ろう。
(b) マリーは私の血肉を分けた子供なのに、別の道を選び、私に背を向けたのだ。

解説

1. 日英語とも人間の不可欠な部分を使って体、人の全体を表しているから、提喩の例である。
2. 英語は名詞句であるが、日本語は通例、「兄弟」(会話例、(a))、「子供」((b))、「娘」「息子」「者」のような名詞をとる。

関連語

日英語とも、「肉親」「近い親戚」と *blood relative, close relative* という関連表現がある。

(1) {血肉を分けた兄弟 / 肉親 / 近い親戚}同士、親の死を乗り越え力を合わせて頑張ろう。

(→(a))

We're brothers. We're {flesh and blood/blood relatives/close relatives}. We'll get through our parent's death together. (→(a))

パンチがきく / phr. 隠喩

{辛いもの / アルコール / スピーチ / 文章}がとても刺激的だ

例文

(a) 彼女はインドの南部出身だから、彼女の作るカレーはおいしいけど、気をつけたほうがいいよ。とにかくパンチがきいているんだから。

463

(b) His political speech really packed a punch, which surprised me because he's actually a very mild-mannered guy.

(c) The new author's novel, which recently won a literary prize, really packs a punch. I think it's very well done.

Notes

1. The English literally means "to hit s.o. very hard," while the Japanese means "s.o.'s punch is effective." The Japanese can be used in boxing matches.
2. The Japanese is most likely a translation of the English.

REL

Punch in the English can be replaced by *wallop*.

(1) She's from Southern India, so she makes delicious curry, but be careful—it really packs a {punch/wallop}! (→ (a))

---

paper tiger / comp. n. / metaphor

{s.o./s.t.} that looks strong but is actually weak

Examples

(a) The administration's support is decreasing exponentially—it's essentially a paper tiger. It probably won't emerge victorious in the next election.

(b) That company president likes to talk big, but his employees don't trust him. He's just a paper tiger.

(c) That country acted like a world power, but in the early 70s, wasn't it just a paper tiger?

Notes

1. A *paper tiger* can be used to describe anything that appears strong but is weak in actuality. By contrast, *hariko no tora* (a papier-mâché tiger) is only used to describe a person or nation.

(1) The provisions of the law had never been used. It felt like a paper tiger to me.
法律の中のその規定は一度も使われたことがなかったから、私はそれは{有名無実/˟張り子の虎}だと思った。

2. *Hariko* is a papier-mâché object made by pasting layers of paper on a wooden model and removing the model after the glue dries.

---

parrot / v. / metaphor

to repeat what s.o. has said, esp. without understanding

Examples

(a) The politician simply parroted whatever his secretary whispered to him.

(b) Everyone's so surprised that that crow can speak, but I think it's really just parroting back what people are saying.

(c) She can't come up with her own ideas, so she just parrots what her parents have told her.

(b) 彼の熱烈な政治演説は実にパンチがきいていて驚きだったけど、日頃の彼はまったくおとなしい、物静かな男なんだよ。

(c) 今度賞を取った新人の小説は、パンチのきいた文章で、なかなかいいと思う。

解説

1. 日本語は"パンチの効き目がある"というのが基本義で、英語は"人を強く打つ"が基本義である。日本語ではボクシングの時には字義通り使える。

2. 日本語は英語からの翻訳の可能性が高い。

関連語

英語の *punch* は *wallop* (ひどい一撃)で置き換えることができる。━📖 REL (1)

P

張り子の虎　/ **n. phr.** ┃ 隠喩

外見は強そうに見えるが実は弱い{人 / 国}

例文

(a) 支持率が落ちる一方の内閣は、まさに張り子の虎だ。今度の選挙は勝てないだろう。

(b) あの社長は大口ばかりたたいているが、社員からの信頼はなく、すでに張り子の虎である。

(c) あの国は世界の強国のような態度を取っていたが、実際は70年代初頭でもう張り子の虎ではなかっただろうか。

解説

1. 英語の *a paper tiger* は外見が強く見えるのに中は弱いものなら何でもいいが、日本語の「張り子の虎」は人か国にしか使えない。━📖 Note (1)

2. 「張り子」は木型に紙を重ねて張り、のりがかわいてから木型を抜き取ったもののことを言う。

オウム返し　/ **comp. n.** ┃ 隠喩

他の誰かが言ったことを意味もわからずそのまま繰り返すこと

例文

(a) その政治家は秘書が耳打ちしたことをオウム返しに述べただけだった。

(b) みんなあのカラスは人間の言葉を話す能力があるって騒いでいるけれど、実は人の言っていることをオウム返しにしているだけだと思うけどね。

(c) 彼女は自分の考えが出せないんだ。それで、両親の言うことをただオウム返しにするだけなんだよ。

465

Notes

1. The English expression uses the noun *parrot* as a verb, but the Japanese means "to respond like a parrot."
2. English also has the simile *{speak/talk} like a parrot*.

(1) She talks like a parrot—she just repeats everything you say.

彼女は人の言うことをオウム返しにすべて繰り返す。

pass (~) / v. / metaphor

to succeed at an exam or screening

Examples

Saya: You sure look happy!

Kenta: That's because I passed my final exam. Now I don't need to take a make-up exam.

Saya: Really? That's great!

- -

(a) Passing the entrance examination for a top university is difficult.

(b) Because he was in debt, he didn't pass the credit card screening process.

Notes

1. In both English and Japanese, the metaphor comes from the image of successfully making it through a place through which one must proceed.
2. In addition to describing the act of succeeding at an exam, inspection, and so on, this metaphor can also describe the approval of a bill or motion. 📖➡ 解説(1)

REL

The Japanese REL, *pasu-suru*, is borrowed from the English and can replace *tōru* in the examples. 📖➡ 関連語(1)

pass (as/for ~) / phr. / metaphor

to be accepted as {s.o./s.t.}

Examples

(a) Though only fifteen, he can pass for twenty.

(b) There are casual shoes that can pass as dress shoes.

(c) He passes for a knowledgeable person in the fashion world.

Note

The basic meaning for both the English and Japanese verbs is "to move through s.t.," but figuratively they can also mean "for {s.o./s.t.} to be taken for {s.o./s.t.} else."

解説

1. 英語は「オウム」という名詞を動詞として使っているが、日本語は「オウム返し」（オウムのような返事の仕方）となっている。
2. 英語には *{speak/talk} like a parrot*（オウムのように話す）という対応する直喩がある。

→📖 Note(1)

（～に）通る   v.   隠喩

試験や審査などに合格する

関 （～に）パスする

例文

さや： うれしそうじゃない。

健太： うん、期末試験に通ったからね。追試、受けなくてもいいんだ。

さや： ほんと？　よかったね。

- -

(a) 一流大学の入学試験に通るのは大変だ。

(b) 彼は借金があって、クレジットカードの審査に通らなかった。

解説

1. 日英語とも、人が何かくぐらなければならないところをうまく通過しているというイメージから比喩が来ている。
2. 試験や審査に合格する以外に、法案や動議が会議で可決する場合にも使える。

(1) 銃規制法案は上院の審議に通らなかった。
　　The Senate failed to pass the gun control law.

関連語

日本語の「（～に）パスする」は英語からの借用語で、例文のすべての「通る」と置き換えることができる。

(1) 一流大学の入学試験に{通る / パスする}のは大変だ。（→(a)）

（～で / として）通る   phr.   隠喩

他の{物 / 人}として受け入れられる

関 （～で / として）通用する

例文

(a) 彼はたった15歳なのに、大人びているから20歳で通る。

(b) よそ行きの靴で通るようなカジュアルシューズがある。

(c) 彼はファッション業界では情報通で通っている。

解説

日英語の基本義は〝何かを通り抜ける〟という意味であり、それが比喩となって、〝あるものが他のものとして受け入れられる〟という意味に転じている。

R⃝E⃝L⃝

Tōru can be replaced by *tsūyō-suru*, but as the latter is of Chinese origin, it is considered more formal. 📖→関連語(1)

pass the baton (on/off) to ~ / phr. metaphor

to hand off s.t. significant to s.o.

REL take (up) the baton; hand ({off/over}) the baton to ~

Examples

(a) Dr. King passed the baton to us. Let's carry it for our lap and then pass it to our children.

(b) He put the project together in 10 years and passed the baton to his subordinates when it got off the ground.

(c) When the right time came, Paul passed the baton to the next generation of leaders whom he had trained.

Notes

1. The Japanese is a translation of the English.
2. The verb *pass (on/off)* can be replaced by *hand (off/over)*.

R⃝E⃝L⃝

One can also say *take (up) the baton* or *(~ kara) baton o uke-toru*, which expresses the same idea from the viewpoint of the recipient.

(1) We took up the baton from Dr. King. (→(a))
われわれはキング牧師からバトンを受け取った。

pawn / n. / metaphor

s.o. who is used by s.o. else in pursuit of a certain goal

Examples

(a) He was just a pawn in some terrible political plot.

(b) She told the media that she was just a pawn in a plot to ruin the president's reputation.

(c) I for one am sick and tired of being treated like a pawn in his plan.

Note

Both the English and Japanese expressions can be used as either metaphors, as in (a) and (b), or similes, as in (c).

関連語

「通る」は「通用する」で置き換えることができる。ただし、「通用する」は漢語のため和語の「通る」より固い表現である。

(1) 彼はたった15歳なのに、大人びているから20歳{で / として}{通る / 通用する}。(→(a))

(〜に)バトンを渡す　phr.　隠喩

意義のあることを他の人に引き継がせる

関 (〜から)バトンを受け取る

例文

(a) キング牧師は私達にバトンを渡してくださった。われわれはそれを持って自分たちの距離を走り、子供達に渡そうではありませんか。

(b) 彼は10年間そのプロジェクトをまとめあげ、軌道に乗ったところで、後輩にバトンを渡した。

(c) 適当な時期が来たとき、ポールは指導者のバトンを自分が育て上げた次世代の指導者に渡した。

解説

1. 日本語は英語の翻訳である。

2. 英語の動詞 pass (on/off) は hand (off/over) で置き換えることができる。

関連語

バトンを受け取る側の視点で表現するときは、日本語では「(〜から)バトンを受け取る」、英語では take (up) the baton で置き換えることができる。📖REL(1)

将棋の駒　n. phr.　隠喩 / 直喩

何かの目的追求のために利用される人

例文

(a) 彼は何か恐ろしい政治的な策略の中で、ただの将棋の駒として使われただけだ。

(b) 彼女は、自分は大統領を失墜させるための将棋の駒として利用されたに過ぎないとメディアに語った。

(c) 彼の計画のために将棋の駒のように扱われるのはもうこりごりだ。

解説

(a)(b)では「将棋の駒」は隠喩だが、(c)では直喩として使われている。

pay attention to ~ / phr. / metaphor

to {watch/listen} to {s.t./s.o.} with one's full attention

Examples

Mike: I hear you're going to New York soon.

Saya: Yeah, but I'm a little worried, because they say that tourists make easy targets for criminals.

Mike: Don't worry. Just pay close attention to what's going on around you, and if someone strange comes near you, turn around and walk away immediately.

(a) He should pay more attention to what his boss tells him.

(b) The most important thing to pay attention to on a first date is not clothing, but your smile.

Note

Pay and *harau* share the basic meaning of "to give money in exchange for s.t. or some service." In this case, they are used metaphorically to express the idea of providing attention to someone or something instead of money.

---

homograph

pay one's respects to ~ / phr. / metaphor

visit s.o. to show one's admiration for {him/her}
～に行って敬意を表する，表敬訪問をする

Example

The prime minister of Japan visited the NYPD Memorial and paid his respects to all those police officers and firefighters who lost their lives.

日本の首相はニューヨーク警察の墓碑を訪ね、命を落とした警官と消防士に敬意を表した。

Penny(-)wise and pound(-)foolish. / phr. / metaphor

to be prudent with small amounts of money but wasteful with larger amounts

Example

I bought this coat on a whim since it was cheap, but the material and craftsmanship are terrible. I wonder if I'm penny wise and pound foolish.

Note

The English and Japanese developed independently of each other in early 17th-century England and late 17th-century Japan, respectively. Both *penny* and *mon* were the smallest monetary units available at the time, with a *pound* currently being worth 100 pennies. Since *hyaku* in the Japanese means "a hundred *mon*," it is very similar to the English.

（〜に）注意を払う　phr.　隠喩

何かを注意深く{見る / 聞く}

例文

マイク：今度、ニューヨークに行くんだって？

さや：そうなの、でも、旅行者は狙われるっていうから、ちょっと心配。

マイク：大丈夫だよ。周りによく注意を払って、変なやつが近づいてきたら、さっと逃げることだね。

- -

(a) 彼は上司が言うことにもっと注意を払うべきだ。

(b) 最初のデートで一番先に注意を払わなければならないことは、着ているものではありません。微笑みなのです。

解説

「払う」と *pay* は"物かサービスに対してお金を与える"という意味を共有している。お金の代わりに比喩的に注意を{誰か / 何か}に与えるのである。

同形異義語

（〜に）敬意を払う　/ phr. /　隠喩

尊敬の気持ちを見せる
show one's respect to s.o.

例文

彼は恩師に敬意を払って、著書の扉に恩師への感謝の言葉をしたためた。
The author paid his respects to his mentor by mentioning him on the title page of his book.

一文惜しみの百知らず　phr.　隠喩

わずかの金を使うのを惜しんで、大きな損失を招く

関 安物買いの銭失い

例文

このコート、安いと思って飛びついて買っちゃったけど、材質も縫製もひどいわ。一文惜しみの百知らずだったかしら。

解説

日英語ともそれぞれ17世紀後期と17世紀初期に独自に出てきている。「文」も *penny* も最小のお金の単位であり、*pound* は *penny* の100倍である。日本語の「百」は「百文」のことであるから、英語ととても近い表現になっている。

REL

The Japanese REL *yasumono-gai no zeni ushinai* (one who buys cheap goods will end up wasting money) is used more often than the main entry. Both expressions have the same meaning. 関連語(1)

per head / phr. / metonymy

for each person

REL a head

Example

The lottery ticket we bought as a group ended up winning us $1,000 per head.

REL

The English and Japanese RELs are *a head* and *hitori-atama*, respectively. 関連語(1)

pie in the sky, (a) / phr. / metaphor

s.t. that is unlikely to come true

REL LOOK castle(s) in the air, (a)

Examples

(a) The plan to build an amusement park on this small plot of land is nothing but a pie in the sky.

(b) This plan to tackle unemployment is not pie in the sky, as was suggested in a recent newspaper editorial. It's for real.

(c) She keeps saying she'll marry a millionaire in the future, but that's just pie in the sky.

Notes

1. While the foods featured in the English and Japanese expressions are different, *pie* and *mochi* (rice cake) are both symbols of their respective countries' cultures.

2. In the Japanese, one cannot eat the *mochi* because it is a drawing, but in the English, the *pie* is imagined as a three-dimensional object floating out of reach.

pile shame on top of shame / phr. / metaphor

to add to one's shame

Example

I want you to make sure you don't let this happen again. That would be piling shame on top of shame.

関連語

日本語には見出しの「一文惜しみの百知らず」よりもよく使われる関連表現として「安物買いの銭失い」がある。この意味は「安いからいいと思って買うとお金を失なうことになる」という意味である。この二つは入れ替えても意味は変わらない。

(1) このコート、安いと思って飛びついて買っちゃったけど、材質も縫製もひどいわ。｛一文惜しみの百知らず / 安物買いの銭失い｝だったかしら。(→例文)

頭割り　comp. n.　換喩
あたまわ　　　　　　　　　　　かんゆ

(費用などを)参加人数で割ること
ひよう　　　　　　さんかにんずう　わ

関 一人頭
ひとりあたま

例文

グループで買った宝くじが当たって、頭割りで1000ドルもらうことになった。
か　たから　あ　　　　あたまわ

関連語

日英語とも、それぞれ「一人頭」*a head* という関連表現がある。

(1) パーティの会費は一人頭3000円にします。
The party's going to come out to 3000 yen a head.

絵に描いた餅　phr.　隠喩
え　か　　もち　　　　　　　　いんゆ

何の役にも立たず、実現不可能なこと
なん　やく　た　　じつげんふかのう

関 LOOK▶空中楼閣
くうちゅうろうかく

例文

(a) この狭い土地に遊園地を作るという計画は絵に描いた餅に過ぎない。
せま　とち　ゆうえんち　つく　　　けいかく　え　か　もち　す

(b) この失業対策は最近の新聞の社説で絵に描いた餅ではないかと書かれたが、そんなことはない。実現可能な企画なのだ。
しつぎょうたいさく　さいきん　しんぶん　しゃせつ　え　か　もち　か　　じつげんかのう　きかく

(c) 彼女は将来大富豪と結婚すると言っているが、それは絵に描いた餅だ。
かのじょ　しょうらいだいふごう　けっこん　い　　え　か　もち

解説

1. 日英語で比喩として出てくる食べ物は異なるが、アメリカは「パイ」で、日本は「餅」といったように、それぞれの国の文化的象徴となる食べ物が使われている。

2. 日本語の「餅」は絵に描いてある二次元の餅で食べられない。一方、英語の「パイ」は空とぶ円盤のように空に浮かぶパイで、三次元の量感はあるが手が届かない、という含みがある。

恥の上塗り　phr.　隠喩
はじ　うわぬ　　　　　　　　いんゆ

さらに恥ずかしい目に合う
は　　め　あ

例文

もうこれ以上、恥の上塗りになるような真似はしないでほしい。
いじょう　はじ　うわぬ　　　　　まね

pillar of strength, a   / n. phr. / metaphor

{s.o./s.t.} that provides support

Example

> After my father died, my elder brother became a pillar of strength for our family.

place in the sun, a   / n. phr. / metaphor

a {position/station} in life that is bright and favorable

Examples

> (a) Life is a struggle to find a place in the sun.
>
> (b) A complete recluse getting picked up by a securities firm and finding his place in the sun—talk about luck.
>
> (c) I'll tell you what little I know about his personal history, but the bottom line is that he deserves a place in the sun.

ANT

> The Japanese ANT is *hi no ataranai basho* (lit. "a place where there is no sunshine").
>
> 反意語(1)

play   / v. / metaphor

unhindered motion (in a machine, etc.)

Example

> If there is no play in a car's steering wheel, driving becomes not only more difficult, but dangerous as well.

play dirty   / phr. / metaphor

act in a {cowardly/unjust} way

Examples

> Mike: This soccer player is always playing dirty.
>
> Kenta: Yeah, winning a game that way is no fun.
>
> -
>
> (a) Our team members said that the other football team played dirty from the very start of the game.
>
> (b) Everyone knows that he played dirty to rise to the very top of the organization.

大黒柱
だいこくばしら　／ **comp. n.** 　隠喩
いんゆ

家や組織の中心となって、その団体を支えている人
いえ　そしき　ちゅうしん　　　　　　　だんたい　ささ　　　　　　ひと

例文

父が死んだ後、兄は一家の大黒柱として、がんばってきた。
ちち　し　　あと　あに　いっか　だいこくばしら

陽の当たる場所
ひ　あ　ばしょ　／ **phr.** 　隠喩
いんゆ

華やかで恵まれた地位や境遇
はな　　めぐ　　　ち い　きょうぐう

反 陽の当たらない場所
ひ　あ　　　　ばしょ

例文

(a) 人生というのは、陽の当たる場所に座ろうとする競争なのだ。
じんせい　　　　　ひ　あ　ばしょ　すわ　　　　　　きょうそう

(b) 世捨人が証券会社に拾われて陽の当たる場所に出てきたのですから、こんなラッ
よすてびと　しょうけんがいしゃ　ひろ　　　　ひ　あ　ばしょ　で
キーな話はありません。
はなし

(c) 私が知っている彼の履歴のほんの一部をこうして並べてみるだけでも、とにかく陽
わたし　し　　　　　かれ　りれき　　　　　いちぶ　　　　　なら　　　　　　　　　　　　ひ
の当たる場所にいるにふさわしい人物だ。
あ　ばしょ　　　　　　　　　　じんぶつ

反意語

日本語の反意語には、「陽の当たらない場所」がある。

(1) 彼らは20年間陽の当たらない場所で働いてきた。
They've been working in an unrewarding environment for the past 20 years.

(〜に)遊びがある
あそ　／ **phr.** 　隠喩
いんゆ

機械などが動くとき、動きに余裕があること
きかい　　　　　うご　　　　　うご　　　よゆう

例文

ハンドルに遊びがない車は、運転しにくいだけでなく、危険でさえある。
あそ　　　くるま　　うんてん　　　　　　　　　きけん

汚いことをする
きたな　／ **phr.** 　隠喩
いんゆ

卑怯なこと、正しくないことをする
ひきょう　　　ただ

例文

マイク：このサッカー選手はいつも汚いことばかりしているね。
せんしゅ　　　きたな

健太：うん、そんなことをして勝っても、ぜんぜんおもしろくないのにね。
けん た　　　　　　　　　　　か

(a) 選手たちによると、そのアメフトのチームは試合のはじめから汚いことをしていた
せんしゅ　　　　　　　　　　　　　　　　　　しあい　　　　　　きたな
そうだ。

(b) 彼が汚いことをして組織のトップまでのぼりつめたことはあまりにも有名だ。
かれ　きたな　　　　　そしき　　　　　　　　　　　　　　　　　　ゆうめい

475

Note

Both the English and Japanese use *dirty* and *kitanai* in the figurative sense of being morally impure, as opposed to describing physical uncleanliness.

play possum / comp. v. / metaphor

to pretend to be {asleep/dead} or not aware of s.t.

Examples

Mrs. S: Kenta, don't lie around. Clean up your room.

Kenta: <zzzzzzzzz>

Mrs. S: Hey, I know you're just playing possum. Get up now.

- -

(a) When Jim's mother came to his bed to check if he was asleep, he played possum.

(b) A lady sitting next to me on the plane kept talking to me, but I couldn't understand her English at all, so I played possum.

Notes

1. The English and Japanese express the same figurative meaning in different fashions. The former says "to feign unresponsiveness like a(n) (o)possum," and the latter "to pretend to be sleep like a raccoon dog, which is believed to be good at feigning sleep." Both *tanuki* and *opossums* are considered to be skilled at feigning sleep. *Possum* is the abbreviated version of *opossum*. *Opossum* is *fukuro-nezumi* (lit. "pouch-mouse") in Japanese. It looks like a mouse, but also has a pouch similar to that of koalas and kangaroos.

2. The Japanese can only mean "to pretend to be asleep," but the English can also mean "to pretend to be dead," as in (1a), or "to pretend not to be aware of s.t.," as in (1b).

(1)a. They say that you should play possum when you are attacked by a bear.
　　熊に襲われたときは、死んだふりをするのがいいそうだ。

b. When the teacher called on him, John played possum.
　　先生が、ジョンの名前を呼んだとき、彼は気がつかないふりをした。

---

homograph

play with fire / phr. / metaphor

to engage in s.t. dangerous
危険を冒す
き けん　おか

Example

When I was young, I used to play with fire by driving over the speed limit and so on.

僕も若い頃には、速度制限を破って運転をするなど、危険を冒したことがある。
ぼく　わか　ころ　　　　せいげんそく ど　　やぶ　　　うんてん　　　　　　　き けん　おか

解 説

英語も日本語も、*dirty*「汚い」を物の汚れとしてではなく、倫理的によくないという意味で使っている点で比喩的である。

たぬき寝入りをする 〔phr.〕 隠喩

眠ったふりをする

例 文

鈴木(妻)：健太、寝ころがってばかりいないで、その辺片付けなさいよ。

健太：グーグーグー

鈴木(妻)：まったく、どうせ、たぬき寝入りでしょ。早く起きなさいよ。

(a) 母親がベッドのところに寝たかどうか見に来たとき、ジムはたぬき寝入りをした。

(b) 飛行機で隣に座っていた婦人が僕にずっと話しかけてきましたが、英語が全然わからなかったので、たぬき寝入りをしました。

解 説

1. 日英語は同じ比喩的意味を違った形で表現している。前者は"寝たふりをするのが上手だと考えられているたぬきのように寝たふりをする"と表現しているのに対して、後者は"オポッサムのように寝たふり、死んだふりをする"と表現している。「たぬき」も *possum* も寝たふりをする動物と考えられている。英語の *possum* は *opossum* の省略形である。*Opossum* は日本語では「ふくろねずみ」と言い、ネズミに似ているが、カンガルーやコアラのように育児嚢を持った動物である。

2. 日本語は"寝たふりをする"という意味しかないが、英語はその意味に加えて"死んだふりをする"と"気がついていないふりをする"という意味がある。—📖 Note(1)

同形異義語

火遊びをする 〔phr.〕 隠喩

分別のないその場限りの情事
to have an affair with s.o.

例 文

既婚者と恋に落ちるというような火遊びはしないほうがいいですよ。結局、傷つくのは、あなただから。

Falling in love with a married man is a bad idea. In the end, you're the one who's going to get hurt.

point / n. / metaphor

a particular detail or element; a particular time or moment; a unit of measurement; the exact or essential fact or idea under consideration; a purpose or objective; a unit of academic credit; a cape (as in a piece of land projecting into a body of water)

REL spot; purpose; strength; weakness

Examples

(a) The fireball was sighted more than 130 km from the point of impact.

(b) At that point in his life, he thought he had already achieved his goal.

(c) Yes, I completely agree with you on that point.

(d) Her strong point was communicating with others.

(e) Math is his weak point.

(f) What is the point of your argument?

(g) What literary point of view is the story written from?

(h) He didn't lose a single point on his English test because he studied really hard.

(i) Sydney is the starting point of the cruise. I heard the ship sails all the way to the South Pole.

(j) The boiling point is the temperature at which a liquid changes into a gas.

Notes

1. The English and Japanese expressions originated from their respective non-metaphorical definitions: "the end of a sharp object; a small mark made by such an object" and "a small mark made by a sharp object," respectively. Both share quite a few metaphorical uses, but there are some differences. For example, in English, *point* can be used to mean "cape" and "purpose/objective," as in (1) below, but *ten* cannot be used this way.

   (1) a. A beautiful lighthouse stands on the point.
       きれいな灯台が{岬 /ˣ点}に立っている。

   b. What's the point of studying Arabic?
       アラビヤ語を勉強する{目的 /ˣ点}は何ですか。

2. In Japanese, *ten* can be used metaphorically in words such as *tenka* (lighting a fire) and *tenken* (examination). 📖→解説(2)

REL

The English RELs *spot* and *purpose* can replace *point* in (a) and Note (1b), respectively. Similarly, *strength* and *weakness* can replace *strong point* in (d) and *weak point* in (e), respectively.

---

point of view; viewpoint / n. phr./comp .n. / metaphor

the perspective one takes on {s.t./s.o.}

Examples

Kenta: I wonder why we can't agree on this.

Karen: We're not disagreeing per se—we're just looking at it from different points of view.

点
てん / n. / 隠喩
いんゆ

特定の空間，特定の時間，注目すべき細部，点数，句読点
とくてい くうかん とくてい じ かん ちゅうもく さい ぶ てんすう く とうてん

例 文

(a) 火の玉を見たという報告は、落下(地)点から130キロ以上離れたところでなされて
ひ たま み ほうこく らっ か ち てん い じょうはな
いた。

(b) 彼は人生のその時点で、目標をすでに達成したと思っていた。
かれ じんせい じ てん もくひょう たっせい おも

(c) ええ、その点ではあなたに完全に賛成します。
てん かんぜん さんせい

(d) 彼女の強い点は、人とのコミュニケーションだ。
かのじょ つよ てん ひと

(e) 数学は彼の弱点だ。
すうがく かれ じゃくてん

(f) あなたの論点は何ですか。
ろんてん なん

(g) そのストーリーは、どんな文学的視点で書かれているのですか。
ぶんがくてき し てん か

(h) 彼は一生懸命勉強したので、英語のテストで一点も失うことはなかった。
かれ いっしょうけんめいべんきょう えい ご いってん うしな

(i) この大型客船の出発点はシドニーです。船は南極点の近くまでも行くそうです。
おおがたきゃくせん しゅっぱつてん ふね なんきょくてん ちか い

(j) 沸点とは、液体が気体に変化する時点の温度のことである。
ふってん えきたい き たい へん か じ てん おん ど

解 説

1. 日英語の見出しはそれぞれ、"尖ったもので作られた小さな印"と、"尖ったものの先、尖った
もので作られた小さな印"という基本義から出てきている。日英語はかなりの比喩表現を共
有しているが、共有していないものもある。例えば、英語には *cape*（岬）、*purpose*（目的）とい
う比喩的な意味があるが、日本語にはない。📖**Note(1)**

2. 日本語では「点火」（火をつける）、「点検」（調べる）のような比喩的な意味がある。

(2)a. 彼はオリンピックの最終ランナーとして聖火台に点火した。

As the last of the Olympic torch bearers, he lit the brazier on the platform.

b. 車は必ず昼間に点検をすべきだ。

You should always try to inspect a car in daylight.

関連語

英語の関連表現のうち *spot* と *purpose* は、それぞれ(a)と Note (1b)の *point* と置き換えること
ができる。*strength* と *weakness* はそれぞれ(d)の *strong point* と(e)の *weak point* と置き換える
ことができる。

視点，観点
し てん かんてん / comp. n. / 隠喩
いんゆ

何かをどこの点から見るかということ
なに てん み

例 文

健太： どうしてこの事に賛成できないのかなあ。
けん た こと さんせい

カレン： 反対なんかしてないわ。私たちは、ただ違った視点から見ているだけよ。
はんたい わたし ちが し てん み

479

(a) When you read a book, you should be able to identify the author's point of view.

(b) A critical analysis takes a viewpoint and attempts to prove its validity.

(c) The book discusses environmental issues from various points of view.

(d) Women and men look at things from different viewpoints.

Notes

1. There is semantic difference between *shiten* and *kanten*. The former means "a camera angle, real or imagined, from which one looks at s.t.," and the latter "a position from which one observes and thinks about s.t." *Shiten* can be used non-metaphorically, but *kanten* is always used metaphorically. 📖→解説(1)

2. *Point of view* is a transliteration of the French *un point de vue*.

poison (for/to) ~, (a) / n. phr. / metaphor
s.t. that is very harmful

Examples

Mr. S: There's been a spike in serious juvenile crimes lately, hasn't there?

Mrs. S: It's probably because they've been spoiled and can't tell right from wrong.

Mr. S: Yeah. Too much love can be a poison.

- -

(a) Drugs are a poison to society.

(b) Television can help children learn, but it can also be a poison.

(c) Alcohol can be a poison or a medicine. In either case, it's best not to drink too much.

R E L

The expression *ki-no-doku(na)* (a regrettable state or situation) etymologically means "a situation that is poison for s.o.'s body and soul." 📖→関連語(1)

polish / v. / metaphor
to make s.t. more refined

Examples

Mrs. S: This pianist plays much better now.

Mr. S: Yeah, she studied abroad in Vienna and polished her skills there.

- -

(a) I'm more the type to polish my mind than polish my car.

(a) 本を読むときには、著者の視点がつかめなければだめだ。

(b) 批判的な分析とは一つの視点をとり、その妥当性を証明しようと試みることだ。

(c) その本は環境問題についていろいろな観点から論じている。

(d) 女性と男性は物事を違った観点から見ることが多い。

解説

1. 「視点」と「観点」には意味上の違いがある。 前者は"何かを見る場合の物理的、心理的なカメラアングル"を、後者は"何かを観察したり、考えたりする場合の立場"を意味する。「視点」は非比喩的にも使えるが、「観点」は比喩的にしか使えない。

(1) カメラマンの{視点 / ×観点}からいうと、この場所は撮影には向かない。
From a photographer's viewpoint, this isn't a good place for taking pictures.

2. 英語の *point of view* は仏語の *un point de vue* の字訳である。

毒 / n. / 隠喩

非常に害になるもの

関 気の毒（な）

例文

鈴木（夫）：最近、未成年の凶悪犯罪が多いね。

鈴木（妻）：甘やかされて育って、善悪の判断がつかないんじゃないの。

鈴木（夫）：うん、親の甘やかし過ぎは、かえって毒だね。

- -

(a) 麻薬は社会の毒だ。

(b) テレビは子供の教育のために役に立つが、毒になることも多い。

(c) お酒は毒にも薬にもなる。飲みすぎは慎みたい。

関連語

日本語の「気の毒（な）」の語源は"ある状況が人の{心 / 体}にとって毒だ"という意味である。

(1) あの人は、火事で家も家族も失ってしまい、本当に気の毒だ。
He lost his house and family in the fire. I feel so sorry for him.

磨く / v. / 隠喩

技術や精神の到達度を高める

例文

鈴木（妻）：このピアニスト、うまくなったわね。

鈴木（夫）：うん、ウィーンに留学して、腕を磨いたね。いい演奏をするね。

- -

(a) 私は車を磨くよりは心を磨くタイプの人間です。

481

(b) When she was a child, I often took my daughter to classical music concerts in order to polish her artistic sensibilities.

(c) Though he was already a guitar and violin virtuoso, he polished not only his skills as a performer, but also as a composer.

Note

Both *polish* and *migaku* can be used metaphorically to mean "to become good at s.t. through constant effort." However, whereas *polish* can also describe the act of refining objects (e.g. "polish an essay"), *migaku* cannot be used in this sense.

(1) I carefully polished my graduation thesis.

卒論の内容を注意深く {推敲した/×磨いた}。

Japanese does have the expression *bun(shō) o migaku*, but as indicated by the definition, this means "to polish one's writing ability."

potbelly　/ comp. n. / metaphor

to have a big stomach

Example

Someone who drinks a lot of beer is likely to end up with a potbelly.

pots and pans　/ n. phr. / synecdoche

utensils for cooking

Examples

(a) When you move, you should be able to unpack your pots and pans right away.

(b) I don't have a toaster or any pots or pans to cook with.

Note

Both the English and Japanese are used as catch-all expressions for cooking utensils. Since a part is being used to represent the whole, this is an example of synecdoche.

pour cold water on ~　/ phr. / metaphor

for {s.o./s.t.} to suddenly discourage {s.o./s.t.}

REL　throw cold water on ~

Examples

(a) When I was told I was being transferred to a local branch just as I was starting to get used to the Tokyo headquarters, I felt as if someone had poured cold water on my dreams.

(b) It's tough watching others pour cold water on his ideas during meetings. He's just trying his best.

(c) With a distinct chill in her voice, Ritsuko poured cold water on her close friend's foolish expectations.

(b) 娘の感性を磨くために私は小さいころからよくクラシックのコンサートに連れて行った。

(c) 彼はすでにギターとバイオリンの達人だったが、演奏家だけでなく作曲家としての腕も磨いた。

解説
日英語とも磨くという行為が努力を通して何かに秀でることを表す。*polish* は能力のみならず「もの」も比喩的に磨くことができるが、「磨く」はこのような意味では使えない。

📖 Note(1)

なお、日本語では「文(章)を磨く」ということができるが、これは定義にあるように(文章の)技術を高めることにあたる。

太鼓腹　/ comp.n.　隠喩

丸く出っ張ったお腹

例文
ビールをたくさん飲む人は、太鼓腹になりがちだ。

鍋釜　/ n. phr.　提喩

炊事用具

例文
(a) 引っ越すときは、鍋釜だけは荷物からすぐに取り出せるようにしておくほうがいい。

(b) 私はトースターも持っていないし、ほかに料理をする鍋釜も持っていない。

解説
日英語ともすべての炊飯用具を指す言葉として使われている。つまり、部分で全体を指すという典型的な提喩のケースである。

{冷や水 / 冷水}を浴びせる　phr.　隠喩

誰かを急に落胆させたり、期待感を萎えさせるような行動をとる

関　(〜に)水を差す

例文
(a) 東京本社での仕事に慣れ始めたところで地方への移動を命じられて、冷や水を浴びせられた気がした。

(b) 彼もがんばっているのだから、会議であんな冷や水を浴びせるような発言をするのはかわいそうだ。

(c) 律子は冷ややかさを増した声音で、親友の脳天気な期待に冷水を浴びせた。

Note

The English can be used in any case where someone/something discourages someone/something else, but the Japanese is used in cases where someone/something discourages someone or someone's success, optimism, or expectations. Therefore, *pour cold water on* ~ in (1) below corresponds to the more straightforward ~ *ni hantai-suru* (to oppose ~) in Japanese.

(1) The executive committee immediately poured cold water on the idea.
　　理事会はその考えに即座に{反対した/ˣ冷水を浴びせた}。

REL

1. *Pour cold water on* ~ can be replaced by *throw cold water on* ~.
(1) The sudden reduction in her paycheck really {poured/threw} cold water on her plans.
　　彼女は給料の控除額に冷や水を浴びせられた気がした。
2. The Japanese REL, ~ *ni mizu o sasu*, means "for s.o. to disrupt s.t. that has been proceeding successfully and cause it to fail." This expression can be used in (2), since the meeting is proceeding smoothly until the mayor interferes, but the main entry cannot. 📖➞ 関連語(2)

---

pour one's heart out to ~　／ phr.　metaphor

to express one's personal {feelings/thoughts} all at once

Examples

Mike: I feel so good! Today I told my section chief everything that's been on my mind.

Colleague: Are you sure pouring your heart out to your boss was a good idea?

Mike: It'll be fine! He probably thinks that's just the way Americans are.

- -

(a) She poured her heart out to you precisely because she trusts you.

(b) Ichiro poured his heart out to her and confessed that he'd been in love with her for the past three years.

Note

The English and Japanese use different verbs. The verb *pour out* means "to cause liquid to flow in a stream," and thus likens one's feelings to a liquid. *Buchimakeru*, however, means "to scatter the contents of a container all over the place."

REL

Kimochi o buchimakeru is replaced by *shinjō o toro-suru* in written Japanese.

📖➞ 関連語(1)

解 説

英語は“{誰か / 何か}が{誰かを落胆させる / 何かを阻止する}”という場合に使えるのに対して、日本語は“{誰か / 何か}が{誰かを落胆させる / 誰かの成功観、楽観、期待を萎えさせる}”という場合に使われる。したがって、(1)のような場合には英語の *pour cold water on ~* は、日本語では「~に反対する」に対応する。━📖 Note(1)

関連語

1. 英語の *pour cold water on ~* は *throw cold water on ~* と置き換えることができる。━📖 REL(1)
2. 日本語には“うまくいっていたことを邪魔してうまくいかないようにする”という意味の「(~に)水を差す」という関連表現がある。(2)では会議はうまく進行していたので「水を差す」は使えるが、「冷や水を浴びせる」は使えない。

(2) 市長はせっかくうまく進行していた会議に{水を差す / ˣ冷水を浴びせる}ような発言をした。
    The mayor gave remarks that poured cold water on the otherwise smooth proceedings.

気持ちをぶちまける　phr.　隠喩

抑えていた{気持ち / 考え}を一気に言う

関 心情を吐露する

例 文

マイク：あ～、すっきりした。今日は、課長に思ってること全部言ってやったよ。
同僚：そんなに気持ちをぶちまけて、大丈夫かな。
マイク：平気さ。アメリカ式だろうくらいに、思ってんじゃないかな。

(a) 彼女はあなたのことを信頼していたからこそ、自分の気持ちをぶちまけたのだ。
(b) 一郎は彼女に、過去3年間も彼女のことを愛していたのだと気持ちをぶちまけた。

解 説

日英語で動詞が異なっている。日本語の動詞「ぶちまける」は“人の気持ちを、容器をひっくりかえして中の物を勢いよくまき散らす”と見なしているのに対して、英語の *pour out* は“液体を流す”という意味なので、人の気持ちを液体であるかのように見なしている。

関連語

日本語の話し言葉では「気持ちをぶちまける」を使うが、書き言葉では「心情を吐露する」が使える。

(1) 彼の書く詩には、素直に心情を吐露したものが多い。
    In many of his poems, he pours his heart out without reservation.

pour money down the drain / phr. / metaphor

to waste money

Examples

Saya: Using millions of yen to build a bridge that practically nobody uses is a real waste of our tax money!

Kenta: Yeah, it's like pouring money down the drain. The locals are saying the same thing.

- - - - - - - - - - - - - - - - - - - -

(a) It looks like they're still pouring money down the drain thanks to that greedy attorney.

(b) Buying lottery tickets is like pouring money down the drain.

Note

Note that the verbs are *pour* in English and *suteru* (to throw away) in Japanese. The expressions are mostly the same otherwise.

pour water into a sieve / phr. / metaphor

to make wasteful efforts that amount to nothing

REL draw water with a sieve

Examples

Kenta: I heard that you started tutoring. How's it going?

Saya: Not well. He's nice, but no matter how hard I try, it's like pouring water into a sieve. He just can't learn!

Kenta: That's because you're a bad teacher.

Saya: Um, rude! But maybe you're right.

- - - - - - - - - - - - - - - - - - - -

(a) Giving advice to the idle is like pouring water into a sieve.

(b) If you don't manage your expenses carefully, you'll just end up pouring water into a sieve and losing money.

Note

Both the English and Japanese examples describe efforts that fail to produce results. In the dialogue, (a), and (b), these efforts are "teaching," "advising," and "making a profit," respectively.

REL

The English and Japanese RELs, *draw water with a sieve* and *zaru de mizu o sukū* (lit. "to scoop up water with a sieve"), are virtually identical.

(1) Giving advice to the idle is like {pouring water into/drawing water with} a sieve. (→(a))
なまけ者に忠告をするのは、{ざるに水を注ぐ/ざるで水をすくう}ようなものだ。

どぶに金を捨てる　/ phr.　隠喩

お金を無駄に使う

例文

さや：こんなほとんど誰も通らないような橋を何億円もかけて作るなんて、税金の無
　　　駄遣いもいいとこね。

健太：うん、まったく金をどぶに捨てるようなもんだね。地元の人でさえ、そう言って
　　　るよ。

- (a) 彼らはあの強欲な弁護士のために相変わらず金をどぶに捨てているようだ。
- (b) 宝くじを買うのはどぶに金を捨てるようなものだ。

解説

日本語では動詞が「捨てる」であるが、英語では *pour*（注ぐ）である。そのほかはほぼ同じである。

ざるに水を注ぐ　/ phr.　隠喩

苦労してまったく無駄なことをする

関　ざるで水をすくう

例文

健太：家庭教師始めたんだって？　どう？

さや：ぜんぜんだめ。いい子なんだけど、いくら教えてもざるに水を注いでる感じ。
　　　ぜんぜん覚えてくれないのよ。

健太：それは、さやの教え方が悪いんだよ。

さや：ま、失礼ね。でも、そうかなあ。

- (a) なまけ者に忠告をするのは、ざるに水を注ぐようなものだ。
- (b) コスト管理をしっかりしなければ、ざるに水を注ぐようなもので、お金は出て行く
　　ばかりだ。

解説

日英語とも各例文の背後には無駄な努力という意味がある。会話例と (a)(b) で、それぞれの
努力は「教えること」「忠告すること」、そして「利益を上げること」である。

関連語

日英語とも、まったく同じ関連表現 *draw water with a sieve* と「ざるで水をすくう」がある。

→ REL(1)

preach to the choir / phr. / metaphor

to talk about s.t. with people who already agree

REL preach to the converted

Examples

(a) When I found out that many were experts on Tibet, I felt like I'd spent most of my time preaching to the choir.

(b) Speaking about the importance of math education to a group of math educators is like preaching to the choir.

Note

Preach to the choir literally means "to give a sermon to a church choir," whereas *shaka ni seppō* literally means "to make the Buddha listen to one of his own sermons."

REL

The English has the REL *preach to the converted*, which literally means "to give a sermon to s.o. who is already a believer." This expression is similar to the Japanese main entry, but it is used less frequently than the English main entry.

(1) Speaking about the importance of math education to a group of math educators is like preaching to the {choir/converted}. (→(b))

(as) pretty as a flower / phr. / simile

very beautiful

Example

The colorful boats floating on the lake were as pretty as flowers strewn upon the water.

(as) pretty as a picture / phr. / simile

very beautiful

Example

The view of the mountains and lakes from here is pretty as a picture.

prick up one's ears / phr. / metaphor

to listen carefully

REL LOOK be all ears

Examples

Karen: Yesterday I heard a terrible argument going on next door. It was really scary!

Saya: Did everything turn out all right?

釈迦に説法　/ phr. / 隠喩

相手が既によく知っていることを説明しようとする

例文

(a) チベットの専門家が大勢いることがわかり、話しているほとんどの時間は「釈迦に説法」という感じだった。

(b) 数学教育者に数学教育の重要性を説くのは、釈迦に説法のようなものだ。

解説

英語の見出し *preach to the choir* の字義通りの意味は"教会の合唱団に説教をする"で、日本語の見出しの「釈迦に説法」の字義通りの意味は"釈迦自身に釈迦が唱えた説法を語って聞かせる"である。

関連語

英語の関連表現 *preach to the converted* の字義通りの意味は"すでに宗教家である人物に説法をする"で日本語の見出しに近い表現だが、使用頻度は英語の見出しよりも少ない。

→📖 REL(1)

P

花のようにきれい　/ phr. / 直喩

とてもきれい

例文

湖に浮かぶカラフルなボートは、まるで湖の上をただよう花のようにきれいだった。

絵のようにきれい　/ phr. / 直喩

とてもきれい

例文

ここから見える山と湖の景色は、絵のようにきれいだ。

聞き耳を立てる　/ phr. / 隠喩

聞きとりにくい{会話/物音}を必死で聞きとろうとする

関 耳をそばだてる, 🔍LOOK 全身を耳にする

例文

カレン： 昨日、隣の部屋で、すっごいけんかしてる声や音が聞こえて、ほんと、恐かったわ。

さや： 大丈夫だったの？

489

Karen: I pricked up my ears to hear what was going on, but things got quiet after a while.

Saya: Good to hear that nothing serious happened.

(a) It's natural for people to prick up their ears when they hear their own name mentioned.

(b) When Tomoe heard the back door open, she pricked up her ears.

Note

Both the Japanese and English metaphors are based on the instinctive, non-verbal behavior of animals such as horses, dogs, and cats that prick up their ears when they hear a sudden sound.

REL

1. The Japanese REL *mimi o sobadateru* (to listen with standing ears) is used much less frequently than *kiki-mimi o tateru*. 📖→ 関連語(1)

2. Both the English and Japanese expressions imply that someone is trying hard to hear something because it is difficult to hear accurately, whether it be someone's words or the sounds that something is making. On the other hand, the RELs *be all ears* and *zenshin mimi da* (to listen to s.t. by making ears out of one's entire body) mean that someone is listening to someone else's words very carefully. 📖→ 関連語(2)

public eye, the / n. phr. / synecdoche

the attention of the general population

Examples

(a) People who are exposed to the public eye should take responsibility for their behavior.

(b) The actress got sick of all the attention surrounding her scandals, so she decided to emigrate to avoid the public eye.

(c) They were growing marijuana at a remote location out of the public eye.

Note

Since *public eye* is not referring to a literal eye, and "eye" represents a part of the whole (public), this is an example of synecdoche.

REL

The Japanese has the REL *seken no me* (lit. "the eye of the world"). In casual contexts such as that of (1a), the REL is used more often than the main entry, but it cannot easily replace the main entry in cases such as (1b). 📖→ 関連語(1)

pull at {s.o.'s/the} heartstrings （心の琴線に触れる）
→ {tug/pull} at {s.o.'s/the} heartstrings

カレン：聞き耳を立てて様子をうかがっていたんだけど、そのうち、静かになったの。

さや：そう、何もなくて、よかったね。

(a) 誰でも自分の名前を言われたら、聞き耳を立てるのは当たり前だ。

(b) 裏口のドアが開く音がしたので、友江は聞き耳を立てた。

解説

日英語の比喩は馬、犬、猫といった動物が急に物音を聞いたときによく見せる「耳を立てる」という非言語的で本能的な行動から出てきた比喩である。

関連語

1. 日本語には「耳をそばだてる」という関連表現がある。これは「聞き耳を立てる」よりもはるかに使用頻度が低い。

(1) 彼女は{聞き耳を立てて / 耳をそばだてて}壁の向こうの会話を聞いていた。
   She pricked up her ears and listened to the conversation through the wall.

2. 見出しは日英語とも、話であれ、物音であれ、聞きにくいので一生懸命聞いていることを表現する。日英語にそれぞれ対応する関連表現に「全身耳だ」と *be all ears* があるが、この表現は"非常に熱心に話を聞くこと"を表す。

(2) 家族がおばあさんの思い出を話しはじめたとき、彼女は全身を耳にして聞いた。
   She was all ears when her family started reminiscing about her grandma.

公共の目　**n. phr.**　提喩

一般の人々（の監視）

関 世間の目

例文

(a) 公共の目にさらされている立場の人間は自分の行動に責任を持つべきだ。

(b) その女優は度重なるスキャンダルに嫌気がさし、公共の目から逃れるために海外への移住を決意した。

(c) この公共の目から隔離された場所で、彼らは大麻の栽培を行っていた。

解説

「公共の目」の「目」の使い方は本当の目ではなく、「目（＝部分）」で「人（＝全体）」を表現しているため、提喩だと解釈される。

関連語

日本語には「世間の目」という関連表現がある。(1a)のような話し言葉では見出しより使用頻度が高いが、(1b)のように見出しと置き換えにくい場合もある。

(1) 日本人って{世間の目 /?? 公共の目}を気にしますよね。
   Japanese people sure care about how they appear in the public eye, don't they?

> **homograph**

pull s.o.'s leg / phr. / metaphor

to {tease/trick} s.o.
かつぐ

Example

John is good at pulling his friend's leg.
ジョンは友達をかつぐのがうまい。

pull ~ {out/up} by the roots / phr. / metaphor

to completely get rid of s.t. bad

REL root out ~

Examples

(a) The new legislation aims to pull corporate corruption out by the roots.

(b) The school administration launched a campaign to pull bullying out by the roots.

(c) We need to root out the mole if we want to stop these leaks.

Notes

1. The English means "to completely get rid of s.t. bad," but the Japanese can also be used to mean "to get rid of s.t. important." 解説(1)

2. The Japanese adverb *ne-kosogi* is followed by verbs, such as ~ *ni suru* (to do to ~) in (a) - (c), *haijo-suru* (to eliminate), and *tori-nozoku* (to eliminate).

3. Because the direct object of the English expression cannot be a tangible object, the following sentence sounds strange. However, the Japanese does not have this restriction.

(2) I heard that his ex-wife {took away his property/×pulled his property out by the roots}.
彼は元の奥さんに、財産を根こそぎ持っていかれたそうだ。

REL

The English REL, *root out*, can be used in the same sense as the main entry, as shown in (a) - (c), but it can also be used to mean "to find/expose s.t. problematic," as shown in (1).

(1) The new legislation aims to root out corporate corruption. (→(a))
新しい法律は、企業の腐敗を見つけて公にすることを目的としている。(→(a))

pull the chestnuts out of the fire / phr. / metaphor

to do s.t. risky for s.o. else's benefit

Examples

(a) Taking charge of the company during this recession is like pulling the chestnuts out of the fire.

(b) The teacher knew that class was the hardest to teach, but she decided to pull the chestnuts out of the fire.

(c) He decided to pull the chestnuts out of the fire and assume the post of minister amidst the political turmoil out of love for his country.

同形異義語

足を引っぱる / phr. / 隠喩

誰かの成功や、何かの進行の邪魔をする
to impede s.o.'s success or progress

例文

彼の行動はひとりよがりで、いつもチームの足を引っぱってしまう。
He always does things his own way and ends up holding his team back.

P

根こそぎ(にする) / phr. / 隠喩

すべて取り除く

例文

(a) 新しい法律は、企業の腐敗を根こそぎにすることを目的としている。

(b) 学校側は、いじめ問題を根こそぎにするためのキャンペーンを始めた。

(c) もし、これらの情報漏洩を止めたかったら、我々は二重スパイを根こそぎにする必要がある。

解説

1. 英語は"何か悪い{物/こと}をすべて取り除く"という意味だが、日本語は"大事な{物/こと}をすべて取り除く"場合にも使える。

(1) 彼らは中米の古代遺跡や伝承を根こそぎ破壊した。
They {destroyed/ˣpulled out by the roots} the traditions and artifacts of Central America.

2. 「根こそぎ」は(a)-(c)のように「〜にする」のほか、「排除する」「取り除く」といった動詞と一緒に使われる。

3. 英語の *pull ~ out by the roots* の目的語は触れられないものでなければならないが、日本語にはそのような制約がない。 —📖 **Note(2)**

関連語

英語の関連表現の *root out ~* は見出しと置き換えができるが、意味は見出しの定義「すべて取り除く」((a)-(c))の他に「何か問題のあることを{見つける/公にする}」((1))という意味もある。 —📖 **REL(1)**

火中の栗を拾う / phr. / 隠喩

自分を犠牲にして敢えて危険をおかす

例文

(a) この不況に社長になるなんて火中の栗を拾うようなものだ。

(b) その教師は、そのクラスが一番教えにくいクラスだと知りながら、火中の栗を拾う決断をした。

(c) 国の行く末を思い、この困難な政治状況で、あえて火中の栗を拾う覚悟で大臣の仕事を引き受けた。

493

> **Note**

> While the English and Japanese use different verbs—*pull out* and *hirou* (to pick up), respectively—their figurative meanings are very similar since both originated from the French expression *tirer les marrons du feu* (lit. "to pull the chestnuts out of the fire"). This expression is found in one of the 243 fables written by French poet Jean de La Fontaine (1621-1695). In the fable, a rat convinces a cat to retrieve chestnuts from a fire. The original lesson that La Fontaine wished to instill in his readers was "beware of deception," but in the English and Japanese interpretations, this lesson becomes "help those in need, even if it means sacrificing yourself." The original source for the expression is said to be Aesop's fables, which La Fontaine borrowed from extensively while adding his own creative touch. But as (a) demonstrates, both the English and Japanese can be used in a negative sense as well.

pull the strings / phr. / metaphor

to manipulate s.t. from behind the scenes

REL string-puller

> **Examples**

Mrs. S: They've been investigating this incident for a while now, but it still hasn't been solved.

Mr. S: Yeah. No use arresting small fry. You've got to catch the one who's pulling the strings.

- - - - - - - - - - - - - - - - - - -

(a) The recent rise in gas prices is definitely the result of someone pulling the strings.

(b) "A" may be the head of that country's cabinet, but it's "B" who's pulling the strings.

(c) If you want to make it in this organization, you need to understand who's really pulling the strings.

> **Notes**

1. Both English and Japanese arose independently from the image of a puppeteer pulling the puppet's strings.

2. The English expression assumes a different meaning when the definite article *the* is not used: "to use one's connections with influential people to obtain a desired outcome." See below for examples.

(1) a. If you want to meet the company president, Mr. Jones can pull some strings for you.
   社長に会いたいんだったらジョーンズ氏が{個人的に働きかけて / ˣ裏で糸を引いて}くれるよ。
   b. I'm trying to pull some strings to get an Egyptian passport.
   僕は{コネを使って / ˣ裏で糸を引いて}エジプトの旅券を手に入れようとしているんだ。

REL

1. In the Japanese, *ura* can be replaced by {*ushiro/kage*} (lit. "the {back/shadows}").

📖→関連語 (1)

2. The RELs for the English and Japanese are *string-puller* and {*ura/ushiro/kage*} *de* {*hito/ito*} *o ayatsuru* (to manipulate {people/strings} from {the back/behind/the shadows}), respectively.

(2) I wonder who {is pulling the strings/the string-puller is} in this war.
   この戦争は、誰が{裏 / 後ろ / 陰}で糸を{引いている / 操っている}のだろうか。

解説

日英語の動詞は、それぞれ、「拾う」と *pull out* (引き出す) で異なっているが、比喩的意味は非常に似ている。それはフランスの詩人ジャン・ド・ラ・フォンテーヌ (1621-1695) の書いた243の寓話の一つに出てくるフランス語の文 *tirer les marrons du feu* (lit. 火の栗を引く) が出典だからである。その寓話はねずみが猫をおだてて火中の栗を拾わせるというもので、ラ・フォンテーヌが読者に伝えたかった教訓は「騙されるな」ということなのだが、日英語とも"自分を犠牲にしても苦境に立っている人を助ける"という解釈になっている。大元の出典はイソップ物語で、ラ・フォンテーヌが広範に、しかも想像力を使って利用したと言われている。しかし、日英語とも (a) のような否定的な用法もある。

P

裏で糸を引く　／ phr.　隠喩

見えないところで、誰かが何かを自分の意のままに動かす

関 {後ろ / 陰} で糸を引く，{裏 / 後ろ / 陰} で {人 / 糸} を操る

例文

鈴木 (妻)：この事件、捜査が長引いてなかなか解決しないわね。

鈴木 (夫)：うん、雑魚ばかり逮捕しても仕方がないよ。裏で糸を引いている人間をつかまえないことには。

(a) 最近のガソリン価格の高騰は誰かが裏で糸を引いているに違いない。

(b) その国の閣僚のトップはAだが、裏でAの糸を引いているのはBだ。

(c) この組織でうまくやりたいのなら、誰が裏で糸を引いているのかをちゃんと理解しておくべきです。

解説

1. 日英語とも、人形師が操り人形の糸を引いて操っているイメージからそれぞれ独自に出てきている。

2. 英語では、定冠詞の *the* をとると、"力を持った友人を使って利益を得る"という意味になることに注意。━📖 **Note (1)**

関連語

1. 日本語の「裏」は「{後ろ / 陰}」と置き換えることができる。

(1) 最近のガソリン価格の高騰は誰かが {裏 / 後ろ / 陰} で糸を引いているに違いない。(→(a))

2. 日英語の関連表現は、それぞれ、「{裏 / 後ろ / 陰} で {人 / 糸} を操る」と *string-puller* である。

━📖 **REL (2)**

495

pushy / adj. / metaphor

aggressively assertive

Examples

Mr. S: She's really succeeded in life, hasn't she?

Mrs. S: Yeah, she made it this far by being pushy. She probably made a lot of enemies along the way, though.

(a) He's pushy and arrogant. He always has to have the last word.

(b) The only thing I don't like about her is that she is pushy.

Note

The English is directly related to the verb *push*, but the Japanese consists of the noun *oshi*, which is derived from the verb *osu* (to push), and *tsuyoi* (strong).

---

homograph

put a lid on ~ / phr. / metaphor

to keep s.t. from increasing further
怒る気持ちを抑える

REL LOOK▶ keep a lid on ~

Example

He was upset, too, but he put a lid on his own anger and tried to focus on the problem at hand.

彼も気が動転したんだけど、怒りを抑えて目前の問題に焦点を合わせようとした。

---

put one's body and soul into ~ / phr. / metaphor

to do s.t. with great passion

Examples

(a) Hideyo Noguchi put his body and soul into his research in order to eradicate yellow fever.

(b) Throughout her life, Mother Teresa put her body and soul into saving those who were suffering from poverty and hunger.

押しが強い / phr. / 隠喩

自己主張がひどく強い

例文

鈴木（夫）：彼女、出世したよね。

鈴木（妻）：そうね、押しの強さで、ここまで上って来られたって感じ。でも、たくさん
敵も作ったでしょうね。

(a) 彼は押しが強くて尊大だ。いつも最後の一言を言いたがる。

(b) 彼女について唯一気に入らないことは、押しが強いという点だ。

解説

日本語では「押し」は動詞「押す」の名詞形で「押し」＋「強い」となっているが、英語では動詞の *push*（押す）と直接結びついている。

同形異義語

（〜に）蓋をする / phr. / 隠喩

まずいことを隠す
to conceal s.t. bad

例文

市長は市職員の不正には蓋をする一方で、市税を上げたり公共事業をカットしたりしようとしている。許せない。

The mayor turned a blind eye to wrongdoings by city officials while trying to raise the municipal tax and curtail public services. I cannot condone such behavior.

身も心も（〜に）打ち込む phr. 隠喩

強い情熱をもって何かをする

例文

(a) 野口英世は黄熱病撲滅のため、身も心も研究に打ち込んだ。

(b) マザー・テレサは生涯を通して、貧困や飢餓に苦しむ人たちの救済に身も心も打ち込んだ。

put down roots (in ~) / phr. / metaphor

to settle down in a place

REL take root (in ~)

Examples

Colleague: When I move to a new town, I only feel like I've really put down roots after I join a local gym and start working out there.

Mike: For me, finding a good bookstore is important. I guess it's different for everyone.

- -

(a) He put down roots in the town of Princeton in 1947, and he taught mathematics at the university until he retired in the mid-70s.

(b) We would love to put down roots in this community and start a family here.

REL

The English and Japanese RELs are *take root (in ~)* and *nezuku*, respectively. *Nezuku* cannot take a human subject, but *ne o orosu* can take both human and nonhuman subjects. As for the English expressions, *put down roots (in ~)* is usually used with a human subject, whereas *take root (in ~)* is used with a nonhuman subject. 📖→ 関連語(1)

put ~ heads together / phr. / metonymy

to share ideas in order to solve a problem

REL Two heads are better than one.

Examples

(a) After their father passed away, his children put their heads together and discussed how to deal with the inheritance.

(b) The high school students put their heads together to come up with ideas for improving the robot they created this summer for the first time.

(c) The villagers put their heads together in preparation for future natural disasters and came up with ideas for preventing damage.

Notes

1. While the English and Japanese use different verbs—*put* and *yose-au* (to draw close to each other), respectively—they are essentially the same metaphor. *Yose-au* often takes the *te*-form, *yose-atte*.

2. *Yose-au* can be used to denote discussions, similar to *giron-suru* (to argue) and *hanasu* (to discuss), but the content being discussed must be serious in nature. The English expression has no such restriction. Since the content of (1) is not serious in nature, the Japanese expression cannot be used. 📖→ 解説(1)

（〜に）根を下ろす　/ phr.　隠喩

定住する

関 （〜に）根付く

例文

同僚：新しい町に引っ越したときって、そこのスポーツジムに入会して運動を始めると、ようやくその土地に根を下ろしたって感じになるね。

マイク：僕はいい本屋を見つけることが重要かな。誰にも違ったやり方があるんだね。

（a） 彼は1947年以来、プリンストンの町に根を下ろし、そこの大学で70年代の半ばまで数学を教えた。

（b） 私達はこの地域社会に根を下ろして、自分達の家庭を築きたいんです。

関連語

日英語の関連表現に、それぞれ「（〜に）根付く」と *take root (in ~)* がある。日本語の関連表現の「根付く」は人間を主語にとれないが、見出しの「（〜に）根を下ろす」は人間でもそれ以外のものでも構わない。一方、英語の見出しの *put down roots (in ~)* は普通は人間を主語にとり、*take root (in ~)* は人間以外のものを主語にとる。

(1)a. ダンは京都に住んで1年もたたないのに、もう地域社会に｛根を下ろして /?? 根付いて｝いる。
Although he has been in Kyoto less than a year, Dan has already put down roots in the community.

　　b. 欧米の習慣で日本に｛根を下ろした / 根付いた｝ものはたくさんある。
Many European and American customs have taken root in Japan.

額を寄せ合う　/ phr.　換喩

複数の人が集まって何か問題点について話し合ったり、相談したりする

関 三人寄れば文殊の知恵，知恵を出し合う

例文

（a） 父が亡くなった後、子供達は遺産相続の方法について額を寄せ合って相談した。

（b） 自分たちがこの夏に初めて作製したロボットの改善案を考えるため、高校生たちは額を寄せ合った。

（c） これからの自然災害に備えて村の住民たちは額を寄せ合って今後の災害防止策を考案した。

解説

1. 日英語はそれぞれ違った動詞、「寄せ合う」と *put*（置く）を使っているが、基本的には同じ比喩表現である。日本語は「寄せ合って」という形で使われることが多い。

2. 日本語は「寄せ合って」と使う動詞が、「議論する」「話し合う」のような議論関係の動詞であり、議論の内容がかなり深刻なものでなければならないが、英語ではこのような制約がない。(1) は話し合いの内容が深刻ではないので、日本語の見出しは使えない。

(1)｛知恵を出し合って /× 額を寄せ合って｝先生の百歳のお誕生日に何を差し上げたらいいかを考えましょう。
Let's put our heads together and figure out what we can give our teacher for his 100th birthday.

499

REL

1. Both English and Japanese have proverbs related to the main entries: *two heads are better than one* and *san-nin yoreba monju no chie*, respectively. The Japanese proverb means "if three people put their heads together, they can generate the wisdom of Manjushri." Manjushri was a disciple of Buddha who was renowned for his wisdom.
2. The Japanese has another REL, *chie o dashi-au* (lit. "to show wisdom to each other").

解説(1)

put ~ on the shelf　*phr.*　metaphor

to postpone s.t.

REL　shelve ~

Examples

Section Chief: Mike, could you look into that matter that was put on the shelf last year?

Mike: Yes, sir.

- -

(a) They've put reforming the law on the shelf for now.

(b) The construction of the new college dorms has been put on the shelf until 2000.

Notes

1. Both the English and Japanese are often used in the passive voice because the agent is usually unspecified.
2. The English can be used to describe someone who has been made unavailable for some reason, as shown in (1), but the Japanese cannot be used this way.

(1) He was put on the shelf due to a knee injury.
彼は膝の怪我で{休まざるを得なかった/*棚上げにされた}。

REL

The English REL, *shelve ~*, has the same meaning as the main entry, but uses the verb *shelve* instead of *put ~ on the shelf*.

(1) The construction of the new college dorms has been {put on the shelf/shelved} until 2000.
(→(b))

put pressure on ~　*phr.*　metaphor

to force s.o. to do s.t.

Examples

Mr. S: Kenta, are you getting yourself prepared to study abroad?

Mrs. S You haven't even started, have you? You're too busy working part-time.

Kenta: Actually, I'm working on it. I really wish you guys would stop putting pressure on me.

- -

関連語

1. 日英語とも関連のことわざの「三人寄れば文殊の知恵」と *Two heads are better than one* がある。字義通りには"複数の頭のほうが一つよりいい"という意味である。「文殊」とは釈迦の弟子の一人でその知恵で知られている。
2. 日本語には「知恵を出し合う」という関連表現もある。📖▶解説(1)

棚上げにする　phr.　隠喩

大事な{問題の解決 /計画の実現}を一時延期して手をつけない

例文

課長：マイク、去年の暮れ以来棚上げにしてある例の案件、もう一度、検討してみてくれるかな。

マイク： はい、承知しました。

- -

(a) 町の法律の改正は、現在のところ棚上げにされている。
(b) 大学の寮の新築工事は2000年まで棚上げされていた。

解説

1. 日英語とも、延期する行為者は不特定多数の場合が多いので、通常受け身文で使われることが多い。
2. 英語は、人がある状況のために何かができない場合にも使えるが、日本語にはそのような使い方はない。📖▶Note(1)

関連語

英語には *shelve ~* という見出しと同じ意味の関連表現がある。*put ~ on the shelf* の代わりに動詞の *shelve* を用いる。📖▶REL(1)

(〜に)プレッシャーをかける　phr.　隠喩

個人に対して何かをするように精神的な圧迫感を与える

関 (〜に)圧力をかける

例文

鈴木(夫)：健太、留学準備の勉強は進んでるのか?
鈴木(妻)：全然よね、健太。バイトばかりしてるでしょ。
健太：ちゃんと考えてるよ。そんな二人揃ってプレッシャーをかけないでほしいな。

- -

501

(a) My parents put pressure on me to find a better job almost every day.

(b) Seems the coach is putting pressure on us so he can lead us to victory.

(c) There's no doubt he put pressure on himself to recover from his injury.

Note

While the Japanese is clearly derived from the English, the English uses the verb *put* while the Japanese uses *kakeru* (to hang).

REL

In addition to the main entry, Japanese has the REL *(~ ni) atsuryoku o kakeru*. *Atsuryoku* is a Sino-Japanese compound that means "pressure." But as demonstrated in the examples above, *(~ ni) puresshā o kakeru* is usually used in personal situations, whereas *(~ ni) atsuryoku o kakeru* is typically used in situations that do not directly apply to oneself. The English expression, on the other hand, does not have any of the aforementioned restrictions. 関連語(1)

put one's (heart and) soul into ~   phr.   metaphor

to completely devote oneself to s.t.

REL   pour one's heart and soul into ~; give one's whole mind to ~

Examples

(a) That artisan put his heart and soul into creating the pot, and it captivated multitudes.

(b) She has put her heart and soul into the project over the past four years.

(c) My job as an astronaut is to tell kids that their dreams can come true, and that there are so many things they can accomplish if they just put their heart and soul into it.

Note

The English and Japanese make metaphorical use of the verbs *put* and *katamukeru* (to {tilt/devote}), respectively.

REL

English has the related expressions *pour one's heart and soul into ~*, and *give one's whole mind to ~*. These expressions can replace the main entry in the example sentences. Japanese has the related expressions *(~ni) sēkon o komeru*, *(~ni) sēkon o sosogu*, and *(~ni) tansē o komeru*. For the first expression, only the verb is different, so it can replace the main entry in all of the example sentences. The second expression, however, means to devote oneself to creating something, so it can only be used in (a). 関連語(1)

(a) 両親はもっといい仕事を探せ、と毎日のようにプレッシャーをかけてくるんだ。

(b) コーチはわれわれにプレッシャーをかけて、勝利に導こうとしているらしい。

(c) 彼は怪我からカムバックしたいと思って、自分にプレッシャーをかけたにちがいないよ。

解説

日本語は、明らかに英語からの借用であるが、動詞が「かける」と put（置く）で異なっていることに注意。

関連語

日本語では、見出しに含まれる借用語「プレッシャー」と並んで漢語系複合語の「圧力」を含んだ「（〜に）圧力をかける」も使える。「（〜に）プレッシャーをかける」は例文のように通常は個人に対して使われるが、「（〜に）圧力をかける」は(1b)のように公的場面で使われることが多い。一方、英語の put pressure on 〜 は個人的な場面でも公的場面でも使える。

(1) a. そんな二人揃って{プレッシャー /^{??}圧力}をかけないでほしいな。（→会話例）

b. 彼は{圧力 /[?]プレッシャー}をかけてニュースの批判性を弱めようとしたことはないと言った。
He has denied putting pressure on the media to make the news less critical.

（〜に）精魂（を）傾ける　phr.　隠喩

一生懸命気持ちを込めて何かをする

関 （〜に）精魂（を）{込める / 注ぐ}，（〜に）丹精（を）込める

例文

(a) あの職人が精魂傾けて作った壺は人々の心を魅了した。

(b) 彼女は過去4年間、そのプロジェクトに精魂を傾けた。

(c) 宇宙飛行士としての私の仕事は、夢は実現するということと、精魂を傾けさえすれば多くのことが遂行できる、ということを子供達に話すことです。

解説

日英語はそれぞれ「傾ける」と put という動詞を隠喩として使っている。

関連語

英語には pour one's heart and soul into 〜, give one's whole mind to 〜 がある。英語の関連表現は put one's heart and soul into 〜 と置き換えることができる。日本語には「（〜に）精魂を{込める / 注ぐ}」と「（〜に）丹精を込める」がある。一つ目は見出しとは動詞が違うだけで、すべての例文で使えるが、二つ目は物作りに真心を込めるという意味なので、(a)でしか使えない。

(1) あの職人が{精魂傾けて / 精魂込めて / 精魂注いで / 丹精込めて}作った壺は人々の心を魅了した。（→(a)）
That artisan {{put/poured} his heart and soul into/gave his whole mind to} creating the pot, and it captivated multitudes. （→(a)）

put the brakes on / phr. / metaphor

to slow down an ongoing activity

Examples

Mr. S: My head is killing me. I had way too much to drink with my buddies last night.

Mrs. S: Honey, maybe you need to put the brakes on the drinking for a while. I know work relationships are important, but you have to think of your health, too.

(a) The automobile company's labor disputes put the brakes on exports.

(b) The government is determined to put the brakes on public spending.

(c) Poor infrastructure is putting the brakes on development of that country.

Note

The English is a driving-related metaphor, with other examples being *get into high gear*, *step on {it/the gas}*, *shift gears*, and so on. The Japanese is clearly borrowed from the English.

REL

The Japanese REL *hadome o kakeru* (lit. "to put a drag on") is an original Japanese expression that can be used to mean "to hinder s.t. bad," as in (1a), but it cannot be used to mean "to hinder s.t. good," as in (1b). 📖→関連語(1)

---

put one's thoughts together (考えをまとめる)→ {get/put} one's thoughts together

---

put up a smokescreen / phr. / metaphor

to do or say s.t. to conceal one's true intentions or behavior

REL be a smokescreen for ~

Examples

(a) I think my husband is having an affair. But whenever I press him, he puts up a smokescreen and evades the issue.

(b) The principal thought that if she told the students what actually happened, they might feel hurt, so she put up a smokescreen when answering their questions.

(c) We have a tendency to lay the blame elsewhere and put up a smokescreen to hide our own faults.

Note

The original meaning of the English and Japanese is "to put up a screen of smoke in battle to prevent the enemy from seeing a military force and its activities." The Japanese expression is borrowed from Chinese.

（〜に）ブレーキをかける　／ phr.　隠喩

何かの進行を{遅くする/止める}

関 歯止めをかける

例文

鈴木（夫）：いやあ、頭が痛い。夕べは同僚とちょっと飲み過ぎちゃったよ。

鈴木（妻）：またですか。あまり飲み過ぎないように、ブレーキをかけてくださいよ。付き合いが大事なことはわかっているけど、自分の体のことも考えなくちゃ。

- (a) 自動車会社の労働争議は、輸出にブレーキをかけた。
- (b) 政府は、公共支出にブレーキをかけるつもりだ。
- (c) 貧しいインフラが、その国の発展にブレーキをかけている。

解説

英語は車の運転に関係する英語の比喩表現、例えば、*get into high gear*（最高調）、*step on the [it/the gas]*（急ぐ）、*shift gears*（扱い方を変える）などの系列に属する。日本語は明らかに英語からの借用である。

関連語

日本語には「歯止めをかける」という日本語本来の表現があるが、これは(1a)のように"何か良くないことを阻止する"という意味では使えるが、"何か良いことを阻止する"(1b)のような場合には使いにくい。

- (1)a. アジア地域にもっと自由で、積極的なニュースメディアがあったら、政治の腐敗に{ブレーキ/歯止め}をかけられるだろう。

  If Asian regions had freer and more proactive news media, it might be possible to put the brakes on corruption in politics.

- b. 貧しいインフラが、その国の発展に{ブレーキ/^{??}歯止め}をかけている。（→(c)）

煙幕を張る　／ phr.　隠喩

本当の意図や行動を隠すために、あいまいな態度をとる

関 〜の煙幕だ, 煙にまく

例文

- (a) 私は夫が浮気していると思うんだけど、問いつめるといつもうまく煙幕を張って逃げるのよね。
- (b) 校長先生は、本当に起きたことを伝えると子供達が傷付くと考えて、子供達の質問に煙幕を張って答えた。
- (c) 私達は責任を他になすりつけ、自分の間違いを隠すために煙幕を張る傾向がある。

解説

日英語とも"戦いのとき、こちらの軍隊とその行動を敵から隠すために幕のように広く煙を拡散させる"という意味である。日本語は中国語からの借用である。

REL

1. The English REL *be a smokescreen for* ~ and the Japanese REL ~ *no enmaku da* are used in the same manner. 📖→ 関連語(1)
2. The Japanese REL *kemu ni maku* is a commonly used expression that means "to boggle s.o.'s mind by bombarding them with things they do not know." 📖→ 関連語(2)

race against time, a / n. phr. / metaphor

attempting to do s.t. quickly to meet a deadline

REL a race against the clock

Examples

Saya: Kenta, how was the TOEFL exam?

Kenta: Not so great. They give you so little time. You only get 15 seconds per question, so there's so much pressure.

Saya: Wow, talk about a race against time.

- - - - - - - - - - - - - - - - - - - -

(a) In the emergency room, doctors are always in a race against time to save people's lives.

(b) When a huge accident or disaster happens, the press is in a race against time to cover the situation accurately.

Note

Note that the English uses the preposition *against*, whereas the Japanese uses the particle *to no* (with).

REL

1. The English REL is *a race against the clock*.
(1) I was working on getting the new program off the ground. From February to September, it was a race against time/the clock.
私は新しい企画を立ち上げようとしていた。2月から9月は{時間/ ×時計}との競争だった。
2. The Japanese REL, *jikan to no tatakai*, is more colloquial than *jikan to no kyōsō*.

📖→ 関連語(2)

rack one's brain(s) / phr. / metaphor

to think very hard (for a long time); often to remember s.t.

REL rack one's head; strain one's wits

Examples

Saya: Hey, Kenta, have you solved this math problem?

Kenta: Nope. I racked my brain, but it was no use.

関連語

1. 日英語とも「〜の煙幕だ」be a smokescreen for ～ という同じ使い方がある。
(1) 彼の微笑みは傲慢さの煙幕にすぎない。
His smile is nothing but a smokescreen for arrogance.
2. 日本語には関連表現として、"相手の知らないようなことばかり言い立てて、相手を圧倒したり、ごまかしたりする"という意味の「煙（けむ）にまく」というよく使う表現がある。
(2) このあいだ、そのことをちらっと聞いてみたら、うまく{煙幕張ってた/煙にまかれちゃった}けど、なんかうれしそうだったよ。
When I tried asking him about it recently, he tried evading the issue, but he looked happy.

時間との競争 （じかんとのきょうそう） n. phr. 隠喩（いんゆ）

締切に追われながら何かをすること（しめきりにおわれながらなにかをすること）

関 時間との戦い（じかんとのたたかい）

例文

さや：健太、TOEFL の試験、どうだった？

健太：あまり、よくなかったよ。ひとつの問題に解答する時間がとても短いんだ。一問、15秒以内なんだよ。プレッシャーが大きくて。

さや：へえ、まさに、時間との競争ね。

(a) 救急医療の現場では、医師は人命を救うためにいつも時間との競争だ。
(b) 大事故や、大災害のときは、報道関係者は時間との競争の中で、現状を正確に報告しなければならない。

解説

日英語で、助詞「との」と前置詞 against（に対して）をそれぞれ使うことに注意。

関連語

1. 英語には a race against the clock（lit. 時計との競争）という関連表現がある。 ─📖 REL（1）
2. 日本語には関連語として「時間との競争」よりも会話的な「時間との戦い」という表現がある。
(2) 救急医療の現場では、医師は人命を救うためにいつも{時間との競争/時間との戦い}だ。
（→（a））

頭を絞る （あたまをしぼる） phr. 隠喩（いんゆ）

何か難しい問題について限界までよく考える（なにかむずかしいもんだいについてげんかいまでよくかんがえる）

関 頭をひねる，知恵を絞る（あたまをひねる，ちえをしぼる）

例文

さや：どう、健太、この数学の問題、解けた？

健太：だめ。必死に頭を絞ったけど、ギブアップ。

Saya: That's sad. My younger brother solved it in five minutes. Then again, I couldn't solve it either.

Kenta: Guess we're both pretty sad.

- - - - - - - - - - - - - - - - - - - -

(a) The people in charge of new product development were racking their brains all day long trying to come up with a name for the new product.

(b) We racked our brains to figure out what steps we could take to implement her suggestions.

Notes

1. Both the English and Japanese expressions can be used to mean "to try hard to solve a problem," but the crucial difference is that, while the English is often used to mean "to try hard to remember s.t.," the Japanese is not used that way, as shown below.

(1) I racked my brains trying to remember her name.
僕は{一生懸命 /⁇ 頭を絞って}彼女の名前を思い出そうとした。

2. The English expression is often used along with "trying to ~" as shown in (a) and Note (1). ┄📖┄ **Note(1)**

3. The English uses the verb *rack* (to torture by stretching the body/limbs), while the Japanese uses the verb *shiboru* (to wring s.t. dry). The Japanese direct object *atama* can mean either "the part of the body that contains the eyes, ears, nose, and mouth" or "the brain matter," while the English simply refers to the brain. Interestingly, the expression *rack one's head*, which replaces *brains* with *head*, can also be used, though it is much less common than the main entry.

REL

Atama o shiboru can be replaced by *atama o hineru* and *chie o shiboru*. Out of these three, *atama o hineru* is used the most frequently. The meaning of the phrase *chie o shiboru* is very close to that of *strain one's wits.* 📖┄ 関連語(**1**)

raise eyebrows / **phr.** **metonymy**

to cause disapproval, worry, shock, etc.

Examples

(a) His strange behavior raised eyebrows among the students in his class.

(b) In a small town like this, wearing anything too flashy will raise eyebrows.

(c) The report I worked so hard on ended up just raising the eyebrows of the section chief and getting thrown back at me.

Note

Both the English and Japanese expressions refer to a non-verbal cue that indicates mild disapproval, among other things. However, the English uses the verb *raise*, which means "to cause {s.t./s.o.} to move to a higher place or level," while the Japanese uses *hiso-meru*, which means "to frown."

REL

The Japanese REL *mayu o tsuri-ageru* (to raise one's eyebrows) is used to refer to someone getting angry. As shown in (1), *mayu o tsuri-ageru* can be used to express anger, but *mayu o hisomeru* cannot. 📖┄ 関連語(**1**)

さや：なさけないわね。私の弟なんか5分よ。ま、私はできなかったけどね。

健太：なんだ。さやもか。

(a) 新製品開発担当者らは新製品の命名のことで終日頭を絞っていた。

(b) 彼女の提案を実現するにはどんな方法があるかと、私たちは頭を絞った。

解説

1. 日英語とも"問題を解決する努力をする"という意味があるが、決定的な違いは英語が"何かを一生懸命思い出そうとする"という意味で頻繁に使われるのに対して、日本語ではそのように使われることはあまりないという点である。➡️📖 Note(**1**)

2. 英語では、(a)とNote(1)のように、*rack one's brains trying to* ~ という文型で使われることが多い。➡️📖 Note(**1**)

3. 日英語は動詞が「絞る」と *rack*（拷問で台の上で体、手足を極限まで引っ張る）で、異なっている。日本語の目的語の「頭」は「目、鼻、口、耳のある体の部分、あるいは脳みそ"という意味であるが、英語 *brain(s)* は「脳」そのものである。興味深いことに、使用頻度は *rack one's brains* よりはるかに低いが、*rack one's head* も可能である。

関連語

日本語の「頭を絞る」は「頭をひねる」「知恵を絞る」と置き換えられるが、3つの中では「頭をひねる」が一番使用頻度が高い。「知恵を絞る」は"能(→脳)から知恵を絞り出す"という意味で英語の *strain one's wits* に対応する。

(1) 彼女は質問に答えようとして｛頭を絞った/頭をひねった/知恵を絞った｝。
She {racked her brain/racked her head/strained her wits} trying to answer the question.

眉をひそめる　*phr.*　換喩

眉根を寄せて、軽い不満、心配、不快、不信、理解不能などの心理を表す

関 眉をつりあげる

例文

(a) 彼の奇妙な行動を見て、クラスの誰もが眉をひそめた。

(b) こんな小さい町では、派手なものを着ると、それが何であれ、人々は眉をひそめますよ。

(c) 頑張ってまとめた報告書を課長に提出したら、課長はただ眉をひそめて私につき返した。

解説

日英語とも、軽い不満を表す表情である。動詞は、日本語では「ひそめる」"眉の間にしわを寄せる"で、英語は *raise* "高い｛ところ/レベル｝に｛何か/誰か｝を上げる"と異なっている。

関連語

日本語には、「眉をつりあげる」という関連表現があるが、これは「眉をひそめる」と違って怒ったときの表情である。下の例文(1)が示すように、日本語の関連表現「眉をつり上げる」は怒りを表現できるが、「眉をひそめる」は怒りを表現できない。

raise the white flag phr. metaphor

to admit one's defeat and surrender

REL hoist the white flag

Examples

(a) After a long war against the government, the tobacco companies finally raised the white flag.

(b) The opponent had no choice but to raise the white flag after the 40-plus player's amazing feat.

(c) The actress's complete lack of emotion forced the director to raise the white flag.

Notes

1. In the West, white is a symbol of peace, and a white flag was typically used in war to indicate that one does not have the will to fight any longer. Japan learned about this Western tradition when the United States' Commodore Matthew Calbraith Perry came to Japan with his black ships to open diplomatic and commercial relations with Japan on July 8, 1853. It is said that he delivered a white flag to the Edo government along with a letter in which he explained that, since Japan could not defeat the U.S., the white flag should be used by Japan to show that it would surrender to the American request to open the country.

2. It is difficult to use the Japanese expression when the context does not make it clear who or what is competing. 📖 解説(**1**)

REL

The English verb *raise* can be replaced by *hoist,* though this is used less frequently. The Japanese verb *kakageru* (to hoist) can be replaced by *ageru* (to raise). 📖 関連語(**1**)

---

homograph

rake in ~ / phr. / metaphor

to gain large amounts of s.t.
簡単に大儲けする
かんたん　おおもう

Example

That lawyer is raking in money as the legal counsel for various companies.
その弁護士は様々な会社の法律顧問として金を集めている。
べんごし　さまざま　かいしゃ　ほうりつこもん　　　　かね　あつ

510

(1) 父は姉の反抗的な態度に{眉をつりあげて/˟眉をひそめて}激怒した。

My older sister's rebellious attitude made her father explode in anger.

白旗を掲げる　　phr.　　換喩

敗北を認めて降参する

関 白旗を上げる

例文

(a) 政府との長い抗争の末、タバコ会社はようやく白旗を掲げた。

(b) 選手の40歳過ぎての快挙に、相手の選手も白旗を掲げるしかなかった。

(c) その女優のあまりのストイックさに、監督も白旗を掲げざるを得なかった。

解説

1. 西洋では白は平和の象徴で、兵士が戦闘を続ける意志のないことを示すために白い旗の形で示した。日本がこの西洋の伝統を学んだのは、ペリー総督が日本との外交通商関係を結ぶために1853年7月8日に黒船に乗ってきたときである。江戸幕府に白旗を届け、親書の中で「日本はアメリカにもちろんかなうわけがないから、白旗は日本が開国に応じることを示すために届ける」と書かれていたという。

2. 日本語では文脈に「争い」の意味が含まれていないと使いにくくなる。

(1) 解析幾何学の第2学期目まで来て、私は{お手上げになった/˟白旗を掲げた}。

I got as far as the second semester of analytical geometry before I raised the white flag.

関連語

日本語の動詞は「上げる」で置き換えられる。英語の動詞は使用頻度はずっと低いが、*hoist*（掲げる）で置き換えることができる。

(1) 政府との長い戦いの末、タバコ会社はようやく白旗を{掲げた/上げた}。(→(a))

After a long war against the government, the tobacco companies finally {raised/hoisted} the white flag. (→(a))

同形異義語

金をかき集める　/ phr. / 隠喩

金をいろいろなところから集める
to gather money from all sorts of places

例文

金が僅かしかなかったので、部屋代を払う金をあちこちからかき集めなければならなかった。

I had so little money that I had to put together money for my rent from here and there.

511

ray of sunshine, a | n. phr. | metaphor

{s.o./s.t.} that lifts others' mood during a difficult time

REL a ray of hope

Examples

(a) Our family has experienced a series of misfortunes, but the baby we had last month has been a ray of sunshine for us.

(b) The discovery of the new drug was a ray of sunshine for those who had been diagnosed with the previously incurable disease.

(c) The fact that the construction business has begun to show life is a ray of sunshine for our country's long-stagnant economy.

Note

While *ray* indicates an actual beam of light, *jō* means "a streak."

REL

The English and Japanese RELs, *a ray of hope* and *kibō no hikari* (lit. "light of hope"), respectively, are very similar to one another.

(1) As long as there's but a single ray of hope for a better future, I want to keep pushing forward.
希望の光がある限り、私は元気を出して前進したいと思う。

reach {a/the} conclusion | phr. | metaphor

to finish deliberations and decide s.t.

REL come to a conclusion

Examples

Mike: Chief, upon completing a very careful review of the data and discussing it with everyone, I've reached the conclusion that it's too early to begin the project. We should hold off a little longer.

Section Chief: Okay. I think we should take your advice this time.

- -

(a) With the Pythagorean theorem, no matter how you try to solve it, you always end up reaching the same conclusion.

(b) After lots of discussion, they both reached the conclusion that it would be best to get divorced.

Notes

1. Both *tassuru* and *reach* are verbs of movement that mean "to get to a point in space."

2. As shown in (b), *reach the conclusion that ~* and *~ to iu ketsuron ni tassuru* are common usages of the main entries.

REL

1. The Japanese can be replaced by *ketsuron ni tōtatsu suru*, though this is more formal and less common than the main entry. 📖➡関連語(1)

一条の光 <ruby>一<rt>いち</rt></ruby><ruby>条<rt>じょう</rt></ruby>の<ruby>光<rt>ひかり</rt></ruby> / n. phr. / 隠喩

苦しいときのわずかな希望

関 希望の光

例文

(a) 我が家にとって不幸が続いたが、先月生まれた赤ちゃんは家族にとって一条の光となった。

(b) その新薬の発見は、かつて不治の病と診断された人々に一条の光を投げかけた。

(c) 建設業界が活気づいていることは、長く低迷するわが国の経済に一条の光となっている。

解説

日本語の「条」(a streak)に対して、英語の *ray* はそれ自体 "一条の光" を意味する。

関連語

日英語ともに「希望の光」と *a ray of hope* という非常に近い関連表現がある。 REL(1)

R

結論に達する <ruby>結<rt>けつ</rt></ruby><ruby>論<rt>ろん</rt></ruby>に<ruby>達<rt>たっ</rt></ruby>する / phr. / 隠喩

結論にたどり着く

関 結論に到達する

例文

マイク: 課長、このプロジェクト、今の段階では早すぎるので、もう少し待ってみたほうがいいと思うんですが。いろいろデータを検討し、皆で話し合った結果、そういう結論に達しました。

課長: そうだね。今回は、君の意見に従ったほうがいいかもしれないね。

(a) ピタゴラスの定理はどんな解き方をしても、最終的には同じ結論に達する。

(b) 長い間話し合った末、二人は離婚するのが一番いいという結論に達した。

解説

1. 日英語の動詞はそれぞれ「達する」*reach* という移動の動詞であり、"空間(の1点)に行き着く" という意味である。

2. (b)のように、日英語とも「～という結論に達する」*reach the conclusion that ~* という文型になることが多い。

関連語

1. 日本語の見出しは「結論に到達する」で置き換えることができる。これは「達する」よりも使用頻度が低く、より書き言葉的である。

(1) ソクラテスは、いかにして為政者は常に統治する者の利益のために統治するという結論に｛達した/到達した｝のだろうか。

How did Socrates reach the conclusion that rulers always rule for the benefit of their subjects?

513

2. The English can be replaced by *come to a conclusion*.

(2) With the Pythagorean theorem, no matter how you try to solve it, you always end up {reaching/coming to} the same conclusion. (→(a))

reach an agreement / phr. / metaphor

to agree after a long negotiation

Examples

(a) After a month of debating the issue, the Diet reached an agreement to raise the consumption tax by 2%.

(b) Even after more than two weeks of the president trying to persuade them, they were unable to reach an agreement about the territorial dispute between Israel and Palestine.

(c) Labor and management have reached a tentative agreement that will avert the strikes slated to begin at midnight tonight.

Note

Both *tassuru* and *reach* are verbs of movement that mean "to get to a point in space." They can be replaced by *come to* and *tōtatsu-suru*, respectively. 📖→解説(1)

{reach/come to} s.o.'s ears / phr. / metaphor

for information to become known to s.o.

Examples

Colleague: Mike, I heard that you landed a big contract.

Mike: Yeah. I'm glad it went so well.

Colleague: Apparently the news reached the president's ears. You might even receive a reward. Congratulations!

Mike: Thanks!

- -

(a) When the rumor about my mentor's retirement reached my ears, I was shocked.

(b) Not a sound reached our ears except the distant booming from the battlefront.

Note

The English can also use the verb *enter*, but this is much less common than *reach* or *come to*. The Japanese uses the verb *hairu* (to enter) much more frequently than *todoku* (to reach), especially in spoken Japanese.

REL

The Japanese REL is *mimi ni ireru*, which means "to tell s.o. about s.t." 📖→関連語(1)

2．英語の見出しは *come to a conclusion* で置き換えることができる。 ➡📖 REL（2）

合意に達する　／ phr.　隠喩

長い交渉の末、同じ意見に到達する

【例文】
(a) 1ヵ月以上にわたる討議の末、議会は2％の消費税アップで合意に達した。
(b) 大統領の2週間以上に及ぶ説得にもかかわらず、イスラエルとパレスチナは領土問題で合意に達することはできなかった。
(c) 労使は、今晩12時に予定されていたストライキを回避する暫定的な合意に達した。

【解説】
「達する」と *reach* はどちらも移動の動詞で、"空間（の1点）に行き着く"という意味である。それぞれ「到達する」と *come to* に置き換えることができる。
(1) 教員組合と市議会は2年契約の更新に関して合意に{達した/到達した}。
The teachers' union and the city council have {reached/come to} an agreement on a new two-year contract.

（〜の）耳に{入る/届く}　／ phr.　隠喩

物音、人の話、うわさなどが聞こえてくる

【関】耳に入れる

【例文】
同僚：マイク、大きい契約が取れたんだって？
マイク：うん、うまくいってよかったよ。

同僚：社長の耳にも入っているらしいよ。社長賞が出るかもな。おめでとう。
マイク：ありがとう。

- -

(a) お世話になった人が退職するといううわさが耳に入り、ショックを受けた。
(b) 戦場から聞こえてくる遠くのドーンという音以外、耳に届く音は何ひとつなかった。

【解説】
英語は日本語の「入る」に対応する動詞 *enter* も使えるが、*reach* と *come to* よりは使用頻度がずっと低い。日本語では「届く」よりも「入る」のほうが特に会話でははるかによく使われる。

【関連語】
日本語には関連表現として「人に情報を知らせる」という意味の「耳に入れる」がある。
(1) 大学院に行きたいので会社を辞めるかもしれないということを上司の耳に入れておいた。
I told my boss in advance that I might leave the company because I want to go to graduate school.

reach the boiling point / phr. / metaphor

for emotions or a situation to get out of control

REL fly into a rage

Examples

(a) We mumble and grumble until things reach the boiling point and we explode in anger.

(b) My father reached his boiling point when he learned that my older sister had eloped with a man who was married with children.

(c) His favorite baseball team was losing by 8 points, but when they made an amazing comeback, his excitement reached the boiling point.

Note

In both English and Japanese, the main entries are usually used to describe anger, but they can also describe someone's passion, as in (c). In addition, the English expression can also be used to describe situations that get out of control.

(1) Tensions with the region have reached a boiling point, and some fear that war is inevitable.
その地域では緊張状態がコントロールできないほど高まり、戦争は避けられないと恐れる者もいる。

REL

1. The English and Japanese RELs are *fly into a rage* and *ikari shintō ni hassuru*, respectively.
📖→関連語(1)

2. Both *reach* and *tassuru* are verbs of movement that mean "to get to a point in space." The Japanese verb can be replaced by *tōtatsu-suru*. 📖→関連語(2)

read between the lines / phr. / metaphor

to try to understand s.o.'s real feelings or intentions from what they say or write

Examples

(a) To understand what Japanese people write, you have to practice reading between the lines. There is tendency for Japanese to use roundabout expressions to say what they mean.

(b) When you are reading literature, sometimes a different perspective reveals itself if you try reading between the lines rather than just what is on the surface.

(c) It is very difficult to read between the lines and understand the text as the writer intended it to be understood.

Notes

1. The English expression can be used to refer to a speaker as well as a writer's intention. But the Japanese can only be used in reference to writing.

(1) Our boss is too polite and indirect. When he talks to you, you always have to read between the lines to understand what he really means.
私たちのボスはばか丁寧で、言い方が遠回しすぎる。彼がものを言うときは、本音を理解するのにいつも{注意深く聞かないと/×行間を読まないと}いけないんだからね。

2. It is quite likely that the Japanese expression *gyōkan* comes from a Chinese compound *zi-li-hang-jian*, where *hang-jian* and *zi-li* mean "between the lines" and "the other side of the Chinese character," respectively.

沸点に達する /phr. 隠喩

{怒り/興奮}が我慢できなくなるほどにまで高まる

関 沸点に到達する，怒り心頭に発する

例文

(a) 私たちはぶつぶつ文句を言い、最後には怒りが沸点に達して爆発するのです。

(b) 姉が妻子ある男性と駆け落ちしたと知って、父の怒りは沸点に達した。

(c) 彼のひいきの野球チームが8点差をひっくり返して逆転した時、彼の興奮は沸点に達した。

解説

日英語ともにこの見出しは普通は怒りを表現するために使われるが、(c)のように情熱を表現する場合にも使われる。また、英語の見出しは、ある状況が制御できなくなる場合にも使われる。➡Note(1)

関連語

1. 日英語には、それぞれ関連語として「怒り心頭に発する」と*fly into a rage* がある。

(1) 姉が妻子ある男性と駆け落ちしたと知って、{父の怒りは沸点に達した/父は怒り心頭に発した}。(→(b))

2. 日本語の「達する」と英語の*reach* はともに"空間(の一点)に行き着く"という意味の動詞である。「達する」は「到達する」に置き換えることができる。➡REL(2)

(2) 私たちはぶつぶつ文句を言い、最後には怒りが沸点に{達して/到達して}爆発するのです。

(→(a))

行間を読む /phr. 隠喩

筆者が文章の中で明言しなかったことを推察して真意を理解する

例文

(a) 日本人の書いた文を理解するには、行間を読む訓練が必要だ。日本人は本当に伝えたいことを遠回しに表現する傾向があるから。

(b) 文学を読んでいるとき、表面に現れているものだけでなく、行間を読んでみると、また別の面が見えてくることがある。

(c) 作者の意図した通りに行間を読むのはとても難しい。

解説

1. 日本語は書き手の意図がわからないときにしか使えないが、英語は書き手だけに限らず話し手の意図がわからないときにも使える。➡Note(1)

2. 日本語の「行間」という表現は中国語の「字裏行間」から来ている可能性が高い。

read s.o.'s face   *phr.* / metaphor

to detect how s.o. feels

REL LOOK▶ read s.o.'s mind

Examples

(a) "I just want to offer you some sort of apology," she said. But I couldn't read her face. Was she being serious?

(b) His power—even with his back to the camera, even when we can't read his face—is terrifying.

Notes

1. *Kao-iro* is a nominal compound that consists of *kao* (face) and *iro* (color). *Kao-iro o yomu* is frequently used, but *kao o yomu*, which more closely resembles the English, is not used as often. 📖→ 解説(1)

2. *Read* can be replaced by *study*, but *study s.o.'s face* emphasizes the attempt to detect someone's feelings, whereas *read s.o.'s face* emphasizes the detection itself.

(2) The poker player studied her opponents' faces carefully and tried to gather information about their hands.
ポーカープレーヤーは、注意深く相手の顔色を読んで、相手の手の中にあるカードの情報を推測しようとする。

REL

Yomu can be replaced by *ukagau*, which means "to be concerned about s.o.'s intentions or feelings." 📖→ 関連語(1)

read s.o.'s mind   / *phr.* / metaphor

to guess what s.o. is thinking

REL read s.o.'s thoughts; LOOK▶ read s.o.'s face

Examples

Karen: Our cat Mimi apparently thinks she's a human.

Kenta: Sounds like the owner is deluding herself.

Karen: No way. Mimi can read my mind. When I'm feeling down, she crawls into my lap to comfort me.

Kenta: That doesn't mean she's reading your mind. She just wants food.

Karen: You're awful.

- - - - - - - - - - - - - - - - - - -

(a) His parents read his mind and not only figured out that he had a girlfriend, but also where they were living.

(b) Con men are usually good at reading other people's minds.

REL

1. The Japanese verb can be replaced by *yomi-toru* (lit. "to read and take s.t."). 📖→ 関連語(1)

顔色を読む / phr. 隠喩

顔の表情を見てその人の気持ちを理解する

関 **LOOK▶** 心を読む, 顔色をうかがう, **LOOK▶** 深読み {し過ぎる / する}

例 文

(a)「あなたにまあちょっと謝りたいだけなのよ。」と彼女は言った。しかし彼女の顔色を読むことはできなかった。本心だったのだろうか。

(b) 彼がカメラに背を向けていて、われわれが彼の顔色を読めないときでさえ、彼の威力の恐ろしさは感じられる。

解 説

1.「顔色」は「顔」と「色」からできている複合名詞である。「顔色を読む」はよく使われるが、英語式の「顔を読む」は「顔色を読む」ほどは使われない。

(1) 彼女は人の{顔色 /² 顔}を読むのが得意らしい。
   She seems to be good at reading faces.

2. 英語の動詞の *read* は *study* で置き換えることができるが、*study s.o.'s face* は相手の気持ちを探ろうと試みる点を強調するのに対して、見出しの *read s.o.'s feelings* は相手の気持ちを感知する時に用いる。**▶📖 Note(2)**

関連語

日本語の「読む」は「うかがう」で置き換えることができるが、意味は「相手の意向や気持ちを気にしたり心配したりする」という意味に変わる。

(1) 子供は母親の顔色をうかがった。
   The child tried to judge his mother's feelings from her facial expressions.

R

心を読む / phr. 隠喩

表情や言動などから、誰かの考えていることを理解する

関 {考え / 心} を読み取る, {胸の内 / 腹(の内)} を読む, **LOOK▶** 顔色を読む,
LOOK▶ 深読み {し過ぎる / する}

例 文

カレン: うちのネコのミミは、自分のこと人間だと思っているみたい。

健太: それは、飼い主の都合のいい錯覚だよ。

カレン: そんなことないわ。ミミは、私の心が読めるのよ。私が元気がないときは、膝に乗ってきてなぐさめてくれるわ。

健太: それは、心を読んでいるんじゃなくて、えさを催促してるんだよ。

カレン: 健太って、ひどいわね。

(a) 彼は両親に心を読まれ、恋人の存在だけでなく、二人の住んでいる所まであてられてしまった。

(b) 詐欺師は、たいてい人の心を読むのが上手だ。

関連語

1. 日本語の動詞は「読み取る」で置き換えることができる。

519

2. The English and Japanese nouns can be replaced by *thoughts* and *kangae/mune no uchi* (lit. "inside one's heart")/*hara (no uchi)* (lit. "inside one's stomach"), respectively.

(2) The parents read their son's {thoughts/mind} and figured out his whereabouts.
彼は両親に{考え / 心 / 胸の内 / 腹(の内)}を読まれ、居場所を見つけられてしまった。
Note that *kangae o yomi-toru* sounds more natural being used figuratively than *kangae o yomu*. 関連語(3)

read too much into ~ / phr. / metaphor

to think that words or actions mean more than they actually do

[REL] 👀 read s.o.'s mind; 👀 read s.o.'s face

Examples

Kenta: Saya, you're too suspicious of others. You read too much into what they're saying.

Saya: And I'd say you're too naïve. You should think more carefully about what others say.

- -

(a) I think the latter part of your discussion reads too much into the issue I was addressing.

(b) This interpretation of the novel reads too much into the writer's intentions.

Notes

1. This expression is metaphorical because the basic meaning of *read* and *yomu* is "to look at and understand the meaning of s.t. that is written."(👀 read one's mind; read s.o.'s face)

2. *Into* in the English is expressed by *fuka-* (deep) in the Japanese.

recharge one's batteries / phr. / metaphor

to rest and restore one's energy

Examples

Mike: I've been busy these days, but now I can finally take a break.

Saya: That's good. Why don't you go to a hot spring for a while and recharge your batteries?

Mike: Yeah, going skiing and visiting a hot spring sounds good.

- -

(a) The basketball player was able to recharge his batteries after a quiet off-season.

(b) Tanned and relaxed, the president said his batteries had been recharged during his month away from Washington D.C.

Note

It is very likely that the Japanese is derived from the identical Chinese compound.

(1) 彼女は本当にあなたの心が{読める / 読み取れる}のです。
　　She can truly read your mind.
2．日英語の名詞はそれぞれ「考え / 胸の内 / 腹（の内）」 *thoughts* で置き換えられる。📖REL(2)
　　また、日本語は「考えを読む」より「考えを読み取る」のほうが比喩として自然である。
(3) 詐欺師は、たいてい人の{心 / 考え}を{読む / 読み取る}のが上手だ。(→(b))

深読み{し過ぎる / する}　comp. v.　隠喩

物事の状況や人の言動、行動を実際以上に解釈する

関 📖 心を読む, 📖 顔色を読む

【例 文】
健太：さやは素直じゃないよ。人が言ってることを深読みし過ぎるよ。
さや：あら、健太がナイーブすぎるのよ。もっと、慎重に人の言ってることを考えたほうがいいわよ。

- -

(a) あなたの後半の議論は、私が問題にしている論点を深読みし過ぎていると思いますよ。
(b) この小説に対する解説は、作者の意図を深読みし過ぎている。

【解 説】
1．この表現は *read* (読む)がその基本義の"書かれたものを見てその意味を理解する"という意味からずれているため比喩的な用法である。(📖 心を読む, 顔色を読む)
2．日本語の「深い」の意味は、英語では *into* で表現されている。

充電する　comp. v.　隠喩

新しい活力を得るために休息をとる

【例 文】
マイク：ここんとこ、忙しかったけど、ようやく休みがとれたよ。
さや：そう、じゃ、しばらく温泉でも行って、充電してきたら。
マイク：うん、温泉スキー旅行なんて、いいね。

- -

(a) そのバスケット選手は静かなオフシーズンを過ごし、来シーズンに向けてしっかり充電できた。
(b) 日焼けしてリラックスした様子で、大統領は首都ワシントンから1か月離れている間に充電できたと言った。

【解 説】
「充電する」は中国語からの借用の可能性が高い。

(as) red as blood / phr. / simile

a deep red color

REL bloodred

Examples

(a) The moon's as red as blood tonight. I've got a bad feeling about this.

(b) That rose is as red as blood.

REL

As *red as blood* and *chi no yō ni akai* can be replaced by *bloodred* and *kesseki-shoku*, respectively. In Japanese, *kesseki-shoku* is a medical term, and *chi no yō ni akai* is normally used in spoken language.

red flag / comp. n. / metaphor

s.t. that indicates imminent danger

Examples

Mrs. S: This morning I went for a physical, and the doctor told me that my blood pressure is a little high.

Kenta: Mom, high blood pressure is a red flag, you know.

Mrs. S: True. I need to be careful.

- -

(a) His strange behavior at work is a red flag. Something must be going on in his personal life.

(b) I don't think I'll take the job. The pay is good, but there are just too many red flags.

Notes

1. Both the English and Japanese expressions make metaphorical use of the color red, which seems to represent danger in many cultures. This is probably because it is the most easily perceptible color.

2. The Japanese uses the noun *shingō* (signal) as its red object, whereas the English uses *flag*. The Japanese expression can be replaced by *kiken-shingō* (lit. "danger signal").

📖― 解説(1)

red scare / comp. n. / metaphor

fear of Communism and other forms of radical left ideology by government or society

Example

With the worsening of the cold war between the U.S. and the Soviet Union in the late 40s, there was a red scare in Hollywood, leading to a large number of people being blacklisted and pushed out of the movie and TV industries.

522

血のように赤い　phr.　直喩

真っ赤

関 血赤色

例文
- (a) 今晩の月は血のように赤い。何か不吉な予感がする。
- (b) あのバラは血のように赤いですね。

関連語
「血のように赤い」と (as) red as blood とは、それぞれ「血赤色」と blood red で置き換えることができる。日本語では「血赤色」は医学用語だが、「血のように赤い」は話し言葉で普通に使われる。

赤信号　n. phr.　隠喩

危険や心配が迫っていることを示すもの

関 LOOK 警鐘，危険信号

例文

鈴木(妻)：今日、定期検診に行ったら、ちょっと血圧が高いって言われたわ。

健太：おかあさん、血圧が高いのは、健康の赤信号だよ。

鈴木(妻)：そうね、気をつけないと。

- (a) 彼の仕事中の変な挙動は、何か個人生活で問題があるという赤信号なのだ。
- (b) 私、その仕事受けないことにしたわ。給料はいいけど、なんか赤信号がいっぱいともっているのよね。

解説
1. 日英語とも赤い色を共有しているが、赤は多くの文化で危険を示すために比喩的に使われているようである。たぶん最も知覚しやすい色のためだろう。
2. 赤いものは英語では flag（旗）で日本語では「信号」であることに注意。日本語は「危険信号」で置き換えることができる。
- (1) 血圧が高いのは、健康の〔赤 / 危険〕信号だよ。（→会話例）

赤狩り　n. phr.　隠喩

国家権力が共産主義者や社会主義者とその協力者を弾圧すること

例文

米ソ冷戦が激化した1940年代後半、ハリウッドでは赤狩りが強行され、多くの人達がブラックリストに載せられて、映画界、演劇界などの表舞台から締め出された。

523

reflect / v. / metaphor

to make apparent or known in s.t. else

Examples

Mike: Has the first draft of our project been approved?

Colleague: No, our idea has been voted down.

Mike: Seriously? I don't like this top-down decision-making. I think their decisions should reflect our views.

Colleague: I think you're right.

- -

(a) The boom in sales of crime prevention tools reflects recent social conditions.

(b) The building reflects the influence of Italian Renaissance architecture.

(c) Nothing reflects the times better than the way young people speak.

Note

The English can also be used non-metaphorically to mean "to mirror s.t.," but the Japanese cannot be used this way. Only the original Sino-Japanese compound has this literal meaning.

(1) The lake's surface reflected the scenic mountains.
湖は水面にきれいな山を{映し出/˟反映}していた。

ride a wave of ~ / phr. / metaphor

to succeed by taking advantage of momentum or circumstances

Examples

Karen: This celebrity has been riding a wave of success lately.

Saya: Yeah, her albums have been huge hits, and she even received an acting award. I heard she's gonna move to Hollywood soon.

- -

(a) The automotive industry has developed significantly by riding a wave of modernization.

(b) He rode a wave of personal popularity to an easy victory in the election.

Note

Ride and *noru* have similar meanings, but they are not exactly the same. *Ride* means "to sit on s.t. mobile," whereas *noru* means "to get onto {s.t./s.o.} that can support one's weight."

反映する / v. 隠喩

影響，状況，思想などが他のものに現れる

例文

マイク: プロジェクトの第1案、通った？

同僚: だめさ。僕達のアイデアは却下されちゃったよ。

マイク: えっ、ほんと？ 上だけで決めないで、もっと僕達の意見も反映させてほしいね。

同僚: そうだね。

(a) 最近の世相を反映して、防犯グッズが大きな売れ行きを見せている。

(b) その建物は、イタリアルネッサンス建築の影響を反映している。

(c) 若者言葉ほど、時代を反映しているものはないだろう。

解説

日本語は非比喩的意味は漢語の語源にしかないが、英語には"鏡のように映す"という非比喩的意味がある。➡📖 Note(1)

R

(〜の)波に乗る / phr. 隠喩

何かの状況をうまく利用することにより、物事が思い通りに進んだり成功したりする

例文

カレン: 最近、このタレント、波に乗ってるわね。

さや: そうね。歌は大ヒットするし、映画でも賞をもらったし。今度、ハリウッドにも進出するんですって。

(a) 自動車産業は近代化の波に乗って大きく成長した。

(b) 彼は人気の波に乗って、選挙で楽々勝利を得た。

解説

「乗る」と ride の基本義は近いが、全く同じではない。「乗る」は"その体重を支えられる{何か / 誰か}の上にあがる"で、ride は"何か動くものの上に座る"である。

525

ride {out the storm/the storm out} / phr. / metaphor

to persevere during a period of difficulty

REL weather the storm

Examples

(a) We have managed to ride out the storm of the financial crisis.

(b) Life has its ups and downs. Though you may be assaulted by fatigue and harsh criticism, you must ride out the storm.

(c) Japan rode out the storm of the atomic bomb and its defeat in World War II and managed to recover with remarkable speed.

Notes

1. Both the English and Japanese are based on the idea of a boat making it safely through inclement weather. When used figuratively, the expressions mean "for {s.o./s.t.} to make it safely through a difficult time." 解説(1)

2. Underlying both the English and Japanese expressions is the conceptual metaphor "life is a voyage." In addition, the English expression is often used to describe sports teams overcoming difficulties, but the Japanese is not used in this manner.

(2) The final minutes of the game seemed to last for hours. But we rode out the storm, and the referee eventually blew his whistle and ended it.

その試合の最後の数分は数時間にも思われた。しかし、われわれは{それ/¹¹ その嵐}を乗り越え、やっと審判の試合終了の笛を聞いた。

REL

The English REL is *weather the storm*, which has the same meaning as the main entry. In this context, *weather* does not refer to atmospheric conditions, but rather making it through a difficult situation.

(1) We have managed to weather the storm of the financial crisis. (→(a))

right-hand man / comp. n. / metaphor

a person who is highly valued and trusted by {his/her} superior

Examples

(a) He was the big-name politician's right-hand man.

(b) Everyone said that he was the company president's right-hand man, but in the end they became enemies.

(c) The first thing you need to do is to find a right-hand man you can rely on.

Note

Hand and *ude*, while similar, have some important differences. The former means "the movable part of a person's arm from the wrist down," and the latter means "the body part between the shoulder and hand."

REL

1. The word *kata-ude* (lit. "one arm") can be used figuratively to mean "a very dependable person." However, unlike *migi-ude* (right-hand man), this term does not indicate a hierarchical relationship. 関連語(1)

526

嵐を乗り越える / phr. 隠喩

{個人 / 機関 / 国}が難局を切り抜ける

例文

(a) われわれはなんとか金融危機の嵐を乗り越えることができた。

(b) 人生には浮き沈みがあります。おそらくあなたは疲労と戦い、残酷な批判を浴びることでしょう。しかし、そのような嵐を乗り越えなければならないのです。

(c) 原爆投下の被害と第二次世界大戦敗戦の嵐を乗り越えて、日本は瞬く間に復興した。

解説

1. 日英語とも"船が悪天候の中を無事に通過する"というのが基本義である。見出しはこの基本義から比喩的な意味、つまり、"{誰か/ ある機関}が困難を無事にくぐり抜ける"という意味が出ている。

(1) エンジンをフルスピードで回転させて船は嵐を乗り越えた。正午には凪がやって来た。
With engines going at full speed, the ship rode out the storm. At noon, the wind died down.

2. 見出しの根底には日英語とも「人生は航海だ」という概念的な比喩が潜んでいる。英語はよくスポーツチームについても使われるが、日本語はそのようには使えない。→📖 Note (2)

関連語

英語には *weather the storm* という見出しと同じ意味の関連表現がある。この場合、*weather* は「天気」ではなく「困難な状況を切り抜ける」という意味の動詞である。→📖 REL (1)

R

右腕 comp. n. 隠喩

上司に高く評価され、信頼されている人

関 片腕

例文

(a) 彼は大物政治家の右腕だった。

(b) 彼は社長の右腕と言われた人物だったが、最後には二人は敵対することになってしまった。

(c) あなたが最初にしなければならないことは、信頼できる右腕を見つけることだ。

解説

「腕」と *hand* は体の部分としては非常に近いが、「腕」は"肩と手の間の部分"で、*hand* は"手首から下の動かせる部分"のことである。

関連語

1. 日本語には関連表現として"とても頼りになる"という意味の「片腕」という比喩表現があるが、「右腕」のように上下関係はない。

527

2. While *kata-ude* can be used in both a literal and figurative sense, "one arm" cannot.

(2) He is my {right-hand/ˣone-arm} man.
彼は私の片腕だ。

right wing/right-wing | comp. n./comp. adj. | metonymy

the more conservative or nationalistic section of a political {party/group/etc.}

[REL] right; right-leaning

[ANT] [LOOK] left wing/left-wing

Examples

(a) It seems every country has right-wingers, left-wingers, and centrists.

(b) Yukio Mishima became absorbed in right wing ideologies in the latter part of his life, and he even organized his own army.

(c) In Japan, you are likely to be denounced as a right-winger if you make statements pertaining to the interests of the nation.

Note

In the French Parliament (post-Revolution), the conservative party used to sit to the right from the perspective of the president. Thus, "right wing" came to serve as metonymy for nationalists.

[REL]

1. *Right wing/right-wing* and *uyoku* can be replaced by *right-leaning* and *migi-yori*, respectively.

(1) This newspaper is rather right-leaning.
この新聞はどちらかというと右寄りだ。

2. In Japanese, sometimes the term *migi* (right) is used in place of *uyoku* (right wing).

📖 関連語(2)

3. The Japanese has another REL, *u-ha* (the right-leaning faction of a party), which is the opposite of *sa-ha* (the left-leaning faction of a party). 📖 関連語(3)

[ANT]

The ANTs for *right wing/right-wing* and *uyoku* are *left wing/left-wing* and *sayoku*, respectively.

(1) Marxism strongly influenced the thoughts of the left wing.
マルクス主義は左翼的思想に多大な影響を与えた。

rise | v. | metaphor

to attain a higher rank; for s.t. to increase in {degree/size/quantity/number/price}

[REL] go up

[ANT] fall

Examples

Karen: I heard that my rent's gonna rise. I don't know what to do.

Kenta: Prices have been rising everywhere. Gas prices have risen a lot, too.

（1）ジョナサン・アイブはアップル創始者のスティーブ・ジョブズの片腕として知られていた。
Jonathan Ive was known as the right-hand man of Steve Jobs, the founder of Apple.
2．日本語の「片腕」は字義通りの意味と"とても頼りになる"という比喩的な意味がある。しかし、
対応する英語の *one arm* は字義通りの意味しかない。 ➡📖 REL(2)

右翼（うよく）　comp. n.　換喩（かんゆ）

保守的で国粋主義的な思想を持った{人 / 政治家 / 政党}

関 右，右寄り，右派

反 左，左寄り，左派， **LOOK** 左翼

例文

（a）どこの国にも、右翼と左翼、そして中道派がいるようだ。

（b）三島由紀夫は、晩年右翼的な思想に傾倒し、自分の軍隊まで組織した。

（c）日本では国の利益に関するような発言をすると、右翼的な考えを抱いていると糾弾
される傾向がある。

解説

もともとは革命後のフランスの国会の議長の席から見て右側に保守派が座っていたので、そ
こから「右翼」は国粋的な人々を示す換喩となった。

関連語

1．「右翼」と *right-wing* は、それぞれ、「右寄り」、*right-leaning* ともいう。 ➡📖 REL(1)

2．日本語では「右翼」と言わずに「右」と言うこともある。

（2）あの政治家は{右翼 / 右}だ。
That politician is a {right-winger/rightist}.

3．日本語にはもう一つ「右派」（cf.「左派」）という関連表現がある。これは党の中の右寄りの
人々を指す。

（3）どんな政党にも多かれ少なかれ、内部には右派も左派も存在するものだ。
Every political party has right and left factions, more or less.

反意語

「右翼」と *right wing/right-wing* の反意語は、それぞれ「左翼」と *left wing/left-wing* である。

➡📖 ANT(1)

上がる（あ）　v.　隠喩（いんゆ）

誰かがより高い地位を得る，{程度 / 大きさ / 量 / 数 / 値段}が増す

反 下がる（さ）

例文

カレン：今度、家賃が上がるんですって。困ったわ。

健太：物価が上がってるからね。ガソリンの値段もすごく上がったよ。

(a) After the new factory was built, production rose significantly, as did the company's profits.

(b) The temperature around here rises and falls in the spring.

Note

In certain Japanese phrases, such as *hi ga noboru* (the sun rises), *kenryoku no za ni noboru* (to rise to power), and *toppu ni noboru* (to rise to the top), *noboru* must be used instead of *agaru*.

REL

Go up can replace *rise* in the English.

(1) Prices have been {rising/going up} everywhere. (→ dialogue)

ANT

The ANTs for *agaru* and *noboru* are *sagaru* (to decrease) and *oriru* (to descend), respectively. However, *hio ga sagaru* is incorrect. *Hi ga shizumu* (lit. "the sun sinks") must be used instead.

rise like a phoenix (from the ashes)   phr.   simile

to make a dramatic comeback

Examples

(a) Our company has gone bankrupt, but we will do whatever it takes to make it rise like a phoenix.

(b) After taking a hiatus due to a serious injury, the pitcher rose like a phoenix from the ashes and won the game today after a one-year absence.

(c) A new World Trade Center rose like a phoenix from the ashes.

Notes

1. The phoenix is a legendary bird from Egyptian mythology that resides in the Arabian desert. It is said that every 500 to 600 years, it reduces itself to ashes on a pyre of wood, only to rise again.

2. While *rise from the ashes* is the typical wording, as shown in (b) and (c), *rise from the flames* can also be used.

(1) The postwar Japanese economy rose like a phoenix from the flames of the war.
戦後の日本経済は戦火の中から不死鳥のように蘇った。

3. In the English, the phrase *from the ashes* is optional, but the corresponding Japanese phrase, *kaijin no naka kara*, is seldom used, and thus not included in the main entry.

4. The Japanese expression is most likely based on the Chinese compound *fushichō* (lit. "undying bird").

rising star   / comp. n. / metaphor

s.o. who is likely to become very successful and famous in {his/her} field

Example

He displayed prodigious talent starting in middle school, and he went on to become a rising star in the flagging sport of volleyball.

(a) 新工場になってから、生産量が格段に上がって、会社の利益も上がった。

(b) この辺では春は気温が上がったり、下がったりする。

解説

日本語は、「日が昇る」「権力の座に昇る」「トップに昇る」のような場合は「昇る」を使い、「上がる」は使えない。

関連語

go up は rise と置き換えることができる。━━📖 REL(1)

反意語

「上がる」の反意語は「下がる」だが、「昇る」の反意語は「降りる」である。ただし、「˟日が降りる」とは言えない。「日が沈む」と言わなければならない。

R

不死鳥のように蘇る   phr.   直喩

困難の極地から復活する

例文

(a) 会社は倒産したが、われわれは一生懸命働いて、会社を不死鳥のように蘇らせるつもりだ。

(b) その投手は大きな怪我から不死鳥のように蘇り、今日、1年ぶりに勝利した。

(c) 新しい世界貿易センターは灰燼の中から不死鳥のように蘇った。

解説

1. フェニックスはエジプトの神話に出てくる伝説の鳥で、アラビアの砂漠に住んでいて、500年か600年おきに自らを香木の中で焼いては蘇ってくるという説などがある。

2. 英語ではフェニックスはふつう(b)(c)のように ashes (灰燼)から蘇るが、flames (炎)から蘇ることもある。━━📖 Note(1)

3. 英語では from the ashes があってもなくてもいいが、日本語ではそれに対応する「灰燼の中から」はまず言わないので見出しにもついていない。

4. 日本語は中国語の「不死鳥」から来ている可能性が強い。

期待の{星 / 新星}   comp. n.   隠喩

これからの活躍を期待されている能力のある人

例文

彼は中学生ながら目覚ましい活躍を見せ、低迷しているバレーボール界の期待の星と騒がれた。

531

risk one's neck / phr. / metaphor

to do s.t. very risky

REL risk one's life; stick one's neck out

Examples

(a) I'm risking my neck by making this deal with Company A.

(b) He risked his neck by appealing directly to his boss.

R E L

1. The Japanese expression has the REL *inochi o kakeru* (to risk one's life). While *risk one's life* is the English equivalent, this sounds less figurative than the Japanese due to the fact that *risk* means "to expose to danger," whereas *kakeru* means "to arch over/hang."

📖 関連語(1)

2. The English also has the REL *stick one's neck out*.

(2) He {risked his neck/stuck his neck out} by appealing directly to his boss. (→(b))

---

homograph

roll one's eyes / phr. / metonymy

to move one's eyes around in a circle in a show of disdain or exasperation
感心しないという気持ちを表す仕草

Example

She rolled her eyes multiple times while Bill was talking—a classic sign of contempt.
ビルが話している間、一度ならず彼女は素早く上を見やった。それは相手をさげすむ典型的な仕草だった。

---

roll up one's sleeves / phr. / metonymy

to get ready for a task

Examples

Kenta: Wow, Mom. You look busy.

Mrs. S: Grandpa is coming in from the countryside, so I've got to roll up my sleeves and get to work on the cooking and the cleaning. Give me a hand, would you?

- - - - - - - - - - - - - - - - - - - -

(a) Okada rolled up his sleeves and resolved to complete the project on time.

Note

The act of rolling up one's sleeves indicates that one is about to get down to a task. The temporal proximity of this act to what follows lends it the properties of metonymy. Note that the Japanese expression is not *sode o makuru* (to roll up one's sleeves), but *ude-makuri o suru* (lit. "to perform arm rolling").

首をかける / phr. / 隠喩
くび

自分の地位や仕事を犠牲にする（覚悟で何かをする）
じぶん　ち い　　しごと　ぎせい　　　　かくご　　なに

関 命をかける
いのち

例 文

(a) 今度のＡ社との取り引きは、首をかける覚悟で取り組むつもりだ。
こんど　　しゃ　　と　ひ　　　　くび　　　かくご　　と　く

(b) 彼は自分の首をかけて、上司に直訴した。
かれ　じ ぶん　くび　　　　じょうし　ちょくそ

関連語

1. 日本語には「命をかける」という関連表現があり、英語の *risk one's life* に対応する。*risk* の基本義は"危険をかける"であり、「かける」の基本義は"何かを高い所からぶらさげる"で、英語より日本語の方が比喩性が高い。

(1) その写真家は、自分の{命をかけて/ˣ首をかけて}戦場写真を撮り続けた。
The photographer risked his life to capture photos of the warzone.

2. 英語には見出しと同じ意味の *stick one's neck out* という関連表現もある。　📖 REL(2)

同形異義語

目を回す / phr. / 換喩
め　まわ　　　　　　　　　　　　かんゆ

ひどく驚く，失神する
おどろ　　しっしん
to be surprised; to lose consciousness

例 文

１億円の宝くじに当たって、驚きと喜びのあまり、母は目を回してしまった。
おくえん　たから　　あ　　　おどろ　よろこ　　　　はは　め　まわ
My mother won a hundred million yen in the lottery, and she was so surprised she fainted.

腕まくりをする / phr. / 換喩
うで　　　　　　　　　　　　　　かんゆ

大きな{仕事／作業}の前に、意気込みや備えの気持ちを表す
おお　　しごと　さぎょう　まえ　いきご　　そな　きも　あらわ

例 文

健太：お母さん、忙しそうだね。
けんた　　かあ　　　いそが

鈴木（妻）：田舎から、おじいちゃんが出てくるのよ。さ、これから、腕まくりをして、
すずき　つま　いなか　　　　　　　　　　　　で　　　　　　　　　　　　　　　うで
料理と掃除。あなたも手伝ってちょうだい。
りょうり　そうじ　　　　　　　てつだ

(a) 岡田は腕まくりをして、プロジェクトを時間通りに完成させる決意をした。
おかだ　うで　　　　　　　　　　　　　　　じかんどお　　かんせい　　　けつい

解 説

日英語ともに、袖を巻き上げる仕草は何かの仕事に一生懸命に取り組む行為に先行する。時間的隣接性と解釈すると、換喩の一種になる。ただ、日本語の表現は「袖をまくる」とは言わず、「腕まくりをする」と言っている点に注意。

533

Rome wasn't built in a day. /phr. /metaphor

important work cannot be achieved in a short time

Examples

Karen: This kanji dictionary is really good.

Mr. S: Yeah, the author is one of the leading authorities when it comes to kanji studies. Apparently it took him 60 years to complete it, though.

Karen: Well, as they say, Rome wasn't built in a day.

(a) It took 30 years for our company to make it this far. Rome wasn't built in a day, after all.

Notes

1. While the proverb itself expresses a historical fact and is thus not metaphorical, it is often used metaphorically, as shown in the examples.

2. The proverb refers to the fact that it took about 500 years, starting in the 6th century BCE, for the Romans to conquer the entire Mediterranean area. The Japanese is clearly a translation of the English, but the English is based on a French proverb recorded in *Li Proverbe au Vilain* (ca. 1190). The English first appeared in Richard Taverner's translation of Erasmus's *Adages* (1545) as *Rome was not bylt on a daie*.

REL

The Japanese REL, *senri no michi mo ippo kara*, literally means "A road of one thousand ri (= about 2,400 miles) starts with the first step." That is, "no matter how big a project you undertake, it starts small."

rub salt {in/into} {the/s.o.'s} wound(s) /phr. /metaphor

for {s.o./s.t.} to make a situation worse

Examples

(a) Her derisive laughter was painful enough, but the abusive language that followed was just rubbing salt in the wound.

(b) Not only was his marriage in tatters, but the company he worked for suddenly went bankrupt. It was as if fate was rubbing salt in his wounds.

REL

The Japanese REL is *naki-ttsura ni hachi* (a bee stings one's crying face). Whereas the main entry implies that someone deliberately inflicts additional pain upon another, this expression implies that the additional pain is a result of bad luck. 関連語(1)

ローマは一日にして成らず　phr.　隠喩

偉大な{仕事 / 成功}は短時間ではできない

関 千里の道も一歩から

例文：

カレン：この漢字の辞書、すごくいいですね。

鈴木(夫)：うん、その学者は漢字研究の最高峰といわれる人だけど、執筆に60年以上かかったそうだよ。

カレン：まさに、「ローマは一日にして成らず」ですね。

(a)「ローマは一日にして成らず」と言いますが、当社もここまで来るのに30年の月日がかかりました。

解説

1. ことわざ自体は歴史的事実なので、比喩性はないが、例文のように比喩的意味で使われる。

2. このことわざはもともとローマ人が全地中海世界を征服するまでに紀元前6世紀から500年ぐらいの長い年月がかかっていることを指している。日本語は明らかに英語からの翻訳であるが、英語も元をただせばフランスの *Li Proverbe au Vilain*（1190年ごろ）に記録されているフランス語版から来ている。英語はエラスムスの『格言』（1545）の Richard Traverner の翻訳に *Rome was not bylt on a daie* として出たのが初出である。

関連語

日本語の類似のことわざとして「千里の道も一歩から」がある。"どんな大きな仕事もまず手近なところから始まる"という意味である。

傷口に塩を{塗る / すり込む}　phr.　隠喩

{誰か / 何か}が{状況 / 状態}を悪化させる

関 泣きっ面に蜂

例文

(a) 彼女のせせら笑いに僕は傷ついた。そのあとの彼女の罵りの言葉は、その傷口に塩をすり込んだ。

(b) 彼の結婚がずたずたになったばかりではない。まるで傷口に塩を塗るかのように、彼の働いていた会社が突然倒産した。

関連語

日本語には「泣きっ面に蜂」という関連表現がある。「何か痛い目にあって泣いているところに更に蜂に刺されて、もっと痛い思いをした」という意味である。見出しは誰かが悪意を持って誰かを傷つけるための行為を重ねて行うのに対し、「泣きっ面に蜂」は「不運が重なる」場合に使われる。

(1) 転んで怪我をした上に、持っていたやかんもひっくり返して、やけどまでしてしまった。まさに{泣きっ面に蜂/[×]傷口に塩をすり込まれたよう}だった。

Not only did I hurt myself falling down, but I also spilled the kettle and burned myself. It's like {a bee stung my crying face/[×]someone rubbed salt into my wounds}.

run one's eyes over / phr. / metaphor

to quickly take a look at s.t.

Examples

(a) Every morning, my dad runs his eyes over the newspaper while eating breakfast before heading off to work.

(b) I ran my eyes over the list of names, but didn't find the name of the person I was looking for.

(c) I ran my eyes over the report for a few minutes before the meeting.

Notes

1. In the English, *run* is a transitive verb, whereas *hashiraseru* is the causative form of *hashiru* (to run).

2. The English can only be used in the context of quickly scanning over written content in order to grasp the main points, as shown in the examples. Thus, while the Japanese can be used in (1a) and (1b), the English cannot. 解説(1)

run in {s.o.'s/the} blood / phr. / metaphor

to be characteristic of one's relatives or ancestors

REL be in one's blood; run in the family

Examples

Saya: Mmmm, this is delicious. Karen, you're a great cook.

Karen: Thanks. My mother and grandmother are even better. I guess culinary skills run in the blood.

- - - - - - - - - - - - - - - - - - - -

(a) He's a third-generation jockey, so horse racing runs in his blood.

(b) Business runs in Morris's blood. At age 11, he began working at his father's consulting firm.

Notes

1. Though the English and Japanese expressions have identical meanings, the Japanese verb is *nagarete iru* (to be flowing) while the English verb is simply *run*.

2. Underlying this expression is the conceptual metaphor "genes are in the blood," which is common to both English and Japanese.

REL

1. The English REL *run in the family* has the same meaning as the main entry.

(1) He's a third-generation jockey, so horse racing runs in {his blood/the family}. (→ (a))

2. The English REL *be in one's blood* means "to be part of one's nature."

(2) Shigeki loves swimming. It's in his blood.
茂樹は水泳が大好きで、{病みつきになっている/[×]水泳の血が流れている}。

（〜に）目を走らせる　phr.　隠喩

何かをすばやく見る

例文

(a) 父は毎朝、朝食を取りながら新聞に目を走らせる。それから、会社に出かける。

(b) 名簿に目を走らせてみたが、目的の人物の名前は見つからなかった。

(c) 私は会議の前に2、3分、報告書に目を走らせた。

解説

1. 日本語の「走らせる」は「走る」の使役形である。英語の *run* は他動詞である。

2. 英語は、何か書かれたものの要点を急いでつかむような文脈でしか使えないが、日本語にはそのような制約がない。

(1)a. 値段に目を走らせるとなんと86,000円！「バッグって、こんなに高いんですか…」

I {glanced at/×ran my eyes over} the price tag. It was 86,000 yen. "How can bags be this expensive?" I wondered.

b. 彼女は周囲にさっと目を走らせた後、目の前に停まった車に急いで乗り込んだ。

After {glancing around at/??running her eyes over} her surroundings, the woman quickly got into the car parked in front of her.

（〜に〜の）血が流れている　phr.　隠喩

親や先祖などから、その特徴的な資質を受け継いでいる

例文

さや：う〜ん、おいしい。カレンって料理上手ね。

カレン：そう、ありがとう。祖母や母はもっとうまいのよ。代々、料理上手の血が流れているみたい。

- -

(a) 彼は祖父から数えて3代目の競馬騎手で、優秀な騎手の血が流れています。

(b) モーリスの体の中にはビジネスの血が流れている。彼は11歳の時に、コンサルティング会社を経営していた父親のために仕事を始めた。

解説

1. 日本語では動詞は「流れている」だが、英語では *run*（走る）である。しかし、比喩全体の意味は同じである。

2. この比喩表現の背後には「遺伝子は血の中にある」という日英共通の比喩的思考が潜んでいる。

関連語

1. 英語には見出しと同じ意味の *run in the family* という関連表現がある。　→📖REL（1）

2. 英語には"何かにとりつかれている"という意味の *be in one's blood* という関連表現がある。

　→📖REL（2）

save face / comp. v. / metaphor

to preserve one's reputation or dignity

[ANT] [LOOK] lose face

Examples

Mike: I'm surprised that the company is donating so much money to NGOs even though it's not doing so well.

Colleague: It probably had to do so in order to save face.

- -

(a) Ogawa wouldn't read his paper at the conference because he knew he wouldn't do well and he wanted to save face.

(b) As a politician, he'll do whatever it takes to save face.

Notes

1. The basic meanings of *save* and *tamotsu* are "to protect {s.o./s.t.} from an undesirable event" and "to maintain s.t.'s condition," respectively. While the meaning of *face* is straightforward, *taimen* is a compound consisting of *tai* (body) and *men* (surface).

2. The Japanese is usually used to mean saving one's own face, but the English can also be used when one allows someone else to save face. In this case, the Japanese expression *kao o tateru* can be used.

(1) In business, sports, or everyday interactions, always allow your opponent to save face. You won. That should be enough. Bragging is counterproductive.
仕事でもスポーツでも日常の付き合いでも、いつも相手の{顔を立てる/˟体面を保つ}ようにしなさい。勝つだけで充分なのです。いばったら逆効果です。

[REL]

Taimen o tamotsu has two RELs: *menboku o tamotsu* (lit. "to keep one's face-eyes") and *mentsu o tamotsu* (lit. "to keep one's face"). The RELs are used with roughly equal frequency, and both are used more frequently than the main entry. [📖→ 関連語(1)

scales fall from s.o.'s eyes, the / phr. / metaphor

to suddenly understand s.t. significant

Examples

(a) When I read Nash's wonderful paper, it was as though the scales fell from my eyes.

(b) All at once the scales fell from her eyes, and she saw this man as he really was.

(c) I was so impressed by his original and straightforward lecture that I felt as if the scales had fallen from my eyes.

Notes

1. This metaphor originated from a story contained in the New Testament of the Bible (ca. 80-90 CE, Acts 9:3-19). In the story, as Saul (later known as Paul) made his way to Damascus, "suddenly a light from the sky flashed around him, and he could no longer see." (9:3) However, because of the power of Christ's spirit, "something like fish scales fell from Saul's eyes, and he was able to see again" (9:18). The English New Testament is a

体面を保つ / phr. 隠喩

世間に対して{誇り / 信用}を持続させようとする

関 面目を保つ, 面子を保つ

反 LOOK▶ 面目を失う

例 文

マイク： うちの会社、厳しい状況なのに、NGO にこんなに多額の寄付をしているんだね。

同僚： うん、会社としての体面を保つためには、断るに断れないんだろうね。

- (a) 小川はうまくできないと自分でも知っていたし、体面を保ちたかったので、学会で論文を発表しようとしなかった。
- (b) 彼は政治家としての体面を保つためなら、何だってやる。

解 説

1. 「保つ」と *save* の基本義は、それぞれ、"現状を維持する"と"よくない出来事から守る"である。英語の *face* の基本義は明らかであるが、日本語の「体面」は「体」+「面」からなる複合語で、かつては「容貌」の意味で使われていた。

2. 日本語は通常、"自分の信用を守る"という意味で使われるが、英語ではそれだけではなく、"他の人の信用を守る"という意味でもよく使われる。この場合、日本語の表現は「顔を立てる」である。─📖 Note(1)

関連語

日本語では関連表現として、「面目を保つ」と、ほぼ同じ使用頻度の「面子を保つ」がある。どちらも見出しより使用頻度が高い。

(1) 小川は、うまくできないと自分でも知っていたし、{体面 / 面子 / 面目}を保ちたかったので、学会で論文を発表しようとしなかった。(→(a))

目から鱗が落ちる / phr. 隠喩

何かがきっかけとなって、突然、物事の実態がよく見え、よく理解できるようになる

例 文

- (a) ナッシュのすばらしい論文を読んだとき、目から鱗が落ちたような感じだった。
- (b) 急に目から鱗が落ちて、彼女はこの人の正体をつかんだ。
- (c) 彼の講義はとても斬新でわかりやすく、目から鱗が落ちたような衝撃を受けた。

解 説

1. この比喩は『新約聖書』の「使徒行伝」(80 〜 90 AD 頃、9 章 3 節から 19 節)にある次の話が出典である。キリストの迫害者の(サウロ、後のパウロ)がダマスカスへ行く途中、「突然、天からの光が彼の周りを照らし、三日間目が見えなくなった」(9 章 3 節)のが、キリストの精霊の力で「目からうろこのようなものが落ち、サウロは元どおり見えるようになった」(9 章 18 節)という話である。英語の『新約聖書』は原語の古代共通ギリシャ語からの翻訳で、今使われている日本語版も同じである。

539

translation of the original Koine Greek, as is the current Japanese translation.

2. *Ga ochiru* is sometimes dropped in casual Japanese speech, with the result being *me kara uroko (da/no)*. 📖➡ 解説(1)

scatter like flies / phr. / simile

for a group of people or animals to suddenly disperse in all directions

REL drop like flies

Examples

(a) The people on the ground scattered like flies when they saw the boxes falling toward them.

(b) The policemen drove the crowd aside, and the people scattered like flies.

(c) Believe me when I say children are afraid of you. Just run down there and they'll scatter like flies.

Note

While the English expression uses *flies* and the Japanese uses *kumo no ko* (baby spiders), both similes use small bugs to express their meaning. In the English, *scatter* is an intransitive verb, while *chirasu* (to cause to scatter) is a transitive (causative) verb.

REL

The English REL *drop like flies* means "to {die/sicken/drop out} in large numbers." The simile *like flies* is commonly used to indicate a great number of people or things.

(1) The flu's really bad this year. People are dropping like flies.
今年はインフルエンザの流行が最悪だ。かかった人々がバタバタと倒れていく。

scratch the surface / phr. / metaphor

to {learn about/examine} only a small part of s.t.

Examples

Saya: Shakespeare's plays may look simple at first glance, but they're really complex, aren't they?

Karen: Definitely. You can't get a sense of their depth if you only scratch the surface.

(a) Our research has barely scratched the surface of genetic complexity.

(b) We thought we understood Afghan culture, but when we went to Afghanistan, we found we had just scratched the surface.

Note

While *surface* and *hyōmen* (lit. "surface-face") have the same meaning, the verbs are somewhat different. *Scratch* means "to make a short line with a pointed object," while *nazoru* means "to trace a model." Still, the expressions have the same overall figurative meaning: "to not go very deeply into s.t."

2．日本語ではくだけた会話ではよく終わりの「が落ちる」が落ちて、「目から鱗{だ / の〜}」となることがある。

(1) 健太：マイク、この記事読んだ？ 世紀の大発見だよね。
マイク：本当、目から鱗だよね。
Kenta: Mike, have you read this article? It's the discovery of the century.
Mike: Yeah, it's like the scales fell from my eyes.

蜘蛛の子を散らすように　phr.　直喩
（く　も　こ　ち）

集まっている人々があっという間に四方に移動する
（あつ　　　　　ひとびと　　　　　　　　　　　　　　しほう　いどう）

例　文

(a) 地上にいる人達は頭上から箱が落ちてきたのを見て、蜘蛛の子を散らすように散らばった。
（ちじょう　　ひとたち　ずじょう　はこ　お　　　　　　み　　くも　こ　　ち　　　　　　　　　ち）

(b) 警官が群集を脇に追いやったので、人々は蜘蛛の子を散らすように散った。
（けいかん　ぐんしゅう　わき　お　　　　　　　　ひとびと　くも　こ　　ち）

(c) 子ども達があなたを恐れているっていうのは、本当なんです。あなたがちょっと走り寄って行っただけで、蜘蛛の子を散らしたように逃げて行きますよ。
（こ　たち　　　　　　おそ　　　　　　　　　　　　　ほんとう　　　　　　　　　　　　　　　はし　よ　い　　　　　くも　こ　ち　　　　　　　　　　に　い）

解　説

日本語は「蜘蛛の子」を、英語は *flies*（ハエ）を使っていて一見違うようであるが、日英語ともに小さな虫を使っている点でとても近い直喩である。日本語の動詞は「散らす」という使役の他動詞であるが、英語の動詞は *scatter*（ちりぢりになる）という自動詞である。

関連語

英語の関連表現 *drop like flies* は"何かが大量に一度に{死ぬ/くずれる / 抜ける}"という意味である。*like flies* という直喩は日常的に用いられ、大勢の人や大量のものを指す。─📖 REL(1)

表面をなぞる　phr.　隠喩
（ひょうめん）　　　（いんゆ）

何かを表面的にだけ見る
（なに　ひょうめんてき　み）

例　文

さや：シェークスピアのストーリーって一見単純そうに見えるけど、すっごく難しいね。
（　　　　　　　　　　　　　　いっけんたんじゅん　　　　み　　　　　　　　　むずか）
カレン：そうね。表面をなぞっただけでは、深いところはなかなか理解できないわね。
（　　　　　　　　ひょうめん　　　　　　　　　　ふか　　　　　　　　　　りかい）

(a) 我々の研究はかろうじて遺伝子の複雑さの表面をなぞったにすぎない。
（われわれ　けんきゅう　　　　　　　いでんし　ふくざつ　ひょうめん）

(b) アフガニスタンの文化を理解していると思っていたが、行ってみると、私達はその表面しかなぞっていなかったことがわかった。
（　　　　　　　　ぶんか　りかい　　　　　　おも　　　　　　　い　　　　　わたしたち　ひょうめん）

解　説

「表面」と *surface* の基本義は同じであるが、「なぞる」と *scratch* の基本義は、それぞれ、"何かを雛形としてその通りたどる"と、"先の尖ったもので短い線を引く"である。しかし、表現全体としては"物事に深く入っていかない"という比喩的意味を共有している。

sea of blood / n. phr. / metaphor

an area covered in blood

REL a pool of blood

Examples

(a) The battlefield was a sea of blood.

(b) It was said the scene of the crime was a sea of blood—all you could do was cover your eyes at such a tragic sight.

(c) The mafia gang violence of the 30s saw outbreaks of killings in various places. It's said that wherever the mafia went, it left behind a sea of blood.

REL

The English and Japanese RELs use *pool*/-*damari* instead of *sea*/*umi*. While the nouns used in the RELs are smaller in scale, they still represent a significant amount of blood.

(1) a. The battlefield was a {sea/ˣpool} of blood. (→ (a))
   戦場は{血の海 /ˣ血だまり}だった。

   b. When the husband returned from work, his wife and daughter were dead, and there was a {pool/ˀsea} of blood on the floor.
   夫が仕事から戻ってきたときに、妻と娘は死んでいた。床は{血の海 / 血だまり}だった。

---

homograph

see eye to eye / phr. / metonymy

to agree fully
同意見だ

Example

We seldom agree, but we see eye to eye on environmental issues.
われわれはめったに意見が合わないんだけど、環境問題については同意見だ。

---

see only one side (of ~) / phr. / metaphor

to not be able to see all aspects of {s.t./s.o.}

Examples

(a) The company president can only see one side of things.

(b) To see only one side of people is the same as seeing things in a negative light.

(c) Religious fanatics can only see one side of issues.

Note

The English and Japanese use the nouns *side* (which can mean both "surface" and "aspect") and *men* (any of the flat surfaces of an object), respectively. Both are spatial concepts used metaphorically.

血の海　n. phr.　隠喩

辺りが血で覆われている状況

関　血だまり

例文

(a) 戦場は血の海だった。

(b) その惨劇は目を覆うばかりで、凶行現場となった銀行は血の海だったという。

(c) 1930年代は、マフィアグループの抗争で、あちこちで殺し合いがあり、彼らが去った後は、辺り一面血の海だったそうだ。

関連語

日英語とも、「海」*sea* の代わりに「溜まり」*pool* という単語を使った関連表現がある。海ほど大きい範囲ではないが、大量に血がある状況を表している。➡📖REL(1)

S

同形異義語

目と目でわかる　/ phr. /　換喩

話さなくてもわかる
for two people to understand each other without verbal communication

例文

私と彼は子供のときからの親友で、何も言わなくても目と目でわかる仲だ。
He and I have been close friends since childhood, so we can understand each other without saying anything.

(〜の)一面しか見ない　phr.　隠喩

{何か / 誰か}の全体を見ることができない

関　(〜の)(一)側面しか見ない

例文

(a) その社長は物事の一面しか見ない、狭い視野の持ち主だ。

(b) 人の一面しか見ないのは、物事を否定的に見るということと同じです。

(c) 宗教の狂信者は、問題の一面しか見ることができない。

解説

日英語はそれぞれ少し意味の違う名詞を使っている。「面」は"何かの平らな表面"という意味で、英語の *side* にはその意味もあるが、「側」の意味もある。両者とも空間概念が隠喩として使われている。

543

REL

The Japanese REL is *(~ no) (ichi)sokumen shika minai.* —📖 関連語（**1**）

---

see stars / phr. / metaphor

to momentarily see flashing lights after hitting one's head

Examples

(a) I bumped into my friend and saw stars.

(b) I saw stars when I fell and bumped my head against the corner of the desk.

Note

While the English may sound more poetic than the Japanese (which literally means "fire comes out of the eyes"), both express the physiological phenomenon experienced when one's head or face is struck.

---

see the light of day / phr. / metaphor

for s.t. to be unveiled to the public

Examples

(a) Because of a lack of funding, our research never saw the light of day.

(b) Thanks to the American literary scholars' research, the ancient diary from medieval Japan finally saw the light of day.

Note

While both the English and Japanese express the same idea, the Japanese is more metaphorical due to its use of *hi no me* (lit. "eye of the sun").

---

homograph

see things in black and white / phr. / metaphor

to have a very simplistic idea of what is {right/wrong}
何かを{書く / 印刷する}，物事を両極端にとらえる

Example

My father tends to see things in black and white, and most of the time his views clash with those of others.

父は物事を両極端にとらえる傾向があるので、たいてい人と意見が衝突するんです。

関連語

日本語には関連表現として「(〜の)(一)側面しか見ない」がある。

(1)a. その社長は物事の一{面 / 側面}しか見ない、狭い視野の持ち主だ。(→(a))
b. 人の一{面 / 側面}しか見ないのは、物事を否定的に見るということと同じです。(→(b))

目から火が出る　phr.　隠喩

頭を強くぶつけたとき、目の前が真っ暗になって光が飛び交うような感じがする

例文

(a) 出合い頭に友達とぶつかって、目から火が出た。
(b) ころんで机の角に頭をぶつけて、目から火が出た。

解説

日本語の見出しより *see stars*(星を見る)という英語のほうが詩的に聞こえるが、日英語とも顔や頭などを強く打たれたときの生理現象を比喩的に表現している。

日の目を見る　phr.　隠喩

今まで人々に知られていなかったものが知られるようになる

例文

(a) 研究費が不足していたため、われわれの研究は日の目を見ることがなかった。
(b) アメリカの文学者達の研究のお陰で、日本の中世の古い日記がようやく日の目を見た。

解説

日英語の意味はまったく同じだが、日本語は英語の *see the light of day* (日の光を見る)と異なり、「日の目」と表現をしているため、より比喩性が高い。

同形異義語

白黒(を)つける　phr.　隠喩

物事の是非をはっきりさせる
to make s.t. clear; to settle once and for all

例文

ついに対決の時が来た。今度の試合こそ白黒をつけて、どちらが強いかを証明するつもりだ。

The time for the showdown has arrived at last. This game will decide once and for all who the better team is.

see through / phr. / metaphor

to understand the true nature of {s.o./s.t.}

Examples

Karen: Today I interviewed a bunch of applicants for an English-teaching job. I'm exhausted.

Mrs. S: Were they mostly young people?

Karen: Actually, a lot of them have considerable experience. But it's hard to see through the image they're projecting when you only meet them once.

(a) The teacher saw through his student's lie about having to go home because of an emergency.

(b) The physicists saw through the errors of the mathematicians.

Note

The English uses the adverb *through*, whereas the Japanese uses the verb *nuku* (to pull [up]).

see which way the wind {blows/is blowing} / phr. / metaphor

to understand how a given situation is changing

REL {know/understand} which way the wind {blows/is blowing}; the winds {have changed/will change}

Examples

(a) In order to see which way the wind blows regarding the economic situation of one's country, one needs to grasp the condition of the global economy.

(b) Land prices have been soaring, and as a result, so have rental prices. So when you rent an apartment, you have to see which way the wind is blowing with regards to the rental market.

(c) A politician must be able to grasp the flow of the times and see which way the wind blows with regards to public opinion.

REL

1. The verbs *see* and *shiru* (to know) can be replaced by *know/understand* and *wakaru* (to understand)/*miru* (to see), respectively. In addition, *kaza-muki* (direction of the wind) can be replaced by *kaze ga dochira no hō ni fuku ka.* 📖→ 関連語 (1)

2. The English and Japanese have the RELs *the winds {have changed/will change}* and *kaza-muki ga kawaru*, respectively.

(2) It is likely that the winds will change course in the economy going forward.
これから経済の風向きが変わることが予想される。

3. In addition, the Japanese has the REL *kaza-muki ga {ii/warui}* (the wind direction {is/is not} in one's favor). 📖→ 関連語 (3)

見抜く   comp. v.   隠喩

隠された本当の意味、事実関係を理解する

例文

カレン：今日は、英語教師志願者の面接をたくさんして、疲れました。

鈴木（妻）：若い人が多いの？

カレン：いえ、実はけっこう経験者もいるんですよ。でも、一度会ったくらいじゃ、どんな考えを持っているかなんて見抜けないですね。

(a) 先生は、急用で帰宅しなければならないという学生の嘘を見抜いた。

(b) その数学者の間違いは、物理学者達によって見抜かれた。

解説

日本語は動詞の「抜く」を、英語は副詞の *through*（貫いて / 抜く）を使っている。

S

風向きを知る   phr.   隠喩

ある状態の変化する方向を知る

関 風向き {を見る / がわかる}、風向きが変わる、風向きが {いい / 悪い}

例文

(a) 自国の経済状況の風向きを知るには世界の経済状態をつかまなければならない。

(b) 地価の高騰により、マンションの価格があがってきているため、部屋を借りるときは家賃相場の風向きを知る必要がある。

(c) 政治家というものは時代の流れをつかんで、世の中の風向きを知ることができなければならない。

関連語

1. 日本語の動詞「知る」と英語の動詞 *see* は、それぞれ、「見る / わかる」*know/understand* で置き換えてもかまわない。なお、「風向き」は「風がどちらの方に吹くか」で置き換えることもできる。

(1) 彼は { 風向き / 風がどちらの方に吹くか } を { 知って / 見て / わかって } から行動するタイプではない。

He doesn't wait around to {know/see/understand} which way the wind is blowing.

2. 日英語には関連表現として「風向きが変わる」*the winds {have changed/will change}* がある。

→ REL (2)

3. 日本語には「風向きが {いい / 悪い}」という関連表現がある。

(3) 今は経済の風向きが悪い。

Right now, the winds aren't blowing in our favor with regards to the economy.

seize {an/the} opportunity　phr.　metaphor

to take advantage of a chance

REL　{find/get/take} an opportunity

ANT　{miss/lose} an opportunity

Examples

(a) After striving every day to beat his own record, he at last seized the opportunity to represent Japan in the Olympics.

(b) When she's back in town, I'll seize the opportunity to propose to her.

(c) We may be in a recession, but we might be able to seize a business opportunity if we leverage our technological capabilities and offer a product no one else can.

Notes

1. *Seize* and *toraeru* both mean "to take hold of {s.t./s.o.}."

2. While the Japanese is used when someone takes advantage of a specific opportunity provided to them, the English can also be used to describe a person actively seeking an opportunity on their own.

(1) More and more students are seizing the opportunity to study abroad.
以前より多くの学生が、留学の機会を{得て/??とらえて}いる。

REL

The English and Japanese have the RELs *{find/get/take} an opportunity* and *kikai o {tsukamu/mitsukeru/eru}*, respectively. While *{find/get/take}* have slightly different meanings, as shown in the examples, *{tsukamu/mitsukeru/eru}* are mostly similar, though it should be noted that *eru* and *toraeru* are used in written Japanese. 　　→関連語(1)

ANT

The English and Japanese ANTs are *{miss/lose} an opportunity* and *kikai o {nogasu/ushinau}*, respectively.

(1) If I don't get a scholarship from the Ministry of Education, I'll {miss/lose} the opportunity to study in the UK.
文科省の奨学金がもらえないと、イギリスに留学する機会を{逃して/失って}しまう。

sell oneself (as ~)　phr.　metaphor

to convince others of one's virtues

REL　sell one's name (as ~)

Examples

Mike: I heard that Tom was just appointed assistant to the department head.

Colleague: It's because that guy's so good at selling himself. If it's English-related work they need, you'd deliver much better results.

Mike: I don't really mind.

機会をとらえる / phr. 隠喩

与えられた機会を利用する

関 機会を{つかむ / 見つける / 得る / 作る}

反 機会を{逃す / 失う}

例文

(a) 彼は日々記録更新のために努力して、ついに日本代表としてオリンピックに参加する機会をとらえた。

(b) 彼女が帰省する機会をとらえて、プロポーズをしてみるつもりだ。

(c) 不況下ではあるが、我が社の高い技術力を生かし、他社にはない商品を売り込んでいけば、ビジネスの機会をとらえることは可能だ。

解説

1. 「とらえる」と *seize* は "{何か / 誰か}をつかむ" という意味を共有している。

2. 日本語は誰かが与えられた機会を利用するときに使われるが、英語はそのような場合だけではなく、誰かが積極的に機会を求める場合にも使われる。 ➡📖 Note(1)

関連語

日英語とも、「機会を{つかむ / 見つける / 得る}」、*{find/get/take} an opportunity* という関連表現がある。英語のそれぞれの動詞の使用は例文のように多少異なった意味になるが、日本語はどの動詞を使用しても意味はほとんど同じである。日本語の「とらえる」と「得る」は書き言葉である。

(1)a. コール首相はすべての隣国の賛同を得てドイツ統一の機会をつかんだ。
   Chancellor Kohl seized the opportunity for German unification with the consent of all of its neighbors.

b. 私は中国ですばらしいビジネスの機会を見つけました。
   I found a tremendous business opportunity in China.

c. われわれは、組織のニーズに合った計画をすすめる機会を得た。
   We got the opportunity to develop a plan tailored to our organization's needs.

d. 彼は論点を明らかにする機会をつかむだろう。
   He will take the opportunity to make his point.

反意語

日英語の反意表現はそれぞれ「機会を{逃す / 失う}」と *{miss/lose} an opportunity* である。

➡📖 ANT(1)

(〜として)自分を売り込む / phr. 隠喩

自分を大事な人として知られるようにする

関 名前を売り込む

例文

マイク: トムが今度部長付きの秘書になったらしいよ。

同僚: まったくあいつは自分を売り込むのがうまいからな。英語関連だったら、マイクのほうがよっぽど実績があるのに。

マイク: ま、いいよ。

549

(a) That presidential candidate had to sell himself as a man of the people.

(b) He is very good at selling himself, which is why he's gotten so many job offers.

Note

Uru (to sell) by itself is insufficient; the compound verb *uri-komu* (lit. "to sell s.t. into") must be used. However, the figurative meaning of the English and Japanese expressions is the same.

REL

The English and Japanese RELs are *sell one's name (as~)* and *~ toshite namae o uri-komu*, respectively. Whereas the main entries mean "to make one's talents known to others," the RELs mean "to spread one's name in order to garner fame."

(1) They were still amateur musicians, so they were trying to sell {themselves/their names} to big-name producers.
彼らはまだ駆け出しのミュージシャンだったので、大物プロデューサーに名前を売り込もうと必死だった。

sell one's body　/ phr. / metaphor

to engage in sexual acts for money

REL　to prostitute oneself

Example

To keep from starving to death, she sold her body just once.

REL

The Japanese has the Sino-Japanese REL *baishun-suru* (lit. "to sell spring"), which corresponds to *to prostitute (oneself)* in English.

sell one's country　/ phr. / metaphor

to betray one's country

Examples

Kenta: I heard that the refugees from that country are treated like traitors who sold their country and that the relatives they left behind are treated horribly.

Mr. S: Yeah. They get scared to death and never tell the truth about where their relatives have disappeared to.

(a) I can't understand how one can sell his country for money.

(b) Their leader would never sell his country to get what he wants.

REL

1. The Japanese REL is *sokoku o uru* (lit. "to sell one's fatherland"), which is used much less frequently than the main entry. 📖→関連語(1)

2. Japanese also has the expression *baikokudo*, which means "an evil person who sells his/ her country." (→ dialogue)

（a）その大統領候補は、大衆の味方として自分を売り込まなければならなかった。

（b）彼は自分を売り込むことがとっても上手なんだ。それで、たくさん仕事の申し込みがあったんだよ。

解説

日本語は「売る」（sell）だけでは不十分で、複合動詞の「売り込む」を使わなければならないが、比喩的意味は同じである。

関連語

日英語とも、関連表現で「〜として名前を売り込む」と *sell one's name (as ~)* がある。見出しが"自分の人間性、才能、能力を知ってもらう"という意味であるのに対し、関連表現は"有名になるために名前を広める"という意味である。 ➡📖 REL（1）

体を売る　phr.　隠喩

性的行為で金銭を得る

関 売春をする

例文

彼女は餓死寸前までいって、一度だけ食べ物のために体を売った。

関連語

日本語には英語の *to prostitute oneself* に当たる「売春する」がある。

（自分の）国を売る　phr.　隠喩

自分の国を裏切るような行為をする

関 祖国を売る，売国奴

例文

健太：あの国からの亡命者は国を売った売国奴として扱われ、国に残った家族はひどい目にあっているらしいね。

鈴木（夫）：うん、それでみんな怖がって、身内がどこに行ったのか、真実を語らないんだろうね。

- - - - - - - - - -

（a）金のために自分の国を売るなんて、どうしてそんなことができるのかわかりません。

（b）彼らの指導者は、自分が求めているものを得るために国を売るような人ではない。

関連語

1．日本語の「祖国を売る」は、「国を売る」より使用頻度は低いが、置き換え可能な関連表現である。

（1）彼らの指導者は、自分が求めているものを得るために{国 / 祖国}を売るような人ではない。

（→（b））

2．日本語には「売国奴」という"自分の国を売った悪い人間"という表現もある。（→会話例）

551

sell one's soul to ~ / phr. / metaphor

to do s.t. immoral or unethical to achieve one's objective

Examples

(a) It is said that he sold his soul to the Devil in exchange for worldly riches.

(b) Left with no other options, Martha decided to sell her soul to the mafia.

send {a ripple/ripples} through(out) ~ / phr. / metaphor

to have a continuous impact on {s.o./s.t.}

REL ripple through(out) ~

Examples

(a) One comment from the company president sent ripples through the project, which had been proceeding without a hitch until then.

(b) This case has the potential to send ripples throughout the nation's legal system.

(c) This year's El Niño could send ripples throughout the ecological system.

Notes

1. Both the English and Japanese expressions usually take an event as their subject.

2. The English and Japanese use similar nouns (*ripple* and *hamon*), but different verbs (*send* and *nagekakeru*).

REL

1. The English REL is *ripple through(out) ~*.

(1) One comment from the company president rippled through the project, which had been proceeding without a hitch until then. (→ (a))

2. The Japanese RELs are *hamon o yobu* (lit. "to call ripples") and *hamon ga {shōjiru/ hirogaru}* (lit. "ripples occur/ripples spread"). 関連語(2)

set one's hand to (~) / phr. / metonymy

to start working on s.t.

REL {put/turn} one's hand to ~

Examples

Mrs. S: Kenta, I see you've left your models half unfinished again.

Kenta: I got tired of making them.

Mrs. S: That attitude's no good. Once you set your hand to something, you should see it through until the end.

- -

(a) My father always did his best at whatever he set his hand to.

(b) There are so many things to do that I don't know what to set my hands to first.

（〜に）魂を売る　phr.　隠喩

自分の目的遂行のために{不道徳／非倫理的}なことをする

例文

(a) 彼は世俗の富と交換に、自分の魂を悪魔に売ったと言われている。

(b) 選択の余地もなく、マーサはマフィアに魂を売る決心をしたのだった。

（〜に）波紋を投げかける　phr.　隠喩

出来事や誰かの行動が否定的な影響を与える

関 波紋を{呼ぶ}、波紋が{生じる／広がる}

例文

(a) 社長の一言が、順調に進んでいたプロジェクトに波紋を投げかけた。

(b) この事件は、国の法体系全体に波紋を投げかける可能性を持っている。

(c) 今年のエルニーニョ現象は生態系に波紋を投げかける恐れがある。

解説

1. 日英語ともに主語が何かの事件であることが多い。

2. 日英語とも名詞は同じ意味の「波紋」と *ripple* を使っているが、動詞は「投げかける」と *send*（送る）で少し異なっている。

関連語

1. 英語は、*ripple through (out), send ripples through (out)* 〜 による置き換えが可能である。

→ REL (1)

2. 日本語には「波紋を呼ぶ」「波紋が{生じる／広がる}」という関連表現がある。

(2) 社長の一言で、順調に進んでいたプロジェクトに波紋が{生じた／広がった}。（→(a)）

（〜に）手をつける　phr.　換喩

何かを始める

関 着手する

例文

鈴木（妻）：健太、模型作り、また途中でほっぽり投げて。

健太：だって、飽きちゃったんだもん。

鈴木（妻）：何言ってるの。いったん手をつけたものは、最後までやりとげなさい。

(a) 父はいったん手をつけたことには、いつも最善を尽くしていた。

(b) やるべきことが多すぎて、どこから手をつけていいのかわからない。

REL

1. In the English, the verb *set* can be replaced by *put* or *turn*.
(1) My father always did his best at whatever he {set/put/turned} his hand to. (→(a))
2. In the Japanese, *te o tsukeru* tends to be replaced by *chakushu-suru* (to launch) in formal contexts. 📖→ 関連語(2)
3. The Japanese expression carries the additional meanings of "to misappropriate money" and "to have an affair with a subordinate." 📖→ 関連語(3)

---

set the stage (for ~) / phr. / metaphor

to prepare for or help facilitate a relatively important {event/project}

Examples

Mike: Looks like the director has finally decided to retire.

Mr. S: Yeah. In reality, the stage was set for his retirement ages ago. It was just a matter of waiting for him to decide to do it.

- - - - - - - - - - - - - - - - - - - -

(a) The U.S.-Russia Summit has set the stage for further dialogue between the two nations.

(b) Technological changes a century ago set the stage for significant economic and social progress.

Note

While *set* (to put {s.t./s.o.} in a certain place) and *yōi-suru* (to make s.t. ready for a particular purpose) have different meanings, the metaphorical meaning of *stage* (a platform for a performance) is identical.

---

shadow of death, the / n. phr. / personification

gloom, such as that due to impending death

Examples

(a) He continued to talk in bed as the shadow of death approached him.

(b) The death row inmate, who had been living under the shadow of death for 15 years, began to dispute the charges and claim his innocence.

(c) He may have been diagnosed with an incurable disease, but he's not afraid of the shadow of death. He is continuing to teach while battling his illness.

Notes

1. The English expression comes from the Old Testament of the Bible (Psalm 23:4): "though I walk through the valley of the shadow of death, I will fear no evil: for thou art with me." The Japanese most likely comes from a translation of this quote.
2. In the context of (a), (b), and (c), both the English and Japanese expressions are personifications of death.

関連語

1. 英語では、動詞の *set* は *put* か *turn* で置き換えることができる。➡📖REL (1)
2. 日本語の「手をつける」は、フォーマルな文脈では「着手する」になる傾向がある。
(2) 政府は、世界の人権を守るという課題に{着手した / ʔ手をつけた}。
　　The government has set its hand to the task of defending human rights throughout the world.
3. 日本語の「手をつける」には、"何かを始める"という意味以外にも、"使ってはいけないお金を使い込む"とか"弱い立場の人と恋愛関係を持つ"のような意味がある。
(3) a. 彼はお客の預金に手をつけて、銀行をクビになった。
　　　He misappropriated a customer's money and got fired from the bank.
　　b. 彼は妻子がいるのに、10歳も年下の部下に手をつけてしまった。
　　　He had an affair with a subordinate 10 years younger than he despite having a wife and kids.

（～の）舞台を用意する　/ phr.　隠喩

比較的大事な{出来事 / 計画}の実現をしやすくするための環境を作る

例 文

マイク： ついにこの監督、引退することになりましたね。

鈴木（夫）： うん、彼がしりぞくための舞台は、もうずっと前から用意されていたんだよ。彼の決心ひとつだったんだね。

- -

(a) 米露首脳会談は、両国が引き続き対話する舞台を用意した。
(b) 1世紀前のテクノロジーの変化は、著しい経済的、社会的な進歩の舞台を用意した。

解 説

「用意する」と *set* の基本義は、それぞれ、"ある目的で何かを準備する"と"{何か / 誰か}をあるところに置く"で、かなり違っているが、「舞台」の比喩的意味は同じである。

死の影　/ n. phr.　擬人化

死が近いという感覚

例 文

(a) 彼は死の影が近づいているのに、ベッドの中で話し続けた。
(b) 15年以上も死の影に怯えて生きてきた死刑囚が、冤罪だと無実を主張し始めた。
(c) 彼は不治の病を宣告されたが、死の影を恐れてはいない。病気と戦いながらも、教壇に立ち続けている。

解 説

1. 英語は聖書（旧約聖書の詩編23：4）の「たとえ私は死の影の谷を歩むとも、わざわいを恐れません。あなたが私と共におられるからです。」から出ている。日本語は聖書の訳から来ている可能性が高い。
2. 日英語とも (a)(b)(c) の文脈では「死の影」は「近くに存在する死」という擬人化表現になっている。

shake one's head phr. metonymy

a gesture that indicates {disagreement/disapproval}

[ANT] nod one's head

[Examples]

(a) I tried my best to persuade my father to let me marry her, but he just kept shaking his head.

(b) When his computer suddenly stopped working, he shook his head and stood up from his desk.

(c) On our first date, I asked if he wanted to ride the rollercoaster, but he just shook his head and stubbornly declined.

[Note]

Both the English and Japanese expressions are used to indicate disagreement, disapproval, or a negative psychological reaction such as anger, disbelief, impatience, and so on.

[ANT]

The English and Japanese ANTs are *nod one's head* and *kubi o tate ni furu* (lit. "to shake one's head vertically")/*unazuku* (to nod one's head), respectively.

(1) When he asked if she would go on a date with him, she nodded her head and said she would love to.
彼が彼女にデートしないかと聞いたら、彼女は{首を縦に振って / うなずいて}「ぜひ！」と言ってくれた。

shallow adj. metaphor

insufficiency or imperfection in {comprehension/knowledge/thoughts/a relationship/history/experience/breathing/sleep/etc.}

[ANT] [LOOK] deep

[Examples]

(a) No matter how well you speak a foreign language, you may be misunderstood if your understanding of the culture is shallow.

(b) If you don't know much about something, it's best to admit it. Pretending that you do by showing off your shallow knowledge is just shameful.

(c) My friend talks big, but he is actually very shallow.

(d) Since I just met him recently, our relationship is still pretty shallow, so I have no idea what kind of person he is.

(e) This university has a shallow history as a research institution, but it has produced great talent over the years.

(f) His experience is still quite shallow, so we can't entrust him with this project.

(g) I could tell that she was very sick because her skin was cold and her breathing was shallow.

(h) My sleep has been shallow recently, so I haven't been getting much rest.

首を横に振る / phr. 換喩

不同意、不承諾など否定的な意志表示を示すジェスチャー

反 首を縦に振る，うなずく

例文

(a) 彼女との結婚について、懸命に説得を試みたが、父は首を横に振るばかりだった。

(b) コンピューターが急に動かなくなったとき、彼は首を横に振って、机から立ち上がった。

(c) 初めてのデートで彼をジェットコースターに誘ったが、彼は嫌がってかたくなに首を横に振っていた。

解説

日英語ともに首を横に振るのは、不同意、不承認、怒り、信じられないという気持ち、いらだちなどの否定的な心理を表す。

反意語

日英語とも、それぞれ「首を縦に振る」「うなずく」と *nod one's head* という反意表現がある。

➡️📖 ANT (1)

浅い / adj. (i) / 隠喩

{理解 / 知識 / 考え / 関係 / 歴史 / 経験 / 呼吸 / 眠り} が {足りない / 不十分である}

反 LOOK▶ 深い

例文

(a) 外国語が話せるようになっても、その文化に対して理解が浅いと、思わぬ誤解を招くことがある。

(b) よく知らなかったら、知らないと言ったほうがいい。浅い知識をひけらかして、知ったかぶりをするのはみっともない。

(c) 私の友人は言うことは大きいが、考えはとても浅い。

(d) 最近知り合ったばかりで、彼との関係はまだ浅いので、どんな人物かよくわからない。

(e) この大学は研究大学としての歴史は浅いが、多くの人材を輩出している。

(f) 彼はまだ経験が浅いので、この仕事をまかせることはできない。

(g) 彼女はひどく病気だったにちがいないよ。だって、皮膚は冷たかったし、呼吸もとても浅かったんだもの。

(h) 最近、眠りが浅くて、よく寝られない。

557

Notes

1. *Shallow* and *asai* mean "having a short distance from the bottom to the surface." The figurative meaning comes from this spatial definition.

2. While the subject of *shallow* can be a person, as in (c), this is not the case for *asai*. Instead, Japanese uses such constructions as *(s.o.) wa (s.t.) ga asai, asahakana* (lit. "shallow-thin"; "thoughtless"), or *senpakuna* (lit. "shallow-thin"; "superficial"), as shown in (1).

(1) People think James is shallow because all he talks about is money.
   ジェームズはお金のことばかり話すので、みんな、彼のことを{浅はかだ/浅薄だ/×浅い}と思っている。

3. The Japanese can also be used to mean "not much time has elapsed since ~ began," but the English does not have this usage. 📖→解説 (2)

ANT

The antonyms for *shallow/asai* are *deep/fukai*, respectively. Both can be used figuratively.

---

sharp / adj. / metaphor/synesthesia

{(climbing) angle/attack/ability to take action/ears/eyes/(power of) judgment/mind/observation/intuition/pain/sound/nuance} is figuratively piercing

REL as {keen/sharp} as a razor; razor-sharp

ANT **LOOK▶** dull

Examples

Doctor: What sort of stomach pain do you have?

Mike: It's a very sharp pain.

- -

(a) It is a joy to teach him because he is so sharp.

(b) Economists have raised sharp questions about the wisdom of government intervention in the stock market.

(c) The president's comments drew sharp criticism from the Republicans.

(d) As soon as the plane took off, it climbed up at an extremely sharp angle.

(e) A sharp winter wind cut through his jacket and clothing.

(f) This situation requires sharp focus.

(g) Biologists must have a sharp eye when it comes to organisms.

(h) At the symposium, we exchanged sharp words over the proper role of government in society.

(i) The aide responded to the press's sharp questions with sharp rejoinders in an effort to defend the president's position.

(j) The Japanese Nobel Prize winner in medicine and physiology has sharp intuition as well as a penetrating intellect.

(k) Dogs have sharp ears, so they can hear very distant sounds.

(l) There was the sharp sound of brakes being applied, and the aircraft stopped with its front wheel in the grassy area.

解 説

1. 「浅い」と shallow の基本義は"底から表面までの距離があまりない"ということで、このような空間的な状況を表す基本義から比喩的な意味が出てきている。

2. 英語の shallow の主語は(c)のように人間でも使えるが、日本語では「浅い」の主語に人間は使えない。日本語では「誰かが何かが浅い」という構文か、「浅はかな」とか「浅薄(せんぱく)な」を使うのが普通である。━📖 **Note(1)**

3. 日本語の"始まりからあまり時間がたっていない"という意味の「浅い」は、英語にはない。

(2) この町に住んで日が浅いが、もうたくさん友達ができた。
   {We haven't been living in this town for very long/ ˣOur days in this town are very shallow}, but we have already made many friends.

反意語

「浅い」shallow の反意表現は、それぞれ、「深い」deep で、どちらの反意表現も比喩的に使える。

S

鋭い（するど） / adj. (i) 隠喩（いんゆ） / 共感覚（きょうかんかく）

{(上昇)角度 / 攻撃 / 行動力 / 耳 / 目 / (状況の)判断力 / 発光体の光 / 頭脳 / 観察 / 直感力 / 痛み / 物音 / 語感}が、あたかもナイフで切るようだ
（（じょうしょう）かくど / こうげき / こうどうりょく / みみ / め / （じょうきょう）はんだんりょく / はっこうたい / ひかり / ずのう / かんさつ / ちょっかんりょく / いた / ものおと / ごかん）

関 かみそりのように {鋭い（するど）/ 切れる（き）}、(頭（あたま）が)切れる（き）

反 鈍い（にぶ）

例 文

医者（いしゃ）：おなかの痛み（いた）はどんな痛み（いた）ですか。
マイク：とても鋭い（するど）痛み（いた）です。

- -

(a) その学生（がくせい）は頭（あたま）が鋭い（するど）から、教えていて楽しいです。

(b) 経済学者（けいざいがくしゃ）たちは政府（せいふ）が株式市場（かぶしきしじょう）に介入（かいにゅう）する考え（かんが）につき、鋭い（するど）疑問（ぎもん）を提示（ていじ）した。

(c) 大統領（だいとうりょう）の発言（はつげん）がもとで、共和党（きょうわとう）から鋭い（するど）批判（ひはん）が出てきた。

(d) 飛行機（ひこうき）は離陸（りりく）するとすぐ非常（ひじょう）に鋭い（するど）角度（かくど）で上昇（じょうしょう）した。

(e) 冬（ふゆ）の鋭い（するど）風（かぜ）が吹（ふ）いてきて、身体（からだ）に切り込（き こ）んでくる感（かん）じだった。

(f) この状況（じょうきょう）には鋭い（するど）注意（ちゅうい）を向（む）けなければならない。

(g) 生物学者（せいぶつがくしゃ）には生命（せいめい）に対（たい）する鋭い（するど）観察眼（かんさつがん）が必要（ひつよう）だ。

(h) シンポジウムでは、社会（しゃかい）での政治（せいじ）の正（ただ）しい役割（やくわり）について鋭い（するど）議論（ぎろん）が交（か）わされた。

(i) 大統領補佐官（だいとうりょうほさかん）は、記者達（きしゃたち）の鋭い（するど）質問（しつもん）に対（たい）し鋭い（するど）返答（へんとう）で切り返（き かえ）して、大統領（だいとうりょう）の立場（たちば）を守（まも）ろうとした。

(j) そのノーベル医学（いがく）・生理学賞受賞者（せいりがくしょうじゅしょうしゃ）は鋭い（するど）直感力（ちょっかんりょく）と洞察力（どうさつりょく）を持（も）っている。

(k) 犬（いぬ）は耳（みみ）が鋭い（するど）ので、かなり遠（とお）くの物音（ものおと）でも聞き分（き わ）けることができる。

(l) ブレーキをかける鋭い（するど）音（おと）がして、飛行機（ひこうき）は機首（きしゅ）の車輪（しゃりん）を緑地帯（りょくちたい）に突っ込（つ こ）んで止（と）まった。

559

(m) Apparently a lot of spices are used in this dish, which lends it a sharp smell.

Notes

1. The metaphorical uses of *sharp* and *surudoi* are nearly identical point for point. The metaphor is derived from the basic meaning of *sharp*, which is "having a fine edge or point that is capable of cutting/piercing." Note that the dialogue and examples (l) and (m) are cases of synesthesia, since the original meaning is transferred to expressions related to senses other than the sense of sight.

2. English and Japanese also have the expressions *sharp wind*/*surudoi kaze*, as shown in (e), and *sharp smell*/*surudoi nioi*, as shown in (m). In Japanese, these expressions are used primarily in written language, such as novels.

3. In English, *sharp* can also mean "chic." This is not the case in Japanese.

(1) He learned the pleasure of wearing a sharp suit as a young musician.
彼は若いミュージシャンとして{粋な / ×鋭い}上着を着る楽しみを覚えた。

REL

1. Both the English RELs, *{keen/sharp} as a razor* and *razor-sharp*, and the Japanese REL, *kamisori no yōni {surudoi/kireru}*, are themselves figurative expressions, but they have the additional meaning of "to be highly intelligent." 📖→関連語(1)

2. When used metaphorically, *kireru* (the potential form of *kiru* [to cut]) means "intelligent."

📖→関連語(2)

---

shine / v. / metaphor

to have a glowing appearance; to be distinguished

REL beam

Examples

Mike: She's really been shining lately, hasn't she?

Colleague: Yeah. Apparently she got a new boyfriend and is doing well at her job.

- - - - - - - - - - - - - - - - - - - -

(a) The children's faces shone with joy when they got a big cake along with presents.

(b) NASA's technical achievements are a shining example for the world.

Note

Both the English and Japanese have the non-metaphorical meaning "for {the sun/a celestial body} to emit light," but they can also mean "for the eyes/face to emit(s) light; for s.o.'s performance/to excel" in a figurative sense.

REL

1. *Hikaru* (to shine/glitter) can be used instead of *kagayaku*. *Hikaru* is used to describe intrinsic qualities (such as talents), whereas *kagayaku* is used to describe external activities (such as accomplishments). 📖→関連語(1)

(m) この料理は香辛料がたくさん使われているようで、鋭い匂いがする。

解説

1. 日英語の「鋭い」と *sharp* の比喩的な使い方はほとんど1対1の対応を見せている。比喩は"切ったり刺したりできるような刃とか尖りのある～"という基本義からの派生である。会話例と、(l)-(m)は基本義の視覚から他の五感と関係した表現に転移した共感覚の例である。
2. 日英語とも「鋭い風」*sharp wind* ((e)) や「鋭い匂い」*sharp smell* ((m)) などの言い方がある。日本語ではこれらの表現は書き言葉的で主に小説の中などに用いられる。
3. 英語の *sharp* には"粋な"という、日本語の「鋭い」にはない意味がある。━📖 **Note(1)**

関連語

1. 日本語の「かみそりのように{鋭い / 切れる}」と英語の *{keen/sharp} as a razor* と *razor-sharp* はいずれも比喩であるが、「非常に理解がはやい」という意味でも使われる。
(1) 彼女は非常に鋭い。かみそりのように切れる。
   She's as sharp as a razor.
2. 日本語の「(頭が)切れる」は、英語の *sharp* 同様に"頭がよい"という意味で使われる。
(2) その学生は頭が{鋭い / 切れる}から、教えていて楽しいです。(→(a))

S

輝く / v. 隠喩

{目 / 顔}がとても明るい，{行動 / 業績 / 才能}が秀でている

関 光っている

例文

マイク： 最近、彼女、輝いているね。

同僚： うん、新しい恋人ができたし、仕事もうまくいっているみたいだしね。

(a) 大きなケーキとプレゼントをもらったとき、子供たちの顔が喜びに輝いた。
(b) NASA の技術上の功績は、世界でも一際輝いている。

解説

日英語の基本義は"{太陽 / 星かそれに類するもの}が光を放つ"であるが、その比喩的な意味は、"目か顔が光を放つ""誰かの行動、才能が秀でている"という意味である。

関連語

1. 日本語の「光る」は「輝く」の代わりに使うことができる。ただし、「光る」は才能のような内在的なものを表すのに対して、「輝く」は何かの業績のように外部から認識できるものに使われる
(1)a. 彼の数学者としての業績は群を抜いて{輝いて /ʔ光って}いた。
   He made many shining achievements as a mathematician.
   b. 大学時代、彼の数学の才能はひときわ{光って /ʔʔ輝いて}いた。
   His mathematical talents really shone in college.

561

2. The English REL, *beam*, is a verb derived from the noun, which means "a ray of light." However, it cannot be used in the sense of something excelling, so it can only replace *shine* in (2a).

(2) a. The children's faces {shone/beamed} with joy when they got a big cake along with presents. (→(a))

   b. NASA's technical achievements are a {shining/ˣbeaming} example for the world. (→(b))

shortsighted / comp. adj. / metaphor

not displaying foresight

REL myopic; nearsighted

ANT farsighted

Examples

Mike: I don't know what to do about our section chief!

Colleague: I know. Someone that shortsighted won't make any progress at all.

- - - - - - - - - - - - - - - - - - - -

(a) The investor's shortsightedness caused him to miss a very profitable opportunity.

(b) We are concerned about the shortsighted planning on the part of the city officials.

(c) Changing jobs is something that you should do only after careful consideration. A shortsighted decision could limit your future prospects.

REL

1. The English has the REL *myopic*. This has the same meaning as the main entry.

(1) We are concerned about {shortsighted/myopic} planning on the part of the city officials.

                                          (→(b))

2. The English also has the expression *nearsighted*, but this is only used in a medical sense.

(2) I've been really nearsighted since I was a kid, so I've always worn glasses.
私は子供の時から強い近視でずっと眼鏡をかけている。

ANT

Farsighted can be used as an ANT for *shortsighted*, but *enshigantekina* cannot be used figuratively. *Saki o mitōseru* (can see ahead) is used instead.

(1) The wise and farsighted leaders of this city planned solutions for environmental problems twenty years ago.
この町の、賢くて{先を見通せる/ˣ遠視眼的な}指導者たちは、20年前に環境問題の解決案をたてていた。

shot in the dark, a / n. phr. / metaphor

a wild guess; an attempt with a low chance of success

Examples

(a) I know this is a shot in the dark, but I called because I thought you might be able to help me.

2. 英語には関連表現として、「光線」という意味の名詞から派生した動詞 *beam*（光線を発射する）がある。しかし、*beam* には "｛行動 / 業績 / 才能｝が優れている" という意味はないから、REL（2a）の *shine* しか置き換えることはできない。➡📖 REL(2)

近視眼的（な） / comp. adj. (na) 隠喩
きん し がん てき　　　　　　　　　　　　　　　　　　　　　　いん ゆ

今見ていることだけを気にして、これからのことは考えない
いま み　　　　　　　　　　　き　　　　　　　　　　　　　　　　　　　　　かんが

【例 文】

マイク： まったく、課長には参っちゃうな。
　　　　　　　　　　か ちょう　　　まい

同僚： ほんと、あんな近視眼的な物の見方してたら、ぜんぜん前に進めないよ。
どうりょう　　　　　　　　　きん し がん てき　もの　み かた　　　　　　　　　　まえ　すす

(a) その投資家は、近視眼的な考え方をしたために、利益の多い投資の機会を逸してし
　　　とう し か　　きん し がん てき　かんが　　　　　　　　　　　り えき　おお　とう し　き かい　いっ
　　まった。

(b) われわれは、市の役人の近視眼的な計画について憂慮している。
　　　　　　　　　し　やくにん　きん し がん てき　けいかく

(c) 転職はよく考えてから実行したほうがいい。近視眼的な判断は将来の展望に支障
　　てんしょく　　　　かんが　　　　　　　じっこう　　　　　　　　きん し がん てき　はんだん　しょうらい　てんぼう　し しょう
　　をきたす。

【関連語】

1. 英語には見出しと同じ意味を持つ *myopic* という関連表現がある。➡📖 REL(1)
2. 英語には *nearsighted* という表現もあるが、医療的な意味しかない。➡📖 REL(2)

【反意語】

英語では *farsighted* が反意表現になるが、日本語の「×遠視眼的」は比喩としては使われない。そのような場合、日本語では「先を見通せる」という。➡📖 ANT(1)

闇夜に鉄砲 / n. phr. 隠喩
やみ よ　てっ ぽう　　　　　　　　　　　　　　いん ゆ

あてずっぽうで何かをする
なに

【例 文】

(a) 闇夜に鉄砲だってことは分かってたけど、あなたなら助けてくれるかもしれない
　　やみ よ　てっ ぽう　　　　　　　　　わ　　　　　　　　　　　　　　　　たす
　　と思って、電話をしたの。
　　　おも　　　　でん わ

563

(b) It's a shot in the dark, but it's probably the most effective thing we can do now.

(c) Opening an overseas branch without carefully researching the local area is like making a shot in the dark.

Note

While the English and Japanese expressions use slightly different words—*dark*/*yamiyo* (a dark, moonless night) and *shot*/*teppō* (gun)—their figurative meanings are very similar.

shoulder (of the road) / n. phr. / metaphor

the border lane on either side of a road

Example

He got into an accident, so he pulled over to the shoulder of the road and waited for the police to arrive.

homograph

shoulder to shoulder (with ~) / phr. / metonymy

close in proximity; in close cooperation
密接に協力する
みっせつ　きょうりょく

Examples

The firefighters worked shoulder to shoulder to put out the blaze.

消防士達は火を消すために密接に協力し合った。
しょうぼうし たち　ひ　け　　　　　みっせつ　きょうりょく　あ

show one's face / phr. / metonymy

to make an appearance

Examples

Mrs. S: Mike, are you leaving already?

Mike: Yeah, there's an important party going on, and I've gotta show my face.

- -

(a) After failing the entrance exam, he never showed his face at class reunions again.

(b) You're always saying you're busy with work, but you should show your cheerful face every once in a while.

Notes

1. While *show one's face* and *kao o miseru* can be used in the sense of "making an appearance," they can also be used literally, as shown below.

(1)a. The man kept his mask on and never showed his face.
男は決して仮面を脱がず、一度も顔を見せなかった。

b. The newborn triplets showed their faces on TV.
生まれたばかりの3つ子の赤ちゃんがテレビで顔を見せた。

(b) 闇夜に鉄砲だけれど、多分今できることとしては一番有効でしょうね。

(c) 現地のことをよく調べもせず海外支店を作ろうなんて、闇夜に鉄砲のようなものだ。

解説

日英語で「闇夜」と *dark* (闇)、「鉄砲」と *shot* (発砲)というように、少し異なる言葉を使っているが、全体の比喩的意味はとても近い。

路肩 / comp. n. / 隠喩

道路の端の盛り上がった部分

例文

事故にあったので、路肩に車を止めて、パトカーの到着を待った。

---

homograph

肩を並べて / phr. / 換喩

立場や力が対等である，対等に何かをする
to be on par with s.o.

例文

彼女は労働者たちと肩を並べて仕事をして、彼らの人望を得た。
She worked side by side with the laborers and won their admiration.

顔を見せる / phr. / 換喩

現れる

関 顔を出す

例文

鈴木(妻)：あら、マイク、もう帰るの。

マイク： ええ、今日は大事なパーティがあるので、これからちょっと顔を見せなければならないんですよ。

(a) 大学入試に失敗した後、彼は二度と高校の同窓会に顔を見せることはなかった。

(b) いつも仕事が忙しいって言ってるけど、たまには元気な顔を見せにいらっしゃい。

解説

1. 「顔を見せる」と *show one's face* は"人の前に現れる"という意味だが、字義通りの解釈も状況では出てくるので注意。 ─📖 Note (1)

565

2. The negative potential forms, *cannot show one's face* and *kao o miserarenai*, can be used to mean "to feel too embarrassed to appear before s.o." depending on the context.

📖→解説(2)

REL

"The Japanese REL, *kao o dasu*, literally means "to put one's face out," and it can be used interchangeably with the main entry in situations such as that shown in (1a). However, in cases such as (1b) where one goes somewhere to engage in an activity, only *kao o dasu* can be used. 📖→関連語(1)

show one's hand / phr. / metonymy

to reveal one's hidden {intentions/plans}

REL lay one's cards on the table

Examples

Section Chief: Have you prepared for tomorrow's meeting?

Mike: Yes. Should I make copies of the budget?

Section Chief: No. I don't want to show our hand before we know what they're planning. Let's wait a bit longer.

Mike: Yes, sir.

- -

(a) Negotiations often fail if you show your hand at the beginning.

(b) People will be more likely to trust you if you show them your hand at the outset.

Notes

1. While *hand* and *te* (arm/hand) have the same basic meaning, *te* can refer to both the entire arm and the hand.
2. The English expression comes from the idea of revealing one's cards during a card game, whereas the Japanese expression comes from the idea of opening a clenched fist to reveal what one is holding. This is a case where the metaphorical expressions have different origins but the same meaning.

REL

1. The English REL is *lay one's cards on the table*.
(1) Negotiations often fail if you {show your hand/lay your cards on the table} at the beginning.

(→(a))

2. The Japanese REL is *te no uchi o akasu*, which means "to clearly {explain/talk about} the hidden {ideas/plans/information/skills} in one's possession." This REL is interchangeable with the main entry. 📖→関連語(2)

566

2．日英語の可能否定形「顔を見せられない」と *cannot show one's face* はいずれも "恥ずかしくて人のところに行けない" という意味になる場合がある。

(2) もしこの試合に負けたら、ファンと後援会の方々に顔を見せられません。
If I lose this game, I won't be able to show my face to my fans and supporters.

関連語

日本語には字義通りの意味の「顔を出す」という関連表現がある。「顔を見せる」と「顔を出す」は、(1a)の場合はどちらを使ってもそれほど意味は違わないが、「顔を出す」には(1b)のように「どこかに行ってそこで何か活動をする」という意味もあり、その場合は置き換えられない。

(1)a. 大学入試に失敗した後、彼は二度と高校の同窓会に顔を{見せる / 出す}ことはなかった。

(→(a))

b. これから会議に顔を{出さ / ˣ見せ}なければならない。
I have to go show my face at the meeting.

手の内を見せる　phr.　換喩

自分の中に秘めている大事な{考え / 計画 / 情報 / 腕前}を他人に教える

関 手の内を明かす

例文

課長：明日の会議の準備はもうできているね。

マイク： はい、予算についてもコピーを作っておきますか。

課長：いや、先方の方針がわかるまで、手の内を見せるわけにはいかないから、それは、ちょっと待ったほうがいいね。

マイク： わかりました。

- - - - - - - - - - - - - - - - - - - -

(a) 始めから手の内を見せてしまうと、交渉はうまくいかないことが多い。

(b) 始めから手の内を見せれば、人に信頼される可能性はもっと高くなるだろう。

解説

1．日本語の「手」と英語の *hand* はほぼ同義であるが、「手」は英語の *arm*（腕）と *hand* の両方を指す場合もある。

2．英語の *show one's hand* はトランプの札を人に見せることから来ているが、日本語の「手の内を見せる」は握った手を開いて中のものを見せることから来ている。つまり、それぞれの比喩が違ったところから由来しているが、同じ比喩的意味を共有している。

関連語

1．英語には *lay one's cards on the table* という関連表現がある。　REL(1)

2．日本語には「自分の中に秘めている大事な{考え / 計画 / 情報 / 腕前}を他人にはっきり{説明する / 語る}」という意味の「手の内を明かす」という関連表現がある。見出しはこの表現と置き換えることができる。

(2) 始めから手の内を{見せて / 明かして}しまうと、交渉はうまくいかないことが多い。(→(a))

567

{show/bare} one's teeth / phr. / metonymy

to act in a threatening manner

Examples

(a) The bloodthirsty killer showed his teeth and came at me.

(b) This river shows its teeth every few years. Last year's hurricane resulted in terrible flood damage.

(c) He shows his teeth whenever someone disagrees with him.

Notes

1. The English uses the noun *teeth*, but the Japanese uses *kiba* (fangs/tusks). As for the verb, the English uses the straightforward *show*, whereas the Japanese uses *muku* (to peel).

2. In (b), the river is personified and used as the subject of the expression.

3. The English can be used literally, but the Japanese cannot.

(1) The child smiled while showing her teeth.
その子は {歯 / ×牙} を見せて笑った。

show the flag （旗ふり役）→ **{wave/show} the flag**

shrug one's shoulders / phr. / metonymy

to lift and contract the shoulders in a show of {indifference/resignation/uncertainty}

Examples

(a) "There's no other choice," she said with an exaggerated shrug of her shoulders.

(b) When the girl's mother told her to stop misbehaving, she shrugged her shoulders in disappointment.

(c) Gail sighed and shrugged her shoulders. "Well, there's nothing you can do about it now."

Note

Japanese people don't shrug their shoulders as often as Westerners do, but when they do, the gesture indicates either resignation, as in (a) and (c), or disappointment/submission, as in (b). This expression can probably be considered a case of metonymy because of the temporal contiguity of the gesture and the psychological state it expresses.

shut one's mouth / phr. / metonymy

to be silent

REL keep one's mouth shut

Examples

(a) The best way to avoid trouble is for me to just shut my mouth and not say another word on the matter.

(b) When I asked the kids who broke the window, they shut their mouths and wouldn't utter a word.

牙をむく / phr. 換喩

攻撃的な姿勢をあらわにする

例文
- (a) 殺人鬼が牙をむいて、襲いかかってきた。
- (b) この川は数年ごとにその牙をむく。去年の台風のときの洪水の被害もひどかった。
- (c) 彼は、自分の意見に反対する者には誰にでも牙をむく。

解説
1. 日本語では「牙」という動物の突出した歯が、英語では人間の歯と同じ *teeth* が使われている。動詞は、日本語は「むく」（表面の皮などを取り去り、中身を出す）が、英語ではもっと直接的に *show*（見せる）が使われている。
2. (b)では「川」が擬人化され、「牙をむく」の主語に使われている。
3. 英語では字義通りに"歯を見せる"で使えるが、日本語ではそのような意味では使えない。

—📖 Note (1)

肩をすくめる / phr. 換喩

仕方がない、恥ずかしいということを身振りや動作で表す

例文
- (a) 彼女は「仕方がないわね」と言って、おおげさに肩をすくめた。
- (b) その女の子は、母親にいたずらを注意されて、肩をすくめた。
- (c) ゲールはため息をついて、肩をすくめた。「もうできることは何もないのよ。」

解説
日本人は西洋人ほどには肩をすくめないが、その動作をするときは同じように(a)と(c)のようにあきらめを表すか、(b)のように落胆の気持ちを表す。この表現は動作が同時に人間の心理を表す、つまり、時間的な近接を表すので換喩の一種として分類できるだろう。

口を閉ざす / phr. 換喩

話すのをやめる，何かについて話さない

関 口を閉じる、口をつぐむ

例文
- (a) もうこれ以上、トラブルを起こさないためには、その問題については口を閉ざして何も言わないのが一番だろう。
- (b) 「だれが窓ガラスを割ったんだ？」と言ったら子供達は口を閉ざして黙っていた。

(c) We used to fight a lot about religion, but I shut my mouth about it and we don't fight anymore.

REL

1. The Japanese RELs, *kuchi o tojiru* and *kuchi o tsugumu*, have the same meaning as the main entry, but the former can also mean "to refuse to talk about s.t." *Kuchi o tojiru* is used much less frequently than *kuchi o tozasu*. *Kuchi o tozasu* can be replaced by *kuchi o tsugumu* when the former means "to not talk about s.t." 📖➡ 関連語(1)

2. The English REL, *keep one's mouth shut*, can be used in the same manner as the main entry, but it can also mean "to avoid revealing s.t. confidential."

(2) If you don't want to make her even angrier, it'd be best to keep your mouth shut.
これ以上、彼女を怒らせたくなかったら、口を閉じたままにしておいたほうがいいよ。

---

shut out / phr. / metaphor

to exclude {s.t./s.o.}

Examples

Mr. S: I heard that a lot of stolen goods show up in online auctions.

Kenta: Yep, you've gotta be careful. What we need are regulations to shut out all the stolen goods.

- -

(a) Takashi spread our secrets around, so we decided to shut him out.

(b) I wanted to attend the party, but they told me to follow the dress code and shut me out.

(c) That group resorted to force in order to shut out the opposition.

Notes

1. The basic meaning for both the English and Japanese is "to close the door so that {s.o./s.t.} cannot come in." *~ out* and *~ dasu* mean "to cause {s.o./s.t.} to proceed from inside to outside," and they are frequently used with verbs other than *shut/shimeru*.

📖➡ 解説(1)

2. This English is also used in Japanese as a borrowed expression. 📖➡ 解説(2)

3. The English is also used to mean "to prevent an opposing team from scoring."

(3) The Yankees shut out the Red Sox 10 : 0.
ヤンキースはレッドソックスに10対0で、シャット・アウト勝ちをした。

(c) 私達は宗教のことでよく喧嘩をしたものですが、宗教について口を閉ざすように
なってからというもの、喧嘩をしなくなりました。

関連語

1. 日本語の関連表現の「口を閉じる」は見出しと同じ「話すのをやめる」という意味の他に、「あ
ることについてあえて話さない」という意味もある。「口を閉じる」は「口を閉ざす」に比べる
と使用頻度がはるかに低い。「口を閉ざす」は「何かについて話さない」という意味の時、「口
をつぐむ」で置き換えられる。

(1) もうこれ以上、トラブルを起こさないためには、その問題については口を{閉ざして/つぐんで
/?? 閉じて}何も言わないのが一番だろう。(→(a))

2. 英語の関連表現 *keep one's mouth shut* は見出しと同じ意味で使えるが、その他に"何かを秘密
にして公にしない"という意味でも使える。📖 **REL(2)**

締め出す   *comp. v.*   隠喩

{誰か/何か}を{組織/グループ}の外に出す

例文

鈴木(夫):ネットオークションって、盗品もけっこう多いらしいね。
健太:そうだよ。気をつけないとね。盗品を締め出す規制が必要だね。

‑ ‑

(a) 隆はわれわれの秘密を他人に漏らしてしまったので、締め出すことにした。

(b) パーティに出席したかったのだが、ドレスコードを指摘され、締め出されてし
まった。

(c) その団体は反対する人間を締め出すために強硬手段に出た。

解説

1. 日英語の基本義は、"戸を締めて{誰か/何か}を入れなくする"である。日本語の「~出す」と
英語の ~ *out* はどちらも"内から外に{誰か/何か}を出させる"という意味である。両者とも
「締める」(shut)以外の動詞ともよく使われる。

(1)a. 彼女はカバンの中から書類を取り出した。
    She took the document out of her bag.
  b. 公園にスズメバチが飛んで来たので、子供達は一斉に逃げ出した。
    Wasps flew into the park, so the children ran out all at once.
  c. ハンターは穴から動物をひきずり出した。
    The hunter drew the animal out of the hole.

2. 日本語でも「シャット・アウト」は借用語として使われている。

(2) すべての誘惑をシャットアウトして、受験勉強に専念した。
    I shut out all temptation and focused on studying for the entrance exam.

3. 英語は"相手チームに点を1点も与えない"という意味でも使う。📖 **Note(3)**

Silence is golden. / phr. / metaphor

not speaking is often the best choice

[REL] Silence is gold.

Examples

Colleague: Now I've done it. I was so blunt that I ended up making the client angry. Silence is golden, let me tell you.

Mike: I'm not so sure about that. It's business, after all. If you don't tell it like it is, things aren't gonna go well.

- -

(a) Whenever we talk, we end up lying. That's why "silence is golden."

(b) The date was going so well that I started talking about my ex. But this made my date really angry, and she ended up leaving early. I guess silence is golden after all.

sink like a {rock/stone} / phr. / simile

to be unable to swim

Example

I sink like a rock, so whenever I go to the beach, I sunbathe but never swim.

sit on one's hands / phr. / metonymy

to not act

Examples

(a) The mayor just sat on his hands and did not take the steps necessary to remedy the situation.

(b) He's ideal for this position because he wants to get things done. He's not the kind of person who will sit on his hands and wait.

Note

The English expression involves the act of sitting on one's hands, but the Japanese involves the act of folding one's arms.

572

沈黙は金（なり） / phr. / 隠喩
話さないのが最善の分別だ

例文

同僚：失敗しちゃったよ。取り引き先にはっきり意見を言って怒らせちゃった。沈黙は金だね。

マイク：それはどうかな。ビジネスなんだから、やっぱり言いたいことは率直に言わないと、うまくいかないんじゃないかな。

(a) 言葉を口に出すと、嘘になってしまう。だから、「沈黙は金なり」なのだ。

(b) デートで調子にのって昔つきあっていた女の子の話をしたら、相手がすっかり腹を立てて、途中で帰ってしまった。やっぱり、沈黙は金だなあ。

S

金づち / n. / 隠喩
ぜんぜん泳げない

例文

私は金づちだから、ビーチで肌を日に焼くだけで、海の中には入らないのよ。

手をこまねく / phr. / 換喩
やるべきことに対して何もせず、そばで眺めている

例文

(a) 市長はただ手をこまねいていただけで、その状況を修復するための満足な処置を取らなかった。

(b) 彼は実行型だからこの役職にぴったりだ。手をこまねいてただ待つというタイプの人間ではないのだから。

解説

日本語は腕をくんでいる動作を、英語は手を尻に敷いて座っている動作を意味している。

sitting duck   / comp. n. / metaphor

{s.o./s.t.} that is vulnerable to attack

Examples

Mrs. S: Hey, are you going out?

Kenta: Yeah. I told the guys that I got paid today, and they asked me to take them to a bar.

Mrs. S: You're just a sitting duck, aren't you?

(a) Having been raised in a reform school and involved in prostitution, gambling, and drugs, she was a sitting duck for sensational journalism.

(b) The elderly are sitting ducks for scams by young people who pretend to be their grandchildren and steal their money. They need to be careful.

(c) Because the politician was frequently involved in scandals, he was a sitting duck for the press.

Notes

1. The English uses *duck* as a metaphor for an easy target, since ducks often sit on the ground. Notice how the Japanese does not specifically refer to a sitting position—it merely says that {s.o/s.t.} is a "good duck."
2. In this expression, *kamo* (duck) is more often written in katakana than in kanji (鴨).

sleep (with ~)   / phr. / metonymy

to have sexual relations with s.o.

Examples

(a) Young people these days are fine sleeping with people they barely know. I wonder if they're worried about STIs?

(b) My grandmother was shocked when she was watching TV with me one day and heard a woman tell a man, "Don't go around acting like we're lovers just because I've slept with you once or twice."

Note

Both *sleep with ~* and *~ to neru* were almost certainly used as euphemisms originally, but nowadays they are simply synonyms for having sexual relations with someone.

（いい）カモ / n. phr. / 隠喩

簡単に{攻撃できる / 騙せる / 利用できる}人

例文

鈴木（妻）：あら、出かけるの？

健太：うん、バイト代が入ったって後輩たちに言ったら、飲みに連れて行ってくれって
せがまれたんだ。

鈴木（妻）：まったく、いいカモにされているんだから。

(a) 彼女は教護院で育ち、売春、ばくち、麻薬などに関わっていたので、扇情的なジャー
ナリズムのいいカモだった。

(b) 高齢者はオレオレ詐欺のカモになりやすいから注意が必要だ。

(c) その政治家はよくスキャンダルを起こすので、マスコミのいいカモだった。

解説

1. 英語で「カモ」はよく地面に座っているのでいい標的になるというところから人の比喩として
使われている。ただし、日本語では英語と違って「座っている」とは表現せず、「いいカモ」と
だけしていることに注意。

2. 日本語の見出しの表記は「カモ」というカタカナ書きのほうが「鴨」という漢字よりもよく使
われている。

（〜と）寝る / phr. / 換喩

夫婦、もしくは、夫婦のように生活している決まったパートナー以外の誰かと性関係を持つ

例文

(a) 最近の若い人達は、たいして相手を知らなくても、簡単に寝てしまうことがある
が、病気が怖くないのだろうか。

(b) ドラマの中で、女が男に「一度や二度寝たくらいで、恋人気取りにならないで」
と言ったので、一緒にテレビを見ていた祖母が驚いていた。

解説

「〜と寝る」も sleep with 〜 も元々は婉曲話法であったにちがいないが、今ではほとんど"〜と
セックスをする"という意味と同義に使われている。

| homograph |

sleep on ~ / phr. / metonymy

to consider s.t. (overnight) before making a decision
今すぐ結論を出さないで、(一晩寝て)もう一度よく考える

| Example |

When I asked her if she would join us on our trip, she said she would sleep on it.
彼女に僕らの旅行に加わるかと聞いたら、一晩よく考えてから決めると言った。

slice of life/slice-of-life   comp. n./adj.   metaphor

a state of life viewed from a certain angle

| Examples |

(a) The novel was a slice-of-life depiction of a world she knew really well.

(b) His first impression of the film was that it was a slice-of-life work that was closer to a documentary than an actual movie.

(c) That photo I loved so much captured a slice of ordinary life in Japan.

| Notes |

1. *Slice* and *danmen* (a fragment) are slightly different in meaning. In English, it is also possible to say *a fragment of life*, but the corresponding Japanese, *sēkatsu no hito-kire*, makes no sense.

2. *Ichimen* and *sokumen* are used more commonly than *danmen*. The former means "one part," whereas the latter means "a part other than the front." 📖→ 解説(**1**)

slip of the tongue, a   / n. phr. /   metaphor

an unintended utterance

REL   a slip of the lip; loosen s.o.'s tongue (about~); a slip of the pen

| Examples |

Saya: You really helped me out today. Thanks a bunch!

Kenta: You're welcome. I wish you were always that honest.

Saya: What did you just say?

Kenta: Oops, sorry! That was just a slip of the tongue.

同形異義語

寝かせる / 寝かす / v. / 隠喩

商品を売らない，資本金を使わない，{酒 / ワイン / 米麹} などを熟成させる
to keep {merchandise/capital} without {selling/using} it; to cause to ferment
{alcohol/wine/malted rice}

例　文

(a) 今の経済状態が落ち着くまで資金を寝かせておこう。

Let's hold off on using the funds until the economy has stabilized.

(b) そのワインはフランスの有名なワインセラーの奥に50年以上も寝かせてあったの
で、途方もない値段がついた。

The wine was incredibly expensive because it was fermented for more
than 50 years in a famous wine cellar in France.

S

{暮らし / 生活}の{断面 / 一面 / 側面} / n. phr. / 隠喩

生活をある観点から見た状態

例　文

(a) 彼女はその小説で、自分がよく知っている暮らしの断面について書いた。

(b) その映画の第一印象は、それが本当の映画というよりは記録映画に近い生の生活の
一面ということだった。

(c) 私が大好きなその写真は、日本の普通の暮らしの側面をとらえていた。

解　説

1. 日英語はそれぞれ名詞の「断面」と *slice* (一切れ)で、多少意味が違う。英語では *a fragment of
life* とも言えるが、日本語では「生活の一切れ」とは言えない。

2. 日本語は「一面」と「側面」の方が「断面」よりも使用頻度がはるかに高い。「一面」は一つの部
分を、「側面」は「正面」ではない部分をそれぞれ示す。

(1) 彼女はその小説で、自分がよく知っている暮らしの{断面 / 一面 / 側面}について書いた。

(→(a))

舌が滑る / phr. / 隠喩

言うべきでないことを間違って言ってしまう

関 口が滑る

例　文

さや：今日は本当に助かったわ。どうもありがとう。

健太：どういたしまして。いつもそうやって素直ならいいんだけどね。

さや：え、何、今の？

健太：あ、ごめん。うっかり舌が滑っちゃった。

577

(a) I didn't mean to say that! It was just a slip of the tongue.

(b) I called my boyfriend John by my ex's name, Mike, but that was just me making an innocent slip of the tongue.

Note

The English is usually used as a noun phrase, while the Japanese is a verb phrase. In the examples, the intransitive verb *suberu* (to slip) is used, but its causative version, *suberaseru* (to cause to slip) can be used in the transitive sense, as shown in (1). The corresponding English is *to make a slip of the tongue*. (1) emphasizes the responsibility of the person who has made the slip of the tongue. 📖→ 解説(1)

REL

1. *A slip of the lip* and *kuchi ga suberu* (lit. "the mouth slips") are RELs for *a slip of the tongue* and *shita ga suberu*, respectively. The English REL is rarely used, but the Japanese REL is used far more often than *shita ga suberu*. 📖→ 関連語(1)

2. The English has the REL *a slip of the pen,* which means "a mistake in s.o.'s writing."

(2) I got an A- instead of an A on my test all because of a simple slip of the pen.
単なる書き間違いだったのに、テストでAの代わりにA-をもらってしまった。

(as) slow as a snail   *phr.* │ simile

for {s.o./s.t.} to be very slow

REL snail's pace; snail-paced

ANT as swift as the wind

Examples

(a) I had to finish my work at the computer lab because my Internet connection at home is as slow as a snail.

(b) This library was supposed to be finished in three years, but the construction has been as slow as a snail, so it's still not done even though it has already been five years.

REL

1. In English, there are two expressions that are very similar to the above: *snail's pace* and *snail-paced.*

(1) I write at a snail's pace./My writing is snail-paced.
僕の書くスピードはかたつむりのようにのろい。

2. The Japanese REL is *gyūho*, which means "for s.t. to be slow and hardly make any progress." 📖→ 関連語(2)

ANT

The English ANT is *as swift as the wind,* and the Japanese ANT is *kaze no yōni hayai.*
📖→ 反意語(1)

(a) そんなことを言うつもりはなかったんだよ。舌が滑っただけさ。

(b) 新しい彼氏のジョンのことを、前の彼氏の名前のマイクと呼んじゃったんだけど、ただ舌が滑っただけだったの。何の意味もなかったのよ。

【解説】

英語はたいてい名詞句で日本語は動詞句になる。例文の日本語の動詞はすべて自動詞の「滑る」だが、その使役形が(1)のように他動詞として使われる場合もある。この場合、英語では *make a slip of the tongue* と言う。(1)では、他動詞のほうが自動詞よりも行為者の責任が強く表現される。

(1) 新しい彼氏のジョンのことを、前の彼氏の名前のマイクと呼んじゃったんだけど、ただ舌{が滑った / を滑らせた}だけだったの。何の意味もなかったのよ。(→(b))

【関連語】

1. 日英語とも、「口が滑る」と *a slip of the lip* という関連表現がある。英語の *a slip of the lip* は見出しよりはるかに使用頻度が低いが、日本語の「口が滑る」は見出しよりはるかに使用頻度が高い。

(1) そんなことを言うつもりはなかったんだよ。{舌 / 口}が滑っただけさ。(→(a))

　　I didn't mean to say that! It was just a slip of the {tongue/lip}.

2. 英語には「書き間違い」という意味の *a slip of the pen* という関連表現がある。 📖REL(2)

かたつむりのようにのろい　*phr.*　直喩

とてものろい，とてもゆっくり進む

【関】牛歩

【反】風のように速い

【例文】

(a) 僕の家のコンピュータの接続スピードがかたつむりのようにのろいので、コンピュータセンターで作業をしなければならなかった。

(b) この図書館は3年で完成する予定だったのに、工事がかたつむりのようにのろく、5年経った今でも未完だ。

【関連語】

1. 英語には関連表現として *snail's pace* と *snail-paced* がある。 📖REL(1)

2. 日本語には「牛歩」という関連表現があり、"物事が遅々として進まない"という意味で使う。

(2) 私の研究は{かたつむりのようにのろく / 牛歩で}、10年かけてもまだ結果が出ない。

　　My research is proceeding at a snail's pace. It's been 10 years and I still haven't produced any results.

【反意語】

日英語の反意表現は、それぞれ、「風のように速い」と *as swift as the wind* である。

(1) 昔は彼女は風のように速く走ったものだ。

　　She used to run as swift as the wind.

sly as a fox / phr. / simile

extremely shrewd

Example

You'd better watch out—she's sly as a fox.

Note

Both the English and Japanese are similes since they use *as* and *yōni*, respectively. However, it is also possible to turn them into metaphors by using only the noun.

(1) He is a fox.
彼はキツネだ。

---

smack one's lips（舌なめずりをする）→ {lick/smack} one's lips

---

small fry / comp. n. / metaphor

a minor person

Example

He's just small fry. Try to find out who the boss is.

(it's a) small world / phr. / metaphor

s.t. said when discovering s.o. shares a mutual acquaintance or meeting s.o. at an unexpected place

Example

My daughter's boyfriend turned out to be the son of one of my former teachers—what a small world we live in!

(s.t.) smell(s) fishy / phr. / metaphor

to be suspicious

REL smell a rat

Examples

Kenta: This job pays 10,000 yen an hour.

Saya: You earn that much just by handing out flyers? Smells fishy to me.

Kenta: Yeah, this is too good to be true.

- -

(a) Something smelled fishy about the way he behaved during the airport security check.

(b) Something about the circumstances surrounding the old couple's death smelled fishy. The detective wondered if there had been foul play.

キツネのようにずる(賢)い / phr. / 直喩

とてもずる賢い

例文

彼女はキツネのようにずるいから、要注意だ。

解説

見出しは日英語とも「ように」*like* が使われている直喩表現である。しかし、「(〜は)キツネだ」*(s.o.) is a fox* と隠喩にして「ずる(賢)い」*sly as* を省略することもできる。━📖 **Note(1)**

S

雑魚 / comp. n. / 隠喩

{地位が低い/重要でない}人

例文

やつは雑魚だ。やつのボスを見つけだせ。

{世界/世間}は{小さい/狭い} / phr. / 隠喩

共通の知り合いがいることがわかる

例文

娘の恋人が、私がお世話になった先生の息子さんだったなんて、世界は狭いなあ。

くさい / adj. (i) / 隠喩

何かが{悪い/変だ/あやしい}と思う

関 うさんくさい, におう

例文

健太：このアルバイト、1時間1万円だって。

さや：ビラ配るだけで、そんなにもらえるなんて、ちょっとくさいわよ。

健太：うん、変だね。

- -

(a) 空港のセキュリティチェックでの彼の行動は、何かくさかった。

(b) その老夫婦の死を取り巻く状況は、何かくさい感じがした。探偵は殺人事件ではないかと思った。

581

Notes

1. The Japanese expression uses the adjective *kusai*, which means "to have a bad odor." The English adjective *fishy*, however, means "to resemble fish in taste/odor." While Japanese has the compound adjective *sakana-kusai*, this simply means "to smell like fish" and cannot be used figuratively to mean "to be suspicious."

2. In Japanese, the noun + *kusai* construction is often used to form similes, such as *han'nin-kusai* (like a criminal) or *obasan-kusai* (like a middle-aged lady).

R E L

The English REL, *smell a rat*, means "to feel that s.t. is wrong/strange." Unlike *smell fishy*, which does not take a person as the subject, this expression must take a person as the subject, as shown in (1). In the Japanese, *kusai* can be replaced by *niou* and *usan kusai*, which consists of *usan* (suspicious) and *kusai* (to smell).

(1) John: The butler's alibi doesn't add up.

Jim: You're right. I think I smell a rat.

ジョン：執事のアリバイはつじつまが合わないな。

ジム：　その通りだ。何か｛（うさん）くさい/におう｝な。

---

smoke out　/ phr. / metaphor

to bring s.t. significant to light

Examples

(a) It's going to take a long time before we can smoke out the truth about the espionage.

(b) Detective Kindaichi is very good at smoking out criminal evidence.

(c) The party failed to smoke out the illegal election activities of the opposition party.

Note

While the English and Japanese expressions have the same metaphorical meaning, they use different verbs. *Aburi-dasu* is a compound verb that means "to hold a picture/text over a flame to reveal the invisible ink," while *smoke out* means "to force s.t./s.o. out using smoke."

(as) {smooth/soft} as {velvet/silk}　/ phr. / simile

very soft and smooth

Examples

(a) This artificial fiber is as smooth as velvet.

(b) The kitten's fur was as soft as silk and pleasing to the touch.

解 説

1. 日本語では「くさい」という意味の形容詞だけだが、英語では *fishy*（魚のような{味 / におい}）という形容詞になっている。日本語にも「魚くさい」という複合形容詞はあるが、字義通りの意味で、"何かが悪いとか、変だとか、あやしいと思う"という比喩的な意味はない。

2. 日本語では「名詞＋くさい」が「犯人くさい」「おばさんくさい」のように、「名詞のようだ」という直喩として使われることもある。

関連語

英語には *smell a rat*（{誰か / 何か}が{変だ / あやしい}と思う）という関連表現がある。この関連表現は主語がものである *smell fishy* と異なり、(1)の例でわかるように主語が人間である。日本語のほうは「うさん」（疑わしい）＋「くさい」からなる「うさんくさい」と「におう」という関連表現がある。「くさい」の例はすべて置き換えることができる。　📖REL(1)

S

あぶり出す / comp. v. / 隠喩

何か大事なことや真実を明るみに出す

例 文

(a) 諜報活動の実態をうまくあぶり出すには、長時間かかる。

(b) 金田一探偵は、犯罪の証拠をあぶり出すのがとてもうまい。

(c) その党は、対抗する党の選挙活動の違法性をあぶり出そうとして失敗した。

解 説

日英語の比喩的意味は共通であるが、使われている動詞は異なる。英語の *smoke out* は"煙で{何か / 誰か}を外に出す"で、日本語の「あぶり出す」は"無色のインクで書いた{絵 / 文}に弱い火を当てて見えるようにする"という意味である。

{ビロード / 絹}のようになめらか / phr. / 直喩

とてもやわらかくてなめらか

例 文

(a) この化学繊維はビロードのようになめらかな手触りだ。

(b) 子猫の毛は絹のようになめらかで、気持ちがいい手触りだ。

583

smooth sailing / phr. / metaphor

easy progress

REL {plain/clear} sailing

Examples

Mrs. S: Mr. Sato must be so happy now that he has married such a wonderful woman.

Mr. S: And that's not all—he was recently promoted. His life is smooth sailing from here on out.

- - - - - - - - - - - - - - - - - - - -

(a) While it was smooth sailing for our economy this year, it looks like it may hit rough waters next year.

(b) If we can complete this project as scheduled and under budget, everything else should be smooth sailing.

(c) It's smooth sailing in the real estate sector. Low interest rates and strong consumer confidence are causing a surge in home purchases.

Note

The English and Japanese expressions have identical meanings. The English is more straightforward, while the Japanese literally means "a favorable tailwind and full sails."

REL

The English has the RELs *plain sailing* and *clear sailing*, which have the same meaning as the main entry but are used less frequently.

(1) While it was {smooth/plain/clear} sailing for our economy this year, it looks like it may hit rough waters next year. (→(a))

smooth (out) the rough edges / phr. / metaphor

to improve s.t.

ANT rough around the edges

Examples

(a) By gaining experience working alongside various people, he, too, smoothed out his rough edges and became nice to his subordinates.

(b) My father used to be short-tempered, but after his grandchild was born, he completely smoothed out his rough edges.

(c) Your personality is decided when you're born. A little bit of hardship isn't enough to smooth out the rough edges.

Notes

1. While the Japanese expression can only be used to mean "for s.o.'s personality to become gentler," the English can also mean "to improve s.t. in some way," as shown in (1a) and (1b).

(1)a. The rough edges of that idea need to be smoothed out.
   そのアイディアは{荒削りのところを整え / ˣ角を取ら}なければならない。

   b. The result was an epic film with all the rough edges smoothed out.
   その結果、{荒削りなところのない / ˣ角の取れた}、叙事詩的な映画が誕生した。

2. *Toreru* (to come off) is an intransitive verb, but *smooth* is used as a transitive verb.

順風満帆
じゅんぷうまんぱん | **n. phr.** | 隠喩
いんゆ

物事が問題なく進む
ものごと　　もんだい　　すす

例文

鈴木（妻）：佐藤さん、すてきな奥さんもらって、幸せね。
すずき　つま　　さとう　　　　　　おく　　　　　　　　しあわ

鈴木（夫）：うん、最近、昇進もしたし、彼の人生は順風満帆だね。
すずき　おっと　　　　さいきん　しょうしん　　　かれ　じんせい　じゅんぷうまんぱん

(a) 我が国の経済は今年は順風満帆だったが、来年は荒れるかもしれない。
　　わ　くに　けいざい　ことし　じゅんぷうまんぱん　　　　らいねん　あ

(b) プロジェクトを計画通り、予算内で終えることができれば、それから先は確実に
　　　　　　　　　けいかくどお　よさんない　お　　　　　　　　　　　　　　さき　かくじつ
順風満帆になる。
じゅんぷうまんぱん

(c) 不動産業は順風満帆だ。低金利と消費者の強い信用とで住宅購入が大波に乗って
　　ふ どうさんぎょう　じゅんぷうまんぱん　ていきんり　しょうひしゃ　つよ　しんよう　じゅうたくこうにゅう　おおなみ　の
いるのだ。

解説

英語は「穏やかな航行」という直接的な表現だが、日本語は字義通りには"都合のいい追い風で帆がいっぱいにはらんでいる"という意味である。

関連語

英語には *plain sailing* と *clear sailing* という見出しと同じ意味を持つ関連表現があるが、使用頻度は見出しより少ない。 ▶📖 **REL(1)**

角が取れる
かど　と | **phr.** | 隠喩
いんゆ

人の性格が穏やかになる，優しくなる
ひと　せいかく　おだ　　　　　　やさ

反 角がある
　　かど

例文

(a) 大勢の人との仕事を経験し、彼も角が取れて部下にもやさしくなった。
　　おおぜい　ひと　　しごと　けいけん　かれ　かど　と　ぶか

(b) 怒りっぽい父親だったが、孫ができてからは、すっかり角も取れた。
　　おこ　　　　ちちおや　　　　　まご　　　　　　　　　　　　　かど　と

(c) 性格は生まれつきのものです。少しばかり苦労したところで、なかなか角なんて取
　　せいかく　う　　　　　　　　　　すこ　　　　　　くろう　　　　　　　　　　　　かど　と
れませんよ。

解説

1. 日本語は"より穏やかで円満になる"という比喩的意味しかないが、英語にはその上に、"何かの質がもっと良くなり、洗練されてくる"という比喩的意味もある。 ▶📖 **Note(1)**

2. 日本語の動詞「取れる」は自動詞だが、英語の動詞 *smooth* は他動詞である。

S

ANT

The English and Japanese ANTs are *rough around the edges* and *kado ga aru*, respectively. The Japanese expression means "to not get along well with others due to one's character," but the English means "to be unrefined." 📖➡ 反意語(1)

(2) His first novel was rough around the edges.
彼の最初の小説は{荒削りだった/ ×角があった}。

---

snake of a line / n. phr. / metaphor

a very long line of people

Examples

(a) When I got to the theater, I was shocked to see the endless snake of a line at the ticket booth.

(b) There was a long snake of a line at airport security.

(c) People have been waiting in a snake of a line since last night to see the Yankees play the Red Sox.

Note

Both the English and Japanese expressions compare the length of a line to a snake. The Japanese is a Sino-Japanese compound consisting of *chō* (long) and *da* (snake). The phrasal version, *nagai hebi no yōna retsu* (a line like a long snake), is not used.

---

snake one's way / phr. / metaphor

for {s.t./s.o.} to move in a winding motion like a snake

REL weave in and out {among/through/of} ~; snake along

Examples

(a) The car in front of me is snaking its way down the road. The driver must be drunk.

(b) The river snakes its way to the ocean.

(c) Westerlies, trade winds, and other winds sometimes snake their way across the globe in a winding motion due to the season and other conditions.

Notes

1. The Japanese expression is limited to describing inanimate objects, but the English can describe people as well. In Japanese, one must use the REL *nū yōni susumu* (to thread one's way) to describe a person. 📖➡ 解説(1)

2. The Japanese comes from the identical Chinese expression.

REL

The English and Japanese RELs are *weave in and out {among/through/of} ~/snake along* and *nū yōni susumu*, respectively.

(1) A taxi driver sped past us and collided with another car as he wove in and out of the traffic.
タクシーの運転手は道路を{蛇行し/縫うように進み}ながら、われわれの車を追い越し、他の車と衝突した。

反意語

日英語の反意表現はそれぞれ「角がある」と *rough around the edges* である。日本語は"性格上つき合いが円滑にいかない"という意味だが、英語は"何か作られたものについて荒削りだ"という意味である。 ━📖 ANT(2)

(1) 彼女は言葉に角があるために友達ができない。
Her way of speaking is rough around the edges, so she has trouble making friends.

長蛇の列 / n. phr. / 隠喩

長い人の列

例文

(a) 劇場に着いたとき、チケット売り場に並んでいる人々の長蛇の列を見てびっくりしてしまった。

(b) 空港のセキュリティチェックは、長蛇の列だった。

(c) ヤンキース対レッドソックスの試合を見るために、きのうの晩から人々は長蛇の列を作って待っていた。

解説

日英語とも、蛇を人の列の長さと比較している。日本語は「長」+「蛇」の漢語系複合語である。「長い蛇のような列」とは言わない。

蛇行する / comp. v. / 隠喩

何かが蛇のように曲がりくねって進む

関 縫うように進む

例文

(a) 前の車が蛇行運転をしているが、恐らくあれは飲酒運転だろう。

(b) 河は蛇行しながら、海へ流れこんでいる。

(c) 偏西風や貿易風のように、風は季節やその他の条件で蛇行して吹くことがある。

解説

1. 日本語では例文にあるように、蛇行するものはふつう人間ではないが、英語では人間であってもかまわない。日本語では人間が主語の場合は「蛇行する」を使わず、(1)のように「縫うように進む」と言わなければならないことに注意。

(1) 牧師は弔いの客の間を{縫うように/×蛇行して}進んだ。
The minister snaked his way through the mourners.

2. 日本語はまったく同形の中国語からの借用である。

関連語

日英語とも、「縫うように進む」/*weave in and out {among/through/of} ~/snake along* という見出しと同じ意味を持つ関連表現がある。━📖 REL(1)

In addition, Japanese has the nominal compound *dakō-unten*, which literally means "snake driving." In English, one could say "weave in and out of traffic," which corresponds to *nū yōni unten-suru*.

snap / v. / metaphor

to suddenly lose one's composure

REL make s.o. sick

Examples

(a) Whenever the boss's subordinates try something new, he always snaps at them and opposes whatever they're doing.

(b) Nowadays, lots of kids snap for no particular reason.

(c) The media often says that kids snap too easily, but it's not just them, right?

Notes

1. The basic meanings of the English and Japanese are "to break suddenly with a sharp sound" and "to be easily separated by a sharp object," respectively. Both can be used as slang expressions that carry the figurative meaning of "to suddenly lose one's composure."

2. The Japanese expression came into vogue in the early 90s, when Japan was suffering from a wave of juvenile crime.

R E L

The English and Japanese RELs are *make s.o. sick* and *mukatsuku*, which are metaphors that mean "to cause s.o. to feel disgust" and "to feel disgusted," respectively.

関連語(1)

snowball / v. / metaphor

for s.t. to increase or expand at an exponential rate

Examples

(a) After the initial round of ads, business began to snowball.

(b) The financial shock dragged down the company's sales, and its debt began to snowball.

(c) Eventually, his debt snowballed to about ¥5,000,000.

Notes

1. The English is a straightforward metaphor, but the Japanese is a simile that literally means "for s.t. to increase like a snowball."

2. Note that the Japanese simile is created using *-shiki ni* (after the style of ~) rather than the usual ~ *no yōni*. 解説(1)

3. *Fueru* is an intransitive verb, but the transitive verb *fuyasu* can also be used when the sentence concerns monetary matters. However, in this case, the *kanji* used is usually 殖 as opposed to 増. 解説(2)

588

なお、日本語の「蛇行運転」は「蛇のようにくねくね曲がって運転する」という意味で使う複合名詞である。英語では「縫うように運転する」に対応する *weave in and out of traffic* も使える。

キレる / v. 隠喩（いんゆ）

我慢（がまん）ができず、簡単（かんたん）に冷静（れいせい）さを失（うしな）う

関 むかつく

例文

(a) あの上司（じょうし）は部下（ぶか）が何（なに）か新（あたら）しいことをしようとすると、いつもキレて反対（はんたい）する。

(b) 最近（さいきん）は何（なに）も特別（とくべつ）の理由（りゆう）がないのにキレる子供達（こどもたち）が大勢（おおぜい）いる。

(c) 「若者（わかもの）はキレやすい」なんて、マスコミでよく言（い）われていますけれど、実際（じっさい）キレるのって若者（わかもの）だけじゃないですよね。

解説

1. 日英語の基本義は、それぞれ"何かが鋭い道具で簡単に2つにわかれる"と"鋭い音を出して何かが壊れる"という意味である。そこから"突然冷静さを失う"という比喩的な意味へ転移して、俗語として使われている。

2. 日本語は90年代初期に青少年の犯罪率の増加に伴い、「切れる若者」として社会問題化して扱われるようになり、「キレる」という表現が一般化した。

関連語

日英語とも、"何かを見たり聞いたりして吐き気をもよおすほど不愉快になる"という意味の「むかつく」と *make s.o. sick* という比喩表現がある。

(1) あの男の顔を見るだけでむかつく。
Just looking at his face makes me sick!

雪（ゆき）だるま式（しき）に増（ふ）える / phr. 直喩（ちょくゆ）

何（なに）かの数（かず）や量（りょう）が加速度的（かそくどてき）に増（ふ）える

関 ねずみ算式（ざんしき）に増（ふ）える

例文

(a) 最初（さいしょ）の広告（こうこく）を出（だ）してからは、仕事（しごと）は雪（ゆき）だるま式（しき）に増（ふ）えた。

(b) 金融（きんゆう）ショックで会社（かいしゃ）の売（う）り上（あ）げが大幅（おおはば）に落（お）ち込（こ）み、負債（ふさい）が雪（ゆき）だるま式（しき）に増（ふ）えた。

(c) 彼（かれ）の借金（しゃっきん）は雪（ゆき）だるま式（しき）に増（ふ）えていき、最後（さいご）には500万円（まんえん）ぐらいまで膨（ふく）らんだ。

解説

1. 英語は「雪だるま」を動詞に使っていて隠喩になっているが、日本語は直喩表現になっている。

2. 日本語の直喩は「～のように」ではなく、「～式に」で表されていることに注意。

(1) 彼の借金は雪だるま{式に/×のように}増えて、最後には500万円ぐらいまで膨らんだ。(→(c))

3. 「増える」は自動詞だが、日本語の場合、財産やお金に関することなら他動詞の「ふやす」も使える。ただし、漢字は「増」よりも「殖」を使用することが多い。

(2) 彼は財産を雪だるま式に殖やした。
He snowballed his assets.

REL

The Japanese REL is *nezumizan-shiki ni fueru* (lit. "to increase in a way similar to how mice breed"), which means "to increase exponentially."

---

soak up / phr. / metaphor
to readily absorb information

Examples

Kenta: Is teaching English fun?

Karen: Yeah, definitely. I get an especially great response when I teach high school students who are interested in American culture. It's amazing how quickly they soak up everything I teach them.

- -

(a) You can soak up anything when you're young, so you should study hard now.

(b) She came to the restaurant as an apprentice and quickly soaked up new cooking techniques. Soon she became so skilled that it looked like she'd be able to open up her own restaurant right away.

Note

The basic meaning of *soak up* and *kyūshū-suru* (to absorb) is "to take in liquid."

(as) soft as {velvet/silk} ({ビロード / 絹} のようになめらか)
→ **(as) {smooth/soft} as {velvet/silk}**

---

sore spot / comp. n. / metaphor
a topic that upsets s.o.

REL sore point; nerve

Examples

Saya: Have you been studying English lately? You haven't given up on going abroad, have you?

Kenta: I've been so busy with my part-time job; I just haven't had the time.

Saya: What're you talking about? There you go again, trying to avoid reality.

Kenta: You really know how to hit a sore spot. But yeah, I guess you're right.

- -

(a) When the topic of tax evasion came up, the politician winced as if they'd hit upon a sore spot, and he quickly changed the subject.

(b) You could say that of all the things that occurred during his presidency, the problems he had with women are his biggest sore spot.

Note

Sore and *itai* are used in a non-physical sense, but their metaphorical use is based on the physical sensation.

関連語

日本語には「ねずみ算式に増える」という関連表現がある。これはねずみが猛烈な勢いで繁殖するさまからきた比喩表現で、数が加速度的に増えるという意味である。

吸収する　/ v. / 隠喩

何か学べることを自分のものにする

例文

健太：英語教えるのって、おもしろい？

カレン：うん、おもしろいよ。特にアメリカの文化に興味を持っている高校生ぐらいの子に教えると、手応えがあるわね。なんでもどんどん吸収して怖いくらい。

- (a) 若いうちは、柔軟で何でも吸収できるのだから、今のうちによく勉強しておきなさい。

- (b) 見習いで店にやってきた彼女は、次々と料理の技術を吸収し、すぐにでも店が開けそうなほどの腕前になった。

解説

「吸収する」も soak up も "水分を吸い取る" というのが基本義である。

痛いところ　/ n. phr. / 隠喩

誰かの {弱点 / 言われたくない部分}

関 痛い点, 泣きどころ

例文

さや：最近、英語の勉強してる？　まだ、留学あきらめてないんでしょ？

健太：アルバイトが忙しくて、それどころじゃないんだよ。

さや：何言ってるの。そうやって、現実逃避しているだけじゃない。

健太：痛いところを突いてくるなあ。ま、実を言うと、そうなんだけどさ。

- (a) その政治家は、話が脱税のことに及ぶと、痛いところに触れられたように、たじろいで話題を変えた。

- (b) 女性問題は、その大統領の在任中に起きた事件の中で、一番痛いところと言えるだろう。

解説

日英語とも「痛い」と sore を非肉体的に使っているが、この比喩的用法は肉体的感覚からきている。

REL

1. The English and Japanese have the RELs *sore point/nerve* and *itai ten*, respectively.
(1) When the topic of tax evasion came up, the politician winced as if they'd hit {a nerve/upon a sore point} and he quickly changed the subject. (→ (a))
その政治家は、話が脱税のことに及ぶと、痛い{ところ / 点}に触れられたように、たじろいで話題を変えた。(→(a))
2. The Japanese REL *naki-dokoro* means both "a scene where people are moved to tears" and "weak point." The latter use coincides with the use of *itai {tokoro/ten}*. 📖→関連語(2)

source of headaches　　n. phr.　metaphor

{s.o./s.t.} annoying or frustrating

REL　thorn in s.o.'s {flesh/side}

Examples

Mr. S: The Yamadas' two older sons didn't have any issues growing up, but the youngest one's apparently the source of a lot of headaches. He doesn't have a job and just spends all his time fooling around.

Mrs. S: No kidding. It must be tough having three sons.

(a) The tax system is a source of headaches for any government.

(b) The spike in gas prices has been a source of headaches for the citizens.

(c) That railroad crossing is a source of headaches for morning commuters because the gates are always down due to all the trains running.

Note

Zutsū no tane literally means "the seed of a headache." The English uses *source* instead of *seed*.

REL

1. The English REL is *thorn in s.o.'s {flesh/side}*, which originated from the New Testament of the Bible (2 Corinthians 12:7). It means "{s.o./s.t.} that constantly causes irritation."
(1) That railroad crossing is a {source of headaches/thorn in the side} for morning commuters because the gates are always down due to all the trains running. (→ (c))
毎朝の通勤者にとって、あの駅の手前の開かずの踏み切りは、頭痛の種だ。(→(c))
2. The Japanese RELs are *atama ga itai* (to have a headache) and ~ *atama o itameru*.

📖→関連語(2)

sow (the) seeds (of ~)　　phr.　metaphor

to lay the groundwork for s.t. to happen

REL　plant (the) seeds (of ~)

Examples

(a) The extremism of religious radicals is always what sows the seeds of strife in the Middle East.

(b) That ideology, which promoted hatred and class struggle, sowed seeds of strife, suspicion, and conflict.

関連語

1. 日英語とも「痛い点」sore point/nerve という関連表現がある。━📖 REL(1)
2. 日本語の関連表現「泣きどころ」は、"人を泣かせるような場面"という意味と"弱点"という意味があり、後者が"痛い｛ところ / 点｝"と意味が重なる。

(2) 彼の｛痛いところ / 痛い点 / 泣きどころ / 弱点｝にうっかり触れたとき、彼は膨れっ面になった。
He gave me a sulky look when I accidentally brought up a sore spot.

頭痛の種　 n. phr. 　隠喩

困ったこと

関 頭が痛い，頭を痛める

例文

鈴木(夫)：山田さんの息子さん、上の二人は問題なく育ったらしいけど、一番下の息子が仕事もせず遊んでばかりいて、頭痛の種らしいよ。

鈴木(妻)：そう、三人も息子さんがいらっしゃると大変ね。

- -

(a) どの政府にとっても、税制は頭痛の種だ。

(b) ガソリンの値上がりは市民にとって頭痛の種だ。

(c) 毎朝の通勤者にとって、あの駅の手前の開かずの踏み切りは、まったくもって頭痛の種だ。

解説

日本語の「頭痛の種」の「種」は、英語では seed (種)ではなく source (源)を用いる。

関連語

1. 英語には thorn in s.o.'s {flesh/side} (lit. ｛肉体 / 脇腹｝に刺さったとげ)という心配、イライラの原因を表す表現がある。これは聖書(新約聖書：コリント人への第2の手紙12章7節)から出てきた表現である。━📖 REL(1)
2. 日本語には関連表現として「頭が痛い」と「頭を痛める」という表現がある。

(2) 仕事がはかどらないので｛頭が痛い / 頭を痛めている｝。
Not being able to make progress with my work is such a headache.

(〜の)種をまく　 phr. 　隠喩

何かの原因を最初に起こす

関 (〜の)種を植え付ける

例文

(a) 中東情勢に争いの種をまくのは、いつも宗教的急進派の過激な行動だ。

(b) 憎しみと階級闘争を唱えた思想は、争い、疑い、対立の種をまいた。

(c) Umeko Tsuda put her heart into sowing the seeds of women's English education, and her efforts would bear amazing fruit in the years to come.

[R][E][L]

Plant (the) seeds (of ~) can replace *sow (the) seeds (of ~)* without changing the meaning. The corresponding Japanese is *(~ no) tane o ue-tsukeru*.

(1) In this book, Genghis Khan is portrayed as a leader who {sowed/planted} the seeds of democracy in Mongolia.

この本では、チンギスハンはモンゴルに民主主義の種を{まいた / 植え付けた}指導者として描かれている。

speak with a forked tongue / phr. / metaphor

to attempt to deceive s.o.

[REL] double-tongued

Examples

Saya: She's always saying something different.

Karen: Yeah, she just says whatever suits her at any given moment. She always speaks with a forked tongue.

Saya: Guess that explains why no one trusts her.

Karen: Exactly.

(a) Many politicians speak with a forked tongue.

(b) He is very effective at speaking with a forked tongue. I wonder how many women he's deceived.

Note

The Japanese literally means "to use two tongues," while the English means "speak with a tongue that is divided into two or more parts like a fork." So the two expressions are fairly close.

[R][E][L]

The English REL, *double-tongued*, comes from the New Testament of the Bible (1 Timothy 3:8).

(1) You can't trust a {person who speaks with a forked tongue/double-tongued person}.

二枚舌を使う人間は信用できません。

spend money like water / phr. / simile

to spend excessive amounts of money

Examples

Karen: You bought a lottery ticket?

Saya: Yeah, this is my first time buying one. I hope I win big. It'd be nice to be able to spend money like water for a change.

Karen: Wow, that doesn't sound like the Saya I know.

(c) 津田梅子が種をまき、深い愛情をもって育てた女子英語教育は、後年、大きな花を咲かせた。

関連語

英語の *plant (the) seeds (of ~)* という関連表現は、意味を変えずに *sow (the) seeds (of ~)* の代わりに使えるが、日本語では「(~の)種を植え付ける」がそれに対応する。 📖 REL(1)

二枚舌を使う /phr. 隠喩
{嘘 / 矛盾したこと}を言う

例文

さや：彼女の話は、本当にころころ変わるね。

カレン：うん、自分に都合がいいように、行き当たりばったりで二枚舌を使うからね。

さや：だから、みんなから信頼されないんだね。

カレン：そういうこと。

- - - - - - - - -

(a) 政治家には二枚舌を使う人が多い。

(b) 彼は本当に二枚舌を使うのが上手だ。何人の女性が彼にだまされたことだろう。

解説

英語の直訳は"フォークのように2つかそれ以上に分かれている舌で話す"で、日本語は"2つの舌"という意味で、両表現は近似している。

関連語

英語には新約聖書(テモテの第一の手紙3章8節)から出た *double-tongued* という関連表現がある。 📖 REL(1)

湯水のように金を使う /phr. 直喩
無駄な{もの / こと}に金を惜し気もなく使う

例文

カレン：あら、宝くじなんか買ったの。

さや：そう、初めて買ってみたんだけど。1等でも当たらないかしら。いっぺん湯水のようにお金を使ってみたいわ。

カレン：さやらしくないこと言うじゃない。

- - - - - - - - -

(a) When he was young, he used to spend money like water on bicycle races.

(b) That mayor started spending money like water right after he was elected, and his wasteful activities put pressure on the city's finances.

Note

Both expressions are based on the idea that *water* and *yumizu* (hot/cold water) are abundant and available everywhere.

spice of life, the   *n. phr.* metaphor

s.t. that colors and enriches human life

Examples

Karen: Music and art really are the spice of life, don't you think?

Saya: That's right. We can live without them, but if you're able to enjoy them, your life is all the richer.

- -

(a) Humor is the spice of life.

(b) Alcohol is said to be the spice of life.

(c) Modern life may be full of stress, but a moderate amount of stress is the spice of life, so you don't want to be completely stress-free.

Note

The Japanese is a translation of the English.

splitting headache   *comp. n.* metaphor

a severe headache

Examples

Mike: You don't look so good, Saya.

Saya: Is it that obvious? I have a splitting headache. I think it's a migraine.

Mike: That sounds bad. You'd better go home and lie down.

- -

(a) I've had a splitting headache for a few days now, and I've been too tired to get out of bed in the morning.

(b) All I can remember is waking up with a splitting headache.

Note

Splitting and *wareru* (to split) both mean "to divide into two or more parts," thus creating the metaphorical image of a head being split in half by severe pain.

(a) 彼は若い頃湯水のように競輪に金を使っていた。

(b) あの市長は当選後すぐに湯水のように金を使い、市の財政を圧迫するような行為を繰り返した。

解説

日英語とも、「湯水」waterはどこにでもいくらでもあるという発想に基づいている。

{人生 / 生活}のスパイス　　n. phr.　隠喩

生活を彩り、豊かにするもの

例文

カレン：音楽や芸術って、ほんと人生のスパイスだね。

さや：そうね。なくても生きていけるけど、楽しむ心を持つと、生活が豊かになるもんね。

- - - - - - - - - - - - - - - - -

(a) ユーモアは人生のスパイスだ。

(b) 酒は人生のスパイスだと言われる。

(c) 現代生活はストレスの固まりだが、適度なストレスは生活のスパイスで、あったほうがいいのだ。

解説

日本語は、英語からの翻訳である。

頭が割れるように痛い　　phr.　直喩

激しい頭痛がする

例文

マイク：さや、顔色が悪いね。

さや：そう？　頭が割れるように痛いのよ。片頭痛だと思う。

マイク：それはよくないね。家に帰って寝たほうがいいよ。

- - - - - - - - - - - - - - - - -

(a) ここ2、3日ずっと頭が割れるように痛い。あまりにも疲れていて、朝ベッドから起きられない。

(b) 私が覚えていることと言ったら、目覚めたとき頭が割れるように痛かったことだけです。

解説

「割れる」とsplittingは"何かが分断される"という意味を共有していて、激しい頭痛で頭が割れるという比喩的なイメージを作っている。

spread rumors / phr. / metaphor

to disseminate gossip

REL spread stories

Examples

Saya: So I heard you have a new girlfriend!

Kenta: Who told you that? She's just a friend.

Saya: Oh really now? So-and-so told me things have been developing pretty nicely.

Kenta: Stop spreading embarrassing rumors about me, would you? You'll ruin my image.

(a) The spread of the Internet has made it much easier to spread rumors.

(b) Whoever throws the world into confusion by spreading rumors about terrorism should be severely punished.

(c) A woman was charged with extorting money from a man by threatening to spread rumors about him.

Notes

1. The basic meaning of *spread* is "to expand and cover more space." The verb *hiromeru* (to propagate) is related to *hirogeru* (to widen) and the adjective *hiroi* (wide).

2. While the verbs in the main entries are both transitive verbs, the intransitive forms (*spread* and *hiromaru*) can be used as well. 📖→解説(1)

REL

The English REL is *spread stories*, which is used somewhat less frequently than the main entry. The Japanese has two RELs: *uwasa o nagasu* (lit. "to cause rumors to flow") and *uwasa o maki-chirasu* (lit. "to scatter rumors"). *Uwasa o maki-chirasu* sounds more colloquial than the main entry, and *uwasa o nagasu* is used more frequently than the main entry. 📖→関連語(1)

spur / v. / metaphor

to cause to act; to stimulate growth or development

Examples

(a) The environmental report stating that people in the city are producing more trash spurred environmentalists' campaign activities.

(b) The governor dismissed claims that the tax cuts had spurred the budget deficit.

(c) Making a new American friend really spurred Yoko's English studies.

Note

The transitive verb *spur* has the same meaning as *hakusha o kakeru*. However, *hakusha* can take either the intransitive verb *kakaru* (to hang), as in (a), or the transitive verb *kakeru* (to hang s.t.), as in (b) and (c).

噂を広める　/ phr.　隠喩
うわさ　ひろ　　　　　　　　　　いんゆ

噂をいろいろなところに伝える
うわさ　　　　　　　　　　　　　つた

関 噂を {流す / まき散らす}
　　うわさ　なが　　　　ち

例文

さや：新しいガールフレンド、できたんだって？
　　　あたら

健太：えっ、どこでそんなこと聞いたの？　ただの友達だよ。
けんた　　　　　　　　　　　　　き　　　　　　　　　ともだち

さや：ほんとかな。結構、いい線いってるって、誰か言ってたよ。
　　　　　　　　けっこう　　　せん　　　　　　だれ　い

健太：変な噂、広めないで欲しいな。もてなくなっちゃうじゃないか。
けんた　へん　うわさ　ひろ　　　　ほ

(a) インターネットの普及によって、噂を広めるのがずっと簡単になった。
　　　　　　　　　　　ふきゅう　　　　　うわさ　ひろ　　　　　　　　かんたん

(b) テロの噂を広めて世の中を混乱に陥れた人物は、厳罰に処せられるべきだ。
　　　　うわさ　ひろ　よ　なか　こんらん　おちい　じんぶつ　げんばつ　しょ

(c) 噂を広めると言って男を脅し金をゆすったかどで、女が告訴された。
　　うわさ　ひろ　　　い　おとこ　おど　かね　　　　　　　　　　おんな　こくそ

解説

1. 英語の *spread* の基本義は"何かがもっと空間に広がるようにする"という意味である。日本語の「広める」は「広げる」「広い」と関係している。

2. 見出しでは他動詞が使われているが、それに対応する自動詞の「広まる」*spread* を使うこともできる。

(1) 噂は人から人へ口伝えで広まる。
Rumors spread from person to person by word of mouth.

関連語

英語には *spread stories*（lit. 話を広める）という関連表現があるが、使用頻度は比較的低い。日本語には二つの関連表現がある。見出しより使用頻度の高い「噂を流す」と、より口語的な「噂をまき散らす」である。

(1) インターネットで噂を {広める / 流す / まき散らす} のがずっと簡単になった。(→(a))
The Internet has made it much easier to spread {rumors/stories}. (→(a))

(〜に)拍車 {をかける / がかかる}　/ phr.　隠喩
はくしゃ　　　　　　　　　　　　　　　いんゆ

すでに進行中の事柄や状態を、何かがより強く進行させる
しんこうちゅう　ことがら　じょうたい　なに　　　　つよ　しんこう

例文

(a) 市民が出すゴミの量が増えているという環境報告で、環境論者達のキャンペーン活動に拍車がかかった。
　　しみん　だ　　　　りょう　ふ　　　　　　　かんきょうほうこく　かんきょうろんじゃたち
　　かつどう　はくしゃ

(b) 知事は、減税が市の財政赤字に拍車をかけたという主張を退けた。
　　ちじ　げんぜい　し　ざいせいあかじ　はくしゃ　　　　　しゅちょう　しりぞ

(c) 親しいアメリカ人の友達ができたことが、洋子の英語の勉強に拍車をかけたようだ。
　　した　　　　　　じん　ともだち　　　　　　　ようこ　えいご　べんきょう　はくしゃ

解説

英語の他動詞 *spur* は日本語の「拍車をかける」と同じ意味である。しかし、日本語の「拍車」は(a)のように自動詞の「かかる」と(b)(c)のように他動詞の「かける」をとることができる。

stabbing pain | comp. n. | metaphor

a sharp pain

REL LOOK▶ sharp

Examples

Mr. S: Doctor, I've been having stomach pains lately.

Doctor: What sort of pain is it?

Mr. S: Well, I get a stabbing pain right about here.

Doctor: All right. Let me examine you.

- -

(a) There are times when I feel a stabbing pain in my eyes. Maybe it's because of my contacts.

(b) The stabbing pain in your cheek is actually being caused by nerve inflammation.

Note

The Japanese expression is a simile, as indicated by the use of *yōna* (like), but the English expression is a metaphor.

stand at a crossroads | phr. | metaphor

to face a critical decision

Examples

Karen: I'm trying to decide whether I should stay in Japan and continue teaching English or not.

Mrs. S: Why? You were saying that you enjoy your work.

Karen: Yeah, but my visa is going to run out soon, and I'm thinking that it's about time I decide what to do. I'm considering going back to the States and enrolling in graduate school, but I'd also like to stay in Japan a bit longer.

Mrs. S: Hmm, sounds like you're standing at a real crossroads. That's a tough decision.

- -

(a) When one stands at life's crossroads, books written by people who have had similar problems sometime give us hints on how to live our lives.

(b) As the number of school-age children continues to decline, Japanese universities are standing at an important crossroads and face far-reaching restructuring.

Note

Crossroads and *kiro* are slightly different in that the former indicates two roads that are crossing, whereas the latter can also indicate two roads that diverge.

REL

1. The verbs *stand* and *tatsu* (to stand) can be replaced by *be* and *iru* (to be), respectively. In Japanese, *tatsu* occurs much more frequently in this expression than *iru*. In English, *be* is more common than *stand*. 📖→関連語(1)

600

刺すような痛み　/ n. phr.　│ 直喩 │

鋭い痛み

関 LOOK▶ 鋭い

例文

鈴木(夫)：先生、最近、時々胃が痛くなるんですが。

医者：どんな痛みですか。

鈴木(夫)：このあたりに刺すような痛みがあります。

医者：そうですか。では、ちょっと診てみましょう。

- (a) 突然、目の中に刺すような痛みを感じることがある。コンタクトレンズがよく合わないのかもしれない。
- (b) 頬に刺すような痛みがあるが、実はその原因は神経の炎症なのである。

解説

日本語のほうは「ような」でわかるように直喩であるが、英語のほうは直喩ではなく、隠喩である。

岐路に立つ　/ phr.　│ 隠喩 │

{人 / 組織 / 国}が、そこから先は決定的な変化が起こるかもしれない重要な時に来ている

関 分岐点に {立つ / いる}

例文

カレン：私、このまま、日本で英語を教え続けようかどうか悩んでるんです。

鈴木(妻)：どうして？　仕事楽しいって言ってたじゃない。

カレン：ええ、それが、もうすぐビザが切れるので、今後、どうしようかと思って。アメリカに戻って、大学院に入ろうかなって。でも、まだ、しばらく日本にもいたいし。

鈴木(妻)：そう、人生の岐路に立っているわけね。難しい選択ね。

- (a) 人生の岐路に立ったときは、同じように悩んだことがある人が書いた本が、いかに生きるかヒントを与えてくれることがある。
- (b) 日本では、就学する子供の数が減ってきて、日本の大学は重大な岐路に立たされており、大幅な改革に直面している。

解説

crossroads と「岐路」では多少意味が異なる。*crossroads* では "2つの道は十字に交叉している" だが、「岐路」は必ずしもそうではなく、"2つの道が枝分かれしている" という意味もある。

関連語

1. 日英語の動詞の「立つ」と *stand* は、それぞれ、「いる」と *be* で代用できる。日本語では「立つ」のほうが「いる」よりはるかに使用頻度が高いが、英語では *be* のほうが *stand* よりはるかに使用頻度が高い。

(1) あなたはできることはすべてやって、今人生の {岐路 / 分岐点} に {立っている / いる} のだ。
    You've done all that you can, and now you {stand/are} at life's crossroads.

601

2. The Japanese has the REL *bunki-ten ni {tatsu/iru}* (lit. "to {stand/be} at a branching point"). 📖➡ 関連語(1)

steal a glance at ~ / phr. / metaphor

to secretly look at {s.t./s.o.}

REL sneak a peek at ~

Examples

(a) The child got really mad at his mother when she stole a glance at his mobile phone.

(b) While talking with his boss, John stole a glance at his watch.

(c) The instructor saw a student stealing a glance at his neighbor's answer sheet and told him to leave the classroom.

Notes

1. The English is a regular verb + direct object construction, but the Japanese is a compound verb that consists of *nusumi* (to steal) + *miru* (to see).

2. The basic meaning of *steal* and *nusumu* is "to take the property of another without permission," so looking at someone's property without permission can be considered an act of visual theft, which lends the expression a figurative meaning.

REL

The English REL, *sneak a peek at ~*, has the same meaning as the main entry.

(1) While talking with his boss, John {stole a glance/sneaked a peek} at his watch. (→(b))

steal s.o.'s heart / phr. / metaphor

to win the love of s.o.

Examples

Karen: How did you and your wife end up getting married?

Mr. S: Well, a friend introduced us. We had a few dates, and by the third date, she'd stolen my heart. So I proposed to her.

(a) The works of Dutch painter Vermeer recently stole my heart.

(b) The cute puppy stole her heart, and she begged her parents to buy him until they finally gave in.

(c) I can still see his smile. That man stole my heart with his smile.

Notes

1. The basic meanings of *steal* and *ubau* are very similar. They mean "to take the property of another without permission" and "to forcibly take s.t. away from s.o.," respectively.

2. This expression can also be used in a passive construction in both English and Japanese.

(1) My heart was stolen by her. (→ dialogue)
私は彼女に心を奪われた。(→ dialogue)

2．日本語には「分岐点に{立つ / いる}」という関連表現がある。　□■→ 関連語（1）

盗み見る　comp. v.　隠喩

人に気づかれないように、こっそり見る

例文

(a) 母親に携帯を盗み見られて、子供はカンカンに怒った。

(b) ボスと話しているときに、ジョンは時計をちらっと盗み見た。

(c) 彼は試験中に隣の学生の解答を盗み見たのが先生に見つかり、教室を出された。

解説

1．英語は「動詞＋直接目的語」という構文であるが、日本語は「盗み」＋「見る」の複合動詞になっている点が異なる。

2．「盗む」と steal の基本義は“人の物をこっそり奪い取る”であるから、誰かのものを許可を得ないで見ることは、視覚的に盗むことであり、比喩になる。

関連語

英語には見出しと同じ意味を持つ sneak a peek at ~ という関連表現がある。　■→ REL（1）

（～の）心を奪う　phr.　隠喩

誰かの気持ちを強く引きつける

例文

カレン：奥様とはどうやって結婚することになったんですか。

鈴木（夫）：まあ、友達の紹介なんですよ。ちょっとデートをして、3回目に会ったとき、彼女に心を奪われ、それで、結婚を申し込んだというわけ。

(a) 僕は最近オランダの画家フェルメールの絵に心を奪われている。

(b) そのかわいい小犬はすっかり少女の心を奪い、彼女はついに両親がその小犬を買い与えてくれるまで、買ってと頼み続けた。

(c) 彼の笑顔がまだ蘇ってくる。彼はその微笑で私の心を奪った男だった。

解説

1．「奪う」と steal の基本義は、それぞれ“無理に取り上げる”と“所有物を許可なしに取る”でかなり近い。

2．日英語とも受け身にすることができる。　■→ Note（1）

stem the tide (of ~) / phr. / metaphor

to stop s.t. (negative) from increasing

Examples

Saya: Is it still true that a lot of people immigrate to the U.S.?

Karen: Yeah. Actually, we have huge numbers of illegal immigrants. We share a border with Mexico, you know. It's not easy to stem the tide of the illegal immigrants from that country.

- -

(a) Their movement is aimed at stemming the tide of reform that began recently.

(b) What can companies and individuals do to stem the tide of junk mail?

Note

The verb *stem* comes from the noun *stem*, and the noun *tide* is used instead of *flow*. By comparison, the Japanese uses the noun *nagare*, which is derived from the verb *nagareru* (to flow), and the verb *tomeru* (to cause s.t. to stop).

REL

1. *Tomeru* can be replaced by the compound verb *kui-tomeru*. 📖→ 関連語(1)
2. There is another Japanese REL, *nagare o seki-tomeru*, which can be used instead of *nagare o tomeru*. 📖→ 関連語(2)

step by step / phr. / metaphor

a little at a time

REL little by little

Examples

Saya: The junior English speech contest was amazing! I was so impressed!

Karen: Thanks! It's all because the kids never gave up and prepared step by step every day.

- -

(a) You have to approach a daunting goal step by step.

(b) When studying a foreign language, it's important to make step-by-step efforts.

(c) The project is advancing step by step.

Notes

1. Both the English and Japanese are usually not used in a negative sense, but rather to indicate gradual (positive) progress.

(1) His illness got worse {little by little/ ×step by step}.
彼の病気は {次第に / ×一歩一歩} 悪くなった。

流れを止める / phr. 隠喩

広範の人々に影響を与えるような状況を止める

関 流れを食い止める，流れを堰き止める

例文

さや：アメリカって今でも移民してくる人が多いんでしょ。

カレン：そうなの。実は、不法移民の数もばかにならないのよ。メキシコなんかとは陸続きだしね。不法移民の流れを止めるのは、容易じゃないのよ。

(a) 彼らの運動はせっかく始まった改革の流れを止めるようなものだ。

(b) 頼みもしない、くだらない迷惑メールの流れを止めるために、会社や個人として何ができるだろうか。

解説

英語では本来名詞である *stem* (堰) を動詞に使い、単なる *flow* (流れ) の代わりに *tide* (潮の流れ) を使っている。一方、日本語では一般的な動詞「流れる」からの派生名詞「流れ」と一般的な動詞「止める」を使っている。

関連語

1. 日本語の動詞「止める」は、「食い止める」で置き換えができる。
(1) 彼らは陣頭に立って、暴力の流れを{止め / 食い止め}ようとしている。
    They are at the forefront of efforts to stem the tide of violence.
2. さらに日本語には、「流れを堰き止める」という関連表現もある。
(2) アメリカは移民法によって、新しい移民の流れを{止める / 堰き止める}ことができた。
    U.S. immigration laws stemmed the tide of new immigrants.

一歩一歩 / phr. 隠喩

(何か時間のかかる、やり甲斐のあることを)少しずつ(する)

関 少しずつ

例文

さや：今日の子供達の英語スピーチコンテスト、すばらしかった。感激したわ。

カレン：そう、どうもありがとう。あの子達がくじけないで、毎日、一歩一歩学んだ結果だわ。

(a) 手ごわい目標には一歩一歩近づいていかなければならない。

(b) 外国語の勉強は一歩一歩の努力が大切だ。

(c) このプロジェクトは、一歩一歩着実に前進している。

解説

1. 日英語とも、否定的なことには普通使われず、何かが段階的にいい方向に進む時に使われる。

📖Note(1)

2. 英語は普通、人間の意図的行動に関してしか使えないから、次の文は英語では不適切であるが、日本語では擬人化の比喩として問題がない。

2. The English usually only refers to intentional actions, so (2) sounds unnatural in English. With the Japanese, however, (2) sounds fine, as it is considered a case of personification. 📖→解説(2)
3. The Japanese literally says "one step, one step," but ˣ*a step by a step* is not acceptable in English.
4. Both the English and Japanese can be used as adverbs, as in the dialogue, (a), and (c), or as noun modifiers, as in (b).

R E L

The English REL, *little by little*, can replace *step by step* in the case of natural phenomena, as in 解説(2), or when expressing something negative, as in Note (1). The corresponding Japanese is *sukoshi zutsu*. 📖→解説(2) ➡📖 Note(1)

stepping stone {to/towards} ~, a 　/ n. phr. 　/ metaphor
means by which s.o. makes progress

Examples

(a) This book is best as a stepping stone towards a better understanding of James Joyce.

(b) Failure is not a stumbling block, but a stepping stone to your next success.

R E L

The Japanese has a REL *fumidai*, which means "s.o. used as a stepping stone to one's own success." It is used in the set phrase *fumidai ni suru* (to make into a stepping stone).

📖→関連語(1)

stick one's nose into ~ 　/ phr. 　/ metaphor
to get involved in s.o. else's affairs

REL　poke one's nose into ~

ANT　keep one's nose out of ~

Examples

Kenta: Wait, Aunt Kimiko is coming again? I don't wanna see her.

Mrs. S: Why not? Isn't she a great aunt? She's so generous!

Kenta: But she sticks her nose into everything. Don't you know that all our relatives hate her?

Mrs. S: True.

- - - - - - - - - - - - - - - - - - - -

(a) Why does Mary feel the need to stick her nose into this mess?

(b) She sticks her nose into everybody else's business. You tell her a little and she finds out a lot.

606

(2) 湖の氷も解け始め、春が{一歩一歩 / 少しずつ}近付いているようだ。

The frozen lake has begun to melt. It seems spring is approaching us {little by little/ ×step by step}.

3. 日本語は「一歩一歩」というように歩数が入っているが、英語では ×a step by a step とは言えないことに注意。

4. 日英語とも、会話例や(a)(c)のように副詞として、あるいは(b)のように名詞修飾語としても使える。

関連語

英語の関連表現 little by little は、解説(2)の自然現象やNote(1)のような否定的なことのときに、step by step と置き換えられる。その場合、日本語は「少しずつ」が使われる。

📖→解説(2) 📖→Note(1)

（〜の）踏み石 　n. phr.　隠喩

進歩のための手段

関 踏み台

例文

(a) この本はジェームズ・ジョイスをもっとよく理解するための踏み石として最適です。

(b) 失敗は、つまづきの石ではなく、次の成功への踏み石となる。

関連語

日本語には「踏み台」"{誰か/ 何か}を一時的に利用する"という意味の関連表現がある。この場合「踏み台にする」という慣用句になる。

(1) 彼は友人を{踏み台 /?? 踏み石}にするのがうまい。

He is good at using his friends as stepping stones.

（〜に）鼻を突っ込む 　phr.　隠喩

他人の事柄に介入する

関 首を突っ込む

例文

健太：え、また、きみ子おばさん、来るの？ 会いたくないな。

鈴木(妻)：どうして、いいおばさんじゃない。気前がいいし。

健太：でも、どんなことにでも鼻を突っ込みたがるから、親戚中から嫌われてるよ。

鈴木(妻)：まあね。

(a) どうしてメアリーは、この泥沼に鼻を突っ込まなければならないと思っているのだろうか。

(b) 彼女は他人のことに鼻を突っ込む。ちょっとでも彼女に話せば、その先をたくさん見つけ出してくる。

Note

The Japanese expression means "to get involved in (another's) affairs when one should not." In other words, the Japanese is always used in a negative sense. This basically holds true in English, though occasionally the English expression can be used to connote involvement that is positive.

REL

1. The Japanese can be replaced by *kubi o tsukkomu* (lit. "to thrust one's neck into ~"), as in (1a). As shown in (1b), this REL can be used in a positive sense, just like the English expression. 📖➡ 関連語(1)

2. The English REL, *poke one's nose into ~*, can replace the main entry when it is used in a negative sense, as in (1a), but it is usually not used in a positive sense, as in (1b).

📖➡ 関連語(1)

ANT

The English ANT is *keep one's nose out of ~*.

(1) I wish that our boss would keep his nose out of our private matters.
ボスが、われわれのプライベートなことに鼻を突っ込まないことを願っています。

(as) still as a statue / phr. / simile

completely unmoving

Example

Modeling for paintings may seem easy, but it's actually quite difficult. Standing as still as a statue for several hours is more tiring than exercise.

homograph

stir s.o. up / phr. / metaphor

to make s.o. excited or angry
かきたてる

Example

The president's speech stirred up the employees and motivated them to work towards their goal.
社長の演説は、目標達成にむけて努力しようという従業員の気持ちをかきたてた。
しゃちょう　えんぜつ　　もくひょうたっせい　　　どりょく　　　　じゅうぎょういん　きも

stir up a hornet's nest / phr. / metaphor

to cause trouble

REL stir up trouble

Examples

(a) He stirred up a hornet's nest by raising the issue of racial discrimination.

解説

日本語は"そうすべきではないのに（他人の）ある状況に入っていく"という意味である。つまり、"常に否定的な介入"を意味している。英語も基本的には日本語と同じだが、時々肯定的な介入でもよい。

関連語

1. 日本語には「首を突っ込む」という関連表現がある。これは(1b)のように、また英語の表現のように、いい意味でも使える。
   (1)a. どうしてメアリーは、この泥沼に{鼻／首}を突っ込まなければならないと思っているのだろうか。（→(a)）
      Why does Mary feel the need to {stick/poke} her nose into this mess?（→(a)）
     b. 僕は労使紛争に{首／ˣ鼻}を突っ込もうと思っています。
      I'm going to {stick/ˀpoke} my nose into this labor-management dispute.
2. 英語は介入が(1a)のように否定的ならば関連表現 *poke one's nose into ~* で置き換えられる。介入が(1b)のように肯定的な場合は普通、置き換えはできない。 📖➡関連語(1)

反意語

英語に *keep one's nose out of ~* という反意表現がある。➡📖 ANT(1)

銅像のように動かない ／ phr. 直喩
どうぞう　　　うご　　　　　　　　　　　ちょくゆ

ぜんぜん動かない
　　　　　うご

例文

絵のモデルの仕事なんて、楽なように見えるけれど、じつは結構大変なのよ。何時間も銅像のように動かないでいるのは、運動するより疲れるわ。

同形異義語

かきまわす ／ comp. v. ／ 隠喩
　　　　　　　　　　　　　　　いんゆ

問題を大きくする
もんだい　　おお
to throw s.t. into confusion

例文

この集まりには、彼は呼ばないほうがいいよ。いつもかきまわすばかりで、建設的な意見はぜんぜん出さないんだから。

You shouldn't invite him to this meeting, because he always just throws things into confusion without providing any constructive feedback.

蜂の巣をつ(っ)ついたような騒ぎ{になる／が起きる} ／ phr. 直喩
はち　す　　　　　　　　　　　　　　　さわ　　　　　　お　　　　　　　　　　ちょくゆ

何か大きな騒ぎが起きる
なに　おお　　　さわ　　お

例文

(a) 彼が人種差別の問題を取り上げたので、蜂の巣をつついたような騒ぎになった。
　　かれ　じんしゅさべつ　もんだい　と　あ　　　　　はち　す　　　　　　　さわ

609

(b) As soon as the news broke about people being infected with a new type of virus, it stirred up a hornet's nest.

(c) The governor stirred up a hornet's nest by raising taxes by 10%.

Notes

1. The English is used to indicate trouble or an otherwise negative reaction, but the Japanese does not have such restrictions. 📖➡ 解説 (1)
2. The Japanese is a simile, while the English is a metaphor.
3. *Tsuttsuita* is the emphatic version of *tsutsuita*.

REL

The English has the REL *stir up trouble*, which has the same meaning as the main entry.

(1) He stirred up {a hornet's nest/trouble} by raising the issue of racial discrimination. (→(a))

---

storm of protest / n. phr. / metaphor

a very strong objection to s.t.

Examples

(a) The legislation caused a storm of protest from the public.

(b) The unpaid salaries caused a storm of protest from the workers.

(c) The Iraq War provoked a storm of protest from many people across the world.

---

stream of consciousness / n. phr. / metaphor

thoughts presented as a continuous flow of images/ideas

Examples

(a) James Joyce's *Ulysses* is written in a stream-of-consciousness style.

(b) Tightness of structure is hard to achieve in a stream-of-consciousness novel.

Note

The phrase *stream of consciousness* is a psychological term originally created by famed American psychologist and philosopher William James (1842-1910). The Japanese is a translation of the English. The translator is thought to have been Sei Ito (1905-1969), a critic and novelist who first used the term in his *On James Joyce's Method: Stream of Consciousness* (1930).

(b) 新種のウィルスによる感染者が出たというニュースが広がったとたん、蜂の巣をつついたような騒ぎが起きた。

(c) 知事が税金を一割上げたときは蜂の巣をつっついたような騒ぎになった。

解説

1. 英語は不満や怒りを表すような騒ぎが起るときにしか使えないが、日本語は必ずしも不満・怒りがなくても使える。

(1) 子供達が野球をしているところにイチローが現れたので、みんな興奮して蜂の巣をつついたような騒ぎになった。
Ichiro's appearance at the children's baseball game {caused a huge commotion/ ×stirred up a hornet's nest}.

2. 日本語は直喩として使われるのに対して、英語は隠喩として使われる。

3. 「つっついた」は「つついた」の強調形である。

関連語

英語には見出しと同じ意味の *stir up trouble* という関連表現がある。 📖 **REL（1）**

S

抗議の嵐 こうぎ あらし / n. phr. / 隠喩 いんゆ

何かに対するとても強い反対 なに たい つよ はんたい

例文

(a) その立法化は、庶民からの抗議の嵐を引き起こした。

(b) 給料の不払いは、労働者から抗議の嵐を引き起こした。

(c) イラク戦争は、世界の多くの人々の間に抗議の嵐を引き起こした。

意識の流れ いしき なが n. phr. / 隠喩 いんゆ

変化して止まない意識を時間軸でとらえたもの へんか や いしき じかんじく

例文

(a) ジェームズ・ジョイスの『ユリシーズ』は意識の流れの文体で書かれている。

(b) 意識の流れの小説では、きっちとした構造は作りにくい。

解説

「意識の流れ」という表現は、もともとは著名なアメリカの心理学者 / 哲学者のウィリアム・ジェームズ（1842-1910）が作った心理学用語である。日本語は英語の翻訳で、批評家 / 作家の伊藤整（1905-1969）の「ジェームズ・ジョイスのメトオド『意識の流れ』に就いて」（1930）が初出のようである。

611

strike oil / phr. / metaphor

to suddenly become very rich

REL strike gold; strike it rich

Examples

Mike: Where are you going for vacation?

Colleague: Las Vegas. I want to see some shows and do a little gambling. Hopefully I'll strike oil.

Mike: Good luck!

- -

(a) They say that he struck oil in the stock market. He built a gorgeous mansion and is now living the high life.

(b) People who strike oil by gambling on things like horse races may become addicted and eventually destroy their lives.

Note

In English, this expression literally means "to find petroleum when boring for it" and presumably getting rich from the discovery. The Japanese expression literally means "to get rich by finding an iron/gold mine."

REL

The English has two RELs: *strike gold* and *strike it rich*. Both tend to be used more frequently than the main entry.

(1) They say that he struck {oil/gold/it rich} in the stock market.

strong / adj. / metaphor

having a powerful {visual/auditory/olfactory/gustatory/tactual/intellectual/ psychological/structural} impact

ANT weak; LOOK have a weakness for ~

Examples

Mrs. S: I heard that Mr. and Mrs. Yamada decided to get a divorce.

Mr. S: I'm not surprised. They never got along very well.

Mrs. S: Mrs. Yamada has a strong personality, after all.

Mr. S: Well, I think the husband is too weak.

- -

(a) He's a strong math student, but his foreign language skills are weak.

(b) This food has a strong sour taste.

(c) The sunshine was strong in Texas.

(d) I don't like the strong smell of this cheese.

(e) These glasses have a really strong prescription.

(f) A strong wind is blowing from the north.

(g) She has a strong sense of responsibility and is relied upon by everybody.

一山当てる / phr. / 隠喩
ひとやまあ　　　　　　　　　いんゆ

投機などで巨額の金をもうける
とうき　　　きょがく　　かね

例文

マイク：休みはどこに行くの？
　　　　やす　　　　　い

同僚：ラスベガス。ショーを見て、ギャンブルをやって、一山当てて来るんだ。
どうりょう　　　　　　　　　　　　み　　　　　　　　　　　　　　　ひとやまあ　　く

マイク：成功を祈るよ。
　　　　せいこう　いの

(a) 彼は株取り引きで一山当てたそうだ。豪邸を建てて、今じゃハイクラスの生活をし
　　かれ かぶと ひ　　ひとやまあ　　　　　　ごうてい　た　　　　いま　　　　　　　　　　せいかつ
　　ている。

(b) 競馬などで一山当てた人は、ギャンブルの深みにはまり、結局身を持ち崩してしま
　　けいば　　　ひとやまあ　ひと　　　　　　　　　　　ふか　　　　　　けっきょくみ　も　くず
　　うかもしれない。

解説

日本語は"鉱山を探し当てて金もうけをする"という字義通りの意味からきていて、英語は"石
油を掘り当てて金もうけをする"という字義通りの意味からきている。

関連語

英語には *strike it rich* (lit. 豊富なそれを打つ＝突然大金持ちになる) と *strike gold* (lit. 金鉱を
打つ＝一山当てる) という関連表現がある。どちらも見出しより使用頻度が高い。

　　　　　　　　　　　　　　　　　　　　　　　　　　　　　　　　　　　━📖 REL(1)

強い / adj. (i) / 隠喩
つよ　　　　　　　　　いんゆ

{視覚的 / 聴覚的 / 嗅覚的 / 味覚的 / 触覚的 / 知的 / 心理的 / 構造的}なインパクトを持つ
しかくてき ちょうかくてき きゅうかくてき みかくてき しょっかくてき ちてき しんりてき こうぞうてき　　　　　　　　　　も

反 LOOK (～に) 弱い
　　　　　　　　よわ

例文

鈴木(妻)：山田さんたち、離婚することに決めたそうよ。
すずき つま　やまだ　　　　　　りこん　　　　　　　き

鈴木(夫)：そう、結局うまくいかなかったか。
すずき おっと　　　けっきょく

鈴木(妻)：奥さん、性格が強いからね。
すずき つま　おく　　せいかく つよ

鈴木(夫)：だんなが弱すぎるんだよ。
すずき おっと　　　　よわ

(a) 彼は数学には強いが、外国語に弱い。
　　かれ すうがく　つよ　　　がいこくご よわ

(b) この料理は酸味が強い。
　　　りょうり さんみ つよ

(c) テキサスの日差しは強かった。
　　　　　　ひざ　　つよ

(d) 私は、このチーズの強い匂いが嫌いです。
　　わたし　　　　　　　　つよ にお　きら

(e) この眼鏡の診断書の度数は、とても強い。
　　　めがね しんだんしょ どすう　　　　つよ

(f) 強い風が北から吹いている。
　　つよ かぜ きた　ふ

(g) 彼女は責任感が強く、だれからも信頼されている。
　　かのじょ せきにんかん つよ　　　　　　　しんらい

(h) The politician has been a strong supporter of free trade.

(i) The players on this team have strong bonds with each other.

(j) He has a strong will and always finishes what he has started.

(k) It takes more than a strong military to conduct a wise foreign policy.

(l) My solution to the math problem bears a strong resemblance to his.

(m) People in his home country have strong expectations that he will eventually receive the Nobel Prize for his research.

(n) The teachers strongly demanded a pay raise.

Notes

1. For the most part, *strong* and *tsuyoi* have similar metaphorical uses, as shown in the examples. But some uses of *strong/tsuyoi* are exclusive to one language. The examples in (1) are cases in which *strong* can be used but *tsuyoi* cannot, and the examples in (2) are cases in which *tsuyoi* can be used but *strong* cannot. 解説(2)

(1) a. This coffee is strong.
   このコーヒーは{濃い / [×]強い}。

   b. My cat is 15 years old, but she's still going strong.
   うちの猫は15歳なんだけど、まだとても{元気だ / [×]強い}。

   c. The market was strong last month.
   先月の市場は{上向きだった / [×]強かった}。

2. In both English and Japanese, *strong/tsuyoi* can also be used in reference to color, as shown in (3). 解説(3)

ANT

Strong and *tsuyoi* can be replaced by their antonyms, *weak* and *yowai*. However, *weak* cannot replace *strong* in (d), and *yowai* cannot replace *tsuyoi* in (d), (h), (l), (m), and (n).

suck {s.t./s.o.} dry   phr.   metaphor

to deprive {s.o./s.t.} of all valuable qualities/possessions

REL   squeeze s.t. out from ~

Examples

(a) He cheated her and sucked her finances dry.

(b) The brokerage firm employee sucked his clients dry and ultimately drove the company itself to bankruptcy.

(c) He sucks people dry of their good intentions no matter where he goes.

Note

The Japanese expression often co-occurs with *hone (no zui) made* (to the bone marrow) to provide emphasis, as shown in (c).

(h) その政治家は、自由貿易を強く支持してきた。

(i) このチームは選手間の結束が強い。

(j) 彼は強い意志を持っていて、一度やり始めたことは必ず完成する。

(k) 賢い外交をするには、強い軍事力以上のものが必要だ。

(l) 私のその数学の問題の解き方は、彼のと強い類似性がある。

(m) 彼の研究はいつかノーベル賞をもらうだろうと、彼の国の人々は強い期待感を持っている。

(n) 教師達は、給料の値上げを強く要求した。

解説

1. 日英語は、例文でわかるように「強い」 strong という形容詞の比喩的な用法のほとんとすべてを共有している。しかし、それぞれの言語固有の使い方もある。(1)の例は英語では使えるが日本語では使えない場合を、(2)の例は日本語では使えるが英語では使えない場合を、それぞれ示している。━📖**Note(1)**

(2) a. 妹は心臓が強い。
   She {is saucy/ ˣhas a strong heart}.

   b. 兄は押しが強い。
   My older brother {is pushy/ ˣhas a strong push}.

   c. 彼は酒に強い。
   He is {a heavy drinker/ ˣstrong in *sake*}.

   d. この合金は熱に強い。
   This alloy is {heat-resistant/ ˣstrong against heat}.

2. 日英語とも「強い」と strong は(3)の例でわかるように、色にも使うことができる。

(3) この絵は色彩が強い。
   This painting has strong colors.

反意語

「強い」と strong の反意表現はそれぞれ「弱い」と weak で、見出しと置き換えることができる。ただし、日本語では(d)、(h)、(l)、(m)、(n)の「強い」は「弱い」と置き換えられない。英語では(d)の strong は weak で置き換えられない。

吸い尽くす / comp. v. / 隠喩

すべてを取ってしまう

関 搾り出す

例文

(a) 彼は彼女をだまして全財産を吸い尽くした。

(b) その証券会社の社員は、顧客の金を吸い尽くして、ついには会社そのものを倒産に追い込んでしまった。

(c) その男はどこに行っても人の善意を骨の髄まで吸い尽くす。

解説

日本語の見出しには(c)のように、「骨(の髄)まで」がつくことがよくある。

615

REL

The English and Japanese have similar RELs: *squeeze s.t. out from ~* and *~ kara ~ o shibori dasu*, respectively. 📖◄ 関連語(1)

---

sunbathe / comp. v. / metaphor

to sit or recline in the sunlight

REL get sunburned; get a (sun)tan

Examples

Saya: The cat looks cozy sitting by the window.

Karen: Yeah, she likes to sit there and sunbathe on nice days.

- - - - - - - - - - - - - - - - - -

(a) Before sunbathing, it's best to apply sunblock.

(b) Eagles sunbathe by lying on rocks and spreading their wings.

Note

The basic meaning of *bathe* and *yoku* is "to pour water on one's body," so it could be said that this expression contains an implied metaphor that likens light to liquid.

REL

The Japanese has five RELs: *(hada ga) kuroku naru* (lit. "[the skin] becomes black"), *hi ni yakeru* (lit. "to be burned by the sun"), *hi ni yaku* (to allow to be burned by the sun), *hiyake-suru* (to be burned by the sun), and *hada o yaku* (to get a tan). The corresponding English expressions are *get sunburned* and *get a (sun)tan*. It should be noted that *sunburn* indicates an inflammation of the skin due to overexposure to the sun, whereas *(sun)tan* simply refers to the browning of the skin. 📖◄ 関連語(1)

---

swallow s.t. {whole/completely} / phr. / metaphor

to accept information uncritically

Examples

Kenta: Mom, don't tell me you bought something useless again.

Mrs. S: But it looked so good when I saw it on the shopping channel.

Kenta: Come on! You can't just swallow those TV ads whole.

- - - - - - - - - - - - - - - - - -

(a) It's dangerous to swallow economists' predictions about the economy whole.

(b) People swallowed what the media was saying completely and treated him like a criminal, even though he had yet to be convicted.

関連語

日英語とも類似の関連表現、「〜から〜を搾り出す」*squeeze s.t. out from ~* がある。

(1) 彼は自分に近づく人から金を簡単に絞り出せるタイプの男だ。

He's the type of guy who can easily squeeze money out of anyone he comes in contact with.

日光浴をする　phr.　隠喩

太陽の光に体をさらす

関 (肌が)黒くなる，日に焼ける，日に焼く，日焼けする，肌を焼く

例文

さや：ネコちゃん、窓辺で、気持ちよさそうね。

カレン：そうなの。天気のいい日は、いつも、あそこで日光浴をするのよ。

(a) 日光浴をする前には、日焼け止めクリームをぬったほうがいいですよ。

(b) 鷲は羽を広げて岩の上にとまり、日光浴をします。

解説

「浴」と *bathe* は"水を浴びる"が基本義であるから、背後に「光は液体だ」という比喩が潜んでいると言えるだろう。

関連語

日本語には「(肌が)黒くなる」「日に焼ける」「日に焼く」「日焼けする」「肌を焼く」の五つの関連表現がある。これらに対応する英語表現は、*get sunburned* と *get a (sun)tan* である。ただし、*sunburn* は太陽に肌をさらしすぎて皮膚が炎症を起こした状態で、一方の *(sun)tan* は単に肌が茶色くなるという意味であることに注意。

(1)a. 冬場は日焼けサロンで{黒くなる / 日に焼ける / 日に焼く / 日焼けする / 肌を焼く}ことにしている。

During the winter, I go to a tanning salon to get a tan.

b. 炎天下で昼寝をして、ひどい日焼けをしてしまった。

I fell asleep under the blazing sun and got terribly sunburned.

鵜呑みにする　phr.　隠喩

人の言うことや情報を無批判に受け入れる

例文

健太：お母さん、またこんな変なもの買っちゃったの。

鈴木(妻)：テレビショッピングで見て、なかなかよさそうだったんだもの。

健太：まったく、すぐ宣伝文句を鵜呑みにするんだから。

(a) 今後の経済の見通しについて経済学者の意見を鵜呑みにするのは危険だ。

(b) 人々は、メディアのもたらす情報を鵜呑みにしてしまい、まだ確定してもいないのに、彼を犯罪者扱いした。

Notes

1. The basic meaning of *swallow* is "to take s.t. through the mouth and into the stomach." When used figuratively, it can mean to accept another's views, teachings, claims, etc., without critical thought.

2. *U-nomi ni suru* comes from the image of a cormorant swallowing fish whole. Cormorants were once used in a traditional form of fishing; the fishermen would use the birds to capture fish and then force them to disgorge their catch.

---

sweat / n. / metonymy

to work hard at s.t.

ANT no sweat

Examples

Mrs. S: How's your new part-time job?

Kenta: The pay's really good, but I have the night shift, so it's really tough.

Mrs. S: So that means you're learning how to earn a living by the sweat of your brow. Good!

- -

(a) They are good at making money without breaking a sweat.

(b) The children break a sweat every Sunday cleaning the local park.

Note

Both English and Japanese use perspiration as a metaphor for hard work. The temporal juxtaposition of hard work and sweat is what makes this expression an example of metonymy.

R E L

The Japanese has the REL *~ ni sē o dasu*, which means "to do s.t. with all one's might."

📖 関連語(1)

A N T

The English has the ANT *no sweat*, which means "no problem."

(1) Doing a double major in math and physics should be no sweat.
数学と物理の二つを専攻するの{はわけはない/ $^{??}$ に汗をかく必要はない}。

---

homograph

sweep s.o. off (of) {his/her} feet / phr. / metaphor

to inspire strong emotions in s.o.
ある感情が高ぶってコントロールがきかない

Example

Her handsome colleague swept her off her feet.
彼女はハンサムな同僚にすっかりまいってしまった。

解説

1. 英語の動詞 *swallow* の基本義は"何かを口を通して胃の中に取り込む"である。それが比喩になると人の意見、教え、主張などをよく考えずに受け入れるという意味になる。

2. 日本語の「鵜呑みにする」は鵜が魚を丸ごと呑むその様子からきている。伝統的な鵜飼いの魚法では、鵜が一度呑み込んだ魚を鵜匠が吐き出させる。

汗を{かく / 流す}　／ phr.　換喩

仕事や勉強などを一生懸命する

関 〜に精を出す

例文

鈴木（妻）：今度のバイト、どう？

健太：うん、バイト代は抜群にいいんだけど。夜中のシフトだし、すっごく大変だよ。

鈴木（妻）：そう。お金のためにはしっかり汗をかかなきゃなんないって、学んでるわけね。結構なことだわ。

- -

(a) 彼らは、汗も流さず金を作るのがうまい。

(b) 子供達は、毎週日曜日に、街の公園の清掃に汗を流している。

解説

日英語とも発汗を一生懸命仕事をすることの換喩として使っている。換喩と考えられるのは仕事と汗が時間的に隣接しているからである。

関連語

日本語には"元気を出して一生懸命何かをする"という意味の「〜に精を出す」という関連表現がある。

(1) もっと仕事に精を出しなさい。
Work with all your might.

反意語

英語では容易に何かができることを *no sweat* という。━📖ANT**(1)**

同形異義語

足({元 / 下})をすくわれる　／ phr.　換喩

油断をしていると、失敗したり裏切られたりする
to be caught off guard and sabotaged/deceived

例文

日本の景気は少しは上向きでこの状態が少しは続きそうだ。しかし、いつ足元をすくわれるかわからない。

There's been a slight uptick in the Japanese economy, and it seems like it will last for a while. But we can't tell when the rug's going to be pulled out from under us.

619

sweet voice comp. n. synesthesia

a voice that is pleasing to the ear

REL sweet-talk s.o. into ~ing

Examples

Saya: Ah, Kenta, what splendid timing. How are you feeling today?

Kenta: Why're you talking in such a sweet voice? You need something, don't you?

Saya: Is it that obvious?

- -

(a) My wife's so cold towards me, yet she always talks to the cat in a sweet voice.

(b) When I hear the sound of your sweet voice, it tickles me from head to toe.

Notes

1. Both the English and Japanese are examples of synesthesia in that an adjective associated with the sense of taste is applied to the sense of hearing.

2. *Sweet* and *amai* are used quite differently, as shown below.

(1) a. You're so sweet!

あなたって、{優しい/ˣ甘い}のね。

b. John is sweet on Karen.

ジョンはカレン{が好きだ/ˣに甘い}。

Amai can be used to mean "too lenient" and "to indulge s.o. too much." 📖 解説 **(2)**

R E L

The English and Japanese RELs are *sweet-talk s.o. into ~ing* and *amai kotoba* (lit. "sweet word"), respectively. 📖 関連語 **(1)**

---

table('s) legs (テーブルの脚) → **{desk/chair/bed/table}('s) legs**

---

tail off phr. metaphor

to gradually decrease

REL taper off

Examples

(a) Business was pretty good at the time, but it tailed off after the global financial crisis.

(b) Though that tennis player used to be considered the best in the world, he, too, would tail off toward the end of his career and struggle to win matches.

(c) The grassroots movement was promising at first, but it tailed off after the leader's death.

Notes

1. The English and Japanese, while close, have some differences. Both use a body part located at the end of the torso—*tail* and *shiri* (hip/buttocks), respectively—but *off* indicates movement away from the *tail*, whereas *subomu* means "to become narrow."

2. The English can be used to indicate a decrease in intensity as well as amount, as shown in (1).

甘い声 / n. phr. / 共感覚

（心中の密かな目的を持って）人をいい気持ちにさせる優しい声

関 甘い言葉

例文

さや：あ、健太、いいとこ、来た。どう、今日のご機嫌は？

健太：なんだよ、いやに甘い声、出しちゃって。何か魂胆があるな。

さや：わかる？

- -

(a) 妻は私にはそっけないが、ネコにはいつも甘い声で話しかける。

(b) 君の甘い声を聞くと、僕の体は爪先から頭までジーンときてしまうんだ。

解説

1. 日英語とも形容詞の比喩的意味は味覚から聴覚への、いわゆる共感覚から出てきている。

2. 日本語の「甘い」と英語の *sweet* は、例文のようにかなり違った意味でも使われるので注意。

—📖 Note (1)

ただし、日本語では、(2)は「甘い」の意味が"寛大"とか"甘やかす"という意味であれば、使うことができる。

(2) ジョンはカレンに甘すぎる。
   John indulges Karen too much.

関連語

日本語には「甘い言葉」、英語には *sweet-talk s.o. into ~ing*（甘い言葉で〜させる）という関連表現がある。

(1) セールスマンの甘い言葉にのせられて、高価な車を買ってしまった。
   The salesman sweet-talked me into buying an expensive car.

尻すぼみになる / phr. / 隠喩

何か勢いのよかったものが終わりに向けて衰える

例文

(a) 一時は調子のよかった商売も、リーマンショックの後は尻すぼみになってしまった。

(b) 世界最強と言われたそのテニス選手も現役の終わりには尻すぼみになって、試合に勝つのに苦労していた。

(c) 最初、勢いのよかった市民運動も、リーダーの死とともに尻すぼみになってしまった。

解説

1. 日英語は近いが同じ表現をとってはいない。動物の「尻」と *tail*（尻尾）、つまり胴体の終わりの部分をそれぞれ使っている。「すぼむ」は"狭くなる"という意味で、*off* は"尻尾を離れる"ことを意味する。

2. 英語は"何かが次第に小さくなっていく"という意味以外に"静まる"という意味もある。

—📖 Note (1)

(1) The thunderstorm tailed off.
雷雨は{静まった／[×]尻すぼみになった}。

REL

The English REL, *taper off*, has the same meaning as the main entry and is used more frequently.

(1) The grassroots movement was promising at first, but it {tailed/tapered} off after the leader's death. (→(c))

{take/do} a 180 (-degree turn)　/ phr. / metaphor

to completely change

Examples

Mike: I can't stand our section chief. He changes his views so quickly.

Colleague: Yeah, he's always doing a 180. These documents are useless now.

(a) Postwar Japan's ideology did a 180-degree turn from militarism to democracy.

(b) He's been living a really unhealthy life. Unless his lifestyle—including his diet—does a 180, he's not going to be around for much longer.

Note

Turn and *tenkan-suru* (lit. "to turn and change") are very similar.

REL

The Japanese REL, *180 do kawaru* (lit. "to change 180 degrees"), is used more frequently than the main entry. 📖→関連語(1)

take a beating (from ~)　/ phr. / metaphor

for {s.o./s.t.} to be severely criticized; to be defeated; to lose a lot of {money/value}

REL take a hammering

Examples

Mike: Hey, I thought you were taking a break and going to Hawaii.

Colleague: Yeah, but I had to postpone it because of an urgent meeting. I took a beating from my wife and kids, too. They complained that they had been looking forward to that trip for a whole year.

(a) He took a beating from the media for his staunch conservatism.

(b) The superintendent's school restructuring plan took a beating from the educator.

Notes

1. The English may not be passive in form, but semantically it is a passive expression like the Japanese. The Japanese usually takes the colloquial adverb *sanzan* (terribly), but it can also take the adverb *koppidoku* (severely), as shown in the dialogue.

622

関連語

英語には見出しと同じ意味の *taper off* という関連表現があり、見出しより使用頻度が高い。

→📖 REL (1)

180度転換する　/ phr.　隠喩

{考え / キャリア / 政策 / 状況}などが完全に変わる

関 180度変わる

例文

マイク：ほんと課長には参るな。すぐに意見を変えるんだから。

同僚：まったく、180度方針転換だもんな。この書類、全部パーだよ。

(a) 戦後日本の思想は軍国主義から民主主義へと180度転換した。

(b) 彼は本当に不健康な生活をしている。食生活を含む生活習慣を180度転換しなければ、長生きはできないだろう。

解説

日本語の動詞「転換する」(lit. 回転して変える)と英語の *turn* は非常に似ている。

関連語

日本語では、「180度変わる」という関連表現があり、「180度転換する」より使用頻度が高い。

(1) 戦後日本の思想は軍国主義から民主主義へと180度{転換した / 変わった}。(→(a))
Postwar Japan's ideology took a 180-degree turn from militarism to democracy. (→(a))

(〜に / から)叩かれる　/ phr.　隠喩

{誰か / 何か}が厳しく批判される

例文

マイク：あれ、休みで、ハワイ行くんじゃなかったですか。

同僚：うん、それが緊急会議で延期。女房、子供にこっぴどく叩かれちゃったよ。1年も前から楽しみにしてたのにって。

(a) 彼はその頑固な保守主義のために、メディアからはさんざん叩かれた。

(b) 教育委員長の学校構造改革計画は、教育者からさんざん叩かれた。

解説

1. 英語の *take a beating (from 〜)* は形は受け身の形ではないが、意味は日本語と同じく受け身である。日本語はたいてい「さんざん」という副詞がつくが、会話例のように「こっぴどく」という副詞も使える。

623

2. A comparison of the figurative meanings of the English and Japanese reveals that the English is much wider in its semantic scope than the Japanese. The Japanese subject must be either a person or something produced by a person, but the English subject can be virtually anything.

(1) a. The drugmaker's shares took a beating, losing 39.6% of their value.
製薬会社の株は〔打撃を受けて/ ˣ さんざん叩かれて〕、39.6％ も下がった。

b. Many economists' reputations also took a beating from the this year's economic turmoil.
経済学者も今年の経済の動揺で〔その評判を失った/ ˣ さんざん叩かれた〕者が大勢いた。

3. The English also has the meaning "to lose a lot of {money/value}."

(2) The stock market took a beating due to the unpredictable behavior of that famous company's CEO.
有名企業の社長の予想できない行動のために、株式市場は打撃を受けた。

R E L

The English has the REL *take a hammering*, which can be used instead of the main entry.

(1) He took a {beating/hammering} from the media for his staunch conservatism. (→ (a))

take a load off one's mind / phr. metaphor

to feel relieved

Examples

(a) Knowing that you were home with my ailing mother and taking care of everything took a load off my mind.

(b) Just knowing that my two-week vacation is starting takes a load off my mind.

(c) Her letter cheered him up. He'd been having some problems with work lately, and assurances like this took a load off his mind.

Notes

1. The English uses the transitive verb *take*, but the Japanese uses the intransitive verb *toreru* (to be taken away).

2. In both the English and Japanese, the person who feels relief must be either the speaker or someone who can empathize with the speaker.

R E L

1. The verb *toreru* can be replaced by *oriru* (to come down) when the expression is used to indicate the relief someone feels when something for which he/she is responsible has been (or is about to be) solved, as in (1a). Note that the verb in (1b) cannot be replaced by *oriru*. 📖→ 関連語(1)

2. In Japanese, the colloquial expression *kata no ni ga oriru* is frequently used. This expression is used when one manages to avoid something one is responsible for.
📖→ 関連語(2)

3. The Japanese can be replaced by the non-metaphorical verb *hotto suru* (to feel relieved) in casual speech. 📖→ 関連語(3)

2. 日英語の比喩的意味を比較すると、英語のほうがはるかに意味領域が広いことがわかる。日本語の場合は主語が人か、人の作り出したものだが、英語では何でも主語になる。

━━📖 Note(1)

3. 英語の見出しには"たくさんのお金や価値を失う"という意味もある。━━📖 Note(2)

関連語

英語には *take a hammering* という関連表現があり、見出しと置き換えることができる。

━━📖 REL(1)

心の重荷が取れる / phr. / 隠喩

安心する

関 心の重荷が下りる, LOOK▶ 肩の荷が下りる, ほっとする

例文

(a) あなたが病気の母と一緒に家にいて、何でも世話をしてくれていることを知っただけで、心の重荷が取れた。

(b) これから2週間のバケーションが始まることを考えただけで、私は心の重荷が取れた。

(c) 彼は彼女の手紙で元気づけられた。最近は仕事のことで問題があったので、このような励ましを受けて心の重荷が取れたのだ。

解説

1. 日本語は自動詞「取れる」を、英語は他動詞 *take* を使っている。

2. 日英語とも、安心する人は、自分か、話者と共感を持てる人に限られる。

関連語

1. 日本語の動詞の「取れる」は次の(1a)のように、何か話し手に責任のある問題が解決|された/されそうな| ときにほっとする場合は、「下りる」で置き換えることができる。(1b)では置き換えられないことに注意。

(1)a. あなたが病気の母と一緒に家にいて、何でも世話をしてくれていることを知っただけで、心の重荷が{取れた/下りた}。(→(a))

 b. これから2週間のバケーションが始まることを考えただけで、私は心の重荷が{取れた/×下りた}。(→(b))

2. 日本語には見出しとよく似た表現で、より使用頻度の高い「肩の荷が下りる」という口語表現がある。この表現は、責任があることが回避できたという場合によく使われる。

(2) あなたが病気の母と一緒に家にいて、何でも世話をしてくれていることを知っただけで、{心の重荷が取れた/肩の荷が下りた}。(→(a))

3. 日本語はくだけた話し言葉では「ほっとする」という非比喩的な動詞で置き換えられる。

(3) あなたが病気の母と一緒に家にいて、何でも世話をしてくれていることを知っただけで、{心の重荷が取れた/ほっとした}。(→(a))

625

take {a/the} long view of ~ / phr. / metaphor

to think about future possibilities instead of focusing only on the present

REL take a broad view

Examples

Mike: You're never going to be good at tennis. I don't get how you're so good at skiing.

Kenta: Hey, don't say that. You have to take the long view, Coach Mike.

- -

(a) Take a long view of your life before deciding your next course of action.

(b) The parents should take the long view when thinking about what would be most helpful to their children.

REL

1. The Japanese has the REL *chōki-tekini miru*, which is often used in economic contexts.

📖 関連語(1)

2. The English has the REL *take a broad view*, which means "to view s.t. from a general perspective in an objective manner."

(2) The book took a broad view of the history of communication.
その本はコミュニケーションの歴史の全体像をとらえている。

take pen in hand / phr. / metonymy

to write s.t.

REL take up one's pen

Examples

(a) I have taken pen in hand to express my gratitude for your kindness.

(b) A few years after he declared his decision not to write any longer, the writer took pen in hand again.

(c) I took pen in hand to thank to you for assisting me with my thesis.

Note

Adding the indefinite article *a* to the English expression makes it non-metaphorical.

(1) My instructor looked at me and said, "Take a pen in hand and write."
先生は私を見て「ペンを手に取って、書きなさい」と言った。

REL

1. The Japanese has two RELs: the Sino-Japanese expression *shippitsu-suru* and *pen o toru*, which replaces *fude* from the main entry with the more colloquial *pen*. 📖 関連語(1)

2. The English has the REL *take up one's pen*. It can be used instead of the main entry.

(2) I have {taken pen in hand/taken up my pen} to express my gratitude for your kindness.

(→(a))

長い目で見る / phr. / 隠喩

現在の状況を短絡的に評価しないで、将来的な可能性を考える

関 長期的に見る

例文

マイク：健太はいつまでたってもテニスが上手にならないな。スキーはあんなにうまいくせに。

健太：ま、そう言わずに、長い目で見てよ。マイクコーチ。

(a) あなたの人生を長い目で見て、何をすべきか決めなさい。

(b) 親は、子供にとって何が一番助けになるかを長い目で見るべきだ。

関連語

1. 日本語には「長期的に見る」という関連表現があり、経済的な文脈で使われることが多い。

(1) 株価の変動については長期的に見る必要がある。
One must take a long view when it comes to fluctuations in stock prices.

2. 英語には *take a broad view* という関連表現がある。"物事の全体像を客観的にとらえる"という意味である。→ REL(2)

筆を執る / phr. / 換喩

あらたまって文章を書く

関 ペンを執る，執筆する

例文

(a) あなたのご親切に感謝を申し上げたいと思い、筆を執りました。

(b) 断筆宣言の数年後、その作家は再び筆を執った。

(c) 卒論のことで先生のご指導に感謝の気持ちを述べたいと思い、筆を執った次第です。

解説

英語では *pen* に不定冠詞 *a* がつくと、比喩表現としては使えない。→ Note(1)

関連語

1. 日本語には「執筆する」という漢語表現と、見出しの「筆」をペンに替えた「ペンを執る」というより口語的な表現もある。

(1) 断筆宣言の数年後、その作家は再び{筆を執った / ペンを執った / 執筆を始めた}。(→(b))

2. 英語には *take up one's pen* という関連表現がある。見出しと置き換えることができる。

→ Note(2)

take shape (as ~) *phr.* metaphor

for s.t. to take on a specific form

Examples

(a) Taoism probably took shape as a religion in China during the second century.

(b) It wasn't until November of 1995 that the initial concept really took shape as an institute.

(c) I think it's fine if my relationship with him stays flexible and doesn't take shape as a marriage.

Note

The Japanese can also assume the form *(~ toiu) katachi o toru* (to take the form of ~). However, *take shape* and *(~ toiu) katachi o toru* are typically used in different ways.

📖 解説(1)

take {s.o.'s side/sides} *phr.* metaphor

to support one party over another in a dispute

REL be on s.o.'s side

Examples

(a) Whenever Dennis and I get into an argument, Mark always takes his side.

(b) Parents shouldn't take sides when their children get into an argument.

Note

Both the English and Japanese are based on the same spatial expression. As such, the expressions reflect the notion that physical proximity breeds empathy.

REL

The English REL, *be on s.o.'s side*, means "to be in support of s.o.'s views," which makes it similar to the main entry.

(1) Whenever Dennis and I get into an argument, Mark {always takes/is always on} his side.

(→(a))

take the bait *phr.* metaphor

to be tricked into doing s.t. that s.o. wants you to do

REL jump at the bait

Examples

(a) To catch the criminal, the police sent him a fake notice saying that he had won the lottery. He foolishly took the bait, and when he showed up, they arrested him.

(b) He was told he would be able to take 25 days off per year, so he took the bait and joined the company, but he ended up only being able to take a week off.

（〜の）形を取る / phr. 隠喩

何かが変化したり、ある状態になる

例文

(a) 道教は中国で2世紀に宗教の形を取ったのだろう。

(b) 最初のアイディアがようやく正式な学会の形を取ったのは、1995年11月だった。

(c) 彼とは結婚という形を取らないで、自由な関係を続けられたらいいと思う。

解説

日本語には「（〜という）形を取る」という構文があるが、英語とこの日本語の構文は一般的に異なる方法で使用される。

(1) このパーティは会員制のみ{の/ という}形を取る。
This party {is/ˣtakes shape as} membership only.

（〜の）側に立つ / phr. 隠喩

争いなどで味方になる

例文

(a) 私とデニスが議論する時は、マークはいつもデニスの側に立つ。

(b) 子供達がけんかをしている時は、親はどちらの側にも立つべきではない。

解説

日英語とも同じ空間的な表現から来ている。つまり、物理的な近接関係は共感の心理を生むということである。

関連語

英語には見出しに近い意味を持つ *be on s.o.'s side* という関連表現がある。

餌に食いつく / phr. 隠喩

誘惑に負ける，何かに惑わされる

関 餌に飛びつく

例文

(a) 犯人を捕まえるために、警察は彼が宝くじに当たったという偽の通知をした。おろかにも彼はその餌に食いつき、現れたときには簡単に逮捕されてしまった。

(b) 彼は年に25日は休暇が取れるという餌に食いついて就職したが、実際は1週間しか取れなかった。

Notes

1. Both the English and Japanese come from the idea of fish eating bait.
2. *Kui-tsuku* means "to bite at s.t. edible" and is more descriptive than *take*, which in this case means "to bring s.t. {near/inside} the body."

REL

The English and Japanese RELs are *jump at the bait* and *esa ni tobi-tsuku*, respectively.

📖→ 関連語(1)

---

take the time (to ~) phr. metaphor

to spend the time required to do s.t. properly

Examples

Colleague: Mike, can you take a look at this English?

Mike: Sorry, I have to finish a report by this afternoon, so I can't afford to take the time to look at that now. Can I do it later?

Colleague: Sure. Whenever you have time, if you don't mind.

- -

(a) When writing a thesis, it's important to take the time to do your research properly.

(b) My daughter is really busy taking care of her family and working full-time, but she still takes the time to come see me and take care of me.

Notes

1. The Japanese expression can also mean "for s.t. to take time." 📖→ 解説(1)
2. On the other hand, the English means "to spend the time required to do s.t. properly."

(2) He was patient and took the time to answer my questions in a manner that I understood.
彼は私の質問に、私がわかるように忍耐強く、時間をかけて答えてくれた。

REL

The Japanese has the REL *jikan o saku*, which means "to spare time for." It can replace *jikan o toru.* 📖→ 関連語(1)

---

take (up) the reins (of ~) phr. metaphor

to take control of s.t., especially an organization or country

REL steer the ship

Examples

Mike: This company has been performing better lately, hasn't it? It was pretty close to going bankrupt, too.

Mr. S: It sure has. Ever since the new president from France took up the reins, it has completely turned things around.

- -

[解 説]

1. 日英語ともに魚が餌に食いつくイメージから来ている。
2. 日本語の「食いつく」の基本義は"食べられる物に噛み付く"で英語の動詞 *take* の基本義は"体表か体内に何かを近づける"である。日本語のほうが英語より描写的だと言える。

[関連語]

日英語とも、それぞれ、関連表現として、「餌に飛びつく」*jump at the bait* がある。

(1) 50％ オフの餌に{食いついて/飛びついて}新製品を買ってみたけれど、質がひどかった。
When I saw that the new product was half off, I {took/jumped at} the bait and bought it, but the quality was terrible.

時間を取る *phr.* 隠喩

何かをするのに時間を{使う/作る}

関 時間を割く

[例 文]

同僚：マイク、ちょっとこの英語、見てくれないかな。

マイク：悪い！　今、ちょっと時間が取れないんだ。午後までに仕上げなきゃいけない報告書があって。後でいいかな。

同僚：うん、じゃ、手のあいたとき、頼むよ。

(a) 論文を書くときは、十分にリサーチする時間を取ることが大切だ。

(b) 娘は家族の世話とフルタイムの仕事で忙しいにもかかわらず、ときどき時間を取って、私の身の回りの世話をしに来てくれる。

[解 説]

1. 日本語には"何かをするのに時間がかかる"という意味もある。

(1) この仕事は時間を取るだけで、あまり成果があがらないので、みんなやりたがらない。
This job just takes up time and doesn't really produce results, so nobody wants to do it.

2. 一方、英語には"時間をかけてゆっくり物事を行う"という意味がある。📖 **Note (2)**

[関連語]

日本語には時間の一部を分けて他のことに使うという意味の「時間を割く」という表現があり、見出しと置き換えができる。

(1) 娘は家族の世話とフルタイムの仕事で忙しいにもかかわらず、ときどき時間を{取って/割いて}、私の身の回りの世話をしに来てくれる。（→(b)）

手綱を取る *phr.* 隠喩

{国家/組織}の指導的立場になる

関 舵を取る

[例 文]

マイク：この会社はこのごろ業績が上がってきましたね。一時は潰れる寸前だったのに。

鈴木(夫)：うん、フランスから来た社長が経営の手綱を取るようになってから、完全に再生したね。

(a) Dr. Kawakami took the reins of the hospital as chief.

(b) The company employees are planning to revitalize business by taking up the reins themselves.

Notes

1. Both the English and Japanese are metaphors that come from the act of using reins to control the horse when horseback riding.

2. The Japanese is used only when someone takes control of {a country/an organization} for a specific purpose, but the English can be used even when there is no specific purpose.

(1) Shirley M. Tilghman, a life scientist, took the reins of Princeton University as president on May 5, 2001.
生命科学者のシャーリイ・ティルマン氏は2001年5月5日にプリンストン大学学長として{就任した/×その手綱を取った}。

REL

1. The English and Japanese have the RELs *steer the ship* and *kaji o toru*, respectively.

关連語 **(1)(2)**

take to (one's) bed / phr. / metonymy

to go to bed, typically with an illness

Examples

(a) I took to my bed for days on end, succumbing to a bout of the flu.

(b) She was never ill for a moment. She took to her bed only four months before her death.

(c) Last night, I took to bed at about 11:30.

Note

Both the English and Japanese expressions mean "to fall ill," as shown in (a) and (b), and "to go to bed," as shown in (c).

homograph

tap s.o.'s shoulder / phr. / metonymy

to draw s.o.'s attention by tapping his/her shoulder
注意を引く

Example

Someone tapped my shoulder, and when I turned around, it was one of my friends from high school.

誰かが肩を叩いたので、振り返ったら、高校の時の仲間だった。

(a) 川上博士は院長として病院経営の手綱を取った。

(b) その会社の労働者たちは自分達で経営の手綱を取って、会社の活性化を計っている。

解説

1. 日英語とも乗馬の時の手綱の使い方から来ている比喩である。

2. 日本語はある特定の目的で国家や組織の指導的立場に立つときにだけ使われるのに対して、英語は特定の目的がない場合も使える。━📖 Note(1)

関連語

1. 日英語には、それぞれ「舵を取る」/*steer the ship* という関連表現がある。

(1) 川上博士は院長として病院経営の手綱を取った。(→(a))

Dr. Kawakami took the reins of the hospital as chief.(→(a))

(2) 川上博士が病院経営の舵を取ったおかげで、病院は前よりもずっと円滑に機能するようになった。

With Dr. Kawakami steering the ship, the hospital has never functioned better.

床につく / phr. / 換喩

寝る, 病気になる

例文

(a) 流感にやられて何日もずっと床についていた。

(b) 彼女は一度も病気をしたことがなかった。死ぬ前の4か月だけ床についた。

(c) 私はきのうの晩、11時半ごろ床についた。

解説

日英語とも(a)(b)のように"病気になる"と(c)のように"寝る"という意味がある。

同形異義語

肩を叩く / phr. / 換喩

会社を辞めさせようとする

to urge s.o. to quit a job

例文

父は、上司に肩を叩かれて、早期退職を促されたらしい。

Apparently my father was urged to retire early by his boss.

633

taste / v./n. / metaphor/synesthesia

to perceive a psychological experience as if by the sense of taste

Examples

(a) Tom lost his mother, and for the first time in his life he tasted profound sorrow.

(b) When the airplane got caught in turbulence and made a sudden nosedive, I had a brief taste of mortal terror.

(c) When Yumi left the parents that had controlled her life for so many years, she tasted freedom and happiness beyond compare.

(d) Before I met her, I had never tasted such happiness.

Note

Both the English and Japanese express the perception of some psychological experience, such as sorrow (as in [a]), fear (as in [b]), freedom (as in [c]), or happiness (as in [d]), in terms of the sense of taste. This type of usage is referred to as synesthesia. In addition, the Japanese can also be used in expressions such as {ongaku/bungaku} o ajiwau (to taste {music/literature}).

tearjerker / comp. n. / metaphor

a story, movie, or other work that makes people cry

Example

I don't usually like tearjerker films and TV shows that deal with illness, but this movie felt different.

tempest in a teapot, a / n.phr. / metaphor

a great uproar over a trivial matter

REL storm in a teacup

Examples

Mrs. S: Disputes have broken out again between the factions of the LDP.

Mr. S: It's all just a tempest in a teapot. It won't have any effect on Japan's political system.

(a) To the heavens, human conflict is just a tempest in a teapot.

(b) Their inheritance dispute is really just a tempest in a teapot. To everyone else, it's just a family feud.

Note

A comparison of the figurative meanings of the English and Japanese expressions shows that the Japanese means "s.t. considered important to insiders but trivial to outsiders," whereas the English means "s.t. considered important that is actually trivial." For this

（〜を）味わう / phr. / 隠喩 / 共感覚

何かの心理的な経験をまるで味覚によるかのように知覚する

例文
- (a) トムは母親を亡くして、人生で初めての深い悲しみを味わった。
- (b) 飛行機が気流に巻きこまれて急降下したときは、一瞬死ぬかと思うような恐怖を味わった。
- (c) 由美は長年自分を支配してきた親の元を離れて、この上ない喜びと自由を味わった。
- (d) 彼女と会うまではこんな幸福（感）を味わったことはなかった。

解説
日英語ともに人間の心理的な体験、例えば、(a)「悲しみ」*sorrow*、(b)「恐怖」*fear*、(c)「自由」*freedom*、(d)「幸福（感）」*happiness* を味覚のように知覚することを表現している。これは共感覚と呼ばれる。また、日本語では「｜音楽 / 文学｜を味わう」のような使い方もできる。

T

お涙頂戴 / n. phr. / 隠喩

簡単に泣ける話

例文
病気を扱った映画やドラマは、お涙頂戴になりがちなので好きではなかったが、この映画は違うと思った。

コップの中の嵐 / n. phr. / 隠喩

内部の者にとっては大事なことが外部の者にとってはささいなこと

例文
鈴木（妻）：また、自民党、派閥争いでもめてるのね。
鈴木（夫）：所詮、コップの中の嵐だよ。日本の政治体制に大した影響はないね。

- (a) 天から見れば、人間が起こす争いなどコップの中の嵐にすぎない。
- (b) 彼らの遺産相続争いなど、所詮、一家族内のコップの中の嵐だ。外から見たらただの内輪もめでしかない。

解説
日英語の比喩的意味を比べるとわかるように、日本語のほうは"外部の者が些細と考えることでも当事者にとっては重要事項だ"という意味で使われるが、英語は"人々が重要だと考えているが実は些細なこと"という意味で使われる。したがって、英語では、内の者と外の者の視点のずれが問題にならない場合でも使えるが、日本語では使えない。その場合は、日本語は「空騒ぎ」を使う。

635

reason, the English can be used even in contexts where conflict between insiders and outsiders is not relevant, while the Japanese cannot. In these cases, *kara-sawagi* (empty fuss) would be used instead. 📖→解説(1)

[R][E][L]

The main entry is typically used in American English. The British English equivalent is *storm in a teacup*.

There is no royal road to ~ / phr. / metaphor

there is no easy way to achieve s.t.

[ANT] there is a royal road to ~

Examples

(a) It is said that Aristotle is the one who told Alexander the Great that there is no royal road to learning.

(b) There is no royal road to success, so the only way to succeed is through constant effort.

(c) It is said that when Euclid was requested by Ptolemy to teach him an easier way of learning geometry, Euclid replied, "There is no royal road to geometry."

Notes

1. As shown in (a) the Japanese often uses *nashi*, an archaic negative form, instead of *nai*. Note that there is no *wa* before *nashi*.

2 *Ōdō* can also be used to mean "the standard/proper way of doing s.t." or "the best of its kind." 📖→解説(1)

[A][N][T]

The proverb is usually used as a negative statement, but it can occasionally be used as an affirmative statement as well.

(1) We endeavor to convince ourselves that there is a royal road to success, but we soon discover that we can omit no steps.
私達は成功には王道があると自分に懸命に言い聞かせてはいるが、ステップを省くわけにはいかないことをすぐ発見するのだ。

homograph

thick-skinned / comp. adj. / metaphor

not easily upset by criticism
物に動じない
もの どう

Example

It isn't true that successful journalists are aggressive and thick-skinned.
成功しているジャーナリストが攻撃的で物に動じないというのはうそだ。
せいこう　　　　　　　　　　　　　　こうげきてき　もの　どう

(1) 予想されていたテロは{空騒ぎ/×コップの中の嵐}に終わった。
The anticipated terrorist attack turned out to be a tempest in a teapot.

関連語

英語の見出しはアメリカ英語で、イギリス英語では *storm in a teacup* になる。

（〜に／の）王道はない　／ phr. ／ 隠喩

何かを達成するためのたやすい方法はない

反 （〜に）王道がある

例文

(a) アレキサンダー大王に「学問に王道なし」と言った人物はアリストテレスだと言われている。

(b) 成功への王道はないのだから、自分で地道な努力を重ねるよりない。

(c) ユークリッドは、プトレマイオスに幾何学への近道を教えてくれと頼まれて、「幾何学に王道はない」と答えたそうだ。

解説

1. 日本語の「王道はない」は文語の「なし」を使って、(a)のように「王道なし」とも言う。「なし」の前に「は」がないことに注意。

2. 日本語では「あることの基準、一番正当な方法、最良の物」という意味で「王道」を使用することがある。

(1) 日本のサービスの王道は、日本の高級旅館で経験できる。
You can experience the pinnacle of Japanese service by staying at a high-class Japanese-style inn.

反意語

この見出しは否定形が使われることが多いが、肯定形を使うこともある。 →📖 ANT(1)

同形異義語

面の皮が厚い　／ phr. ／ 隠喩

図々しい
shameless

例文

彼は面の皮が厚いこと、この上ない。平気で借金をして、返そうともしない。
He has no shame at all, borrowing money and not even trying to pay it back.

thorny path, {a/the}   / comp. n. / metaphor

a difficult situation

Examples

(a) Life is a thorny path, but we can get through it as long as we have love.

(b) Japan's economy has been on a thorny path since the bubble burst.

(c) Buoyed by a lofty sense of purpose, the leaders of democratic nations have all trod the thorny path of politics.

Notes

1. The basic meanings of *path* and *michi* are "a route for traveling along" and "a route that connects two points for use by people or vehicles," respectively. While *thorny* is an adjective, *ibara* is a noun that means "thorn."

2. The English expression can be used with a number of verbs, including *walk*, *tread*, and *follow*. The Japanese is typically used with *tadoru*, as shown in (b), and *ayumu*, as shown in (c).

throw in the towel   / phr. / metaphor

to give up

REL throw {in/up} the sponge

Examples

(a) No one threw in the towel at that football game. They fought until the end.

(b) I would be delighted to see that dictator throw in the towel.

(c) There were quite a few times when I wanted to throw in the towel. But thanks to my friends, I pulled through.

Notes

1. The English expression comes from boxing, where a coach would throw a towel into the ring to concede defeat.

2. The Japanese is a direct translation of the English.

REL

1. *Throw {in/up} the sponge*, another boxing expression, can replace *throw in the towel*, though this is used much less frequently than the main entry.

(1) No one {threw in the towel/threw {in/up} the sponge} at the football game.
そのフットボールの試合では誰もタオルを投げずに最後まで戦った。

2. The Japanese REL, *saji o nageru* (lit. "to throw the spoon"), means "for a doctor to give up on a patient; for s.o. to give up on s.t." This comes from the idea of a doctor ceasing treatment and throwing away the spoon used to prepare a patient's medicine because the patient is beyond saving. *Saji o nageru* can replace the main entry when used in the sense that someone is giving up on something, such as in (c), but not when someone is giving up in a competition. In fact, *saji o nageru* is used more frequently than the main entry when indicating that someone is giving up on something. 📖→ 関連語(2)

茨の道 / n. phr. 隠喩
いばら みち

試練の多い人生
しれん おお じんせい

例文

(a) 人生は茨の道だが、「愛」さえあれば乗り越えられる。
じんせい いばら みち あい の こ

(b) 日本の経済は、バブル崩壊後は茨の道を辿ってきた。
にほん けいざい ほうかいご いばら みち たど

(c) 民主国家の指導者たちは、高邁な目標を持ってそれぞれに茨の道を歩んできた。
みんしゅこっか しどうしゃ こうまい もくひょう も いばら みち あゆ

解説

1. 「道」と path の基本義は、それぞれ、"人や車が通るための2点を結ぶルート"と"歩く小道"である。「茨」は名詞であるが、thorny は"とげのある"という意味の形容詞である。

2. 日本語では一般的に(b)の「辿る」や(c)の「歩む」のような動詞が使われる。英語では walk、tread、follow などの動詞と共に使うことができる。

T

タオルを投げる / phr. 隠喩
な いんゆ

負けを認めて、もうそれ以上挑戦しない
ま みと いじょうちょうせん

関 さじを投げる
な

例文

(a) そのフットボールの試合では誰もタオルを投げずに最後まで戦った。
しあい だれ な さいご たたか

(b) あの独裁者がタオルを投げれば喜ぶね、僕は。
どくさいしゃ な よろこ ぼく

(c) 何回もタオルを投げたいと思ったんですが、友達のおかげで、がんばってやり通しました。
なんかい な おも ともだち とお

解説

1. 英語は、ボクシングでコーチが負けを認めたときにリングにタオルを投げ込むことからきている。

2. 日本語は英語からの直訳である。

関連語

1. 英語にはボクシングからきている他の表現、throw {in/up} the sponge があり、見出しと置き換えられるが、使用頻度ははるかに低い。📖 **REL (1)**

2. 日本語には"医者が患者の治療をあきらめる。誰かが何かについてあきらめる"という意味の「さじを投げる」という関連表現がある。これは「医者がもう助からない患者の治療をあきらめて、薬を調合するために使うさじを捨てる」ということからきている。「さじを投げる」は(c)のように、誰かとの戦いではなく、何かをあきらめるような場合には見出しと置き換えることができる。また、何かをあきらめる場合の使用頻度は「さじを投げる」の方が見出しよりはるかに高い。

(2) 何回も{タオルを投げ/さじを投げ}たいと思ったんですが、友達のおかげで、がんばってやり通しました。(→(c))

{throw/bring} s.t. into (sharp) relief / phr. / metaphor

to make s.t. evident

Examples

(a) The discussion threw into sharp relief the president's views on Medicare.

(b) It can be said that the rapid development of social media is throwing social isolation in modern society into relief once again.

(c) The train accident brought the importance of safety into sharp relief.

Notes

1. Both the English and Japanese use the basic meaning of *relief* and *uki-bori*, which is "a sculpting technique in which forms are clearly distinguished from a surrounding plane."

2. Western relief sculpture originated between the era of Alexander the Great (4th century BCE) and the Hellenistic period. Some say Japanese relief sculpture originated in the Kamakura period (1185-1333) through Chinese influence, but some argue that it originated in the Jomon period.

3. The English uses the verbs *throw* (as in [a] and [b]), and *bring* (as in [c]), while the Japanese uses *sareru* (as in [a]), *suru* (as in [b]), *and naru* (as in [c]).

throw oneself into ~ / phr. / metaphor

to engage in s.t. with enthusiasm

Examples

(a) The best way to learn a foreign language is for you to throw yourself into a situation where you have to use it.

(b) Those who followed in Gandhi's footsteps often threw themselves into politics.

(c) In this region, even young children throw themselves into the fighting for the sake of waging holy war.

Note

The Japanese can only be used in written language, but the English can be used in both spoken and written language.

throw up one's hands / phr. / metonymy

a problematic situation that one cannot do anything about

Examples

Kenta: Saya, how was the exam? Was it hard?

Saya: I had to throw up my hands. It took me two hours to finish like only half the exam.

Kenta: No way! If it gave you that much trouble, I probably would've turned in blank sheets.

浮き彫りに{する / される / なる}　phr.　隠喩

関連した出来事によって、ものの実態が自然に明らかになる

例文

(a) その議論で、大統領の医療保険に関する見解が鋭く浮き彫りにされた。

(b) ソーシャルメディアの急速な発展は、現代社会における個人の孤独を改めて浮き彫りにしたと言える。

(c) その電車事故で、安全性の重要さが浮き彫りになった。

解説

1. 日英語とも「浮き彫り」と *relief* の基本義、"形と像が回りの平面からはっきり区別されるような彫刻という美術の技術"の比喩的用法である。

2. 西欧の浮き彫り彫刻品は、紀元前4世紀のアレクサンダー大王の時代からヘレニズム文明の時代にかけて出てきたのに対して、日本では鎌倉時代(1185-1333)に中国の影響で出てきたという説もあるが、縄文時代まで遡るという説もある。

3. 英語で使われる動詞は(a)と(b)のように *throw*（投げる）か、(c)のように *bring*（もたらす）であるのに対して、日本語では(a)「される」、(b)「する」、(c)「なる」が使われる。

T

(〜に)(自分の)身を投じる　phr.　隠喩

価値があると思うものに最大限の努力を払う

例文

(a) 外国語の一番の習得法は、その言語を使わねばならない状況に自分の身を投じることだ。

(b) ガンジーの跡を継いだ人達は、しばしば政治に自分の身を投じた。

(c) この地域では、幼い子供達までが聖戦の名の下に戦いに身を投じているのだ。

解説

日本語は書き言葉でしか使えないが、英語は話し言葉でも書き言葉でも使える。

お手上げ　comp. n.　換喩

何かの問題に対してどうすることもできない状況

例文

健太：ね、試験、どうだった？　難しかった？

さや：もう、お手上げ！　2時間かかって半分ぐらいしか書けなかったわ。

健太：うそ！　さやでもそんなに難しいんなら、僕なんか白紙状態だな。

641

(a) "This is a load of garbage!" He turned away and sighed, as if throwing up his hands in defeat.

(b) Their son's behavior was totally out of control, and the situation seemed hopeless, so they threw up their hands.

Note

Both the English and Japanese express a feeling of resignation, but the English refers to a gesture in which the palms are turned upward and the arms are raised outward in an indication of exasperation. The Japanese has no accompanying gesture.

{tides are/tide is} {turning/changing}, the   phr.   metaphor

for a situation, trend, or public opinion to change

REL LOOK▸ turn the tide

Examples

(a) Because of her courageous remarks, the tide of the conference turned.

(b) The tide is turning in favor of renewable energy.

(c) As a linguist, I have a strong interest in how the tides have been turning recently in the field of neuroscience.

Notes

1. The verb in the English expression most commonly takes the progressive tense, though it can take other tenses as well depending on the context. Note that the subject of the Japanese expression is *nagare* (to flow) as opposed to *tide*.

2. Both the English and Japanese expressions mean "for a situation, trend, or public opinion to change," but the Japanese can also mean "for the flow of movement to change."

📖→ 解説(1)

REL

1. The English has the REL *turn the tide*, which is a transitive version of the main entry that means "to cause a reversal in a situation."

(1) A single brave soldier turned the tide of battle.
一人の勇気ある兵士が戦いの流れを変えた。

2. In addition, the Japanese entry has a transitive version as well: *nagare o kaeru*.

📖→ 関連語(2)

(a)「ゴミの山じゃないか！」彼はお手上げといわんばかりに、顔をそむけて嘆いた。

(b) 彼らは息子のあまりの横暴ぶりに、お手上げの状態で、なすすべもなかった。

解説

日英語とも「あきらめ」の気持ちを表す表現だが、英語では両手を広げて手の平を上に向ける仕草をすることでより強い感情を示すことがある。日本語では仕草はともなわない。

流れが変わる / phr. 隠喩

{世論 / 傾向 / 動き / 経過} が変わる

関 **LOOK** 流れを変える

例文

(a) 彼女の勇気ある発言で会議の流れが変わった。

(b) 流れは再生可能エネルギーに賛同する方向に変わっている。

(c) 言語学者として最近の脳科学の発展の流れが変わってきていることに関心を持っている。

解説

1. 英語表現の動詞はほとんどの場合進行形が使われているが、背景によっては他の時制も用いることができる。また、日本語の表現の主語は「流れ」であるのに対して、英語は tide (潮) である。

2. 日英語とも、"状況、傾向、大衆の意見などが変化する"の意味も持つ。さらに日本語では、"何かの動きが変化する"という意味でも使用できる。

(1)a. この通りにデパートができてから、客の流れが変わった。
   Ever since a department store was built on this street, the flow of customers has changed.
  b. タイムアウトの後、試合の流れが変わった。
   After the time-out, the tide of the game turned.

関連語

1. 英語には見出しの自動詞を他動詞に変えた *turn the tide* という関連表現がある。意味は「状況を逆転させる」である。━📖 **REL (1)**

2. 日本語には、見出しの自動詞が他動詞になった「流れを変える」という表現がある。

(2) 彼女の勇気ある発言{で会議の流れが変わった / は会議の流れを変えた}。(→(a))

643

tie the knot (with ~) / phr. / metaphor

to get married; to perform a wedding ceremony

Examples

(a) 32 years ago today, my hubby and I tied the knot.

(b) The daughter of a famous singer tied the knot with an Oscar-winning actor on Saturday in a ceremony on the Big Island.

(c) I'm not the one who got married. My older bother Takuya's the one who tied the knot with Takako.

Notes

1. The only meaning the English and Japanese share is "to get married." In addition to this meaning, the English can mean "to preside over a wedding ceremony," and the Japanese can mean "for {people/countries/organizations/cultures} to have a close relationship."

　　　　　　　　　　　　　　　　　　　　　　　　　　　　　📖← 解説(1)

(2) The pastor tied the knot for the couple.
　　牧師が二人{の結婚の司式をした/[×]を結んだ}。

2. *Tie* means "to fasten s.t. to s.t. else with string," while *musubareru* means "for two {people/things} to be fastened."

Time and tide wait for no man. / phr. / personification

things will not wait when one is late

Examples

Mrs. S: Kenta, don't you have school today?

Kenta: Yeah, but I'm playing hooky.

Mrs. S: Excuse me? You'd better study while you're still young. Haven't you heard the expression "Time and tide wait for no man"?

- -

(a) Time and tide wait for no man. You should study abroad while you're still young and engage in intellectual exchange.

(b) Time and tide wait for no man, so seize the opportunity being presented to you.

Notes

1. The basic meanings of *tide* and *saigetsu* are "the rising and falling of the sea" and "years (and months)," respectively.

2. The Japanese expression is from a poem by famous Chinese poet Tao Yuanming (365-427).

3. The subject is personified in both the English and Japanese. Note that the English takes the alliterative phrase *time and tide* as its subject.

4. *Matazu* is the archaic negative present end-form of *matsu* (to wait).

結ばれる /v. 隠喩

結婚する，複数の{人 / 国 / 組織 / 文化}が互いに非常に近い関係になる

例文

(a) 32年前の今日、私はうちの人と結ばれたのよ。

(b) 有名歌手の娘とオスカーを受賞している俳優がハワイのビッグアイランドで土曜日に挙式をして結ばれた。

(c) 結婚したのは僕じゃないんだ。貴子と結ばれたのは兄貴の卓也なんだ。

解説

1. 日英語共通の意味は"結婚する"だけである。日本語には"複数の{人 / 国 / 組織 / 文化}が密な関係になる"という意味があり、英語には"結婚式を執り行う"という意味が、それぞれある。➡📖 Note(2)

(1) A社とB社の間で技術提携が結ばれた。
   Company A and Company B have {established a technological partnership/ˣtied the knot}.

2. 「結ばれる」と tie の基本義は、"2人か2つのものがひもでつなぎ合わせられる（「結ぶ」の受け身形)"と"ひもで何かを何かにゆわえつける"である。

歳月人を待たず /phr. 擬人化

人が何をしていようと時間は過ぎていってしまう

例文

鈴木(妻)：健太、今日は、学校行かないの？

健太：うん、今日は、サボり。

鈴木(妻)：何言ってるの。若いうちにちゃんと勉強しなきゃだめよ。歳月人を待たずって言うでしょ。

(a) 歳月人を待たず。若いときから海外に留学して知的越境をすることが大事だ。

(b) 歳月人を待たず、ですから、与えられた機会はつかみなさい。

解説

1. 「歳月」と tide の基本義は、それぞれ"年月"と"海の干満"である。

2. 日本語は中国の有名な詩人、陶淵明(365-427)の詩がその出典である。

3. 英語も日本語も主語が擬人化されている。英語のほうでは頭韻を踏んだ time and tide が使われている点に注意。

4. 「待たず」は古文で使う「待つ」の否定、現在終止形である。

Time is a great healer. *phr.* personification

Emotional pain subsides with the passage of time

REL Time heals all wounds.

Examples

Saya: What's wrong? You look sad.

Karen: Yeah, my boyfriend dumped me, so I'm not feeling too great.

Saya: I'm sorry to hear that... I know it hurts now, but time is a great healer, you know.

Karen: I sure hope so. But it feels like I'll never get over this.

- -

(a) When it comes to trauma and sorrow, time is a great healer. All you have to do is wait as time quietly passes by.

(b) They say time is a great healer, but it has been 32 years and I still feel the pain of losing you.

REL

The English has the REL *time heals all wounds*. It has the same metaphorical meaning as the main entry.

(1) I'm sorry to hear that... I know it hurts now, but {time is a great healer/time heals all wounds}, you know. (→ dialogue)

Time is money. *phr.* metaphor

time is valuable

Examples

Colleague: How long are these guys gonna keep talking? We're busy, you know.

Mike: I know, right? Every minute and every second counts. Don't they know that time is money?

Colleague: I heard that you say the exact same thing in English, too. Humans really do think the same way regardless of nationality, don't they?

- -

(a) I'd love to go on watching TV all day long, but as they say, time is money!

(b) Going by bus takes too long. It might be a bit expensive, but let's take a taxi. Time is money, after all.

Notes

1. The Japanese is a translation of the English.

2. The copula *nari* is an archaic form of *da*, *dearu* and *desu*, but it is still used in proverbs and the like.

時がいやしてくれる phr. 擬人化

時が経てば、{悲しみ/苦しみ/憎しみ}がやわらぐ

例文

さや：どうしたの、元気ないね。

カレン：うん、彼にふられちゃった。けっこう落ち込んでるの。

さや：そう。今はつらいと思うけど、そのうち、時がいやしてくれるわよ。

カレン：そうだといいけど。なんかそんな日は来そうもない気がするわ。

- (a) あなたの心の傷も、悲しみも時がいやしてくれるでしょう。静かに時の過ぎ行くのを待っていればいいのです。
- (b) 時がいやしてくれると人は言いますが、あなたを亡くして32年、まだそのときの苦しみを感じています。

関連語

英語には *time heals all wounds*（lit. 時は心の傷をいやす）という関連表現がある。見出しと同じ意味を持つ比喩である。 ━ REL(1)

時は金なり phr. 隠喩

時間はお金と同じように価値があるから無駄にしてはいけない

例文

同僚：あいつら、いつまでだべってんだろうね。この忙しいのに。

マイク：ほんと、1分1秒を争うときなのに。「時は金なり」だよ。

同僚：英語でもそう言うらしいね。人間の考えることは万国共通だな。

- (a) 僕はね、一日中テレビを見ていたいんだけど、言うだろ、「時は金なり」って。
- (b) バスで行くのは時間がかかります。ちょっと高いですが、タクシーで行きましょう。「時は金なり」です。

解説

1. 日本語は英語の翻訳である。
2. 「なり」という言葉は、「だ」「である」「です」の文語的表現であるが、今でもことわざなどで使われる。

647

time is ripe ({for/to} ~), the   *phr.*   metaphor

the prime time for doing s.t. has come

Examples

Mrs. S: Aren't you and Keiko going to get married? You've been seeing each other for a long time.

Friend: I want to. We've been dating for five years, and I feel the time is ripe for marriage, but she isn't so enthusiastic about the idea.

- -

(a) It's a bit too early, so let's put the plan into action when the time is ripe.

(b) There's no such thing as "the time is ripe." Nothing happens unless you make it happen.

(c) I am confident that the time is ripe for initiating dialogue between the two countries.

Notes

1. *Time* means "the continuum of events that proceed from past to present to future." *Ki* means "the right time for doing s.t. significant."

2. The Japanese can only be used when referring to something of significance, but the English can be used even when referring to something relatively insignificant.

(1) The time is ripe for starting a fall vegetable garden.

秋の菜園を始める{のにちょうどよいころだ/ˣ機が熟した}。

REL

Ki ga jukusu can be replaced by *toki ga jukusu*. The former is more formal than the latter, but it is used more frequently. 📖→ 関連語(1)

(only) time will tell   *phr.*   personification

s.t. will become known after time has passed

Examples

(a) One hope is that our prime minister will succeed in revitalizing the Japanese economy. Only time will tell if this is going to happen.

(b) We pray that the new president will live up to our expectations. But only time will tell, and all we can do is wait and see.

(c) Time will tell whether or not a child is gifted. There's no point in worrying when the child is less than five years old.

Note

The English tends to be used with the emphatic adverb *only*, as shown in (a) and (b).

REL

In Japanese, *toki dake ga oshiete kureru* (only time will tell) can be replaced by the REL *toki nomizo shiru* (only time knows). The latter sounds more like a proverb than the former. 📖→ 関連語(1)

（〜のための）機が熟す　*phr.*　隠喩

何かを始めるのにちょうどいい時期になる

関 時が熟す

例文

鈴木（妻）：けい子さんとはご結婚はまだ？　もう、長いおつきあいでしょ。
友達：ええ、今年で5年目ですし、そろそろ機は熟したという気もするんですが、あっちがあまり乗り気じゃなくて。

- (a) この計画は今はまだ時期尚早なので、もう少し機が熟すのを待ってから行動に移そう。
- (b) 機が熟すなどということはない。自分から始めなければ何事も始まらないのだ。
- (c) 2か国間の対話を始めるための機が熟したものと確信しています。

解説

1. 「機」と *time* の基本義は、それぞれ "なにか意義あることをするのにいい時" と "過去から現在を通って未来への連続体" である。
2. 日本語は何かかなり大事な事柄の好機がやってきたときにしか使えないが、英語はそれほど大事ではない事柄のときでも使える。━ Note (1)

関連語

日本語の「機が熟す」は「時が熟す」と置き換えることができる。前者は後者よりフォーマルだが、使用頻度ははるかに高い。

(1) ｛機 / 時｝が熟すなどということはない。（→(b)）

時（だけ）が教えてくれる　*phr.*　擬人化

時間がたたないと結果はわからない

関 時のみぞ知る

例文

- (a) 首相が日本の経済に活を入れることに成功することを願っているが、その結果は時だけが教えてくれる。
- (b) 新しい大統領がわれわれの期待を裏切らないでくれれば、と祈っている。時が教えてくれるから、待ってみなければならない。
- (c) 子供に優れた才能があるかないかは時が教えてくれる。5歳以下のときはそんなに期待しても仕方がない。

解説

英語は(a)(b)のように強調の副詞 *only* と一緒に使われる傾向がある。

関連語

日本語の「時だけが教えてくれる」は関連表現の「時のみぞ知る」と置き換えることができる。後者のほうがより慣用句的である。

(1) 来年はどうなるのだろう。｛時だけが教えてくれる / 時のみぞ知る｝。
　　What'll happen next year? Only time will tell.

tip of the iceberg, the / n. phr. / metaphor

a very small part of some larger issue or problem

Examples

Mr. S: This article says cybercrime is starting to become a problem again.

Kenta: The crimes being reported are just the tip of the iceberg. I'm sure there are a lot more crimes being committed that no one knows about.

Mr. S: True. We'll probably be seeing a lot more in the future.

- -

(a) That illegal payment was only the tip of the iceberg. A lot more problems were discovered with the company's books.

(b) So far, only one politician has been arrested for bribery. But many agree that this is only the tip of the iceberg.

Notes

1. Both the English and Japanese expressions are metaphors based on the idea that one can only see a fraction of an iceberg, since the majority is hidden underwater. *Tip* means "the very end of a pointed object," and *ikkaku* means "one corner." *Iceberg* and *hyōzan* both consist of *ice + mountain*; *berg* comes from the German word for *mountain*.

2. The expressions almost always appear in the following forms: *be {only/just} the tip of the iceberg* and *hyōzan no ikkaku ni suginai*, as shown in the examples.

3. It is very likely that *hyōzan no ikkaku* comes from the Chinese expression 冰山一角 .

to death / adv. phr. / metaphor

to a very high degree

REL dead; be dying to do; be dying for ~

Examples

Saya: Mike, how was yesterday's party?

Mike: It was no fun at all.

Saya: Really? Weren't you excited about all the girls who were supposed to show up?

Mike: Yeah, but all they talked about was fashion and shopping. I was bored to death.

- -

(a) John jumped out of nowhere wearing a gorilla mask and scared me to death.

(b) I was thrilled to death to see my girlfriend after such a long time apart.

(c) After walking 20 kilometers without eating anything, I felt like I was starving to death.

Notes

1. *Shinu hodo* can be followed by an adjective that denotes an emotional state, as shown in (1). The English expression cannot be used this way, however. ⬛📖→解説(1)

氷山の一角 / n. phr. / 隠喩

ある事のほんの一部しか観察されていない事柄

例文

鈴木(夫)：この記事によると、またインターネットを使った犯罪が問題になっているね。

健太：そんなの氷山の一角にすぎないよ。インターネットを使った犯罪は、現実に知られているより、はるかに多いと思うね。

鈴木(夫)：そうだね。これから、もっと増えるだろうしね。

(a) その不正支出は氷山の一角にすぎなかった。その後、この会社の帳簿ではるかに多くの不正が見つかったのだ。

(b) 今までのところ、収賄容疑で逮捕されたのは政治家一人だった。しかし、これは氷山の一角だということで大方の意見が一致している。

解説

1. 日英語とも、氷山はその一角しか海上に現れていないという認識に基づく比喩である。「一角」と tip の基本義は、"一つの角"と"先が尖ったものの一番先の部分"である。「氷山」も iceberg も「氷＋山」から来ているが、英語の berg は「山」を意味するドイツ語から来ている。

2. 日英語とも、例文でわかるように、ほとんどきまって「氷山の一角にすぎない」be {only/just} the tip of the iceberg という文型をとる。

3. 日本語の「氷山の一角」は中国語の「氷山一角」から来た可能性が高い。

死ぬほど / adv. / 隠喩

おおげさに感情を表現する誇張表現

例文

さや：マイク、昨日のパーティ、どうだった？

マイク：ぜんぜん面白くなかったよ。

さや：あら、そう。女の子達が大勢来るって楽しみにしてたんじゃないの？

マイク：そうだけど。みんな、ファッションや買い物の話ばかりで、死ぬほど退屈しちゃったね。

(a) ジョンがゴリラのマスクをかぶって飛び出してきたので、死ぬほどびっくりした。

(b) 彼女に久しぶりに会えて死ぬほどうれしかった。

(c) 何も食べずに20キロも歩いたので、死ぬほどお腹がすいた。

解説

1. 日本語では主に(1)のように心理状態を表す形容詞の前で使う。一方、英語では形容詞の後では使えない。

(1)a. 正直なところ、死ぬほど寂しかった。

To be honest, I was {dead lonely/ ×lonely to death}.

   b. 映画はとっても面白かった。とってもね。ほんと、死ぬほどおかしかったんだ。

The movie was really funny. It really was. By the end, I {almost died laughing/ ×was amused to death}.

651

2. *Shinu hodo* literally means "to the extent that one will die." The adverbial phrase verb + *hodo* means "to the extent that one (verb)." 📖 解説 **(2)**

3. *Dead/shi(nda)* can be used to personify nouns. Some examples include *dead volcano/shika-zan*, *dead company/shinda kaisha*, *dead language/shigo*, and *dead custom/shinda shūkan*.

REL

1. The colloquial adjective *dead* can be used in the same manner as ~ *to death*.

(1) a. I am dead serious.

   僕は死ぬほど真剣なんだ。

   b. The entrance examination was dead easy.

   入学試験は死ぬほど易しかった。

2. The English also has the RELs *be dying for/be dying to do*, which cannot be translated into Japanese using *shinu hodo* ~.

(2) I'm dying for a brand new start.

   私はまったく始めから{出直したいんです/[×]死ぬほど出直したいんです}。

---

to the ends of the earth / adv. phr. / metaphor

to a very remote location; to the furthest extent possible

Examples

(a) I found that I couldn't go a day without looking at her. I would follow her to the ends of the earth.

(b) This isn't any ordinary trip. It's an adventure to the very ends of the earth.

(c) Travel by train has a unique atmosphere that isn't available in travel by car, bus or plane. The track that extends as far as the ends of the earth. Scenery from the window that runs away with time. Encounters with people who I happen to sit with on the train.

Note

Both the English and Japanese come from the original ancient Greek version of *The Acts of the Apostles* in the New Testament (Chapter 1:8), in which it is written, "You will be witnesses for me...to the ends of the earth."

REL

The Japanese can be replaced by *kono yo no hate made*. 📖 関連語 **(1)**

---

to the marrow / adv. phr. / metaphor

thoroughly

REL ~ to the core; ~ to the bone; ~ to the backbone

Example

It was so cold outside that I was chilled to the marrow.

Note

In addition to expressing cold, *hone no zui made* can also be used as an intensifier that means "thoroughly." 📖 解説 **(1)**

2．日本語の「死ぬほど」は"死ぬ程度に"という意味である。「Ｖ＋ほど」は"（人が）Ｖするほどに"という意味の副詞句である。

(2) あの先生の講義はあくびが出るほどつまらない。

　　lit. "The professor's lectures are boring to the extent that one yawns."

　　(=The professor's lectures are terribly boring.)

3．日英語の「死（んだ）」dead は「死火山」dead volcano、「死んだ会社」dead company、「死語」dead language、「死んだ習慣」dead custom のように擬人化表現として使える。

関連語

1．英語では形容詞の dead (死んだ) も話し言葉で、~ to death の比喩的意味で使える。━📖REL(1)

2．英語には be dying to do; be dying for ~ という関連表現があるが、日本語の「死ぬほど～」を使って翻訳はできない。━📖REL(2)

地の果てまで ／ phr. ／ 隠喩

"どこまでも"という意味を表す誇張表現

関 この世の果てまで

例文

(a) 僕は１日でも彼女の顔を見ないと気が済まないんです。彼女の後なら地の果てまでついて行きます。

(b) これは普通の観光旅行ではありません。地の果てまで訪ねて行く冒険旅行です。

(c) 鉄道旅行には、クルマ、バスや飛行機にはない独特の旅の雰囲気がある。地の果てまで延びる線路。時とともに流れ行く車窓風景。車内で偶然隣り合わせた人との出会い。

解説

日英語とも新約聖書『使徒行伝』(1:8)の「また地の果てまで、私の証人となる」の原典の古代ギリシャ語から来ている。

関連語

日本語は「この世の果てまで」で置き換えることができる。

(1) 彼女の後なら｛地の／この世の｝果てまでついて行きます。(→(a))

骨の髄まで ／ phr. ／ 隠喩

徹底的に

例文

外は本当に寒くて、骨の髄まで凍えてしまった。

解説

英語の見出しはほとんどの場合「寒さ」を強調する場合に使われるが、日本語では「寒さ」以外を表す場合にも使える。

(1) 彼は骨の髄まで真面目だ。

　　He is serious to the core.

653

toot one's own horn （ほらを吹く） → {blow/toot} one's own horn

touch {on/upon} ~ / phr. / metaphor
to {speak/write} about s.t. briefly

Examples
- (a) The professor touched briefly on the poems' content and then, without further commentary, spent the rest of the time talking about the poet's background.
- (b) The article about the plane crash listed the names of the people who died, but it does not touch upon the cause of the crash.
- (c) The discussions also touched upon exchange programs, including a plan to exchange specialists between the two countries.

Note
> Both the English and Japanese expressions are metaphorical extensions of the original tactile meaning of *touch* and *fureru*, "to come into contact with s.t. physical."

trace / v. / metaphor
to investigate a sequence of (historical) events

Examples
- (a) The Smithsonian Museum traces the evolution of animals from the Ice Age to the present day.
- (b) If you trace the history of Middle Eastern conflicts, you'll discover that some of the causes occurred over 2,000 years ago.
- (c) Each year on August 15th, groups gather at various locations all throughout the country to trace the history of the war.

Note
> The non-metaphorical meaning of the expression is "to attempt to find something or someone that was lost."

trade friction / comp. n. / metaphor
tension between two countries due to a trade imbalance

Examples
- (a) It is important to minimize trade friction between the two nations.
- (b) Agricultural products are often one of the causes of trade friction.

Note
> *Friction* and *masatsu* mean "a resistant force produced when two objects in contact with one another move in opposing directions." The Japanese is a translation of the English.

{〜に / について} 触れる / phr. 隠喩

何かについて（短く）{話す / 書く}

例文

(a) 教授は詩の内容に簡単に触れただけで、詳しい解説はせず、残りの時間は作者の背景を説明した。

(b) 飛行機事故の記事には、死亡した乗客の名前は書いてあったが、事故の原因については触れていなかった。

(c) その討議では、二国間の専門家の交流を含む計画についても触れた。

解説

日英語ともに触覚動詞「触れる」/touch の基本義 "物に触れる" という意味からの比喩表現である。

跡をたどる / phr. 隠喩

（歴史的な）出来事をさかのぼって調べる

例文

(a) スミソニアン博物館では、氷河期から現在までの動物の進化の跡をたどることができる。

(b) 中東戦争の跡をたどっていくと、紀元前にすでにその原因が起きていたことがわかる。

(c) 毎年、8月15日には、戦争の跡をたどる集会が各地で開かれる。

解説

「跡をたどる」の本来の意味は、"いなくなった人や物を見つけようとする" である。

貿易摩擦 / n. phr. 隠喩

二国間の貿易収支の不均衡のために生じる政治的、経済的対立

例文

(a) 両国間の貿易摩擦を最小限にとどめることは重要である。

(b) 農産物が貿易摩擦の一因になることが多い。

解説

「摩擦」も friction も、基本義は "2つの接触した物が反対方向に動くときに生じる負の力" である。日本語は英語の翻訳である。

transparency / n. / metaphor

a state in which information is readily accessible

Example

> There were doubts about the transparency of the approval process for the new medicine.

treat s.o. like a slave / phr. / simile

to make s.o. work like a slave would

Examples

> Karen: What's wrong, Mike? You seem really upset.
>
> Mike: I just can't believe the way my boss treats people. He treats his subordinates like slaves!
>
> Karen: Can't you just tell him not to treat you like that?
>
> Mike: If I said that, I'd be in a ton of trouble!

- - - - - - - - - - - - - - - - - - - -

> (a) The CEO treated his employees like slaves and was hated by everybody.
>
> (b) Cinderella was treated like a slave by her stepmother.

Note

> Japanese has the compound noun *dorē-atsukai*. (→dialogue)

trigger / v./n. / metaphor

for {s.t./s.o.} to cause s.t.

Examples

> Kenta: Karen, you don't look so good.
>
> Karen: Yeah, I have a bit of a headache. Sometimes my head starts hurting like this on days when the weather isn't so great.
>
> Kenta: Really? Maybe it's triggered by changes in the air pressure.
>
> Karen: Could be.

- - - - - - - - - - - - - - - - - - - -

> (a) Sudden drops in the value of stocks can often trigger a panic in the economy.
>
> (b) The incident served as a trigger for nationwide riots.

Notes

> 1. *Trigger* can be used as either a noun or a transitive verb, and both can be used metaphorically. *Hikigane ni naru* is an intransitive expression that means "to become a trigger." Both the English verb and the Japanese expression are derived from nouns that mean "a lever used to release a bullet."

透明性 / n. phr. / 隠喩

組織や団体の内容や行動が公であること

例文

新薬の認可の過程について、透明性が疑われている。

奴隷のように扱う / phr. / 直喩

誰かを自分の意のままに扱う

例文

カレン： どうしたの？　マイク、そんなにぷりぷりして。

マイク： まったく、うちの課長、人使い、荒いんだよな。部下をまるで奴隷のように扱うんだから。

カレン： 奴隷扱いしないでくださいって、言ったら？

マイク： そんなこと言ったら、大変だよ。

- - - - - - - - - - - - - - - -

(a) その社長は社員を奴隷のように扱い、みんなに嫌われていた。

(b) シンデレラは継母に奴隷のように扱われた。

解説

日本語には「奴隷扱い」という複合名詞もある。(→会話例)

引き金になる / phr. / 隠喩

何かが起こるきっかけとなる

例文

健太： カレン、なんだか元気ないね。

カレン： うん、ちょっと頭が痛いの。天気が悪くなる日は、時々、こんなふうに頭が痛くなるのよ。

健太： へえ、気圧の変化が引き金になるのかなあ。

カレン： たぶん。

- - - - - - - - - - - - - - - -

(a) 経済恐慌は株価の暴落が引き金になることが多い。

(b) その事件が引き金となって、全国的な暴動が起きた。

解説

1. 英語の*trigger*は名詞としても他動詞としても比喩的に使用できる。日本語の「引き金になる」（become a trigger）は自動詞の表現である。日英語とも、銃の弾丸を発射させる金具の呼称（「引き金」と*trigger*）に由来する表現である。

2. The English expression can take both animate and inanimate nouns as its subject, but the Japanese can only take inanimate nouns.

(1) Hitler triggered the Second World War with his hatred for Jews.

ヒットラーはユダヤ人に対する憎しみをもとに、第二次世界大戦の{引き金を引いた/[×]引き金となった}。

3. The Japanese verb *naru* (to become) usually takes the particle *ni*, but it tends to be replaced by *to* in written Japanese, as shown in (b).

{tug/pull} at {s.o.'s/the} heartstrings　phr.　metaphor

for s.t. to move s.o.'s deepest emotions

REL　touch s.o.'s heartstrings

Examples

(a) Your presentation was not only motivational, but it also pulled at our heartstrings.

(b) The devotion she displayed in collaborating with the talented musicians tugged at my heartstrings and made me tear up.

(c) More than any of her previous works, the songs in this album pulled at my heartstrings.

Note

Both the English and Japanese are based on an image of someone playing a string instrument and the listener being moved by the performance. However, the English uses the verbs *tug* and *pull*, while the Japanese uses *fureru* (to touch).

REL

The verbs *tug at* and *pull at* can be replaced by *touch*, as shown in (1), though the former two verbs are used much more frequently.

(1) More than any of her previous works, the songs in this album {tugged at/pulled at/touched} my heartstrings. (→(c))

turn one's back on ~　phr.　metonymy

to take an indifferent attitude towards {s.o./s.t.}; to refuse to accept {s.t./s.o.}

REL　turn a cold shoulder to ~; give ~ the cold shoulder

Examples

Mr. S: You do Skype meetings at your company, right?

Mike: Yeah, we use Skype a lot. But sometimes it's hard to hear what's being said, so some people complain about it, especially when English is being used.

Mr. S: Really? Sounds like they're turning their back on the times.

Mike: I couldn't agree more.

2. 英語の *trigger* は、主語に物も人も取れるのに対して、日本語の「引き金になる」は物しか取れない。主語が人の場合は「引き金を引く」となる。➡️📖 Note(1)

3. 日本語の「なる」は助詞の「に」をとるのが通例であるが、書き言葉では(b)のように、「と」になる場合もある。

心の琴線に触れる　／ phr.　隠喩
（こころ　きんせん　ふ）　　　　　　（いんゆ）

何かが誰かの心を感動させる
（なに　　だれ　　こころ　かんどう）

例文

(a) あなたの発表はやる気を起こさせてくれただけではなく、私達の心の琴線にも触れました。

(b) 彼女はすばらしい音楽家たちとともに献身的な協力をしてくれた。それは私の心の琴線に触れ、思わず感謝の涙が出た。

(c) このアルバムの曲は、これまでのどの作品よりも心の琴線に触れた。

解説

日英語ともに、人が弦楽器を奏でていて、それを聞く人が感動している様子がもととなっている。ただし、日英語で異なる動詞「触れる」(touch) と *tug/pull* が使われている。

関連語

英語では動詞の *tug at/pull at* は *touch* によって置き換えることができるが、*tug at/pull at* のほうがはるかに使用頻度が高い。➡️📖 REL(1)

（〜に）背を向ける　／ phr.　換喩
（せ　む）　　　　　　　　　（かんゆ）

{誰か / 何か}に冷淡な態度を取る, 従うことをこばむ
（だれ　なに）　　　　（れいたん　たいど　と）　　（したが）

例文

鈴木(夫)：マイクの会社ではスカイプを使った会議はするんでしょ。
（すずき　おっと）　　　　　　　　　　　　（かいしゃ）　　　（つか）　　　（かいぎ）

マイク：ええ、頻繁に。でも、声が聞き取りにくかったりするので、いやがる人達もいますよ。特に英語の会議だと。
（ひんぱん）　　　（こえ）（き）（と）　　　　　　　　　　　　　　（ひとたち）
（とく　えいご　かいぎ）

鈴木(夫)：へえ、それは随分、時代の流れに背を向けているねえ。
（すずき　おっと）　　　　（ずいぶん　じだい　なが）　　（せ　む）

マイク：ええ、本当に。
（ほんとう）

(a) He could not imagine turning his back on his faith and going on with his life.

(b) When I was young, I turned my back on my parents' love for me and ran away from home, but now that they are both dead, I really regret it.

(c) She never turns her back on a friend in need.

Notes

1. Turning one's back on someone is universally regarded as a gesture that expresses one's indifference or refusal to talk.

2. In the English, replacing the preposition *on* with *to/towards* tends to express the literal gesture of turning one's back toward someone. In the Japanese, *senaka* is almost never used, and the expression *~ ni senaka o mukeru* can usually only be interpreted literally. In (1), using *senaka* invites a literal interpretation, though there are cases where the non-verbal behavior indicates the person's psychological state. 📖➝解説(1)

REL

The English has two RELs: *turn a cold shoulder to ~* and *give ~ the cold shoulder.* They mean "to show dislike for s.o./s.t." and "to treat s.o/s.t. very coldly," respectively.

(1)a. The leader of the group gave us the cold shoulder.
グループの指導者はわれわれに冷たい{そぶり/ˣ背}を見せた。

b. The public loved the movie, but the critics turned a cold shoulder to it.
一般の人々はその映画をとてもいいと思ったが、批評家たちは{冷たくあしらった/ˣ冷たい背を見せた}。

turn back the clock / phr. / metaphor

to make s.t. return to an earlier state

REL push back the clock

Examples

(a) If you could turn back the clock 20 years, what would you do?

(b) We can't turn back the clock. But we can rebuild the areas hit by the disaster.

(c) I met up with an old ex of mine, and it felt as if we had turned back the clock.

Notes

1. While the Japanese refers explicitly to a clock's hands *(tokē no hari)*, the English verb *turn back* refers to them implicitly.

2. *Moto ni* means "back to the original time."

REL

The English can be replaced by *push back the clock*, but this is not used as frequently as the main entry.

(1) We can't {turn/push} back the clock. But we can rebuild the areas hit by the disaster.
(→(b))

(a) 宗教に背を向けて生きることなど、彼には考えられないことだった。

(b) 若い頃、両親の愛に背を向けて家を飛び出してしまったが、２人が亡くなった今は、とても後悔している。

(c) 彼女は、困っている友達に背を向けたことが一度もない。

解 説

1. 誰かに背中を向ける身ぶりは、普遍的にその人に無関心か、話したくないという意志を表現している。

2. 英語の *on* を *to/towards* に変えると比喩ではなく、字義通り "背を誰かに向ける" という解釈になる。また、日本語の見出しでは「背中」は滅多に使われない。したがって、「(〜に) 背中を向ける」は通常、字義通りの解釈しかできない。(1) の例で「背中」を使えば、それは言語としては字義通りの解釈であるが、同時にその動作をした人間の心理を表す場合もある。

(1) 彼女は最近、僕に {背 / ?背中} を向けるようになった。
Lately she has begun turning her back on me.

関連語

英語には *turn a cold shoulder to ~* (lit. 冷たい肩を向ける) と *give ~ the cold shoulder* (lit. 冷たい肩を与える) という二つの関連表現がある。それぞれ「{誰か / 何か} が嫌いという気持ちを示す」と「{誰か / 何か} をとても冷たくあしらう」という意味である。 →📖 REL (1)

時計の針を (元に) 戻す　/ phr. / 隠喩

過去に戻ってやりなおす

例 文

(a) もし時計の針を20年ぐらい元に戻せたら、何がしたいですか。

(b) 時計の針は戻せない。だけど、災害地の復興は可能だ。

(c) 昔の恋人に再会して、まるで時計の針を戻したかのような時を過ごした。

解 説

1. 日本語は「時計の針」を明示しているが、英語では *turn back* (回し戻す) という動詞で非明示的に時計の針を表現している。

2. 日本語の「元に」というのは "元の時間" という意味である。

関連語

英語は *push back the clock* で置き換えることができるが、使用頻度は *turn back the clock* よりもはるかに低い。 →📖 REL (1)

661

homograph

turn s.o.'s stomach / phr. / metaphor

for s.t. to make s.o. feel sick
気分を悪くする，気分が悪くなる

Example

The ice cream turned my stomach.
アイスクリームを食べたら気分が悪くなった。

turn the tide phr. metaphor

to cause a reversal in a situation

REL LOOK {tides are/tide is} {turning/changing}, the

Examples

(a) Our team was behind during the first half of the game, but we persevered and managed to turn the tide during the second half.

(b) His bold remarks turned the tide of the meeting and led to a resolution.

(c) That one bold step initiated by the educator turned the tide of education for girls and women in this country.

Note

The English can mean "to change the direction of s.o.'s life," but the Japanese cannot be used in this sense.

(1) This book has turned the tide for me.
この本は私の人生の{方向/×流れ}を変えた。

REL

Both the English and Japanese are transitive expressions. The intransitive versions are *the {tides are/tide is} {turning/changing}* and *nagare ga kawaru*, respectively. 関連語(1)

turning point, {a/the} / comp. n. / metaphor

a time when a significant change occurs

REL {a/the} crossroads; (critical) juncture

Examples

(a) He believes that people in their sixties are at a turning point in their lives.

(b) There was a turning point in our marriage when my husband got into a motorcycle accident in 1999.

(c) The fashion industry now stands at an important turning point. Many firms that used to be successful have been experiencing poor performance.

Note

The location at which the turning occurs is described as a *point* in the English and *kado* (corner) in the Japanese.

662

【同形異義語】

腹を立てる　/ phr. / 隠喩
　はら　た　　　　　　　　　いんゆ

怒る
おこ
to get angry

【例文】

父は兄がいつまでも働かないことに腹を立て、家から追い出してしまった。
ちち　あに　　　　　　　　はたら　　　　　　　はら　た　　いえ　　お　だ
My father got angry at my older brother for refusing to work, so he drove him out
of the house.

流れを変える　/ phr. / 隠喩
　なが　　か　　　　　　　　いんゆ

{試合 / 戦争}などの勝ち負けや、何かの進行方向を変える
しあい　せんそう　　　　か　ま　　　なに　　しんこうほうこう　か

【関】【LOOK】流れが変わる
　　　　　　　　なが　　か

【例文】

(a) 我々のチームは試合の前半は負けていたが、あきらめないで頑張って、後半戦で試
　　われわれ　　　　　　しあい　ぜんはん　ま　　　　　　　　　　　　　　がんば　　　　　こうはんせん　し
　　合の流れを変えた。
　　あい　なが　か

(b) 彼の勇気ある発言が会議の流れを変えて、結論を導いた。
　　かれ　ゆうき　　　はつげん　かいぎ　なが　か　　　けつろん　みちび

(c) その教育者が初めて取った大胆な行動は、この国の女子教育の流れを変えた。
　　　　きょういくしゃ　はじ　と　　だいたん　こうどう　　　　くに　じょしきょういく　なが　か

【解説】

英語は"人生の方向を変える"という意味があるが、日本語にはそのような意味はない。

📖Note(1)

【関連語】

日英語とも他動詞表現だが、その自動詞表現は関連表現の「流れが変わる」the {tides are/tide is} {turning/ changing} である。

(1) その教育者が初めて取った大胆な行動のお陰で、この国の女子教育の流れが変わった。(→(c))
　　Thanks to one bold step initiated by the educator, the tide of girls' and women's education changed. (→(c))

曲がり角　/ n. phr. / 隠喩
　ま　　かど　　　　　　　　いんゆ

何かが著しく変わる時
なに　いちじる　か　　とき

【関】節目, 分岐点, 転(換)期, ターニングポイント
　　　ふしめ　ぶんきてん　てん かん き

【例文】

(a) 彼は60代は人生の曲がり角だと信じている。
　　かれ　　だい　じんせい　ま　かど　　しん

(b) 夫が1999年にバイク事故に遭ったときが私たちの結婚生活の曲がり角になった。
　　おっと　　　ねん　　　　じこ　あ　　　　　わたし　　けっこんせいかつ　ま　かど

(c) ファッション業界は今重要な曲がり角に立っている。これまで活躍してきた企業の
　　　　　　　ぎょうかい　いまじゅうよう　ま　かど　た　　　　　　　　かつやく　　　　　きぎょう
　　多くが業績不振に苦しんでいる。
　　おお　ぎょうせきふしん　くる

【解説】

曲がるところが日本語では「角」で、英語ではpoint(点)である。

663

REL

1. The Japanese expression has the REL *fushime*. Unlike *magari-kado*, which refers to turning points in an individual's life, *fushime* refers to life-changing events that most people experience, such as becoming an adult, getting married, retiring, and so on.
📖→ 関連語(1)

2. The English can be used regardless of the nature of the events that follow the turning point, but the Japanese can only be used when the situation after the turning point is assumed to be negative or neutral. When the situation is positive, the expression *tenkan-ki* is used. *Bunki-ten* and *tāningu pointo* can be used in a neutral sense. 📖→ 関連語(2)

3. The English expression has the RELs *{a/the} crossroads* and *(critical) juncture*. Both expressions describe a point at which an important decision must be made.

(3) a. When my boyfriend proposed to me, I felt like I was at a crossroads. I didn't know what to do.
彼が私に結婚を申し込んだ時、私は人生の分岐点にいると感じたの。どうしたらいいか分からなかったわ。

b. Negotiations between the two superpowers have reached a critical juncture.
双方の超大国の交渉は大切な節目を迎えていた。

---

twilight (of one's life/career/etc.), the / n. phr. / metaphor

toward the end of s.t.

REL one's later years; one's twilight years

Examples

(a) When I reach the twilight of my life, I want to be able to look back and think about what a good life I had.

(b) Copernicus's book *On the Revolution of Celestial Spheres* was printed during the twilight of his life.

REL

1. Both *the twilight of one's life* and *jinsē no tasogare* are used in poetic written language. In spoken language, they are replaced by *one's later years* and *ban'nen*, respectively.
📖→ 関連語(1)

2. The English REL *one's twilight years* can replace the main entry.

(2) When I reached {the twilight of my life/my twilight years}, I want to be able to look back and think about what a good life I had. (→(a))

---

twist logic / phr. / metaphor

to engage in false reasoning

Examples

(a) She twists logic to fit her mood of mind, lashing out at anyone nearby.

関連語

1. 日本語には関連表現として「節目」という言葉がある。「曲がり角」がある個人的な変わり目を意味するのに対し、「節目」は人生においてすべての人が決まって迎える変わり目、例えば、成人になる、結婚する、退職することなどを表す。

(1) 結婚は人生の{節目 / ⁷曲がり角}である。
Marriage is a turning point in life.

2. 英語ではある時点の後の状況がよくても悪くても使えるが、日本語は状況が悪いか中立の場合にしか使えない。状況がよくなる場合は、「転(換)期」という。「分岐点」や「ターニングポイント」は中立的な意味で使える。

(2) 司法試験合格が私の人生の{分岐点 / 転(換)期 / ターニングポイント / ×曲がり角}だった。
Passing the bar exam was the turning point of my life.

3. 英語には {a/the} crossroads (lit. 交差点で) と (critical) juncture (lit. 重大な岐路) という関連表現がある。どちらも重要な決定をしなければならない時点を表している ➡📖 REL (3)

人生の黄昏(時)
じんせい たそがれ とき / **n. phr.** **隠喩**
いんゆ

人生の終わりに近い時期
じんせい お ちか じき

関 晩年
ばんねん

例文

(a) 人生の黄昏を迎えたときに、振り返って、いい人生だったと思えるような生き方をしたいものだ。
じんせい たそがれ むか ふ かえ じんせい おも い かた

(b) コペルニクスの『天球の回転について』という本が活字になったのは、まさに彼の人生の黄昏時だった。
てんきゅう かいてん ほん かつじ かれ じんせい たそがれどき

関連語

1. 「人生の黄昏」と twilight of one's life は詩的な書き言葉で使われ、話し言葉では、それぞれ「晩年」と one's later years が使われる。

(1) 彼は{人生の黄昏(時)/ 晩年}には、ダーウインの進化論の頑強な反論者としてよく知られるようになった。
In {the twilight of his life/his later years}, he became best known for his staunch opposition to Darwinian evolution.

2. 英語の関連表現 one's twilight years (lit. 黄昏の年月) は見出しと置き換えられる。

➡📖 REL (2)

(屁)理屈をこねる
へ りくつ / **phr.** **隠喩**
いんゆ

いろいろと無理な理屈を言う
む り りくつ い

例文

(a) 彼女は自分の気分に合うように屁理屈をこねて、近くにいる人なら誰にでも突っかかって行く。
かのじょ じぶん きぶん あ へりくつ ちか ひと だれ つ い

665

(b) He always uses twisted logic and never actually does anything.

(c) He's always twisting logic to prove his points.

Note

> Both *twist* and *koneru* (to knead) are manual actions that are used as transitive verbs that take *logic*/*rikutsu* as their object to yield a figurative meaning.

uncrowned {king/queen} / comp. n. / metaphor
s.o. who possesses the power but not the title

Example

> He may have relinquished his post, but he is an uncrowned king in the business world who wields considerable influence.

(right) under s.o.'s nose / phr. / metaphor
for s.t. to be or happen right in front of s.o.

Examples

> Saya: Did you hear that one of the students in the class next door got expelled for cheating?
>
> Kenta: Really? How did the teacher find out?
>
> Saya: Well, the student was doing it right under her nose, so it wasn't that hard.

(a) The keys were right under my nose, but I'd been looking for them for 10 minutes.

(b) I pretended not to notice the religious persecution going on right under my nose.

Notes

> 1. The English uses *nose* while the Japanese uses *me* and *hana*, but both expressions have the meaning "for s.t. to be or happen near s.o."
> 2. In addition to meaning "right in front of s.o." or "near," as shown in (a), the main entries also imply that the discovery is unexpected.

(b) 彼は、いつも理屈をこねてばかりいて、全然実行しようとしない。

(c) 彼は自分の言い分を正当化しようとして、いつも屁理屈をこねる。

解説

「こねる」も *twist*（巻きつける、よじる、よる）も手の動作を表す。それが「理屈」の他動詞として使われると比喩的な意味が出てくる。

無冠の帝王 / **n. phr.** / 隠喩

非常に有能で実力があるにも関わらず、大きな賞をもらったことがない人

例文

彼はポストをしりぞいた今も、無冠の帝王として業界に影響を与えている。

目と鼻の先 / **n. phr.** / 隠喩

すぐ近く

例文

さや：ねえ、隣のクラスの子がカンニングをして学校を辞めさせられたって、聞いた？

健太：ほんと？ 先生、どうやってそれ見つけたの？

さや：その学生、先生の目と鼻の先でやったんですって。だから、すぐ見つかっちゃった。

- - - - - - - - - - - - - - - - - - - -

(a) 鍵は僕の目と鼻の先にあったのに、10分も探していたんだ。

(b) 私は自分の目と鼻の先で宗教上の迫害が起きていることに目をつぶっていた。

解説

1. 英語では「鼻」、日本語では「目と鼻」が用いられているが、どちらの表現も"何かがすぐ近くにある"という意味は同じである。

2. 日英語とも(a)のように「すぐ近く」とか「そば」といった意味に加えて、何かを発見してそれが予想外だったという含意がある。

homograph

underdog / comp. n. / metaphor

s.o. at a disadvantage
不利な状況にある人

Example

I always like to cheer for the underdog in boxing matches.

ボクシングの試合では、私はいつも負けそうな方の選手を応援してしまう。

Notes

1. The Japanese, which literally means "a losing dog," makes the idea of losing explicit, whereas the English does not.

2. *Underdog* does not necessarily mean that someone is at a disadvantage, but rather that people perceive that person to be at a disadvantage. Moreover, unlike the Japanese, there is no implication that an underdog has an undesirable personality. 📖▶ 解説(1)

(2) In this rugby match between Japan and New Zealand, Japan will be the underdog, but it may still have a chance to win.

この日本対ニュージーランドのラグビーの試合は、日本 {に勝ち目はない/ ×が負け犬だ} が、日本が勝つチャンスがないわけではない。

REL

The Japanese has the REL *makeinu no tōboe* (lit. "far cries of a losing dog"), which means "to be unwilling to admit defeat" or "to put up a brave front." There is no corresponding expression in English. 📖▶ 関連語(1)

use one's head / phr. / metaphor

to think hard

REL use one's {noggin/noodle}

Examples

Saya: This math quiz is for elementary school students, but it's pretty hard. I can't figure it out.

Kenta: Let me see... Oh, these are a cinch. Try using your head more.

Saya: What?! You're the last person I want to hear that from!

(a) When I was little, my brother would always tell me to use my head.

(b) This problem may look difficult, but you should be able to solve it if you use your head a bit.

Notes

1. Because both *head* and *atama* can mean "brain," *use one's head* and *atama o tsukau* can be used to mean "to think hard to solve a problem."

2. In both English and Japanese, this figurative expression is often used when chiding or criticizing someone.

同形異義語

負け犬 / comp. n. / 隠喩

争いに負けて逃げ出した人
a loser

関 負け犬の遠吠え

例 文

勝負の世界は勝つか負けるかしかない。自分で負けたと思い込んだら始めから負け犬になってしまう。

In the world of competition, it's win or lose. If you think you're going to lose, you're a loser from the beginning.

解 説

1. 日本語は「負ける犬」ということで「負ける」が明示されているが、英語はそうではない。
2. 英語の *underdog* は負けた人のことではなくて、負けると思われている人を指す。日本語のように否定的な性格を意味しない。 ━ Note (2)
(1) ボクシングの試合であえなくノックアウトになったチャンピオンは負け犬となって退場した。
The boxing champion who, tragically, got knocked out during the match, left the ring a {loser/ˣunderdog}.

関連語

日本語では負け惜しみを言ったり、強がりを言ったりすることを「負け犬の遠吠え」と言う。英語ではこれに対応する表現はない。
(1) こんなに試合で負けては、どんな言い訳を言っても負け犬の遠吠えさ。
We lost the game so badly that any excuses we make would just make us sound like sore losers.

U

頭を使う / phr. / 隠喩

よく考える

例 文

さや： この小学生の算数クイズ、けっこう難しくて、わからないな。
健太： どれどれ。あっ、こんなの簡単じゃない。もっと、頭を使わなきゃ。
さや： あら、健太にそんなこと言われたくないわね。

- -

(a) 子供の頃、兄はよく私に頭を使えと言ったものだ。
(b) この問題は難しそうに見えますが、ちょっと頭を使ったら解けるはずです。

解 説

1. 「頭」も *head* も "脳"の意味があるので、「頭を使う」*use one's head* はともに "よく考えてうまく問題を解決する"という意味になる。
2. 日英語ともこの比喩表現は、人をいさめたり、批判したりする文脈で使われることが多い。

669

R E L

Head in the English expression can be replaced by *noggin* or *noodle* without changing the meaning.

(1) When I was little, my brother would always tell me to use my {head/noggin/noodle}. (→(a))

vegetative state / comp. n. / metaphor

a state of impaired consciousness in which s.o. cannot perform voluntary acts

Examples

(a) Chieko believes her father is in a vegetative state with no hope of recovery.

(b) Before she got into a car accident and fell into a vegetative state, she was a happy and energetic child.

(c) The neurosurgeon who examined him predicted he would either die or fall into a vegetative state.

Notes

1. English and Japanese have the expressions *vegetable* and *shokubutsu-ningen*, respectively. They can be used to refer to someone in a vegetative state, though it should be noted that some may find this insensitive.

2. It is possible that *shokubutsu-jōtai* is derived from *vegetative state*.

vicious {circle/cycle} / comp. n. / metaphor

a situation in which trying to solve one problem results in new problems

ANT virtuous {circle/cycle}

Examples

Kenta: Mom, I thought you were on a diet.

Mrs. S: I am, but if I don't eat for a while, I end up eating too much when I do eat.

Kenta: Sounds like a vicious circle to me. Wouldn't it be better to just eat a moderate amount instead of starving yourself?

(a) Let's break that vicious cycle in which you can't get a job without experience and you can't get experience without a job.

(b) In illness or old age, people tend to stop using their bodies as much, which causes their legs and backs to weaken to the point where it becomes even harder for them to move around. Many people have eventually become bedridden due to this vicious circle.

Notes

1. While the basic meanings of the components of the English and Japanese expressions are different, the figurative meanings are identical. The basic meanings of the adjective *vicious* and the noun *aku* (evil) are "marked by vice or immorality" and "s.t. evil," respectively; the basic meanings of *circle* and *junkan* are "a round plane figure made of points which are equidistant from the center" and "a repeated circular movement," respectively.

関連語

英語の見出しの head は意味を変えずに noggin（脳）か noodle（スラングで頭の意味。麺という意味ではない）と置き換えられる。 **REL (1)**

植物状態 / n. phr. / 隠喩
しょくぶつじょうたい　　　　　　　　　いんゆ

脳はほとんど働いていないが、呼吸をして生き続けている状態
のう　　　　　はたら　　　　　　　　　こきゅう　　　　い　つづ　　　　　じょうたい

例文

(a) 智恵子は、父親は回復の見込みのない植物状態だと思っている。
ちえこ　　ちちおや　かいふく　みこ　　　　　しょくぶつじょうたい　　おも

(b) 彼女は自動車事故で大怪我をして植物状態になる前は、幸せな元気いっぱいの子供
かのじょ　じどうしゃじこ　おおけが　　　　しょくぶつじょうたい　　　まえ　しあわ　　げんき　　　　　こども
だった。

(c) 彼を診断した神経外科医は、彼は死ぬか、植物状態になるかのどちらかだろうと予
かれ　しんだん　　しんけいげかい　　かれ　し　　　しょくぶつじょうたい　　　　　　　　　　　　　　よ
測した。
そく

解説

1. 日英語には、それぞれ「植物人間」と vegetable という表現があり、意味は見出しとほぼ同じである。放送禁止用語なので、公での使用は避けた方がよい。

2. 日本語の「植物状態」は英語の vegetative state の直訳の可能性が高い。

悪循環 / n. phr. / 隠喩
あくじゅんかん　　　　　　　　　いんゆ

二つ以上の問題が互いに悪い影響を与え合って、際限なく事態を悪化させること
ふた　いじょう　もんだい　たが　　わる　えいきょう　あた　あ　　　　さいげん　　じたい　あっか

反 好循環
こうじゅんかん

例文

健太：お母さん、ダイエットしてるんじゃなかったっけ？
けんた　　かあ

鈴木（妻）：そうなんだけど、しばらく食べないでいると、食べ始めたとき、かえって食
すずき　つま　　　　　　　　　　　　　　　　た　　　　　　た　はじ　　　　　　　　　　た
べすぎちゃって、駄目ね。
だめ

健太：悪循環だね。我慢しないで、適度に食べたほうがいいんじゃない？　身体にも悪
けんた　あくじゅんかん　　がまん　　　　てきど　た　　　　　　　　　　　　　　からだ　　わる
いよ。

(a) 「仕事がないから経験がない。経験がないから仕事がない」という悪循環を断ち
しごと　　　　　けいけん　　　けいけん　　　　しごと　　　　　　あくじゅんかん　た
切ろう。

(b) 老後や病後にあまり身体を動かさないでいると、足腰が弱り、動き回るのが難し
ろうご　びょうご　　　　からだ　うご　　　　　　　　あしこし　よわ　　うご　まわ　　　むずか
くなる。この悪循環で、ついに寝たきりになってしまう人がかなりいるという。
あくじゅんかん　　　　　ね　　　　　　　　　　ひと

解説

1. 日英語の構成素の基本的な意味は違っているが、比喩的意味は共通である。名詞の「悪」と形容詞の vicious の基本義は、それぞれ、"悪いこと" と "不道徳な性格の" である。「循環」と circle（円）の基本義は、それぞれ、"円周的な反復運動" と "中心から等距離にある点の連続からなる平面図" である。

2. *Vicious* is an adjective derived from the noun *vice* (*akutoku*), so there is a high possibility that the Japanese is a translation of the English. In Chinese, 悪循環 is written 悪性循環, but if the Chinese were borrowed as-is, it would sound like a medical term.

[A][N][T]

The English and Japanese ANTs are *virtuous {circle/cycle}* and *kō-junkan*, respectively.

📖→ 反意語(1)

---

viewpoint (視点 / 観点) → **point of view/viewpoint**
　　　　　　　　 してん　かんてん

---

voice / n. / metaphor

a formal expression of {thoughts/feelings/opinions}; a part in a decision-making process

Examples

Mike: The section chief was the only one who spoke during the meeting yesterday.

Colleague: True. None of us has a chance to chime in.

Mike: I wish he would listen to the voice of the people working under him for once.

- -

(a) We'll make sure your voice is heard at this meeting.

(b) Listening to students' voices should allow instructors to be better teachers.

(c) This system allows a minority to have a strong voice in government.

Notes

1. *Kisetsu* (season) and *nenrē* (age) can be personified in Japanese. Each is considered to have its own *koe* (voice) that serves as a harbinger of its arrival, as shown in (1). While *voice* can be used to personify seasons in English, especially in more formal or poetic contexts, it is seldom used to personify age. 📖→ 解説(1)

2. The English main entry can also mean "a say in a decision."

(2) The great thing about a small company is that every employee has a voice in company-related matters.

小規模企業のいいところは、すべての従業員が社業に関する事柄の決定に自分の意見を反映できることである。

---

one's voice cracks / phr. / metaphor

one's voice suddenly changes in pitch

Example

I could barely listen to the aria that opera singer performed today. Her voice cracked on the high notes. She obviously didn't practice enough.

2. 英語の *vicious* は *vice*（悪徳）から派生している形容詞なので、日本語は英語の翻訳の可能性が高い。中国語は「悪循環」を「悪性循環」というが、これを日本語にそのまま借用したら、意味は医学用語になる。

反意語

日英語共に、「好循環」と *virtuous {circle/cycle}* という反意語がある。

(1) 運動を定期的にすると、食欲は出る、体は丈夫になる、気分は明るくなる、人付き合いもよくなる、といった好循環を生む。

Regular exercise will result in a virtuous {circle/cycle} of benefits, including good appetite, increased physical strength, a cheerful mood, and healthy relationships.

声（こえ）　n.　隠喩（いんゆ）

公式に表明された｛考え／気持ち／意見｝
こうしき ひょうめい かんが きも いけん

例文

マイク：昨日の会議は課長ばっかり話していたね。
きのう かいぎ かちょう

同僚：ほんと、口をさしはさむ間もなかったね。
どうりょう くち ま

マイク：もっと、部下の声を聞いてもらいたいね。
ぶか こえ き

- -

(a) この会議ではあなたがたの声を聞けるようにします。
かいぎ こえ き

(b) 教師は学生たちの声に耳を傾ければ、よりよい授業ができるはずだ。
きょうし がくせい こえ みみ かたむ じゅぎょう

(c) この体制のおかげで、政治に少数派の声を反映できるようになった。
たいせい せいじ しょうすうは こえ はんえい

解説

1. 日本語では季節や年齢が擬人化されて「声」を持っていると考えられ、それぞれ近づく気配を意味する(1)のような例がある。一方、英語でも詩的な文脈で季節が擬人化されて「声」を持っているように表現することがあるが、年齢が擬人化されることはめったにない。

(1) a. 秋の声を聞くとなんとなく寂しくなる。
 When I {hear the voice/feel the signs} of autumn, I begin to feel somewhat lonely.

 b. 70の声を聞いて、めっきり体力の衰えを感じるようになった。
 As I {turned/×heard the voice of} seventy, I began to feel like my physical strength was rapidly fading away.

2. 英語の見出しには「ある決断に含まれる自分の意見」という意味もある。　📖 Note (2)

声が割れる（こえ わ）　phr.　隠喩（いんゆ）

声の調子が悪くなったり、はずれたりする
こえ ちょうし わる

関 声がつぶれる，声が割れる，音が割れる
こえ こえ わ おと わ

例文

今日のオペラ歌手のアリアは聞けたものではなかった。高音部になると突然声が
きょう き こうおんぶ とつぜんこえ

割れてしまった。練習不足が見え見えだった。
わ れんしゅうぶそく み み

REL

The Japanese has the RELs *koe ga tsubureru*, *koe ga kareru*, and *oto ga wareru*. While the first two both describe an abnormality resulting from vocal strain, *koe ga tsubureru* means that one loses one's voice, whereas *koe ga kareru* means that one's voice sounds hoarse. *Oto ga wareru* describes an abnormal sound and is often used with regards to audio equipment, string instrument performances, and so on. 📖→ 関連語(1)

walk a tightrope   *phr.*   metaphor

to be in a situation that requires caution, especially one that requires balancing between two extremes

REL walk a {thin/fine} line

Examples

Colleague: Man, I'm going to have to borrow money using my credit card again this month. I might go bankrupt at this rate.

Mike: You're walking a tightrope by doing that. I'd stop if I were you.

Colleague: I know, but...

(a) The company is walking a tightrope by taking out loans from the bank as it teeters on the edge of bankruptcy.

(b) Starting a new business during the current recession is like walking a tightrope.

Notes

1. The Japanese is a metaphor if the verb *suru* (to do) is used, as in *tsuna-watari o suru*, but expressions without *suru*, such as *tsuna o wataru*, are not metaphorical. By contrast, *walk a tightrope* without the verb *to do* can be used metaphorically, but *do tightrope walking* cannot.

2. The English expression is often used in the form *walk a tightrope between ~ and ~*, which conjures the image of a person nearly losing their balance while suspended between the two ends. The Japanese cannot be used in this manner.

(1) It appears that we may need to walk a tightrope between cancer and aging if we are to seek any meaningful extension of the human life span.
人の寿命を有意義に伸ばそうと思うと、癌と老化の{両方に注意をはらう/間で$^{??}$綱渡りをする}必要があるようだ。

REL

1. The metaphorical meaning of *hakuhyō o fumu* is close to that of *tsuna-watari o suru*. However, the former means "to find oneself in dangerous circumstances," while the latter means "to take action despite being in a dangerous situation." *Abunai hashi o wataru*, an expression related to both of them includes nuance that "s.o. dares to do s.t. dangerous."

2. The English REL, *walk a {thin/fine} line*, means to balance the needs/demands of two competing groups or ideas. It is thus more specific in scope than the main entry, which can also refer generally to situations in which one must be careful.

関連語

日本語には「声がつぶれる」「声がかれる」「音が割れる」という関連表現がある。前の二つは、どちらものどを酷使して声に異常が出た場合に使われるが、「声がつぶれる」は声が出なくなることを意味し、「声がかれる」は声がなめらかに出なくなることを意味する。「音が割れる」は「音の調子がはずれる」ことで、普通は音声機器や弦楽器演奏の不具合の時に使われる。

(1)a 昨日、大声でひいきのサッカーチームを応援していたら、声が{つぶれて/かすれて}しまった。
I was cheering so wildly for my favorite soccer team yesterday that {I lost my voice/my voice got hoarse}.

  b. パソコンのスピーカーのボリュームを大きくしても、音が割れて聞こえるだけで、なかなかいい音声は得られない。
Even if I turn up the volume on my computer's speakers, the sound becomes grainy and I can't get good sound quality.

綱渡り（をする） / phr. 隠喩

非常に危険な状況で前に進む

関 LOOK▶ 薄氷を踏む, 危ない橋を渡る

例文

同僚：あ～あ、今月もまたカードで借金か。そのうち、カード破産するかな。

マイク：そんなクレジットカードで綱渡りをするような生活、やめたほうがいいよ。

同僚：うん、わかってるんだけど。

- -

(a) その会社は倒産寸前の中で、銀行から融資を受けながら綱渡り状態を続けている。

(b) 今の経済不況で新しい事業を始めるのは、危ない綱渡りをするようなものだ。

解説

1. 日本語では「綱渡りをする」のように「する」を使うと比喩表現になるが、「綱を渡る」のように「する」を使わないと比喩表現ではなくなる。ところが、英語では逆に*walk a tightrope*のように*do*を使わないと比喩表現になるが、*do tightrope walking*のように、*do*を使うと比喩ではなくなる。

2. 英語は*walk a tightrope between ~ and ~*という形でよく使われる。これは綱の両端の間で平衡感覚を失いかけている人のイメージを想起させる。しかし、日本語はそのようには使えない。

→📖 Note(1)

関連語

1. 「薄氷を踏む」は「綱渡りをする」に近い比喩であるが、前者は"やむをえず危険な状況に立つ"で、後者は"危険を冒して行動する"という意味である。また、「危ない橋を渡る」には、"あえて危険なことをする"というニュアンスが含まれる。

2. 英語には*walk a {thin/fine} line*（lit.「細い/かすかに見える」線の上を歩く）という関連表現がある。二つのグループや意向の要求が均衡を保つという意味で、一般的に注意すべき状況を表す場合、つまり見出しよりより細心の注目が必要な場合に使われる。

walk the same path as ~ ((~と)同じ道を歩む)→ {follow/walk} the same path as ~

walking {dictionary/encyclopedia}, a　comp. n.　personification

s.o. with a lot of knowledge, especially about a particular subject

Examples

Saya: You sure know a lot about American baseball, Kenta.

Kenta: When it comes to the Major League, I'm a walking dictionary. Actually, that's how I got interested in English in the first place.

Saya: But when it comes to English, you still rely on actual dictionaries, don't you?

- -

(a) Chris, from my perspective at least, is a walking dictionary of the Japanese language.

(b) Kazuo is a walking dictionary of classical music.

Notes

1. In the Japanese, the dictionary is portrayed as being alive, whereas in English it is portrayed as walking. However, both convey the same figurative meaning: "a person who is very knowledgeable (about a particular subject)."

2. *Jibiki* is an archaic form of *jisho* that is rarely used outside of this expression. Note that the expression ˣ*iki-jisho* does not exist.

R E L

The Japanese has the RELs *mono-shiri* (one who knows a lot), *haku-gaku* (one who is well-educated), and *haku-shiki* (one with wide knowledge). They are all examples of metonymy. The main difference between the *iki-jibiki* and the aforementioned expressions is that they imply knowledge that encompasses several areas. Thus, one can say {*nihon-go/ kurashikku ongaku*} *no iki-jibiki da* ([s.o. is] a walking {dictionary/encyclopedia} of {the Japanese language/classical music})," but one cannot say {*nihon-go/kurashikku-ongaku*} *no* {ˣ*mono-shiri*/ˣ*haku-gaku*/ˣ*haku-shiki*} *da*.

wall　/ n. / metaphor

an obstacle that prevents one from proceeding; a barrier or defense

REL **LOOK▶** build a wall around oneself; **LOOK▶** hit {a/the} wall; **LOOK▶** the walls have ears.; **LOOK▶** wallflower

Examples

Kenta: You went to listen to Professor Mori's lecture, right?

Saya: Yeah, there were a lot of people there.

Kenta: Fitting for the guy who broke through the wall of harmful traditions. He sure attracts a lot of attention.

- -

676

生き字引 / n. phr. 擬人化

ある分野に関して知り尽くしている人

関 物知り, 博学, 博識

例文

さや：健太って、ほんとアメリカ野球のこと詳しいね。

健太：大リーグの生き字引って呼んでほしいね。そもそも英語が好きになったきっかけなんだから。

さや：でも、英語のほうは本物の辞書にお世話になりっぱなしね。

(a) クリスは、僕から見れば、日本語の生き字引だ。

(b) 和男はクラシック音楽の生き字引なのです。

解説

1. 日本語では「辞書が生きている」と表現し、英語では「辞書が歩いている」と表現しているが、"何でも詳しく知っている人"という比喩の意味は同じである。

2. 日本語の「字引き」という言葉は、「辞書」より古い単語で、この表現以外ではめったに使われないが、「˟生き辞書」という言葉はない。

関連語

日本語には「生き字引」の関連表現として「物知り」「博学」「博識」がある。「物知り」は"広く何でも知っている人"、「博学」は"学問的なことをよく知っている人"、「博識」は"知識が広い人"であり、すべて換喩である。「生き字引」と決定的に違う点は、これらは知識の分野が決まっていない点である。だから、「｜日本語／クラシック音楽｜の生き字引だ」とは言えるが,「｜日本語／クラシック音楽｜の｜˟物知り／˟博学／˟博識｜だ」とは言えない。

W

壁 / n. 隠喩

前に進むことを阻む障害, 大きすぎて超えられない境界や防壁

関 **LOOK▶**（自分の）回りに壁を築く, **LOOK▶**壁にぶつかる
LOOK▶壁に耳あり, **LOOK▶**壁の花

例文

健太：森教授の講演、聞きに行ったんだって？

さや：うん、人がたくさん来てたよ。

健太：そうか、悪しき伝統の壁を破った人だもんね。みんな注目してるね。

677

(a) Harry Potter is an entertaining tale about a boy who uses his magical powers to overcome the various walls that he encounters.

(b) When the investigation team started to probe into the cabinet member's corruption, they faced a thick wall of nondisclosure.

[R][E][L]

1. In Japanese, *kabe* (wall) can be used to express a target or limit that cannot be exceeded, but English typically uses *ceiling* to express this idea.

(1) After working at the company for years, he hit a {ceiling/ ×wall} and couldn't get promoted any further.
何年かその会社で働いた後、彼はそれ以上は昇進不可能という壁にぶちあたった。

2. The English and Japanese have the RELs *build a wall around oneself/(jibun no) mawari ni kabe o kizuku* and *hit {a/the} wall/kabe ni butsukaru*. In these expressions, *wall* and *kabe* are used in the same sense as they are used in the main entry. 📖→関連語(2)

wallflower | comp. n. | metaphor

s.o. who stays on the outskirts of social functions because {he/she} is shy or unpopular

[Example]

He invited her to the hall and tried to get her to dance, but she preferred to be a wallflower.

The walls have ears. | phr. | personification

one should be careful about what one says, because s.o. may be listening

[Examples]

Mike: Wait, we shouldn't talk about the new project here.

Colleague: You're right. The walls have ears. Shall we go somewhere else?

Mike: Let's do that.

(a) The walls have ears. Don't think for a minute that, despite all your precautions, no one is going to get into your place and install a listening device.

(b) They say that the walls have ears, but in Palestine, the walls seem to talk. Wherever you look, the walls have political and occasionally social messages written on them.

[Notes]

1. According to the *Nihon Kokugo Daijiten* (Dictionary of the Japanese Language), *kabe ni mimi ari* first appeared during the Kamakura Period in the *Heike Monogatari* (Tale of the Heike). And according to the *Oxford English Dictionary*, *the walls have ears* was first used in Thomas Shelton's translation (1620) of Miguel de Cervantes's *Don Quixote* in the sentence "they say that the walls have ears."

2. The Japanese expression ends with the verb *ari*, which is an archaic form of *aru* (to exist).

(a) ハリーポッターは、少年が何度も困難の壁に突き当たっては、魔法の力でそれを乗り越えていくというとても楽しいお話だ。

(b) 捜査当局が閣僚の汚職を追及しようとしたとき、黙秘の厚い壁に直面した。

関連語

1. 日本語では壁 (wall) を「大きすぎて超えられない目標や限界」を意味する場合にも用いるが、その場合英語では *ceiling* が用いられる。━📖 **Note (1)**

2. 日英語には関連表現として「(自分の)回りに壁を築く」*build a wall around oneself* と「壁にぶつかる」*hit {a/the} wall* がある。この二つの比喩表現では「壁」*wall* の意味は見出しと同じである。

(2) a. 彼は自分の周りに壁を築いて、誰もよせつけない。
　　 He builds a wall around himself and keeps anyone from approaching.

　 b. 人生の大きな壁に{突き当たった / ぶつかった}とき、あなたは誰に相談しますか。
　　 Who do you consult when you hit a wall?

壁の花 / n. phr. 隠喩

パーティなどで中心から外れている目立たない人

例 文

彼は彼女を誘ってホールで踊らせようとしたが、彼女は壁の花でいる方を好んだ。

壁に耳あり phr. 擬人化

誰かが話を聞いているかもしれないから、よく注意したほうがいい

例 文

マイク： ちょっと、ここでその新しいプロジェクトの話はまずいよ。

同僚： そうだね。「壁に耳あり」だからね。場所を変えようか。

マイク： うん。

- -

(a) 「壁に耳あり」ですよ。どんなに用心しても、誰かがあなたの場所に入り込んで、盗聴器を備え付けるなんてことは十分あり得ることですよ。

(b) 普通の格言では「壁に耳あり」って言われているけれど、パレスチナでは壁はものを言うらしい。どこを見ても壁に政治的、時には社会的なスローガンが書いてあるんだ。

解 説

1. 『日本国語大辞典』によると「壁に耳あり」の日本語の初出は鎌倉時代の『平家物語』である。『オクスフォード英語大辞典』によると、英語の初出はセルバンテス作『ドン・キホーテ』の、トマス・シェルトンによる英訳(1620)に出てくる「壁に耳がある、と言われている」である。

2. 日本語は文語的表現の「あり」になっているが、その現代語形は「ある」である。

3. Japanese also has the expression *kabe ni mimi ari, shōji ni me ari* (the walls have ears and the sliding doors have eyes), which includes *shōji* (paper sliding door), a symbol of Japanese culture. This expression is generally more common than the main entry.

war of nerves   n. phr.   metaphor

a conflict in which psychological tactics are employed

REL   a battle of nerves; a battle of wits; psychological warfare

Examples

Kenta: Karen, what are you watching so intently?

Karen: A professional tennis match. At this level of competition, it's less about skill and more about winning the war of nerves.

Kenta: True.

(a) Auctioneering is not for the faint-hearted. It's a war of nerves.

(b) The war of nerves between the criminal, who's holed up with a hostage, and the police has been going on for a while.

REL

1. The English has the REL *a battle of nerves*, which can be used instead of the main entry.
(1) The {war/battle} of nerves between the criminal, who's holed up with a hostage, and the police has been going on for a while. (→ (b))
2. The English and Japanese have the RELs *psychological warfare/shinri-sen* and *a battle of wits/zunō-sen*, respectively. The former is characterized by the use of tactics that disrupt the enemy's emotional state, whereas the latter describes a showdown characterized by intellect. 関連語(2)

warm   adj.   metaphor/synesthesia

affectionate; cordial; soft

REL   hot

ANT   LOOK cold

Examples

Saya: Karen told me that she volunteers at a nursing home every week by teaching English to senior citizens.

Kenta: She comes off as cold at first, but I guess she's really a warm person underneath.

Saya: She said that every time she goes there, she receives such a warm welcome, which makes her feel that it's really worth doing.

----

3. 日本語には「障子」という日本の文化的な特徴を加えた「壁に耳あり、障子に目あり」という表現がある。一般的には見出しより、この表現の方がよく使われる。

神経戦 （しんけいせん） / comp. n. / 隠喩（いんゆ）

相手を心理的に負かそうとする戦い
（あいて）（しんりてき）（ま）（たたか）

関 頭脳戦，心理戦
（ずのうせん）（しんりせん）

例文

健太：カレン、何、真剣に見てんの？
（けんた）（なに）（しんけん）（み）

カレン：プロのテニスマッチ。ここまでくると、技術の戦いというより神経戦ね。
（ぎじゅつ）（たたか）（しんけいせん）

健太：そうだね。
（けんた）

(a) 競売は気が弱い人のすることではない。神経戦なのだから。
（きょうばい）（き）（よわ）（ひと）（しんけいせん）

(b) 人質を取って立てこもった犯人と警察の間では長時間の神経戦が続いている。
（ひとじち）（と）（た）（はんにん）（けいさつ）（あいだ）（ちょうじかん）（しんけいせん）（つづ）

関連語

1. 英語には *a battle of nerves*（lit. 神経の戦い）という関連表現があって、見出しと置き換えられる。━━ REL (1)

2. 日英語とも、「心理戦」*psychological warfare* と「頭脳戦」*a battle of wits* という関連表現がある。前者は敵の感情を乱す戦術を用いることを表現しており、後者は知能を使う戦いという意味である。

(2) a. 将棋や碁のプロ棋士の戦いでは心理戦を制した方が勝つと言われている。

   In professional chess and *go* matches, it is said that the one who wages psychological warfare more effectively wins.

 b. 彼はチェスゲームでコンピュータとの戦いに勝利し、世紀の頭脳戦を制した。

   He won the chess game against the computer, emerging victorious in the biggest battle of wits of the century.

温（暖）かい / 温（暖）かな （あたた） / adj.(i) / 隠喩（いんゆ） / 共感覚（きょうかんかく）

思いやりのある，やさしい，やわらかな
（おも）

関 熱い，暑い
（あつ）（あつ）

反 寒い，LOOK 冷たい
（さむ）（つめ）

例文

さや：カレンって、毎週、高齢者養護施設でボランティアで英語教えてるんだって。
（まいしゅう）（こうれいしゃようごしせつ）（えいごおし）

健太：そう。彼女、ちょっと冷たそうに見えるけど、本当は温かい人なんだね。
（けんた）（かのじょ）（つめ）（み）（ほんとう）（あたた）（ひと）

さや：毎回、施設でとても温かい歓迎を受けて、やりがいがあるって言ってたわ。
（まいかい）（しせつ）（あたた）（かんげい）（う）（い）

681

(a) A child brought up in warm family environment often grows up to be a considerate person.

(b) I want a carpet with warm colors, such as red and yellow, to make my room seem more welcoming.

(c) I love the warm feeling of stroking a cat's soft fur while it purrs in my arms.

Notes

1. When used metaphorically, *warm* can be used either before or after a noun, but *atatakai* tends to be used before a noun.

(1)a. John is very warm.
   ジョンは{とても温かい人だ/⁇とても温かい}。
   b. The reception was very warm.
   {とても温かい歓迎を受けた/⁇歓迎はとても温かかった}。

However, using *atatakai* as part of a predicate is perfectly grammatical if it is used in a construction that takes the form of *(s.o.) wa (s.t.) ga (adjective)* (s.t. is an innate part of s.o.). 📖→ 解説(2)

2. There are two kanji used for *atatakai*: 暖 (*on*-reading = *dan*) and 温 (*on*-reading = *on*). The former is used when referring to atmospheric warmth, as in *atatakai heya* (暖かい部屋 [warm room]), and the latter is often used in metaphorical expressions, as in *atatakai kokoro* (温かい心 [warm heart]) and *atatakai hito* (温かい人 [warm person]). However, there are some cases where the kanji used depends on the situation, such as *atatakai iro* (暖かい色 [warm color]), *atatakai seien* (暖かい声援 [warm encouragement]), *atatakai kimochi* (暖 / 温かい気持ち [warm feelings]), and *atatakai nomi-mono* (温かい飲み物 [warm drink]). Which kanji is used depends on the situation.

REL

1. There are two Chinese characters used for *atsui*: 暑い and 熱い . The former is used when referring to high atmospheric temperature, as in *atsui natsu* (暑い夏 [hot summer]), and the latter is used when referring to something other than atmospheric temperature, as in *atsui ocha* (熱いお茶 [hot tea]). While 暑い cannot be used metaphorically, 熱い can. Examples include *atsui shisen* (熱い視線 [passionate gaze]), *atsui naka* (熱い仲 [mutual attraction]), *atsui omoi* (熱い思い [passion]), and so on.

2. *Hot* means "to have a high temperature," and it can be used figuratively in expressions such as *hot-tempered*, *hot news*, and *hot as a pepper*, among others.

ANT

The ANTs for *atatakai* (温かい / 暖かい [warm]) as a metaphorical adjective are *tsumetai* (冷たい [cold]) and *samui* (寒い [cold]). *Tsumetai* can be often used figuratively, as in *tsumetai hito* (cold person), *tsumetai taido* (cold attitude), *tsumetai me* (cold stare), and other expressions. *Samui* can also be used figuratively, but not as the antonym of *atatakai*. It is often used figuratively to express something that is insufficient or unsatisfactory, such as in *futokoro ga samui* (strapped for cash), *samui fun-iki* (cold atmosphere), and *samui jōdan* (bad joke). 📖→ 反意語(1)

(a) 温かい家庭環境の中で育てられた子供は、思いやりのある子に育つことが多い。

(b) 部屋をもっと居心地よくするために、赤や黄色のような暖かい色のカーペットが欲しい。

(c) 柔らかい猫を撫でて腕の中でゴロゴロいうときに感じる、暖かい気持ちが好きなの。

【解 説】

1. *warm* が比喩として使われる場合、*warm* は名詞の前後に使えるが、「温(暖)かい」が比喩として使われる場合は名詞の前に使われる傾向がある。 ━📖 **Note(1)**
しかし、日本語において、誰かが何かを自分の一部として所有していることを表す構文では、述部に「温(暖)かい」を使っても問題はない。

(2) ジョンは心がとても温かい。
lit. As for John, his heart is very warm. (→ John has a very warm heart.)

2. 「あたたかい」の漢字は「暖」「温」のどちらも使用され、音読みは「暖→ダン」と「温→オン」である。「暖かい部屋」などのように大気のあたたかさを表す場合には「暖」が一般的である。また、「温かい心」「温かい人」のような比喩的表現には「温」が使われることが多い。ただし、「暖かい色」「暖かい声援」「暖/温かい気持ち」「温かい飲み物」のような例もあり、どちらの漢字を使用するかは場合によって異なる。

【関連語】

1. 日本語の「あつい」の漢字は「暑い」と「熱い」がある。前者は「暑い夏」のように気温が高い時、後者は「熱いお茶」のように気温以外のものの温度が高い時に用いられる。「暑い」は比喩的に使用されないが、「熱い」は「熱い視線」「熱い仲」「熱い思い」のように比喩的にも使用される。

2. 英語の *hot* は "高温だ" という意味だが、*hot-tempered*(短気な)、*hot news*(最新の注目を集めているニュース)、*hot as a pepper*(とうがらしのように辛い)などの表現では比喩的に使われる。

【反意語】

比喩的な意味の「温(暖)かい」の反意表現は「冷たい(寒い)」である。「冷たい」は「冷たい人」「冷たい態度」「冷たい目」「冷たい心」などのように比喩的によく使われる。「寒い」も「温(暖)かい」の反意表現としてではないが、比喩的に使われることがある。「懐が寒い」「寒い頭髪」「寒い雰囲気」「寒い冗談」などのように、何かが十分ではなかったり、何かに満足できないことを表す時に使用される。

W

683

warm the bench / phr. / metaphor

to not have a chance to play during a game

REL bench warmer

Example

> I don't want to just warm the bench; I want to participate in matches sometimes.

wash one's hands of ~ / phr. / metaphor

to abandon; to refuse to be responsible

Examples

> Colleague: How did they respond?
>
> Mike: The response was lackluster. I'm not so sure we can turn this into a successful business.
>
> Colleague: If it looks like it'll take too much time, then maybe we should just wash our hands of the whole thing.

- -

(a) I haven't washed my hands of her yet. I'm thinking of having a heart-to-heart talk with her.

(b) There are times when even I just want to wash my hands of the dangerous sport of boxing.

(c) Pilate could not find Jesus guilty of wrongdoing and washed his hands of his execution.

Note

> While both the English and Japanese use the word *hand* (*te*), the verbs *wash* and *hiku* (to pull) are quite different.

REL

> The Japanese has the REL *(~ kara) ashi o arau* (to wash one's feet of ~), which can be used to mean "to abandon criminal activity," "to distance oneself from bad influences," or "to quit one's job (regardless of whether it is good or bad)." 📖➡ 関連語(1)

watch one's mouth / phr. / metonymy

to be careful about what one says

REL watch one's tongue; watch what one says; watch one's step

Examples

> Mike: Kimura sure put up a fight during today's meeting, didn't he?
>
> Colleague: Yeah. He made good points, but he should have watched his mouth.
>
> Mike: Yeah. His arguments were correct, but they definitely angered the section chief.

- -

ベンチを温（暖）める　phr.　隠喩

試合の出番がなくて、控えの選手でいること

関 ベンチウォーマー

例文

いつもベンチを暖めてばかりいないで、たまには試合に出てみたいなあ。

（～から）手を引く　phr.　隠喩

何かとの縁を切る，何かの責任をとらなくなる

関 （～から）足を洗う

例文

同僚：先方の反応はどう？

マイク：あまり、ぱっとしないね。ビジネスに持ち込めるかどうか微妙なところだね。

同僚：あまり時間がかかるようなら、この仕事からは手を引いたほうがいいかもね。

(a) まだ彼女との関係から手を引いていないんだよ。じっくり彼女と話し合おうと思っているところなんだ。

(b) 僕だって危険なボクシングから手を引きたいと思うことがあるんだよ。

(c) ピラトはイエスに罪があるとは思えなかったので、彼の刑執行から手を引いた。

解説

日英語とも「手」が共通に使われているが、動詞は「引く」と wash（洗う）で全然違う。

関連語

日本語には「（～から）足を洗う」という関連表現があり、"悪事をやめる""悪い仲間から離れる""悪業か正業かに関係なく職を辞する"という意味がある。

(1) 彼はやくざから足を洗った。
He washed his hands of the *yakuza* (=Japanese mafia).

口に気をつける　phr.　換喩

言うべきでないこと、余計なことを言わないようにする

関 口を慎む

例文

マイク：今日の会議、木村の反論、すごかったね。

同僚：うん。でも、これからはもうちょっと口に気をつけるほうがいいかもね。

マイク：うん、彼の言うことは正論なんだけどね。課長、かなり頭に来てたね。

W

(a) I made my dad really angry. Maybe I should've watched my mouth.

(b) Who do you think you're talking to? You better watch your mouth!

Notes

1. In the English, the verb is *watch*, but in the Japanese it is *ki o tsukeru* (to be careful).
2. Because words come from the mouth, *mouth* and *kuchi* are used as metonymy for human speech.

REL

1. The English and Japanese have the RELs *watch one's tongue* and *kuchi o tsutsushimu*, respectively. Both are used less frequently than the main entries. 📖▶関連語(1)
2. The English has the RELs *watch what one says* and *watch one's step*. The former has the same meaning as the main entry, but the latter can apply to all sorts of actions, not just speech.

(1) a. You'd better watch what you say—the boss might be listening.
言うことには気をつけた方がいいよ。ボスが聞いているかもしれないから。

b. You'd better watch your step in that class. I heard the teacher's really strict.
その授業では、行動に気をつけた方がいいよ。先生がすごく厳しいらしいから。

{wave/show} the flag　/ phr. / metaphor

to show support for s.t.

REL flag waver

Examples

(a) Now that our course has been determined, we can't afford to have the wrong type of person start waving the flag for us.

(b) His role is waving the flag for government policies.

Note

In both English and Japanese, the non-metaphorical meaning is "to signal by waving a flag."

REL

The English compound *flag waver* can often mean "patriot," but the Japanese compound *hata-furi* does not have this meaning.

(1) "Flag waver" is sometimes interpreted as "conservative."
「愛国者」は時に「保守主義者」と捉えられることがある。

way　/ n. / metaphor

a manner or method by which s.o. does s.t.; a course leading to an objective

Examples

(a) I usually go my own way regardless of others' opinions.

(b) Everyone has their own best way of doing things, but sometimes it takes a long time to find it.

(c) Because the illness has progressed this much, there is no way to treat it other than surgery.

(a) ずいぶん父を怒らせてしまった。口に気をつけるべきだったかもしれない。

(b) 誰に向かって物を言っているんですか？　口に気をつけなさい。

【解説】

1. 動詞は日本語では「気をつける」であるが、英語では *watch*（見守る）である。

2. 言葉は口から発声するものなので、「口」*mouth* が言葉の換喩として使われている。

【関連語】

1. 関連表現として、日本語には「口を慎む」、英語には *watch one's tongue* があるが、どちらも見出しの方が使用頻度が高い。

(1) エリックは口{に気をつけ/ を慎ま}ないと訴えられてしまう。
　　 If Eric doesn't watch his {mouth/tongue}, he's going to end up with a lawsuit.

2. 英語には *watch what one says*（lit. 言うことを見なさい）と *watch one's step*（lit. 足下を見なさい）という関連表現がある。前者は見出しと同じ意味を持つが、後者は話すことのみならず、様々な動作に使用される。 ➡📖 REL (1)

旗ふり役　/ comp. n. / 隠喩
はた　　やく　　　　　　　　　　　　　　いんゆ

集団の先頭に立って人々に働きかけながら物事を推し進める人
しゅうだん　せんとう　た　　ひとびと　はたら　　　　　ものごと　お　すす　ひと

【例文】

(a) 我々の方向性は決まったが、とんでもない奴が旗ふり役になると困る。
われわれ　ほうこうせい　き　　　　　　　　やつ　はた　やく　　　　こま

(b) 彼はいつも政府が示した政策の旗ふり役を務めている。
かれ　　　　せいふ　しめ　せいさく　はた　やく　つと

【解説】

日英語とも基本義は "旗を振って信号を送る" である。

【関連語】

英語の名詞句 *flag waver* はよく「愛国者」という意味で使われるが、日本語の「旗ふり役」にはその意味はない。 ➡📖 REL (1)

道　/ n. / 隠喩
みち　　　　　いんゆ

何かをする仕方、手段や方法
なに　　　しかた　しゅだん　ほうほう

【例文】

(a) 私は、他の人の意見がどうあろうと、たいていは我が道を行く。
わたし　ほか　ひと　いけん　　　　　　　　　　わ　みち　い

(b) 誰にでも最善の道がある。ただ、それを見つけ出すのに時々長い時間がかかる。
だれ　　さいぜん　みち　　　　　　　　　み　だ　　　ときどきなが　じかん

(c) ここまで病状が悪化したら手術するよりほかに道はないだろう。
びょうじょう　あっか　しゅじゅつ　　　　　　　みち

687

Notes
1. Both *way* and *michi* can be used figuratively to describe the manner or method by which someone does something.
2. Both *way* and *michi* are used figuratively in such idiomatic expressions as *go one's (own) way/{waga/jibun} no michi o iku*, as shown in (a); *(one's) own best way (of doing s.t.)/saizen no michi*, as shown in (b); and *there is no way other than ~/~ yori hoka ni michi wa nai*, as shown in (c).
3. *Michi* can also mean "field" and "ethics." 📖→解説(1)

weather vane / comp. n. / metaphor

describes s.o. whose opinions and ideas change easily

Example

He's just like a weather vane. His attitude and opinions change by the day.

Note

A weathercock is an object shaped like a rooster that measures the speed and direction of the wind. Because it changes its direction so often, it is used to describe people whose attitudes and opinions change often.

weave through ~ / phr. / metaphor

to move through s.t. in a winding manner

[REL] [LOOK] snake one's way

Examples

(a) The car was weaving through the pouring rain on a road through the mountains.

(b) The bus wove through the city for about 30 minutes before we arrived at the glittering harbor.

(c) She hurriedly weaved through the crowd looking for her friend.

Note

The basic meaning of both *weave* and *nū* contains the idea of "moving in a zigzag motion." Applying this idea to objects, such as roads and vehicles, gives rise to the figurative meaning.

weight off one's shoulders, a（肩の荷が下りる）
→ **{load/weight} off one's shoulders, a**

解 説

1. 日英語とも人の歩く「道」と *way* が誰かが何かをする仕方、手段や方法の比喩になっている。
2. 日英語ともに「道」と *way* は(a)の「｜我が/自分の｜道を行く」*go one's (own) way*、(b)の「最善の道」*(one's) own best way (of doing s.t.)*、(c)の「〜よりほかに道はない」*there is no way other than〜* のように慣用句で使用される。
3. 日本語には他に、"分野""物事の道理"という比喩的意味もある。

(1)a. 何か困った時は、その道の専門家に聞いてみるのもいいことだ。
   When you get stuck, you should ask a professional in the field.

  b. 盗みは人の道に外れる行為だ。
   Stealing is an act that goes against morality.

風見鶏 _{かざみどり} / comp. n. / 直喩 _{ちょくゆ}

意見や考えが簡単に変わる _{いけん} _{かんが} _{かんたん} _か

例 文

彼は風見鶏のように、日によって態度や意見が変わる。
_{かれ} _{かざみどり} _ひ _{たいど} _{いけん} _か

解 説

風見鶏とは鶏をかたどった風向計のことで、風向きによって首の向きがくるくる変わることから、人の態度や意見がくるくる変わるという比喩が出てきた。

(〜を){縫うように/縫って} _ぬ _ぬ / phr. / 直喩/隠喩 _{ちょくゆ} _{いんゆ}

何か(特に乗り物)が障害物を避けて曲がりながら進む _{なに} _{とく} _の _{もの} _{しょうがいぶつ} _さ _ま _{すす}

関 **LOOK▶** 蛇行する _{だこう}

例 文

(a) 車は土砂降りの山中を縫うように進んでいた。
   _{くるま} _{どしゃぶ} _{さんちゅう} _ぬ _{すす}

(b) バスは半時間ぐらい町の中を縫うように走り、輝くばかりの港に着いた。
   _{はんじかん} _{まち} _{なか} _ぬ _{はし} _{かがや} _{みなと} _つ

(c) 彼女は友達を捜そうとして雑踏を縫うように急いだ。
   _{かのじょ} _{ともだち} _{さが} _{ざっとう} _ぬ _{いそ}

解 説

日英語の動詞の「縫う」、*weave*（織る）はどちらも基本義に"ジグザグ運動(左右に交互に折れ曲がりながら進む動き)"を含んでいる。そこから道や乗り物がジグザグに進むことを見出しのように表現するようになった。

W

welcome {s.o./s.t.} with open arms   *phr.* **metonymy**

to welcome {s.o./s.t.} wholeheartedly

REL greet {s.o./s.t.} with open arms

Examples

Mrs. S: I heard that my sister's son Hiroshi got a job.

Mr. S: Good for him! It's impressive that he found a job during this recession.

Mrs. S: Maybe studying computer science gave him an advantage.

Mr. S: I bet you're right. IT companies welcome applicants like him with open arms.

- - - - - - - - - - - - - - - - - - - -

(a) His new teammates didn't necessarily welcome him with open arms, but they recognized him as a member of the team.

(b) We welcomed the new peace initiative in the Middle East with open arms.

Notes

1. Both the English and Japanese metaphors are based on the literal gesture of opening both arms to welcome someone.

2. *Moro-te* has the same meaning as *ryō-te* (both hands).

REL

1. The English can be replaced by *greet {s.o./s.t.} with open arms*, but this expression is less frequent than the main entry.

(1) We {welcomed/greeted} the new peace initiative in the Middle East with open arms.

(→(b))

2. The Japanese has two RELs, *moro-te o agete {sansē/sandō}-suru* and *moro-te o agete yorokobu*. 📖→ 関連語(2)

where one stands (on ~)   *phr.* **metaphor**

s.o.'s view or an attitude about s.t.; s.o.'s situation or status

REL one's position on ~

Examples

Mrs. S: When juveniles commit crimes, the victim's information gets leaked while penetrator's privacy is completely protected. I just don't get it.

Mr. S: Yeah, they should change where they stand on juvenile crime. They should take the feelings of the victims' family into consideration. It's not fair to only protect the criminal's privacy.

- - - - - - - - - - - - - - - - - - - -

(a) We don't know where the politician stands on the issue of nuclear reactor safety.

(b) Nobody knows where she stands on environmental issues.

(c) As the parent of a child who has been bullied, I'd like to ask where you stand on the issue of bullying.

もろ手を挙げて歓迎する　/ phr.　換喩

誰かや何かを心から迎える

関 もろ手を挙げて {賛成 / 賛同} する，もろ手を挙げて喜ぶ

例 文

鈴木(妻)：姉の息子の弘、就職決まったそうよ。

鈴木(夫)：それはよかったね。この不況に、大したもんだ。

鈴木(妻)：コンピュータサイエンスを専攻したから強いのかもね。

鈴木(夫)：その通りだな。IT 関連企業は、もろ手を挙げて歓迎だからね。

(a) 新しいチームメートは、彼のことをもろ手を挙げて歓迎したわけではなかったが、チームの一員としては認めた。

(b) われわれは中東の新しい平和の第一歩をもろ手を挙げて歓迎した。

解 説

1. 日英語とも、"両手を挙げて歓迎する"という字義通りの解釈から出てきた比喩である。
2. 「もろ手」の意味は"両手"である。

関連語

1. 英語は *greet {s.o./s.t.} with open arms* (lit. もろ手を挙げて挨拶する)と置き換えられるが、使用頻度ははるかに低い。 ➡ REL(1)
2. 日本語には「もろ手を挙げて {賛成 / 賛同} する」「もろ手を挙げて喜ぶ」という関連表現がある。

(2)a. 彼らは私の意見にもろ手を挙げて{賛成 / 賛同}してくれた。
　　 They readily agreed with my opinion.

　 b. 彼が入学試験にパスしたとき、彼の両親はもろ手を挙げて喜んだ。
　　 When he passed the entrance examination, his parents were overjoyed.

({〜についての / の})立場　/ phr.　隠喩

{〜について / の}意見や態度，置かれた状況や地位

関 (〜に {関する / 関しての}) 立場，スタンス

例 文

鈴木(妻)：少年犯罪って、被害者の情報は垂れ流しで、加害者のプライバシーは完全に守られていて、本当に納得いかないわ。

鈴木(夫)：うん、メディアは少年犯罪の扱いについての立場を改めるべきだね。被害者の親族の気持ちも考えて取材すべきだな。加害者側だけそっとしておくなんてのは、不公平だね。

(a) その政治家が原子力発電の安全性についてどのような立場を取っているかはわからない。

(b) 誰も彼女の環境問題についての立場を知らない。

(c) お子さんがいじめにあった親御さんとして、いじめ問題についての立場を聞かせてください。

691

Note

The Japanese uses the compound noun *tachiba* (lit. "standing-place"), whereas the English uses the verb *stand*.

REL

Japanese possesses two slightly related yet more formal expressions: *(~ ni kansuru) tachiba* and *(~ ni kanshite no) tachiba*. The English REL, *one's position on ~*, has essentially the same meaning as the main entry. 📖▶ 関連語(1)

Where there's a will, there's a way. /phr. / metaphor

if one wants s.t. badly enough, one can find the means of obtaining it

Example

Kenta: Man, my TOEFL score was terrible as usual. I think I may have to give up on the idea of studying abroad.

Saya: What are you talking about? Don't say that. Where there's a will, there's a way. If you just keep at it, your wish will come true.

Kenta: That's easy for you to say.

Saya: Don't be so negative. Keep trying.

Note

The Japanese is a translation of the English.

REL

The Japanese has the REL *sēshin-ittō nani-goto ka narazaran*, which means "if one single-mindedly focuses on s.t., one can achieve it."

Where there's smoke, there's fire. /phr. / metaphor

rumors won't spread unless there is some truth to them

REL There's no smoke without fire.

Examples

Mike: So are Takahashi and Kanda going to get married?

Colleague: Apparently so, but it's still just a rumor.

Mike: I can't believe it. Don't they always fight like cats and dogs?

Colleague: Well, they say where there's smoke, there's fire. When it comes to romance, you just never know.

- -

(a) I heard that the prime minister received treatment in a special cancer ward. I don't know if it's true, but where there's smoke, there's fire.

解 説

日本語は「立場」という複合名詞を使っているが、英語は動詞の *stand*（立つ）を使っている。

関連語

日本語には「｛～について / の｝立場」よりややフォーマルな「（～に｛関する / 関しての｝）立場」という表現もある。英語の関連表現 *one's position on ~* も、見出しと基本的に同じ意味を持っている。

(1) 誰も彼女の環境問題に｛ついての / 関する / 関しての｝立場を知らない。(→(b))
Nobody knows {where she stands/her position} on environmental issues.

意志あるところに道あり　phr.　隠喩

何かが本当に欲しければ、それを手にする手段を見つけることができる

関 精神一到何事か成らざらん

例 文

健太：あ～あ、TOEFL の点数は相変わらずだし、もう留学はあきらめたほうがいいいかもな。

さや：何言ってるのよ。「意志あるところに道あり」っていうじゃない。強く念じて努力すれば、願いは必ずかなうわよ。

健太：さやはそうだろうけど。

さや：情けないこと言ってないで、頑張りなさいよ。

解 説

日本語は英語からの翻訳である。

関連語

日本語には「精神一到何事か成らざらん」という関連表現がある。意味は「気持ちを統一して物事にあたれば、どんなことでも成し遂げられないことはない」である。

火のないところに煙は立たない　phr.　隠喩

まったく事実ではないことに噂は出てこない

例 文

マイク：今度、高橋さんと神田さん、結婚するんだって？

同僚：らしいね。噂だけだけど。

マイク：信じられないな。犬猿の仲だと思ってたけど。

同僚：火のないところに煙は立たないってね。男女の仲なんて、いつどうなるかわかんないさ。

(a) 総理大臣が特別癌病棟で治療を受けたということを聞いたが、事実関係はわからない。しかし、火のないところに煙は立たない。

(b) Some years ago, they were accused of using chemical weapons against the enemy. That accusation may not be based on fact, but I think where there's smoke, there's fire.

Note

Because the Japanese literally means "where there's no fire, there's no smoke," the viewpoints of the English and Japanese are different. It should also be noted that the affirmative English sentence is straightforward compared to the Japanese, which is rather indirect because it utilizes a double negative construction.

REL

The English can be replaced with *There is no smoke without fire*, but the main entry is more common.

(1) He denied having an affair with his secretary, but as they say, {where there's smoke, there's fire/there's no smoke without fire}.
彼は秘書との情事を否定したが、しかし、火のないところに煙は立たないのだ。

---

whiplash / comp. n. / metaphor

injury resulting from a sudden jerking motion of the head

Example

Yesterday I was rear-ended and suffered a whiplash injury.

(as) white as snow / phr. / simile

pure white

Example

Snow White had skin as white as snow.

---

win s.o.'s heart / phr. / metaphor

to make s.o. fall in love with you

REL **LOOK** capture s.o.'s heart; **LOOK** steal s.o.'s heart

Examples

(a) I like this girl. I want to be more than just friends. But I don't know how to win her heart.

(b) She dated people like Stephen A. Douglas and Abraham Lincoln. Lincoln won her heart, and the two were married in 1842.

(c) He won her heart and got the consent of her parents, but not yet his own father's.

(b) 数年前に彼らは敵に対して化学兵器を使ったと非難された。その非難は事実に基づいていないかもしれないが、火のないところに煙は立たないと思う。

解説

英語の直訳が"煙のあるところに火がある"となることでもわかるように、日英語には視点の違いがある。さらに、日本語は二重否定で表現の仕方が間接的であるが、英語は肯定文で、より直接的である。

関連語

英語は日本語の見出しにより近い *There's no smoke without fire.* に置き換えることができるが、見出しのほうがよく使われている。📖 **REL(1)**

むち打ち症 / comp. n 隠喩

頭部が突然前後にふられることで首を痛めること

例文

昨日、運転中に後ろから追突されて、むち打ち症になってしまった。

雪のように白い / phr. 直喩

とても白い

例文

白雪姫の肌は雪のように白かった。

心を勝ち取る / phr. 隠喩

誰かが喜ぶことをして、愛してもらうようにする

関 心を射止める, **LOOK▶** 心を捕らえる, **LOOK▶** (〜の)心を奪う

例文

(a) 僕はこの女の子が好きなんです。友達以上のつきあいがしたいんです。でも、どうやったら彼女の心を勝ち取れるかがわかりません。

(b) 彼女はスティーブン・ダグラスやアブラハム・リンカーンのような人々とデートしました。そして、リンカーンが彼女の心を勝ち取り、1842年に二人は結婚したのです。

(c) 彼は彼女の心を勝ち取り、彼女の両親の同意も得た。しかし、自分の父親の同意がまだだった。

REL

1. The English and Japanese expressions have the RELs *{capture/steal} s.o.'s heart* and *kokoro o toraeru*, respectively. The Japanese REL must be used when the subject is inanimate, as in (1) below. The subject of the English REL can be animate or inanimate.

(1) a. In 1928, Samuel Beckett moved to Paris, and the city quickly {won/captured/stole} his heart.
   1928年にサミュエル・ベケットはパリに引っ越し、この町は彼の心を{とらえました/⁇勝ち取りました}。

   b. Whichever design you choose, our beautiful Valentine's Day gift boxes are sure to {win/capture/steal} her heart!
   どのデザインをお選びになっても私どもの美しいバレンタインデーの贈り物の箱は必ずや彼女の心を{とらえる/⁇勝ち取る}でしょう。

2. The Japanese has another REL, *kokoro o itomeru* (lit. "to shoot s.o.'s heart"), which comes from the idea of Cupid shooting an arrow into someone's heart. While this expression employs a different image, it has the same meaning as *kokoro o kachitoru* and can be used to replace this expression. 📖← 関連語(2)

---

witch hunt / comp. n. / metaphor

an attempt to locate and harass those with unpopular views

Examples

(a) The government and police began a witch hunt with the aim of annihilating labor unions.

(b) During McCarthy's communist witch hunt in the 1950s, communists and those suspected of sympathizing with them were arrested.

(c) Group consciousness gone awry can sometimes lead to violent witch hunts.

Notes

1. The term *witch hunt* originally referred to the medieval and early-modern European practice, by those in power and those associated with the Church, of searching for individuals who held heretical views and persecuting them for practicing witchcraft and conspiring with demons, which often culminated in their being burned at the stake. Those victimized by these hunts were often scapegoats, and it is estimated that between two and three million people were killed as a result of this persecution. Many victims were poor, non-white, practitioners of non-Christian faiths, or otherwise removed from mainstream society. Joan of Arc, the French heroine renowned for her exploits during the Hundred Year's War, was burned at the stake as well. The Salem Witch Trials that took place in Massachusetts from 1692 to 1693 are another famous example of this persecution. The expression eventually took on the figurative meaning of singling out a person or group and damaging their reputation, regardless of the veracity of the claims against them.

2. The Japanese is a translation of the English.

関連語

1. 日英語には、それぞれ、「心を捕らえる」{capture/steal} s.o.'s heart という関連表現がある。日本語の関連表現の場合、(1)のように主語が人以外のときは「心を捕らえる」を使わなければならない。英語でも同じ発想の {capture/steal} s.o.'s heart が使えるが、主語に制限はない。

📖 REL (1)

2. 日本語には「心を射止める」という関連表現もある。キューピッドが人の心に矢を射るという連想からきている。この表現は、イメージは違うが実質上は「心を勝ち取る」と同じ意味で、置き換えることができる。

(2) 彼は彼女の心を {勝ち取り／射止め}、彼女の両親の同意も得た。(→(c))

魔女狩り
まじょがり / n. phr. / 隠喩 いんゆ

権力者や多数派が(政治的に)異端分子として見なす人物に制裁を加える
けんりょくしゃ たすうは せいじてき いたんぶんし み じんぶつ せいさい くわ

例文

(a) 労働組合を撲滅させようとした政府と警察は、魔女狩りを始めた。
ろうどうくみあい ぼくめつ せいふ けいさつ まじょがり はじ

(b) 1950年代のマッカーシーの魔女狩りによって、共産党のシンパやそれと関係を持ったと疑われ捕えられた人々がいる。
ねんだい まじょがり きょうさんとう かんけい もと うたが とら ひとびと

(c) 集団妄想は、時に魔女狩りのような暴挙を生むものだ。
しゅうだんもうそう とき まじょがり ぼうきょ う

解説

1. 「魔女狩り」とは、もともとの意味は、中世から近世初期までのキリスト教圏において、"権力の座にいる者とキリスト教会とが、異端的見解を実践している者を、悪魔と結託して魔術を行う魔女であるかのように捕らえ、拷問や一方的な裁判の末に、火あぶりの刑で死刑に処した"ことを指す。当時の犠牲者は200万人とも300万人とも言われるが、そのほとんどは、下層階級や異教徒、非白人などの社会的弱者であった。百年戦争の時の功績で有名なフランス女性の英雄ジャンヌ・ダルクも火あぶりの刑に処せられた。1692年から1693年にマサチューセッツ州で起きたセイラム魔女裁判も有名な例である。このことに端を発し、比喩的意味、すなわち"ある特定の人物を名指しし、実証可能かどうかわからない疑惑でその人物の社会的名誉を傷つけたり、引きずり下ろそうとしたりする"に発展した。

2. 日本語は英語からの直訳である。

with (a) heavy heart / phr. / metaphor

with much sorrow

ANT with a light heart

Examples

(a) I still think of the victims of the Great Earthquake with a heavy heart.

(b) I've been following that incident with a heavy heart.

(c) I read the book with heavy heart, made acutely aware of just how much sorrow, pain, and unspeakable horror war could etch into our hearts.

REL

The Japanese REL *omoi kokoro de* is more similar to the English than the main entry, but it is not used often. 📖→関連語(1)

ANT

The English and Japanese share similar ANTs: *with a light heart* and *karoyakana kimochi de*, respectively. Japanese also has the expression *karui kimochi de*, in which the adjective *karui* corresponds to *light*, but this cannot be used as an ANT of *omoi kimochi de* because it means "without thinking about s.t. seriously." 📖→反意語(1)

with one's tail between one's legs / phr. / metaphor

feeling ashamed and dejected, especially after a defeat

REL turn tail

Examples

Saya: I took part in a debate competition today at the university.

Karen: They have debate competitions in Japan?

Saya: Yeah, they've been catching on recently. The other team was so well-prepared that we left with our tails between our legs.

- -

(a) The director yelled at him until he had tears in his eyes and slunk away with his tail between his legs.

(b) They always come to each World Cup with great expectations, only to leave with their tails between their legs.

Note

Both the English and Japanese expressions come from the image of a dejected dog slinking away with its tail between its legs. Note that the Japanese does not mention *between one's legs*. It uses the verb *maku* (to coil) instead.

REL

The English REL, *turn tail*, means "to run away, typically out of fear."

(1) In a state of panic, she turned tail and fled.
パニック状態になって、彼女はしっぽを巻いて逃げた。

重い気持ちで / phr. 隠喩

とても暗く、悲しい気持ちを抱く

関 重い心で

反 軽やかな気持ちで

例文
- (a) 私は今でも大震災の被災者のことを重い気持ちで思い出します。
- (b) 私は重い気持ちでその事件の経過を追っている。
- (c) 戦争がいかに悲しみや痛み、言いようのない思いを深く深く心に刻み込むのか、重い気持ちでその本を読み通しました。

関連語

日本語には「重い心で」という、より英語の見出しに近い関連表現があるが、使用頻度は低い。

(1) 私は今でも大震災の被災者のことを重い{気持ちで／心で}思い出します。(→(a))

反意語

日英語とも「軽やかな気持ちで」*with a light heart* という同じ反意表現がある。なお、日本語には「軽い気持ちで」という表現があるが、"真剣に考えないで"という意味で、「重い気持ちで」の反意表現としては使えない。

(1) 以前は毎朝重い気持ちで起きていたが、運動を始めてからは{軽やかな／[×]軽い}気持ちで起きられるようになった。

I used to wake up every morning with a heavy heart, but now that I've started exercising, I can start each day with a light heart.

しっぽを巻く / phr. 隠喩

負けて、元気なく逃げ出す

例文

さや：今日、大学でディベートの試合に出たんだけどね。

カレン：日本でも、ディベートってするの？

さや：最近ね。相手チームはよく訓練してるから、練習不足のわれわれはしっぽを巻いて退散っていう感じだったわ。

- (a) 彼は所長に怒鳴りつけられて、最後には目に涙を浮かべ、しっぽを巻いて帰っていった。
- (b) 彼らはワールドカップの試合にはいつも大いなる期待をもってやって来るのだが、結局しっぽを巻いて去って行く。

解説

日英語とも、しょげた犬が足の間にしっぽを入れて、こそこそ逃げる様子から出てきた表現である。日本語は「足の間に」とは表現せず、「巻く」という動詞を使っていることに注意。

関連語

英語の関連表現 *turn tail* (lit. しっぽをまわす)は、"恐怖から逃げ出す"という意味である。

REL (1)

(see) with unclouded eyes / phr. / metaphor

to see things without prejudice

Examples

(a) If we are to know the truth, we must be able to see with unclouded eyes.

(b) His clarity of vision enables him to examine all sides of a matter with unclouded eyes.

(c) When you can no longer understand someone, you have no choice but to reevaluate that person with fresh and unclouded eyes, as if you two were meeting for the first time.

Note

Both the English and Japanese expressions are used most frequently with the verbs *see* and *miru*, respectively, but other verbs can be used as well, such as *examine* (*shiraberu*), as shown in (b), and *evaluate* (*hyōka-suru*), as shown in (c).

---

within a hair's breadth （間一髪で） → {by/within} a hair's breadth
かんいっぱつ

woman of the hour, the （時の人） → {man/woman} of the hour, the
とき　ひと

---

s.o.'s words carry weight / phr. / metaphor

s.o.'s words have a significant impact

Examples

(a) "It really made me realize that money can't buy happiness." That someone who had worked so hard to become rich said this made his words carry weight.

(b) He is a man of few words, but his words carry weight.

(c) That politician's speech is too long, and his words don't carry weight at all.

Note

S.o.'s words carry weight and *kotoba ni omomi ga aru* have different literal meanings, but their metaphorical meanings are essentially the same.

REL

The Japanese REL, ~ *no kotoba wa omoi*, can replace the main entry. 📖→ 関連語(1)

700

曇りのない目（で見る） / phr. 隠喩

物事を偏見なく見る

例文

(a) 真理を知りたければ、曇りのない目で見ることができなければならない。

(b) 彼にははっきりとしたビジョンがあるので、物事をあらゆる角度から曇りのない目で調べることができる。

(c) 相手が理解できなくなったら、初めてその人に会ったときのように、新鮮な曇りのない目で再評価するしかない。

解説

日英語とも、それぞれ「見る」see と一緒に使うことが多いが、(b)(c)のように他の動詞も自由に使える。また、日英語とも「見る」と see だけではなく「調べる」examine、「評価する」evaluate などといった認知を表す動詞も使える。

言葉に重みがある / phr. 隠喩

{話し手 / 書き手}の言葉に威厳と説得力がある

関 ～の言葉は重い

例文

(a) 「幸せはお金では買えないんだとつくづく思ったよ」。苦労して金持ちになった彼の言葉には重みがあった。

(b) 彼は言葉数の少ない人だけれど、彼の言葉には重みがある。

(c) あの政治家の演説は長いだけで、言葉に重みがない。

解説

英語の *s.o.'s words carry weight* の本来の意味は"言葉が重みを運ぶ"ということだが、日本語と発想が非常に近い。

関連語

日本語には「～の言葉は重い」という関連表現があり、見出しと置き換えができる。

(1) 仕事についての先輩の言葉 { には重みがあった / は重かった}。
The words of advice my mentor gave me about my job carried weight.

work addict / comp. n. / metaphor

a person who works too hard

REL workaholic

Examples

Colleague: Mike, can you stay late and help me today?

Mike: Sure, let's get this work done tonight.

Colleague: I see you've become a work addict too! I was hoping that you wouldn't imitate us Japanese on this point.

Mike: Says the guy who's always dumping work on me.

- -

(a) There are many work addicts in Japan who have sacrificed their family, hobbies, and friends.

(b) Recently my husband's been saying that his job is his hobby, but I wonder what a work addict like him is going to do after retirement.

REL

Starting in the 1970s, *workaholic* (work + a + [alco]holic) became more common than *work addict*, and Japanese borrowed this expression in turn (*wākahorikku*).

(1) I consider myself a {work addict/workaholic}, but that doesn't necessarily mean that I'm doing a good job.
私は自分のことを{仕事中毒 / ワーカホリック}だと思っているが、良い仕事をしているとは限らない。

work one's fingers to the bone / phr. / metaphor

to work very hard

REL work one's {tail/butt} off

Examples

(a) Kobayashi worked her fingers to the bone to make sure the project was finished on time.

(b) The farmer worked his fingers to the bone to turn this land into a productive farm.

(c) The new secretary is a good-natured guy who works his fingers to the bone.

Note

The English and Japanese expressions share the same metaphorical meaning, though they have different literal interpretations. Whereas the English literally means that "someone uses their fingers so much that they are whittled down to just the bones," the Japanese means that "someone works very hard without sparing either flesh or bone.

REL

1. The Japanese has the REL *mi o ko ni shite hataraku* (lit. "to work and turn one's body into powder"). 関連語(1)

2. The English has the REL *work one's {tail/butt} off*, which has the same meaning as the main entry, though it should be noted that *work one's butt off* may be considered crude.

仕事中毒 / n. phr. / 隠喩

私生活を犠牲にして、仕事ばかりしている{人 / 状態}

関 ワーカホリック

例文

同僚：マイク、今日も残業につきあってくれるの。

マイク：そう、今日中にこの仕事片付けちゃおうよ。

同僚：ついにマイクも仕事中毒になってしまったか。そんなところは、日本人のまね
をしないで欲しかったけど。

マイク：そんなこと言って、仕事回してくるの誰だよ。

(a) 日本には仕事中毒になって家庭や趣味や交友関係を犠牲にしてしまっている人が
多い。

(b) 夫は最近「オレの趣味は仕事だ」なんて言ってるけど、彼のような仕事中毒が定年
退職したら、何やるんだろう。

関連語

英語は1970年代から *workaholic*（work + a + [alco]holic）を使うほうが多くなっている。
日本語はこれを「ワーカホリック」として借用している。 📖 **REL(1)**

W

骨身を惜しまず働く / phr. / 隠喩

一生懸命働く

関 身を粉にして働く

例文

(a) 小林はプロジェクトが予定通り終わるように、骨身を惜しまず働いた。

(b) 農夫は骨身を惜しまず働いて、この土地を豊かな農地にした。

(c) 新しい秘書は気だてはいいし、骨身を惜しまず働く。

解説

日英語とも"一生懸命働く"という比喩的意味を共有しているが、英語のほうは"指を使って
あまりにも働き過ぎてそれが骨だけになってしまう"というように表現しているのに対して、
日本語のほうは"自分の体と骨を惜しみなく使って働く"というように表現している。

関連語

1. 日本語には、「身を粉にして働く」（lit. 身体が粉になってしまうほど働く）という関連表現があ
る。

(1) 父は子供達全員に高等教育を受けさせるため、{骨身を惜しまず / 身を粉にして}働いた。
The father worked his fingers to the bone to put all of his children through high school.

2. *work one's [tail/butt] off* は見出しと同じ意味を持つ関連表現であるが、このうち *work one's
butt off* は、品がないと見なされることがあるので注意。

703

work hand in hand (with ~) / phr. / metonymy

to do s.t. together with s.o.

REL go hand in hand (with ~)

Examples

(a) We work hand in hand with partners from a wide variety of industries around the world.

(b) We historians worked hand in hand with archaeologists every step of the way.

(c) Japan has to work hand in hand with neighboring Asian countries in order to contribute to improvement in the region.

Note

Work hand in hand (with ~) has the same figurative meaning as ~ to te ni te o totte ~, though the verb totte (to take) is absent in the English.

REL

1. The English has the REL go hand in hand (with ~), which means "for s.t. to accompany s.t. else," but there is no corresponding Japanese REL.

(1) a. Terrorism goes hand in hand with drugs.
テロリズムは麻薬と対になりやすい。
b. Romantic dinners and proposals go hand in hand.
ロマンティックな夕食とプロポーズはうまく合う。

2. The Japanese has the REL te ni te o tazusaete, which can be substituted for the main entry in all the examples, but it is used much less frequently. 📖→ 関連語(2)

work like a horse / phr. / simile

to work very hard

REL workhorse

Examples

Karen: I'm so exhausted! I wonder if I should quit my teaching job.

Saya: But don't you like teaching?

Karen: Yeah, it's an interesting job, but there are so many things that come with teaching, you know? I work like a horse from morning till evening, but there's just no end to it.

- -

(a) I feel like I've been working like a horse all year long.

(b) The new department head had already garnered a reputation for being a terrible person. He would get up at six o'clock every morning and work like a horse, and he insisted that his subordinates do the same.

Note

The only difference between the English and Japanese is that the English uses horse and the Japanese uses basha-uma (a carriage horse).

REL

The English has the REL workhorse, which is a noun used to describe someone or some-

704

手に手を取って   phr.   換喩
て　　て

一緒に何かをする
いっしょ　　なに

関 手に手を携えて
て　て　　たずさ

例 文
(a) 私達は世界中のさまざまな企業と、手に手を取ってやっています。
わたしたち　せ かいじゅう　　　　　　　　　　　　　　　き ぎょう　　　て　て　と

(b) 私達歴史家は、全行程にわたり考古学者と手に手を取って仕事をしてきた。
わたしたちれきし か　　ぜんこうてい　　　　　こう こ がくしゃ　て　て　と　　し ごと

(c) 日本は近隣のアジア諸国と手に手を取って、アジアをよりよくするために貢献し
に ほん　きんりん　　　　　　しょこく　て　て　と　　　　　　　　　　　　　　　　　　こうけん
なければならない。

解 説
英語の *work hand in hand (with ~)* は日本語の「(~と)手に手を取って(~をする)」と比喩的な
意味は同じだが、日本語の動詞の「取って」は英語には出てこない。

関連語
1. 英語には *go hand in hand (with ~)* という関連表現がある。"一つのことがもう一つのことを
伴う"という意味である。日本語にはそれに対応する関連表現はない。━📖 **REL(1)**
2. 日本語には「手に手を携えて」という関連表現があり、見出しと置き換え可能であるが、使用
頻度は低い。
(2) 私達歴史家は、全行程にわたり考古学者と{手に手を取って / 手に手を携えて}仕事をしてき
た。(→(b))

馬車馬のように働く   phr.   直喩
ば　しゃうま　　　　　　　　はたら　　　　　　　　　ちょく ゆ

一生懸命、必死に働く
いっしょうけんめい　ひっ し　はたら

例 文
カレン: あ～あ、疲れたな。もう、教師の仕事、辞めようかな。
つか　　　　　　　きょう し　し ごと　や

さや: だって、教えること好きなんでしょ。
おし　　　　　す

カレン: うん、それはおもしろいんだけど、付随する仕事がすごくって。馬車馬のよ
ふ ずい　し ごと　　　　　　　　ば しゃうま
うに朝から晩まで働いても、ぜんぜん終わらないんだもん。
あさ　　ばん　　はたら　　　　　　　　　　お

(a) 一年中ずっと馬車馬のように働いてきた感じがします。
いちねんじゅう　　ば しゃうま　　　　はたら　　　　かん

(b) 新しい部長は恐ろしい人間だという評判がすでに立っていた。朝は6時に起き、
あたら　　ぶ ちょう　おそ　　　にんげん　　　ひょうばん　　　た　　　　あさ　　じ　お
馬車馬のように働き、部下にも同じように働くことを要求した。
ば しゃうま　　　　はたら　ぶ か　　おな　　　　　　はたら　　　　ようきゅう

解 説
日英語の唯一の違いは日本語は「馬車馬」で、英語はただ *horse* (馬)が使われている点である。

関連語
英語の関連表現 *workhorse* (lit. 使役馬)は、疲れることなく働き続ける人や物を表現するとき
に使われる。日本語では「働き蜂」がそれにあたる。━📖 **REL(1)**

705

thing that works tirelessly. The Japanese equivalent is *hataraki-bachi* (worker bee).

(1) That guy is a workhorse. He stays in the office until midnight almost every day.
あいつはまったく働き蜂さ。ほとんど毎日、深夜までオフィスにいるよ。

work under ~ / phr. / metaphor

to have s.o. overseeing one's work

Examples

Friend: Have you worked under Professor Mackey?

Karen: Yeah, I did a couple of years back. He was wonderful. I learned a lot from him. Unfortunately, I won't have another chance to work under such a great professor.

- -

(a) From May to June of 1991, I worked under the supervision of department chief Kobayashi.

(b) I'm currently working under Professor Smith in the Department of Computer Science.

Notes

1. *Under* is a spatial preposition, while *shita/moto* (under/below) is a spatial noun. Their spatial definitions can be expanded figuratively to suggest "being supervised or controlled by s.o."

2. The kanji 下 can be read as either *shita* or *moto*, though the latter is more appropriate for written Japanese.

The world revolves around s.o. / phr. / metaphor

s.o.'s situation is more important than other people's

REL s.o.'s world revolves around {s.o./s.t.}

Examples

Mrs. S: Auntie is so self-centered.

Mr. S: She thinks the world revolves around her. Let's just avoid her.

- -

(a) The emperor was an arrogant young ruler who thought the world revolved around him.

(b) Jo still believes the world revolves around him and can't imagine that anything else could be more important.

Notes

1. The English is usually preceded by verbs such as *think*, as in the dialogue and (a), or *believe*, as in (b). Similarly, the Japanese is usually followed by verbs such as *omou* (to feel), as in the dialogue, *kangaeru* (to think), as in (a), and *shinjiru* (to believe), as in (b).

2. Note that the Japanese expression uses *jibun o chūshin ni* (making oneself the center), whereas the English uses *around s.o.*

REL

The English REL is *s.o.'s world revolves around {s.o./s.t.}*, which means that someone or something is very important in someone's life.

（〜の）下で働く　**phr.**　隠喩

｛雇用者/上司｝の支配の及ぶところで仕事をする

例文

友達：カレン、マッキー先生の下で働いたことあるの？

カレン：うん、何年か前にね。すばらしい先生で本当に多くのことを学んだわ。あんな先生の下で働けるチャンスはもう二度とないわね、残念だけど。

(a) 1991年の5月から6月まで、小林部長の監督の下で働きました。

(b) 現在私はコンピュータサイエンス学科のスミス教授の下で働いている。

解説

1. 日英語の「下」と under（下）はそれぞれ空間を表す名詞、前置詞であるが、"〜によって｛監督/コントロール｝される"という比喩的な意味に拡張している。

2. 「下」という漢字は「した」とも「もと」とも読めるが、後者のほうがより書き言葉的である。

世界は自分を中心に回っている　**phr.**　隠喩

とても自己中心的である

例文

鈴木（妻）：本当にあの叔母は自分勝手で我がままなんだから。

鈴木（夫）：世界は自分を中心に回っていると思ってんだよ。ほっとこう。

(a) 皇帝は高慢な若い為政者で、世界は自分を中心に回っていると考えていた。

(b) ジョーは今でも世界は自分を中心に回っていると信じていて、自分よりもっと大切なものが一つでもあることが想像できない。

解説

1. 英語では通例、会話例と(a)のように think（考える）か、(b)のように believe（信じる）といった動詞が先行する。日本語でも会話例のように「思う」、(a)のように「考える」や、(b)のように「信じる」が後続することが多い。

2. 英語は「自分を中心に」とは言わず、around s.o.（自分のまわりを）と言っていることに注意。

関連語

英語の関連表現の s.o.'s world revolves around ｛s.o./s.t.｝（lit. ｛誰か/何か｝が｛誰か/何か｝の周りを回る）は誰かの人生において、とても大切な人や物を意味する。　**REL(1)**

(1) Ever since she became a mother, Susan's world has revolved around her baby boy.
母親になってからというもの、スーザンの世界は息子の周りだけで回っている。

worst-case scenario, the / n. phr. / metaphor

the worst possible state of affairs

ANT the best-case scenario

Examples

Kenta: The World Cup has finally started, but we probably can't expect much from the Japan team, can we?

Mr. S: I hope they at least make it to the final round. I'd like them to avoid the worst-case scenario of being eliminated during the qualifying rounds.

- -

(a) We have to be prepared for the worst-case scenario, in which the smallpox virus is spread and triggers a global pandemic.

(b) If a company is prepared for the worst-case scenario, then it is ready to deal with smaller mishaps as well.

Note

The Japanese expression is a direct translation of the English. Note, however, that the Japanese does not mention *case*.

REL

Shinario (scenario) can be replaced by *suji-gaki* (outline/plot), but the latter is used infrequently. 📖→関連語(1)

ANT

The English ANT, *the best-case scenario*, is used as frequently as *the worst-case scenario*, but *saizen no shinario* is used much less frequently than *saiaku no shinario*.

(1) The best-case scenario is one where all parties evaluate the current situation realistically as well as how it may change in the short and long term.
最善のシナリオは関係者が現実的に現状を評価し、その短期的、長期的変化を評価するということだ。

最悪のシナリオ / n. phr. / 隠喩

予想し得る最も悪い状態

関 最悪の筋書き

反 最善のシナリオ

例文

健太：いよいよワールドカップが始まったけど、今回の日本チームはあまり期待できないね。

鈴木(夫)：せめて、決勝ラウンドに残れればよしだな。予選ラウンド落ちなんていう、最悪のシナリオだけは回避してほしいね。

- -

(a) 天然痘ウィルスが散布されて世界的に流行するといった、最悪のシナリオに備えておかなければならない。

(b) 会社が最悪のシナリオに備えておけば、小さな災難にも応じる準備ができていることになる。

解説

日本語は英語からの直訳である。ただし、日本語には英語の *case*(場合)はないことに注意。

関連語

日本語では「シナリオ」を「筋書き」と置き換えることはできるが、使用頻度は低い。

(1) 会社が最悪の{シナリオ/筋書き}に備えておけば、小さな災難にも応じる準備ができていることになる。(→(b))

反意語

日本語の反意語の「最善のシナリオ」の使用頻度は「最悪のシナリオ」よりもはるかに低いが、英語の反意語の *the best-case scenario* は *the worst-case scenario* 同様よく使われている。

→ ANT(1)

W

709

■日本語見出し・五十音順索引・Japanese Entry/Syllabary Index

あ

愛の巣 あい す	love nest	413
青筋を立てて怒る あおすじ た おこ	burst a blood vessel	123
青二才 あお にさい	greenhorn	287
赤狩り あか が	red scare	523
赤字 あかじ	be in the red	51
赤信号 あかしんごう	red flag	523
赤ちゃん言葉 あか ことば	baby talk	29
(トンネルの先に)明かりが見える さき あ み	light at the end of the tunnel	385
上がる あ	rise	529
明るい面を見る あか めん み	look on the bright side (of ~)	403
明るみに出る あか で	come to light	165
(~の)アキレス腱 けん	Achilles' heel	19
悪循環 あくじゅんかん	vicious {circle/cycle}	671
悪夢 あくむ	bad dream, a	31
あごがはずれる{ほど/くらい/ぐらい}	one's jaw drops	351
浅い あさ	shallow	557
足が凍りつく あし こお	{get/have} cold feet	271
(~の)足かせ{に/と}なる あし	be a fetter on ~	37
足が地に着いている あし ち つ	have one's feet on the ground	307
(~を)味わう あじ	taste	635
足({元/下})をすくわれる あし もと もと	sweep s.o. off (of) {his/her} feet	619
足を引っぱる あし ひ	pull s.o.'s leg	493
足を踏み入れる あし ふ い	get one's foot in the door	261
汗を{かく/流す} あせ なが	sweat	619
(~に)遊びがある あそ	play	475
(~に~を)与える あた	give s.t. to {s.o./s.t.}	271
温(暖)かい/温(暖)かな あた あた あた あた	warm	681
~の頭 あたま	head of ~	317
頭数 あたまかず	head count	315
頭が真っ白になる あたま ま しろ	one's mind goes blank	425
頭が割れるように痛い あたま わ いた	splitting headache	597
頭越し(に) あたまご	go over s.o.'s head	277
頭に叩き込む あたま たた こ	beat ~ into s.o.'s head	73
頭の上を通り過ぎる あたま うえ とお す	go over s.o.'s head	277
頭の後ろに(も)目がついている あたま うし め	have eyes in the back of one's head	305
頭のてっぺんから爪先まで あたま つまさき	from head to toe	255
頭割り あたまわ	per head	473
頭を{空/空っぽ}にする あたま から から	{empty/clear} one's head (of)	219
頭を絞る あたま しぼ	rack one's brain(s)	507
頭を使う あたま つか	use one's head	669
頭を冷やす あたま ひ	keep a cool head	355
新しい血 あたら ち	new blood	441
後味が悪い あとあじ わる	leave a bad taste (in one's mouth)	375
後の祭り あと まつ	day after the fair, a	183
あと一押し ひとお	one more push	453
跡をたどる あと	trace	655

■日本語見出し・五十音順索引・Japanese Entry/Syllabary Index

穴があったら入りたい あな　はい	crawl into a hole and die	171
（〜に）穴をあける あな	make a hole in ~	415
穴を埋める あな　う	fill {a/the} hole(s)	241
あぶり出す だ	smoke out	583
甘い声 あま　こえ	sweet voice	621
飴と鞭 あめ　むち	carrot-{and/or}-stick	141
操り人形（だ） あやつ　にんぎょう	be a puppet	39
嵐の前の静けさ あらし　まえ　しず	calm before the storm, the	131
嵐を乗り越える あらし　の　こ	ride {out the storm/ the storm out}	527
暗雲が漂う あんうん　ただよ	dark clouds ~ (on the horizon)	181
暗礁に乗り上げる あんしょう　の　あ	on the rocks	447
暗中模索（する） あんちゅうもさく	grope in the dark	289

い

生き返る い　かえ	come back to life	163
生き字引 い　じびき	walking {dictionary/ encyclopedia}, a	677
息を呑む いき　の	breathtaking	111
石頭の いしあたま	bull-headed	121
意志あるところに道あり い　し　みち	Where there's a will, there's a way.	693
意識の流れ いしき　なが	stream of consciousness	611
石のように固い いし　かた	(as) hard as (a) rock	295
椅子から（転げ）落ちる い　す　ころ　お {ほど/くらい/ぐらい}	fall {off/out of} one's chair	233
椅子の脚 い　す　あし	chair('s) legs	187
（椅子の）背（もたれ） い　す　せ	back	29

痛いところ いた	sore spot	591
一条の光 いちじょう　ひかり	ray of sunshine, a	513
一枚岩 いちまいいわ	monolithic	427
（〜の）一面しか見ない いちめん　み	see only one side (of ~)	543
一文惜しみの百知らず いちもん　お　ひゃく　し	Penny(-)wise and pound(-)foolish.	471
一石二鳥 いっせき　に　ちょう	kill two birds with one stone	363
一銭の価値もない いっせん　か　ち	not worth a dime	445
一線を越える いっせん　こ	cross (over) {a/the} line	173
（〜を）一掃する いっそう	make a clean sweep of ~	413
（〜と）一体{と/に}なる いったい	become one with ~	75
{〜が/で}いっぱい	full of ~; ~ is full	257
一匹狼 いっぴきおおかみ	lone wolf	401
一歩一歩 いっぽ　いっぽ	step by step	605
一歩先を行く いっぽ　さき　い	be one step ahead	57
一歩先を行く いっぽ　さき　い	one step ahead (of ~)	453
犬かき いぬ	dog paddle	197
犬死する いぬじに	die like a dog	189
犬のように忠実 いぬ　ちゅうじつ	(as) faithful as a dog	227
茨の道 いばら　みち	thorny path, {a/the}	639
（〜の）イロハ	ABCs of ~, the	17

う

（〜に）餓える う	be starved {for/of} ~	63
浮き彫りに{する/される /なる}	{throw/bring} s.t. into (sharp) relief	641
動く（動き） うご　うご	move	433

711

（〜を）失う うしな	lose ~	405
有頂天{だ/になる} うちょうてん	float on air	247
腕まくりをする うで	roll up one's sleeves	533
鵜呑みにする うの	swallow s.t. {whole/completely}	617
馬面 うまづら	horse face	337
（〜を）生む う	breed	111
埋もれる う	be buried in ~	45
右翼 うよく	right wing/right-wing	529
浦島太郎{のよう/みたい}な うらしまたろう	like (a) Rip Van Winkle	391
裏で糸を引く うら いと ひ	pull the strings	495
裏取り引き うらと ひ	backroom ~	31
裏も表も{知っている/知る} うら おもて し し	know ~ inside (and) out	365
瓜二つ うりふた	like two peas in a pod	391
噂を広める うわさ ひろ	spread rumors	599

え

餌に食いつく えさ く	take the bait	629
（〜の）餌食{に/と}なる えじき	fall prey to ~	235
絵に描いた餅 え か もち	pie in the sky, (a)	473
絵のようにきれい え	(as) pretty as a picture	489
炎上する えんじょう	flame	245
煙幕を張る えんまく は	put up a smokescreen	505

お

〜王 おう	king	365
黄金時代 おうごんじだい	golden age	281

（〜に/の）王道はない おうどう	There is no royal road to ~	637
オウム返し がえ	parrot	465
狼少年 おおかみしょうねん	cry wolf	175
大口をたたく おおぐち	have a big mouth	301
陸に上がった河童{のよう/みたい}な おか あ かっぱ	like a fish out of water	387
お金を崩す かね くず	break (a bill)	103
押しが強い お つよ	pushy	497
遅咲き（の花） おそざ はな	late bloomer	367
お手上げ て あ	throw up one's hands	641
おとぎ話（のような） ばなし	(sound) like a fairy tale	387
お山の大将 やま たいしょう	king of the hill	365
同じ線である おな せん	along the same lines	25
（〜と）同じ道を歩む おな みち あゆ	{follow/walk} the same path as ~	253
同じ屋根の下で暮らす おな やね した く	live under the same roof	397
お涙頂戴 なみだちょうだい	tearjerker	635
汚名 おめい	bad name	33
重い気持ちで おも きも	with (a) heavy heart	699
温室育ち おんしつそだ	hothouse; hothouse flower	339

か

カードを握る にぎ	hold (all) the cards	331
飼い犬に手を噛まれる か いぬ て か	bite the hand that feeds you	85
怪物 かいぶつ	monster	429
〜返す かえ	~ back	29

■日本語見出し・五十音順索引・Japanese Entry/Syllabary Index

蛙の面に{水/小便} かえる つら みず しょうべん	like water off a duck's back	393
顔色を読む かおいろ よ	read s.o.'s face	519
顔が曇る かお くも	one's face clouds (over)	225
顔に書いてある かお か	be written all over one's face	69
顔に泥を塗る かお どろ ぬ	get egg all over one's face	261
顔を曇らせる かお くも	one's face clouds (over)	225
顔を見せる かお み	show one's face	565
(〜に)かかっている	hang {on/upon} ~	293
輝く かがや	shine	561
かきまわす	stir s.o. up	609
嗅ぎ回る か まわ	nose around	443
(〜の)鍵を握る かぎ にぎ	hold the key (to ~)	333
(〜の)核心に迫る かくしん せま	get to the core of ~	269
(〜の)影におびえる かげ	be afraid of one's own shadow	41
(〜に)影を落とす かげ お	cast a shadow over ~	143
かごの(中の)鳥 なか とり	caged bird	129
過去を葬る かこ ほうむ	bury the past	123
風見鶏 かざ み どり	weather vane	689
風向きを知る かざ む し	see which way the wind {blows/is blowing}	547
舵のない船{のような/みたい}な かじ ふね	like a ship without a rudder	389
風{のよう/みたい}に かぜ	like the wind	391
片思い かたおも	one-sided love	455
(〜の)形を取る かたち と	take shape (as ~)	629

かたつむりのようにのろい	(as) slow as a snail	579
肩に(のし)かかる かた	fall (squarely) on s.o.'s shoulders	235
肩の荷が下りる かた に お	{load/weight} off one's shoulders, a	397
(〜に)傾く かたむ	lean toward(s) ~	373
肩を叩く かた たた	tap s.o.'s shoulder	633
肩を落とす かた お	drop one's shoulders	211
肩をすくめる かた	shrug one's shoulders	569
肩を並べて かた なら	shoulder to shoulder (with ~)	565
型を破る かた やぶ	break the mold	109
勝ち馬に乗る か うま の	get on the bandwagon	265
火中の栗を拾う か ちゅう くり ひろ	pull the chestnuts out of the fire	493
カットする	cut	177
角が取れる かど と	smooth (out) the rough edges	585
金づち かな	sink like a {rock/stone}	573
金が物を言う かね もの い	Money talks.	425
金をかき集める かね あつ	rake in ~	511
壁 かべ	wall	677
壁にぶつかる かべ	hit {a/the} wall	329
壁に耳あり かべ みみ	The walls have ears.	679
壁の花 かべ はな	wallflower	679
神の仕業 かみ しわざ	act of God, an	19
(いい)カモ	sitting duck	575
からすの足跡 あしあと	crow's-feet	175

713

体を売る からだ う	sell one's body	551
空約束 そらやくそく	empty promise	219
殻を破る から やぶ	come out of one's shell	165
(〜の)側に立つ がわ た	take {s.o.'s side/ sides}	629
(〜にとって(の))癌(だ) がん	be cancerous to 〜	47
間一髪で かんいっぱつ	{by/within} a hair's breadth	125
棺桶に片足を突っ込む かんおけ かたあし つ こ	have one foot in the grave	311
考えが動く かんが うご	be moved	55
考えをまとめる かんが	{get/put} one's thoughts together	267
観点 かんてん	point of view; viewpoint	479
顔面蒼白{になる/だ} がんめんそうはく	face turns white	227

き

機会をとらえる き かい	seize {an/the} opportunity	549
(〜のための)機が熟す き じゅく	time is ripe (for/to 〜), the	649
聞き耳を立てる き みみ た	prick up one's ears	489
刻み付けられる きざ つ	be engraved in 〜	51
(〜を)築く きず	build	117
傷口に塩を{塗る/すり込む} きずぐち しお ぬ こ	rub salt {in/ into} {the/s.o.'s} wound(s)	535
傷口をなめる きずぐち	lick one's wounds	383
規則を曲げる きそく ま	bend the rules	77
期待の{星/新星} き たい ほし しんせい	rising star	531
汚いことをする きたな	play dirty	475
(〜の気持ち)を傷つける きも きず	hurt s.o.'s feelings	339

キツネのようにずる(賢)い がしこ	sly as a fox	581
絹のようになめらか きぬ	(as) {smooth/soft} as {velvet/silk}	583
牙を抜く きば ぬ	draw {s.o.'s/s.t.'s} teeth	205
牙をむく きば	{show/bare} one's teeth	569
気分が沈む き ぶん しず	one's heart sinks	321
基本に立ち返る き ほん た かえ	go back to the basics	275
気持ちが動く き も うご	be moved	55
気持ちが沈む き も しず	one's heart sinks	321
(自分の)気持ちを隠す じ ぶん き も かく	hide one's feelings	327
気持ちをぶちまける き も	pour one's heart out to 〜	485
脚光を浴びる きゃっこう あ	be {under/in} the spotlight	67
吸収する きゅうしゅう	soak up	591
窮鼠猫を噛む きゅうそねこ か	A doomed mouse will bite a cat if he has no choice.	197
行間を読む ぎょうかん よ	read between the lines	517
共通の基盤 きょうつう き ばん	common ground	167
興味を引く きょうみ ひ	draw s.o.'s interest	203
〜{から/と/に}距離を置く きょり お	distance oneself from 〜	193
キレる	snap	589
岐路に立つ き ろ た	stand at a crossroads	601
木を見て森を見ず き み もり み	can't see the forest for the trees	137
近視眼的(な) きん し がんてき	shortsighted	563
禁断の果実 きんだん か じつ	forbidden fruit	253

714

■日本語見出し・五十音順索引・Japanese Entry/Syllabary Index

金の卵 きん　たまご	(goose that lays the) golden egg, the	281

く

空中楼閣 くうちゅうろうかく	castle(s) in the air, (a)	145
空腹 くうふく	empty stomach, (on) an	221
釘付けになる くぎづ	nail down	433
くさい	(s.t.) smell(s) fishy	581
腐ったリンゴ くさ	bad apple	31
草の根（の〜） くさ　ね	grass roots; grassroots 〜	285
下り坂 くだ　ざか	be over the hill	59
口伝えで くちづた	by word of mouth	129
口止め料 くち ど　りょう	hush money	341
口に気をつける くち　き	watch one's mouth	685
唇を噛む くちびる　か	bite one's lip	83
口を閉ざす くち　と	shut one's mouth	569
口を開く くち　ひら	open one's mouth	459
（自分の）国を売る じ ぶん　くに　う	sell one's country	551
苦杯をなめる くはい	drink (from) {a/the} bitter cup (of 〜)	207
（〜の）首が飛ぶ くび　と	heads {will/are going to} roll	317
首をかける くび	risk one's neck	533
首を横に振る くび　よこ　ふ	shake one's head	557
蜘蛛の子を散らすように く も　こ　ち	scatter like flies	541
曇りのない目（で見る） くも　め　み	(see) with unclouded eyes	701
暗い くら	dark	179
暮らしの{断面/一面/側面} く　だんめん いちめん そく めん	slice of life/slice-of-life	577

（〜に）狂っている くる	be mad about 〜	53

け

（〜に）敬意を払う けいい　はら	pay one's respects to 〜	471
計画を立てる けいかく　た	build a plan	119
計算高い けいさんだか	be calculating	45
警鐘 けいしょう	alarm, {an/the}	23
けだもの	beast, a	71
血縁関係 けつえんかんけい	blood-relationship	93
血肉を分けた〜 けつにく　わ	one's own flesh and blood	463
結論に達する けつろん　たっ	reach {a/the} conclusion	513
（〜の）解毒剤（だ） げ どくざい	be an antidote to 〜	41
煙と消える けむり　き	go up in smoke	279
犬猿の仲だ けんえん　なか	fight like cats and dogs	239
健康（的）な けんこう　てき	healthy	319
建設的な意見 けんせつてき　い けん	constructive criticism	169
権力にしがみつく けんりょく	cling to power	155
剣を交える けん　まじ	cross swords with 〜	175

こ

恋に落ちる こい　お	fall in love with 〜	231
恋は盲目 こい　もうもく	Love is blind.	411
合意に達する ごうい　たっ	reach an agreement	515
抗議の嵐 こうぎ　あらし	storm of protest	611
公共の目 こうきょう　め	public eye, the	491
攻撃する こうげき	attack	27
（〜の）洪水 こうずい	flood of 〜, a	249

715

鋼鉄のように硬い	(as) hard as steel	295
声	voice	673
声が割れる	one's voice cracks	673
呉越同舟	be in the same boat	53
超える	beyond	79
氷のように冷たい	(as) cold as ice	161
心（が）温まる	heartwarming	325
心が痛む	one's heart aches for s.o.	319
心が狭い	narrow-minded	437
心の痛み	ache in one's heart	17
心の重荷が取れる	take a load off one's mind	625
心の琴線に触れる	{tug/pull} at {s.o.'s/ the} heartstrings	659
心の声に従う	follow one's heart	253
心の底から	from the bottom of one's heart	255
（〜の）心を奪う	steal s.o.'s heart	603
心を勝ち取る	win s.o.'s heart	695
心を捕らえる	capture s.o.'s heart	139
（〜に）心を開く	open one's heart (to ~)	455
（〜に）心を開く	open one's mind (to ~)	457
心をよぎる	cross one's mind	173
心を読む	read s.o.'s mind	519
骨子	bare bones of ~, the	35
コップの中の嵐	tempest in a teapot, a	635

（〜の）言葉に踊らされる	dance to s.o.'s tune	179
言葉に重みがある	s.o.'s words carry weight	701
この世を去る	leave this {life/ world}	375
五里霧中	(all) in a {fog/haze}	343
壊れた家庭	broken home	115
壊れたレコード{のよう/ みたい}	broken record	117

さ

最悪のシナリオ	worst-case scenario, the	709
歳月人を待たず	Time and tide wait for no man.	645
最後に笑う	have the last laugh	313
最前線に立つ	be on the front lines	55
賽は投げられた	The die is cast.	189
財布が軽い	light purse	385
財布の底をはたく	bet one's bottom dollar	79
財布のひもを握る	hold the purse strings	333
雑魚	small fry	581
刺すような痛み	stabbing pain	601
さびつく	be rusty	61
左翼	left wing/left-wing	377
ざるに水を注ぐ	pour water into a sieve	487
猿真似	Monkey see, monkey do.	427
（〜と言って）騒ぐ	make noise (about ~)	419

716

■日本語見出し・五十音順索引・Japanese Entry/Syllabary Index

三角関係 さんかくかんけい	love triangle	413

し

幸せの星のもとに生まれ しあわ　ほし　う る	be born under a lucky star	43
時間との競争 じかん　きょうそう	race against time, a	507
時間を稼ぐ じかん　かせ	buy time	125
時間をつぶす じかん	kill time	361
時間を取る じかん　と	take the time (to ~)	631
仕事中毒 しごとちゅうどく	work addict	703
紙上で しじょう	on paper	447
（～に）自信をなくす じしん	lose confidence (in ~)	407
地滑り的勝利 じすべ　てきしょうり	landslide (victory)	367
自尊心を傷つける じそんしん　きず	hurt s.o.'s pride	339
時代の{先/先端}を行く じだい　　さきせんたん　い	ahead of the times	23
舌が滑る した　すべ	slip of the tongue, a	577
舌がもつれる した	{get/be} tongue- tied	269
（～の）下で働く した　はたら	work under ~	707
舌なめずりをする した	{lick/smack} one's lips	381
舌の先まで出かかってい した　さき　で る	be on the tip of one's tongue	57
しっぽを巻く ま	with one's tail between one's legs	699
視点 してん	point of view; viewpoint	479
死ぬほど し	to death	651
死の影 し　かげ	shadow of death, the	555
（～に）縛られる しば	be tied up with ~	65

自分だけの世界に じぶん　　せかい	in a world of one's own	343
（自分で）自分の首をしめ じぶん　じぶん　くび る	cut one's own throat	177
（～として）自分を売り込 じぶん　う　こ む	sell oneself (as ~)	549
締め出す し　だ	shut out	571
釈迦に説法 しゃか　せっぽう	preach to the choir	489
十字架を背負う じゅうじか　せお	carry {a/one's} cross	141
十字砲火 じゅうじほうか	crossfire	175
じゅうたん爆撃 ばくげき	carpet-bomb	141
充電する じゅうでん	recharge one's batteries	521
出世の階段を上がる しゅっせ　かいだん　あ	climb the ladder of success	155
十中八九 じゅうちゅうはっく	nine (times) out of ten	443
順風満帆 じゅんぷうまんぱん	smooth sailing	585
将棋の駒 しょうぎ　こま	pawn	469
状況が許せば じょうきょう　ゆる	circumstances permitting	151
冗談が過ぎる じょうだん　す	{be/go} beyond a joke	43
冗談はさておき じょうだん	joking aside	353
情熱（の炎） じょうねつ　ほのお	flame(s) of passion	245
将来が明るい しょうらい　あか	future {looks/is} bright	259
勝利に酔う しょうり　よ	be intoxicated with victory	53
勝利の栄冠を得る しょうり　えいかん　え	be crowned with victory	47
植物状態 しょくぶつじょうたい	vegetative state	671
知らぬが仏 し　　ほとけ	Ignorance is bliss.	341

717

白旗を掲げる しらはた かか	raise the white flag	511
尻すぼみになる しり	tail off	621
白か黒か しろ くろ	black and white	87
白黒(を)つける しろくろ	see things in black and white	545
神経戦 しんけいせん	war of nerves	681
神経に障る しんけい さわ	get on s.o.'s nerves	263
神経を{静/鎮}める しんけい しず しず	calm s.o.'s nerves	133
人生のスパイス じんせい	spice of life, the	597
人生の黄昏(時) じんせい たそがれ どき	twilight (of one's life/career/etc.), the	665
心臓が{止まる/止まりそ しんぞう と と うになる}	one's heart stops	323
死んだ し	be dead	47
新天地を切り開く しんてんち き ひら	break new ground	107
侵入 しんにゅう	invasion	347
芯まで腐っている しん くさ	be rotten to the core	59
神話 しん わ	myth	433

す

(～のために)水火も辞さ すい か じ ない	go through fire and water (for ~)	279
水晶のように透き通って すいしょう す とお いる	(as) clear as crystal	153
吸い尽くす す つ	suck {s.t./s.o.} dry	615
頭痛の種 ずつう	source of headaches	593
(～を)捨てる す	dump	215
頭脳流出 ず のうりゅうしゅつ	brain drain	101
頭脳労働者 ず のうろうどうしゃ	brain worker	101
すべての道はローマに通 みち つう ず	All roads lead to Rome.	25

(～に)すべての目が注が め そそ れる	all eyes are on ~	25
スポット(ライト)を浴び あ る	be {under/in} the spotlight	67
炭のように黒い すみ くろ	(as) black as coal	87
鋭い するど	sharp	559

せ

生活のスパイス せいかつ	spice of life, the	597
生活の{断面/一面/側面} せいかつ だんめん いちめん そくめん	slice of life/slice-of-life	577
成功の階段を上がる せいこう かいだん あ	climb the ladder of success	155
(～に)精魂(を)傾ける せいこん かたむ	put one's (heart and) soul into ~	503
生死の境 せい し さかい	between life and death	79
聖戦 せいせん	holy war	335
青天のへきれき せいてん	bolt {from/out of} the blue, a	95
世界は自分を中心に回っ せ かい じ ぶん ちゅうしん まわ ている	The world revolves around s.o.	707
{世界/世間}は{小さい/ せ かい せ けん ちい 狭い}	(it's a) small world	581
背筋がぞくぞくする せ すじ	chill runs down one's spine, a	149
狭い せま	narrow	435
(～に)背を向ける せ む	turn one's back on ~	659
線 せん	line	395
全身を耳にする ぜんしん みみ	be all ears	41
全体像をつかむ ぜんたいぞう	get the (whole) picture	267
洗脳する せんのう	brainwash	101
(一)線を引く いっ せん ひ	draw {a/the} line (between ~ and ~)	201

■ 日本語見出し・五十音順索引・Japanese Entry/Syllabary Index

そ

総決算の時 そうけっさん とき	day of reckoning, the	183
象牙の塔 ぞうげ とう	ivory tower	349
その上（に） うえ	on top of that	451

た

第一歩 だいいっ ぽ	first step, the	245
大海の一滴 たいかい いってき	drop in the bucket, a	211
大黒柱 だいこくばしら	pillar of strength, a	475
太鼓腹 たい こ ばら	potbelly	483
態度を硬化させる たい ど こうか	harden s.o.'s attitude	295
台風の目（の中にいる） たいふう め なか	(in the) eye of the {storm/hurricane}	223
体面を保つ たいめん たも	save face	539
ダイヤの原石 げんせき	diamond in the rough, a	187
タオルを投げる な	throw in the towel	639
高い たか	high	327
蛇行する だこう	snake one's way	587
（〜に/から）叩かれる たた	take a beating (from ~)	623
畳の上で死ぬ たたみ うえ し	die in one's bed	187
（{〜についての/の}）立場 たち ば	where one stands (on ~)	691
手綱を締める た づな し	keep a tight {rein/leash} on ~	359
手綱を取る た づな と	take (up) the reins (of ~)	631
（〜に）脱帽する だつぼう	one's hat is off to ~	297
棚上げにする たな あ	put ~ on the shelf	501
たぬき寝入りをする ねい	play possum	477

ち

（〜の）種をまく たね	sow (the) seeds (of ~)	593
（〜に）魂を売る たましい う	sell one's soul to ~	553

（自分を）小さく感じる じ ぶん ちい かん	feel small	239
{〜に/と}近い ちか	close to ~	159
近い ちか	near	439
血が凍る ち こお	blood freezes	91
（〜に〜の）血が流れている ち なが	run in {s.o.'s/the} blood	537
知識が（幅）広い ち しき はば ひろ	have (a) wide knowledge of ~	315
血と汗と涙 ち あせ なみだ	blood, sweat, and tears	93
血の海 ち うみ	sea of blood	543
地の果てまで ち は	to the ends of the earth	653
血のように赤い ち あか	(as) red as blood	523
血は水よりも濃い ち みず こ	Blood is thicker than water.	91
（〜に）注意を払う ちゅうい はら	pay attention to ~	471
注意を引く ちゅうい ひ	draw s.o.'s attention	203
宙に浮いたままだ ちゅう う	be up in the air	67
（〜を）鳥瞰する ちょうかん	(take a) bird's eye view of ~	83
長蛇の列 ちょうだ れつ	snake of a line	587
血を沸き立たせる ち わ た	make s.o.'s blood boil	417
沈黙は金（なり） ちんもく きん	Silence is golden.	573

つ

（〜に）ついていく	follow	251
（〜を）つかむ	grasp	283

719

机の脚	desk('s) legs	187
(～に)包まれる	be wrapped in ~	69
つなぐ	connect	167
(～を)つなぐ橋	bridge between	113
綱渡り(をする)	walk a tightrope	675
角(を)突き合わせる	lock horns (with ~)	399
冷たい	cold	161
強い	strong	613
面の皮が厚い	thick-skinned	637

て

手	hand	291
帝国	empire, {an/the}	217
(～で)手(が)いっぱい	have one's hands full (with ~)	307
テーブルの脚	table('s) legs	187
手が要る	need a hand	441
～的な味わい	flavor	247
てこ	leverage	381
手近に	close at hand	157
鉄の意志	iron will	349
鉄砲玉のように	like a bullet out of a gun	385
鉄面皮{の/な}	brazen-faced	103
(～を)手に入れる	get one's hands on ~	263
手に負えない	get out of hand	265
(～の)手に落ちる	fall into the hands of ~	233
手に手を取って	work hand in hand (with ~)	705
手の内を見せる	show one's hand	567

手元に{ある/(おいて)おく/持っている}	have (s.t.) on hand	309
手元に置く	keep s.t. on hand	361
(～に)照らして{みる/考える}	in light of ~	345
(～に)手を貸す	{lend (s.o.)/give s.o.} a hand	379
手をこまねく	sit on one's hands	573
(～に)手をつける	set one's hand to (~)	553
手をつなぐ	join hands	353
(～から)手を引く	wash one's hands of ~	685
手を汚す	dirty one's hands	191
点	point	479
(～の)点数を稼ぐ	earn points (with ~)	215
天の恵み	manna from heaven	421

と

同一線上にある	along the same lines	25
銅像のように動かない	(as) still as a statue	609
胴体着陸	belly landing	77
堂々巡りをする	go {around/round} in circles	273
透明性	transparency	657
遠い	distant	195
(～で/として)通る	pass (as/for ~)	467
(～に)通る	pass (~)	467
時がいやしてくれる	Time is a great healer.	647
時が教えてくれる	(only) time will tell	649

■日本語見出し・五十音順索引・ Japanese Entry/Syllabary Index

時の人 <small>とき ひと</small>	{man/woman} of the hour, the	419
時は金なり <small>とき かね</small>	Time is money.	647
毒 <small>どく</small>	poison (for/to) ~, (a)	481
時計の針を(元に)戻す <small>と けい はり もと もど</small>	turn back the clock	661
床につく <small>とこ</small>	take to (one's) bed	633
年を感じる <small>とし かん</small>	feel one's age	237
隣の芝生は{青い/青く見える} <small>となり しばふ あお あお み</small>	The grass is (always) greener (on the other side of the fence).	283
(~に)飛びつく <small>と</small>	jump at ~	355
(~(へ)の)扉を開く <small>とびら ひら</small>	open the door {to/for} ~	459
どぶに金を捨てる <small>かね す</small>	pour money down the drain	487
ドミノ現象 <small>げんしょう</small>	domino effect, {a/the}	197
共食い(の~) <small>とも ぐ</small>	dog eat dog/dog-eat-dog	195
友達を作る <small>ともだち つく</small>	make {a friend/friends}	415
鳥のように自由 <small>とり じ ゆう</small>	(as) free as a bird	255
鳥肌が立つ <small>とりはだ た</small>	{get/have} goose bumps	271
奴隷のように扱う <small>ど れい あつか</small>	treat s.o. like a slave	657

な

長い目で見る <small>なが め み</small>	take {a/the} long view of ~	627
流れ <small>なが</small>	flow	249
流れが変わる <small>なが か</small>	{tides are/tide is} {turning/changing}, the	643
流れに逆らう <small>なが さか</small>	against the tide (of ~)	21

流れを変える <small>なが か</small>	turn the tide	663
流れを止める <small>なが と</small>	stem the tide (of ~)	605
鍋釜 <small>なべかま</small>	pots and pans	483
名前が大きい <small>な まえ おお</small>	big-name	81
波風を立てる <small>なみかぜ た</small>	make waves	419
(~の)波に乗る <small>なみ の</small>	ride a wave of ~	525
鳴り物入りで宣伝する <small>な もの い せんでん</small>	beat the drum for ~	73

に

苦い経験 <small>にが けいけん</small>	bitter experience	85
逃がした魚は大きい <small>に さかな おお</small>	The biggest fish is always the one that got away.	81
肉眼 <small>にくがん</small>	naked eye(s), {the/one's}	435
日光浴をする <small>にっこうよく</small>	sunbathe	617
鈍い <small>にぶ</small>	dull	213
二枚舌を使う <small>に まいじた つか</small>	speak with a forked tongue	595
鶏が先か卵が先か(の問題) <small>にわとり さき たまご さき もん だい</small>	chicken and egg problem, {a/the}	147

ぬ

(~を){縫うように/縫って} <small>ぬ ぬ</small>	weave through ~	689
盗み見る <small>ぬす み</small>	steal a glance at ~	603
濡れねずみ <small>ぬ</small>	look like a drowned rat	403

ね

寝かせる/寝かす <small>ね ね</small>	sleep on ~	577
根こそぎ(にする) <small>ね</small>	pull ~ {out/up} by the roots	493
猫の首に鈴をつける <small>ねこ くび すず</small>	bell the cat	75
ねじがゆるんでいる	have a screw loose	301

721

寝た子を起こすな	Let sleeping dogs lie.	381
熱しやすく冷めやすい	blow hot and cold	95
熱波	heat wave	325
根深い	deep-rooted	185
眠りに落ちる	fall asleep	229
(～と)寝る	sleep (with ~)	575
(～に)根を下ろす	put down roots (in ~)	499

は

ハードルを越える	clear {a/the} hurdle(s)	151
灰色の部分	gray area	285
(～の)バイブル(だ)	be the bible ({for/ of} ~)	63
鋼のように硬い	(as) hard as steel	295
(～に)拍車{をかける/が かかる}	spur	599
爆弾発言をする	drop a bomb(shell)	209
白鳥のように{優美/優 雅}	(as) graceful as a swan	281
薄氷を踏む	(tread) on thin ice	449
禿げ山	bald mountain	35
恥の上塗り	pile shame on top of shame	473
馬車馬のように働く	work like a horse	705
裸の王様	emperor's (new) clothes, the	217
旗ふり役	{wave/show} the flag	687
蜂の巣をつ(っ)ついたよ うな騒ぎ{になる/が起き る}	stir up a hornet's nest	609

(～と)波長が合う	be on the same wavelength (as ~)	55
ハト派	dove	199
(～に)バトンを渡す	pass the baton (on/ off) to ~	469
～の花(形)	flower of ~ , the	251
鼻が利く	have a nose for ~	301
話が飛ぶ	(the) conversation jumps	169
鼻の差で	by a nose	127
花のようにきれい	(as) pretty as a flower	489
(～に)鼻を突っ込む	stick one's nose into ~	607
羽のように軽い	(as) light as a feather	383
羽を{もがれる/もぎ取ら れる}ようだ	clip s.o.'s wings	157
バブルが弾ける	bubble bursts, the	117
(～に)波紋を投げかける	send {a ripple/ ripples} through(out) ~	553
腹を立てる	turn s.o.'s stomach	663
張り子の虎	paper tiger	465
針の目	eye of a needle	223
歯を食いしばる	grit one's teeth	289
反映する	reflect	525
(～の)反対にあう	meet with opposition (from ~)	423
パンチがきく	pack a punch	463
パンドラの箱を開ける	open (a) Pandora's box	459

ひ

| 火遊びをする | play with fire | 477 |

■日本語見出し・五十音順索引・Japanese Entry/Syllabary Index

引き金になる	trigger	657
(〜に)引き込まれる	be drawn into 〜	49
引きずり込む	drag into	201
額に汗して	by the sweat of one's brow	127
額を寄せ合う	put 〜 heads together	499
火付け役	firebrand	243
羊の皮をかぶった 狼	be a wolf in sheep's clothing	39
一息で	in one breath	345
一握り(の〜)	handful of 〜, a	293
一山当てる	strike oil	613
火に油を注ぐ	add fuel to the fire	19
陽の当たる場所	place in the sun, a	475
火のないところに煙は立たない	Where there's smoke, there's fire.	693
日の目を見る	see the light of day	545
秘密を守る	keep a secret	359
ひも付きの〜	have strings attached (to 〜)	313
冷や汗をかく	break (out) {into/in} a cold sweat	105
180度転換する	{take/do} a 180(-degree turn)	623
{冷や水/冷水}を浴びせる	pour cold water on 〜	483
氷河期	ice age	341
病気で倒れる	fall ill	229
氷山の一角	tip of the iceberg, the	651
表面上	on the surface	449
表面をなぞる	scratch the surface	541

ひよこ	chicken	147
昼間のように明るい	(as) bright as day	113
ビロードのようになめらか	(as) {smooth/soft} as {velvet/silk}	583
(〜に)火をつける	{build/light} a fire under 〜	119
びんの首	neck of a bottle	439

ふ

深い	deep	185
深みにはまる	be in deep water	51
深読み{し過ぎる/する}	read too much into 〜	521
武器を置く	lay down one's arms	371
腹心の友	bosom buddy	99
袋のねずみ	(to be caught) like a rat in a trap	389
不死鳥のように 蘇 る	rise like a phoenix (from the ashes)	531
(〜の)舞台を用意する	set the stage (for 〜)	555
二心	double-minded	199
豚に真珠	cast (one's) pearls before swine	145
(〜に)蓋をする	keep a lid on 〜	357
(〜に)蓋をする	put a lid on 〜	497
沸点に達する	reach the boiling point	517
筆を執る	take pen in hand	627
(〜の)踏み石	stepping stone {to/towards} 〜, a	607
プライドを傷つける	hurt s.o.'s pride	339
振り返ってみる	look back on 〜	401
古傷	old wound(s)	447

723

（〜に）ブレーキをかける	put the brakes on	505
（〜に）プレッシャーをかける	put pressure on ~	501
{〜に/について}触れる	touch {on/upon} ~	655

へ

下手な鉄砲も数撃{てば/ちゃ}当たる	Even a bad shot hits the mark given enough tries.	221
ベッドの脚	bed('s) legs	187
ベンチを温（暖）める	warm the bench	685

ほ

{法/法律}を破る	break the law	109
貿易摩擦	trade friction	655
方向	direction	191
法（律）の網	meshes of the law, the	425
吠える犬は噛まない	Barking dogs {never/seldom} bite.	35
墓穴を掘る	dig one's own grave	191
母語	mother tongue	429
母国	motherland	429
ほこりをかぶる	gather dust	259
骨と皮（ばかりだ）	be (nothing but) skin and bones	61
骨無し	have no {backbone/spine}	309
骨の髄まで	to the marrow	653
骨身に沁みる	bone-chilling	97
骨身を惜しまず働く	work one's fingers to the bone	703
（〜に）骨を埋める	lay (down) {one's/s.o.'s} bones	369

骨を折る	break one's neck	105
炎が（〜を）なめ尽くす	{fire licks/flames lick} at ~	243
ほらを吹く	{blow/toot} one's own horn	95
ぼろ雑巾のよう（になる）	limp as a (wet) rag	395
本の虫	bookworm	99

ま

曲がっている	crooked	171
曲がり角	turning point, {a/the}	663
（〜{に/の}）幕を下ろす	bring the curtain down on ~	115
負け犬	underdog	669
魔女狩り	witch hunt	697
瞬く間に	in the blink of an eye	347
（〜の）窓（だ）	be the window {of/on/to} ~	65
的を射る	hit the mark	331
（〜を）招く	invite	349
（〜に）魔法をかける	cast a spell {on/over} ~	143
眉をひそめる	raise eyebrows	509
（自分の）回りに壁を築く	build a wall around oneself	121

み

（〜を）見失う	lose sight of ~	411
磨く	polish	481
右腕	right-hand man	527
右の耳から（入って）左の耳に（抜ける）	go in one ear and out the other	275

■日本語見出し・五十音順索引・Japanese Entry/Syllabary Index

(〜を)見下す	look down {on/upon} ~	401
水と油	oil and water	445
水も漏らさない	hold water	335
(〜を)満たす	fill (s.t. with)	241
道	way	687
道を切り開く	clear {a/the} path for ~	153
〜{の/に}道を(切り)開く	open the way {to/for} ~	461
蜜月期間	honeymoon (period/phase), {a/the}	337
(将来の)見通しが暗い	future {looks/is} black	257
緑	green	287
見抜く	see through	547
身の毛がよだつ	one's hair stands on end	291
(〜の)耳に{入る/届く}	{reach/come to} s.o.'s ears	515
(自分の)耳を疑う	can't believe one's ears	135
(〜に)耳を貸す	lend {s.o. an ear/an ear to s.o.}	379
身も心も(〜に)打ち込む	put one's body and soul into ~	497
見る目がある	have an eye for ~	303
(〜に)(自分の)身を投じる	throw oneself into ~	641
実を結ぶ	bear fruit	71

む

無冠の帝王	uncrowned {king/queen}	667
無血(の〜)	bloodless ~	95

無神経(な)	have some nerve	311
結ばれる	tie the knot (with ~)	645
むち打ち症	whiplash	695
胸が張り裂ける	break s.o.'s heart	105
胸焼け	heartburn	323

め

目が飛び出る{ほど/くらい/ぐらい}	eyes pop out of one's head	225
(〜に)目{が開かれる/を開く}	open one's eyes to ~	455
目が回る	make one's eyes spin	417
目が回る	make s.o.'s head spin	417
目から鱗が落ちる	scales fall from s.o.'s eyes, the	539
目から火が出る	see stars	545
目覚める	awake to ~	27
目玉商品	eye-catcher	225
(〜の)メッカ	mecca {for/of} ~, {a/the}	423
目と鼻の先	(right) under s.o.'s nose	667
目と目でわかる	see eye to eye	543
目には目を	eye for an eye, an	221
目の保養	feast one's eyes on ~	237
(自分の)目を疑う	can't believe one's eyes	137
(〜に)目を落とす	drop one's eyes (to ~)	209
(〜に)目をつける	have {an/one's} eye on ~	305

725

目を{つぶって/つむって}てもできる	can do s.t. with one's eyes closed	135
(〜に)目をつぶる	close one's eyes to ~	159
(〜の)芽を摘む	nip ~ in the bud	443
(〜に)目を通す	look through ~	405
(〜に)目を走らせる	run one's eyes over	537
目を回す	roll one's eyes	533
面目を失う	lose face	409

も

盲点	blind spot	89
もう一押し	one more push	453
燃え尽きる	be {burned/burnt} out	45
文字通り(に)	literally	397
(〜を){持つ/持っている}	have	297
(〜の)下で働く	work under ~	707
もやしのような	beanpole	71
漏れる	leak (out)	371
もろ手を挙げて歓迎する	welcome {s.o./s.t.} with open arms	691
諸刃の 剣	double-edged sword	199
問題外	out of the question	461

や

やけどする	get burned (by s.o.)	261
(〜に)優しい	be easy on ~	49
山のような	mountain of ~, a	431
闇夜に鉄砲	shot in the dark, a	563

ゆ

雪だるま式に増える	snowball	589
雪のように白い	(as) white as snow	695
指一本動かさない	lift a finger	383
湯水のように金を使う	spend money like water	595
夢がある	dream of ~	205
夢が破れる	one's {dream is/ dreams are} shattered	207

よ

(〜の)夜明け	dawn of ~ , the	181
呼びかける	call on	131
(〜に)弱い	have a weakness for ~	303

ら

ライオンのように勇敢	(as) brave as a lion	103
裸眼	naked eye(s), {the/ one's}	435
楽に息がつける	can breathe easy	133

り

(屁)理屈をこねる	twist logic	665
(〜の)リトマス試験紙(だ)	be a litmus test for ~	37
理論を組み立てる	construct a theory	169

れ

冷血(な)	cold-blooded	163
冷静さを失う	lose one's cool	409
冷戦	cold war	163
(〜という)レッテルを貼る	label ~ (as)	367
連鎖反応	chain reaction	147

■日本語見出し・五十音順索引・Japanese Entry/Syllabary Index

ろ

ローマは一日にして成らず <small>いちにち</small><small>な</small>	Rome wasn't built in a day.	535
路肩 <small>ろ かた</small>	shoulder (of the road)	565

わ

我が家は我が城 <small>わ や わ しろ</small>	A man's home is his castle.	421
罠に落ちる <small>わな お</small>	fall into {a/the} trap	231
笑い上戸 <small>わら じょうご</small>	laughing drunk	369
(溺れる者は)わらをもつかむ <small>おぼ もの</small>	A drowning man will clutch at a straw.	213
悪口を言う <small>わるぐち い</small>	bad-mouth	33

727

■ English Entry Index・英語見出し索引

A

ABCs of ~, the	16
ache in one's heart	16
Achilles' heel	18
act of God, an	18
add fuel to the fire	18
against the tide (of ~)	20
ahead of the times	22
alarm, {an/the}	22
all eyes are on ~	24
All roads lead to Rome.	24
along the same lines	24
attack	26
awake to ~	26

B

baby talk	28
~ back	28
back	28
backroom ~	30
bad apple	30
bad dream, a	30
bad-mouth	32
bad name	32
bald mountain	34
bare bones of ~, the	34
bare one's teeth	568
Barking dogs {never/seldom} bite.	34
be a fetter on ~	36
be a litmus test for ~	36
be a puppet	38
be a wolf in sheep's clothing	38
be afraid of one's own shadow	40
be all ears	40

be an antidote to ~	40
be beyond a joke	42
be born under a lucky star	42
be buried in ~	44
be {burned/burnt} out	44
be calculating	44
be cancerous to ~	46
be crowned with victory	46
be dead	46
be drawn into ~	48
be easy on ~	48
be engraved in ~	50
be in deep water	50
be in the red	50
be in the same boat	52
be intoxicated with victory	52
be mad about ~	52
be moved	54
be on the front lines	54
be on the same wavelength (as ~)	54
be on the tip of one's tongue	56
be one step ahead	56
be over the hill	58
be rotten to the core	58
be rusty	60
be (nothing but) skin and bones	60
be starved {for/of} ~	62
be the bible ({for/of} ~)	62
be the window {of/on/to} ~	64
be tied up with ~	64
be tongue-tied	268
be {under/in} the spotlight	66
be up in the air	66

■ English Entry Index・英語見出し索引

be wrapped in ~	68	bookworm	98
be written all over one's face	68	bosom buddy	98
beanpole	70	brain drain	100
bear fruit	70	brain worker	100
beast, a	70	brainwash	100
beat ~ into s.o.'s head	72	(as) brave as a lion	102
beat the drum for ~	72	brazen-faced	102
become one with ~	74	break (a bill)	102
bed('s) legs	186	break s.o.'s heart	104
bell the cat	74	break (out) {into/in} a cold sweat	104
belly landing	76	break one's neck	104
bend the rules	76	break new ground	106
bet one's bottom dollar	78	break the law	108
between life and death	78	break the mold	108
beyond	78	breathtaking	110
big-name	80	breed	110
The biggest fish is always the one that got away.	80	bridge between	112
		(as) bright as day	112
(take a) bird's eye view of ~	82	bring s.t. into (sharp) relief	640
bite one's lip	82	bring the curtain down on ~	114
bite the hand that feeds you	84	broken home	114
bitter experience	84	broken record	116
black and white	86	bubble bursts, the	116
(as) black as coal	86	build	116
blind spot	88	build a fire under ~	118
blood freezes	90	build a plan	118
Blood is thicker than water.	90	build a wall around oneself	120
blood-relationship	92	bull-headed	120
blood, sweat, and tears	92	burst a blood vessel	122
bloodless ~	94	bury the past	122
blow hot and cold	94	buy time	124
blow one's own horn	94	by a hair's breadth	124
bolt {from/out of} the blue, a	94	by a nose	126
bone-chilling	96	by the sweat of one's brow	126

729

by word of mouth	128	close to ~	158
C		cold	160
caged bird	128	(as) cold as ice	160
call on	130	cold-blooded	162
calm before the storm, the	130	cold war	162
calm s.o.'s nerves	132	come back to life	162
can breathe easy	132	come out of one's shell	164
can do s.t. with one's eyes closed	134	come to s.o.'s ears	514
can't believe one's ears	134	come to light	164
can't believe one's eyes	136	common ground	166
can't see the forest for the trees	136	connect	166
capture s.o.'s heart	138	construct a theory	168
carpet-bomb	140	constructive criticism	168
carrot-{and/or}-stick	140	(the) conversation jumps	168
carry {a/one's} cross	140	crawl into a hole and die	170
cast a shadow over ~	142	crooked	170
cast a spell {on/over} ~	142	cross (over) {a/the} line	172
cast (one's) pearls before swine	144	cross one's mind	172
castle(s) in the air, (a)	144	cross swords with ~	174
chain reaction	146	crossfire	174
chair('s) legs	186	crow's-feet	174
chicken	146	cry wolf	174
chicken and egg problem, {a/the}	146	cut	176
chill runs down one's spine, a	148	cut one's own throat	176
circumstances permitting	150	**D**	
clear one's head (of)	218	dance to s.o.'s tune	178
clear {a/the} hurdle(s)	150	dark	178
clear {a/the} path for ~	152	dark clouds ~ (on the horizon)	180
(as) clear as crystal	152	dawn of ~, the	180
climb the ladder of success	154	day after the fair, a	182
cling to power	154	day of reckoning, the	182
clip s.o.'s wings	156	deep	184
close at hand	156	deep-rooted	184
close one's eyes to ~	158	desk('s) legs	186

■ English Entry Index・英語見出し索引

diamond in the rough, a	186
die in one's bed	186
The die is cast.	188
die like a dog	188
dig one's own grave	190
direction	190
dirty one's hands	190
distance oneself from ~	192
distant	194
do a 180(-degree turn)	622
dog eat dog/dog-eat-dog	194
dog paddle	196
domino effect, {a/the}	196
A doomed mouse will bite a cat if he has no choice.	196
double-edged sword	198
double-minded	198
dove	198
drag into	200
draw {a/the} line (between ~ and ~)	200
draw s.o.'s attention	202
draw s.o.'s interest	202
draw {s.o.'s/s.t.'s} teeth	204
dream of ~	204
one's {dream is/dreams are} shattered	206
drink (from) {a/the} bitter cup (of ~)	206
drop a bomb(shell)	208
drop one's eyes (to ~)	208
drop in the bucket, a	210
drop one's shoulders	210
A drowning man will clutch at a straw.	212
dull	212

dump	214

E

earn points (with ~)	214
emperor's (new) clothes, the	216
empire, {an/the}	216
empty one's head (of)	218
empty promise	218
empty stomach, (on) an	220
Even a bad shot hits the mark given enough tries.	220
eye for an eye, an	220
eye of a needle	222
(in the) eye of the {storm/hurricane}	222
eye-catcher	224
eyes pop out of one's head	224

F

one's face clouds (over)	224
face turns white	226
(as) faithful as a dog	226
fall asleep	228
fall ill	228
fall in love with ~	230
fall into {a/the} trap	230
fall into the hands of ~	232
fall {off/out of} one's chair	232
fall (squarely) on s.o.'s shoulders	234
fall prey to ~	234
feast one's eyes on ~	236
feel one's age	236
feel small	238
fight like cats and dogs	238
fill (s.t. with)	240
fill {a/the} hole(s)	240
fire licks at ~	242

731

firebrand	242
first step, the	244
flame	244
flame(s) of passion	244
flames lick at ~	242
flavor	246
float on air	246
flood of ~, a	248
flow	248
flower of ~, the	250
follow	250
follow one's heart	252
follow the same path as ~	252
forbidden fruit	252
(as) free as a bird	254
from head to toe	254
from the bottom of one's heart	254
full of ~; ~ is full	256
future {looks/is} black	256
future {looks/is} bright	258

G

gather dust	258
get burned (by s.o.)	260
get cold feet	270
get egg all over one's face	260
get one's foot in the door	260
get goose bumps	270
get one's hands on ~	262
get on s.o.'s nerves	262
get on the bandwagon	264
get out of hand	264
get the (whole) picture	266
get one's thoughts together	266
get to the core of ~	268

get tongue-tied	268
give s.o. a hand	378
give s.t. to {s.o./s.t.}	270
go {around/round} in circles	272
go back to the basics	274
go beyond a joke	42
go in one ear and out the other	274
go over s.o.'s head	276
go through fire and water (for ~)	278
go up in smoke	278
golden age	280
(goose that lays the) golden egg, the	280
(as) graceful as a swan	280
grasp	282
The grass is (always) greener (on the other side of the fence).	282
grass roots; grassroots ~	284
gray area	284
green	286
greenhorn	286
grit one's teeth	288
grope in the dark	288

H

one's hair stands on end	290
hand	290
handful of ~, a	292
hang {on/upon} ~	292
(as) hard as (a) rock	294
(as) hard as steel	294
harden s.o.'s attitude	294
one's hat is off to ~	296
have	296
have a big mouth	300

■ English Entry Index・英語見出し索引

have a nose for ~	300
have a screw loose	300
have a weakness for ~	302
have an eye for ~	302
have {an/one's} eye on ~	304
have cold feet	270
have eyes in the back of one's head	304
have one's feet on the ground	306
have goose bumps	270
have one's hands full (with ~)	306
have no {backbone/spine}	308
have (s.t.) on hand	308
have one foot in the grave	310
have some nerve	310
have strings attached (to ~)	312
have the last laugh	312
have (a) wide knowledge of ~	314
head count	314
head of ~	316
heads {will/are going to} roll	316
healthy	318
one's heart aches for s.o.	318
one's heart sinks	320
one's heart stops	322
heartburn	322
heartwarming	324
heat wave	324
hide one's feelings	326
high	326
hit {a/the} wall	328
hit the mark	330
hold (all) the cards	330
hold the key (to ~)	332
hold the purse strings	332

hold water	334
holy war	334
honeymoon (period/phase), {a/the}	336
horse face	336
hothouse; hothouse flower	338
hurt s.o.'s feelings	338
hurt s.o.'s pride	338
hush money	340

I

ice age	340
Ignorance is bliss.	340
(all) in a {fog/haze}	342
in a world of one's own	342
in light of ~	344
in one breath	344
in the blink of an eye	346
invasion	346
invite	348
iron will	348
ivory tower	348

J

one's jaw drops	350
join hands	352
joking aside	352
jump at ~	354

K

keep a cool head	354
keep a lid on ~	356
keep a secret	358
keep a tight {rein/leash} on ~	358
keep s.t. on hand	360
kill time	360
kill two birds with one stone	362
king	364

733

king of the hill	364
know ~ inside (and) out	364

L

label ~ (as)	366
landslide (victory)	366
late bloomer	366
laughing drunk	368
lay (down) {one's/s.o.'s} bones	368
lay down one's arms	370
leak (out)	370
lean toward(s) ~	372
leave a bad taste (in one's mouth)	374
leave this {life/world}	374
left wing/left-wing	376
lend (s.o.) a hand	378
lend {s.o. an ear/an ear to s.o.}	378
Let sleeping dogs lie.	380
leverage	380
lick one's lips	380
lick one's wounds	382
lift a finger	382
light a fire under ~	118
(as) light as a feather	382
light at the end of the tunnel	384
light purse	384
like a bullet out of a gun	384
(sound) like a fairy tale	386
like a fish out of water	386
(to be caught) like a rat in a trap	388
like a ship without a rudder	388
like (a) Rip Van Winkle	390
like the wind	390
like two peas in a pod	390
like water off a duck's back	392

limp as a (wet) rag	394
line	394
literally	396
live under the same roof	396
load off one's shoulders, a	396
lock horns (with ~)	398
lone wolf	400
look back on ~	400
look down {on/upon} ~	400
look like a drowned rat	402
look on the bright side (of ~)	402
look through ~	404
lose ~	404
lose confidence (in ~)	406
lose one's cool	408
lose face	408
lose sight of ~	410
Love is blind.	410
love nest	412
love triangle	412

M

make a clean sweep of ~	412
make {a friend/friends}	414
make a hole in ~	414
make s.o.'s blood boil	416
make one's eyes spin	416
make s.o.'s head spin	416
make noise (about ~)	418
make waves	418
man of the hour, the	418
manna from heaven	420
A man's home is his castle.	420
mecca {for/of} ~, {a/the}	422
meet with opposition (from ~)	422

■ English Entry Index・英語見出し索引

meshes of the law, the	424
one's mind goes blank	424
Money talks.	424
Monkey see, monkey do.	426
monolithic	426
monster	428
mother tongue	428
motherland	428
mountain of ~, a	430
move	432
myth	432

N

nail down	432
naked eye(s), {the/one's}	434
narrow	434
narrow-minded	436
near	438
neck of a bottle	438
need a hand	440
new blood	440
nine (times) out of ten	442
nip ~ in the bud	442
nose around	442
not worth a dime	444

O

oil and water	444
old wound(s)	446
on paper	446
on the rocks	446
on the surface	448
(tread) on thin ice	448
on top of that	450
one more push	452
one step ahead (of ~)	452

one-sided love	454
open one's eyes to ~	454
open one's heart (to ~)	454
open one's mind (to ~)	456
open one's mouth	458
open (a) Pandora's box	458
open the door {to/for} ~	458
open the way {to/for} ~	460
out of the question	460
one's own flesh and blood	462

P

pack a punch	462
paper tiger	464
parrot	464
pass (~)	466
pass (as/for ~)	466
pass the baton (on/off) to ~	468
pawn	468
pay attention to ~	470
pay one's respects to ~	470
Penny(-)wise and pound(-)foolish.	470
per head	472
pie in the sky, (a)	472
pile shame on top of shame	472
pillar of strength, a	474
place in the sun, a	474
play	474
play dirty	474
play possum	476
play with fire	476
point	478
point of view	478
poison (for/to) ~, (a)	480
polish	480

735

potbelly	482	ray of sunshine, a	512
pots and pans	482	reach {a/the} conclusion	512
pour cold water on ~	482	reach an agreement	514
pour one's heart out to ~	484	reach s.o.'s ears	514
pour money down the drain	486	reach the boiling point	516
pour water into a sieve	486	read between the lines	516
preach to the choir	488	read s.o.'s face	518
(as) pretty as a flower	488	read s.o.'s mind	518
(as) pretty as a picture	488	read too much into ~	520
prick up one's ears	488	recharge one's batteries	520
public eye, the	490	(as) red as blood	522
pull at {s.o.'s/the} heartstrings	658	red flag	522
pull s.o.'s leg	492	red scare	522
pull ~ {out/up} by the roots	492	reflect	524
pull the chestnuts out of the fire	492	ride a wave of ~	524
pull the strings	494	ride {out the storm/the storm out}	526
pushy	496	right-hand man	526
put a lid on ~	496	right wing/right-wing	528
put one's body and soul into ~	496	rise	528
put down roots (in ~)	498	rise like a phoenix (from the ashes)	530
put ~ heads together	498	rising star	530
put ~ on the shelf	500	risk one's neck	532
put pressure on ~	500	roll one's eyes	532
put one's (heart and) soul into ~	502	roll up one's sleeves	532
put the brakes on	504	Rome wasn't built in a day.	534
put one's thoughts together	266	rub salt {in/into} {the/s.o.'s} wound(s)	534
put up a smokescreen	504	run one's eyes over	536

R

race against time, a	506	run in {s.o.'s/the} blood	536
rack one's brain(s)	506		
raise eyebrows	508	save face	538
raise the white flag	510	scales fall from s.o.'s eyes, the	538
rake in ~	510	scatter like flies	540

S

save face	538
scratch the surface	540
sea of blood	542

■ English Entry Index・英語見出し索引

see eye to eye	542
see only one side (of ~)	542
see stars	544
see the light of day	544
see things in black and white	544
see through	546
see which way the wind {blows/is blowing}	546
seize {an/the} opportunity	548
sell oneself (as ~)	548
sell one's body	550
sell one's country	550
sell one's soul to ~	552
send {a ripple/ripples} through(out) ~	552
set one's hand to (~)	552
set the stage (for ~)	554
shadow of death, the	554
shake one's head	556
shallow	556
sharp	558
shine	560
shortsighted	562
shot in the dark, a	562
shoulder (of the road)	564
shoulder to shoulder (with ~)	564
show one's face	564
show one's hand	566
show one's teeth	568
show the flag	686
shrug one's shoulders	568
shut one's mouth	568
shut out	570
Silence is golden.	572
sink like a {rock/stone}	572

sit on one's hands	572
sitting duck	574
sleep (with ~)	574
sleep on ~	576
slice of life/slice-of-life	576
slip of the tongue, a	576
(as) slow as a snail	578
sly as a fox	580
smack one's lips	380
small fry	580
(it's a) small world	580
(s.t.) smell(s) fishy	580
smoke out	582
(as) smooth as {velvet/silk}	582
smooth sailing	584
smooth (out) the rough edges	584
snake of a line	586
snake one's way	586
snap	588
snowball	588
soak up	590
(as) soft as {velvet/silk}	582
sore spot	590
source of headaches	592
sow (the) seeds (of ~)	592
speak with a forked tongue	594
spend money like water	594
spice of life, the	596
splitting headache	596
spread rumors	598
spur	598
stabbing pain	600
stand at a crossroads	600
steal a glance at ~	602

737

steal s.o.'s heart	602	tearjerker	634
stem the tide (of ~)	604	tempest in a teapot, a	634
step by step	604	There is no royal road to ~	636
stepping stone {to/towards} ~, a	606	thick-skinned	636
stick one's nose into ~	606	thorny path, {a/the}	638
(as) still as a statue	608	throw in the towel	638
stir s.o. up	608	throw s.t. into (sharp) relief	640
stir up a hornet's nest	608	throw oneself into ~	640
storm of protest	610	throw up one's hands	640
stream of consciousness	610	{tides are/tide is} {turning/changing}, the	642
strike oil	612	tie the knot (with ~)	644
strong	612	Time and tide wait for no man.	644
suck {s.t./s.o.} dry	614	Time is a great healer.	646
sunbathe	616	Time is money.	646
swallow s.t. {whole/completely}	616	time is ripe ({for/to} ~), the	648
sweat	618	(only) time will tell	648
sweep s.o. off (of) {his/her} feet	618	tip of the iceberg, the	650
sweet voice	620	to death	650

T

table('s) legs	186	to the ends of the earth	652
tail off	620	to the marrow	652
take a 180(-degree turn)	622	toot one's own horn	94
take a beating (from ~)	622	touch {on/upon} ~	654
take a load off one's mind	624	trace	654
take {a/the} long view of ~	626	trade friction	654
take pen in hand	626	transparency	656
take shape (as ~)	628	treat s.o. like a slave	656
take {s.o.'s side/sides}	628	trigger	656
take the bait	628	tug at {s.o.'s/the} heartstrings	658
take the time (to ~)	630	turn one's back on ~	658
take (up) the reins (of ~)	630	turn back the clock	660
take to (one's) bed	632	turn s.o.'s stomach	662
tap s.o.'s shoulder	632	turn the tide	662
taste	634	turning point, {a/the}	662

■ English Entry Index・英語見出し索引

twilight (of one's life/career/etc.), the	664	whiplash	694
twist logic	664	(as) white as snow	694

U

uncrowned {king/queen}	666	win s.o.'s heart	694
(right) under s.o.'s nose	666	witch hunt	696
underdog	668	with (a) heavy heart	698
use one's head	668	with one's tail between one's legs	698

V

vegetative state	670	(see) with unclouded eyes	700
vicious {circle/cycle}	670	within a hair's breadth	124
viewpoint	478	woman of the hour, the	418
voice	672	s.o.'s words carry weight	700
one's voice cracks	672	work addict	702

W

walk a tightrope	674	work one's fingers to the bone	702
walk the same path as ~	252	work hand in hand (with ~)	704
walking {dictionary/encyclopedia}, a	676	work like a horse	704
wall	676	work under ~	706
wallflower	678	The world revolves around s.o.	706
The walls have ears.	678	worst-case scenario, the	708
war of nerves	680		
warm	680		
warm the bench	684		
wash one's hands of ~	684		
watch one's mouth	684		
wave the flag	686		
way	686		
weather vane	688		
weave through ~	688		
weight off one's shoulders, a	396		
welcome {s.o./s.t.} with open arms	690		
where one stands (on ~)	690		
Where there's a will, there's a way.	692		
Where there's smoke, there's fire.	692		

739

参 考 文 献

Bredin, Hugh (1984) "Metonymy" *Poetics Today* 5(1): 45–58.

Cameron, Lynne (2003) *Metaphor in Educational Discourse Continuum.* London: Continuum.

Fass, Dan (1997) *Processing metonymy and metaphor.* London: Ablex.

Hasegawa, Yoko (2012) *The Routledge Course in Japanese Translation.* London and New York: Routledge.

Lakoff, George, and Mark Johnson (1980) *Metaphors We Live by.* Chicago: Chicago University Press.

Lakoff, George, and Mark Turner (1989) *More than Cool Reason: A Field Guide to Poetic Metaphor.* Chicago: Chicago University Press.

Lazar, G. (1996) "Using Figurative Language to Expand Students Vocabulary" *ELT Journal* 50: 43–51.

Low, G. D. (1988) "On Teaching Metaphor" *Applied Linguistics* 9(2): 125–147.

MacLennan, Carol H. G. (1994) "Metaphors and Prototypes in the Learning Teaching of Grammar and Vocabulary" *International Review of Applied Linguistics in Language Teaching* 32(2): 97–111.

Makino, Seiichi (2007) "The Japanese Pluralizer *-tachi* as a Window into the Cognitive World" In S. Kuno, S. Makino, and S. Strauss eds. *Aspects of Linguistics: In Honor of Noriko Akatsuka,* 109–120. Tokyo: Kurosio Publishers.

Makino, Seiichi and Michio Tsutsui (2008) *A Dictionary of Advanced Japanese Grammar.* Tokyo: The Japan Times.

Ortony, Andrew (1979) *Metaphor and Thought.* Cambridge: Cambridge University Press.

Ricoeur, Paul (2014) *The Rule of Metaphor: The Creation of Meaning in Language.* Published on-line.

Riddle, E. (1999) "Metaphor and Prototypes in Vocabulary and Grammar" *TESOL'99: Avenues to Success Program Archive March* 9–13, 1999, New York.

Taylor, John (1989) *Linguistic categorization: Prototypes in linguistic theory.* Oxford: Clarendon Press.

東眞須美 (2014)『比喩の理解（シリーズ言語学と言語教育 32)』東京：ひつじ書房.

岡まゆみ (2004)「メタファーは OPI 判定のマーカーとなりうるか？」*Proceedings of the 3rd International Symposium on OPI.*

岡まゆみ (2005)「メタファー指導が日本語教育にもたらすもの」鎌田修他編『言語教育の新展開：牧野成一教授古稀記念論集（シリーズ言語学と言語教育 4)』181–200. 東京：ひつじ書房.

岡まゆみ (2014)「メタファーが内包する文化相互理解の可能性と日本語教育におけるメタファーの活用」筒井通雄他編『日本語教育の新しい地平を開く：牧野成一教授退官記念論集（シリーズ言語学と言語教育 30)』21–38. 東京：ひつじ書房.

川上誓作編集 (1996)『認知言語学の基礎』東京：研究社.

楠見孝編 (2007)『メタファー研究の最前線』東京：ひつじ書房.

佐藤信夫 (1978)『レトリック感覚』東京：講談社.

瀬戸賢一 (1995)『メタファー思考：意味と思考のしくみ』講談社新書. 東京：講談社.

瀬戸賢一 (1995)『空間のレトリック』東京：海鳴社.

瀬戸賢一編著 (2003)『ことばは味を超える：美味しい表現の探求』東京：海鳴社.

瀬戸賢一 (2005)『よくわかる比喩：ことばの根っこをもっと知ろう』東京：研究社.

瀬戸賢一 (2017)『時間の言語学：メタファーから読み解く』ちくま新書. 東京：筑摩書房.

中村明 (1977)『比喩表現辞典』東京：角川書店.

中村明 (2006)『文の彩り：顔・姿・心を描く名表現』東京：岩波書店.

中村明 (2007)『日本語の文体・レトリック辞典』東京：東京堂出版.

中村明 (2013)『比喩表現の世界　日本語のイメージを読む』筑摩選書. 東京：筑摩書房.

鍋島弘治朗 (2011)『日本語のメタファー』東京：くろしお出版.

波多野完治 (1958)『ことばと文章の心理学』東京：新潮社.

深谷昌弘・田中茂範 (1996)『コトバの〈意味づけ論〉：日常言語の生の営み』東京：紀伊国屋書店.

牧野成一 (1978)『ことばと空間』東京：東海大学出版会.

牧野成一 (1980)『くりかえしの文法』東京：大修館書店.

牧野成一 (2006)「談話における換喩の認知言語的分析」日本語教育国際研究大会，コロンビア大学.

山梨正明 (1988)『比喩と理解（認知科学選書 17）』東京：東京大学出版会.

レイコフ G.・ジョンソン M.（1986)『レトリックと人生』（渡部昇一ほか訳）東京：大修館書店.

■著者紹介

牧野成一
まきの せいいち

現職	イリノイ大学アジア研究センター・言語学科名誉教授、プリンストン大学東洋学科日本語・言語学名誉教授
最終学歴	イリノイ大学大学院言語学博士
教歴	イリノイ大学教授、プリンストン大学教授を経て名誉教授
著書	Some Aspects of Japanese Nominalizations (Tokai University Press, 1968);『ことばと空間』(東海大学出版会, 1978);『ウチとソトの言語文化学』(アルク, 1996);『くりかえしの文法』(大修館書店, 1980) ;『日本語学習 基礎英日辞典』(講談社インターナショナル, 2002);『日本語基本文法辞典』『日本語文法辞典 [中級編][上級編]』(共著, ジャパンタイムズ, 1986/1995/2008)、ほか研究論文多数
その他	瑞宝中綬章受賞 (2014)

Seiichi Makino

Current position	Professor Emeritus of Japanese and Linguistics, Center for Asian Studies, University of Illinois at Urbana-Champaign; Professor Emeritus of Japanese and Linguistics, Department of East Asian Studies, Princeton University
Highest degree	Ph.D. in Linguistics, University of Illinois at Urbana-Champaign
Teaching history	Professor, University of Illinois; Professor, Princeton University
Major publications	*Some Aspects of Japanese Nominalizations* (Tokyo: Tokai University Press, 1968); *Language and Space* (Tokyo: Tokai University Press, 1978); *Roles of Inside and Outside in Linguistic and Cultural Studies* (Tokyo: ALC PRESS INC., 1996); *Grammar of Repetition* (Tokyo: Taishukan, 1980); *Kodansha's Basic English-Japanese Dictionary* (Kodansha International, 2002); *A Dictionary of Basic Japanese Grammar*; *A Dictionary of Intermediate Japanese Grammar*; *A Dictionary of Advanced Japanese Grammar* ([Co-authored with Michio Tsutsui], Tokyo: The Japan Times, 1986/1995/2008); and many other papers on linguistics and pedagogy
Other	The Order of the Sacred Treasure, Gold Rays with Neck Ribbon (2014)

岡 まゆみ
おか

現職	ミシガン大学アジア言語文化学科日本語プログラムディレクター, ミシガン大学夏期日本語教授法コース主任講師
最終学歴	ロチェスター大学大学院教育学修士課程修了
教歴	上智大学非常勤講師, コロンビア大学専任講師, プリンストン大学専任講師, ミシガン大学専任講師を経て現職
著書	『中上級者のための速読の日本語 [第2版]』(ジャパンタイムズ, 2013) ;『上級へのとびら』(共著、くろしお出版, 2010) ;『きたえよう漢字力』(共著、くろしお出版, 2010) ;『中級日本語を教える 教師の手引き』(くろしお出版, 2011) ;『これで身につく文法力』(共著、くろしお出版, 2012)、ほか研究論文多数

Mayumi Oka

Current position	Director, Japanese Language Program, Department of Asian Languages and Cultures, University of Michigan; Head Lecturer, Japanese Pedagogy Course, Summer Language Institute, University of Michigan
Highest degree	M.A. in Education, University of Rochester
Teaching history	Part-time Lecturer, Sophia University, Japan; Lecturer, Columbia University; Lecturer, Princeton University; Lecturer, University of Michigan
Major publications	*Rapid Reading Japanese [Second Edition] Improving Reading Skills of Intermediate and Advanced Students* (Tokyo: The Japan Times, 2013); *TOBIRA Gateway to Advanced Japanese Learning Through Content and Multimedia* (Tokyo: Kurosio Publishers, 2009); *Power up Your KANJI* (Tokyo: Kurosio Publishers, 2010); *Teaching Intermediate Japanese Teacher's Guide* (Tokyo: Kurosio Publishers, 2011); *Grammar Power : Exercises for Mastery* (Tokyo: Kurosio Publishers, 2012); and many other papers on linguistics and pedagogy

■英文校閲

グレン・ラシュリー／ Glenn Lashley

2007年にハーバード大学英米文学部を卒業。
英米文学学士号を取得。2013年にミシガン
大学日本学研究センターにて日本学修士号
を取得。現在は東京在住でフリーランスの
編集者、翻訳者として活躍中。

Glenn Lashley received a B.A. in English
and American Literature and Language from
Harvard University in 2007 and an M.A.
in Japanese Studies from the University of
Michigan in 2013. He currently lives and works
in Tokyo as a freelance editor and translator.

■校閲協力：藤田 侊一郎

日英共通メタファー辞典
A Bilingual Dictionary of English and Japanese Metaphors

2017年 11月27日　　第1刷 発行

[著者]	牧野成一 岡まゆみ
[発行人]	岡野秀夫
[発行所]	くろしお出版 〒113-0033　東京都文京区本郷3-21-10 Tel：03・5684・3389　　Fax：03・5684・4762 URL：http://www.9640.jp　　Mail：kurosio@9640.jp
[装丁]	庄子結香（カレラ）
[印刷]	藤原印刷

Ⓒ 2017 Seiichi Makino, Mayumi Oka, Printed in Japan
ISBN 978-4-87424-745-7 C3581

乱丁・落丁はお取り替えいたします。本書の無断転載・複製を禁じます。